Dictionary of Literary Biography

Dictionary of Literary Biography Documentary Series

Dictionary of Literary Biography Yearbooks

Concise Series

Dictionary of Literary Biography® • Volume Two Hundred Ninety-Six

Twentieth-Century European Cultural Theorists, Second Series

Twentieth-Century European Cultural Theorists, Second Series

Edited by
Paul Hansom
University of Southern California

A Bruccoli Clark Layman Book

Detroit • New York • San Diego • San Francisco • Cleveland • New Haven, Conn. • Waterville, Maine • London • Munich

THOMSON

GALE

Dictionary of Literary Biography
Volume 296: Twentieth-Century European Cultural Theorists,
Second Series
Paul Hansom

LIBRARY OF CONGRESS CATALOGING-IN-PUBLICATION DATA

Twentieth-century European cultural theorists. Second series / edited by Paul Hansom.
   p. cm. — (Dictionary of literary biography ; v. 296)
"A Bruccoli Clark Layman Book."
Includes bibliographical references and index.
   ISBN 0-7876-6833-8
   1. Critics—Europe—Bio-bibliography. 2. Philosophers—Europe—
Bio-bibliography. I. Hansom, Paul. II. Series.

PN74.T85 2004
801'.95'0940904—dc22   2004004913

Printed in the United States of America
10 9 8 7 6 5 4 3 2 1

To our immediate duties:
without these we are nothing

Contents

Plan of the Series

. . . Almost the most prodigious asset of a country, and perhaps its most precious possession, is its native literary product—when that product is fine and noble and enduring.

Mark Twain*

The advisory board, the editors, and the publisher of the *Dictionary of Literary Biography* are joined in endorsing Mark Twain's declaration. The literature of a nation provides an inexhaustible resource of permanent worth. Our purpose is to make literature and its creators better understood and more accessible to students and the reading public, while satisfying the needs of teachers and researchers.

To meet these requirements, *literary biography* has been construed in terms of the author's achievement. The most important thing about a writer is his writing. Accordingly, the entries in *DLB* are career biographies, tracing the development of the author's canon and the evolution of his reputation.

The purpose of *DLB* is not only to provide reliable information in a usable format but also to place the figures in the larger perspective of literary history and to offer appraisals of their accomplishments by qualified scholars.

The publication plan for *DLB* resulted from two years of preparation. The project was proposed to Bruccoli Clark by Frederick G. Ruffner, president of the Gale Research Company, in November 1975. After specimen entries were prepared and typeset, an advisory board was formed to refine the entry format and develop the series rationale. In meetings held during 1976, the publisher, series editors, and advisory board approved the scheme for a comprehensive biographical dictionary of persons who contributed to literature. Editorial work on the first volume began in January 1977, and it was published in 1978. In order to make *DLB* more than a dictionary and to compile volumes that individually have claim to status as literary history, it was decided to organize volumes by topic, period, or

From an unpublished section of Mark Twain's autobiography, copyright by the Mark Twain Company

genre. Each of these freestanding volumes provides a biographical-bibliographical guide and overview for a particular area of literature. We are convinced that this organization—as opposed to a single alphabet method—constitutes a valuable innovation in the presentation of reference material. The volume plan necessarily requires many decisions for the placement and treatment of authors. Certain figures will be included in separate volumes, but with different entries emphasizing the aspect of his career appropriate to each volume. Ernest Hemingway, for example, is represented in *American Writers in Paris, 1920–1939* by an entry focusing on his expatriate apprenticeship; he is also in *American Novelists, 1910–1945* with an entry surveying his entire career, as well as in *American Short-Story Writers, 1910–1945, Second Series* with an entry concentrating on his short fiction. Each volume includes a cumulative index of the subject authors and articles.

Since 1981 the series has been further augmented by the *DLB Yearbooks*, which update published entries, add new entries to keep the *DLB* current with contemporary activity, and provide articles on literary history. There have also been nineteen *DLB Documentary Series* volumes, which provide illustrations, facsimiles, and biographical and critical source materials for figures, works, or groups judged to have particular interest for students. In 1999 the *Documentary Series* was incorporated into the *DLB* volume numbering system beginning with *DLB 210: Ernest Hemingway*.

We define literature as the *intellectual commerce of a nation:* not merely as belles lettres but as that ample and complex process by which ideas are generated, shaped, and transmitted. *DLB* entries are not limited to "creative writers" but extend to other figures who in their time and in their way influenced the mind of a people. Thus the series encompasses historians, journalists, publishers, book collectors, and screenwriters. By this means readers of *DLB* may be aided to perceive literature not as cult scripture in the keeping of intellectual high priests but firmly positioned at the center of a nation's life.

DLB includes the major writers appropriate to each volume and those standing in the ranks behind them. Scholarly and critical counsel has been sought in deciding which minor figures to include and how full their entries should be. Wherever possible, useful references are made to figures who do not warrant separate entries.

Each *DLB* volume has an expert volume editor responsible for planning the volume, selecting the figures for inclusion, and assigning the entries. Volume editors are also responsible for preparing, where appropriate, appendices surveying the major periodicals and literary and intellectual movements for their volumes, as well as lists of further readings. Work on the series as a whole is coordinated at the Bruccoli Clark Layman editorial center in Columbia, South Carolina, where the editorial staff is responsible for accuracy and utility of the published volumes.

One feature that distinguishes *DLB* is the illustration policy–its concern with the iconography of literature. Just as an author is influenced by his surroundings, so is the reader's understanding of the author enhanced by a knowledge of his environment. Therefore *DLB* volumes include not only drawings, paintings, and photographs of authors, often depicting them at various stages in their careers, but also illustrations of their families and places where they lived. Title pages are regularly reproduced in facsimile along with dust jackets for modern authors. The dust jackets are a special feature of *DLB* because they often document better than anything else the way in which an author's work was perceived in its own time. Specimens of the writers' manuscripts and letters are included when feasible.

Samuel Johnson rightly decreed that "The chief glory of every people arises from its authors." The purpose of the *Dictionary of Literary Biography* is to compile literary history in the surest way available to us–by accurate and comprehensive treatment of the lives and work of those who contributed to it.

The *DLB* Advisory Board

Introduction

This volume continues a project begun in *DLB 242: Twentieth-Century European Cultural Theorists, First Series,* to provide biographies of the men and women who wrestled with the complex theoretical problems of twentieth-century culture. With few exceptions, the men included here focus their critical attention on the idea and nature of the human "subject," and how that subject is created and maintained. While arguably an abstract categorization, the subject is synonymous with our notions of the person, with the psychoanalytic categorizations of the patient, and with the target of socio-historical forces, more commonly known as audiences or masses. These theorists place the subject within, and in opposition to, the external world of objects and explore the continual dialogue produced between man and his cultural environment, making the human subject the grounding point for much of the cultural theory of the twentieth century. Their work collectively may be read as the struggle to answer a triad of questions: what do we know, how do we know it, and how do these ways of knowing affect us?

While their language is often complex and their concepts sometimes quite dense, these theories have their philosophical roots in the Enlightenment and in part represent both an affirmation of and departure from those investigations. The decentering of God and his replacement by rational man began a general movement toward theoretical abstraction concerning human knowing. René Descartes, Thomas Hobbes, and Benedict de Spinoza placed the logical and rational human subject at the center of the universe, while Gottfried Wilhelm Leibniz explored the nature and limits of the observing "I" in the world. If the scientific revolution in the same period insisted on categorical, verifiable, and evidential truths, the philosophical revolution developed a metaphysical system that structured the world as a series of indeterminate negotiations. Immanuel Kant conceived of the mind itself as an ordering principle, a prime mover in the creation of the world, and claimed that the world appeared as it did because the mind ordered it so. Consequently, the human world was not an eternal structure but a continual representation, placing the subject at the center of his own meaning-creation processes.

The twin conundrums of knowing the world (phenomenology) and the forms in which the world is known (hermeneutics) occupied theorists at the dawn of the twentieth century. Edmund Husserl, writing against what he saw as a spiritual crisis in the heart of man, argued for a reaction against nineteenth-century scientific rationalism in his *Logische Untersuchungens* (1900–1901; translated as *Logical Investigations,* 1970) and *Ideen zu einer reinen Phänomenologie und phänomenologischen Philosophie* (1913; translated as *Ideas: General Introduction to Pure Phenomenology,* 1931). By positing a phenomenological approach, Husserl explored the nature of human awareness, insisting on a transcendental subjectivity, where the connections between man and the world could be clearly developed into a schematized philosophical system. Husserl's phenomenology was modified by one of his pupils, Martin Heidegger. Hailed as the most important philosopher of the twentieth century, Heidegger largely rejected the transcendental relation to the world and chose to focus on the nature of human being, attempting to create by analogy a philosophical understanding of the nature of modern life itself. Because existence is always experienced in the world, Heidegger claimed the foundation of our humanness was practically bound up with others in that world, and these relations constituted life itself. Because the world is not an object circling independently of perception, however, he posited that humans can never fully objectify reality (and therefore study it), because they are simultaneously subject and object of the world. In *Sein und Zeit* (1927; translated as *Being and Time,* 1962), Heidegger sought to displace the human subject from its imaginary position of dominance and suggested that existence itself can never be grasped as a finished object.

Other theorists emerging from the German philosophical tradition included Hans-Georg Gadamer, who developed the modern conception of hermeneutics, or the theory of interpretation. Concerned with the human subject as maker and structurer of meaning and consciousness, in *Wahrheit und Methode* (1960; translated as *Truth and Method,* 1975) Gadamer explored how people perceive and understand categories such as truth and beauty and the underlying premises that construct them as categories. Concerned with pointing out the limits of scientific observation, Gadamer posited the "dialogue" approach to meaning, whereby people make their understanding of the world by creating a series of narrative story lines. Hermeneutics offered an awareness of interpretive limits and possibilities, suggesting the world was continually open, and by asking questions people became open to experiencing the world.

Problems of knowing and being naturally led to the exploration of the ethical position of human beings in that world. For Franz Brentano and Emanuel Lévinas, the ethical question became a basic philosophical premise. In his *Investigations of the Psychology of the Sense* (1907) and *On the Classification of Psychological Phenomena* (1911), Brentano argues the mental realm had a dimension of intentionality, that man could directly influence the world and how it is perceived. In the same vein, Lévinas's *Existence and Existents* (1947) and *The Humanism of the Other Person* (1972) claimed that the ethical form of understanding actually preceded ontology, or being. Just because everyday encounters with others were encounters with a realm absolutely beyond one's understanding, this "unknowingness" did not necessarily mean the other person was beyond relation. It was the ethical realm that provided a bridge to others, and this bridge represented the nature and extent of human obligation to each other. Lévinas provided a concrete moral philosophy based on ready needs, needs that were largely the ethical expectations people have of themselves in the world.

Lévinas was enormously influential on the French existentialist Jean-Paul Sartre. Also heavily influenced by Husserl and Heidegger, Sartre interrogated the notion of perception and agreed that the world existed only within human experience, and since for him existence precedes essence, consciousness creates the world. If such were the case, so Sartre's existentialism reasoned, man could make the choice of existing as he wished, by developing the most ethical form of consciousness. In such works as *L'Etre et le néant* (1943; translated as *Being and Nothingness,* 1956) and *L'Existentialisme est un humanisme* (1946; translated as *Existentialism and Humanism,* 1948), Sartre offered a principle of reason to support life and morality, a philosophy of acting well in the world, in order to promote a better, more ethical life.

Providing the materialist bridge for existentialist theory, Ernst Bloch translated the idea of the ethical into the political and social realms. Writing after the German defeat of 1918, Bloch sought to develop a metaphysics that would counteract the spiritual impoverishment he witnessed in his culture. He waged a battle against the crass commercialism and mechanization of European society by insisting on rehabilitating the utopian ideal, thereby reviving the possibility of faith in the future. His philosophy of hopefulness was most clearly developed in *Geist der Utopie* (1918; translated as *The Spirit of Utopia,* 2000) and later in *Das Prinzip Hoffnung* (1954–1959; translated as *The Principle of Hope,* 1986) and *Tübinger Einleitung in die Philosophie* (1963–1964; partly translated as *Philosophy of the Future,* 1970), in which Bloch argues society should build itself "into the blue," thus moving beyond the more traditional Marxist analyses, which tended toward the deterministic.

In addition to developing their own cultural theories, many were instrumental in outlining "sociology" as a new form of knowledge, and their studies and classifications sought to provide an understanding of the forms and nature of organized, urban experience. For example, in "Die protestantische Ethik und der Geist des Kapitalismus" (1920; translated as *The Protestant Ethic and the Spirit of Capitalism,* 1930) Max Weber explored European modernity, paying particular attention to the parallels between spiritual and economic development and structures. Similarly, "sociologists" such as Georg Simmel and Maurice Merleau-Ponty developed new stylistic elements in their own critiques, capturing the disorientation of the era by working through the fragmented essay or aphorism to represent this social experience accurately. Interested in the dialectical relations between seemingly unrelated social phenomena, they reached the conclusion that social values that appeared unified were in fact products of antagonistic forces. In short, the social realm was less a solid structure than a constant struggle.

The collapse of the German Empire after World War I and the rise of the Weimar Republic thrust the country into a new phase of its cultural development. The experience of modernity brought about new conditions of social organization and ushered in the rise of standardization and bureaucratization, resulting in a profound alienation and redefinition of the individual as a social and psychological being. Critics such as Siegfried Kracauer sought to study the growth of German mass culture, especially movies and radio, and the impact it had on the collective psyche of the populace. For Kracauer, these new devices had enormous social and psychological consequences, most of which were ignored. Despite the material boon offered by modern society, Kracauer discerned an evacuation of human vitality and the emergence of a transcendental loneliness at the heart of this modern culture. By paying attention to fragments of German mass culture, Kracauer explored the systems motivating social behavior and mentality. In works such as *Das Ornament der Masse* (1963; translated as *The Mass Ornament,* 1995) and *From Caligari to Hitler: A Psychological History of the German Film* (1947), Kracauer hoped to reveal the complex zeitgeist of a troubled nation. Similar work was also carried out by Max Horkheimer, one of the founding members of the Institute for Social Research, better known as the Frankfurt School. Though avowedly Marxist in orientation, Horkheimer's analysis of Hitlerian culture and the mechanisms of totalitarian thought produced a massive body of interdisciplinary work linking aesthetics, economics, law, philosophy, psychology, and sociology. In constructing a theory of modern experience, Horkheimer wanted to cut through mass ideology to show the political nature of lived relations. Horkheimer's *Dialektik der Aufklärung* (1947; translated as *Dialectic of Enlightenment,* 1972), co-authored with Theodor W. Adorno, and *Zur Kritik der instrumentellen Vernunft* (1967; translated as *Critique of Instrumental Reason,* 1974) both became seminal documents within the later schools of cultural studies and critical theory. Despite his theoretical complexity, Horkheimer's analysis pointed out the disturbing, dehumanizing trends found within mass culture, most notably the problems of "right thinking" and the growing specialization and instrumentality of contemporary society. For Horkheimer and his Frankfurt School, modernity included the seeds of a profoundly antihumanist politics and was responsible for both the fundamental decay of Enlightenment ideals and the disappearance of reason and morality from social life.

This deep pessimism could also be found in the work of Erich Fromm, who was also developing a critical-psychological analysis of the culture at large. Though deemed too simplistic by the more sophisticated theoreticians of the Frankfurt School, Fromm emerged as a profound humanist, keen to explore contemporary character types and the lurking problems of authoritarian personality inherent in contemporary society. His *Escape from Freedom* (1941) and *The Sane Society* (1955) argue that the increasing bureaucratization of both German and American society was producing significantly new personality types in order to cope with the society at large. The resulting pathology of normalcy led him to declare modern life as a form of insanity, whereby freedom was distrusted and even feared.

Theorists such as Franz Fanon focused on the imperial dimensions of European identity, exploring the specific relations between the colonial subject and the colonizing power, the nature of identity construction within the realm of the colonial, and the ways in which the colonial subject came to view themselves as actually colonized. By concentrating on experience within French North African colonies, primarily Algeria, Fanon analyzed the means by which life under occupying forces generated submissive identities for colonial Arab subjects. Interested in the interplay between racism and social justice and the interdependence of politics and economic relations, Fanon laid the foundation for the study of the specific links between race and capitalism. *Peau noir, masques blancs* (1952; translated as *Black Skin, White Masks,* 1967) and *Les Damnés de la terre* (1961; translated as *The Wretched of the Earth,* 1963) became key texts in the liberation politics of Third World and postcolonial studies.

The twentieth-century crises of politics and modernity were understandably manifest within the psychological realm. Sigmund Freud was instrumental in developing this new field of psychoanalytical study, whereby the effects of these cataclysmic changes could be revealed by analysis of the structures and symbols of the human mind. As Freud was a practicing psychologist and theorist, his work became a lifelong project that evolved with revisions, rejections, and expansions of his theories over time. Not content with focusing solely on individual cases, in his *Totem und Tabu* (1913; translated as *Totem and Taboo,* 1918) and *Das Unbehagen in der Kultur* (1930; translated as *Civilization and Its Discontents,* 1930) he explores the larger problems of psychic disturbance in everyday culture and within civilization in general. At the core of Freud's work lay the claim that all human beings must repress the "pleasure principle" in favor of the "reality principle" in order to become socialized, and that individual progress through this process had important psychological consequences. For most, the effects were not particularly bothersome. For a minority, however, the repression was excessive and thus produced illness, more commonly known as neurosis. In *Die Traumdeutung* (1900; translated as *The Interpretation of Dreams,* 1913) he explores the imagery produced by unconscious mental structures; in *Der Witz und seine Beziehung zum Unbewussten* (1905; translated as *Wit and Its Relation to the Unconscious,* 1916) he examines the ways in which a slip of the tongue or joke telling could indicate certain emotional and psychical conditions. Freud was also fascinated by the nature of human sexuality and motivation and the ways in which erotically charged experiences of the early infant life within the family were vital to the development of an adult identity. This gave rise to his notorious concepts of the Oedipus complex and penis envy. The unconscious remained central to human identity for Freud, and his development of the psychoanalytical method to deal with these difficulties remains a major contribution to human study. The enormous impact of Freud's work on the popular culture of the twentieth century is evident in the survival of many of his models, theories, and practices.

Yet, Freud was not without challengers. His erstwhile pupil and colleague Carl Gustav Jung broke with him to develop alternate theories of the unconscious and their cultural implications. The split over Freud's concentration on infantile sexual development allowed Jung to explore the transcultural aspects of human identity by merging the psychoanalytic with studies of anthropology, mythology, and comparative religion. In works such as *On the Psychology of the Spirit* (1948) and *Man and His Symbols* (1964) Jung sought the patterns underlying what he understood to be the human collective unconscious.

The other significant departure from Freudian orthodoxy came with French psychoanalyst Jacques Lacan's work. A radical post-Freudian, Lacan's criticisms proved to be so provocative that he was expelled from the International Psychoanalytical Association in 1959. In response, he established his own Ecole Freudienne in 1964. A notoriously difficult writer and theorist, Lacan became one of the most influential poststructuralist critics by integrating psychoanalytical theory with linguistics. In his enormously influential essay collection *Ecrits* (1966; partly translated as *Ecrits: A Selection,* 1977), Lacan argued that the unconscious was structured like a language and that human beings derived their identity by simultaneously acquiring language.

Attempts to determine and identify the structures beneath social activity and organization also had their counterparts within the fields of linguistics and literary study. For structuralists and poststructuralists alike, the linguistic theories of Ferdinand de Saussure laid the essential groundwork for their general approaches and suggested an essential interplay between language and the object it describes. All theorists in this area shared two common assumptions: that language is open-ended, informed by the interplay of cultural ideologies and codes; and most importantly, that language can be "deconstructed." The ability to look at language from a variety of perspectives and the recognition of its importance as an elemental component of gender identity influenced many feminist poststructuralists such as Hélène Cixous, Julia Kristeva, and Luce Irigaray. These theorists posited a specifically "feminine" writing language and genre that was a more accurate reflection of women's condition within culture. Irigaray's *Ce sexe qui n'en est pas un* (1977; translated as *This Sex Which Is Not One,* 1985) and *Speculum de l'autre femme* (1974; translated as *Speculum of the Other Woman,* 1985) outline the potential of "female writing" as a radical departure from male-centered language discourse and attempt to link female biology to distinctly female expressions and constructions.

With the exception of Jacques Derrida, the most influential poststructuralist thinker was Roland Barthes, who delved into the pop-cultural realm to develop a system of analytical reading commonly known as semiology, in which words, images, and cultural phenomena are "deciphered" to determine the codes and ideologies underlying social life. Barthes foregrounds culture as a metalanguage that not only generates meaning but also illustrates the conflicts that occur around the production of that meaning. His most popularly accessible work, *Mythologies* (1957; translated, 1972), provides a witty series of essays and observations on the ideological structures behind popular and high-cultural phenomena such as the striptease and fighter pilots. His *Eléments de semiologie* (1964; translated as *Elements of Semiology,* 1967), a more theoretical linguistic approach derived from Saussure's work, proved to be the manifesto of the French structuralist movement.

Barthes eventually abandoned this rigid structuralist approach in favor of a looser methodology. His revolutionary essay "La mort de l'auteur" (The Death of the Author, 1968) and groundbreaking study *S/Z* (1970; translated, 1974) inaugurated a wholly new way of reading literature. By exploring the differences between the "lisible," or readerly, text, which makes its readers into passive consumers, and the "scriptible," or writerly, text, which makes the reader into an active participant in the production of meanings within the text, Barthes drew attention to the creative plurality of language and determined the continual reader-writer transactions that take place during the act of reading. Barthes argued for the abandonment of the "genius author" category and shifted critical focus to the reader, who becomes vital in the exchange and production of meaning. He continued to explore the function of language in the creation of reality throughout his poststructuralist phase, producing such idiosyncratic masterworks as *Le plaisir du Texte* (1973; translated as *The Pleasure of the Text,* 1975) and *Roland Barthes par Roland Barthes* (1975; translated as *Roland Barthes by Roland Barthes,* 1977), which further challenge the conventional distinctions between critic and creator, fiction and nonfiction, and the literary and nonliterary.

Poststructuralists also worked within the broader realms of culture and history, exploring the development of contemporary institutional epistemologies, or knowledge systems. Michel Foucault and Gilles Deleuze developed new, interdisciplinary approaches to the human sciences, in which the traditional all-knowing subject, or cogito, was forced from center stage in favor of determining discourses. Deleuze and Felix Guattari's *Capitalisme et schizophrénie: Mille Plateaux* (1980; translated as *A Thousand Plateaus: Capitalism and Schizophrenia,* 1987) attempts to produce new concepts for the categories of logic and sense by celebrating the indeterminate elements of nonbeing and the indefinable qualities of the "aliquid." Deleuze also interrogated traditional psychoanalytical categories and criticized them for codifying and confining all human activity within the arena of the family. His and Guattari's *Capitalisme et schizophrénie:*

L'anti-Oedipe (1975; translated as *Anti-Oedipus: Capitalism and Schizophrenia,* 1977) shows how capitalism liberates desire through production and commodification and argues that this liberation is essentially reterritorialized within the institutional parameters of the family, religion, and class relations, for example. Though not necessarily in opposition to these social forces, this desire produces a schizophrenic energy, and Deleuze celebrates these schizoid tendencies as paradigms for new social and psychological energies.

Other postmodernist theorists such as Jean Baudrillard, Jean-Francois Lyotard, and Guy Debord turned their attention to contemporary culture, shifting their focus onto the actual system of consumer culture itself, offering compelling analyses of how people are structured by their contemporary moment. For the postmodernists, culture literally takes on a life of its own. While Debord identified this phenomenon in his *La Société du spectacle* (1967; translated as *The Society of the Spectacle,* 1970), Baudrillard characterized the postmodern as overarching dominance of media and technological developments, which together produce new forms and perceptions of reality–a "hyperreality" in fact–that replace the world people know. Interested in advanced industrial society and its communications technologies such as television and digital enhancement, Baudrillard addresses this new cultural language and its disorienting spatiotemporal relations. In *La société de consommation* (1970; translated as *The Consumer Society,* 1998), *Simulacres et simulation* (1981; translated as *Simulacra and Simulation,* 1994), and *Ecran Total* (1997; translated as *Screened Out,* 2002), Baudrillard theorizes the landscape of the late twentieth century, where reality itself has become a tenuous concept at best and where unreality has become the structuring element of the world.

If the postmodernists and their poststructuralist cousins show readers anything, it is the abiding necessity for cultural definition and redefinition and the need to be flexible in understanding human subjectivity. Theory is not only a vital and expansive part of the philosophical realm, it is now central to undergraduate and graduate education found in most European and American universities, cutting across the curriculum to inform the humanities, the sciences, the social sciences, and the fine arts. There seems little doubt that twenty-first-century cultural developments will have their own theorists, and these theorists will, as Bloch suggested,

"build themselves into the blue." What this future theory looks like, however, is somewhat hazy; yet, as intellectual history makes clear, and what this volume shows, is that certain questions always remain central.

–*Paul Hansom*

Acknowledgments

This book was produced by Bruccoli Clark Layman, Inc. Charles Brower was the in-house editor.

Production manager is Philip B. Dematteis.

Administrative support was provided by Ann M. Cheschi and Carol A. Cheschi.

Accountant is Ann-Marie Holland.

Copyediting supervisor is Sally R. Evans. The copyediting staff includes Phyllis A. Avant, Caryl Brown, Melissa D. Hinton, Philip I. Jones, Rebecca Mayo, Nadirah Rahimah Shabazz, and Nancy E. Smith.

Editorial associates are Jessica Goudeau, Joshua M. Robinson, and William Mathes Straney.

In-house prevetter is Catherine M. Polit.

Permissions editor and database manager is Amber L. Coker.

Layout and graphics supervisor is Janet E. Hill. The graphics staff includes Zoe R. Cook and Sydney E. Hammock.

Office manager is Kathy Lawler Merlette.

Photography supervisor is Paul Talbot. Photography editor is Scott Nemzek.

Digital photographic copy work was performed by Joseph M. Bruccoli.

Systems manager is Donald Kevin Starling.

Typesetting supervisor is Kathleen M. Flanagan. The typesetting staff includes Patricia Marie Flanagan, Mark J. McEwan, and Pamela D. Norton.

Walter W. Ross is library researcher. He was assisted by the following librarians at the Thomas Cooper Library of the University of South Carolina: Jo Cottingham, interlibrary loan department; circulation department head Tucker Taylor; reference department head Virginia W. Weathers; reference department staff Laurel Baker, Marilee Birchfield, Kate Boyd, Paul Cammarata, Joshua Garris, Gary Geer, Tom Marcil, Rose Marshall, and Sharon Verba; interlibrary loan department head Marna Hostetler; and interlibrary loan staff Bill Fetty, Nelson Rivera, and Cedric Rose.

Twentieth-Century European Cultural Theorists, Second Series

Dictionary of Literary Biography

Gaston Bachelard

(27 June 1884 – 16 October 1962)

Alison Ross
Monash University

BOOKS: *Essai sur la connaissance approchée* (Paris: Vrin, 1928);

Etude sur l'évolution d'un problème de physique: La propagation thermique dans les solides (Paris: Vrin, 1928);

La valeur inductive de la relativité (Paris: Vrin, 1929);

Le pluralisme cohérent de la chimie moderne (Paris: Vrin, 1932);

L'intuition de l'instant: Etude sur la "Siloë" de Gaston Roupnel (Paris: Stock, 1932);

Les intuitions atomistiques: Essai de classification (Paris: Boivin, 1933);

Le nouvel esprit scientifique (Paris: Alcan, 1934); translated by Arthur Goldhammer as *The New Scientific Spirit* (Boston: Beacon, 1984);

La dialectique de la durée (Paris: Boivin, 1936); translated by Mary McAllester Jones as *The Dialectic of Duration* (Manchester, U.K.: Clinamen, 2000);

L'expérience de l'espace dans la physique contemporaine (Paris: Alcan, 1937);

La formation de l'esprit scientifique: Contribution à une psychanalyse de la connaissance objective (Paris: Vrin, 1938);

La psychanalyse du feu (Paris: Gallimard, 1938); translated by Alan C. M. Ross as *The Psychoanalysis of Fire* (Boston: Beacon, 1964);

Lautréamont (Paris: Corti, 1939; enlarged, 1986); translated by Robert S. Duprée (Dallas: Dallas Institute of Humanities and Culture Publications, 1986);

La philosophie du non: Essai d'une philosophie du nouvel esprit scientifique (Paris: Presses Universitaires de France, 1940); translated by G. C. Waterston as *The Philosophy of No: A Philosophy of the New Scientific Mind* (New York: Orion, 1968);

L'eau et les rêves: Essai sur l'imagination de la matière (Paris: Corti, 1942); translated by Edith R. Farrell as

Gaston Bachelard (from Jean Claude Margolin, Bachelard, *1974; Thomas Cooper Library, University of South Carolina)*

Water and Dreams: An Essay on the Imagination of Matter (Dallas: Pegasus Foundation, 1983);

L'air et les songes: Essai sur l'imagination du mouvement (Paris: Corti, 1943); translated by Farrell and C. Freder-

3

ick Farrell as *Air and Dreams: An Essay on the Imagination of Movement* (Dallas: Dallas Institute of Humanities and Culture Publications, 1988);

La terre et les rêveries du repos: Essai sur les images de l'intimité (Paris: Corti, 1948);

La terre et les rêveries de la volonté: Essai sur l'imagination des forces (Paris: Corti, 1948); translated by Kenneth Haltman as *Earth and Reveries of Will: An Essay on the Imagination of Matter* (Dallas: Dallas Institute of Humanities and Culture Publications, 2002);

Le rationalisme appliqué (Paris: Presses Universitaires de France, 1949);

L'activité rationaliste de la physique contemporaine (Paris: Presses Universitaires de France, 1951);

L'actualité de l'histoire des sciences (Alençon: Alançonnaise, 1951);

Le matérialisme rationnel (Paris: Presses Universitaires de France, 1953);

La poétique de l'espace (Paris: Presses Universitaires de France, 1957); translated by Maria Jolas as *The Poetics of Space* (New York: Orion, 1964);

Notice sur la vie et les travaux d'Edouard Le Roy, 1870–1954, lue dans la séance du 15 février 1960 (Paris: Firmin-Didot, 1960);

La poétique de la rêverie (Paris: Presses Universitaires de France, 1960); translated by Daniel Russell as *The Poetics of Reverie: Childhood, Language and the Cosmos* (New York: Orion, 1969);

La flamme d'une chandelle (Paris: Presses Universitaires de France, 1961); translated by Joni Caldwell as *The Flame of a Candle* (Dallas: Dallas Institute of Humanities and Culture Publications, 1988);

Le droit de rêver (Paris: Presses Universitaires de France, 1970); translated by J. A. Underwood as *The Right to Dream* (New York: Grossman, 1971);

Fragments d'une poétique du feu, edited, with an introduction and notes, by Suzanne Bachelard (Paris: Presses Universitaires de France, 1988); translated by Kenneth Haltman as *Fragments of a Poetics of Fire* (Dallas: Dallas Institute of Humanities and Culture Publications, 1990).

Collections: *Etudes,* edited by Georges Canguilhem (Paris: Vrin, 1970);

Epistémologie, edited by Dominique Lecourt (Paris: Presses Universitaires de France, 1971);

L'engagement rationaliste, edited by Canguilhem (Paris: Presses Universitaires de France, 1972).

Editions in English: *On Poetic Imagination and Reverie: Selections from the Works of Gaston Bachelard,* translated and edited by Colette Guadin (Indianapolis: Bobbs-Merrill, 1971);

Gaston Bachelard, Subversive Humanist: Texts and Readings, translated and edited, with introductory notes, by

Mary McAllester Jones (Madison: University of Wisconsin Press, 1991).

OTHER: "Physique et mathématique," in *Septimana Spinozana: Acta conventus oecumenici in memoriam Benedicti de Spinoza diei natalis trecentesimi Hagae Cornilis habiti* (The Hague: Nijhof, 1933), pp. 74–84;

"Valeur morale de la culture scientifique," in *VI-e Congrès international d'éducation morale: Résumés des communications présentée au congrès Cracovie, 1934* (Cracovie: Comité de organisateur du Congrès, 1934);

"Critique préliminaire du concept de frontière épistémologique," in *Actes du huitième Congrès international de philosophie à Prague* (Prague: Orbis, 1936), pp. 3–9;

Martin Buber, *Je et tu: La vie en dialogue,* preface by Bachelard (Paris: Aubier, 1938);

"La Psychologie de la Raison," in *Les conceptions modernes de la Raison,* Publications de l'Institute international de collaboration philosophique (Paris: Hermann, 1939), pp. 28–34;

"La Psychanalyse de la connaissance objective," in *Annales de l'Ecole des Hautes-Etudes de Gand,* volume 3 (Ghent: Ecole des Hautes-Etudes, 1939), pp. 3–13;

"Univers et Réalité," in *Travaux du deuxième Congrès des Sociétés de Philosophie françaises et de langue française (Lyon, les 13–15 avril 1939)* (Lyon: Neveu, 1939);

"La pensée axiomatique," in *Etudes philosophiques* (Ghent: Ecole de Hautes-Etudes, 1939), pp. 21–22;

"L'image littéraire," in *Domaine français* (Geneva: Editions des Trois Collines, 1943), pp. 245–256;

"La philosophie de la mécanique ondulatoire," in *Vingtième anniversaire de la Mécanique ondulatoire: Plaquette Commémorative* (Paris: Gauthier-Villars, 1944);

"Une rêverie de la matière," in José Corti, *Rêves d'encre: Vingt-cinq images* (Paris: Corti, 1945);

Jean Cavaillès, *Sur la logique et la théorie de la science,* preface by Bachelard (Paris: Presses Universitaires de France, 1947);

"Le problème philosophique des méthodes scientifiques," in *Actes du Congrès d'histoire des sciences* (Paris: Hermann, 1949);

"The Philosophic Dialectic of the Concepts of Relativity," translated by Forrest W. Williams, in *Albert Einstein, Philosopher-Scientist,* edited by Paul Arthur Schilpp (Evanston, Ill.: Library of Living Philosophers, 1949), pp. 563–580;

"L'idonéisme ou l'exactitude discursive," in *Etudes de philosophie des sciences, en hommage à Ferdinand Gonseth à l'occasion de son soixantième anniversaire* (Neuchâtel: Griffon, 1950), pp. 7–10;

Gabrielle Ferrières, *Jean Cavaillès, philosophe et combattant (1903-1904)* (Paris: Presses Universitaires de France, 1950)–includes essay by Bachelard;

Patrick Mullahy, *Oedipe: Du mythe au complexe. Exposé des théories psychanalytiques,* preface by Bachelard (Paris: Payot, 1951);

Albert Ginet, *Berceuse pour aucun sommeil,* preface by Bachelard (Perpignan: A. Vinas, 1951);

Albert Flocon, *Traité du burin,* preface by Bachelard (Paris: Blaizot, 1952);

Jean-Edouard Spenlé, *Les grandes maîtres de l'humanisme européen,* preface by Bachelard (Paris: Corrêa, 1952);

Paul Diel, *Le symbolisme dans la mythologie grecque: Etude psychoanalytique,* preface by Bachelard (Paris: Payot, 1952);

"La Vocation scientifique et l'âme humaine," in *L'Homme devant la science: Texte des conférences et des entretiens* (Neuchâtel: La Baconnière, 1953), pp. 1–29;

Juliette Boutonier, *Les dessins des enfants,* preface by Bachelard (Paris: Scarabée, 1953);

Albert Burloud, *Psychologie de la sensibilité,* preface by Bachelard (Paris: Colin, 1954);

"Le nouvel esprit scientifique et la creation des valeurs rationnelles," in *Encyclopédie française, tome 19: Philosophie, Religion* (Paris: Société nouvelle de l'Encyclopédie française, 1957), pp. 14-14–14-15;

"Cosmos et Matière," in Laure Garcin, *Peintures récentes et dessins* (Paris: Galerie 93, 1957);

"Lyrisme et silence," in *Max Picard zum siebzigsten Geburtstag,* edited by Wilhelm Hausenstein and Benno Reifenberg (Erlenbach-Zurich: Rentsch, 1958), pp. 155–157;

Jules Duhem, *Histoire des origines du vol à réaction,* preface by Bachelard (Paris: Nouvelles Editions Latines, 1959);

Jean Revol, preface by Bachelard (Brussels: Museum of Fine Arts, 1961);

Roger Plin, *dessins, sculptures,* preface by Bachelard (Paris: Paul Cézanne Gallery, 1961);

Simon Segal, *Segal ou l'ange rebelle,* edited by Waldemar George, preface by Bachelard (Geneva: Cailler, 1962).

SELECTED PERIODICAL PUBLICATIONS–UNCOLLECTED: "La richesse d'inférence de la physique mathématique," *Scientia: Revue internationale de Synthèse scientifique* (1928): 44;

Review of Francis Warran, *L'oeuvre philosophique de Hoené Wronski: Textes, commentaires et critiques,* in *Revue de Synthèse* (April–October 1934): 252–253;

"Lumière et substance," *Revue de Métaphysique et de Morale,* 41 (1934): 343–366;

"Pensée et langage," *Revue de Synthèse,* 8 (1934): 81–86, 237–249;

"Idéalisme discursive," *Recherches philosophiques,* 35, no. 4 (1934): 21–29;

"Le surrationalisme," *Inquisitions,* no. 1 (1936);

"Logique et épistémologie," *Recherches philosophiques,* 6 (1936–1937): 410–413;

"La continuité et la multiplicité temporelle," *Bulletin de la Société française de philosophie,* 37 (1937): 53–81;

"Un livre d'un nommé R. Descartes," *Archeion,* 19 (1937): 161–171;

Review of Armand Petitjean, *Imagination et réalisation,* in *Nouvelle Revue Française,* 48 (1937): 455–456;

"La psychanalyse du feu," *Nouvelle Revue Française,* 51 (1938): 225–238;

"Le bestiaire de Lautréamont," *Nouvelle Revue Française,* 53 (1939): 711–734;

"Lautréamont mathématicien," *L'usage de la parole,* 1 (December 1939): 15;

"La déclamation muete," *Exercice du Silence* (1942);

Review of Pierre Ducasse, *Méthode et intuition chez Auguste Comte: Essai sur les origines intuitives du positivisme,* in *Revue philosophique de la France et de l'Etranger,* 132 (1942–1943): 85–90;

Review of Stéphane Lupasco, *L'expérience microphysique et la pensée humaine, Revue philosophique de la France et de l'Etranger,* 132 (1942–1943): 155–158;

"L'imagination aérienne: Les Constellations," *Poésie,* 43, no. 15 (1943): 5–12;

"Le ciel bleu et l'imagination aérienne," *Confluences,* 3, no. 25 (1943): 417–460;

"La philosophie scientifique de Léon Brunschvicg," *Revue de Métaphysique et de Morale,* 50 (1945): 77–84;

"Lautréamont, poète du muscle et du cri," *Cahiers du Sud,* no. 275 (1946): 31–38;

"Le vin et la vigne des Alchimistes," *Formes et Couleurs,* no. 1 (1946);

"Le complexe d'Atlas," *Formes et Couleurs,* no. 2 (1946);

"La maison natale et la maison onirique," *Lettres,* 23 (1947): 5–17;

"La philosophie dialoguée," *Dialectica,* 1 (1947): 11–20;

"De la nature du rationalisme," *Bulletin de la Société française de philosophie,* 44, no. 2 (1950): 45–86;

"Les tâches de la philosophie des sciences," *Informations philosophiques,* 1, no. 1 (1951): 1–9;

"Le cosmos du fer," *Derrière le Miroir,* nos. 90–91 (October–November 1956);

"Lettre à Vandercammen," *Marginales* (February 1958): 160–163;

"Message de Gaston Bachelard," *Cahiers Internationaux du Symbolisme,* no. 1 (1963): 5–6.

Gaston Bachelard occupies a pivotal position in twentieth-century French intellectual life. His works and reputation span the two fields that, in modern European culture, are generally considered antitheses: poetics and science. In each of these fields Bachelard carved out a distinctive reputation characterized by his rejection of the methodological conventions of his precursors and contemporaries. The significance of his work can be gauged by the extension of his influence beyond the philosophy of science and poetics and into the philosophy of the human sciences (as in the work of Michel Foucault), the literary criticism of scholars such as Roland Barthes and Jacques Derrida, and the history of science (as exemplified by Georges Canguilhem). In contrast to his centrality within French intellectual culture, the uneven translation of Bachelard's work into English has linked his name in Anglo-American cultures to his works on poetics rather than science. This uneven process of translation has hampered his reception within the Anglo- American tradition of the philosophy of science, despite the continuing currency of many of his ideas for this field.

Gaston Bachelard was born in Bar-sur-Aube, a small town in Champagne, France, on 27 June 1884. His parents kept a small tobacco and newspaper shop in the main street close to where his father's family had worked as shoemakers. While there was no tradition nor emphasis upon competitive academic culture within his family, as a child Bachelard excelled at school and showed a particular talent for the study of literature. Largely self-taught, his academic path was only determined when Bachelard was in his late thirties. Before he studied philosophy, Bachelard's early adulthood was spent working for the postal service, serving in the Signals Corps during World War I, and working as a teacher of science and mathematics at the Collège de Bar-sur-Aube.

Bachelard left Bar-sur-Aube in 1902 but returned to his native town seventeen years later to study at the conclusion of World War I. From the time he left until the outbreak of the war Bachelard worked as a teaching assistant in the provinces at Sézanne Collège (1902) and as a postal clerk at Remiremont from 1903 to 1905. He did his military service as a telegraphist at Pont-à-Mousson from 1905 to 1907, and worked in the administrative section of the postal service at the Gare de l'Est station in Paris from 1907 to 1913. While in this latter post Bachelard studied for and received his *licence* (bachelor's degree) in mathematical science from the Lycée Saint-Louis in 1912. In 1913, with the intention of studying to become an engineer and with the aid of a scholarship in mathematics from the Lycée Saint-Louis, he took leave from his position to prepare for the examination for engineering students in telegraphy. Bachelard never became an engineer, however, and did not complete any further formal study for nearly nine more years.

While on his leave, on 8 July 1914 Bachelard married a schoolteacher from his region, whose name has been lost to posterity. His studies and his married life were interrupted, however, when Bachelard was mobilized on 2 August 1914. After the war, in which he served for thirty-eight months in a combat unit and was awarded the Croix de Guerre for his service in the trenches, he abandoned his aspirations for engineering and in 1919 began to teach physics and chemistry at the Collège de Bar-sur-Aube. On 20 June 1920 his wife died, a few months after giving birth to their only child: a daughter, Suzanne. Bachelard never wrote of his wartime experiences nor his bereavement; during this tumult he received his *licence* in philosophy after one year of study in 1920. Now in his mid thirties, Bachelard rapidly advanced in his philosophy career. He became qualified to teach philosophy as an *agrégé* (state-certified teacher) in 1922 and, at the age of forty-three, he completed two *theses d'Etat* (doctoral theses) from the Sorbonne in 1927: *Essai sur la connaissance approchée* (An Essay on Knowledge by Approximation) and *Etude sur l'évolution d'un problème de physique: La propagation thermique dans les solides* (A Study on the Evolution of a Problem of Physics: Heat Transfer in Solids). In this same year Bachelard began to teach part-time at the Université de Dijon, while still working at the Collège de Bar-sur-Aube.

In 1930 Bachelard left Bar-sur-Aube and his position as a teacher there to take up a full-time appointment as professor of philosophy at the Faculty of Letters at the Université de Dijon. During his time at Dijon, Bachelard formed a strong friendship with Gaston Roupnel, a physicist whose interests, like Bachelard's, extended beyond his scientific field. Bachelard met Roupnel, whose novel *Siloë* (1927) later became the occasion for a work of his own, in 1927. At Dijon, Bachelard prefigured the path of his later career at the Sorbonne by teaching, in addition to philosophy, French literature to foreign students.

During his ten years at Dijon, Bachelard published eight books as well as many articles, reviews, and conference papers. The books composed during this period fell into two main areas: epistemology and studies of consciousness and time. In the area of epistemology Bachelard established his reputation for polemic, attacking the prevailing philosophy of science, which, he argued, was an inadequate tool to understand the radical innovations of twentieth-century science. His early works on consciousness and time had a similar refrain: he documented the break twentieth-century science represented from previous conceptions of "ordinary consciousness." Henri Bergson and Edmund Husserl were marked as early adversaries to Bachelard's chosen emphasis on the interruptions to ordinary consciousness that Albert Einstein's theory of relativity entailed for physics. Bergson and Husserl each advanced philosophical positions that were critical of the evidence of ordinary consciousness, but neither developed a position able to accommodate twentieth-century science. Husserl's phenomenology was conceived as an inquiry into the faculty and process of the constitution of objects of perception. This focus on perception was the source of the limitations of phenomenology for the philosophy of science. Husserlian phenomenology aimed to describe objects in a way that freed them from conceptual presuppositions, but its fidelity to the appearance of the object was incompatible with the shift in physics to nonperceptual data.

Bachelard's *La dialectique de la durée* (translated as *The Dialectic of Duration*, 2000), published in 1936, had the popular philosophy of Bergson as its main target. Bergsonian philosophy used a conception of continuous time to oppose the "limited knowledge" of science. The main contrast in Bergson's thought was between time as duration and time perceived through practical consciousness. The "intuition" defended by Bergson's philosophy was of a knowledge unable to be attained by inference or observation. The independence of intuition from reason or experience qualified it as a concrete knowledge of an interrelated whole prior to the abstractions and fragmentation of modern science. The hostility of Bergson to science made him a constant target of critique in Bachelard's epistemology. Following from Bachelard's 1932 work *L'intuition de l'instant: Etude sur la "Siloë" de Gaston Roupnel* (The Intuition of the Instant: A Study of Gaston Roupnel's "Siloë"), in which the intuition of Bergsonism is opposed to the discontinuous time of contemporary physics (the "instant"), in *La dialectique de la durée* Bachelard applies his conception of dialectical knowledge as the identification of the binding character of prescientific experience on knowledge to Bergson. In each book Bachelard defends and develops his own conception of scientific rationalism against the movement that he, and the supervisors of his doctoral theses from the Sorbonne, Abel Rey and Léon Brunschvicg—saw as a form of anti-intellectualism. Rationalism in Bachelard's eyes is a struggle against those easy intuitions that constitute obstacles to the counterintuitive, mathematic basis of modern science. Bergson's faith in intuition as a route to the attainment of "true knowledge" defends the certainty of immediacy that modern science interrupts. For Bachelard, not only is the intuitive the source of obstacles for scientific development; it also consists of a private form of knowledge that is removed from the institutionally framed interactions between scientists that are the practice and "proof" for the techniques of modern science. In the final chapter of *La dialectique de la durée* Bachelard coins the phrase "l'analyse de rythme" (rhythm-analysis) to explain how the discontinuities of modern physics and other sciences can be brought into a rhythm of life. The poetic rhythm that he finds in Surrealism is used by

Bachelard with his daughter, Suzanne, and three unidentified colleagues at the Collège de Bar-sur-Aube, where he taught physics and chemistry from 1919 until 1930 (from Jean Claude Margolin, Bachelard, 1974; Thomas Cooper Library, University of South Carolina)

Bachelard as a model for the relation between the effort of critique required by intellectual knowledge and the repose that follows and complements it.

In 1938 Bachelard published two books. The first, *La formation de l'esprit scientifique: Contribution à une psychanalyse de la connaissance objective* (Formation of the Scientific Spirit: A Contribution to the Psychoanalysis of Objective Knowledge), links his conception of epistemology with the task of reconceptualizing cognitive acts, and the second, *La psychanalyse du feu* (translated as *The Psychoanalysis of Fire*, 1964), was a source of controversy at the Sorbonne, where Bachelard's interest in the topic of the poetic imagination was greeted with suspicion. In *La formation de l'esprit scientifique*, Bachelard argues for a conception of the development of knowledge as a dialectical engagement with previous knowledge. The errors against which scientific knowledge develops have a partly psychological basis, and dealing with the epistemological obstacles of what he termed the "pre-scientific mind" requires dismantling the privilege of immediate experience and the modern philosophical value placed on generality in knowledge. Bachelard's epistemology of post-Einsteinian science located the break between modern science and ordinary knowledge as a function of the mathematicism of science. This mathematicism and the break it represents with the "pre-scientific mind" requires of reason a polemical role in relation to ordinary knowledge. This polemic is also internal to science, however, and the epistemologist accordingly must conduct a "psychoanalysis" of the scientific mind in order to identify in it and clear from it the sedimentations of prescientific conceptualizations.

La psychanalyse du feu, one of Bachelard's best-known books on the poetic imagination, is a marked contrast to these epistemological questions. Discontent with what he later saw as a confused account of poetic truth, Bachelard claimed that of all his works it was this one that he wished to rewrite. In it he argues that fire is not simply an epistemological obstacle but a law under which dreams and poetic images are linked to the four elements. His argument in this work, which advances a conception of poetic truth that his epistemology classifies as an obstacle, was perhaps less sensational than its effect. Bachelard's appointment to the Sorbonne as Rey's successor in the prestigious chair of the history and philosophy of science two years later, in 1940, coincided with what many of his new colleagues feared was a shift in his intellectual interests from the sciences to poetics. In the first year of his appointment, and despite the fact that the chair was dedicated to science, it became clear that Bachelard's publishing and teaching would accommodate both of his interests. Prior to leaving Dijon, Bachelard published *La psychanalyse du feu* in 1938; then in 1939 he published a book on the Comte de Lautréamont (translated, 1986), the topic of many of his literature classes there, as well as one of his best-known works in the field of epistemology: *La philosophie du non: Essai d'une philosophie du nouvel esprit scientifique* (translated as *The Philosophy of No: A Philosophy of the New Scientific Mind,* 1968). The *non* in the French title of this work refers to the major scientific renovations of "ordinary" experience of space and time (non-Euclidean geometry and non-Newtonian physics). Bachelard establishes here the limited determination, or historically provisional nature, of scientific concepts. The present state of science and the norms of what counts as scientific are not to be treated as a completed doctrine, nor is past science to be queried for its failure to embody these norms. What Bachelard terms "the new scientific spirit" is here envisaged as a polemical rationalism that does not so much dispense with Newtonian physics as confine it to a limited terrain of operationality. Here Bachelard develops a conception of regional rationalism that became hugely influential for the work of

Canguilhem in the life sciences and Foucault in the human sciences. In his advocacy for this rationalism Bachelard criticizes the modern, specifically Kantian tradition of philosophical concepts of reason and the subject insofar as they posit universal conditions that the course of the developments within the contemporary sciences are incompatible with. The significant distinction drawn here, and in Bachelard's subsequent works on science, is that scientific knowledge proceeds by the rectification of the old science it breaks with, and that this rectification is blocked by the tradition of epistemology–current in the French academy and represented by the influential epistemology of Emile Meyerson–that works on the model of a universal reason. Philosophy, Bachelard argues, needs to subordinate the concepts of its historical practice to the current practice of science.

After *La philosophie du non* Bachelard turned once more to poetry and specifically the problem of defining the poetic image. The interrelation between these two fields of Bachelard's work has been a source of contention among scholars. While references to literary figures and especially poets appear in his works on science, Bachelard's writing on poetry, like his work on science, is an attempt to read literature as a break with "ordinary consciousness." In his treatment of the poetic image Bachelard discovered the material sources of the rational mind. In his conception of material imagination he argues that the human relation to matter is structured by a drive to intellectuality. The origins of poetic images of matter are less a function of instinct than a threshold phenomena of rational consciousness. These images precede contemplation and contribute, as does science, to a break with the given. In the four books he published in this field in the 1940s–*L'eau et les rêves: Essai sur l'imagination de la matière* (1942; translated as *Water and Dreams: An Essay on the Imagination of Matter,* 1983); *L'air et les songes: Essai sur l'imagination du mouvement* (1943; translated as *Air and Dreams: An Essay on the Imagination of Movement,* 1988); *La terre et les rêveries de la volonté: Essai sur l'imagination des forces* (1948; translated as *Earth and Reveries of Will: An Essay on the Imagination of Matter,* 2002); and *La terre et les rêveries du repos: Essai sur les images de l'intimité* (Earth and Reveries of Rest: An Essay on Images of Intimacy, 1948)–Bachelard outlines a material account of the imagination. Against literary criticism, which Bachelard charged with having become distant from the experience of reading literature, he attributes to poetic images the quality of novelty that sustains for the reader an experience of possibility. In the link Bachelard forges between the image and possibility he dismantles the status of the image in idealism as a representation in order to conceive of it as an act. The agency of the image is measured by its ability to puncture reality in favor of the possible. One of the premises behind Bachelard's work on the poetic image is the association of literature with mere fabrications. His work on the poetic image distinguishes accordingly between *rêve* (dream, or escapism) and the *reverie* (daydream) that re-creates and surpasses the real.

Between 1949 and 1957 Bachelard continued to write and teach on poetics but again tended to concentrate his energies on problems of post-Einsteinian epistemology. In works such as *Le matérialisme rationnel* (Rational Materialism, 1953) Bachelard grapples with the implications for the history of science of the radical innovations of twentieth-century science. The conventional practice of the history and epistemology of science and the ordinary understanding of reality together transport to science a false concept of historical continuity. The discontinuous nature of contemporary scientific development with other forms of understanding, as well as the accelerated time of contemporary science, in which internal epistemological breaks are the norm, has significant implications for the philosophy of science. Among these implications Bachelard identifies an idea that he uses to great effect within his poetics: just as the poetic image carries a novelty that is obscured by the received frameworks of literary criticism, so too it is only at the level of particular examples that the philosophy of science can give general lessons. Bachelard's final works on epistemology left some of his critics unsatisfied. If he is credited with explaining the constitutive role of errors in scientific knowledge and the operation of such knowledge as an obstacle to the future course of scientific development, critics have found such reflections insufficient to the task Bachelard set himself: namely, to develop an historical epistemology adequate to the new science.

After his retirement in 1955 Bachelard returned again to the problems of the poetic imagination, publishing three books in this field: *La poétique de l'espace* (1957; translated as *The Poetics of Space,* 1964), *La poétique de la rêverie* (1960; translated as *The Poetics of Reverie: Childhood, Language and the Cosmos,* 1969), and *La flamme d'une chandelle* (1961; translated as *The Flame of a Candle,* 1988). In these works he emphasizes the poetical role of language. *La poétique de l'espace* is one of Bachelard's most influential texts on poetics. In it he gives a clear account of the principles orientating his poetics. These principles all emanate from his interest in the shared nature of the effect of the poetic image. From the force of the poetic image follows Bachelard's distrust of the causal explanations of the image in psychoanalysis and psychology. These latter are unable to access the novelty that structures the ontology of the poetic image.

Bachelard's interest in the particular image, detached from the explanations of its significance by meaning-orientated discourses, is also to be distinguished from the comprehensive approach to poetry in literary criticism. Where Bachelard finds literary criticism closed

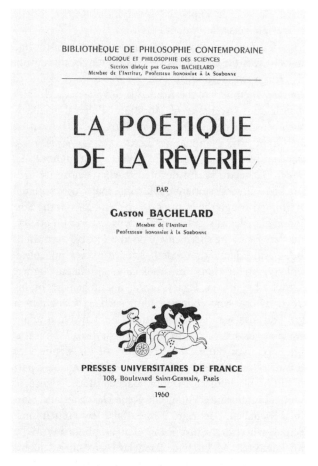

BIBLIOTHÈQUE DE PHILOSOPHIE CONTEMPORAINE
LOGIQUE ET PHILOSOPHIE DES SCIENCES
Section dirigée par Gaston BACHELARD
Membre de l'Institut, Professeur honoraire à la Sorbonne

LA POÉTIQUE
DE LA RÊVERIE

PAR

GASTON BACHELARD

Membre de l'Institut
Professeur honoraire à la Sorbonne

PRESSES UNIVERSITAIRES DE FRANCE
108, Boulevard Saint-Germain, Paris
—
1960

Title page for the second of three works Bachelard published on the poetic imagination in the late 1950s and early 1960s. It was translated in 1969 as The Poetics of Reverie: Childhood, Language and the Cosmos *(Thomas Cooper Library, University of South Carolina).*

to the significance of the poetic image, he is drawn back—against his earlier distrust—to the pertinence of phenomenology. While the phenomenological conception of consciousness constitutes an obstacle to the course of scientific development, its attitude of suspension is well suited to the novel force of the poetic image. In contrast to Husserlian phenomenology, however, Bachelard's "phenomenology" is made to accommodate the linguistic form of the image. But psychoanalysis, rather than phenomenology, serves as a negative model for his mature poetics. In his introduction to this work Bachelard criticizes psychoanalysis for trying to explain "the flower by the fertilizer." In this image, in Bachelard's view, the contrast between the novelties of science and poetry are at their clearest. The profound changes new ideas install in contemporary science have been measured against and tested through a body of historically accepted ideas. The novelty of poetic acts, in contrast, is not able to be measured, tested, or explained by a past. Rather, poetic images are acts that originate a world.

Gaston Bachelard's appointment to the Sorbonne in 1940 was the last of his career. He taught there until his retirement in 1955. In 1955 he was elected as one of the forty members of the Académie des Sciences Morales et Politiques (Academy of Moral and Political Sciences) of the Institut de France, and in 1961 he was awarded the Grand Prix National des Lettres for *La flamme d'une chandelle* by a unanimous jury vote. Throughout his career Bachelard was a devoted teacher whose lectures touched a diverse student population, many of whom tell of sitting through the lectures on epistemology at the Sorbonne in order to secure a spot for his lectures on poetry. His defense of the specificity of poetry, like his account of the specific demands modern science makes on epistemology, made him an unusually influential figure. Bachelard's strange legacy is the inimitableness of his ideas. Those who followed him, such as Canguilhem and Foucault, tended to extend his influence and adapt his ideas into areas of their own expertise. While this influence may mute the recognition of his significance outside of France, within France, where his texts are part of the high-school curriculum, Bachelard is a figure of national significance. Alongside René Descartes and Cardinal Richelieu, Bachelard is one of the few French intellectuals who has the distinction of an amphitheater in the Sorbonne named for him. Bachelard was buried in his hometown of Bar-sur-Aube three days after his death on 16 October 1962. He was survived by his daughter, Suzanne, who herself went on to teach philosophy at the Sorbonne.

Bibliographies:

Jean Rummens, "Gaston Bachelard: Une bibliographie," *Revue Internationale de Philosophie,* 17 (1963): 492–504;

H. Choe, *Gaston Bachelard: Epistemologie. Bibliographie* (Frankfurt am Main & New York: Lang, 1994).

Biography:

Jean Claude Margolin, *Bachelard* (Paris: Seuil, 1974).

References:

Hervé Barreau and others, *Bachelard: Exposés* (Paris: Union Générale d'Editions, 1974);

Maurice Blanchot, "Vaste comme la nuit," *Nouvelle Revue Française,* 93 (1959): 684–695;

Georges Bouligand and others, *Hommage à Gaston Bachelard: Etudes de philosophie et d'histoire des sciences* (Paris: Presses Universitaires de France, 1957);

Georges Canguilhem, "L'Histoire des sciences dans l'œuvre épistémologique de Gaston Bachelard," *Annales de l'Université de Paris,* 33 (1963): 24–39;

Mary Ann Caws, *Surrealism and the Literary Imagination: A Study of Breton and Bachelard* (The Hague: Mouton, 1966);

Robert Champigny, "Gaston Bachelard," in *Modern French Criticism: From Proust and Valéry to Structuralism,* edited by John K. Simon (Chicago: University of Chicago Press, 1972), pp. 175–191;

C. G. Christofides, "Gaston Bachelard's Phenomenology of the Imagination," *Romantic Review,* 52 (1961): 36–47;

Jacques Gagey, *Gaston Bachelard; ou, La conversion à l'imaginaire* (Paris: Rivière, 1969);

Jean Hyppolite, "Gaston Bachelard ou le romantisme de l'intelligence," in *Hommage à Gaston Bachelard* (1957);

Bruno Latour and G. Bowker, "A Booming Discipline Short of Discipline: Social Studies of Science in France," *Social Studies of Science,* 17, no. 4 (1987), pp. 715–748;

Dominique Lecourt, *Bachelard; ou, Le jour et la nuit: Un essai du matérialisme dialectique* (Paris: Grasset, 1974);

Lecourt, *Marxism and Epistemology: Bachelard, Canguilhem, and Foucault,* translated by Ben Brewster (London: New Left Books, 1975);

Mary McAllester, "Gaston Bachelard: Towards a Phenomenology of Literature," *Forum for Modern Language Studies,* 12 (April 1976): 91–104;

McAllester, "Polemics and Poetics: Bachelard's Conception of the Imagining Consciousness," *Journal of the British Society for Phenomenology,* 12 (January 1981): 3–13;

Walter Privitera, *Problems of Style: Michel Foucault's Epistemology,* translated by Jean Keller (Albany: State University of New York Press, 1995), pp. 1–25;

Jean-Pierre Roy, *Bachelard; ou, Le concept contre l'image* (Montreal: Presses de l'Université de Montréal, 1977);

Vincent Therrien, *La révolution de Gaston Bachelard en critique littéraire: Ses fondements, ses techniques, sa portée. Du nouvel esprit scientifique à un nouvel esprit littéraire* (Paris: Klincksieck, 1970);

Mary Tiles, *Bachelard: Science and Objectivity* (Cambridge & New York: Cambridge University Press, 1984);

Michel Vadée, *Bachelard; ou, Le nouvel idéalisme épistémologique* (Paris: Editions sociales, 1975);

Marcel Voisin, *Bachelard* (Brussels: Editions Labor, 1967).

Roland Barthes

(12 November 1915 – 26 March 1980)

Frederick Luis Aldama
University of Colorado, Boulder

BOOKS: *Le Degré zéro de l'ecriture* (Paris: Seuil, 1953); translated by Annette Lavers and Colin Smith as *Writing Degree Zero* (London: Cape, 1967; New York: Hill & Wang, 1968); republished with *Nouveaux essais critiques* (Paris: Seuil, 1972);

Michelet par lui-même (Paris: Seuil, 1954); translated by Richard Howard as *Michelet* (Oxford & New York: Hill & Wang, 1987);

Mythologies (Paris: Seuil, 1957); translated by Lavers as *Mythologies* (London: Cape, 1972; New York: Hill & Wang, 1972);

Sur Racine (Paris: Seuil, 1963); translated by Howard as *On Racine* (New York: Hill & Wang, 1964);

Essais Critiques (Paris: Seuil, 1964); translated by Howard as *Critical Essays* (Evanston, Ill.: Northwestern University Press, 1972);

La Tour Eiffel, by Barthes and André Martin (Paris: Delpire, 1964); translated by Howard as *The Eiffel Tower and Other Mythologies* (New York: Hill & Wang, 1979);

Eléments de semiologie (Paris: Seuil, 1964); translated by Lavers and Smith as *Elements of Semiology* (London: Cape, 1967; New York: Hill & Wang, 1968);

Critique et vérité (Paris: Seuil, 1966); translated by Katrine Pilcher Keuneman as *Criticism and Truth* (London: Athlone, 1987; Minneapolis: University of Minnesota Press, 1987);

Système de la mode (Paris: Seuil, 1967); translated by Howard and Matthew Ward as *The Fashion System* (New York: Hill & Wang, 1983; London: Cape, 1985);

L'Empire des signes (Geneva: Albert Skira, 1970); translated by Howard as *Empire of Signs* (New York: Hill & Wang, 1982; London: Cape, 1983);

S/Z (Paris: Seuil, 1970); translated by Richard Miller as *S/Z* (New York: Hill & Wang, 1974; London: Cape, 1975);

Sade, Fourier, Loyola (Paris: Seuil, 1971); translated by Miller as *Sade, Fourier, Loyola* (New York: Hill & Wang, 1976);

Roland Barthes (from The Grain of the Voice: Interviews 1962–1980, *translated by Linda Coverdale, 1985; Thomas Cooper Library, University of South Carolina)*

Analyse structurale et exégèse biblique: Essais d'interprétation, by Barthes and others (Neuchâtel: Delachaux & Niestlé, 1971); translated by Alfred M. Johnson Jr. as *Structural Analysis and Biblical Exegesis: Interpretational Essays* (Pittsburgh: Pickwick, 1974);

Le Degré zéro de l'ecriture suivi de nouveaux essais critiques (Paris: Seuil, 1972); translated by Howard as *New Critical Essays* (New York: Hill & Wang, 1980);

Le plaisir du texte (Paris: Seuil, 1973); translated by Miller as *The Pleasure of the Text* (New York: Hill & Wang, 1975; London: Cape, 1976);

Roland Barthes par Roland Barthes (Paris: Seuil, 1975); translated by Howard as *Roland Barthes by Roland Barthes* (New York: Hill & Wang, 1977; London: Macmillan, 1977);

Fragments d'un discours amoureux (Paris: Seuil, 1977); translated by Howard as *A Lover's Discourse: Fragments* (New York: Hill & Wang, 1978; London: Cape, 1979);

Arcimboldo, text by Barthes (Paris & Milan: F. M. Ricci, 1978);

Leçon: Leçon inaugurale de la Chaire de sémiologie littéraire du Collège de France, prononcée le 7 janvier 1977 (Paris: Seuil, 1978);

Sollers écrivain (Paris: Seuil, 1979); translated by Phillip Thody as *Sollers Writer* (London: Athlone, 1987); translation republished as *Writer Sollers* (Minneapolis: University of Minnesota Press, 1987);

La chambre claire: Note sur la photographie (Paris: Gallimard, 1980); translated by Howard as *Camera Lucida: Reflections on Photography* (New York: Hill & Wang, 1981);

Littérature et réalité (Paris: Seuil, 1982);

L'obvie et l'obtus (Paris: Seuil, 1982); translated by Howard as *The Responsibility of Forms: Critical Essays on Music, Art, and Representation* (New York: Hill & Wang, 1984; Oxford: Blackwell, 1986);

All Except You: Paul Steinberg (Paris: Reperes, 1983);

Le Bruissement de langue (Paris: Seuil, 1984); translated by Howard as *The Rustle of Language* (New York: Hill & Wang, 1986; Oxford: Blackwell, 1986);

L'Aventure Sémiologique (Paris: Seuil, 1985); translated by Howard as *The Semiotic Challenge* (New York: Hill & Wang, 1988; Oxford: Blackwell, 1988);

Incidents (Paris: Seuil, 1987); translated by Howard as *Incidents* (Berkeley: University of California Press, 1992).

Collection: *Œuvres complètes,* 3 volumes, edited by Eric Marty (Paris: Seuil, 1993–1995).

Editions in English: *Image, Music, Text,* selected and translated by Stephen Heath (New York: Hill & Wang, 1977; London: Fontana, 1977);

A Barthes Reader, edited, with an introduction, by Susan Sontag (New York: Hill & Wang, 1982; London: Cape, 1982).

In 1976 Roland Barthes was appointed chair of literary semiology and elected to the Collège de France—the highest position in the French academic system. His lifelong pursuit of formally interpreting the sign systems that make up culture from literature and biography to wrestling and restaurant menus was finally fully recog-nized. Together with the French academy's acknowledgment of Barthes's force as a seminal intellectual figure, these two events reflect also his worldwide recognition as a critic, writer, and thinker. Put simply, if Barthes had not developed his particular strain of "semiology"—a system for decrypting social life as ideologically motivated textual signs, springing from Ferdinand de Saussure's theories of how language signifies—contemporary scholarship in the humanities would not be the same. Barthes extended de Saussure's linguistic theory to include all textual representations in everyday life. His massive intellectual range and production—writing dozens of critical studies on literature and modern-day culture as well as metaphysical meditations beginning in the early 1950s and ending with his death in 1980—have been a constant source of inspiration for a wide range of theoretical endeavors, such as narratology and the multifaceted interdisciplinary scholarship that informs literary hermeneutics, poststructuralism, and cultural studies.

Roland Gérard Barthes was born on 12 November 1915 in Cherbourg, France. When Barthes was born, his Protestant, middle-class mother, Henriette Barthes (née Binger), was twenty-two years old, and his Catholic father, Louis Barthes, whom he never knew, was thirty-two; one month before Barthes's first birthday, his father was killed serving as a navy officer in World War I. As a boy, Barthes followed his mother to Paris. Much to his mother's chagrin, she took up work as a bookbinder to support herself and her young son. As a boy, Barthes left Paris during his school holidays and spent time with his father's family in the peaceful town of Bayonne in the Gascony region of southwest France. With his paternal aunt and grandmother, he learned to draw, paint with watercolors, and play the piano. He was especially fond of listening to his grandmother's stories and reading novels and history books—all of which fed his imagination and satisfied his huge appetite for knowledge. During this period Barthes first began to conceive of himself as an intellectual and a writer.

As a teenager Barthes had already become enamored with Marcel Proust and Honoré de Balzac. Reading such authors supplied him with the critical lens through which he could interpret life close to home. He learned from these authors how to "read" his family with a critical eye. He mentions in an interview in 1971 for *Tel Quel* (scripted by Jean Thibaudeau) that his visits to Bayonne played "a Proustian role in my past—a Balzacian role, too, since I heard there, over many visits, the discourse of a certain type of provincial bourgeoisie, which from an early age I found more diverting than oppressive." Reading and studying literature as a teenager helped him to understand otherwise indescribable feelings that had weighed heavily on him, such as the reason for his family's conflicts. He learned to see these conflicts, for example, not so much as the difference between his mother's Protestantism and his paternal family's provincial bourgeois Catholicism but as his family's playing out of class and religious roles generally. Barthes began to develop an awareness of how language–the Parisian cosmopolitan dialect as opposed to the provincial bourgeois Bayonne dialect–carries implicit class prejudices. These prejudices became even clearer to Barthes when his mother's love affair with a man named André Salzedo in Bayonne became known to the paternal family. On 11 April 1927 Barthes's half brother, Michel Salzedo, was born, and his mother was cut off completely from the paternal family; the family's underlying class and religious prejudices were now made explicit. One of Barthes's biographers, Louis-Jean Calvet, aptly sums up: "This period was to leave young Roland bitter, and his feelings of bitterness remained with him throughout his life. All his friends could sense a kind of aggression, resentment or bitterness." Reading did not help heal the wound left after young Barthes was cut off from his father's family and from holidays filled with reading, painting, and playing the piano. The causes for the pain–the mother's banishment was just the excuse the family needed to exercise their class and religious superiority–were long lasting for the young, sensitive Barthes and later found more formal shape in his theoretical texts.

As a teenager Barthes used his piano-playing skills to make money as an instructor while attending lycée, where he pursued a deep interest in literature and philosophy, studying for his *baccalauréat* (university entrance exams) at different high schools in Paris. Barthes excelled at his studies and intended to pass the *baccalauréat* with high grades, with the hope of bringing him one step closer to realizing his ultimate goal: to take his exams for the *aggrégation* (France's highest degree for lycée teachers and professors of undergraduates). The realization of this goal was curtailed, however, when, just before taking his exams for the *baccalauréat*, he was diagnosed with tuberculosis. On 10 May 1934 Barthes was told that he suffered from haemoptysis, a condition that left him with a lesion on his left lung that then led to pulmonary tuberculosis. Instead of taking the exams for the *baccalauréat* with his peers that spring, he was sent away to a sanatorium in the town of Bedous in the Pyrenees. After months of treatment and convalescence, Barthes passed his *baccalauréat* in the fall of 1934. Shortly after passing the exam, however, he took another turn for the worse and was readmitted for more treatment. He was finally deemed fit enough to return to Paris, and in the fall of 1935 he began studying for a degree in classics. In the

1971 interview with *Tel Quel*, Barthes recalls how "being good at literature I had planned, up until my illness, to go to the *Ecole normale supérieure;* but when I returned to Paris in 1935 I settled for a degree in classics; a meager investment for which I compensated by forming the Classical Theater Group of the Sorbonne with Jacques Veil."

Illness, however, again interrupted Barthes's studies for his *licence* in classical letters at the Sorbonne between 1935 and 1939 with frequent trips to French and Swiss sanatoriums for tuberculosis patients. His studies thus proved a difficult (most town libraries, except those in Switzerland, refused to lend books to tuberculosis patients) and long process. Regardless of difficulty of pursuing his studies, he managed to continue reading and thinking about writers such as Gustave Flaubert, Proust, André Gide, Paul Valéry, Charles Baudelaire, and Walt Whitman, who were some of the writers he returned to later in his life. During one period of treatment in a sanatorium, Barthes met the figure who helped him focus and think through more deeply problems of class and language that had plagued him since his childhood in Bayonne: Trotskyist typographer Georges Fournié, who introduced Barthes to Marxism. Fournié's socialist bent appealed to Barthes, who was at the time deeply engaged with Jean-Paul Sartre's *Qu'est-ce que la littérature?* (1947; translated as *What Is Literature?,* 1949). He remarks in the 1971 interview with *Tel Quel* how this identifies a period when he became "a Sartrean and a Marxist." When he returned to Paris, however, in spite of his newfound engagement with Marxism, he did not take up with the French Communist Party nor participate in trade-union organization. Rather, his brand of Marxism was expressed in his scholarly pursuits and theoretical inquiries.

Barthes experienced a series of relapses of pulmonary tuberculosis in October 1941 and again in July 1943. Though he was deemed physically unfit and unable to participate in World War II, he was also forced to delay taking his exams for the *avocational licence* in grammar and philology. He passed this exam in the fall of 1943 and then began looking for work. Though he held several piecemeal high-school teaching jobs, it was not until 1948 that he secured a university-level teaching position at the French Institute in Bucharest, Romania. This appointment was followed in 1950 by a one-year appointment as a "reader" (lecturer) for the Service de l'enseignement des relations culturelles (Service for the Teaching of Cultural Relations) at the University of Alexandria in Egypt. Barthes arrived in Alexandria filled with ideas on class ideology and language but lacked a methodology for holding them together. His friendship with a fellow lecturer, A. J.

Barthes's mother, Henriette, née Binger. His father, Louis, was killed in World War I a month before Barthes's first birthday in 1916 (photograph by Robert David; from Louis-Jean Calvet, Roland Barthes: A Biography, *translated by Sarah Wykes, 1995; Thomas Cooper Library, University of South Carolina).*

ically reproduce dominant ideologies. As such, Barthes also turned to Claude Levi-Strauss's groundbreaking structuralist approach to cultural anthropology, knowing that a focus on structures would help him discover a theoretical approach to literature—and culture—that would help him answer questions such as those posed by Sartre: What is the role of the writer, of literature, and of the reader? His first forays into literary interpretation began with essays that analyzed Proust, Balzac, François-Auguste-René de Chateaubriand, and Gide. Barthes started moving away from those general questions that gravitate around the writer and his relationship to language and audience, as per Sartre, and sought to uncover the author/reader relationship as it is constructed by the formal structures and styles of the text.

In 1947 Barthes published the first of these essays in the journal *Combat*—whose first editor was one of Barthes's most admired writers, Albert Camus. Seeing promise in Barthes's early essays, the editor of the cultural section of *Combat,* Maurice Nadeau, published them—an act that opened doors into Parisian intellectual circles for the otherwise unknown Barthes. In 1953 Barthes collected these essays along with new essays to publish as the book *Le Degré zéro de l'ecriture* (translated as *Writing Degree Zero,* 1967). He would have preferred being published by the prestigious French publishing behemoth, Gallimard, who had published Sartre, but they refused, so he went with the smaller, but more radically progressive, Editions du Seuil. Barthes's small book was heralded as a brilliant and groundbreaking approach to reading language and literature within an historical and cultural context. It caught the critical favor of many powerful scholars, including his original champion Nadeau, who wrote in a July 1953 issue of *Les Lettres nouvelles* (New Letters) that Barthes's scholarly debut was remarkable, with an analysis of literature that offers "new 'views' on language . . . with all of the scientific exactitude that the subject can stand." Other French theorists such as Maurice Blanchot and Gérard Genette also wrote favorably of Barthes's book. Genette, who pursued his own interest in narrative structure, wrote in a review essay titled "L'envers des signes" (Obverse of Signs), collected in *Critical Essays on Roland Barthes* (2000), that *Le Degré zéro de l'ecriture* marked a radical shift in narrative analysis with its semiological approach, which reveals "a much vaster world than that of literature" and provides a "rhetoric" for understanding "the world of *communication,* of which the press, the cinema, and advertising are the most obvious and best-known forms."

With *Le Degré zéro de l'ecriture* Barthes introduces a wide-ranging, radically new method for studying literature. Barthes also introduced his colleagues to the possi-

Greimas, helped change this circumstance. Greimas introduced Barthes to the father of modern linguistics, de Saussure, as well as to the theoretical achievements of linguists Roman Jakobson and Louis Hjelmslev. While studying de Saussure, Jakobson, and Hjelmslev, Barthes conversed endlessly and enthusiastically with Greimas about the function and structure of everyday speech acts and literary language.

Barthes showed a special interest in the figurative function of metaphor and metonymy. He was drawn to linguistics as the theoretical model that promised a radical break from a belletristic approach to literature. In Alexandria he began formally to bring together linguistic theory with a Marxist analysis to reveal how the deep structures of a literary text exist within and uncrit-

bility of studying–unlike the scholarship of his day, which analyzed a small cadre of revered dead writers–living, contemporaneous authors such as Alain Robbe-Grillet, Michel Butor, Philippe Sollers, and Raymond Queneau. In response to these texts, Barthes began to develop a "meta-language" that brought together and caused "*friction* between literary language and critical language," according to Genette's pronouncement in "Obverse of Signs." To uncover just how a given literary text signifies, Barthes proposes that the scholar defamiliarize those formal structures and linguistic codes that make up the text. Here, Barthes elaborates on the concept of the signifier/signified/sign relationship developed by de Saussure and later elaborated by Jakobson and Hjelmslev. To this end he identifies the sign not as a natural phenomenon of language but as arbitrarily constructed and manipulated by ideological interest. For example, he looks at linguistic structures and styles of nineteenth-century authors such as Flaubert and Balzac to analyze their use of realism, which renders reality coherent and "real" but also, as Barthes reveals, covers over and renders "natural" a bourgeois agenda.

Barthes contrasts this analysis with a reading of twentieth-century authors such as Sollers who employ what he identifies as "le degré zéro de l'ecriture" (writing degree zero)–a colorless style that bares the artificial, ideologically biased ordering of reality in the literary text. Clearly, Barthes favored such zero-degree writers, whose prose destabilizes dominant ideological systems. Moreover, he championed otherwise academically neglected writers such as Sollers because of their use of style and language that self-reflexively points to the artifice of the text and denaturalizes those nineteenth-century literary texts that traditionally render universal and coherent the relationship between the word and reality *hors texte* (beyond the text). The zero-degree writing exhibited by Queneau and Robbe-Grillet (as well as the earlier modernists Proust and Louis-Ferdinand Céline) destroys, for example, the descriptive depth of the adjectival phrase in order to foreground language as an "empty" system and an artificial construct; style and language need not naturalize hierarchies of class difference. Influenced by Bertolt Brecht's concept of the *verfremdungeffekt* (distance effect) in drama, Barthes considered this method of breaking a text down into its constituent linguistic units (signifier/signified/sign) and its subsequent reconstruction as a way to reveal the rules by which the text functions in its "natural," "ideologically innocent" state. Indeed, after Brecht's Berliner Ensemble toured Paris in 1954, Barthes wrote an editorial titled "La Révolution brechtienne" that appeared in *Théâtre Populaire* in 1955; it was collected in *Essais Critiques* (1964). Both methods, according to Barthes, func-

tioned to denaturalize the textual sign and remind its audience that bourgeois culture is an effect of history and not a manifestation of nature. Thanks to zero-degree writing, Barthes concluded, "the human problem is disclosed and delivered without bias, and the writer is always an honest man."

Barthes chose to use a more iconoclastic essay form to introduce his new approach to literary analysis. Since many of the chapters that make up *Le Degré zéro de l'ecriture* were originally published as articles in journals and magazines, the book is presented as a collection of essays. Barthes deliberately chose, however, to break from the conventions of scholarship that privilege the well-documented and archived model of analysis–books with chapters, footnotes, bibliographies, and indexes–and that focus on the same canon of dead authors. He chose instead to write without extratextual citation and to use a less pedantic and rigid essay form to try out (in French *essai* means "to try out") his ideas. Like Robbe-Grillet and Queneau, who denaturalize a nineteenth-century realism used as a means to normalize bourgeois ideology, he used his essay to challenge academic institutional conventions. In both content (his efforts to denaturalize the sign) and in form (his less academic essay style) Barthes sought to destabilize his reader's "naturalized" perception of dominant social and cultural norms, hence, his celebration of writers who use a colloquial, spoken French rather than those traditionally identified as composing the backbone of French literary history, who use the stiff and stale language of the "passé historique" (past historic). For example, he describes the preterit as presupposing "a world which is constructed, elaborated, self-sufficient, reduced to significant lines, and not one which has been sent sprawling before us, for us to take or leave."

Barthes sidestepped the concept of *clarté* (clarity), which he believed to be inherent in a classical conception of a directly accessible sign, and avoided using the footnote, emphasizing the need for the reader of his criticism to think things out for himself. Often, too, his personalized and subjective style announces his own subjective presence and particular tastes that determine the focus of his interpretations. He chose the essay form to offer his readers a rigorous yet self-reflexively subjective analysis. In both the form and content, then, Barthes sought to challenge the concept that the scholarly text leads de facto to universal truths and understanding. For Barthes, language and therefore the literary work is a text that cannot carry a universal truth; it simply provides a situation about which one makes *truths*. If, as Barthes proposes, the sign is that which stands for something else and if the world is made up of signs, then all signs, all texts, can be interpreted as lacking in truth–including his own methods of analysis. As such, he deflated both the traditional scholarly essay that created the illusion of making natural and coherent the representation of truth of the linguistic sign and the institution of reading literature that overly revered dead canonical authors. He sought to complicate the act of interpreting and reading to enliven the literary works themselves.

In 1954 Barthes deepened his development and application of a semiological metalanguage in his first book-length study, *Michelet par lui-même* (translated as *Michelet,* 1987). Here, Barthes continues to use a meditative essay style, not to write a biography or a history filled with facts and events, but to identify the nineteenth-century historian and author of *Histoire de France* (History of France, 1833–1867), Jules Michelet, as a complex psychological figure with certain obsessions. He begins the book by explaining that "the reader will not find either a history of Michelet's ideas, or a history of his life, still less an explanation of one by the other." Indeed, this "little book," as Barthes calls it, grew out of an earlier interest in those passages in Michelet's work that were filled with literary allusion and that used a narrative technique common to fictional narratives; this interest began when Barthes was drawn to Michelet's Romantic histories while convalescing as a young adult in a Swiss sanatorium, where he began indexing sentences that resonated with significance. In organizing *Michelet par lui-même* Barthes similarly clusters together thematic obsessions that he sees recurring in Michelet's work into categories such as "feminary" or "bestiary," for example. By organizing the book into a series of Michelet's obsessions, Barthes attempts to go against the grain of traditional French scholarship that worshiped Michelet and emptied him of meaning, seeking instead to anchor him back in his body–a body that also reflected a complex literary psyche. In a similar gesture, Barthes inscribes in the margins of *Michelet par lui-mème* a variety of categories that identify his own presence and tastes. For Barthes the critic, like his subject, is not beyond the corporeal.

When *Michelet par lui-même* first appeared, it received mixed reviews and created a rift between the formation of a new, progressive, intellectual "Left" and an old-guard, conservative "Right." For Albert Béguin, Barthes's idiosyncratic, pleasure-themed analysis of Michelet proved a breath of fresh air. In his essay "Pre-criticism," collected in *Critical Essays on Roland Barthes,* Béguin concludes, "I hope that Roland Barthes, with the same diviner's rod at the tip of his fingers will one day traverse Balzacian territory." Critics affiliated with *Combat* also applauded Barthes. In "Michelet Not Dead," another essay collected in *Critical Essays on Roland Barthes,* Lucien Febvre writes: "I consider Roland Barthes's book to be one of the most lively and astute

pieces of writing ever devoted to Michelet." Many critics, however, such as the prestigious literary historian Sorbonnard Raymond Picard, forcefully resisted *Michelet par lui-même,* attacking Barthes's highly unorthodox method of interpreting the revered historian. Picard made this attack more formal in 1965 with his publication of *Nouvelle critique ou nouvelle imposture?* (translated as *New Criticism or New Fraud,* 1969).

After publishing *Michelet par lui-même,* Barthes broadened his analytic purview to include not just biographical subjects and literary works but also cultural texts more generally. Driven by the desire to reveal how different texts work as *discours* (discourse) to manipulate people in their everyday life, he began to apply his semiological method to reveal as a construct "la naturalité de signe" (the naturalness of the sign) by emphasizing the artificial nature of all communication systems. In 1957 he published a collection of essays–previously written for *Les Lettres nouvelles*–titled *Mythologies* (translated, 1972). Here, his leftist and Sartrean-based study of the life of signs within society takes on subjects such as wrestling, striptease, advertising, newspapers and magazines, and photography as examples of modern-day "mythologies" that transmit a bourgeois ideology. (Again, Barthes's unorthodox style and controversial subject matter meant that the more established and conservative publisher Gallimard rejected the book, and once again the more progressive Editions du Seuil agreed to publish it.) A myth, according to Barthes, is the translation of an artificially constructed bourgeois ideology into "natural" laws; myths confuse culture and history with nature to reinforce and make normal social stereotypes. Here, Barthes considers it the job of the critic to use the semiological method to decode discourses–language systems–present in these different phenomena that make up everyday life in France, and to expose these myths as delusions. For example, he opens *Mythologies* with the statement: "I resented seeing Nature and History confused at every turn, and I wanted to track down, in the decorative display of *what-goes-without-saying,* the ideological abuse which, in my view, is hidden there."

Barthes then delves into critical readings of wrestling, for example, which he interprets not as an innocent sport but rather as a spectacle that reproduces a conflict between Good (a white-costumed wrestler) and Evil (a black-costumed wrestler) and subtly coerces the audience into participating in a form of moralism that ultimately reproduces destructive class hierarchies. He reads the striptease not as an act of disrobing but as a larger reflection of a society that naturalizes the hyper-sexualizing and disempowering of women. For Barthes, the exercise of decoding such cultural texts involves identifying the primary message–stripping or wrestling,

The Institut Français des Hautes Etudes in Bucharest, Romania, where Barthes held his first university-level teaching position from 1948 to 1950 (photograph by Philippe Rebeyrol; from Louis-Jean Calvet, Roland Barthes: A Biography, *translated by Sarah Wykes, 1995; Thomas Cooper Library, University of South Carolina)*

for example—then uncovering how this primary message functions to conceal a secondary message. Thus, he seeks to identify the "factual" system of representation in which objects are given meaning and then to analyze how this "factual" system (the fact of wrestling, for example) solicits emotional responses to seduce its audience and cover over ideology. The audience takes sides (the "good" side) and therefore naturalizes bias and prejudice.

Barthes similarly interprets a photograph of a black soldier saluting in French army fatigues. Here, he reads the picture as a sign that appears within the historical context of the Algerian war of independence and thus that naturalizes the process of realigning an older image (codes of costume and gesture traditionally associated with the appearance of a white soldier) with a new image (the black soldier) to create a new concept in the viewer's mind: French imperialism is good for both Africans and French. In the other essays that make up the collection, Barthes further decrypts how cultural iconography and activities circulate as myths and distort reality for ideological effect. In the article "La

Grand tromperie" (The Great Hoax), first published in *La Nouvelle Revue français* (1957), then collected in *Critical Essays on Roland Barthes,* Maurice Blanchot sums up Barthes's combining of linguistics and phenomenology to decipher the "hidden center of meanings by going towards them according to a movement which mimes that of their constitution and also by a sort of sovereign negligence, capable of leaving aside the presuppositions of all naïve knowledge." In *Mythologies,* Barthes seeks self-consciously to employ a semiological analysis to open his readers' eyes to all facets of life and its underlying textual codes that work in the interest of the bourgeoisie.

The publication of *Le Degré zéro de l'ecriture* and *Michelet par lui-même* did not guarantee Barthes a steady place in the French academy. His unorthodox approach made it difficult for him to secure funding for his next projects. For example, the Centre national de recherche scientifique (National Center for Scientific Research) refused to fund his proposal to study the French fashion system. By the early 1960s, however, the academy—with much pressure from a rising and powerful cadre of new scholars—had begun to change what it considered legitimate subjects of study. During this period Barthes, along with Leo Spitzer and others, put together a colloquium on modern literature in the Belgian town of Liège, from where they launched the attack against the insularism of French universities (evidenced by the fact that professors were unfamiliar with the work of the Russian formalists, with Anglo-Saxon New Criticism, and with German research) and against a university system that was still preoccupied with excavating origins in a traditional literary historical fashion. Also, Barthes began finding common intellectual ground with certain prominent intellectuals, such as Georges Friedmann, Claude Brémond, and Edgar Morin, as well as with the younger scholars Christian Metz, Tzvetan Todorov, and Jean-Claude Milner—all of whom wrote for the review *Communications* and who sought to make visible the coherent semiological goals of the *nouvelle critique* (new criticism).

Barthes's election in 1960 as director of studies of "Sociology of signs, symbols and representation" in the economics and social sciences department at the Ecole pratique des hautes études moved his semiological approach from the margins of academia to its center. Though Barthes's idiosyncratic analysis of literature kept him out of literature departments in France, his position at the French Ecole pratique des hautes études provided him with the funding and research opportunities to continue his work—and to build a team of like-minded scholars. During this period, Barthes published his second book-length biographical study, *Sur Racine* (1963; translated as *On Racine,* 1964), not so much because of a personal draw to this writer but because it allowed him yet again to apply his semiological approach to the much-worshiped dramatist and poet Jean Racine. Barthes interpreted Racine's characters as figures that act out elemental myths and archetypal conflicts between primitive forces; he read Racine's biography, filled with family jealousies, as the central motivating force in his plays. Here Barthes launches into a redefinition of tragedy as spatially constructed in relation to three tragic sites: the chamber, the antechamber, and the outside world. Tragedy itself exists between the inner chamber (the interior, psychological place) and the exterior, social spaces. He removes traditional considerations of drama according to concepts of process and duration, proposing in its place that drama—and tragedy in particular—exists spatially and beyond time and history. Like his earlier interpretation of Michelet, Barthes calls attention to the deficiencies in literary and biographical scholarship on Racine, denouncing the traditional use of literary monographs as commentaries to reproduce an aura of genius around the author. For Barthes, then, Racine is less the genius

that traditional scholarship identifies and more a figure whose theater of the Comédie Française is a spectacle that transmits deeper social manipulations and ideological motives. History and biography take on a secondary role in Barthes's "anthropology" of Racine, focusing instead on how this figure represents through language and theatrical convention dominant myths and ideologies.

After Barthes published *Sur Racine,* the more traditional literary and historical scholars were up in arms. Already filled with vitriol after the publication of *Michelet par lui-même,* Picard published a book-length attack on Barthes, *Nouvelle critique ou nouvelle imposture.* Picard critiques harshly Barthes's semiological and iconoclastic analytic method employed both in *Michelet par lui-même* and *Sur Racine,* exclaiming how he uses a "show-off kind of criticism," filled with pretentious neologisms and jargon that promise "a rigor that his thought belies." Picard calls Barthes an academic fraud and identifies his scholarship as careless and misguided—typical, in Picard's mind, of the scholarship characterized by the practitioners of the *nouvelle critique.* In response to Picard's attack, in 1966 Barthes published a collection of essays titled *Critique et vérité* (translated as *Criticism and Truth,* 1987), in which he lays out programmatically what the goals of the study of literature might be: to formalize an interpretative framework sensitive to the multiple interpretations of a text and to account for the underlying logic of its signs as governed by a set of rules that exist independently of the author. More vehemently than ever, Barthes uses de Saussure's theory of language as social phenomenon to discuss the role of the author who has the choice to select and combine elements of this system to destabilize received meaning. (In his earlier *Eléments de semiologie* [1964; translated as *Elements of Semiology,* 1967] Barthes also uses this semiological approach to analyze how food and clothing signify in French society according to the rules of the signifier/signified/signification relationship.) After Barthes proposed that *langue* (language) functions as a system of conventions one could identify in literature and that *parole* (word) identifies the potential for the individual to act against predetermined systems, the writer and critic alike could use language to effect social change.

Though Picard and other scholars thought they would obtain a swift victory over Barthes, the outcome was quite the opposite. With his publication of the forceful *Critique et vérité,* which firmly positioned him within the *nouvelle critique,* Barthes proved a great rhetorician (well versed in all the procedures of persuasion such as voice, tone, and argument) who curried tremendous support from up-and-coming powerful figures such as Genette, Sollers, Todorov (*Théorie de la littéra-*

ture, 1966), Julia Kristeva (who introduced Barthes to Mikhail Bakhtin's postformalist theory of intertextuality), and others affiliated with the review *Tel Quel.* "L'affaire Picard," as it became known, put Barthes on the map as a symbol of counterestablishment scholarship in a period when posters of Mao Tse-Tung, Che Guevara, and Nikolai Lenin plastered hallway corridors at the Sorbonne, and intellectuals and college students were in the media limelight decrying French imperialism. Fellow semiologist and innovative novelist Serge Doubrovsky's response to Picard's attack appeared in his book, *Porquoi la nouvelle critique* (1966) and reflects well this general climate. He identifies Picard as representative of a backward scholarship that threatens to put humanistic scholarship "back three centuries" and that reveals "sprouting beneath the pomp of academic caps, the donkey ears of obscurantism." Indeed, "l'affaire Picard" helped centrally situate Barthes in the progressive academic limelight and glued together the common bond between him and other critics of the *nouvelle critique.*

By the late 1960s the divide between the intellectual Left and Right in the French academy that appeared in "l'affaire Picard" had deepened. By this time, as well, Barthes had himself become famous as a successful director of semiology *(chef de travaux)* at the Ecole pratique des hautes études and had added to his list of critically lauded publications such books as *La Tour Eiffel* (1964; translated as *The Eiffel Tower and Other Mythologies,* 1979) and *Système de la mode* (translated as *The Fashion System,* 1983). When *Système de la mode* appeared in 1967, Barthes expanded his semiological approach to literature and biography to include French fashion. In this exhaustive study, Barthes proved to the world how semiotics could be applied to analyze preexisting constructions of cultural objects such as clothing. He maintains that in the "discourse" of clothing, fashion magazine advertising works at the level of denotation and connotation to create a language system that signifies independent of the wearer. According to Barthes, to make for a better society, one should be aware that sartorial choices participate in a class- and gender-based ideological system. After the publication of *Système de la mode,* Barthes wrote the hugely influential essay "L'effet de réel" (The Reality Effect). First published in *Communications,* volume 11 in 1968, Barthes turned to literature, but this time to identify an "effet de réel" wherein even the seemingly most insignificant details have significance in that they function to cover over the deeper ideology of a given text. Indeed, Barthes considered that the "tyrannical constraints of what we must call aesthetic verisimilitude" conceal an underlying worldview that is prevalent at the moment when the text is written.

Barthes around the time his first book, Le Degré zéro de l'ecriture *(1953; translated as* Writing Degree Zero, *1967), was published (photograph by Robert David; from Louis-Jean Calvet,* Roland Barthes: A Biography, *translated by Sarah Wykes, 1995; Thomas Cooper Library, University of South Carolina)*

That same year, in his essay "La mort de l'auteur" (The Death of the Author; first published in *Aspen Magazine* [1967]), Barthes radically expanded his concept of the "reality effect" with the introduction of his concept of the "death of the author." In this controversial essay he suggests that, if the "real" in narrative realism is a way to cover over ideology, then one must identify the author as participating within a larger system governed by ideology. He replaces the concept of *auteur* (author), which connotes creative genius, with that of *scripteur* (writer), which defines the author as simply an entity invested with the possibility of putting together certain combinations of words and sentences. The reader would now be free to interpret the text without the constraints of the traditional method of discerning the author's intention. With Barthes's "mort de l'auteur" he authorized the reader to interpret the literary text idiosyncratically, marking the birth of the polysemic reading that is beyond the control of the author and that is written and rewritten in the act of reading. He concluded this essay: "We now know that a text is not a line of words releasing a single 'theological' meaning (the 'message' of an Author-God) but a multidimensional space in which a variety of writings, none of them original, blend and clash."

In the 1970s Barthes was caught up in the sweep of the poststructuralist wave. The new school of thought known as deconstruction had found a place in philosophy and history departments and was gaining momentum in France. In 1966 Michel Foucault had published his best-selling *Les Mots et les choses: Une archéologie des sciences humaines* (translated as *The Order of Things: An Archeology of the Human Sciences,* 1970) and Jacques Lacan had published the first volume of his *Ecrits* (*Writings;* translated, 1977), and in 1967 Jaques Derrida had published *De la grammatologie* (translated as *Of Grammatology,* 1976). In a series of lectures on Balzac's *Sarrasine* (1831) between 1968 and 1969, Barthes had successfully tested a deconstructive conceptual grid that moved away from his earlier structuralist-based semiological method.

In 1970 Barthes published *L'Empire des signes* (translated as *Empire of Signs,* 1982), in which he formally critiques his earlier semiological analysis, identifying it as naive and lacking a more radically articulated awareness that all language and therefore all experience is a textual construct. After several trips to Japan, Barthes fixated on the idea of a nation constructed through a language and metaphysical system that confounds a westerner's mastery. In his eighty meditations on, for example, sumo wrestling, the figure of the geisha, the handwritten kanji character, the philosophy of Zen, and the emptiness of haiku, Barthes undertakes a "reading" of Japan as a textual construct that defies mastery. For Barthes, Japan is a world made up of signs that he cannot interpret and therefore of a cultural system that resists mastery. It is a world that he holds above that of the West, where sign systems simply give the illusion of a subject's grasping of reality through language. Unlike his earlier, more scientifically based semiotics, *L'Empire des signes* is a journey into what Barthes identifies as "the untranslatable"; the Western subject experiences a shock in which, he writes, "everything Occidental in us teeters and the rights of the 'father tongue' vacillate." According to Barthes, Japan is made of signs that operate under a completely different system and metaphysical premise than those of the West, with its belief in the universal concept of language, truth, and the supremacy of the individual. Japan is a sign system that resists singular, definitive interpretation; it is a polysemous

text made up of signs that unfix meaning and resist being controlled by their referent. Barthes's Japan is about the collective and the experience of the infinite play of signifiers that unfold into nothingness.

In a similar deconstructive move away from his earlier semiotics-based analysis, Barthes transformed his lectures on Balzac's *Sarrasine,* given at the Ecole pratique des hautes études, into a book, *S/Z* (1970; translated, 1974). In an impressive 80,000-word study of the 10,000 words that make up Balzac's novella, Barthes seeks to point readers and critics away from an impulse to make a text cohere and make sense. By dividing up his analysis into 561 numbered fragments, Barthes aptly displays that reading should not follow the text but should instead open up the possibility for digression. For Barthes, it is in the digression—and not in the attempt to control a text such as *Sarrasine*—that interpretation and meaning can occur: "If a reading attempts to describe a given text, something different than the text is produced. . . . Hence, reading operates somewhere between the reader and the text as an activity and creativity whose historicity cannot be understood on the same planes as those of reader and text." Although Barthes still identifies structures in *S/Z,* he does so to insist on the destruction of the seeming unity of the text. He innovates five codes for deconstructing the different linguistic and cultural elements that regulate how the text signifies: the "hermeneutic" regulates the posting and solving of a mystery; the "semic" controls how the signified-signifier-signification relationship connotes meaning; the "symbolic" is concerned with processes of transformation of meaning through language substitution within the text; the "proairetic" controls the plot and actions of the text; and the "referential" codifies the references of the text to a reality *hors texte.* Barthes provocatively reads against the grain of traditional literary interpretation, reading the referential code in *Sarrasine* not as a reference to an extratextual or historical reality *hors texte,* but to what Barthes calls the *doxa:* stereotypes, notions of human psychology, and behavior characteristic of Balzac's epoch. As such, Balzac is simply quoting and not destabilizing the ideological underpinnings of this era.

At first, Barthes identifies *Sarrasine* as a text with a "limited plurality," or as a *lisible* (readerly) rather than a *scriptible* (writerly) text. By the time he finishes reading *Sarrasine* sentence by sentence according to the five codes, however, he disrupts its seeming unity as a *lisible* text. With his aim of "de-originating" the text accomplished, he affirms the primacy of the reader's presence in producing the text. Barthes identifies the reader as a "plurality of other texts, of codes which are infinite" that can either actively produce or simply consume the text. The more the text is *scriptible,* the more the reader can engage it in a process of infinite meaning-making. The *scriptible* text has a greater degree of the semic code present, which invests it with a greater degree of polysemy and openness; however, as Barthes proves, even a *lisible* text such as *Sarrasine*, which is seemingly constrained, can include a variety of different voices and complex levels of conflict and contradiction. Finally, Barthes identifies the writer's "self" as a convention of the text that he or she writes; the writer's "self is a 'creature of paper'" or else an "effect of language." In a poststructural maneuver, then, the text, reader, and author are textual (grammatical) constructs that intersect with cultural codes and that ultimately do not refer to an objective reality. According to Barthes, if the text, the reader, and the author can be found everywhere, then they lack a substantive presence. He concludes that "text," "reader," and "author" are illusory constructs.

Barthes's close reading of codes to destabilize traditional understandings of the text (reader, author, and narrative) continues in his 1971 book *Sade, Fourier, Loyola* (translated, 1976). In *Sade, Fourier, Loyola* Barthes focuses on the Marquis de Sade, Charles Fourier, and Saint Ignatius of Loyola—or as he identifies them, "the evil writer, the great utopian, and the Jesuit saint"—all of whom create new *logothétes* (systems of language) that rupture sign systems and defy the reader's impulse to control and contain their texts. Each writer is interesting to Barthes because each advocates some form of exclusion from the world; each divides, reorders, and theatricalizes language and representation. These *logothétes* use these different orders to destabilize the traditional author's use of language to refer to the "real" of reality outside the text. Rather, they use language to refer to a reality that could never exist beyond the text: Sade's thousands of sex acts, Fourier's Age of Harmony, Loyola's God. In reading Sade, Barthes identifies a Sadean grammar (his stylized tableaux that describe postures, figures, operations, and scenes that exist independently of reality) that calls attention to a reader's process of trying to make sense of that which is represented textually but is impossible to experience in the world outside the text. He also calls attention to how this Sadean grammar plays with a nonmimetic language to engage the reader's imagination and frustrate comprehension simultaneously. Such writer-intellectuals as Sade, Fourier, and Loyola are aware that language mediates understanding of reality, so they invent texts that foreground the meaning-making process, based on the arbitrary relationship between the signifier/signified and the sign, to complicate the referential function of their text and to frustrate the reader's attempt to master its meaning. Finally, Barthes also acknowledges his own participation within conventions of language manipulated by ideology, self-consciously identifying his own

Barthes the year he published Sade, Fourier, Loyola *(1971), which he described as a book about "the evil writer, the great utopian, and the Jesuit saint" (from* The Grain of the Voice: Interviews 1962–1980, *translated by Linda Coverdale, 1985; Thomas Cooper Library, University of South Carolina)*

analysis as an impossible process of interpreting a text that is itself an untranslatable transcript or reality.

In this poststructuralist phase, Barthes no longer considered that the analysis of universal structures that govern language was a viable tool to decrypt the text, the individual, and society. Instead, he turned to investigations that focused on the indeterminate space of the body. In 1973 he published *Le plaisir du texte* (translated as *The Pleasure of the Text*, 1975), in which he offers a series of meditations on the corpus of the text and the reader's body and their different respective modes of pleasuring and experiencing pleasure. Barthes declared of the body: "We have several of them; the body of anatomists and physiologists, the one science sees or discusses: this is the text of grammarians, critics, commentators, philologists (the pheno-text). But we also have a body of bliss consisting solely of erotic relations, utterly distinct from this first body: it is another contour, another nomination. . . . The pleasure of the text is irreducible to physiological need." The focus on pleasure was a way for Barthes to vitalize it as a site of study traditionally neglected in studies of literature and philosophy and repressed in Western society generally. Barthes identifies two different forms of pleasure: *Jouissance* is pleasure that disrupts conventions and that overturns authorized pleasures that middle-class conservatives lay claim to; it is beyond language. And *plaisir* is the authorized pleasure, where the individual is conscious of his or her enjoyment; it is a pleasure that can be articulated through language. Barthes sets these two forms of experiencing pleasure not just in the reading of the text, but in its own articulation of pleasure. So the "texte de plaisir" gives pleasure, but it is an illusory one because it functions within the dominant social relations that shape subjectivity; on the other hand, the "texte de jouissance" refuses to exist within dominant conventions and therefore causes a certain vertigo and a sense of fragmentation and loss of subjectivity. For Barthes, any given text will have more or less *plaisir* or *jouissance*. If the text has an excess of *jouissance,* it will have more moments identifiable as perverse, fetishistic, and not culturally respectable. If it has an excess of *plaisir,* it will have moments that convey a sense of pleasure as being reproducible within the reader and society at large. He writes: "The pleasure of the text is that moment when my body pursues its own ideas–for my body does not have the same ideas I do." Finally, his investigation of the pleasures of the text allows him to generate a critique of a society that represses and suppresses individual, pleasuring bodies.

More and more Barthes turned his readings of literature and culture from that recognized as criticism and interpretation to the more subjective form of narrative fictional expression. At one point, he even likened his role as a critic to that of a *scripteur* of novels. In 1975 he published *Roland Barthes par Roland Barthes* (translated as *Roland Barthes by Roland Barthes,* 1977), in which he presents a series of fragmented meditations on his life as reapprehended through his body's experiences. According to Barthes, because he experiences the world through language, his body is inseparable from language. This premise allows him to launch into meditations on how language intersects with a metaphysical probing of subjectivity–a subjectivity that he then deconstructs through his own articulation of how codes of language function to convey certain meanings, for example, in the reprinted photographs of himself in the book. Moreover, *Roland Barthes par Roland Barthes* is Barthes's innovative exercise in writing an autobiography that self-reflexively performs autobiography as spectacle–a series of fragments and displaced modes of representation covered over, made seamless, and natu-

ralized as "real" in the genre traditionally. As François Dosse sums up in volume one of *History of Structuralism:* "He wanted to present himself as an essential language effect more than a reference to any extra-textual nature. This subject was to produce a Barthes-effect, a polyphonic, mobile image of multiple compositions and recompositions in which only a few hints were given for a freely interpretable score." For Barthes, the writing of a self-reflexive autobiography ultimately leads him to read his own body and love (for his mother in particular) as polysemous and forever indeterminate.

Barthes's preoccupation with writing books that were more subjectively driven and novel-like continued with his publication in 1977 of *Fragments d'un discours amoureux* (translated as *A Lover's Discourse: Fragments,* 1978). In this best-selling book–his interview with the popular television book program *Apostrophes* boosted sales tremendously–which grew out of a series of lectures conducted during a seminar on Johann Wolfgang von Goethe's *Die Leiden des jungen Werthers* (Sorrows of Young Werther, 1774) over a two-year period, Barthes explored the nature of love and passion as clustered into "figures" of the lover's discourse and identified by themes such as "Absence" (Behavior), "Contacts" (Contacts), "Corps" (Bodies), "Démons" (Demons), "Exil" (Exile), "Fâcheux" (Unfortunate), "Nuages" (Clouds) and "Je-t-aime" (I love you). Here, Barthes explores not just the pain of love but the perverse pleasure derived from being in an unbearable and intractable romantic relationship. Barthes reads the love affair as analogous with the reader's intractable engagement with the text. Just as the lover finds himself in need of interpreting the ambiguous signs of the actions of *l'amoureurt* (the loved one) or *l'objet aime* (the loved object), the reader likewise engages with the literary (or critical) text. Both lover and reader are dissatisfied with mere surfaces, so both attempt to understand their texts from within. Where the lover wants to control the text, however, the reader attempts to engage and actively produce rather than simply consume the text. Barthes deliberately uses a fragmented style and fills out the marginalia of *Fragments d'un discours amoureux* with intertextual references to Balzac, Lacan, and Goethe to discourage the reader from consuming rather than producing meaning.

In his 1980 publication of *La chambre claire: Note sur la photographie* (translated as *Camera Lucida: Reflections on Photography,* 1981) Barthes turns more forcefully to himself as the subject of textual decoding. Here, his deconstructive tendency crystallizes in his use of a fragmented, self-reflexive, and allusive prose style, as if to say that one can read Barthes but can never know Barthes. (He uses this same technique in his autobiography, *Roland Barthes par Roland Barthes.*) Inspired by his deep feelings of abandonment and trauma over his mother's death, this book (developed from an earlier essay, *Le message photographique* [The Photographic Message], published in *Communications,* 1961) takes the form of a treatise devoted to photography—not photographic history, but how the photograph can be understood as a series of snapshots of history experienced on a personal level. For Barthes, the multiple meanings of the frozen image are ultimately contained by the overwhelming presence of death. According to Barthes, that which appears in the image is already dead. Here, Barthes uses the term *studium* to identify the scientific approach of misreading a photograph as fact and *punctum* to identify the resistance of the photograph to such a scientific approach. Barthes's identification of the *punctum*—that small point that captures the eye—in a series of images connects his body and soul to the image/object. For Barthes, such photographs, with their revealing minor elements, stand out from the rest and are not to be possessed but rather emotionally relished and enjoyed. Barthes also distinguishes between "folle on sage" (mad or tame) photographs. The tame photograph is one in which the realism remains "relative, tempered by aesthetic or empirical habits." In the mad photograph the realism "is absolute, and so to speak, original, obliging the loving and terrified consciousness to return to the very letter of Time: a strictly repulsive movement which reverses the course of the thing, and which I shall call, in conclusion, the photographic *ecstasy.*" As such, different degrees of madness and tameness determine if a photograph calls attention to the unreality of the experience of its physical expression and the viewer's possession. More generally, the photograph allows Barthes to meditate on consciousness and the imagination: the process of negating consciousness as the world is emptied of ordinary qualities and transformed into a created, aesthetic object.

At the end of his life, Barthes was only interested in writing on objects, texts, or themes that inspired meditations on his subjective experience of the world. The posthumously published *Incidents* (1987; translated, 1992) was also such a subjective and fragmented meditation that focused on his gay sexual experiences in North Africa. His earlier development and employment of a semiological metalanguage to decode sign systems that gravitated around literature, food, clothing, and advertising had completely disappeared. Barthes now preferred to theorize the raw experiences of life. As Jonathan Culler summarizes Barthes's career as a critic in his *Roland Barthes* (1983): "Each time Barthes urged the merits of some new, ambitious project—a science of literature, a semiology, a science of contemporary myths, a narratology, a history of literary signification, a science of divisions, a typology of textual pleasure—he

Paperback cover for the U.S. edition of the 1977 English translation of Roland Barthes par Roland Barthes *(1975), a collection of fragmentary autobiographical meditations (Thomas Cooper Library, University of South Carolina)*

swiftly passed on to something else. Abandoning what he had set in motion, he often wrote wryly or disparagingly about his prior preoccupations." At the end of his career as a thinker and writer, he had shifted from a Sartrean/ Marxist linguistic interpretation of signs in his innovative readings of culture and society to a more self-reflexive mode of meditating on the self and the world.

By the time of his death on 26 March 1980, Barthes was an internationally recognized intellectual figure. His early struggle to open the eyes of the French academy to his different brands of interdisciplinary scholarship had succeeded. He had been the first chairman of literary semiology at the Collège de France and as such had attained the highest position in the French academic system. From the 1970s until his death (from pulmonary complications that resulted from being hit by a truck while crossing the road in front of the Collège de

Barthes on 7 January 1978, presenting the inaugural lecture after his appointment to the first chair of literary semiology at the Collège de France (from Louis-Jean Calvet, Roland Barthes: A Biography, *translated by Sarah Wykes, 1995; Thomas Cooper Library, University of South Carolina)*

France), his books sold well and his lectures were packed with students, schoolteachers, and preeminent academics. One of his former students, Kristeva, recalled in her essay "La voix de Barthes" (Barthes's Voice) (collected in *Critical Essays on Roland Barthes*) that he had a special gift for seducing audiences with a lecture style that was soft-spoken and that combined erudition with popular culture, metaphysical meditation with topics such as love and passion. Sollers, in an essay included in *Critical Essays on Roland Barthes,* identified Barthes as "one of the rare great writers of our time," who "invented sequence-writing, flexible montage, the block of prose in a fluid state, musical classification, the vibrant utopia of detail, a solid basis of a finally bearable (discreet) transformation of human relations, the syntactic *satori,* the irruption of language into the truth of language." By the end of the 1970s he had become one of France's most sought-after academics and theorists.

As a scholar and teacher, Barthes stirred peoples' minds. Through his books he gave impulse for others to do their own work. His impact on scholarship has been long lasting and far-reaching. His initial interest in textual structures stimulated the work of Genette, who

gave life to the field of narratology; Barthes's early work also had a huge impact on the young Todorov, who went on to develop tools to analyze narrative structure and genre. Theorists of genre more generally have used Barthes's identification of the vertical (paradigmatic) and horizontal (syntagmatic) process of textual production as a way to study, for example, the difference between a novel and a short story, showing how stories use metaphor to encode primary myths, satisfy paradigms of narrative closure, and balance a verticalized meaning (expository mode) with a horizontalized event-sequence (narrative mode). Across the Atlantic Ocean, Barthes's work helped form the generation that followed the New Critics, which includes Robert Scholes, Susan Sniader Lanser, and Seymour Chatman. The American critic Wayne Booth, in his *Critical Understanding* (1979), called him "the man who may well be the strongest influence on American criticism today."

Barthes's "La mort de l'auteur" helped open the door to what is now known as reader-response theory. As a result, signs replaced words, texts displaced works. Meaning was less a production of definition or authorial intention than what came to be known as textuality and a practice of reading that is well characterized by Umberto Eco's notion of the *opera aperta* (open work). His interrogation of traditional disciplinary bound-aries–psychology, linguistics, history, literature–as well as his later critique of universals and truths helped pave the way for ethnic and gender-based scholarship of the 1980s. This important debt is also visible in cultural studies, a field of literary scholarship that revisits old texts by embedding them within systems of other cul-tural texts. Without Barthes, feminist theory might not look the same. His "death of the author" liberated the woman reader in feminist scholarship; and his denatu-ralizing of social, sexual, and gender codes, along with his critique in *Le plaisir du texte* of the textual pleasure traditionally identified as a heroic masculine climax, also helped shape the feminist scholarship that set out to denaturalize patriarchal text systems. According to Gilles Philippe's 1996 catalogue of scholarly essays on Barthes, there are more than a thousand studies that focus on his work.

As a whole, Roland Barthes's semiological theo-ries and more personalized meditations attempt to artic-ulate the subject's relationship to and negotiation with history and society. Though there is much that Barthes is critical of, his work in toto has a certain utopian impulse; the sense that there might be a way–either through language, the body, or pleasure–that people might relate differently to one another and to the world they struggle to inhabit.

Interviews:

Le grain de la voix: Entretiens 1962–1980 (Paris: Seuil, 1981); translated by Linda Coverdale as *The Grain of the Voice: Interviews 1962–1980* (London: Cape, 1985; New York: Hill & Wang, 1985);

Jean Thibaudeau, "Responses: Interview with *Tel Quel*," translated by Vérène Grieshaber, in *The Tel Quel Reader,* edited by Patrick Ffrench and Roland-François Lack (London & New York: Routledge, 1998), pp. 249–267.

Bibliography:

Joan Nordquist, comp., *Roland Barthes: A Bibliography* (Santa Cruz, Cal.: Reference and Research Ser-vices, 1994).

Biography:

Louis-Jean Calvet, *Roland Barthes 1915–1980* (Paris: Flammarion, 1990); translated by Sarah Wykes as *Roland Barthes: A Biography* (Bloomington: Indiana University Press, 1995).

References:

Réda Bensmaïa, *The Barthes Effect: The Essay as Reflective Text,* translated by Pat Fedkiew (Minneapolis: University of Minnesota Press, 1987);

Wayne Booth, *Critical Understanding* (Chicago: Univer-sity of Chicago Press, 1979), pp. 69–70;

Jonathan Culler, *Roland Barthes* (New York: Oxford University Press, 1983);

François Dosse, *Le chant du cygne, 1967 à nos jours,* vol-ume 2 of *Histoire du structuralisme* (Paris: La Décou-verte, 1992); translated as *History of Structuralism,* 2 volumes (Minneapolis: University of Minnesota Press, 1997), pp. 98–105;

Serge Doubrovsky, *Pourquoi la nouvelle critique: Critique et objectivité* (Paris: Mercure de France, 1966); trans-lated by Derek Coltman as *The New Criticism in France* (Chicago: University of Chicago Press, 1973);

Lucien Febvre, "Michelet Not Dead," translated by Diana Knight, in *Critical Essays on Roland Barthes,* edited by Knight, pp. 31–33;

Gérard Genette, "L'envers des signes," in his *Figures: Essais,* volume 1 (Paris: Seuil, 1966), pp. 185–204;

Diana Knight, ed., *Critical Essays on Roland Barthes* (New York: G. K. Hall, 2000);

Julia Kristeva, "La voix de Barthes," *Communications,* 36 (1982): 119–122;

Michael Moriarty, *Roland Barthes* (Stanford, Cal.: Stan-ford University Press, 1991);

Maurice Nadeau, "Le degré zéro de l'écriture," *Lettres Nouvelles,* 1–5 (1953): 591–599;

Gilles Philippe, *Roland Barthes,* Bibliographie des Ecri-vains français, no. 3 (Paris & Rome: Memini, 1996);

Sorbonnard Raymond Picard, *Nouvelle critique ou nouvelle imposture?* (Paris: Pauvert, 1965); translated by Frank Towne as *New Criticism or New Fraud* (Pull-man: Washington State University Press, 1969);

Phillipe Sollers, "R.B.," *Tel Quel,* 47 (1971): 19–26;

Tzvetan Todorov, "Late Barthes," in *Critical Essays on Roland Barthes,* edited by Knight, pp. 123–128.

Jean Baudrillard

(27 July 1929 –   )

Jean Arnold
University of California, Riverside

BOOKS: *Le système des objets: La consommation des signes,* Bibliothèque Médiations, no. 93 (Paris: Denoël-Gonthier, 1968); translated by James Benedict as *The System of Objects* (London & New York: Verso, 1996);

La société de consommation: Ses mythes, ses structures, Collection "Le point de la question," no. 4 (Paris: S. G. P. P., 1970); translated as *The Consumer Society: Myths and Structures* (London & Thousand Oaks, Cal.: Sage, 1998);

Pour une critique de l'économie politique du signe (Paris: Gallimard, 1972); translated by Charles Levin as *For a Critique of the Political Economy of the Sign* (London & St. Louis: Telos, 1981);

Le Miroir de production; ou, L'illusion critique du matérialisme historique, Collection "Mutations-Orientations," no. 27 (Paris: Casterman, 1973); translated by Mark Poster as *The Mirror of Production* (St. Louis: Telos, 1975);

L'échange symbolique et la mort (Paris: Gallimard, 1976); translated by Iain Hamilton Grant as *Symbolic Exchange and Death* (London & Thousand Oaks, Cal.: Sage, 1993);

L'Effet Beaubourg: Implosion et dissuasion, Collection Débats (Paris: Galilée, 1977); translated by Rosalind Krass and Annette Michelson as "The Beaubourg-Effect: Implosion and Deterrence," *October,* 20 (1982): 3–13;

Oublier Foucault, Collection "L'espace critique" (Paris: Galilée, 1977); translated by Nicole Dufresne as "Forgetting Foucault," *Humanities in Society,* 3 (1980): 87–111;

L'Ange de stuc (Paris: Galilée, 1978);

A l'ombre des majorités silencieuses, ou, La fin du social, suivi de L'extase du socialisme, Cahiers d'Utopie, no. 4 (Fontenay-sous-Bois: Imprimerie Quotidienne, 1978); translated by Paul Foss, John Johnston, and Paul Patton as *In the Shadow of the Silent Majorities, or, The End of the Social, and Other Essays,* Foreign Agents Series (New York: Semiotext(e), 1983);

Jean Baudrillard (photograph by S. Bassouls/Sygma; from the dust jacket for America, *1988; Richland County Public Library, Columbia, South Carolina)*

De la séduction, Collection "L'espace critique" (Paris: Galilée, 1979); translated by Brian Singer as *Seduction,* New World Perspectives (New York: St. Martin's Press, 1990);

26

Simulacres et simulation, Collection Débats (Paris: Galilée, 1981); selections translated by Foss, Patton, and Philip Beitchman as *Simulations,* Foreign Agent Series (New York: Semiotext(e), 1983); translated by Sheila Faria Glaser as *Simulacra and Simulation* (Ann Arbor: University of Michigan Press, 1994);

Les stratégies fatales (Paris: Grasset & Fasquelle, 1983); translated by Beitchman and W. G. J. Niesluchowski as *Fatal Strategies,* edited by Jim Fleming (New York: Semiotext(e) / London: Pluto, 1990);

La gauche divine: Chronique des années 1977–1984 (Paris: Grasset, 1985);

Amérique (Paris: Grasset, 1986); translated by Chris Turner as *America* (London & New York: Verso, 1988);

L'Autre par lui-même: Habilitation, Collection Débats (Paris: Galilée, 1987); translated by Bernard Schutze and Caroline Schutze as *The Ecstasy of Communication,* edited by Sylvère Lotringer (Brooklyn, N.Y.: Autonomedia, 1988);

Cool Memories, 1980–1985 (Paris: Galilée, 1987); translated by Chris Turner (New York & London: Verso, 1990);

Cool Memories II, 1987–1990 (Paris: Galilée, 1990); translated by Turner (Durham, N.C.: Duke University Press, 1996);

La transparence du mal: Essai sur le phénomènes extrêmes, Collection "L'espace critique" (Paris: Galilée, 1990); translated by James Benedict as *The Transparency of Evil: Essays on Extreme Phenomena* (London & New York: Verso, 1993);

Enrico Baj: Transparence du kitsch (Paris: Editions de la Différence/Galerie Beaubourg, 1990);

La guerre du Golfe n'a pas eu lieu (Paris: Galilée, 1991); translated, with an introduction, by Patton as *The Gulf War Did Not Take Place* (Bloomington: Indiana University Press, 1995; Sydney: Power Publications);

L'illusion de la fin, ou, La grève des événements, Collection "L'espace critique" (Paris: Galilée, 1992); translated by Turner as *The Illusion of the End* (Stanford, Cal.: Stanford University Press, 1994; Cambridge: Polity Press, 1994);

Figures de l'altérité, by Baudrillard and Marc Guillaume (Paris: Descartes, 1994);

La pensée radicale (Paris: Sens & Tonka, 1994); translated by David Macey as "Radical Thought," *Parallax: A Journal of Metadiscursive Theory and Cultural Practices,* 1 (September 1995): 53–62;

Le crime parfait, Collection "L'espace critique" (Paris: Galilée, 1995); translated by Turner as *The Perfect Crime* (London & New York: Verso, 1996);

Fragments: Cool Memories III, 1990–1995 (Paris: Galilée, 1995); translated by Emily Agar (London & New York: Verso, 1997);

Ecran Total, Collection "L'espace critique" (Paris: Galilée, 1997); translated by Turner as *Screened Out* (London & New York: Verso, 2002);

Illusion, désillusion, esthétiques (Paris: Sens & Tonka, 1997);

Car l'illusion ne s'oppose pas á la réalité . . . (Paris: Descartes, 1998);

Le complot de l'art, suivi de Entrevues à propos du "Complot de l'art" (Paris: Sens & Tonka, 1999);

L'échange impossible (Paris: Galilée, 1999); translated by Turner as *Impossible Exchange* (London & New York: Verso, 2001);

Jean Baudrillard: Fotografien, Photographies, Photographs, 1985–1998, edited by Peter Weibel (Ostfildern-Ruit: Hatje / Graz: Neue Galerie Graz / New York: Distributed Art Publishers, 1999);

Sur la photographie (Paris: Sens & Tonka, 1999);

Cool Memories IV, 1995–2000 (Paris: Galilée, 2000); translated by Turner (London & New York: Verso, 2003);

Mots de passe (Paris: Pauvert, 2000);

Les objets singuliers: Architecture et philosophie, by Baudrillard and Jean Nouvel (Paris: Calmann-Lévy, 2000); translated by Robert Bononno as *The Singular Objects of Architecture* (Minneapolis: University of Minnesota Press, 2002);

The Vital Illusion, edited by Julia Witwer, Wellek Library Lectures (New York: Columbia University Press, 2000);

Le ludique et le policier: Et autres textes parus dans Utopie, 1967/78 (Paris: Sens & Tonka, 2001);

Télémorphose: Précédé de L'élevage de poussière (Paris: Sens & Tonka, 2001);

Power inferno, Collection "L'espace critique" (Paris: Galilée, 2002);

L'esprit du terrorisme, Collection "L'espace critique" (Paris: Galilée, 2002); translated by Turner as "The Spirit of Terrorism," in *The Spirit of Terrorism and Other Essays* (London & New York: Verso, 2003), pp. 1–34.

Edition: *La société de consommation: Ses mythes, ses structures,* preface by J. P. Mayer, Idées-poche, no. 316 (Paris: Gallimard, 1985).

Editions in English: *The Evil Demon of Images* (Sydney: Power Institute of Fine Arts, University of Sydney, 1987);

Forget Foucault & Forget Baudrillard: An Interview with Sylvère Lotringer, Foreign Agent Series (New York: Semiotext(e), 1987);

Jean Baudrillard: Selected Writings, translated by Jacques Morrain and others, edited, with an introduction, by Mark Poster (Cambridge: Polity Press, 1988; Stanford, Cal.: Stanford University Press, 1988; revised and expanded, 2001);

Revenge of the Crystal: Selected Writings on the Modern Object and Its Destiny, 1968–1983, edited and translated by Paul Foss and Julian Pefanis (London & Concord, Mass.: Pluto/Power Institute of Fine Arts, University of Sydney, 1990);

The Uncollected Baudrillard, translated by Sophie Thomas and others, edited by Gary Genosko (New York: Sage, 2001);

The Spirit of Terrorism and Other Essays (London & New York: Verso, 2003).

OTHER: "The Implosion of Meaning in the Media and the Implosion of the Social in the Masses," translated by Mary Lydon, in *The Myths of Information: Technology and Postindustrial Culture,* edited, with an introduction, by Kathleen Woodward (London: Routledge & Kegan Paul, 1980; Madison: Coda / Milwaukee: Center for Twentieth Century Studies, University of Wisconsin, 1980), pp. 137–148;

Sophie Calle, *Suite vénitienne* (Paris: Etoile, 1983); translated by Danny Barash and Danny Hatfield (Seattle: Bay Press, 1988)–includes "Please Follow Me" by Baudrillard;

"The Precession of Simulacra," translated by Paul Foss and Paul Patton, in *Art after Modernism: Rethinking Representation,* edited by Brian Wallis, Documentary Sources in Contemporary Art, no. 1 (New York: New Museum of Contemporary Art / Boston: Godine, 1984), pp. 253–281;

"The Structural Law of Value and the Order of Simulacra," translated by Charles Levin, in *The Structural Allegory: Reconstructive Encounters with the New French Thought,* edited, with an introduction, by John Fekete, Theory and History of Literature, no. 11 (Minneapolis: University of Minnesota Press, 1984), pp. 54–73;

"Beyond Right and Wrong or the Mischievous Genius of Image," translated by Laurent Charreyron and Amy Gerstler, in *Resolution: A Critique of Video Art,* edited by Patti Podesta (Los Angeles: Los Angeles Contemporary Exhibitions, 1986);

"The Year 2000 Has Already Happened," translated by Nai-fei Ding and Kuab-Hsing Chen, in *Body Invaders: Panic Sex in America,* edited by Arthur Kroker and Marilouise Kroker, CultureTexts (New York: St. Martin's Press / London: Macmillan / Montreal: New World Perspectives, 1987), pp. 34–44;

"Hot Painting: The Inevitable Fate of the Image," in *Reconstructing Modernism: Art in New York, Paris, and Montreal, 1945–1964,* edited by Serge Guilbaut (Cambridge, Mass.: MIT Press, 1990), pp. 17–29;

"When Bataille Attacked the Metaphysical Principle of Economy," translated by David James Miller, in *Ideology and Power in the Age of Lenin in Ruins,* edited by Arthur Kroker and Marilouise Kroker, CultureTexts (New York: St. Martin's Press, 1991), pp. 135–138;

"Biosphere II," in *Des mondes inventés: Les parcs à thème?* edited by Anne Marie Eyssartel and Bernard Rochette (Paris: Editions de la villette, 1992), pp. 126–130;

"Transpolitics, Transsexuality, Transaesthetics," translated by Michel Valentin, in *Jean Baudrillard: The Disappearance of Art and Politics,* edited by William Stearns and William Chaloupka (New York: St. Martin's Press, 1992; London: Macmillan, 1992);

"The Masses: The Implosion of the Social in the Media," translated by Marie Maclean, in *The Polity Reader in Cultural Theory* (Cambridge: Polity Press/ Blackwell, 1994);

"The Consumer Society," in *The Polity Reader in Social Theory* (Cambridge: Polity Press/Blackwell, 1994), pp. 362–366;

"The System of Collecting," in *The Cultures of Collecting,* edited by John Elsner and Roger Cardinal (London: Reaktion, 1994; Cambridge, Mass.: Harvard University Press, 1994), pp. 7–24;

"On Consumer Society," in *Rethinking the Subject: An Anthology of Contemporary European Social Thought,* edited by James D. Faubion (Boulder, Colo.: Westview Press, 1995), pp. 193–203;

"No Pity for Sarajevo," "The West's Serbianization," and "When the West Stands in for the Dead," translated by James Patterson, in *This Time We Knew: Western Responses to Genocide in Bosnia,* edited by Thomas Cushman and Stjepan G. Meštrović (New York & London: New York University Press, 1996);

"The Hysteresis of the Millennium," in *The Year 2000: Essays on the End,* edited by Charles B. Strozier and Michael Flynn (New York: New York University Press, 1997);

Luc Delahaye, *L'Autre,* text by Baudrillard (London: Phaidon, 1999).

TRANSLATIONS: Bertolt Brecht, *Dialogues d'exiles,* translated by Baudrillard and Gilbert Badia (Paris: L'Arche, 1956);

Peter Weiss, *La persécution et l'assassinat de Jean-Paul Marat: Représentés par le groupe théatral de L'hospice de Charenton sous la direction de Monsieur de Sade: Drame en deux actes* (Paris: Seuil, 1965);

Weiss, *L'instruction: Oratorio en onze chants* (Paris: Seuil, 1966);

Weiss, *Chant du fantoche lusitanien* (Paris: Seuil, 1968);

Weiss, *Discours sur la genèse et le déroulement de la très longue guerre de libération du Vietnam: Illustrant la nécessité de la lutte armée des opprimés contre leurs oppresseurs ainsi que la volonté des Etats-Unis d'Amérique d'anéantir les fondements de la révolution* (Paris: Seuil, 1968);

Karl Marx and Friedrich Engels, *L'Ideologie allemande: Critique de la philosophie allemande la plus récente dans la personne de ses représentants Feuerbach, B. Bauer et Stirner, et du socialisme allemand dans celle de ses différents prophètes,* edited by Badia, translated by Baudrillard and others (Paris: Editions Sociales, 1968);

Wilhelm E. Muhlmann, *Messianismes révolutionnaires du tiers-monde,* Bibliothèque des sciences humaines (Paris: Gallimard, 1968);

Engels, *Le Role de la violence dans l'histoire* (Paris: Editions Sociales, 1969).

SELECTED PERIODICAL PUBLICATIONS–
UNCOLLECTED: "Beyond the Unconscious: The Symbolic," translated by Lee Hildreth, *Discourse,* 3 (1981): 60–87;

"Fatality or Reversible Imminence: Beyond the Uncertainty Principle," translated by Pamela Park, *Social Research,* 49, no. 2 (Summer 1982): 272–293;

"La Fin des passions historique" ["La gauche divine I"], *Le Monde,* 21 September 1983, pp. 1, 10;

"Social: La Grande Illusion" ["La gauche divine II"], *Le Monde,* 22 September 1983, p. 10;

"What Are You Doing after the Orgy?" *Traverses,* 29 (October 1983): 2–15;

"Clone Story or The Artificial Child," translated by Paul Foss, *ZG,* 11 (Summer 1984): 16–17;

"L'an 2000 ne passera pas," *Traverses,* 33/34 (January 1985): 8–16; translated as "The Year 2000 Will Not Take Place," in *Futur*Fall: Excursions into Post-Modernity,* edited by E. A. Grosz and others (Sydney: Power Institute of Fine Arts Press, 1986), pp. 18–28;

"The Child in the Bubble," *Impulse,* 11, no. 4 (Winter 1985): 12–13;

"Softly, Softly," translated by Malcolm Imrie, *New Statesman,* 113 (6 March 1987): 44;

"USA 80s," translated by Mark A. Polizzotti, *Semiotext(e),* 13 (1987): 47–50;

"The Reality Gulf," *Guardian,* 11 January 1991, p. 25;

"The Virtual Illusion: Or the Automatic Writing of the World," *Theory, Culture & Society,* 12, no. 4 (November 1995): 97–107;

"De l'exorcisme en politique ou la conjuration des imbeciles," *Liberation,* 7 May 1997, p. 7.

Jean Baudrillard's many published works span more than three decades of the late twentieth century and have been translated into many languages; the extensive length of his bibliography is just one indication of the intense interest he incites as he publishes his penetrating views of Western culture. He has been described variously as "one of the world's major thinkers," "one of France's leading intellectuals," and "one of the most frequently cited contemporary social theorists." Critics have further noted Baudrillard's incalculable influence on postmodern thought; Richard J. Lane, for instance, writes in *Jean Baudrillard* (2000) that he "is not only one of the most famous writers on the subject of postmodernism, but he somehow seems to embody postmodernism itself." Introduced on one occasion, with some levity, as a "post-modern bogeyman," Baudrillard is someone who tells people what they may not want to hear, what they may doubt can even be true–at least to the literal extent he expresses it–and what they nevertheless recognize as penetrating in its conceptualization of lived experience within contemporary postmodernity. Baudrillard has filled the role of theorist with color and verve, using extravagant–even apocalyptic–rhetoric in his portrayals of late-twentieth-century culture.

Jean Baudrillard was born at 7:00 A.M. on 27 July 1929, in Reims, France, to Raymonde LeBrun and Marius Baudrillard. His parents worked as *fonctionnaires,* or civil servants; his mother, Raymonde, was a postal worker, and his father, Marius, worked as a gendarme, or policeman. His paternal grandparents were Julienne Legendre and Isidore Baudrillard; his maternal grandparents, Simone Hattat and Ernest LeBrun, worked a farm just north of Reims, in Seraincourt, Ardennes. The immediate family of Baudrillard's youth experienced the urbanization of workers so prevalent in the middle of the twentieth century; his early environment thus was focused on the family household and its domestic arrangement rather than the farm fields of his grandparents. His early impressions of this household can be traced to his first book, *Le système des objets: La consommation des signes* (1968; translated as *The System of Objects,* 1996), in which he writes, "What gives the houses of our childhood such resonance in memory is clearly this complex structure of interiority, and the objects within it serve for us as boundary markers of the symbolic configuration known as home. . . . The social sign of property and psychological sign of the immanence of the family, make this traditional space into a closed transcendence." Throughout his writings Baudrillard connects the imaginative worlds of psychology and symbolic meaning to the external world of objects and landscape. In his view symbolic meaning inhabits the material world, because, as he describes in *Cool Memories II, 1987–1990* (1990; translated, 1996), "all situations are inspired by an object, a fragment, a present obsession, never by an idea." In *Cool Memories,*

Dust jacket for the English translation of Amérique *(1986), in which Baudrillard characterizes the United States as a postmodern utopian society (Richland County Public Library, Columbia, South Carolina)*

1980–1985 (1987; translated, 1990), Baudrillard explains that "immateriality of signs is alien to me, as it is to a race of peasants with whom I share an . . . ancestral belief in the real." Baudrillard is keenly aware that as a theorist, his ideas are situated within his life experience and embedded in his historical time and place; calling attention to the way his received values and formative experiences form a basis for his theories reveals his responsive morality with respect to a larger truth.

Baudrillard attended the Lycée de Reims, where he worked hard at his studies. He recalls in an interview with Mike Gane and Monique Arnaud published in *Baudrillard Live: Selected Interviews* (1993):

I was the first member of the tribe, so to speak, to do some studying. . . . I was not brought up in an intellectual milieu–there was nothing around me–my parents were what they were, not even petit bourgeois, or perhaps very lowly petit bourgeois. It was not a cultural environment. So I had to compensate for this by working extremely hard at the Lycée.

In 1958, at the age of twenty-nine, Baudrillard began teaching German in secondary schools, where he specialized in German social theory and literature, reading Friedrich Nietzsche in German. At the time Baudrillard's leftist political opinions, like those of Roland Barthes and Jean-Paul Sartre, led him to oppose French colonial policy in Algeria. By 1962 he had published some literary reviews, including one on Italo Calvino. In 1966 an event changed the outward course of Baudrillard's life: sociologist Henri Lefebvre brought him to study at the Faculté de Paris, Sorbonne. Here Baudrillard filled the positions of *assistant, maitre-assistant* (master assistant), and *maitre de conferences en sociologie* (master of lectures in sociology) at the Université Paris X–Nanterre over a period of twenty years.

In May 1968, two years after his arrival in Paris, Baudrillard experienced the Parisian student political revolt, a public event he later characterized as "a fatal event." In *Oublier Foucault* (1977; translated as "Forgetting Foucault," 1980), he writes about revolution that "when it comes it is to hide the fact that it is no longer meaningful." In hindsight, he recalls in "Dropping out of History," a 1983 interview with Sylvère Lotringer included in *The Uncollected Baudrillard* (2001), he viewed May 1968 as a "pure event which comes without explanation or referent, . . . an event that we have been unable to rationalize and exploit–and from which we have been able to conclude nothing." Baudrillard has argued that, from May 1968 forward, Western culture has lost its historical sense, so that public events can no longer be ascribed to causes; rather, these events occur randomly and without reason. "For me," he states in *Oublier Foucault,* "events are no longer those of the subject; they reach a point where they function all by themselves." Here, and throughout Baudrillard's work, "culture" refers not to the arts but to a sum of the practices, meanings, and production in the human environment, a total way of life.

Baudrillard remained at the Université Paris for twenty years, from 1966 to 1986. His first accomplishment was to complete his *thèse de troisiéme cycle de la sociologie* (thesis of the third cycle of sociology) in 1966, which was published two years later as *Le système des objets*. Also in the same year, he published a French translation of Karl Marx and Friedrich Engels's "Die deutsche Ideologie" (The German Ideology, 1845–1846). He completed his *thèse principale* (principal thesis) at the Sorbonne in February 1986, eighteen years later. After receiving his final degree, Baudrillard directed l'IRIS (Institut de Recherche et d'information Socioeconomique) at the University of Paris–IX Dauphine, from October 1986 to October 1990. During the late 1980s he began to travel widely, creating photographs of objects from various world locations. Because he was spending increasing amounts of time on travel, interviews, and publication, he retired from teaching sociology at the Université Paris X–Nanterre in 1987. He has devoted his energies to lecturing, writing, teaching, photography, and publication since then.

Baudrillard has drawn his cultural analyses from an unusual breadth of sources, combining ideas from different disciplines while defining his own position over and against those ideas. He has drawn from–and been at variance with–Marx, Ferdinand de Saussure, Georg Wilhelm Friedrich Hegel, Jacques Lacan, Georges Bataille, Barthes, and Jean-François Lyotard, for example. When asked, in an unpublished 1999 interview with Jean Arnold, about what friends and enemies he has made throughout his working life, he preferred to pinpoint his "enemies," describing their qualifications for this role. First, Baudrillard alienated the French university establishment after the publication of *Oublier Foucault* in 1977. Michel Foucault had focused upon cultural order and power as the reality principle for Western culture in *Les Mots et les choses: Une archéologie des sciences humaines* (1966; translated as *The Order of Things: An Archeology of the Human Sciences,* 1970), and in such theoretical classics as *Surveiller et punir: Naissance de la prison* (1975; translated as *Discipline and Punish: The Birth of the Prison,* 1977) and *Histoire de la sexualité* (1976–1984; translated as *The History of Sexuality,* 1978–1986). Baudrillard simply states in *Oublier Foucault* that "if it is possible at last to talk with such definitive understanding about power, sexuality, the body, and discipline . . . it is because at some point *all this is here and now over with,*" for "you can only reveal a phenomenon if it is already disappearing." Foucault occupied a position of power in the academy, such that the contents and even the title of this book alienated an important part of the university. While Foucault had depicted a culture with underlying order, Baudrillard described the proliferating objects and images of that culture. As a "renovation within ruination," Baudrillard wrote in *Cool Memories,* his postmodernity brought an "end of final evaluations."

Baudrillard also alienated feminists after the publication of *De la séduction* in 1979 (translated as *Seduction,* 1990). The dissension is not hard to imagine as one reads some of the text from his work: "Freud was right: there is but one sexuality, one libido–and it is masculine. Sexuality has a strong, discriminative structure centered on the phallus, castration, the Name-of-the-Father, and repression. There is none other. . . . Either the structure remains the same, with the female being entirely absorbed by the male, or else it collapses. . . ." This "discriminative structure" in gender relations leaves no foundation or space for feminist thought, in which women could be perceived as having power or agency to determine their own point of view or life plan. Yet, Baudrillard vehemently defended his position in an interview with Suzanne Moore and Stephen Johnstone published in *Marxism Today* in January 1989 and collected in *Baudrillard Live:* "I am not in agreement with hardline feminist ideology, which says that woman as seducer is a degrading role. In my view the strategy of seduction is a happy, liberating power for women." Believing as he does that personal experience resides at the origin of theory, Baudrillard allows readers to suspect that his personal life has included its own transcendent experiences of seduction. The epigraph for the year 1980 in *Cool Memories, 1980–1985,* "The first day of the rest of your life," designates a period following three transcendent, once-in-a-lifetime experiences: the "stunning impact of the deserts and California, . . . the woman whose beauty stunned me the most . . . and whose loss wounded me the most, [and] the best book—or two—I shall ever write" are all in his past; *Cool Memories, 1980–1985* "is where the rest of life begins." While personal human relations in his life have remained unrepresented in his publications, Baudrillard does mention his two children, Gilles and Anne.

In his next phase, Baudrillard felt there had been a "break with the left" after publishing "La gauche divine" (The Divine Left) in *Le Monde* on 21 and 22 September 1983. Even earlier, however, his reaction to the May 1968 student riots across France—in which he had taken part—had left him with the sense that no revolution could ever succeed, that the time for political opposition was at an end. One might add that while Baudrillard began his work on objects with criticism of Marxist thought about the commodity, by 1972, with the publication of *Pour une critique de l'économie politique du signe* (translated as *For a Critique of the Political Economy of the Sign,* 1981), he criticized Marxist ideology of the Left.

Finally, Baudrillard mentioned a distancing from both Lefebvre and Pierre Bourdieu. His mentor, Lefebvre, was rooted in sociological study; yet, Baudrillard eventually enlarged his own analysis far beyond disciplinary bounds toward a culturewide critique, a move that required mastery of several disciplines. If, as James Ferguson noted in his introduction of Baudrillard before his 1999 Wellek Library Lecture at the University of California, Irvine, "The Murder of the Real" (published as *The Vital Illusion,* 2000), sociologists have perceived him as a "post-modern bogeyman," such views arise from Baudrillard's rejection of the idea of total cultural structure, a vital assumption on which sociologists base their research. Baudrillard also eventually nullified Bourdieu's discussion on aesthetics and class "distinction." In the interview with Arnold, Baudrillard noted that "it is difficult to distinguish what is art and what is not art. There will always be artists and art, but maybe the rules of the game are confused. Art is a form without value."

In summing up this discussion enumerating his enemies, Baudrillard's words themselves from *Cool Memories* give his perspective about these relations over time, and about his ultimate hopes for interaction of ideas in the field of European cultural theory:

> The tangled web of hatreds, of complicities, of rivalries between different schools of thought and of changes in mood causes each atom in the intellectual world . . . to prefer . . . itself, while all the atoms detest each other. . . . The fact that certain disconcerting effects of beauty and truth may spring forth from time to time . . . remains a miraculous paradox.

Indeed, Baudrillard has evaluated a variety of fields of thought in late-twentieth-century Western culture, and by defining his differences from other thinkers he has established an honored place and a discursive space located solidly within their midst.

Over the course of his career Baudrillard's work has developed in three general phases: First, his work on objects and their systems of signification as they form a cultural code; second, the metaphysical concept of seduction; and finally, the concept of simulation and its function in the contemporary age of information. Although the trajectory of these topics arcs from structural analysis of the culture, toward transcendence, and back toward description of the contemporary power of the image, these phases are unified by their concern for the role of the object—as opposed to the subject—in contemporary cultural experience.

Baudrillard defines the object as the locus of the real, and its ontology thus becomes an important site for the construction of cultural meaning in his works. This orientation toward the object arises from the background of his grandparents' labor as peasants, and his parents' urban household: his immersion in a material world was the starting point of his thought. Baudrillard is also quick to point out that his birthplace, Reims, is also the town where the symbolist poet Arthur Rimbaud lived. In Rimbaud's symbolist poetry of "unmediated vision," in Paul de Man's words, the fusion of objects with the subject's imagination took precedence. The privileged position of the object "remains unchallenged among the inheritors of romanticism," de Man notes in *The Rhetoric of Romanticism* (1984). For symbolists and Baudrillard alike, to take the part of the object is to challenge the centuries-old Cartesian view that meaning is determined entirely by the subject. To expand cultural awareness away from the human subject toward the ontology of the object—whether that object is person, animal, or thing—is also to initiate a monumental conceptual and ethical shift. No longer can the consequences of a subject's self-assertive practices go unexamined: imperialism, misogyny, conspicuous consumption, or environmental destruction must be understood as impositions upon "objects" in the external world. The centuries-long Western preoccupation with the subject—or the many concepts that support the point of view of the subject, such as humanism, Enlightenment rationalism, the self, and consciousness—has thus been questioned. If earlier symbolist poets had collapsed the subject and object, however, Baudrillard sets them in opposition; he then focuses upon the object. More than one type of object beckons his interest, as he tells Nicholas Zurbrugg in an interview published in *Eyeline* (11 August 1990) and collected in *Baudrillard Live:* "the non-aesthetic object, the banal object, or the metaphysical object." He further explains in *The Vital Illusion,* "At the moment when the subject discovers the object—whether it is an 'Indian' or a virus—the object makes a reversible, but never innocent, discovery of the subject. . . . knowledge, defined conventionally, always proceeds in the same direction, from the subject to the object. But today processes of reversion are emerging everywhere—in areas from anthropology to viral pathology." Baudrillard wants to look beyond the blind spots of one-way rationalist thought, which locates the source of truth inside the subject's mind. Yet, he cautions,

> I won't transform the object into a supersubject. But it would seem that something has escaped us. Definitively. This is not because our science and technologies are not advanced enough; on the contrary. The closer we come, through experimentation, to the object, the more it steals away from us and finally becomes undecidable. And do not ask where it has gone. Simply the object is *what escapes the subject*—more we cannot say, since our position is still that of the subject and of rational discourse. . . . That, if there is any, is the secret of the universe.

When science and rationalism can no longer lead the human subject toward an unveiling of the mysteries of all that exists within and outside the human mind, it is time to expand one's range of thought toward the object—person, land, nature, thing—to learn what mysteries it holds.

In surveying a progression of Baudrillard's ideas in particular works, one should begin by recognizing that his interest in culturewide critique arose from his graduate training in sociology, which placed emphasis on interpretation of communal trends. When he launched his career, his first three books—*Le système des objets, Pour une critique de l'économie politique du signe,* and *Le Miroir de production; ou, L'illusion critique du matérialisme historique* (1973; translated as *The Mirror of Production,* 1975)—focused upon objects and their meanings. Baudrillard's ongoing interest in objects circulating through the culture begins with a critique of Marxist commodity analysis. He rejected Marx's limited view of the commodity as a product of narrowly economic practices, preferring to consider the commodity/object as a sign with culturewide significance.

Under the tutelage of Lefebvre, Baudrillard's third-cycle thesis, defended in 1966, surveys household objects as cultural artifacts that serve as sites for ideological production. In *Le système des objets* Baudrillard demonstrates that domestic objects express a range of human experience: power, passion, or privilege. These objects can also take aberrant forms: gizmos and gadgets that suggest functionality for its own sake; the unique object that symbolizes personal relations; the antique that suggests origination; or the stylized object that represents industrialization. Baudrillard's ultimate goal in this work is to form a working concept of "consumption," the defining activity that shapes contemporary Western culture. The critique was based on the principle that "everything that cannot be invested in human relationships is invested in objects," so that the proliferation of household objects shows the relative poverty of communal ties in the culture. Objects, including household pets, serve to assuage loneliness and fear of death; these objects also respond to the psychology of control, desire, or narcissism. Indeed, ownership of an object allows the object to function as a mirror. Baudrillard notes that even though the "exchange value . . . of an object is a function of cultural and social determinants, its absolute singularity . . . arises from the fact of being possessed by me—and this allows me, in turn, to recognize myself in the object as an absolutely singular being."

The owned object bestows an identity upon the human subject from a seemingly objective, "real" world; paradoxically, as mirror, "the object . . . sends back not real images, but desired ones," in Baudrillard's analysis. The automobile is one of the most important objects in the system of objects that operates as a whole environment, for it functions as a technology replete with psychological gratification. It supplies the physical elation of movement that constantly negotiates the relation between time and space and mediates between the object system of the household and the larger culture. Each auto differentiates itself from other cars through an endless array of parts, colors, sizes, and interior design, so that it operates in a wide public arena as a sign of class and status. Of all commodities circulating in the culture, the automobile most clearly reveals how a visual language of signs functions through infinite variation, and how the object responds to the psychological needs of its owner.

Baudrillard's next two books, *La société de consommation: Ses mythes, ses structures* (1970; translated as *The Consumer Society: Myths and Structures,* 1998) and *Pour une critique de l'économie politique du signe,* further developed his

JEAN BAUDRILLARD

■

SIMULACRA
AND
SIMULATION

Translated by Sheila Faria Glaser

MICHIGAN

Paperback cover for the 1994 English translation of the 1981 collection of essays on contemporary culture in the information age (Richland County Public Library, Columbia, South Carolina)

critique of material culture through a reading of objects/ commodities as signs. In *La société de consommation* Baudrillard stresses the use of consumer objects as parts of a whole system of meaning, and their collection in each household altogether as an "inseparable totality." Baudrillard links production and consumption within the culture, whereas Marx had separated them into discrete spheres of economic activity. In further contrast to Marx, Baudrillard argues that the commodity does not depend for its existence upon utility; instead, it has become "a distinctive and idle substance, a luxury, and an item, among others, in the general display of consumables." Therefore, "we have reached the point where 'consumption' has grasped the whole of life," Baudrillard argues. Through marketing, display cases, advertising, the credit card, and the shopping mall, consumption organizes everyday life and structures subjective experience. In the consumer society, the consumer is no longer free to choose the objects he owns. Instead, the consumer chooses in conformity to values systematized by the society, class, and subculture; possessions vary to reflect one's position in the social hierarchy and cultural milieu. Baudrillard drives home his point: "the liberty and sovereignty of the consumer are nothing more than a mystification. The well-preserved mystique of satisfaction and individual choice (primarily supported by economists), whereby a 'free' civilization reaches its pinnacle, is the very ideology of the industrial system."

Unlike the field of economics that presupposes a consumer's freedom of choice, Baudrillard assumes the consumer lives within a code that is ruled by the system of objects. If Western culture once formed its social hierarchies according to land and title, it now forms its hierarchies according to ownership and display of objects. Consumption then becomes based not on need but on membership in a group. The consumer needs what has been produced in order to reflect a certain status within the society: production now determines needs, rather than needs dictating production. In fact, because needs arise from production, the consumer society reaffirms the puritan ideology that had been in place at the beginning of the Industrial Revolution: the puritan work ethic values successful production as a sign of divine salvation made manifest in empirical reality. Indeed, this extension of puritanism "is what makes consumption the powerful factor of integration and social control we know it to be," states Baudrillard.

In addition to describing the coercion that this system of objects perpetrates upon the individual consumer, Baudrillard elaborates on the system of signs from which these objects draw their meaning. He explains the connection between the Saussurian linguistic system and Freudian concepts of object relations that inhabit the society of the consumer:

> the flight from one signifier to another is no more than the surface reality of a *desire,* which is insatiable because it is found on a lack. And this desire, which can never be satisfied, signifies itself locally in a succession of objects and needs. . . . Pleasure . . . appears . . . as the individual rationalization of a process whose objectives lie elsewhere. . . . The system of consumption is based on a code of signs (object/signs) and differences, and not on need and pleasure.

The pleasure consumers experience in driving a luxury car, for instance, would serve a deeper need of the cultural system that is "designed to assure a certain type of communication," for use of status symbols places the consumer in a group that defines itself by possession of these symbols. Baudrillard cites John Kenneth Galbraith as claiming that "the individual serves the industrial system not by supplying it with saving and the resulting capital; he serves it by consuming its products. On no other matter, religious, political, or moral, is he so elaborately and skillfully and expensively instructed."

Pour une critique de l'économie politique du signe reexamines Marx's idea that the commodity is separated into "use value" and "exchange value." When Marx separates these two qualities of an object, he falls prey to the ideology of utilitarian values, according to Baudrillard. As Marx attempts to validate the commodity/ object as natural by evaluating its use value, he is blind to the fact that "use" is culturally determined; for example, watches and computers may be useful in some cultures but not in others. To believe in need and use as the raison d'être of an object is to subject oneself to the tyranny of the culture through its system of objects, which imposes cultural order. Baudrillard thus argues that even concepts of utility change from one period to another. He presents this problem in Marx's critique as a blind spot that undermines the whole Marxian argument about the goals of the laboring class. Furthermore, if Marx believes the laboring class should make more money to buy more goods, he supports the basic assumptions of capitalism, which supports the system of objects.

Le Miroir de production further develops Baudrillard's arguments against Marxism as espoused in *Pour une critique de l'économie politique du signe*. Production and consumption mirror and mutually inform one another in a unified system that cannot be broken down into dual functions of the political economy, as Marx had described it. Yet, Baudrillard perceives an even more fatal weakness in Marx; as described by the translator of *The Mirror of Production*, Mark Poster, the weakness comes not from Marx's "effort to outline a revolutionary social theory . . . but in the failure of historical materialism to attain this end." The whole capitalist idea of labor, which Marx upholds and extends under the rubric of communism, presupposes a "rationalist intentionality for human action." Baudrillard finally sums up his argument against Marxism in this way: "Marxism is the projection of the class struggle and the mode of production onto all previous history; it is the vision of the future 'freedom' based on the conscious domination of nature. These are extrapolations of the economic . . . , [and] Marxist critique is led despite itself to reproduce the roots of the system of political economy."

While appearing to mount a revolution against capitalism, Marxism simply mirrors its more basic assumptions, and "to project . . . the world of production . . . everywhere else is a theoretically fraudulent

operation" that "bears the stigmas of the rigidity and the silence that it imposes on its object," Baudrillard argues. Marxism is therefore complicit with Adam Smith's concept of abstract social labor and the sale of labor, so that the individual is alienated from his or her own body. Instead, Baudrillard wants to break out of this mode of thought, for all these economic debates entertain the false assumption that a human is solely "the subject of the labor system." In addition, Marx's critique of capitalism falsifies the status of slavery by reconceptualizing the transcendent terms of freedom and repression entirely in terms of labor power. The relegation of the idea of "freedom" to an economic definition used for the purpose of opposing slavery has diminished the Western cultural horizon, such that now "the ideology of freedom remains the weak point of our Western rationality." The purpose of pointing out this diminution in the idea of freedom, as Baudrillard does in *Cool Memories, 1980–1985,* is that this narrow definition precludes any perception of the ways in which cultural systems can tyrannize individual lives: "As for freedom, it will soon cease to exist in any shape or form. Living will depend upon absolute obedience to a strict set of arrangements, which it will no longer be possible to transgress. The air traveler is not free. In the future, life's passengers will be even less so: they will travel through their lives fastened to their (corporate) seats."

As Baudrillard questions the ideas behind a binary opposition of freedom and servitude, he writes in *Le Miroir de production*: "The old form of voluntary servitude was that of free men using that freedom paradoxically to turn themselves into serfs. The new voluntary servitude is that of men obeying the demand that they be free." More revolutionary than Marx, he questions the general economic assumptions that Western culture operates upon. Baudrillard thus defines Western culture as "the mirror of production" itself.

As Baudrillard ends this first stage of thought, he has established the object as the site of the real and described the culture that communicates through consumer objects. At this time he had added the political Left in France to his growing list of "enemies" because he rejected revolution and asked not how the culture should be narrowly engaged in producing a quantity of commodities but why. In the second stage of his work, he finds that the one point of transcendence within the material culture is the seduction of the subject by the object. Seduction involves a psychic attraction to the illusion of the Other, for the seductive object acts like a mirror that entices, absorbs, and deceives the subject. Seduction is a way for the subject to get beyond ordinary consciousness and to experience a metaphysical plane in an immanent, phenomenal world. Indeed, Baudrillard argued in an interview with Lotringer (published in *Forget Foucault & Forget Baudrillard: An Interview with Sylvère Lotringer,* 1987) that his "point of view is completely metaphysical." Seduction typically originates in the object/Other and is projected from the visual surface of that image. The prime example Baudrillard cites is the mythological Narcissus, who falls in love with his own image reflected in the watery surface of the pond. The image "absorbs and seduces him, which he can approach but never pass beyond," he writes in *De la séduction.* Baudrillard differentiates the mirror of Narcissus from the mirror of Lacan's mirror stage, which establishes an identity for the subject within the external culture. Baudrillard's mirror of seduction features the object as the subject's internal illusion; the object reflects the subject's gaze and convinces the subject that this image is inevitable, because it is meant just for him. Seduction tends to undermine order, according to Baudrillard, because it "represents mastery over the symbolic universe, while power represents only mastery of the real universe." Seduction inhabits a metaphysical realm outside of everyday experience, because it "cannot possibly be represented, because in seduction the distance between the real and its double, and the distortion between the Same and the Other, is abolished." Seduction is what remains for a subject who eschews narrowly rational views, preferring instead a transcendental experience of that which escapes the mind: the object.

While the idea of seduction seems to hold resonance for the workings of the marketplace—underlying the effects of advertising, sales, fashion, and furnishings—Baudrillard's idea of seduction also appears in a problematic light for feminists on both sides of the Atlantic. In fact, Gane notes of Baudrillard's theory of seduction in *Baudrillard: Critical and Fatal Theory* (1991) that its "major target is modern feminism." For instance, Baudrillard objects to Luce Irigaray's detailed descriptions of female sexual experience because he wishes to focus upon woman as seductress, the one who weaves illusion in a metaphysical realm. Here Baudrillard imagines woman elevated to "pure object," a position of great power, in his view.

It is important to understand the essentialism of both Irigaray and Baudrillard; Irigaray attempts to define in an innovative manner what is or could be "woman" for a culture that has always silenced women because of its ruling masculine, patriarchal interests and power. Baudrillard, on the other hand, attempts to conceptualize the image of woman as the essence of a seductive, metaphysical realm that enchants the male subject. In an implied reference to Irigaray's feminist critique, he writes in *De la séduction:* "Anatomy is not destiny, nor is politics: seduction is destiny. It is what remains of a magical, fateful world, a risky, vertiginous

and predestined world; it is what is quietly effective in a visibly efficient and stolid world." Although French feminism has concentrated admirably and innovatively on defining a positive essence for woman in a culture that has too long ignored this subject position, its critique has operated on the assumption that the sexes are always different. By contrast, American feminists have concentrated more on gaining political and economic power for women, a medium that they would share with men.

Yet, Baudrillard argues for the redeeming qualities of seduction; in a society that lives in an immanent realm of objects, seduction is the only route to metaphysical experience, in his view. Sadie Plant's interpretation in her essay "Baudrillard's Woman: The Eve of Seduction" (1993), however, argues that Baudrillard's "seduction becomes the guarantor: as long as seduction is possible, there must be a subject to be seduced. And this subject is masculine, as Baudrillard is quick to admit and happy to assume, while that which seduces is its *'missing dimension,'* the feminine." Plant further explains that, for Baudrillard, feminist "woman's insistence that she too must have meaning and purpose, desires and discourses of her own is a misguided rejection of her own and only powers. These are the powers of the secret and the artificial, that which is undecidable and manifest in ritual, game, ceremony, and seduction." Here, Baudrillard has imposed his subject/object opposition onto man/woman relations as a continuation of his critique of the object.

In a third stage, Baudrillard's work expansively describes the contemporary power of the image through the electronic media. In *Simulacres et simulation* (1981; translated as *Simulacra and Simulation,* 1994), Baudrillard arrives at a description of contemporary culture of the information age, the age of media-generated images. Proliferating information denies ultimate reality, because it substitutes a plethora of data for meaning, a trend reinforced by images generated by the media. In each case the physical object has receded in importance, replaced instead by virtual objects. In his introduction to *Jean Baudrillard: Selected Writings* (1988), Poster notes that in *Simulacres et simulation* "the distinction between object and representation, thing and idea are no longer valid." In addition, one finds a collapse of other previous conceptual oppositions, such as nonfiction and fiction, truth and lie, artificial and real. Baudrillard argues that meanings simply dissipate as Western culture loses its reference to the real by "substituting the sign of the real for the real." Because simulacra present a model or an imagined image as real, and because no critical distance in viewing the image can be maintained, simulacra dictate definitions of what is real; as a result, the category of "real" becomes radically destabilized, changed by all kinds of imaginative simulations. Through the media of television, computer screen, and cinema, reality is determined and deployed through the reproduced image to a culture that constructs these simulacra in its imagination as virtually real. The image generates a world of hyperreality to which "the masses" generally submit. After all, as Charles Levin notes in *Jean Baudrillard: A Study in Cultural Metaphysics* (1996), "it takes a certain vision to resist the lure of vision." By way of explanation about the hyperreal in contemporary culture, Baudrillard writes in the title essay of *Simulacre et simulation:* "Today abstraction is no longer that of the map, the double, the mirror, or the concept. Simulation is no longer that of a territory, a referential being, or a substance. It is the generation by models of a real without origin or reality: a hyperreal." Recognizing the power of the image generated by the media, Baudrillard then asks: "Are the mass media on the side of power in the manipulation of the masses, or are they on the side of the masses in the liquidation of meaning, in the violence perpetrated on meaning, and in fascination?"

Most critics of Baudrillard will ask how one is to read this type of cultural criticism. While Baudrillard's discussion borders at times on the hallucinatory—without proof and often without example—the ideas are still perceptive. The reader thus corroborates with the text by producing his or her own ideas that may support or reject the argument, subjectively evaluating the validity of Baudrillard's concepts. Yet, Poster argues with acuity in his introduction to *Jean Baudrillard: Selected Writings* that Baudrillard's later work "is invaluable in beginning to comprehend the impact of new communication forms on society. He has introduced a language-based analysis of new kinds of social experience, experience that is sure to become increasingly characteristic of advanced societies. . . . For critical theorists, Baudrillard represents the beginning of a line of thought, one that is open to development and refinement by others." Baudrillard's oeuvre over a period of three decades focuses upon the interpretation of objects as they function as cultural signs rather than on the pure physicality of the objects themselves. Baudrillard also sees a transcendent experience of seduction within an empirical Western culture that is based in materiality. Finally, he critiques contemporary media and its realm of virtual reality.

Baudrillard has thus captured in words an apocalyptic version of what many cultural critics call the postmodern imaginary, as he proposes and affirms an extreme form of Western cultural identity. If postmodernism features a disappearance of both the subject and any point of referentiality, then Baudrillard might consent to inclusion in this broad category; yet, he might chafe at postmodern labels, too, for his later concern with seduction, cultural metaphysics, and analysis of the spread of information have little to do with other postmodern thought. Ultimately, his innovative concepts push back limits to thought, as he eschews any contemporary nostalgia for passing cultural symbolic systems or concepts that totalize the culture, naming instead new cultural processes and circumstances. In *Cool Memories II* he describes his postmodern vision with typical hyperbole as "the first truly universal conceptual conduit, like jeans or Coca-Cola. It has the same virtues in Vancouver or Zanzibar, Chicago or Budapest."

Some critics such as Poster, Gane, and Levin have recognized the soft spot in Baudrillard's methods that feature unproved description of cultural systems: his later works include "abstraction due to the lack of backgrounding" in Gane's view, or a "lack of . . . sustained, systematic analysis" according to Poster. As if in answer, Baudrillard himself argues in *Cool Memories, 1980–1985* that "there is nothing worse than this obligation to research, to seek out references and documentation that has taken up residence in the realm of thought and which is the mental and obsessional equivalent of hygiene." Moving beyond questions of methodology, however, Baudrillard's grand achievement has been to bring a wholeness of vision to the field of cultural critique at a time when most knowledge and interpretation has splintered cultural analysis into specialized, partial domains. He protests in *Cool Memories II* that "concepts . . . are under house arrest, under the fierce control of each discipline."

One of Baudrillard's descriptions of an anonymous writer in *Cool Memories II* well fits his own work: "He illuminates the landscape of society with an intense, ultrasensitive light and brings out a strange, hyperreal relief—a coherent reading, precisely like the light of a laser." Because of Baudrillard and his cultural theory, "culture" can no longer be defined as just capitalist or communist, democratic or totalitarian, revolutionary or reactionary, baroque or classical in its art, music, or literature, for each of these categories of analysis is but a small part of the total human experience in any given period. Culture may no longer be spoken of as specialized by its economic form, as a politically ideological form, as a linear historical narrative, or as a specialized expression of discrete or applied aesthetics. The ways of talking about culture will be more inclusive to the wholeness of human experience because of Baudrillard.

Baudrillard has also critiqued "America" as the site of pure postmodernism, particularly in his *Amérique* (1986; translated as *America,* 1988). As a latter-day Alexis de Tocqueville looking with a traveler's curiosity and insight into American culture, his commentary has defined and expressed the American postmodern, postcapitalist, technologically based angst for the West.

*Dust jacket for the published version (2000) of "The Murder
of the Real," Baudrillard's 1999 Wellek Library Lecture
at the University of California, Irvine (Richland County
Public Library, Columbia, South Carolina)*

Like de Tocqueville, he sees the negative foundations
of the "greatness" of the United States, for American
culture features violence and banality along with its
freedom and power. Baudrillard argues that the United
States is a utopian society, a status that explains its "lack
of need for metaphysics and the imaginary." European
thought becomes reality when it crosses the Atlantic;
however, Americans "build the real out of ideas," he
notes. By contrast, Europeans "transform the real into
ideology." Baudrillard argues that Americans consistently attempt to put their utopian ideals into practice,
so that "If America were to lose this moral perspective
on itself, it would collapse. This is not perhaps evident
to Europeans, for whom America is a cynical power
and its morality a hypocritical ideology. We remain
unconvinced by the moral vision Americans have of
themselves, but in this we are wrong." He sees American culture with sympathy as well as insight, viewing
the culture of the West and of California as the advance
guard of Euro-Western culture: "Today, all the myths
of modernity are American. . . . In Los Angeles, Europe
has disappeared." Yet, California "has invented nothing: it has taken everything from Europe and served it
up again in a disfigured, meaningless form, with an
added Disneyland glitter." Here, Baudrillard's rhetoric
reaches a state of incantatory rhythm: "World center of
sweet madness, mirror of our dejecta and our deca-

dence. . . . parody of cities, the parody of technology in
Silicon Valley, the parody of oenology, the parody of
religion."

In *The Vital Illusion* he explains the dynamics of his
travel experience: "since the world drifts into delirium,
we must adopt a delirious point of view." In the process
of writing, however, Baudrillard reveals conscious control of his rhetoric, for he points to the fact that "all this
is true, since the text itself resembles the hysterical ste-
reotype it confers upon California." Travel promotes
an experience heavily weighted toward visual impression of a place rather than lived experience in a place,
and Baudrillard is aware of the ways in which this circumstance affects his perspective: "one of the pleasures
of travel is to dive into places where others are compelled to live and come out unscathed, full of the mali-
cious pleasure of abandoning them to their fate. [In
California], even their local happiness seems tuned to a
secret resignation. It never compares, at least, with the
freedom to leave." His perceptions of the United States
are thus the insights of one who views the culture with
a fresh perspective; yet, his perceptions differ from
those who possess long-lived experience of a region.
His own words in *Cool Memories II* reveal the middle
ground for his analysis: "it isn't enough to have seen a
town; you have to have [at least] gone through it."

In his critique of the United States, Baudrillard
conflates the American landscape with theory in order
to give form to his ideas about postmodernity. One
example of this conceptual dynamic resides in his
descriptions of the desert of the Southwest, which forms
an empty landscape corresponding to the lack of meaning in postmodernity. "American culture is heir to the
deserts," and as a "sublime form," the desert suggests
"a mental frontier where the projects of civilization run
into the ground. . . . We should always appeal to the
desert against the excess of signification, of intention
and pretention in culture," he asserts in *Cool Memories II*.
The desert thus serves culture as a panacea for the
overabundance of information and the glut of images in
a media-driven, postmodern age.

Jean Baudrillard has also fused meaning with
landscape as he connects one of his concepts to the
geography of the Continental Divide. In *Fragments: Cool
Memories III, 1990–1995* (1995), he demonstrates ways
in which human thought may be structured like that
natural border:

> In man, it is these thoughts, and not the rivers, that
> divide themselves. Like the image of the continental
> waters, these thoughts separate subtly, and in a way
> quite unpredictable, in opposite directions to utterly
> lose themselves in some impersonal ocean. . . .
> It is on this same imaginary line, on the same invisi-
> ble crest, that are separated for ever the left and the

right, man and woman, good and bad, and one language from another. If there is no center of the world, there is always, by contrast, the origin of this line of demarcation traced by nature. . . .

Here Baudrillard reveals a core belief in a source that produces binary oppositions, rather than believing in a single center of meaning. Throughout his career he has considered these oppositional patterns–subject/object, man/woman, good/evil, metaphysical/physical. As a photographer, writer, lecturer, and teacher, he seeks the origins of these thought patterns through deep cultural analysis.

Interviews:

Christian Descamps, "Jean Baudrillard et la séduction," in *Entretiens avec Le Monde 3: Idées contemporaines,* edited by Descamps (Paris: Le Découverte/Le Monde, 1984);

"Le regard de Jean Baudrillard: Le bonheur made in U.S.A.," *Magazine Littéraire* (December 1985): 225–248;

Suzanne Moore and Stephen Johnstone, "Politics of Seduction," *Marxism Today,* 33 (January 1989): 54–55;

"Interview with John Johnston," *Art Papers,* special issue on "The End of the End" (January–February 1989): 4–7;

Pierre Archaud, "The Politics of Performance: Montand, Coluche = Le Pen?" *New Political Science,* 16–17 (Fall–Winter 1989): 23–28;

Paul Ramblai, "Travels in Hyperreality," in *French Blues: A Not-So Sentimental Journey through Lives and Memories in Modern France* (London: Heinemann, 1989), pp. 166–169;

John Strand, "An Interview with Jean Baudrillard," *Art International,* 12 (Autumn 1990): 55–57;

Dianne Hunter, "Interview with Jean Baudrillard," in *Image and Ideology in Modern/Postmodern Discourse,* edited by David B. Downing and Susan Bazargan (Albany: State University of New York Press, 1991), pp. 287–291;

Baudrillard Live: Selected Interviews, edited, with an introduction, by Mike Gane (London & New York: Routledge, 1993);

Roy Boyne and Scott Lash, "Symbolic Exchange: Taking Theory Seriously: An Interview with Jean Baudrillard," *Theory, Culture and Society,* 12, no. 4 (November 1995): 79–95;

Judith Williamson, "An Interview with Jean Baudrillard," translated by Brand Thumin, in *The Block*

Reader in Visual Culture (London & New York: Routledge, 1996);

Rex Butler, "Baudrillard's List," in *Jean Baudrillard: Art and Artefact,* edited by Nicholas Zurbrugg (Thousand Oaks, Cal. & London: Sage, 1997), pp. 43–50;

Paul Sutton, "Endangered Species? An Interview with Jean Baudrillard," *Angelaki OAE,* 2, no. 3 (1997): 217–224;

Entrevues à propos du "Complot de l'art": Avec Geneviève Breerette, Catherine Franklin, Françoise Gaillard, Ruth Scheps (Paris: Sens & Tonka, 1997);

Philippe Petit, *Le paroxyste indifférent: Entretiens avec Philippe Petit* (Paris: Grasset, 1997); translated by Chris Turner as *Paroxysm: Interviews with Philippe Petit* (London & New York: Verso, 1998);

François L'Yvonnet, *D'un fragment l'autre: entretiens avec François L'Yvonnet* (Paris: Albin Michel, 2001).

Bibliographies:

Richard G. Smith, "Following Baudrillard: A Bibliography of Writing on Jean Baudrillard," in *Jean Baudrillard: Art and Artefact,* edited by Nicholas Zurbrugg (Thousand Oaks, Cal. & London: Sage, 1997), pp. 168–179;

Eddie Yeghiayan, comp., "Jean Baudrillard: A Bibliography," *The Wellek Library Lecturers Bibliographies* (1999) <http://sun3.lib.uci.edu/~scctr/Wellek/baudrillard/index.html>.

References:

Rex Butler, *Jean Baudrillard: The Defence of the Real* (Thousand Oaks, Cal. & London: Sage, 1999);

Mike Gane, *Baudrillard: Critical and Fatal Theory* (London & New York: Routledge, 1991);

Douglas Kellner, *Jean Baudrillard: From Marxism to Postmodernism and Beyond* (Stanford, Cal.: Stanford University Press, 1989);

Kellner, ed., *Baudrillard: A Critical Reader* (Oxford & Cambridge, Mass.: Blackwell, 1994);

Richard J. Lane, *Jean Baudrillard* (London & New York: Routledge, 2000);

Charles Levin, *Jean Baudrillard: A Study in Cultural Metaphysics* (New York: Prentice Hall/Harvester Wheatsheaf, 1996);

Sadie Plant, "Baudrillard's Woman: The Eve of Seduction," in *Forget Baudrillard?* edited by Chris Rojek and Bryan S. Turner (London & New York: Routledge, 1993).

Maurice Blanchot

(22 September 1907 – 20 February 2003)

Sara Guyer
University of Oregon

See also the Blanchot entry in *DLB 72: French Novelists, 1930–1960.*

BOOKS: *Thomas l'Obscur: Roman* (Paris: Gallimard, 1941);

Comment la littérature est-elle possible? (Paris: José Corti, 1942); translated by Michael Syrotinski as "How Is Literature Possible?" in *The Blanchot Reader,* edited by Michael Holland (Oxford: Blackwell, 1995), pp. 49–60;

Aminadab (Paris: Gallimard, 1942); translated by Jeff Fort (Lincoln: University of Nebraska Press, 2002);

Faux Pas (Paris: Gallimard, 1943); translated by Charlotte Mandell (Stanford, Cal.: Stanford University Press, 2001);

Le Très-Haut (Paris: Gallimard, 1948); translated by Allan Stoekl as *The Most High* (Lincoln: University of Nebraska Press, 1996);

L'Arrêt de mort (Paris: Gallimard, 1948); translated by Lydia Davis as *Death Sentence* (Barrytown, N.Y.: Station Hill, 1978);

La Part du feu (Paris: Gallimard, 1949); translated by Mandell as *The Work of Fire* (Stanford, Cal.: Stanford University Press, 1995);

Lautréament et Sade (Paris: Editions de Minuit, 1949);

Thomas l'Obscur: Nouvelle version (Paris: Gallimard, 1950); translated by Robert Lamberton as *Thomas the Obscure* (New York: Lewis, 1973);

Au moment voulu (Paris: Gallimard, 1951); translated by Davis as *When the Time Comes* (Barrytown, N.Y.: Station Hill, 1985);

La Ressassement éternel (Paris: Editions de Minuit, 1951); enlarged as *Après Coup, précedé par, Le Ressassement éternel* (1983); translated by Paul Auster as *Vicious Circles: Two Stories and "After the Fact"* (Barrytown, N.Y.: Station Hill, 1983);

Celui qui ne m'accompagnait pas (Paris: Gallimard, 1953); translated by Davis as *The One Who Was Standing Apart from Me* (Barrytown, N.Y.: Station Hill, 1993);

L'Espace littéraire (Paris: Gallimard, 1955); translated by Ann Smock as *The Space of Literature* (Lincoln: University of Nebraska Press, 1985);

Le Dernier Homme (Paris: Gallimard, 1957; revised, 1977; revised again, 1979); translated by Davis as *The Last Man* (New York: Columbia University Press, 1987);

La Bête de Lascaux (Paris: GLM, 1958; enlarged edition, Montpellier: Fata Morgana, 1982); translated by Leslie Hill as "The Beast of Lascaux," *Oxford Literary Review,* 22 (2001): 9–18;

Le Livre à venir (Paris: Gallimard, 1959); translated by Charlotte Mandell as *The Book to Come* (Stanford, Cal.: Stanford University Press, 2003);

L'Attente l'oubli (Paris: Gallimard, 1962); translated by John Gregg as *Awaiting Oblivion* (Lincoln: University of Nebraska Press, 1997);

L'Entretien infini (Paris: Gallimard, 1969); translated by Susan Hanson as *The Infinite Conversation* (Minneapolis: University of Minnesota Press, 1993);

L'Amitié (Paris: Gallimard, 1971); translated by Elizabeth Rottenberg as *Friendship* (Stanford, Cal.: Stanford University Press, 1997);

Le Pas au-délà (Paris: Gallimard, 1973); translated by Lycette Nelson as *The Step Not Beyond* (Albany: State University of New York Press, 1992);

La Folie du jour (Montpellier: Fata Morgana, 1973); translated by Davis as *The Madness of the Day* (Barrytown, N.Y.: Station Hill, 1981);

L'Ecriture du désastre (Paris: Gallimard, 1980); translated by Smock as *The Writing of the Disaster* (Lincoln: University of Nebraska Press, 1986);

The Gaze of Orpheus, and Other Literary Essays, translated by Davis, edited by P. Adams Sitney, preface by Geoffrey Hartman (Barrytown, N.Y.: Station Hill, 1981);

De Kafka à Kafka (Paris: Gallimard, 1981);

The Sirens' Song: Selected Essays, translated by Sacha Rabinovitch, edited by Gabriel Josipovici (Bloomington: Indiana University Press, 1982; Brighton: Harvester, 1982);

Après Coup, précédé par, Le Ressassement éternel (Paris: Editions de Minuit, 1983); translated by Auster as "Vicious Circles," in *Vicious Circles: Two Fictions and "After the Fact"* (Barrytown, N.Y.: Station Hill, 1983);

La Communauté inavouable (Paris: Editions de Minuit, 1983); translated by Pierre Joris as *The Unavowable Community* (Barrytown, N.Y.: Station Hill, 1988);

Le Dernier à parler (Montpelier: Fata Morgana, 1984); translated by Joseph Simas as "The Last One to Speak," *ACTS: A Journal of New Writing,* 8/9 (1988): 228–239;

Michel Foucault tel que je l'imagine (Montpellier: Fata Morgana, 1986); translated by Jeffrey Mehlman as "Michel Foucault as I Imagine Him," in *Foucault/Blanchot* (New York: Zone Books, 1987), pp. 61–109;

Sade et Restif de la Bretonne (Brussels: Editions Complexe, 1986);

Joë Bousquet (Montpellier: Fata Morgana, 1987);

Une voix venue d'ailleurs: Sur les poèmes de Louis-René des Forêts (Paris: Ulysse, fin de siècle, 1992);

L'instant de ma mort (Montpellier: Fata Morgana, 1994); translated by Rottenberg as *The Instant of My Death* (Stanford, Cal.: Stanford University Press, 2000);

The Blanchot Reader, edited by Michael Holland (Oxford, Blackwell: 1995);

Les Intellectuels en question: Ebauche d'une réflexion (Paris: Fourbis, 1996); translated by Holland as "Intellectuals under Scrutiny: An Outline for Thought," in *The Blanchot Reader,* pp. 206–227;

Pour L'Amitié (Paris: Fourbis, 1996); translated by Leslie Hill as "For Friendship," *Oxford Literary Review,* 22 (2001): 25–38;

The Station Hill Blanchot Reader: Fiction and Literary Essays, translated by Auster, Davis, and Lamberton, edited by George Quasha (Barrytown, N.Y.: Station Hill, 1998);

Henri Michaux, ou le refus de l'enfermement (Tours: Farago, 1999);

Ecrits Politiques 1958–1993 (Paris: Scheer, 2003).

Maurice Blanchot has written only infrequently about his life. He has refused to be photographed, interviewed, or seen. This extreme discretion marks a body of writing that has touched everything of importance in modern European philosophy and literature, and, as Geoffrey Hartman has argued in his preface to Blanchot's *The Gaze of Orpheus, and Other Literary Essays* (1981), will be recognized to have "made French 'discourse' possible."

Blanchot is the author of significant works on George Wilhelm Friedrich Hegel, Friedrich Nietzsche,

Martin Heidegger, Georges Bataille, Michel Foucault, and Emmanuel Lévinas, as well as the marquis de Sade, Friedrich Schlegel, Friedrich Hölderlin, Rainer Maria Rilke, comte de Lautréament, Stéphane Mallarmé, Franz Kafka, René Char, and Paul Celan. These lists are not exhaustive. Blanchot also had a major influence on contemporary literary theorists and philosophers, above all Jacques Derrida, Foucault, Gilles Deleuze, Sarah Kofman, Hélène Cixous, and Paul de Man, all of whom have devoted texts to Blanchot. Moreover, Blanchot has influenced several contemporary artists and writers working across media, including Jean-Luc Godard, Marguerite Duras, Paul Auster, and Gary Hill.

Blanchot's invisibility, coupled with the significant influence of his work, led some late-twentieth-century critics to question the relationship between writing that sounds like a "voice that comes from elsewhere" (the title of one of Blanchot's late works) and the life of its author. More specifically, they have struggled to articulate the relation between a measured, even reserved oeuvre and its author's involvement with several extremist publications in the 1930s and 1940s. They have sought to understand Blanchot's complex, anti-Hitlerian nationalism in relation to his later politics, especially his strong stance against the Algerian War in 1958, his commitment to the creation of an international literary review, his participation in the students' and writers' groups of May 1968, and his enduring support of Israel. In letters, essays, introductions, and the autobiographical narrative *L'instant de ma mort* (1994; translated as *The Instant of My Death,* 2000), Blanchot willingly has acknowledged the bare facts of his life. Yet, these facts may have little or no relation to the works that rigorously engage the question of literature—works that seem to be written by no one, works that conceive of the writer as one who speaks from beyond the grave.

From his first volume of criticism, *Comment la littérature est-elle possible?* (1942; translated as "How Is Literature Possible?," 1995) to *L'instant de ma mort,* Blanchot rendered literature a question. Not only did he put literature in question, but in "La littérature et la droit de la mort" (Literature and the Right to Death), which first appeared in two installments in *La Nouvelle Revue Française* in 1949, he asks the reader to suppose that "Literature begins when literature becomes a question." Blanchot thus demonstrated that literature is uncontainable, reconcilable neither with the life of an author (hence his autobiographical reticence) nor with political ends (hence his critique of "engaged" writing). In his major contributions to literary theory, Blanchot also rendered literature a philosophical question, thus opening the field in which theorists such as Derrida,

Foucault, Jean-Luc Nancy, and Philippe Lacoue-Labarthe came to work.

Yet, it is not only as an essayist and critic but also as a writer of fictional narratives that Blanchot's influence on literary theory can be felt. Jean-Paul Sartre, Derrida, Lévinas, Foucault, Kofman, and J. Hillis Miller, for example, have devoted theoretical essays to readings of Blanchot's fiction. Their insight as literary theorists has at one time or another found an inaugural point in Blanchot's narratives. If a brief survey of the contemporary theorists indebted to Blanchot indicates his influence as a thinker, and if a catalogue of his works indicates his range as a writer, an account of Blanchot's friendships—with, among others, Lévinas, Bataille, Char, Robert Antelme, and Dionys Mascolo—and of his political involvement from the early 1930s to May 1968, when he withdrew from the public sphere, frames the life of this foremost theorist.

Maurice Leon Alexandre Blanchot was born 22 September 1907 in Quain in Saône-et-Loire, France, to Marie Mercey and Joseph Blanchot. He was the fourth child, after George (1895), Marguerite (1897), and René (1901). His family was Catholic and well-off. As a child—and later as an adult—Blanchot was in constantly poor health. Perhaps the most significant of his ailments began in 1922, when he was fifteen years old. An error during surgery on his abdomen left him with a rare blood disease—similar to the blood poisoning that one of the main characters in his best-known fiction, *L'Arrêt de mort* (1948; translated as *Death Sentence*, 1978), suffers. Like these characters and those in so many other of Blanchot's works who "outlive" their deaths, Blanchot himself suffered throughout his life—not only from this childhood ailment, but from asthma, vertigo, insomnia, and exhaustion as well.

Upon finishing his baccalaureate in 1923 or 1924, Blanchot enrolled at the University of Strasbourg, where he studied philosophy, classical and German literatures, sociology, psychology, and history. Perhaps most important, at Strasbourg, Blanchot met—and became lifelong friends with—Lévinas, a Lithuanian Jew some years his senior. In the final sentences of *Pour L'Amitié* (translated as "For Friendship," 2001), first published as the introduction to Mascolo's *A la recherche d'un communisme de pensée* (In Search of a Communism of Thought, 1993) and republished separately in 1996, Blanchot explains that Lévinas was the one friend whom he addressed intimately, that is, using the intimate second-person pronoun *(tutoiement)*. He explains that "this happened not because we were young, but by a deliberate decision, a covenant I hope never to break."

At Strasbourg, Blanchot introduced Lévinas to French literature, including the works of Marcel Proust and Paul Valéry, about which Lévinas later wrote. More significant, Lévinas introduced Blanchot to German philosophy. In particular, because of Lévinas, Blanchot read the phenomenology of Edmund Husserl. During these years Blanchot also encountered the fundamental ontology of Lévinas's teacher Heidegger. In a footnote to a 1988 letter to Catherine David, published in *Le Nouvel Observateur,* Blanchot recalled that in 1927 or 1928 Lévinas helped him to understand Heidegger's recently published magnum opus, *Sein und Zeit* (1927; translated as *Being and Time,* 1962). Blanchot explained to David that his encounter with Heidegger's philosophy of Being produced a "real intellectual shock" and that Lévinas's critical translation of Heidegger had a major influence on his work, recognizable from *Thomas l'Obscur* (Thomas the Obscure, 1941) to *L'Ecriture du désastre* (1980; translated as *The Writing of the Disaster,* 1986). The effect of this friendship with Lévinas can be felt in all of Blanchot's critical writing. Perhaps this influence can be witnessed most prominently, however, in Blanchot's interrogation of "the impossibility of dying." In readings of Kafka, Hölderlin, Rilke, and Hegel, indeed in critical rereadings of some of the works that Heidegger treats in his later essays on poetry, Blanchot responds to Heidegger's account of man as "Being-towards-death" and to Heidegger's understanding of death as the "possibility of impossibility." Blanchot demonstrates over and over again that these literary writers do not indicate an awareness of the possibility of death, but rather the insistence of the impossibility of dying. Blanchot articulates this logic only in the late 1940s—in the first versions of the essay "Literature and the Right to Death" and in the *récit* (narrative) *L'Arrêt de mort* (1948; translated as *Death Sentence,* 1978). Yet, Blanchot's most important theoretical developments emerged because of this initial meeting at Strasbourg.

Around 1929 Blanchot and Lévinas both left Strasbourg for Paris. In Paris, Blanchot took up studies, this time at the Sorbonne. He received a *diplome d'études supèrieures* (diploma of superior studies) for his thesis on "Conception du dogmatisme chez les sceptiques" (The Skeptics' Conception of Dogmatism). He also undertook to study medicine at Sainte-Anne, with specialties in neurology and psychiatry, but abandoned these plans before long, becoming an avid journalist by day and a writer by night.

Beginning in 1931, Blanchot contributed countless articles, signed and unsigned, to various French newspapers and magazines. Initially, his articles appeared in publications associated with the anti-Hitlerian Far Right, later with the Vichy government, and by the end of the 1940s he wrote for all of the major French literary reviews (including *La Nouvelle Revue Française,* under the guidance of Jean Paulhan; *Critique,* founded by Bataille; and *L'Arche* [The Arch], run by André Gide).

Blanchot's first published article, "François Mauriac et ceux qui étaient perdus" (François Mauriac and the Lost Ones), appeared on 28 June 1931 in *La Revue française politique et littéraire* (French Review of Politics and Literature), a bimonthly magazine associated with the right-wing group Action Française. This first piece was followed by an article on Mohandas Gandhi in *Les Cahiers mensuels* (July 1931) and by regular front-page articles in the conservative, anti-parliamentary daily *Journal des débats politiques et littéraires* (Journal of Political and Literary Debates), beginning on 18 August 1931 with an article titled "Comment s'emparer du pouvoir?" (How to Seize Power?). Blanchot soon became editor of the foreign desk at the *Le Journal des débats,* and he became the editor in chief of the newspaper itself around 1934. He held this position until July 1940 (immediately following the German occupation of France and the establishment of a separate, collaborationist government in Vichy), when the newspaper relocated to Clermont and was authorized by the Vichy government. Prior to collaboration, and at the time of Blanchot's editorship, *Le Journal des débats* was a more-or-less mainstream, if elitist and highly conservative, paper, known since the French Revolution as an intellectual forum for the right wing.

During this period Blanchot also contributed to *La revue française* (The French Review) and several smaller papers and reviews. These included *Le Rempart* (The Rampart), an outlet of the Jeune Droite (Young Right) edited by Paul Lévy; *Aux Écoutes,* another of Lévy's ventures, for which Blanchot also served as editor in chief; *Combat,* a nationalist monthly; and *L'Insurgé / politique et social* (The Insurrectionist / Political and Social), an anticommunist, weekly offshoot of *Combat.* Unlike *Le Journal des débats,* these publications promoted an extremist brand of nationalism, and on occasion verged upon fascism.

In the pages of *L'Insurgé,* in essays on Rilke, revolution, and other literary and political topics–almost none of which were collected in books–Blanchot first came to describe the critical terrain that he inhabited in the later essays that define his career as a critic. Here, also, he published articles deeply critical of contemporary, liberal politics in France, articles that called for a response to Adolf Hitler's rise to power in Germany and the overthrow of what, in his opinion, was the dissolution of the French nation by the compromised Popular Front. These publications led late-twentieth-century Anglo-American literary critics, convinced of Blanchot's importance as a thinker and writer, to question the relation between his political involvement in the 1930s and his apparently radical leftist position in

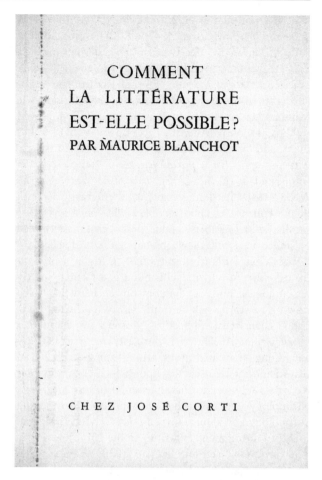

COMMENT
LA LITTÉRATURE
EST-ELLE POSSIBLE?
PAR MAURICE BLANCHOT

CHEZ JOSÉ CORTI

Paperback cover for Maurice Blanchot's first volume of literary criticism, published in 1942 and translated in 1995 as "How Is Literature Possible?" (Olin Memorial Library, Wesleyan University)

the 1950s and 1960s. Moreover, these articles have led critics to wonder whether Blanchot in the 1930s and 1940s was merely a right-wing nationalist or whether his position also was anti-Semitic. Few of the hundreds of articles that Blanchot published during these years seem to include explicitly anti-Semitic statements. Yet, two damning articles on Léon Blum, the Jewish president of the liberal Popular Front government, did appear in *L'Insurgé.* Several other articles–given the individuals that Blanchot mentions in them, above all, Charles Maurras, the founder of the highly reactionary Action Française, a well-known anti-Semite, and a convicted collaborator–have been understood to be fascist and implicitly anti-Semitic. Yet, there is inadequate evidence that Blanchot was a committed anti-Semite or a fascist.

While establishing his career as a journalist, Blanchot also composed two brief narratives, "L'Idylle" (1936; translated as "The Idyll," 1985) and "Le dernier mot" (The Last Word). Blanchot claimed that he initially did not plan to publish these texts, yet they both appeared in journals in 1947 ("L'Idylle" in the first issue of *La Licorne* [The Unicorn]; "Le dernier mot" in *Fontaine* [Fountain]) and are collected in the 1952 volume *Le ressassement éternel*. (Eternal Returnings, translated by Anster as *Vicious Circles*). In 1983 Editions de Minuit again published these works–this time followed by "Après Coup" (After the Fact), an essay that situates them, and "L'Idyll" in particular, in relation to Auschwitz–as *Après Coup, précédé par, Le Ressassement éternel* (translated as *Vicious Circles: Two Stories and "After the Fact,"* 1983). "Le dernier mot" is an enigmatic account of the collapse of language. "L'Idylle," in a style that recalls Kafka or Albert Camus, describes a man's exiled existence in a village where happiness is the law. In "Après Coup" Blanchot states that "L'Idylle" is a story from before Auschwitz. This point is a factual, strictly chronological one, but he goes on to claim that from now on all stories will be from before Auschwitz. Blanchot's claim recalls Theodor Adorno's statement that "Poetry after Auschwitz is barbaric" but recasts it by suggesting that henceforth the distinction between before and after Auschwitz, upon which claims such as Adorno's rely, cannot be understood in terms of strict chronology. For Blanchot, Auschwitz interrupts all chronology and all narrative, a point to which his eventual turn to fragmentary writing in the 1970s and 1980s bears witness. Yet, in the late 1930s, having completed–and left unpublished–"L'Idylle" and "Le dernier mot," Blanchot devoted his efforts to his first major fictional work: the novel *Thomas l'Obscur*.

In May 1940 Germany invaded France, and Blanchot's direct involvement with the radical Right came to an end. By the close of that year he had quit his editorial post at the now reactionary *Journal des débats*. Yet, he continued to write a weekly column, "Chronique de la vie intellectuel" (Chronicle of Intellectual Life), until the demise of the newspaper in 1944. Blanchot's regular contribution to a collaborationist paper indicated an activist logic that at the time many of his peers found highly suspect. In *Pour L'Amitié,* Blanchot explains that rather than abandon a group or publication tainted by the collaborationist regime, he aimed to redirect these groups, above all Jeune France, from the inside and "to use the association against itself." The project ultimately proved a failure.

At about the time of his resignation as editor of the *Le Journal des débats*, Blanchot was approached by Pierre Drieu de la Rochelle, who invited him to become head of *La Nouvelle Revue Française*, the magazine formerly run by Paulhan, which the Germans took control of in June 1940. The idea was that Drieu de la Rochelle, the collaborator, would remain the visible head of the publication, while Blanchot would run it as a strictly lit-

erary publication. Blanchot, however, realized that this decision would have been a grave compromise, and he reports in *Pour L'Amitié* having turned down the offer by saying "I can't invite people to contribute to a journal in which I would not myself want to be published." During the period that followed, Blanchot published his first books–three novels and two volumes of collected essays. He also met Bataille and Mascolo, two of the friends that had an enduring effect on his work.

Just as Blanchot's encounter with Lévinas radically changed his relation to philosophy, his encounter with Bataille, a novelist, theorist, and librarian, coincides with a profound change in his politics. Blanchot became friends with Bataille in the early 1940s and commemorates their friendship explicitly in the final chapter of his 1971 volume, *L'Amitié* (translated as *Friendship,* 1997), as well as in his many analyses of and references to Bataille elsewhere. It is perhaps because of Bataille that Blanchot recast his intellectual and political project of refusal as a radical calling into question.

Pierre Prevost introduced Blanchot and Bataille at the end of 1940. From the autumn of 1941 until March 1943 they met regularly as part of two working groups organized to discuss Bataille's work in progress, *L'Expérience intérieure* (1943; translated as *Inner Experience,* 1988). Bataille considered a conversation with Blanchot to be the point of origin of the project. While *L'Expérience intérieure* outlines the possibility of atheological ecstasy, of a radical calling into question of the self that does not rely upon an authority, it also links this "contestation" (another term for which Bataille thanks Blanchot) to community. Bataille's community is not based on an organic–or even a claimed–identity but rather a community of those who "live" contestation, in other words, "those who have nothing in common," because they have called all self-identity into question. This understanding of community differs radically from the mythic community of a nation that Blanchot had advocated only a few years earlier. In 1943 Blanchot reviewed *L'Expérience intérieure* in his weekly column and called it, in the words of Nietzsche, "A work entirely apart." He repeats this evaluation in the 1962 essay "L'experience-limite" (translated as "Limit-Experience," 1993), later included in *L'Entretien infini* (1969; translated as *The Infinite Conversation,* 1993), and in 1983 Blanchot elaborates his discussion of community in *La Communauté inavouable* (translated as *The Unavowable Community,* 1988), devoted to Bataille–by way of Nancy–as well as to another friend, the novelist Duras.

In 1941 *Thomas l'Obscur*, Blanchot's first novel, was published. Bataille quotes passages from the novel in *L'Expérience intérieure,* as does Lévinas in *De l'existence à l'existant* (1947; translated as *Existence and Existents,* 1978). Both friends had read the novel in manuscript. Gallimard published Blanchot's second novel, *Aminadab* (translated, 2002) in September 1942. While Camus and Paulhan were among the reviewers that responded to the novel warmly, Sartre reviewed it in 1943 in a somewhat retaliatory tone, noting critically its resemblance to the works of Kafka. In this same year, at the suggestion of Mascolo, a member of the French Resistance and philosopher with whom Blanchot had became friends, *Faux Pas* (translated, 2001), Blanchot's first volume of essays, appeared.

Faux Pas collects many of the reviews Blanchot had published in the *Journal des débats* along with three pieces from *L'Insurgé* and an article on Lautréament that first ran in the *La Revue française des idées et des œuvres* (French Review of Ideas and Works). In *Pour L'Amitié* Blanchot recalls that he had saved no copies of these articles, sent into "the unoccupied zones by secret channels," and he imagines that Mascolo likely saved these texts and presented them to the publisher Gaston Gallimard with the suggestion of a published volume. While the essays in *Faux Pas* primarily treat nineteenth- and twentieth-century philosophy and literature, and while most of them already had appeared in the *Le Journal des débats,* the censorship board then active in occupied France refused its publication twice before the book finally appeared in December 1943.

During the final months of the occupation Blanchot returned to his family home, "the Chateau," in the Loire. There, in the summer of 1944, he had an "experience" that came to orient his thought of experience itself. As Blanchot recalls in *L'instant de ma mort,* the Allies had arrived in France, and the Germans responded "with useless ferocity." In June a lieutenant knocked on the door, ordered everyone–including Blanchot's sister, aunt, mother, and sister-in-law–outside, and commanded Blanchot to stand against a wall before a firing squad. As the soldiers lined up to shoot him, a battle was heard to begin nearby. The lieutenant left to investigate, and the soldiers–who turned out not to be Germans, as the family had thought, but Russians–allowed Blanchot to flee into the woods. This survival of the instant of certain death is what Blanchot calls "lightness" in *L'instant de ma mort* and what elsewhere–in his essays, fiction, and fragments–he calls the impossibility of dying. When the lieutenant returned, Blanchot had disappeared. After escaping, however, he witnessed another injustice. Although the lieutenant searched his family home and stole "a sort of thick manuscript" that was never returned, "the Chateau," because it belonged to the wealthy, remained standing, while all of the surrounding farms were destroyed by flames. In 1994 Blanchot admits that he was left ashamed by the injustice of class privilege and suggests that by 1944 his politics already were in transition, a

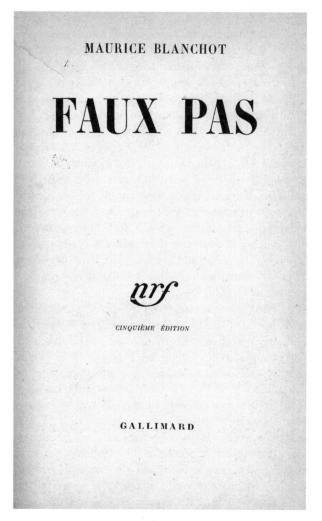

MAURICE BLANCHOT

FAUX PAS

nrf

CINQUIÈME ÉDITION

GALLIMARD

Title page for Blanchot's 1943 volume, a collection of reviews and essays that had appeared in periodicals such as L'Insurgé *and the* Journal des débats *(Robert W. Woodruff Library, Emory University)*

transition the effects of which were borne out first in 1958 and then in 1968. Blanchot's experience in Quain exemplified the thought of inner experience and the irremissibility of existence that with Bataille and Lévinas he already had begun to articulate. His writing changed to reflect this "experience" of death.

Blanchot returned to Paris and Parisian literary life in the autumn of 1944. He wrote for several journals including Gide's *L'Arche,* Sartre's *Les Temps Modernes* (Modern Times), Bataille's *Actualité* (Actuality), *Critique* (Bataille's more influential journal, for which Blanchot was permitted to write on anything he wished), *Carrefour* (Crossroads), and *Paysage Dimanche.* He sat on juries for literary prizes. At this point he began to frame his most important critical essays, including "Literature and the Right to Death," which appeared in two parts in *Critique* before becoming the final essay in *La Part du Feu* (1950, translated as *The Work of Fire,* 1995), a volume that collects many of the essays Blanchot published during this period.

La Part du Feu opens with two essays on Kafka and, like *Faux Pas,* includes essays on major figures in French letters. Just as the most important essay in *Faux Pas* is *Comment la littérature est-elle possible?,* the most significant essay in the volume is "La littérature et la droit de la mort." Here, Blanchot read Lévinas with Hegel and Kafka with Mallarmé and Paulhan in order to demonstrate that literature effects what Hegel called "a life that endures and maintains itself in death," a life for which negativity does not lead to sublimation but indicates the impossibility of dying and the irrevocability of being. In this essay, language and literature mark the site where genuinely philosophical questions—that is, questions of finitude and negativity—emerge.

Blanchot's divided 1948 narrative *L'Arrêt de mort* takes up this thought of the impossibility of dying, as does the narrative titled "Un récit?" (A Narrative?), which appeared in the journal *Empédocle* in 1949 and later was published as *La folie du jour* (1973; translated as *The Madness of the Day,* 1981). *L'Arrêt de mort* takes place in 1938; it is a work dated by the war and by history. Formally and thematically, it is concerned with the condition of irremissibility or survival. The narrator, a journalist and writer condemned to death, returns to J., a dying woman who does not die but whose pulse, finally, "scatters like sand"; *L'Arrêt de mort* also tells of the many women that the narrator encounters during his days and nights. The *récit* is divided into two narratives whose relation is never fully articulated and that, therefore, never properly end or begin. Upon its initial publication *L'Arrêt de mort* was reviewed by Bataille in *Critique,* Maurice Nadeau in *Combat,* and Pierre Klossowski in *Le Temps Modernes.* Some years later, Derrida analyzed it—alongside Percy Bysshe Shelley's *The Triumph of Life* (1822)—in "Living On: Borderlines."

This indeterminate negativity of *L'Arrêt de mort,* understood as a writer's "double dying," constitutes Blanchot's *L'Espace littéraire* (1955; translated as *The Space of Literature,* 1985). In essays on Rilke, Kafka, and Mallarmé, Blanchot elaborates this structure, distinguishing between the death that these writers seek in their work, the possible death, and what he calls "that other death which is death without end, the ordeal of the end's absence." Yet, in elaborating this distinction, he shows that the search for death as a possibility in writing gives way to death as the impossibility of dying. This impossibility does not mean that death in the world lies in wait, however, for *L'Espace littéraire* demonstrates that death remains what one already has lost. If death is still to come, its arrival will not allow for an experience of death, for that experience remains without subjects.

In contemplating the Orpheus myth—in a chapter, "Le regard d'Orphée (The Gaze of Orpheus), that he calls the center of attraction of *L'Espace littéraire*—Blanchot articulates the impossibility of dying most explicitly. Drawing not only from Ovid but also from Rilke, the author of *Die Sonette an Orpheus* (1923; translated as *Sonnets to Orpheus,* 1936), Blanchot explains that Orpheus descends into the underworld to retrieve the dead Eurydice through song and returns her to the world of the living. He promises not to look back until they have left Hades; yet, unable to resist, he turns back to gaze upon her and loses Eurydice to death a second time. This turn, in which one fails to raise the dead because one wants to catch a glimpse of death, for Blanchot marks the beginning of writing. In *L'Espace littéraire,* and especially those sections devoted to Rilke and Hölderlin, Blanchot responds to Heidegger's studies of poetry. This response is referred to explicitly in the titles of his chapters, including "La littérature et l'expérience originelle" (Literature and the Original Experience), but also in his choice of texts, for Blanchot considers the same poems that Heidegger does in his essay "Wozu Dichter?" (1946; translated as "What Are Poets For?," 1971).

At about the same time that the first versions of the essays included in *L'Espace littéraire* began to appear in journals, Blanchot composed two further fictional narratives: *Au moment voulu* (1951; translated as *When the Time Comes,* 1985) and *Celui qui ne m'accompagnait pas* (1953; translated as *The One Who Was Standing Apart from Me,* 1993). A third novel, *Le Dernier homme* (translated as *The Last Man,* 1987), was published in 1957, although as early as 1955 excerpts from the book appeared in journals, including *La Nouvelle Nouvelle Revue Française, Botteghe Oscure,* and *Monde Nouveau* (New World).

During this period, Blanchot wrote from Eze, where from 1949 to 1957—as he describes on the opening page of *Une voix venue d'ailleurs: Sur les poèmes de Louis-René des Forêts* (A Voice from Elsewhere: On the Poems of Louis-René des Forêts, 1992)—he lived in a small room with two windows: one affording a view of Corsica, the other of Cap Ferat. Despite his isolation, friendship remained central for Blanchot. In 1953 he published *La Bête de Lascaux* (translated as "The Beast of Lascaux," 2001), devoted to Char's poem "La Bête innomable" (The Unnameable Beast, 1952) and the discovery in 1940 of seventeen-thousand-year-old cave paintings in the south of France. The essay appeared first in *La Nouvelle Nouvelle Revue Française,* then in 1958 and again in 1982 was published as a short volume, by which time Bataille's own book on Lascaux and the birth of art also had been published. *La Bête de Lascaux* was the first of many texts that Blanchot devoted to Char. He develops his account of the fragment and the neuter in later essays that engage Char's poetry. Char also contributed to this exchange when, in 1955, he published "Le Mortel Partenaire" (translated as "The Mortal Partner"), a prose poem.

In 1957, three days after Blanchot's fiftieth birthday, his mother died. Touched by this loss, he initially returned to Paris to stay with his brother René and in the summer of the following year decided to remain permanently in Paris, moving to a Left Bank apartment on the corner of rue Madam and rue de Vaugirard. In *Pour l'Amitié* Blanchot attributes his return to Paris to Charles de Gaulle's return to power. In response to de Gaulle's return, Blanchot visited Mascolo at the publishing house Gallimard, not to discuss his books in progress—*Le Livre à venir* (The Book to Come), another collection of essays, appeared with Gallimard in the following year, 1958—but rather to discuss politics, specifically the war in Algeria, which had begun in May.

During this meeting Blanchot also met, for the first time, Antelme, the author of *L'espèce humaine* (1947; translated as *The Human Race,* 1992), a testimonial account of Buchenwald and Dachau. At the time of his arrest in Paris, Antelme had been active in the French Resistance. He was married to Duras, and a close friend of Mascolo helped to organize his precarious return from Dachau to Paris. According to Christophe Bident, Blanchot likely read *L'espèce humaine* in 1950, and the book had a major influence on him. Indeed, in response to the question posed by a Polish magazine "What is the influence that the war had on literature after 1945?" Blanchot composed a brief text on "Guerre et littérature" (War and Literature), later collected in *L'Amitié,* in which he explains that "the books stemming from the experience of which the camps were the place forever without place have kept their dark radiance: not read and consumed in the same way as other books" and identifies Antelme's book as "the simplest, the purest, and the closest to this absolute that it makes us remember." In addition to "Guerre et littérature," Blanchot devoted several others to Antelme—most significantly, "L'espèce humaine," a chapter of *L'Entretien infini.* Blanchot understood Antelme to demonstrate that the human is "the indestructible that can be infinitely destroyed." This logic of survival in destruction—conceived alongside Lévinas's ethics—ultimately led Blanchot to the phrase "the writing of the disaster."

Blanchot reentered public life by publishing two explicitly political articles in the journal *Le 14 Juillet* (14 July). The first, "Le Refus" (translated as "Refusal"), is written in the first-person plural. It appeared initially in the second issue of the journal (October 1958) and later

MAURICE BLANCHOT

L'attente l'oubli

nrf

GALLIMARD

Title page for Blanchot's philosophical exploration of communication (1962; translated as Awaiting Oblivion, *1997) in the form of a dialogue in which a woman demands that a man act in a way that will make it possible for her to speak to him (Hodges Library, University of Tennessee)*

in *L'Amitié.* The essay calls not only for a refusal of "the worst" but for the refusal of what appears "reasonable." "La perversion essentielle" (The Essential Perversion) appeared the following June. In this article, which Char hailed in a brief note published in the December 1966 issue of *La Nouvelle Revue Française,* Blanchot identifies the "essential corruption of political power" that attends de Gaulle's role as sovereign.

The refusal of de Gaulle that instigated Blanchot's return to politics in 1958 was succeeded by the refusal of the Algerian War in 1960. In September, Blanchot, along with Mascolo, Antelme, and André Breton, co-authored the "Déclaration sur le droit à l'insoumission dans la guerre d'Algérie" (translated as "A Declaration Concerning the Right of Insubordination in the Algerian War," 1960). The text supported those Frenchmen who refused to take up arms against

Algerians, which is to say, those who refused to maintain the colonial force of France, as well as those who chose to fight for the Algerians. Blanchot discusses the declaration in a 1960 interview with Madeleine Chapsal, which first appeared in *Le Droit à la insoumission (le dossier des 121)* (The Right of Insubordination [The Dossier of the 121]) and was translated in *The Blanchot Reader* (1995), in which he explains that he chose to sign—indeed to compose—this text "as a writer . . . not as a political writer, nor even as a citizen involved in the political struggle, but as an apolitical writer who felt moved to express an opinion about problems that concern him essentially." Blanchot aligns writing with responsibility as separate from politics, suggesting that ethical questions, or questions of responsibility, are more essential than political questions. Yet, this statement also implies that an ethical response can lead to activist, or "political," engagements. Moreover, this gesture—the sovereign decision of insubordination—responds to what two years earlier Blanchot had identified as the "essential perversion" of sovereignty. The call for responsibility articulated in the "Manifeste de 121," so called because it was signed by 121 writers and intellectuals, was a call for a mode of nonperverse power. Two magazines agreed to publish the manifesto—*Lettres nouvelles* (New Letters) and *Les Temps Modernes*—and both were immediately banned and confiscated. The text did appear in the United States in 1960, published in the *Evergreen Review,* and news of the manifesto spread throughout Europe.

Between 1958 and 1968 Blanchot became involved in several related political projects. Perhaps the most ambitious was an international review that he imagined along with Italo Calvino, Pier Paolo Passolini, and Elio Vittorini in Italy; Günter Grass, Hans-Magnus Enzensberger, Ingeborg Bachmann, and Uwe Johnson in Germany; and Roland Barthes, Michel Leiris, des Forêts, Duras, Antelme, and Mascolo in France; as well as other writers in these countries and in Poland, England, and the United States. The project failed. A dossier that appeared in the journal *Lignes* in 1990 collects all of the documents related to the review, including Blanchot's articulation of its mission and its practice. These texts have theoretical importance, not least because they anticipate many of the discussions of cosmopolitanism and globalization that came to preoccupy literary theory in the late 1990s.

In these documents Blanchot explains that translation would have been a major aspect of the "Revue Internationale," and he goes so far as to state that "in a certain sense, the translator would be the real writer of this review." By understanding translation as writing, rather than a secondary form of transmission, and by taking Hölderlin's translations of Sophocles' tragedies

as a model, Blanchot in 1960 imagined a possibility of writing and publication that remains radical and—at least on the scale that the "Revue Internationale" promised—unrealized.

Blanchot attributed the failure of the review to the August 1961 division of Berlin by the Berlin Wall, an event that he examines in the brief but important 1961 text "The Name Berlin." This text is remarkable not only for the way that it describes the problem of division in relation to writing but also because, like the texts Blanchot imagined would appear in the "Revue Internationale," it is written by translators. The text appeared for the first time in Italian translation in 1964, was translated from Italian to English in 1982, was then translated from Italian to French—the original French text had been lost—by Hélène Jelen and Nancy, and was also translated into German. Parallel translations of the essay into French (by Jelen and Nancy), English (by Aris Fioretos), Russian (by Mikhail Yampolsky), and German (by Werner Hamacher) appeared in a 1994 volume of the American journal *Modern Language Notes.*

As Blanchot became newly involved in politics, his texts became increasingly fragmentary. In *L'Attente l'oubli* (1962; translated as *Awaiting Oblivion,* 1997), Blanchot undoes (or multiplies) the division between fiction and philosophy. In this fragmentary narrative he treats the possibility and impossibility of address and the minimal condition of speaking to another person—if one exists. Thus, over and over again the woman in the volume addresses a man, asking him to act in such a way that she can speak to him. This demand—which already assumes the situation for which it asks—promises a thinking community marked neither by identity nor by any quality shared by individuals, a community that in *La Communauté inavouable* Blanchot associates not only with Duras and with Bataille but also with the political activities in which he came to be involved in 1968.

In the early part of 1968 Blanchot and Derrida met for the first time. François Fédier had invited them both to contribute works to a volume of essays devoted to Jean Beaufret, a French philosopher who was closely linked to Heidegger and whose anti-Semitism recently had been discovered. In response to this discovery, Derrida withheld his submission, and Blanchot dedicated his to Lévinas. Together Blanchot and Derrida wrote a letter to Fédier and the contributors to the volume, but they later discovered that the letter was not delivered. Only two years earlier Derrida had published his first volumes, works that indicate a clear debt to Blanchot and that also influenced Blanchot's work, in particular the essays included in *L'Entretien infini.* Also during this period, the first critical collection devoted to Blanchot was published. In June 1966, four years after Bataille's death, Blanchot was the subject of a rare special issue of *Critique* that included essays by Jean Starobinski, Georges Poulet, de Man, Foucault, Roger Laporte, and Lévinas, as well as a poem by Char. The essays included in the volume, along with Derrida's essays, collected in the 1986 volume *Parages,* remain some of the most significant critical engagements with Blanchot's writing. The special issue of *Critique* signaled, already in 1966, the importance of Blanchot's thought for philosophy and criticism.

While the "Beaufret Affair," as Bident calls it, was taking place, Blanchot, along with Antelme, Mascolo, and Duras, thrust himself—joyously, according to Lévinas—into the events of May 1968. In addition to speaking at public protests and participating in the general strike, in May and June of that year Blanchot wrote several declarations, including statements of solidarity with the student movement and of political refusal. These letters—two of which appeared in *Le Monde*—were signed by the most renowned artists and writers of the day, including Sartre and Simone de Beauvoir and the movie directors Godard, François Truffaut, Alain Resnais, and Jacques Rivette, as well as many philosophers and critics. Other statements were signed by the Comité d'action étudiants-écrivains (Students-Writers Action Committee), the group in which Blanchot played an active part.

In October 1968 Blanchot—along with Mascolo, Duras, and Antelme—formed *Comité: Bulletin publié par le Comité d'Action étudiants-écrivains au service du Mouvement* (Committee: Bulletin Published by the Students-Writers Action Committee in Service to the Movement). The first and only issue of *Comité* included eighteen brief, unsigned texts written by Blanchot. Here Blanchot elaborated—in a language that recalled both his political writing of the 1930s and 1940s and his critical writing of the 1950s and 1960s—his call for refusal and revolution. *Comité* also included Blanchot's most explicit—and influential—engagements with Marxism: "Lire Marx" (Reading Marx), which later appeared in *L'Amitié* under the title "Le trois paroles de Marx" (Marx's Three Voices), "Three Readings of Marx," and the brief "Communisme sans Heritage" (translated as "Communism without a Heritage" in *The Blanchot Reader*). In the latter essay, Blanchot opposes a form of ecstasy—"the call to go out, into an outside that is neither another world nor what lies behind the world"—to patriotism, which he finds indistinguishable from nationalism. While these texts marked Blanchot's enthusiastic return to public politics, shortly after their appearance Blanchot withdrew entirely from that public.

In the section of *La Communauté inavouable* titled "Mai 68" (May '68) and in the opening lines of his homage *Michel Foucault tel que je l'imagine* (1986; translated as *Michel Foucault as I Imagine Him,* 1987) Blanchot

MAURICE BLANCHOT

L'écriture du désastre

nrf

GALLIMARD

Title page for Blanchot's 1980 collection of fragmentary reflections on writers such as Emmanuel Lévinas, Georg Wilhelm Friedrich Hegel, and Franz Kafka, translated in 1986 as The Writing of the Disaster *(Hodges Library, University of Tennessee)*

acknowledges the almost utopian eventfulness of May 1968. He explains that for a brief instant one could speak freely, without authority or right. Yet, *Comité* failed after only a single issue, and soon thereafter Blanchot disappeared from public life. Blanchot's departure from politics has been attributed to the turn by the Left against the state of Israel and against Zionism, a turn that Blanchot understood as indistinguishable from anti-Semitism and that would have coincided with the discovery of Beaufret's anti-Semitism. This disappointment alone does not seem to account adequately for Blanchot's abandonment of the public sphere.

Blanchot's departure was radical. After 1968 he never met Lévinas again, nor did he see Mascolo, Antelme, Duras, Derrida, or any of his other friends, although he did occasionally speak with them on the telephone or correspond by letter. From this point on he refused to expose his life or his face to photographers, interviewers, biographers, or journalists in search of the author, who belongs, to use Blanchot's own idiom, not to the day, but to the night of invisibility. To avoid publicity also was to avoid the confusion that photographs or biographical accounts cannot help but render. At about the time of his disappearance, Blanchot developed a new form of writing–fragmentary and preoccupied with ethics as a question of responsibility–that defined his work in the 1970s and 1980s. Indeed, these two changes are related. Blanchot had discovered that each time his life touched history, each time he submerged himself in public activity, he suffered a profound and certain failure. To abandon the public was to recognize its limits and susceptibility to misdirection. Blanchot thus did not disappear simply to protect one secret or another but to protect himself against the unforeseeable and potentially dangerous outcome of political activism. In other words, his withdrawal from public politics involved an explicit act of responsibility and coincided with a turn to questions of responsibility in his late work. This does not mean that after 1968 Blanchot no longer spoke about historical events–he addressed Salman Rushdie's exile, Nelson Mandela's imprisonment, and Heidegger's Nazism. These texts derive from ethical positions rather than political affiliations, however.

This anonymity and fragmentary quality characterize *L'Entretien infini,* a volume, like *L'Attente l'oubli,* that undoes the division between narrative and critical voices. The book consists of revised versions of essays written prior to 1968 and opens with an anonymous conversation that is interrupted and recovered throughout the text. Essays–on Antelme, Bataille, Kafka, Nietzsche, and Char–sometimes open with or culminate in the fragmentary exchange between interlocutors. These conversations leave in question the authorial voice by multiplying it in a way that frustrates attempts to establish certain authority.

In 1970 Blanchot published *Le Dernier à parler* (published as a book in 1984 and translated as "The Last One to Speak," 1988), a brief essay on Celan, whose poetry bears witness to the indelible marks of the Shoah on language. The next year, *L'Amitié* appeared. *L'Entretien infini, Le dernier à parler,* and *L'Amitié* are the first texts of Blanchot's post-1968 period. They indicate the itinerary that Blanchot undertook from the early 1970s and 1980s, in which fragmentation, friendship, and the thought of disaster distinguish his late work.

In *Le Pas au-délà* (1973; translated as *The Step Not Beyond,* 1992) and in *L'Ecriture du désastre,* Blanchot radicalizes this style and publishes volumes composed entirely of fragments. These texts–which resemble the

Jena Romantics' fragments more than they do Nietzsche's aphorisms, although Schlegel, Novalis (Friedrich Leopold, Baron Von Hardenberg), and Nietzsche all are treated within them–withhold continuity and theorize the interruptions that they perform. Here also Blanchot's preoccupation with thinking and writing after Auschwitz becomes apparent.

When fragments from *L'Ecriture du désastre* first appeared, they bore the subtitle "in the margin of Emmanuel Lévinas's books." Yet, not only Lévinas's thought but also Antelme's testimony, his survival, and the translation of philosophical accounts of man that it opened allowed Blanchot to articulate his final and perhaps most important critical project. *L'Ecriture du désastre* is Blanchot's third volume entirely composed of fragments. In reflections on writers such as Lévinas, Hegel, Char, Kafka, Celan, Schlegel, and Antelme, Blanchot came to situate his work historically, while recognizing that in relation to disaster, history is suspended. The volume opens with a statement in which Blanchot translates his earlier accounts of the impossibility of dying as well as the survival of the human in destruction that Antelme articulates: "The disaster changes everything, all the while leaving everything intact." The disaster is never reduced to a name of a place or event. Rather it names a radical, unaccountable negativity after which nothing will remain the same, yet after which there is no ground from which to recognize this change. Thus, the disaster has no witness and precludes all experience: these privations are the essence of the disaster. While the concept of disaster had already emerged in Blanchot's readings on Kafka and in his own narratives, the full scope of this development was voiced only in the fragments of the 1980 volume.

After *L'Ecriture du désastre,* published when Blanchot was seventy-three years old and already quite frail, most of Blanchot's publications were editions of earlier works or extremely brief homages. *Le Dernier à parler* appeared in a volume of its own, as, in 1987, did a brief text that Blanchot had written decades earlier on the novelist Joë Bousquet. The text on Berlin was published, as was a collection of Blanchot's many essays on Kafka, *De Kafka à Kafka* (From Kafka to Kafka, 1981), and *Après Coup, précedé par, Le Ressassement éternel.* Blanchot also wrote brief, if important, texts for (and about) Foucault, des Forêts, Derrida, Lévinas, and Jean-François Lyotard, as well as several letters–in lieu of solicited essays–that appeared in journals and magazines in Europe and the United States. Without question, the most important publishing event of this late period occurred in 1994 with Blanchot's return to narrative in the autobiographical *L'instant de ma mort.*

Derrida's *Demeure: Maurice Blanchot* (translated as *Demeure: Fiction and Testimony,* 2000), a close analysis of

L'instant de ma mort (and Blanchot's work more generally), appeared as an essay in *Passions de la littérature: Avec Jacques Derrida* (Passions for Literature: With Jacques Derrida, 1966) and then as a book in 1998. It is the most important of the many works on Blanchot that proliferated in the 1980s and 1990s. Lacoue-Labarthe also devoted an essay to *L'instant de ma mort* (presented at a 1997 conference in honor of Derrida), and taken together, these analyses indicate the centrality of Blanchot's notion of the *récit* for any contemporary account or testimony.

While Blanchot published little in the 1990s, it is the decade in which a critical discourse on the author fully emerged. In the early 1990s the journals *Lignes* and *L'esprit createur* (The Creator Spirit) devoted special issues to Blanchot, and at a 1993 International Blanchot Conference in London, which led to the publication of *Maurice Blanchot: The Demand of Writing* (1996), American, British, and French scholars, including Laporte, gathered to examine Blanchot's oeuvre. In the mid and late 1990s, Gerald Bruns, Leslie Hill, Thomas Carl Wall, John Gregg, Timothy Clark, and Steven Ungar published books about Blanchot, and between 1997 and 2001, *Furor, Revue des Sciences Humaines* (Review of Human Sciences), *L'œil de bœuf* (The Eye of the Ox), *Yale French Studies,* and *The Oxford Literary Review* published special issues devoted to Blanchot's writing. Two English-language anthologies—one devoted to Blanchot's fiction, the other to his critical writing—and Bident's biography, *Maurice Blanchot: Partenaire invisible* (1998), also appeared during this period. Some of these works sought to expose the secrets of Blanchot's life and his work. Others have borne witness to the rigor—at once infectious and alienating—that marks Blanchot's writing. Yet, in one way or another, each of these works makes abundantly clear that to read Blanchot—even, and perhaps especially, to read *L'instant de ma mort*—is to encounter the question of literature, a question that Blanchot's work poses with still unmatched force.

On 20 February 2003, Blanchot died at home in Yvelines, France. He was ninety-five years old. His body was cremated.

During his lifetime, Maurice Blanchot worked simultaneously at the margins and the center of contemporary critical theory. On the one hand, he was virtually unknown, an author whose most important works were occasional pieces, book reviews or fragments, and someone who—after the events of 1968—never made a public appearance; on the other hand, his work in its enigmatic difficulty and its undeniable force has influenced generations of thinkers among whom Bataille, Lévinas, Derrida, Foucault, Nancy, de Man, Jean Starobinski, and Gilles Deleuze are only the most

Maurice Blanchot
L'instant
de ma
mort

Fata Morgana

Paperback cover for the 1994 book, translated as The Instant of My Death *(2000), in which Blanchot describes how he escaped what appeared to be certain death by a Russian firing squad in June 1944 (Robert W. Woodruff Library, Emory University)*

well known. As a thinker, but above all, a writer, Blanchot's influence remains to be calculated; indeed, it may ultimately prove incalculable—for so many philosophers and theorists write "with" him, yet do so without ever mentioning his name.

Biography:
Christophe Bident, *Maurice Blanchot: Partenaire invisible* (Paris: Champ Vallon, 1998).

References:
Avec Dionys Mascolo, special issue, *Lignes,* 33 (1998): 84–89, 111–184, 208–221;
Georges Bataille, *L'Expérience intérieure* (Paris: Gallimard, 1943); translated by Leslie Anne Boldt as *Inner Experience* (Albany: State University of New York Press, 1988);
Christophe Bident, *Reconnaissances: Antelme, Blanchot, Deleuze* (Paris: Callman-Levy, 2003);
Bident and Pierre Villar, eds., *Maurice Blanchot: récits critiques* (Paris: Léo Scheer, 2003);

Gerald L. Bruns, *Maurice Blanchot: The Refusal of Philosophy* (Baltimore: Johns Hopkins University Press, 1997);

Françoise Collin, *Maurice Blanchot et la question de l'écriture* (Paris: Gallimard, 1971);

Jacques Derrida, *Demeure: Maurice Blanchot* (Paris: Galilée, 1998); translated by Elizabeth Rottenberg as *Demeure: Fiction and Testimony* (Stanford, Cal.: Stanford University Press, 2000);

Derrida, *Parages* (Paris: Galilée, 1986);

Derrida, *Politiques de l'amitié: Suivi de L'oreille de Heidegger* (Paris: Galilée, 1994); translated by George Collins as *The Politics of Friendship* (London & New York: Verso, 1997);

Disastrous Blanchot, special issue, *Oxford Literary Review*, 22 (2001);

Dossier Maurice Blanchot, special issue, *Relantir Travaux*, 7 (Winter 1997);

L'Enigme Blanchot, special issue, *Magazine littéraire*, 424 (October 2003);

Michel Foucault, *La Pensée du dehors* (Montpellier: Fata Morgana, 1986); translated by Brian Massumi as "Maurice Blanchot: The Thought from Outside," in *Foucault/Blanchot* (New York: Zone Books, 1987), pp. 7–58;

Carolyn Bailey Gill, ed., *Maurice Blanchot: The Demand of Writing* (London & New York: Routledge, 1996);

John Gregg, *Maurice Blanchot and the Literature of Transgression* (Princeton: Princeton University Press, 1994);

Ullrich Haase and William Large, *Maurice Blanchot* (London & New York: Routledge, 2001);

Leslie Hill, *Bataille, Klossowski, Blanchot: Writing at the Limit* (Oxford: Oxford University Press, 2001);

Hill, *Blanchot: Extreme Contemporary* (London & New York: Routledge, 1997);

Sarah Kofman, *Paroles Suffoquées* (Paris: Galilée, 1987); translated by Madeleine Dobie as *Smothered Words* (Evanston, Ill.: Northwestern University Press, 1998);

Philippe Lacoue-Labarthe, *Agonie terminée, agonie interminable (Sur Maurice Blanchot)* (Paris: Galilée, 2004);

Roger Laport, *A l'extrême pointe: Bataille et Blanchot* (Paris: Fata Morgana, 1994), pp. 31–67; expanded as *A l'extrême pointe: Proust, Bataille, Blanchot* (Paris: POL, 1998), pp. 64–95;

Emmanuel Lévinas, *Autrement qu'être; ou, Au-delà de l'essence* (The Hague: Nijhoff, 1974); translated by Alphonso Lingis as *Otherwise Than Being; or, Beyond Essence* (The Hague & Boston: Nijhoff, 1981);

Lévinas, *De l'existence à l'existant*, revised edition (Paris: Vrin, 1978); translated by Lingis as *Existence and Existents* (The Hague: Nijhoff, 1978);

Lévinas, *Sur Maurice Blanchot* (Paris: Fata Morgana, 1975); translated by Michael B. Smith as "On Maurice Blanchot," in *Proper Names* (Stanford, Cal.: Stanford University Press, 1996), pp. 125–170;

Lévinas, *Totalité et infini: Essai sur l'extériorité* (The Hague: Nijhoff, 1961); translated by Lingis as *Totality and Infinity: An Essay on Exteriority* (Pittsburgh: Duquesne University Press, 1969);

Joseph Libertson, *Proximity: Blanchot, Bataille, and Communication* (The Hague: Nijhoff, 1982);

Lire Blanchot I, special issue, *Gramma*, 3/4 (1976);

Lire Blanchot II, special issue, *Gramma*, 5 (1976);

Maurice Blanchot, special issue, *Critique*, 229 (June 1966);

Maurice Blanchot, special issue, *Furor*, 29 (1999);

Maurice Blanchot, special issue, *Lignes*, 11 (September 1990);

Maurice Blanchot, special issue, *L'œil de bœuf: Revue Littéraire Trimentrielle*, 14/15 (May 1998);

Maurice Blanchot, special issue, *Revue des Sciences Humaines*, 253 (1999);

J. Hillis Miller, *Versions of Pygmalion* (Cambridge, Mass.: Harvard University Press, 1990), pp. 179–210;

Jean-Luc Nancy, *La communauté désoeuvrée* (Paris: Bourgois, 1986); translated by Peter Connor and others as *The Inoperative Community*, edited by Connor (Minneapolis: University of Minnesota Press, 1991);

The Place of Maurice Blanchot, special issue, *Yale French Studies*, 93 (1988);

Diane Rubenstein, *What's Left? The Ecole Normale Supérieure and the Right* (Madison: University of Wisconsin Press, 1990);

Jean-Paul Sartre, "*Aminadab*, or the Fantastic Considered as a Language," in his *Literary and Philosophical Essays*, translated by Annette Michaelson (London: Hutchinson, 1968), pp. 56–72;

Steven Shaviro, *Passion and Excess: Blanchot, Bataille and Literary Theory* (Tallahassee: Florida State University Press, 1990);

Ann Smock, *What Is There to Say?* (Lincoln: University of Nebraska Press, 2003);

Steven Ungar, *Scandal and Aftereffect: Blanchot and France since 1930* (Minneapolis: University of Minnesota Press, 1995);

Thomas Carl Wall, *Radical Passivity: Lévinas, Blanchot, and Agamben* (New York: State University of New York Press, 1999).

Ernst Bloch

(8 July 1885 – 4 August 1977)

John T. Hamilton
Harvard University

BOOKS: *Geist der Utopie* (Munich & Leipzig: Duncker & Humblot, 1918; revised edition, Berlin: Cassirer, 1923); translated by Anthony A. Nassar as *The Spirit of Utopia* (Stanford, Cal.: Stanford University Press, 2000);

Vademecum für heutige Demokraten (Bern: Freie Verlag, 1919);

Thomas Münzer als Theologe der Revolution (Munich: Wolff, 1921);

Durch die Wüste: Kritische Aufsätze (Berlin: Cassirer, 1923);

Spuren (Berlin: Cassirer, 1930);

Erbschaft dieser Zeit (Zurich: Oprecht & Helbling, 1935); translated by Neville Plaice and Stephen Plaice as *Heritage of Our Times* (Oxford: Polity Press, 1991; Berkeley: University of California Press, 1991);

Freiheit und Ordnung: Abriss der Sozial-Utopien (New York: Aurora, 1946);

Subjekt-Objekt: Erläuterungen zu Hegel (East Berlin: Aufbau, 1949); chapter 9 translated by John Lamb as "The Dialectical Method," *Man and World*, 16 (1983): 281–313;

Avicenna und die Aristotelische Linke (Berlin: Rütten & Loening, 1952);

Christian Thomasius: Ein deutscher Gelehrter ohne Misere (Berlin: Aufbau, 1953);

Das Prinzip Hoffnung, 3 volumes (East Berlin: Aufbau, 1954–1959); translated by Neville Plaice, Stephen Plaice, and Paul Knight as *The Principle of Hope,* 3 volumes (Cambridge, Mass.: MIT Press, 1986; Oxford: Blackwell, 1986);

Differenzierungen im Begriff Fortschritt (Berlin: Akademie, 1956);

Naturrecht und menschliche Würde (Frankfurt am Main: Suhrkamp, 1961); translated by Dennis J. Schmidt as *Natural Law and Human Dignity* (Cambridge, Mass.: MIT Press, 1986);

Philosophische Grundfragen: Zur Ontologie des Noch-Nicht-Seins (Frankfurt am Main: Suhrkamp, 1961);

Verfremdungen, 2 volumes (Frankfurt am Main: Suhrkamp, 1962, 1964);

Tübinger Einleitung in die Philosophie, 2 volumes (Frankfurt am Main: Suhrkamp, 1963, 1964); volume 1 translated by John Cumming as *A Philosophy of the Future* (New York: Herder & Herder, 1970);

Literarische Aufsätze (Frankfurt am Main: Suhrkamp, 1965); translated by Andrew Joron and others as *Literary Essays* (Stanford, Cal.: Stanford University Press, 1998);

Atheismus im Christentum: Zur Religion des Exodus und des Reichs (Frankfurt am Main: Suhrkamp, 1968); translated by J. T. Swann as *Atheism in Christianity: The Religion of the Exodus and the Kingdom* (New York: Herder & Herder, 1972);

Philosophische Aufsätze zur objektiven Phantasie (Frankfurt am Main: Suhrkamp, 1969);

Politische Messungen, Pestzeit, Vormärz (Frankfurt am Main: Suhrkamp, 1970);

Im Christentum steckt die Revolte, by Bloch and Adelbert Reif (Zurich: Die Arche, 1971);

Das Materialismusproblem—seine Geschichte und Substanz (Frankfurt am Main: Suhrkamp, 1972);

Vorlesungen zur Philosophie der Renaissance (Frankfurt am Main: Suhrkamp, 1972);

Experimentum Mundi: Frage, Kategorien des Herausbringens, Praxis (Frankfurt am Main: Suhrkamp, 1975);

Zwischenwelten in der Philosophiegeschichte: Aus Leipziger Vorlesungen (Frankfurt am Main: Suhrkamp, 1977);

Tendenz, Latenz, Utopie (Frankfurt am Main: Suhrkamp, 1978);

Fabelnd denken: Essayistische Texte aus der "Frankfurter Zeitung" (Tübingen: Klöpfer & Meyer, 1997);

Leipziger Vorlesungen zur Geschichte der Philosophie, 4 volumes (Frankfurt: Suhrkamp, 2000);

Logos der Materie: Eine Logik im Werden, edited by Gerardo Cunico (Frankfurt: Suhrkamp, 2000).

Editions and Collections: *Religion im Erbe: Eine Auswahl aus seinen religionsphilosophischen Schriften* (Frankfurt am Main: Suhrkamp, 1959); translated by E. B. Ashton as *Man on His Own: Essays in the Philosophy of Religion* (New York: Herder & Herder, 1970);

Werkausgabe, 17 volumes (Frankfurt am Main: Suhrkamp, 1959–1978);

Über Karl Marx (Frankfurt am Main: Suhrkamp, 1968); translated by John Maxwell as *On Karl Marx* (New York: Herder & Herder, 1971);

Widerstand und Friede: Aufsätze zur Politik (Frankfurt am Main: Suhrkamp, 1968);

Die Kunst, Schiller zu sprechen und andere literarische Aufsätze (Frankfurt am Main: Suhrkamp, 1969);

Karl Marx und die Menschlichkeit: Utopische Phantasie und Weltveränderung (Reinbek bei Hamburg: Rowohlt, 1969);

Über Methode und System bei Hegel (Frankfurt am Main: Suhrkamp, 1970);

Pädagogica (Frankfurt am Main: Suhrkamp, 1971);

Recht, Moral, Staat (Pfullingen: Neske, 1971);

Das antizipierende Bewusstsein (Frankfurt am Main: Suhrkamp, 1972);

Vom Hasard zur Katastrophe: Politische Aufsätze aus den Jahren 1934–1939 (Frankfurt am Main: Suhrkamp, 1972);

Ästhetik des Vor-Scheins, 2 volumes, edited by Gert Ueding (Frankfurt am Main: Suhrkamp, 1974); translated in part by Jack Zipes and Frank Mecklenburg as *The Utopian Function of Art and Literature* (Cambridge, Mass.: MIT Press, 1988);

Zur Philosophie der Musik (Frankfurt am Main: Suhrkamp, 1974); translated by Peter Palmer as *Essays on the Philosophy of Music* (Cambridge & New York: Cambridge University Press, 1985);

Abschied von der Utopie? edited by Hanna Gekle (Frankfurt am Main: Suhrkamp, 1980);

Kampf, nicht Krieg: Politische Schriften 1917–1919, edited by Martin Karol (Frankfurt am Main: Suhrkamp, 1985).

The work of Ernst Bloch stands as one of the most significant contributions to twentieth-century philosophy and cultural theory. Elaborated across more than seven decades of publication, lecturing, and teaching, his innovative formulations of utopianism, materialism, and Marxist theory have touched upon a remarkable variety of subjects, disciplines, and art forms. Consequently, his influence is as broad as it is profound, reaching work in literature and aesthetics, speculative and practical philosophy, religious studies and liberation theology, music and music history, social theory, and political science. This kind of extensive applicability is grounded in the nature of his unrestricted, highly literary approach to philosophy. It is perhaps best reflected by the sheer diversity of the close friendships and professional associations that he enjoyed throughout his long and productive life, many of whom include the most important authors, artists, composers, and intellectuals of the century. The conversation, encompassing the entire spectrum of the humanities, goes on. With the publication of a complete edition of his works in seventeen volumes (*Werkausgabe,* 1959–1978), his multifaceted investigations and analyses continue to participate in many of the most pressing issues and discussions of contemporary thought, both inside the academy and out.

Ernst Simon Bloch was born on 8 July 1885 in Ludwigshafen, Germany, an entirely industrial suburb made up of smokestacks, blast furnaces, merchant ports, and working-class families, which distinguished it from the culturally sophisticated and well-to-do city of Mannheim, which lay on the opposite side of the Rhine. The son of assimilated Jewish parents—his mother, Berta (née Feitel), and his father, Markus, who worked as an inspector for the Imperial Railways—Bloch grew up consciously aware of these two poles of nineteenth-century capitalism. For him, life essentially defined itself between the distressed conditions of laborers and the affluence of the bourgeoisie or, as he later described it in *Erbschaft dieser Zeit* (1935; translated as *Heritage of Our Times,* 1991), between "the realities and the ideals of the industrial age." Finding little stimulation in his upbringing and schooling in Ludwigshafen, Bloch early on learned to escape and seek out more enticing worlds. Like many of his generation, he turned to the adventure novels of Karl May, whose characters could be fleshed out by the exotic appearance of the wayfaring men sailing into port. He also fled into the heady realms of German idealist philosophy, discovered within the grand halls of the castle library in Mannheim.

These childhood attractions remained an integral part of Bloch's mature thinking. Indeed, he readily admitted (as quoted in Silvia Markun's *Ernst Bloch in Selbstzeugnissen und Bilddokumenten,* 1977) that "There is only Karl May and Hegel, anything in between is an impure mixture." That is to say, the general pattern of his intellectual career was already being established, represented beneath the rubrics of Ludwigshafen and Mannheim—an urban allegory that could readily articulate dialectical tensions: between bourgeois and proletariat dreams; political and spiritual concerns; new and old worlds. Much later, this vision served as a corrective to the kind of populist socialism prevalent in the Eastern Bloc. If he experienced firsthand the dehumanization denounced by Marx on one side of the river, he discovered on the other side the spiritual and cultural dimension generally overlooked by a vulgar Marxism bound too tightly to a schematic, economic explication of social conditions. For him, tradition was not simply a cause for suspicion but a necessary source of attraction as well. As Jürgen Habermas observed in "Ernst

Bloch: A Marxist Schelling" (1983), "Bloch wants to glean ideas from the ideologies, to salvage whatever may be true in false consciousness."

The self-styled duality of his early education seems to have motivated and structured Bloch's university studies. In an interview from 1959, quoted in Peter Zudeik's *Der Hintern des Teufels: Ernst Bloch–Leben und Werk* (The Back of the Devil: Ernst Bloch–Life and Work, 1985), he remarked on the inspiring coexistence of the two cities: "This ensemble of industry and colorful aura might well have manifested itself in the search for a philosophy that would not be divided between understanding and aura." It therefore comes as no surprise that, when he entered the University of Munich in 1905, he chose a course of study that would maintain a juxtaposition of objective and subjective investigations, which he found in a curriculum devoted to philosophy and psychology headed by Professor Theodor Lipps. Lipps's slightly romanticized, phenomenologically based research pointed Bloch, in 1907, to the University of Würzburg, where he continued his work under the direction of Oswald Külpe, a leading exponent of psychological trends in epistemology, aesthetics, and the history of philosophy. Here, Bloch further broadened his studies to include *Germanistik* (German Philology and Literature), music, and physics. It was also at Würzburg that he first came into contact with an esoteric group of young Zionists captivated by the Cabala. An offshoot of the various youth movements circulating through Germany at the time, this particular group was interested in the possibility of deploying Jewish mysticism as a political-intellectual strategy against the rationality of the mainstream authority of the university.

Out of this rich ferment emerged a document that proved to be of fundamental importance in the development of Bloch's own philosophy–a manuscript he wrote at the age of twenty-two, "Über die Kategoire Noch-Nicht" (On the Category Not-Yet). Later described as the "origin" of his philosophy, the category of the *Not-Yet* reformulated epistemological and ontological conceptualizations by introducing an "anticipatory consciousness" that provided knowledge of concrete potentiality–knowledge as "not-yet-conscious." It was an exhilarating discovery, which not only propelled Bloch's dissertation on the shortcomings of current academic philosophy and its neo-Kantianism, but also gained him entrance into Georg Simmel's prestigious, private colloquium in Berlin.

Simmel's weekly meetings focused primarily on *Lebensphilosophie* (philosophy of life), a powerful trend within Wilhelminian culture explicitly opposed to positivism and the restrictive program of the neo-Kantian school. Spiritually indebted to the work of Friedrich

ERNST BLOCH

ERBSCHAFT DIESER ZEIT

1935

VERLAG OPRECHT & HELBLING ZÜRICH

Title page for Bloch's analysis of German culture during the Weimar era (translated as Heritage of Our Times, *1991), completed shortly before his expulsion from Switzerland in 1934 because of his Communist affiliations (Earl Gregg Swem Library, College of William and Mary)*

Nietzsche, Wilhelm Dilthey, Henri Bergson, and Max Scheler, *Lebensphilosophie* placed a radical emphasis on creativity, youth, and the obscurity of the immediate. In a word, it dealt with the idea of the *Erlebnis* (experience of the lived moment) against an overrefined, determinist–indeed, devitalized–notion of reality. The sociological implications were obvious, for *Lebensphilosophie* sought nothing less than an entire rebirth of cultural life, a reanimation of an impoverished world. On this basis it fed directly into the burgeoning movements of the avant-garde, from symbolism and Stefan George's circle to Dada experimentation and Expressionism.

In addition to allowing Bloch to develop the creative, if not subversive, aspects of philosophical speculation, Simmel's group brought him into contact with the young Hungarian György Lukács. Their friendship flourished immediately, fueling an enthusiasm that soon took them to Heidelberg. There, in 1912, they infiltrated Max Weber's seminar, flaunting an oracular and rather pompous manner that intentionally upset university sobriety. Lukács brought his friend into contact with the great tradition of Russian novelists just as avidly as Bloch prompted a profound engagement with the history of German philosophy for Lukács. First, through daily meetings and then through extended correspondence, each exerted a lasting influence on the other. In later years Bloch readily acknowledged the significance of Lukács's thinking for his early work, while pointing out his own influence on the latter's groundbreaking text, *Die Theorie des Romans* (1920; translated as *The Theory of the Novel*, 1971).

Also around this time, Bloch found a second companion, Else von Stritzky, a sculptress from Latvia, whom he married in June 1913. A sickly woman from a wealthy family, she displayed an intense passion for the writings of Christian mystics and clearly nourished Bloch's attraction to Gnosticism. As the threat of war grew ever more pronounced, the couple relocated to a country home where, after a serious operation, Else could convalesce in peace. Here in relative isolation, devoted to his ailing wife, Bloch experienced a renewed sense for religion and the spiritual. His involvement in more worldly matters was now limited to participating in the pacifist movements headed by Karl Jaspers and Gustav Radbruch. This new alliance eventually caused Bloch to break with Lukács, who decided to join the armed forces at the outbreak of World War I in 1914. When the friends' paths came to cross again, their exchanges frequently turned into bitter antagonism.

With financial matters secured by his father-in-law's business interests in Riga, Bloch sat out most of the war in relative tranquillity, in a beautiful home set in the rural Bavarian village of Grünwald. Here, brimming with fervor and eager to respond to the European debacle, he wrote his first book, *Geist der Utopie* (1918; translated as *The Spirit of Utopia*, 2000). Some four hundred pages in length, the book was an inspired amalgamation of everything that had formed his thinking up to that point, with a revolutionary zeal unmistakably Marxist in tone. Its syncretic energy brought elements of societal critique, art history, Messianism, and mystical doctrine into line with a rather innovative, irrationalist theorization of music and music history—the working title, which remained unchanged until Bloch's publisher convinced him otherwise, had been "Musik und Apokalypse." It made an immediate and striking impression, albeit among a select group of German intelligentsia. Simmel, who had first read the work in manuscript for Bloch's publisher, Duncker and Humblot, openly recognized its genius; and the

composer Otto Klemperer, to whom Simmel passed the musicology sections for review, readily concurred. The lyric poet Margarete Susman, whom Bloch met through Simmel's circle in Berlin and to whom he dedicated his next book, *Thomas Münzer als Theologe der Revolution* (Thomas Münzer as a Theologian of the Revolution, 1921), praised it as a "new German metaphysics" that could enlighten a nation impoverished and darkened by war. In a similar vein, a young Theodor W. Adorno, who came across the work directly after completing his *Abitur* (high-school exit examination), was instantly captivated. He later reminisced in his essay "Henkel, Krug und frühe Erfahrung" (The Handle, the Pot, and Early Experience, 1991) how this first encounter with Bloch constituted an altogether seminal experience—"Dark as a gateway, with a muffled blare like a trumpet blast."

Bloch's primary intention was to battle against the commercialization, mechanization, and consequent nihilism of late-capitalist society by providing a philosophical rehabilitation of utopian thought. To this end he adopted the idiosyncratic, Expressionist style that became his trademark. Gnomic, aphoristic utterances gave way to effusions in dense, if not turgid, prose, saturated with metaphors and freely associative imagery. Throughout, the particular and the episodic, no matter how digressive, were privileged over the general and the abstract. Bloch's model was the montage technique developed by Expressionist artists, an approach that perfectly corresponded to the fragmentation of the surrounding world. His earlier insight into the category *Not-Yet* was served well by this method of parceling and defamiliarization, which, as Adorno recognized, sought to "break through the encrusted surface of life," as he put it in his essay "Blochs Spuren" (Ernst Bloch's *Spuren*, 1991). In this way Bloch could not only point to the self-destructiveness of Wilhelminian culture but also, in face of the resultant, postdiluvian clearing, modify the emptiness of mere presence by the possibilities that lie within it. Philosophy, Bloch wrote in *Geist der Utopie*, would then bring into focus the "function of utopia, maintained against misery, death, the husk-realm of mere physical nature":

> To find it, to find the right thing, for which it is worthy to live, to be organized, and to have time: that is why we go, why we cut new, metaphysically constitutive paths, summon what is not, build into the blue, and build ourselves into the blue, and there seek the true, the real, where the merely factual disappears—*incipit vita nova*.

The new life that begins in the wake of the general catastrophe is grounded in the human capacity to install ourselves in a present structured not by the past but by the future—what he meant by "bauen uns ins Blaue hinein" (build ourselves into the blue). Whereas Bloch's intention was unambiguously Marxist in its negatively charged critique, it went far beyond conventional socialist analyses by moving past merely economic explications of social conditions, positively introducing a demonstration of artistic, if not genial, potentiality.

By the time *Geist der Utopie* appeared in print, Bloch had immigrated to Switzerland with his wife, Else, who had become increasingly sick. In Bern he came into contact with a dynamic group of artists working against the war efforts. This circle, which included the Dada anarchist Hugo Ball and the acclaimed author Hermann Hesse, had been publishing a weekly paper, *Die Freie Zeitung* (The Free Paper), which almost exclusively leveled criticism at Kaiser Wilhelm. By the end of the war, Bloch, under various pseudonyms, contributed more than one hundred articles, later published in the collection *Kampf, nicht Krieg: Politische Schriften 1917–1919* (Struggle, not War: Political Writings, 1917–1919, 1985), the majority of which focused on the same basic message, namely, that a German victory would only serve Prussian militarism, not Germany. Also from this period of self-imposed exile came Bloch's initial reactions to the October Revolution in Russia, primarily in the article "Lenin, der 'rote Zar'" (Lenin, the "Red Czar," 1918) and then in a pamphlet, *Vademecum für heutige Demokraten* (Handbook for Today's Democrats, 1919). His cautious praise, tempered by a critical assessment of Bolshevist politics, proved to be highly interesting, given his later endorsement of Soviet Communism and the Stalinist regime.

The signing of the Versailles treaty and Else's worsening condition brought the Blochs back to Germany. Within a year and a half, after many extended cures and hospital stays, she was dead. Bloch was devastated. He withdrew altogether from society and limited his writing to the project clearly inspired by his wife's ardent interest in Christian mysticism, published toward the end of 1921—*Thomas Münzer als Theologe der Revolution*. A portrayal of the life and work of the heretical preacher and visionary of the Peasants' Revolt of 1525, this book not only provided Bloch with the opportunity to demonstrate the politically subversive capacities of religious thinking, but also allowed him to give fuller expression to the theistic impulse that was only mildly evident in his earlier work. This new turn, which incidentally set itself against a simplistic denouncement of religion in the name of Marxism, also led many to mistake Bloch's position. For example, it led the journalist Siegfried Kracauer to compare the book to the work of Martin Buber, a charge with which Bloch was especially uncomfortable. Neither a

call for Judaic renewal nor a treatise against Jewish assimilation, Bloch referred to his Münzer book simply as a "coda" to *Geist der Utopie,* a concrete depiction of "revolutionary romanticism" that served his own burgeoning, universalist chiliasm.

Bloch's reputation as a profound and rather heterodox exponent of socialist theory flourished in the Weimar Republic. He established himself in Berlin, where he contributed regularly to the prominent journals of the city and kept in close contact with some of the most influential thinkers of the era, including Walter Benjamin, Bertolt Brecht, Adorno, Klemperer, and Kracauer. These were busy years for Bloch. A second, ill-fated marriage in 1922 to the painter Linda Oppenheimer ended in separation within the year. In 1923 Bloch published an entirely revised and expanded version of *Geist der Utopie,* dedicated to Else's memory, and also oversaw the appearance of a collection of early essays, *Durch die Wüste: Kritische Aufsätze* (Through the Desert: Critical Essays). Frequent travel across Europe and North Africa included an extended stay in 1924 with Benjamin on the island of Capri, where the two monitored each other's experiments with hashish. Toward the end of the decade, the friends met up again in Paris, where Benjamin, through his association with fellow Marcel Proust translator Franz Hessel, was beginning to incorporate techniques of urban strolling, or *flânerie,* and autobiographical reminiscence as a provocation toward political change.

Benjamin's writings from this time, primarily the mosaic-like prose of *Einbahnstraße* (1928; translated as "One-Way Street," 1979) and *Berliner Chronik* (first published in 1970; translated as "A Berlin Chronicle," 1978), have their direct counterpart in the philosophical anecdotes of Bloch's next book, *Spuren* (Traces, 1930). Although originally conceived during his years of Swiss exile, the book arguably was motivated by the relationship with Benjamin, who like Bloch appreciated the exploration of everyday material as a search for the Not-Yet. Forgoing any sustained narration, Bloch pursued his method of discerning within the present the intrusion of the future, which would disrupt the alienating reifications fixed by dominant social conditions.

The Nazi takeover of the German government in March 1933 clearly marked the beginning of a new phase in Bloch's life: a period of hounded exile that ultimately drove him to the United States. In 1934 he married the woman who shared his life until his death, Karola Piotrkowska, an architect from Poland with a deep commitment to the German Communist Party (KPD). The couple's political activism, devoted to the Marxist defeat of fascism, rendered their immigrant

ERNST BLOCH

DAS PRINZIP HOFFNUNG

ERSTER BAND

AUFBAU-VERLAG BERLIN
1954

Title page for the first volume of Bloch's three-volume magnum opus (1954–1959; translated as The Principle of Hope, *1986), written during his years as an émigré in Cambridge, Massachusetts (Jean and Alexander Heard Library, Vanderbilt University)*

status highly precarious among the Swiss authorities. Before their expulsion, Bloch completed his next book, *Erbschaft dieser Zeit,* which, by means of analyses of Weimar culture, offered an explication of the rise of fascism as well as a critique of the failings of communism in giving the people a viable alternative. Unfortunately, according to Bloch, National Socialism *did* respond to basic human needs and was able to safeguard its political victories by manipulating an ideology that satisfied the masses' hunger, no matter how deceptively. Communism must respond by cooperating with the avant-garde in literature and the arts and thereby provide society with material that would assist in the realization of a better future. Along these lines, while living in Paris the following year, 1935, Bloch joined Brecht for the International Congress for the Defense of Culture, where he presented his paper "Dichtung und sozialistische Gegenstände" (Literature

and Socialist Objects), published as "Marxismus und Dichtung" (Marxism and Poetry) in *Literarische Aufsätze* (1965; translated as *Literary Essays,* 1998).

Bloch's intense struggle against fascism, which he understood as the necessary consequence of Western capitalism in decay, forced him into dogged justifications of Soviet Union policy. Bloch seemed willing to abandon his formerly critical, unconventional rewriting of Marxist theory in order to uphold what he believed to be the only possible combatant in the world against the Nazis' terrible power. This position, taken to the dubious extreme of unstinting support for Stalinism, threatened his expected post at the Institut für Sozialforschung (Institute for Social Research), then housed at Columbia University. Nonetheless, chased from Vienna, then Paris and Prague, the Blochs finally fled to New York in 1938, one year after the birth of their son, Jan Robert. Adorno had been enthusiastic about having Bloch join the institute, but the director, Max Horkheimer, felt that his pro-Soviet politics, especially in the wake of the Moscow Show Trials of 1936–1937, would necessarily compromise his critical sharpness. Bloch was therefore denied the academic position that had been the economic basis for his emigration, and he remained without a steady income for the entire eleven years of his exile. Despite his early pleas arguing that German refugees learn the language and appreciate the culture of their new host country, Bloch grew ever more critical of American life and never mastered English. Consequently, he stayed home to write, incessantly and in relative isolation, while Karola found whatever work she could, first as a door-to-door insurance agent in the Bronx, then as a waitress. After a brief stay in Marlborough, New Hampshire, in 1942, through the recommendation of a friend the Blochs rented a house in Cambridge, Massachusetts, where Karola finally received an offer to work for a local architectural firm.

Bloch made use of his time, simultaneously working on various large-scale projects on a broad range of subjects, for which he accumulated thousands of pages in manuscript. The work that most clearly represents his American exile, however, remains his magnum opus, composed over the course of many years in the reading room at the Widener Library at Harvard College: *Das Prinzip Hoffnung* (1954–1959; translated as *The Principle of Hope,* 1986). Fundamentally against all concepts of stasis or inert totality, the general thrust of the book posits the idea of hope as the means to prevent the future from being foreclosed by a predetermined thinking—as he repeatedly formulated it: "Denken heißt überschreiten" (Thinking means stepping beyond).

Similar to the introduction to *Geist der Utopie,* Bloch's starting point is the radical vacuity of being, which is in fact already agitated by the pull of the future. His writing has retained the lapidary style of Expressionism: "WE START OUT EMPTY.–I move. From early on we are searching. All we do is crave, cry out. Do not have what we want." Significantly, while this gambit certainly resembles the move Martin Heidegger makes through his conceptualization of anxiety, Bloch overrides Heidegger's famous explication of human existence as "Sein-zum-Tode" (Being-unto-Death) by positing an inexhaustibly open-ended expansion of life. For yet another postwar generation bordering on nihilism–this time beneath the auspices of a popularized existentialism–Bloch furnished a valid, optimistic alternative.

The first of the three volumes of *Das Prinzip Hoffnung* is divided into three parts, dealing with the process that should lead humans from existential hunger, through expectation, to a "revolutionary interest" that will usher in the historically new–what Bloch refers to as the *Novum.* Accordingly, he must first distinguish his forward-aimed drives from the regressive drives of psychoanalysis, which bind the subject despotically to the past. Sigmund Freud's notion of repression, Alfred Adler's psychology of the Will, and–in especially salty terms–the phylogenetic primitivism of Carl Gustav Jung, whom Bloch calls the "psychoanalytic Fascist," are all discredited in turn as methods of stagnation. Instead, one should develop an "anticipatory consciousness" focused not on romanticized hallucinations or self-deceptions but on perfectly realizable possibilities for a better society. In place of the dark night dreams of repressed desires or collective memories, Bloch advocated concentrating on the proleptic force of the daydream. Bondage to the past is dissolved through a fresh emphasis on fairy tales, travelogues, movies, and theater.

The second volume consists of a single part devoted entirely to an overview of historical utopias–medical, social, technological, architectural, and artistic. Here, all the great proponents of utopian thinking are discussed at length: from Solon and Plato; through Augustine, Joachim di Fiore, and Thomas More; to Sir Francis Bacon, Charles Fourier, and Henri de Saint-Simon. Throughout, Bloch redefines human freedom metaphorically in terms of the "aufrechter Gang" (upright gait), an existential capacity to counter obstruction and carry oneself further. Here, emphasis is placed on the messianic vision of di Fiore, which, after Marx, may be understood in its proper humanist (in other words, atheistic) sense and finally be enacted.

This victory of optimism over nihilism is given its full expression in the third volume of *Das Prinzip*

Hoffnung, titled "Identität" (Identity). In promulgating a refreshed Prometheanism, illustrated in the main by the figure of Johann Wolfgang von Goethe's Faust, Bloch reestablishes the divine on an altogether human plane. Not heaven but earth is the locus of the future, an immanent transcendence that essentially transforms the world of the here and now into an "extra-territorial" place. Not-Yet-Consciousness thereby enacts a socialist liberation by seeing what can be in what merely is. The necessary condition–and the principal problem–of Bloch's enterprise is the infinitude of the future. Fundamentally inexhaustible, the societal content must somehow come to terms with the eschatological force of the project. To this end Bloch adopts a short line from *Faust* (1808) that formulates the need for perpetual corrections and redefinition: "Verweile doch, du bist so schön" (Stay awhile, you are so beautiful). In this passage Bloch allows Faust's radical unrest to infiltrate the dialectical plot of Georg Wilhelm Friedrich Hegel's *Die Phänomenologie des Geistes* (1807; translated as *Phenomenology of Mind,* 1910). The result is a chiliasm–a faith in the eventual arrival of the timeless Absolute–that is thoroughly situated within the sphere of human temporality. This irradiation of human time by the infinite drives the book all the way to its concluding chapter. Here, in Marxist terms, Bloch reintroduces the categories of Not-Yet-Conscious and Not-Yet-Become to show how Faustian creativity will prevent an eschatology that would dry up human possibility and thereby establish a "real democracy." This realizable but forever tentative, experimental society will be nothing less than a world free from oppression, exploitation, and humiliation–a true beginning at the end of a history of alienation, named in the final resounding word of the book, now rescued from Nazi desecration: *Heimat* (homeland).

That the United States could never be home for the Blochs became more apparent as the country edged closer to its ideological confrontation with the Soviet Union. Bloch never did improve his English nor temper his stand against what he perceived as the "fascism" of American culture–indeed, *Das Prinzip Hoffnung* includes scathing attacks on everything from jazz and Hollywood to the Ku Klux Klan. Furthermore, Karola never gave up her work for the Communist Party, a fact that, given the increasing paranoia of U.S. government agencies, left the family in a precarious situation, even if citizenship had been granted in 1945. Bloch was no doubt ready, therefore, to accept an offer to take over the chair of philosophy at the Karl Marx University in Leipzig. In 1949 the family moved to East Germany, and Bloch, at the age of sixty-four, for the first time in his life began work as a university professor.

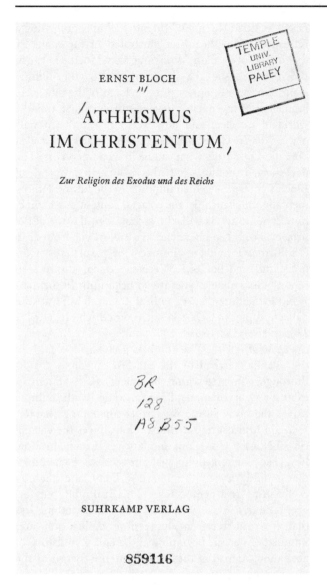

ERNST BLOCH
in

ATHEISMUS
IM CHRISTENTUM

Zur Religion des Exodus und des Reichs

*Title page for Bloch's 1968 work of biblical interpretation,
translated as* Atheism in Christianity: The Religion
of the Exodus and the Kingdom *(1972), which
became a seminal text in the field of liberation
theology (Samuel Paley Library,
Temple University)*

The new career proved highly successful. His frank criticism of state politics, tolerated for the moment, made him a popular lecturer, while the quantity and rapidity of his publications, reaped from his decade-long exile, gave him the aura of a most prolific scholar and thinker. Each year brought out another full-length study: a critical examination of Hegel's epistemology, *Subjekt-Objekt: Erläuterungen zu Hegel* (Subject-Object: Commentaries on Hegel, 1949); a book on Aristotle's materialism as transmitted by his medieval commentators, *Avicenna und die Aristotelische Linke* (Avicenna and the Aristotelian Left, 1952); an extended

essay on the eighteenth-century German scholar Christian Thomasius, *Christian Thomasius: Ein deutscher Gelehrter ohne Misere* (Christian Thomasius: A German Scholar without Misery, 1953); and, beginning in 1954, all three volumes of *Das Prinzip Hoffnung*. In addition to this intense activity, Bloch resumed his old friendship with Lukács, with whom he founded the academic journal *Deutsche Zeitschrift für Philosophie* (German Magazine for Philosophy).

This enormous success, however, did not hinder the state Communist Party (the SED) from pressuring Bloch to moderate his heterodox Marxism. As the political crises of the Khrushchev years unfolded, the conflicts between the aged philosopher and the dogmatic politicians became more and more pronounced. By 1957 Bloch had been forced to retire from his university position and was officially prohibited from holding public lectures. Undeterred, Bloch turned to West Germany, where he continued to give talks and publish papers. With the construction of the Berlin Wall in 1961, the Blochs, who had been vacationing in Munich at the time, decided to stay in the Federal Republic, where a professorship in philosophy at the University of Tübingen awaited.

Denounced as a traitor by the East and held suspect as a longtime critic of the West, Bloch delivered his inaugural lecture to a crowded hall on "a question of particular relevance": "Kann Hoffnung enttäuscht werden?" (Can Hope Be Disappointed? published in *Literarische Aufsätze*). That Bloch admitted this possibility in no way signaled an intellectual resignation. On the contrary, it demonstrated the necessarily open-ended, unfinished quality of his utopian project. In fact, the disappointment Bloch suffered from the failings of the Socialist state inspired another decade and a half of an unflagging commitment to writing, teaching, and political activism. His book on the varying traditions of the concept of natural rights, *Naturrecht und menschliche Würde* (1961; translated as *Natural Law and Human Dignity,* 1986), was followed in quick succession by an extended exegesis on Not-Yet-Being, *Philosophische Grundfragen: Zur Ontologie des Noch-Nicht-Seins* (Fundamental Questions in Philosophy: On the Ontology of Not-Yet-Being, 1961), two volumes of essays titled *Verfremdungen* (Defamiliarizations, 1962, 1964), and two volumes of material from his university lectures, *Tübinger Einleitung in die Philosophie* (Tübingen Introduction to Philosophy, 1963, 1964), the first volume of which was translated as *A Philosophy of the Future* (1970).

Bloch's association with two of his theology colleagues at Tübingen, Jürgen Moltmann and Johannes Metz, motivated the publication of his *Atheismus im Christentum: Zur Religion des Exodus und des Reichs* (1968;

translated as *Atheism in Christianity: The Religion of the Exodus and the Kingdom,* 1972). This work, which was begun in the United States, served as a seminal text for the burgeoning liberation theology of Latin America. In accordance with his radical reinterpretation of the Judeo-Christian tradition begun in *Das Prinzip Hoffnung,* the transcendent, otherworldly realm of religion is to be located on earth, which should now be understood as "extra-territorial." Explicitly contrasting the Pauline reading of the Crucifixion and Resurrection, Bloch comprehends Christ's Incarnation *in time* as the triumph of the human over an illusory, deceptive timelessness. Immanence thereby reintroduces the religious impulse into Marxist theory—not as an opiate but as an instrument for social change.

Equally critical now of both United States and Soviet policies, Ernst Bloch vehemently supported the Prague Spring and protested against the Vietnam War. Meanwhile, his publications continued to appear, including a book on the history of materialism, *Das Materialismusproblem—seine Geschichte und Substanz* (The Problem of Materialism—Its History and Substance, 1972), and a theoretical investigation into Marxist categories, *Experimentum Mundi: Frage, Kategorien des Herausbringens, Praxis* (Experimentum Mundi: Question, Categories of Elaboration, Practice, 1975). In addition to his untiring activism, while maintaining a busy lecture schedule, he managed to oversee and revise the seventeen volumes of his collected works, published by Suhrkamp. To the end of his days he remained a vibrant, critical, and continually innovative voice. His final words attest to this vitality and perfectly illustrate the tenacious theme of his life's work, which had always expressed a desire to "venture beyond" while remaining within the realm of objective, concrete possibility. They also recall the infinite generosity of his thinking, focused as it was on reaching others so that, collectively, the goal of a better world may be attained. On 4 August 1977, as he succumbed to heart failure at the age of ninety-two, Bloch simply confessed: "Ich kann nicht mehr" (I'm no longer able).

Letters:

Briefe: 1903–1975, 2 volumes, edited by Karola Bloch and others (Frankfurt am Main: Suhrkamp, 1985);

Bloch and Arnold Metzger, *Wir arbeiten im gleichen Bergwerk: Briefwechsel 1942–1972,* edited by Karola Bloch, Ilse Metzger, and Eberhard Braun (Frankfurt am Main: Suhrkamp, 1987);

Bloch and Wieland Herzfelde, *"Wir haben das Leben wieder vor uns": Briefwechsel 1938–1949,* edited by Jürgen Jahn (Frankfurt am Main: Suhrkamp, 2001).

Interviews:

Arno Münster, ed., *Tagträume vom aufrechten Gang: Sechs Interviews mit Ernst Bloch* (Frankfurt am Main: Suhrkamp, 1977).

Bibliographies:

Siegfried Unseld, *Ernst Bloch zu ehren: Beiträge zu seinem Werk* (Frankfurt am Main: Suhrkamp, 1965), pp. 397–403;

Renate Kübler, *Über Ernst Bloch* (Frankfurt am Main: Suhrkamp, 1968), pp. 133–150;

Thomas Wren, "An Ernst Bloch Bibliography for English Readers," *Philosophy Today,* 15 (1970): 272–273;

Burghart Schmidt, *Materialien zu Ernst Blochs "Prinzip Hoffnung"* (Frankfurt am Main: Suhrkamp, 1978);

Joan Nordquist, *Ernst Bloch: A Bibliography* (Santa Cruz, Cal.: Reference and Research Services, 1990).

Biographies:

Silvia Markun, *Ernst Bloch in Selbstzeugnissen und Bilddokumenten* (Reinbek bei Hamburg: Rowohlt, 1977);

Karola Bloch, *Aus meinem Leben* (Pfullingen: Neske, 1981);

Peter Zudeick, *Der Hintern des Teufels: Ernst Bloch—Leben und Werk* (Moos: Elster, 1985);

Vincent Geoghegan, *Ernst Bloch* (London & New York: Routledge, 1996).

References:

Theodor W. Adorno, "Ernst Bloch's *Spuren,*" in *Notes to Literature,* volume 1, edited by Rolf Tiedemann, translated by Shierry Weber Nicholsen (New York: Columbia University Press, 1991), pp. 200–215;

Adorno, "The Handle, the Pot, and Early Experience," in *Notes to Literature,* volume 2, edited by Tiedemann, translated by Nicholsen (New York: Columbia University Press, 1991), pp. 211–219;

Klaus Berghahn, "A View through the Red Window: Ernst Bloch's *Spuren,*" in *Modernity and the Text: Revisions of German Modernism,* edited by Andreas Huyssen and David Bathrick (New York: Columbia University Press, 1989), pp. 200–215;

Karola Bloch and Adelbert Reif, eds., *"Denken heißt überschreiten": In memoriam Ernst Bloch, 1885–1977* (Cologne & Frankfurt: Europäische Verlagsanstalt, 1978);

Jamie O. Daniel and Tom Moylan, eds., *Not Yet!: Reconsidering Ernst Bloch* (London & New York: Verso, 1997);

John Dickinson, "The Ambiguous Quest: Ernst Bloch's Early Love," *Bloch-Almanach,* 16 (1997): 158–198;

Jürgen Habermas, "Ernst Bloch: A Marxist Schelling," in his *Philosophical-Political Profiles,* translated by Frederick Lawrence (Cambridge, Mass.: MIT Press, 1983), pp. 61–77;

Detlef Horster, ed., *Ernst Bloch zum 90. Geburtstag. Es muss nicht immer Marmor sein. Erbschaft aus Ungleichzeitigkeit* (Berlin: Wagenbach, 1975);

Wayne Hudson, *The Marxist Philosophy of Ernst Bloch* (New York: St. Martin's Press, 1982);

Frederic Jameson, "Ernst Bloch and the Future," in his *Marxism and Form: Twentieth-Century Dialectical Theories of Literature* (Princeton: Princeton University Press, 1971), pp. 116–159;

Michael Landmann, "Talking with Ernst Bloch: Korèula, 1968," *Telos,* 25 (1975): 183–184;

Anson Rabinbach, "Between Enlightenment and Apocalypse: Benjamin, Bloch and Modern German Jewish Messianism," *New German Critique,* 34 (1985): 78–124;

Rabinbach, "Unclaimed Heritage: Ernst Bloch's *Heritage of Our Times* and the Theory of Fascism," *New German Critique,* 11 (1977): 5–21;

Sándor Rádnoti, "Lukács and Bloch," in *Lukács Reappraised,* edited by Agnes Heller (New York: Columbia University Press, 1983), pp. 63–75;

Gérard Raulet, "Critique of Religion and Religion as Critique: The Secularized Hope of Ernst Bloch," *New German Critique,* 9 (1976): 77–86;

Richard Roberts, "An Introductory Reading of Ernst Bloch's *The Principle of Hope,*" *Journal of Literature and Theology,* 1 (March 1987): 89–112;

Burghart Schmidt, *Ernst Bloch* (Stuttgart: Metzler, 1985);

George Steiner, "Forward Dreams," *TLS: The Times Literary Supplement* (3 October 1975): 1128;

Gert Ueding, *Glanzvolles Elend: Versuch über Kitsch und Kolportage* (Frankfurt am Main: Suhrkamp, 1973);

Jack Zipes, ed., Special Section on Ernst Bloch, *New German Critique,* 45 (1988).

Papers:
The majority of Ernst Bloch's papers are held in the Bloch Archive in Ludwigshafen, Germany. Correspondence with György Lukács is in the Lukács Archive, Budapest, Hungary; and correspondence with Siegfried Kracauer is in the Kracauer Nachlaß, Schiller National Museum, Marbach am Neckar, Germany.

Franz Brentano

(16 January 1838 – 17 March 1917)

Frances Gray
University of New England

BOOKS: *Von der mannigfachen Bedeutung des Seienden nach Aristoteles* (Freiburg im Breisgau: Herder, 1862); translated by Rolf George as *On Several Senses of Being in Aristotle* (Berkeley: University of California Press, 1975);

Die Psychologie des Aristoteles, insbesondere seine Lehre vom nous poietikos (Mainz: Franz Kirchheim, 1867); translated by George as *The Psychology of Aristotle: In Particular His Doctrine of the Active Intellect,* edited by George (Berkeley: University of California Press, 1977);

Psychologie vom empirischen Standpunkte, 2 volumes (Leipzig: Duncker & Humblot, 1874); translated by Antos C. Rancurello, D. B. Terrell, and Linda L. McAlister as *Psychology from an Empirical Standpoint,* edited by Oskar Kraus (London: Routledge & Kegan Paul / New York: Humanities Press, 1973);

Über die Gründe der Entmutigung auf philosophischem Gebiete: Ein Vortrag gehalten beim Antritte der philosophischen Professur an der k.k. Hochschule zu Wien am 22. April 1874 (Vienna: Braumüller, 1874);

Was für ein Philosoph manchla Epoche macht: Vortrag zum Besten des Lesevereins der deutschen Studenten Wiens (Vienna: Hartleben, 1876);

Neue Räthsel, as Änigmatias (Vienna: Gerold, 1879);

Über den Creatianismus des Aristoteles (Vienna: Gerold, 1882);

Offener Brief an Herrn Professor dr. Eduard Zeller aus Anlass seiner Schrift über die Lehre des Aristoteles von der Ewigkeit des Geistes (Leipzig: Duncker & Humblot, 1883);

Vom Ursprung sittlicher Erkenntnis (Leipzig: Duncker & Humblot, 1889); translated by Cecil Hague as *The Origin of Knowledge of Right and Wrong* (Westminster: Constable, 1902; revised, 1961);

Das Genie (Leipzig: Duncker & Humblot, 1892);

Das Schlechte als Gegenstand dichterischer Darstellung (Leipzig: Duncker & Humblot, 1892);

Über die Zukunft der Philosophie (Vienna: Hölder, 1893);

Die vier Phasen der Philosophie und ihr augenblicklicher Stand (Stuttgart: Cotta, 1895); translated by Balazs M. Meze and Barry Smith as "The Four Phases of

From Oskar Kraus, Franz Brentano: Zur Kenntnis seines Lebens und seine Lehre, *1919; Thomas Cooper Library, University of South Carolina*

Philosophy and Its Present Condition," *Philosophy Today,* 43, no. 1 (Spring 1999): 14–28;

Meine letzten Wünsche für Österreich (Stuttgart: Cotta, 1895);

63

Noch ein Wort über das Ehehinderniss der höheren Weihen und feierlichen Gelübde (Vienna: Manz, 1895);

Zur eherechtlichen Frage in Österreich: Krasnopolskis Rettungsversuch einer verlorenen Sache (Berlin: Guttentag, 1896);

Krasnopolskis letzter Versuch (Leipzig: Arndt, 1896);

Neue Vertheidigung der Spanischen Partie (Vienna: "Wiener Schachzeitung," 1900);

Untersuchungen zur Sinnespsychologie (Leipzig: Duncker & Humblot, 1907);

Änigmatias: Neue Rätsel (Munich: Oskar Beck, 1909);

Aristoteles und seine Weltanschauung (Leipzig: Quelle & Meyer, 1911); edited and translated by George and Roderick Chisholm as *Aristotle and His World View* (Berkeley: University of California Press, 1978);

Aristoteles Lehre vom Ursprung des menschlichen Geistes (Leipzig: Veit, 1911);

Von der Klassifikation der psychischen Phänomene (Leipzig: Duncker & Humblot, 1911);

Die Lehre Jesu und ihre bleibende Bedeutung, edited by Alfred Kastil (Leipzig: Meiner, 1922);

Versuch über die Erkenntnis, edited by Kastil (Leipzig: Meiner, 1925);

Die vier Phasen der Philosophie und ihr augenblicklicher Stand, nebst Abhandlungen über Plotinus, Thomas von Aquin, Kant, Schopenhauer und Auguste Comte, edited by Kraus (Leipzig: Meiner, 1926);

Vom sinnlichen und noetischen Bewußtsein (Psychology III), edited by Kraus (Leipzig: Meiner, 1928); translated by Margarete Schättle and McAlister as *Sensory and Noetic Consciousness: Psychology from an Empirical Standpoint III* (London: Routledge & Kegan Paul/Humanities Press, 1981);

Über die Zukunft der Philosophie, edited, with an introduction and commentary, by Kraus (Leipzig: Meiner, 1929);

Vom Dasein Gottes, edited by Kastil (Leipzig: Meiner, 1929); translated by Susan F. Krantz as *On the Existence of God: Lectures Given at the Universities of Wurzburg and Vienna, 1868–1891* (Dordrecht & Boston: Nijhoff, 1987);

Wahrheit und Evidenz, edited by Kraus (Leipzig: Meiner, 1930); translated by Chisholm, Ilse Politzer, and Kurt R. Fischer as *The True and the Evident* (London: Routledge & Kegan Paul, 1966; New York: Humanities Press, 1966);

Kategorienlehre, edited by Kastil (Leipzig: Meiner, 1933); translated by Chisholm and Norbert Guterman as *The Theory of Categories* (The Hague & Boston: Nijhoff, 1980);

Grundlegung und Aufbau der Ethik, edited by Franziska Mayer-Hillebrand (Bern: Francke, 1952); translated by Elizabeth Schneewind as *The Foundation and Construction of Ethics* (London: Routledge &

Kegan Paul / New York: Humanities Press, 1973);

Religion und Philosophie: Ihr Verhältnis zueinander und ihre gemeinsamen Aufgaben, edited by Mayer-Hillebrand (Bern: Francke, 1954);

Die Lehre vom Richtigen Urteil, edited by Mayer-Hillebrand (Bern: Francke, 1956);

Grundzüge der Ästhetik, edited by Mayer-Hillebrand (Bern: Francke, 1959);

Geschichte der Griechischen Philosophie, edited by Mayer-Hillebrand (Bern: Francke, 1963);

Die Abkehr vom Nichtrealen, edited by Mayer-Hillebrand (Bern & Munich: Francke, 1966);

Philosophische Untersuchungen zu Raum, Zeit, und Kontinuum, edited by Stephen Körner and Chisholm (Hamburg: Meiner, 1976); translated by Smith as *Philosophical Investigations on Space, Time, and the Continuum* (London & New York: Croom Helm, 1988);

Deskriptive Psychologie, edited by Chisholm and Wilhelm Baumgartner (Hamburg: Meiner, 1982); translated by Benito Müller as *Descriptive Psychology* (London & New York: Routledge, 1995);

Über Aristoteles: Nachgelassene Aufsätze, edited by George (Hamburg: Meiner, 1986);

Geschichte der Philosophie der Neuzeit, edited by Klaus Hedwig (Hamburg: Meiner, 1987).

OTHER: "Unbekannte Manuskripte Franz Brentanos," in *Horizons of a Philosopher: Essays in Honor of David Baumgart,* edited by Joseph Frank, Helmut Minkowski, and Ernest J. Sternglass (Leiden: Brill, 1963), pp. 34–49;

"On the Concept of Truth," translated by Roderick M. Chisholm and Kurt R. Fischer in *Readings in the Theory of Knowledge,* edited by John V. Canfield and Franklin H. Donnell Jr. (New York: Appleton-Century-Crofts, 1964), pp. 261–284.

SELECTED PERIODICAL PUBLICATIONS–UNCOLLECTED: "Auguste Comte und die positive Philosophie," *Chilianeum: Blätter für katholische Philosophie, Kunst, und Leben,* new series 2 (1869): 15–37;

"Der Atheismus und die Wissenschaft," anonymous, *Historisch-politische Blätter f. d. katholische Deutschland,* 72 (1873): 853–872, 916–929;

"Herr Horwicz als Rezensent: Ein Beitrag zur Orientierung über unsere wissenchaft-lichen Kulturzustände," *Philosophische Monatshefte,* 4 (1875), pp. 180–187;

"Über ein optisches Paradoxon," *Zeitschrift für Psychologie und Physiologie der Sinnesorgane,* 3 (1892): 349–358; 5 (1893): 61–82;

"Das Recht auf den Selbstmord," *Deutsche Zeitung* (Vienna), 6 September 1894;

"Zur Lehre von den optischen Täuschungen," *Zeitschrift für Psychologie und Physiologie der Sinnesorgane,* 6 (1894): 1–7;

"Zur Lehre von der Empfindung," *Dritter internationaler Congress für Psychologie in München* (1897): 110–133;

"Über voraussetzunglose Forschung," anonymous, *Münchner Neueste Nachrichten,* 573 (15 December 1901);

"Thomas von Aquin," *Neue Freie Presse,* 18 April 1908;

"Zur Lehre von Raum und Zeit," *Kant-Studien,* 25 (1920): 1–23;

"Religion und Philosophie," *Philosophie und Leben,* 1 (1925): 333–339;

"Über Prophetie," *Jahrbuch der Charakterologie,* 2–3 (1926): 259–264;

"Zur Klassifikation der Künste," *Hochschulwissen Heft,* 2 (1926): 57–62;

"Gegen entia rationis, sogenannte irreale oder ideale, Gegenstände," *Philosophische Hefte,* 2 (1929): 257–274;

"Das Franz Brentano-Gutachten Über die päpstliche Infallibilität," *Archiv für mittelrheinische Kirchengeschichte* (1955): 295–334.

In 1998 *The Brentano Puzzle,* edited by Roberto Poli, was published. This collection, the proceedings of a conference by the same name, posed the question of Franz Brentano's importance to philosophy. Yet, the idea behind the conference was to work through the puzzle that surrounds Brentano's apparent invisibility as a nineteenth-century thinker. There seems to be no doubt about his intellectual legacy into the twenty-first century: his scholarly work in both philosophy and psychology is profoundly influential. His place as an esteemed twentieth-century cultural theorist is guaranteed by what now might be thought of as his cross-disciplinary contributions through his passionate engagement in the intellectual life of the late nineteenth century. Brentano is rarely mentioned as a great philosopher of that century, however, in spite of his philosophical significance. Whether that significance should be couched in terms of his philosophical contributions as a thinker in his own right or because of his pedagogical legacy is moot.

During the twentieth century, the development of a philosophical psychology inspired by Brentano's seminal idea, that of intentional inexistence, was responsible for generating vigorous philosophical debate. Simultaneously, Brentano's work laid the foundation for the study of psychology. Indeed, he is regarded as a father of empirical psychology. He wrestled with his Catholic faith for much of his life. He was ordained a Catholic priest, a vocation he abandoned after ten years. Nonetheless, he was regarded by Catholic liberals as a significant contributor to Catholic intellectual

Brentano's best-known pupil, the philosopher and psychologist Alexius Meinong, who began studying under Brentano at the University of Vienna in 1874 (from Howard O. Eaton, The Austrian Philosophy of Values, *1930; Thomas Cooper Library, University of South Carolina)*

life in Austria at the end of the nineteenth century. Philosopher, psychologist, theologian, and radical, Brentano was a charismatic figure, profoundly intellectual and devoted to learning and to his students.

Franz Clemens Honoratus Hermann Brentano was born in Marienberg on 16 January 1838, the second child of Christian Franz Brentano and Emilie Genger (née Reichelsheim). Christian Brentano, an émigré from Tremezzo, Italy, was a well-known Catholic intellectual and writer. His father, Peter Anton Brentano, fathered twenty children from three different marriages. Franz was born, therefore, into a large and well-connected European family with strong Germanic and Italian roots.

Christian Brentano had married late in his life, in 1835, when he was fifty-one years old. He fathered five children. It is difficult to assess the effect his death in

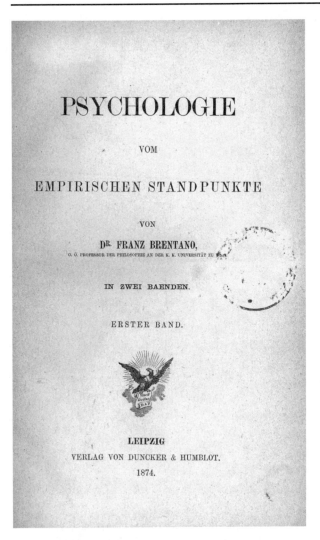

PSYCHOLOGIE

VOM

EMPIRISCHEN STANDPUNKTE

VON

DR. FRANZ BRENTANO,
O. Ö. PROFESSOR DER PHILOSOPHIE AN DER K. K. UNIVERSITÄT ZU WIEN.

IN ZWEI BAENDEN.

ERSTER BAND.

LEIPZIG
VERLAG VON DUNCKER & HUMBLOT.
1874.

Title page for Brentano's best-known work (translated as
Psychology from an Empirical Standpoint,
1973), in which he develops his theory of the
intentionality of mental acts in the context of
the histories of philosophy and psychology
(Kent State University Library)

1851 had on his young family. Franz Brentano developed a strong and loving relationship with his mother, and they mutually supported each other until her death in 1881. According to Oskar Kraus, Brentano's major biographer, his relationship with his mother was close both emotionally and intellectually. Brentano was born into a family with a rich intellectual heritage; his younger brother, Ludwig Josef, later became famous as a scholar, political economist, and pacifist.

Franz Brentano was educated in the Royal Bavarian Gymnasium in Aschaffenburg. He studied in the general education program at the Lyceum in Aschaffenburg between 1855 and 1856 before attending university. Brentano's student career involved his attendance at several universities. He studied at the University of Munich from 1856. In 1858, he moved to Würzburg for one semester and then to Berlin for 1858 and 1859. Having developed a passionate interest in the Scholastic Thomas Aquinas during his youth, Brentano elected to read Aristotle under the guidance of Friedrich Trendelenburg in Berlin. Trendelenburg, a German philosopher and philologist, was a leader in the study of Aristotle.

During his time in Berlin, Brentano's relationship with his aunt Bettina Brentano von Arnim flourished. She was able to draw out Brentano's poetic and romantic disposition. Himself a translator of verse and a budding poet, he was undoubtedly inspired by his somewhat unorthodox aunt. He was able also to deepen his acquaintance with the von Savignys, the family into which another aunt, Kunigunde, had married. Both of these extended familial relationships helped encourage Brentano's cultural and intellectual growth.

Brentano moved to the Academy in Münster for 1859 and 1860, again embracing the study of Scholastic philosophy as a pupil of the German Catholic philosopher Franz Jacob Clemens. The rediscovery of Aristotle's work in the eleventh and twelfth centuries had heavily influenced medieval philosophical thought and theology. Medieval Scholasticism had succeeded in maintaining a presence in nineteenth-century German philosophy and theology courses. Given this background, it is no accident that Aristotle is perhaps the major philosophical and theological authority on whom Brentano drew in the development of his own philosophy.

In 1862 Brentano's first work was published. *Von der mannigfachen Bedeutung des Seienden nach Aristoteles* (translated as *On Several Senses of Being in Aristotle,* 1975) argues that Aristotle's categories are not mere linguistic devices. Rather, the categories (substance, quantity, quality, relation, time, place, position, state, action, and affection), under which all thinking falls, derive from a single origin. Brentano shows in this work how the categories can be deduced and classified. The book was met with great enthusiasm for its scholarship and novelty of approach to Aristotle. Brentano was awarded a doctorate in absentia from the University of Tübingen in this same year, on July 17.

Feeling the call to a religious vocation, Brentano stayed at the Dominican Monastery at Graz during 1862 but left after a short time. His leaving Graz did not mean that he no longer felt the call to religious life, however. He went on to study theology in Munich and at the Theological Seminary in Würzburg and was ordained a Roman Catholic priest on 6 August 1864. Almost two years later, in July 1866, Brentano became a *privatdozent* (lecturer or assistant) in philosophy at the University of Würzburg. As an assistant he received no fixed salary; yet, the position was significant in Brentano's career, providing an opportunity for him to teach and to continue with his research. He wrote an (unpublished) thesis on Friedrich Schelling, "Darstellung und Kritik der Lehre Schellings in den drei Studien" (Exposition and Critique of Schelling's Teachings in Their Three Phases). This was followed by his habilitation, for which he wrote *Die Psychologie des Aristoteles, insbesondere seine Lehre vom nous poietikos* (1867; translated as *The Psychology of Aristotle: In Particular His Doctrine of the Active Intellect,* 1977). Brentano had expanded his interests beyond the boundaries of pure philosophy, in which metaphysical questions took center stage. He was now entering new territory for him, the study of psychology, a study obviously influenced by his reading of both Aristotle and of the Scholastics.

In 1866 Brentano began teaching courses on the history of philosophy, logic, metaphysics, and psychology. Carl Stumpf, who was a major influence in the development of the psychology of music and Gestalt psychology, was among his first students. In 1867, Anton Marty, the Swiss philosopher best known for his work in philosophy of speech, became a student of Brentano. Marty developed a strong and lasting intimate relationship with Brentano, both personally and professionally.

Stumpf and Marty formed the core of an intellectual circle around Brentano, which also included Hermann Schell and Gelehrten Ernst Commer. As Catholic intellectuals, Schell, a future leader of the Catholic Modernist Movement, and Commer, a conservative, were theological opponents later in their lives. The circle included Georg Friedrich von Hertling, who became prime minister and foreign minister of Bavaria and then chancellor of Germany in 1917–1918. Brentano was Hertling's first philosophy teacher. Inspired by Brentano, Hertling wrote a dissertation at the University of Berlin, *De Aristotelis notione Unius* (On Aristotle's Notion of the One, 1864), and a book, *Materie und Form und die Definition der Seele bei Aristoteles* (Matter and Form and the Definition of Soul in Aristotle, 1871).

Brentano's writing and teaching careers gained momentum. His essay on Johann Adam Möhler's *Kirchengeschichte* (Church History, 1867–1868) appeared in the second volume of an 1867 critical collection edited by Pius Bonifatius Gams. In his teaching, he began to formulate the idea that philosophy develops through four phases or stages. Philosophy, he maintains, ascends in the first stage and then descends in a deteriorating spiral. His theory deals with what he identified as ancient, medieval, and modern philosophy, a classification that, with some modifications, is still acknowledged by most philosophers. Georg Wilhelm Friedrich Hegel had similarly systematized the history of philosophy,

albeit in terms of memorializing it as the history of human experience and thus human consciousness, but with a tendency toward progression. Hegel regarded his own philosophy as the culmination of philosophical thinking. In Brentano's schema, it is legitimate to infer that the four stages are cyclic, repeating themselves through further epochs.

In 1869 Brentano's essay "Auguste Comte und die positive Philosophie" (Auguste Comte and Positivist Philosophy) was published in the journal *Chilianeum: Blätter für katholische Philosophie, Kunst, und Leben.* Comte was the founder of positivism, the idea that knowledge arises from observation and that one cannot know unobservable physical objects. Brentano, who was disenchanted by the idealism of Schelling and Hegel, embraced Comte's empirical approach, attracted by its implicit realism. With Brentano's developing views on psychology as an empirical science, he naturally found the work of Comte intellectually attractive.

Meanwhile, Brentano had also been struggling with the twin demands of his religious faith and his metaphysical commitments, a struggle that had begun when he was a young man. According to his pupil Stumpf, Brentano had never been a supporter of the Jesuits, the most influential religious order close to the seat of papal power. The Jesuits had been founded in an atmosphere of Counter Reformation zeal and were always privileged in relation to moral and theological matters in the eyes of Rome. The debate over the question of papal infallibility peaked in 1869, with the Jesuits giving the idea of papal infallibility their full support. The concept was not fully endorsed, however, in Germany and among other Catholic intellectuals in England, Hungary, and France.

Brentano had been successful in disengaging his metaphysical critique of religious belief from his teaching, thus, in a sense, protecting him from his doubts about the Roman Catholic Church and his own place in religion. The question of papal infallibility focused anew his theological troubles, however. He was persuaded by the bishop of Mainz to write a position paper against papal infallibility, "Das Franz Brentano Gutachten über die päpstliche Infallibilität" (Franz Brentano's Opinion on Papal Infallibility). This paper was well argued and became an influential document in the arguments of the German church against the dogma.

For Brentano, the time had come when he could no longer ignore his own wrestling with reason and faith. His inner voice of reason won him over, and once the doctrine of papal infallibility was declared, he could pretend no longer that he was a faithful and undoubting son of the Church. Brentano must have been fully aware of the implications of his stand: his academic appointment was, in part, held by virtue of his priesthood. His leaving

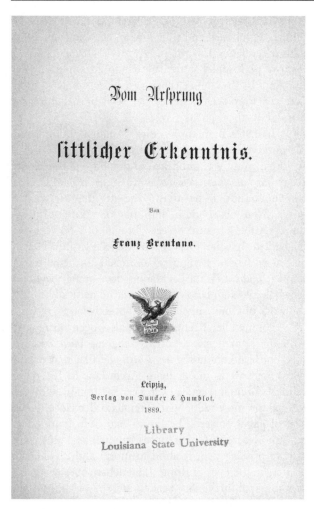

Vom Ursprung

sittlicher Erkenntnis.

Von

Franz Brentano.

Leipzig,
Verlag von Duncker & Humblot.
1889.

Title page for Brentano's treatise on the nature of goodness, translated in 1902 as The Origin of Knowledge of Right and Wrong *(Hill Memorial Library, Louisiana State University)*

the priesthood echoed through the rest of his life and separated him from many of his supporters (for example, Hertling). On the other hand, he was able to persuade Stumpf to leave the priesthood also in 1870, and in this episode one might recognize the impact Brentano's convictions had on his loyal admirers.

Academically, Brentano remained a rising star. He was appointed professor *extraordinarius* in his absence in England during 1872. He was also writing the book that has brought probably his greatest and lasting fame in both psychology and philosophy, *Psychologie vom empirischen Standpunkte* (1874; translated as *Psychology from an Empirical Standpoint,* 1973).

Brentano left the priesthood in 1873. Because leaving the priesthood meant that he was in effect excommunicated, he found himself in an invidious position. Not only did he lose his academic status as a professional, affiliated philosopher, he lost the commu-

nity into which he had grown and which had supported him for nearly twenty years.

The aspect of Brentano's lifework for which he is most remembered is elucidated in *Psychologie vom empirischen Standpunkte.* Brentano's championing of Comte and his heavy bias toward Aristotelianism emerges as a central feature of this work. His discussion of mental and physical phenomena in the context of the histories of philosophy and psychology is thorough and insightful. Critical to his discussion is his claim that there are no positive interpretations of mental phenomena. Rather, the mental has been defined in terms of what it is not in relation to the physical. Brentano found this position theoretically unsatisfactory.

Using a notion he appropriated from Scholastic philosophy and rehabilitating Aristotle, he argues that the mental does have at least one affirmative feature, intentionality. For him, the distinguishing mark of mental phenomena is intentional inexistence which means that mental phenomena are always directed toward some object, they are always *about* something. Mental phenomena can thus be thought of as having immanent objectivity or directedness: their content is immediately here now. He noted that his idea that mental phenomena always display reference to a content is ambiguous. In so noting, Brentano testifies to his awareness of the potential controversy over the meaning of what he is proposing. He has lengthy footnotes to his text, including a reference to Aristotle's discussion of mental inexistence, which highlight that awareness. History has shown that his intuition was right. The status of the mental object, what it is that has immanent objectivity, has engendered compelling debate since the publication of the book. Further, that the mental does actually have the irreducible status that he attributes to "it" has also caused enormous controversy. Some physicalist reductionists (those who argue that there are only physical objects or at least that mental language can be reduced to physical language), for example, claim that the mental actually *is* the physical; others interested in supervenience claim that there is only the material, but that mental language is irreducible to material language even though the referent of mental language and physical language is identical.

Losing his position at Würzburg, Brentano found a post in Austria at the University of Vienna in 1874. Since he had been antagonistic to the idea of Otto von Bismarck's unification of Germany without Austria, it was of some comfort to him that he was able to secure the Vienna position. He continued teaching and publishing in Austria, enculturated into Viennese life and pleasures. He wrote poetry and learned chess, about which he wrote the book *Neue Vertheidigung der Spanischen Partie* (New Moves in the Spanish Game of Chess,

1900). During this period, Alexius Meinong, the founder of object theory who is regarded by many as Brentano's most famous pupil, became a student of Brentano in 1874. Meinong developed Brentano's idea of intentional inexistence and posited the existence of nonexistent objects. The status of such objects has created much philosophical speculation and disagreement. One of its first critics was Brentano himself. Meinong remained in Vienna until 1882 as a *privatdozent,* then moved to Graz, first as professor *extraordinarius* and then as professor *ordinarius.*

In 1880 Brentano married, an event that caused him further anguish. Kraus notes that the Austrian Legal Code denied the sacrament of marriage to former priests. Again, Brentano found himself having to relocate to avoid controversy, something he did not quite manage. He resigned from his professorial post in Vienna, applied for Saxon citizenship, and moved to Leipzig. He and Ida Lieben were married in a civil ceremony in Leipzig on 16 September 1880. He was allowed, eventually, to return to Vienna, in 1881, but as a *privatdozent,* a demotion from his professorship. He had been promised a professorship, but because, it is thought, of pressure from a conservative Catholic priesthood, the position failed to materialize.

Brentano remained in Vienna until 1895. His pupils included Sigmund Freud. His empirical approach to psychology and his emphasis on association and intentionality greatly influenced Freud. Rudolph Steiner, Christian von Ehrenfels, and Jan Twardowski, all of whom contributed significantly to philosophy and psychology during the late nineteenth and early twentieth centuries, were also students of Brentano. Of particular note is Edmund Husserl, the founder of phenomenology, who became a student of Brentano in 1884. Husserl's "Erinnerungen an Franz Brentano" (Reminiscences of Franz Brentano), included in Kraus's *Franz Brentano: Zur Kenntnis seines Lebens und seine Lehre* (Franz Brentano: An Acknowledgment of His Life and Teachings, 1919), reveals a fascination with philosophy that was enhanced by his contact with Brentano. Husserl loved and respected his teacher, but his work took a turn away from Brentano's; according to him, Brentano had difficulty in coming to terms with his pupils whose work developed independently of his.

Brentano began taking his summer holidays at a house he purchased in 1887, in Schönbühl on the Danube, a practice he continued for many years. In 1888 Johannes Christian Michael, his only child, was born. The following year, *Vom Ursprung sittlicher Erkenntnis* (translated as *The Origin of Knowledge of Right and Wrong,* 1902), an ethical treatise that explores the nature of goodness, appeared. G. E. Moore, the English metaphysical and ethical realist, in his review of this text in

Brentano in old age (from Howard O. Eaton, The Austrian Philosophy of Values, *1930; Thomas Cooper Library, University of South Carolina)*

the *International Journal of Ethics* (1903), argued that Brentano's work was groundbreaking. This book reveals Brentano's realism. Philosophically speaking, realism is the idea that there is existence independent of human thought. Antirealist arguments about ethics, morals, and ontology suggest that they are constructed through social practice or even determined by what is known and what are the limits of human thinking and language systems. Brentano argues, as does Moore, that goodness is a natural property independent of any truths about what exists. Brentano's commitment to ethical realism complements and perhaps inspired Moore's.

Four years later, in 1893, Ida Lieben died. Her death was an enormous blow to Brentano. Driven by the frustration of not gaining a professorship, Brentano left Vienna in 1895 and went to Italy, his family's place of origin. His somewhat nomadic existence took him to itinerant posts in Rome, Palermo, and Florence. He remarried in 1897. His second wife, Emilie Rueprecht, was with him until his death in 1917. They had no children. Little is written about Emilie. Except in reference to her marriage to Brentano, no birth or death dates are available in the literature.

Although Brentano suffered from near blindness, he continued to write philosophy. *Untersuchungen zur Sinnespsychologie* (Inquiry into Sense Psychology) appeared in 1907. He completed *Von der Klassifikation der psychischen Phänomene* (On the Classification of Psychological Phenomena) in 1911. Between 1911 and 1917, he continued to compose philosophy by dictating his essays. These essays appeared as appendices in volume one of the 1924 edition, edited by Kraus, of *Psychologie vom empirischen Standpunkte*. The purpose of these essays was both explanatory and clarificationary.

In 1915, because of Italy's involvement in World War I, Brentano moved to Zurich, where he died on 17 March 1917 after a bout of appendicitis. The sheer volume of the work and the range of subject material, from philosophy to psychology to theology to ethics to politics, suggests the magnitude of Franz Brentano's mind and his breadth of vision. He loved the intellectual life passionately. Clearly, he was an intellectual hero to many of his students; he had a wonderful, profound intelligence; and his pedagogical inspiration was instrumental in helping to form some of the greatest minds of Europe over the past century.

Letters:

"Briefe Franz Brentanos an Hugo Bergman," edited by Hugo Bergman, *Philosophy and Phenomenological Research*, 7 (1946): 83–158;

Philosophenbriefe: Aus der wissenschaftlichen Korrespondenz von Alexius Meinong mit Franz Brentano, edited by Rudolf Kindinger (Graz: Academische Druck- und Verlagsantalt, 1965).

Bibliography:

Paolo Gregoretti, *Franz Brentano: Bibliografia completa, 1862–1982* (Trieste: University Press of Trieste, 1983).

Biography:

Oskar Kraus, *Franz Brentano: Zur Kenntnis seines Lebens und seine Lehre. Mit Beiträgen von C. Stumpf und E. Husserl* (Munich: Beck, 1919).

References:

Liliana Albertazzi, *Introduzione a Franz Brentano* (Rome: Laterza, 1999);

Elisabeth Baumgartner and Wilhelm Baumgartner, "Comments on Jacquette's 'Brentano's Scientific Revolution,'" *Southern Journal of Philosophy*, supplement, 40 (2000): 223–229;

Michael Benedikt, "Leibniz and Brentano: Two Philosophers Concerning Catastrophes and Their Solutions," *History of European Ideas*, 20, nos. 4–6 (February 1995): 931–936;

Johannes Brandl, "The Legacy of Franz Brentano," *Philosophical and Phenomenological Research*, 57, no. 3 (September 1997): 697–702;

Deborah Brown, "Immanence and Individuation: Brentano and the Scholastics on Knowledge of Singulars," *Monist*, 83, no. 1 (January 2000): 22–46;

Roderick M. Chisholm, *Brentano and Meinong Studies* (Amsterdam: Rodopi, 1982);

Raul Corrazon, *Franz Brentano's Ontology* <http://www.formalontology.it/brentanof.htm> [accessed 10 February 2004];

Howard O. Eaton, *The Austrian Philosophy of Values* (Norman: University of Oklahoma Press, 1930);

Dale Jacquette, "Brentano's Scientific Revolution in Philosophy," *Southern Journal of Philosophy*, supplement, 40 (2002): 193–222;

John Macnamara and Geert-Jan Boudewijnse, "Brentano's Influence on Ehrenfels's Theory of Perpetual Gestalts," *Journal for the Theory of Social Behaviour*, 25, no. 4 (December 1995): 401–417;

Linda L. McAlister, ed., *The Philosophy of Brentano* (London: Duckworth, 1976);

Benito Muller, "Proterosis, Proteraesthesis and Noticing a Red Tint: An Essay Concerning Franz Brentano's Descriptive Psychology," *Brentano Studien*, 9 (2000–2001): 267–278;

Roberto Poli, ed., *The Brentano Puzzle* (Aldershot & Brookfield, Vt.: Ashgate, 1998);

Barry Smith, *Austrian Philosophy: The Legacy of Franz Brentano* (Chicago: Open Court, 1994);

Smith, "Boundaries: An Essay in Mereotopology," in *The Philosophy of Roderick M. Chisholm*, edited by Lewis E. Hahn (Chicago: Open Court, 1997);

Smith, *The Philosophy of Franz Brentano* <http://ontology.buffalo.edu/smith/articles/brentano/> [accessed 10 February 2004];

Amie L. Thomasson, "Phenomenology and the Development of Analytic Philosophy," *Southern Journal of Philosophy*, supplement, 40 (2002): 115–142;

Wojciech Zelaniec, "Disentangling Brentano: Why Did He Get Individuation Wrong?" *Brentano Studien*, 7 (1997): 455–463.

Papers:

Franz Brentano's papers are held in archive at Houghton Library of the Harvard College Library, Harvard University, Cambridge, Massachusetts.

Guy Debord

(28 December 1931 – 30 November 1994)

Tom Lavazzi
City University of New York–Kingsborough

BOOKS: *Fin de Copenhague,* by Debord and Asger Jorn ([Copenhagen?]: Bauhaus Imaginiste, 1957);

Memoires: Structures Portantes d'Asger Jorn, by Debord and Jorn (Paris: Internationale Situationniste, 1959);

Contre le cinéma (Aarhus, Denmark: Institute Scandinave de Vandalisme Comparé, 1964);

La Société du spectacle (Paris: Buchet-Chastel, 1967); translated as *The Society of the Spectacle* (Detroit: Black and Red, 1970; revised, 1973);

Internationale situationniste: Bulletin centrale edité par les sections de l'Internationale situationniste (Amsterdam: Van Gennep, 1970);

La véritable scission dans l'Internationale, by Debord and Gianfranco Sanquinetti (Paris: Champ Libre, 1972); translated by Michel Prigent and Lucy Forsyth as *The Veritable Split in the International: Theses on the Situationist International and Its Time* (London: B. M. Piranha, 1974);

Œuvres cinématographiques complètes: 1952–1978 (Paris: Champ Libre, 1978); partly translated by Richard Parry as *Society of the Spectacle and Other Films* (London: Rebel Press, 1992);

Préface à la quatrième édition Italienne de "La Société du Spectacle" (Paris: Champ Libre, 1979); translated by Prigent and Forsyth as *Preface to the Fourth Italian Edition of "The Society of the Spectacle"* (London: Chronos, 1983);

Ordures et décombres: Déballés à la Sortie du Film: In girum imus nocte et consumimur igni (Paris: Champ Libre, 1982);

Considérations sur l'assassinat de Gérard Lebovici (Paris: Lebovici, 1985); translated by Robert Greene as *Considerations on the Assassination of Gerard Lebovici,* edited by Greene (Los Angeles: TamTam, 2001);

Le "Jeu de la Guerre": Relevé des positions successives de toutes les forces au cours d'une partie, by Debord and Alice Becker-Ho (Paris: Lebovici, 1987); translated by Len Bracken as "The Game of War," in his *Guy Debord: Revolutionary* (Venice, Cal.: Feral House, 1997), pp. 240–251;

Guy Debord (from <www.notbored.org/debord.html>)

Commentaires sur la société du spectacle (Paris: Lebovici, 1988); translated by Malcolm Imrie as *Comments on the Society of the Spectacle* (New York & London: Verso, 1990);

Panégyrique, Tome Premier (Paris: Lebovici, 1989); translated by James Brook as *Panegyric: Volume I* (New York & London: Verso, 1991);

In girum imus nocte et consumimur igni (Paris: Lebovici, 1990); translated by Forsyth (London: Pelagian, 1991);

"Cette Mauvaise Réputation . . ." (Paris: Gallimard, 1993);

Le déclin et la chute de l'économie spectaculaire-marchande (Paris: Jean-Jacques Pauvert aux Belles Lettres, 1993);

Des Contrats (Cognac: Le Temps qui'il fait, 1995);

Panégyrique, Tome Second (Paris: Fayard, 1997).

Edition: *In girum imus nocte et consumimur igni: Suivi de Ordures et décombres* (Paris: Gallimard, 1999).

Editions in English: *The Society of the Spectacle,* translated by Richard Parry (London: Rebel Press Aim, 1987);

The Society of the Spectacle, translated by Donald Nicholson-Smith (New York: Zone Books, 1994);

Complete Cinematic Works: Scripts, Stills, Documents, translated and edited by Ken Knabb (Oakland, Cal.: AK, 2003).

PRODUCED SCRIPTS: *Hurlements en Faveur de Sade,* motion picture, Films Lettristes, 1952;

Sur le passage de quelques personnes à travers une assez courtre unité de temps, motion picture, Dansk-Fransk Experimentalfilmskompagni, 1959;

Critique de la Separation, motion picture, Dansk-Fransk Experimentalfilmskompagni, 1961;

La Société du Spectacle, motion picture, Simar Films, 1973;

Réfutation de tous les jugements, tant elogieux qu'hostiles, qui ont été portes sur le film "La Société du Spectacle," motion picture, Simar Films, 1975;

In girum imus nocte et consumimur igni, motion picture, Simar Films, 1978;

GuyDebord: Son Art et Son Temps, television, by Debord and Brigitte Cornand, Canal +, 9 January 1995.

OTHER: "Methods of Detournement" (by Debord and Gil Wolman), "Primary Problems in the Construction of a Situation," and "Perspectives for Conscious Alterations in Daily Life," in *Situationist International Anthology,* edited by Ken Knabb (Berkeley, Cal.: Bureau of Public Secrets, 1981), pp. 8–14, 43–45, 68–75;

"Two Accounts of the Derive," "Unitary Urbanism at the End of the 1950s," and "The Situationists and New Forms of Action in Politics and Art," in *On the Passage of a Few People through a Rather Brief Moment in Time: The Situationist International, 1957–1972,* edited by Elisabeth Sussman (Cambridge, Mass. & Boston: MIT Press/Institute of Contemporary Art, 1989), pp. 135–139, 143–147, 148–153;

Guy Debord présente Potlatch: 1954–1957, edited by Debord (Paris: Gallimard, 1996).

SELECTED PERIODICAL PUBLICATIONS–UNCOLLECTED: "To Put an End to Nihilistic Comfort," *Lettrist International,* 3 (1953): n.p.;

"Exercise in Psychogeography," *Potlatch,* 2 (1954): 12;

"Economically Weak," *Potlatch,* 15 (1954): 57;

"The Big Sleep and Its Clients," *Potlatch,* 16 (1955): 61–62;

"The Value of Education," *Potlatch,* 16, 17, 18 (1955): 64–65, 71–72, 76–77;

"Architecture and Play," *Potlatch,* 20 (1955): 86–88;

"Why Lettrism?" by Debord and Gil J. Wolman, *Potlatch,* 22 (1955): 97–103;

"One Step Back," *Potlatch,* 28 (1957): 139–141;

"Still More Effort if You Want to Be Situationists," *Potlatch,* 29 (1957): 143–146.

Guy Debord was an experimental motion-picture maker, founder and autocratic head of the Situationist International, ideologue-cum-activist, and "Doctor of Nothing" (as he labels himself in his mock autobiography, *Panégyrique, Tome premier,* 1989 [translated as *Panegyric: Volume I,* 1991]). His dialogic cinematic technique and insightful analysis of postmodern, commodity-driven society have had a formative impact on both artists and theoreticians of contemporary, image-obsessed culture.

Debord was born in Paris on 28 December 1931. In 1939, shortly after his father, Martial (a pharmacist), died of tuberculosis and just before the German occupation of France, Debord moved to Nice with his mother, Paulette, and maternal grandmother, Lydie Rossi. While in Nice, Paulette fell in love with an Italian driving-school principal, Domenico Bignoli, their affair culminating in two half siblings for Debord: Michele (born in 1940), whose aimless life ended in suicide (1976) from an overdose of drugs and alcohol, and Bernard (born in 1940). A few years after her breakup with Bignoli, Paulette married a notary, Charles Labaste, whom she had met while he was vacationing in Nice, partially supported by a family inheritance; Debord gained a stepsister and stepbrother, Chantel and Bernard. In 1950 Debord joined the Lettrists, a group of Paris-based avant-garde artists led by Romanian poet and motion-picture maker Isidore Isou (Jean Cocteau awarded Isou's movie *Traité de bave et d'éternité* [The Drivel and Eternity Treatise] the avant-garde prize at Cannes that same year), and soon after married novelist Michele Bernstein (many of whose stories are based on her life with Debord); he married Alice Becker-Ho, his second wife, in 1970. After taking university exams, Debord moved back to Paris in 1951 but never attended university; residing in an inexpensive hotel on rue Racine, he spent his days and nights reading, writing, working on motion-picture projects, wandering the streets of Paris, and debating politics with fellow Lettristes while drinking wine and mixes of beer and rum at Chez Moineau and other popular Left Bank locations.

Debord split with Isou's Lettrist movement in 1952, forming Lettrist International with Bernstein and moviemaker Gil J. Wolman. Shortly before Debord left the movement, the Lettrist journal *Ion* published "Prolegomenes a tout cinema futur" (Prolegomena to All Future Cinema, April 1952), an essay in which he acknowledges the impact on his own work of the movement. In the same April issue, *Ion* published the text version of Debord's first major movie, *Hurlements en Faveur de Sade* (Howlings in Favor of Sade, 1952), while the image montage was still under construction, yielding an insight into Debord's aesthetic stance and process: critique precedes spectacle. Films Lettristes produced the ninety-minute black-and-white movie later that year. Though Debord originally planned to orchestrate nonsense words and images, in the style of the Lettrists, the final version of the motion picture is constructed as a multivoice discourse, collaging a variety of rhetorical modes—personal and journalistic, theoretic and poetic, legalistic and self-reflexive (that is, commenting on the production of the movie itself)—without any "imagery" in the conventional sense. As in all of Debord's movies, the disembodied voices interact syncretically, by juxtaposition and association, rather than in direct dialogue; they are voice-overs, but in this case, voices over a void: an absence of images. In an attempt to evade the spectacular trap of cinema and keep viewers uncomfortably self-conscious of the illusionistic, introjected quality of all imagery, the only "images" to be had are those described on the soundtrack, and even the sonic illusion proves ultimately unsustainable, the movie ending in twenty-four minutes of blackness and silence.

Hurlements en Faveur de Sade had its first full screening in Paris at the Latin Quarter Club on 13 October 1952; a previous showing that year at another avant-garde cinema club was disrupted by an irate audience and management. According to Len Bracken's *Guy Debord: Revolutionary* (1997), though there were parodies of the movie in the months following the October screening (including an ad for a mock performance that would consist of turning off the lights in the theater for fifteen minutes), *Hurlements en Faveur de Sade* has since been reappraised as a hallmark of avant-garde moviemaking and Situationist praxis. The script of *Hurlements en Faveur de Sade* is included in *Œuvres cinématographiques complètes: 1952–1978* (Complete Cinematographic Works: 1952–1978, 1978) and was first translated to English in *Society of the Spectacle and Other Films* (1992), along with Debord's other motion-picture scripts, with the exception of *In girum imus nocte et consumimur igni* (We Spin Around in the Night and Are Consumed by Fire, 1978), which was published in a separate, critical edition in 1990, and *Guy Debord: Son Art et Son Temps* (Guy Debord: His Art and His Times, 1995), a collaboration, not available in text form, with Brigitte Cornand for French experimental television.

Isidore Isou, whose group of avant-garde artists, the Lettrists, Debord joined in 1950 (from Len Bracken, Guy Debord: Revolutionary, *1997; Thomas Cooper Library, University of South Carolina)*

Though suffering from severe depression—he attempted suicide in 1953—Debord remained fairly active over the next four years, publishing several articles, some of which he produced collaboratively along with other Lettrist International members in the two journals of the new movement, *Internationale Lettriste* and *Potlatch*. In 1957 Debord merged his Paris-based Lettrist International with the Psychogeographic Society of London and the Movement for an Imaginist Bauhaus (a Belgian, Italian, and Scandinavian collective organized in 1953 by painter Asger Jorn) to form the Situationist International, an artists' collective whose aesthetic is rooted in the social. Debord and Jorn collaborated on two art books, *Fin de Copenhague* (End of Copenhagen, 1957), and *Memoires: Structures Portantes d'Asger Jorn* (Memoirs: Bearing Structures of Asger Jorn, 1959).

Fin de Copenhague (published by Jorn's Bauhaus Imaginiste) utilized collage and action painting techniques to critique city planning in Jorn's native Copenhagen. *Memoires* (first published by Debord's Internationale Situationniste but financed by Jorn) collages found and autobiographical material—including sentence fragments (in varying ink densities and font styles), black-and-white photographs, architectural diagrams, images of fortresses from various cultures and historical periods, map fragments of Paris neighborhoods, and cartoons—with abstract, free-form, linear color drawings; to discourage commodification, the original "anti-book," as Debord categorized it, was bound in sandpaper. The sentence fragments are by turns imagistic and poetically evocative, abstractly theoretical or critical, and intimate or matter-or-fact, posing as bits of dialogue taken out of context. Some compositions are open, free-breathing, almost tranquil, while others are disruptive, dense, and jumbled, as text and imagery mutually interfere.

Opening with a grainy, full-page head shot of Debord, *Memoires* is divided into three sections, corresponding to hallmark periods in Debord's life—"Juin 1952" (June 1952), "Décembre 1952" (December 1952), and "Septembre 1953" (September 1953). *Hurlements en Faveur de Sade* was first screened on 30 June 1952, and the first congress of the Lettristes International took place on 7 December 1952. The summer of 1953 was a period of soul-searching for Debord. He chalked "Never Work" on a wall on rue de Seine. In an article ("To Put an End to Nihilistic Comfort") in the August 1953 issue of *Internationale Lettriste,* perhaps foreseeing the ultimate futility of the Situationist program even before the movement was founded, Debord stated that "every revolutionary program" should be based on "a certain idea of happiness even if we know it by losing it"; in the same issue, he revealed plans for a new movie, "La Belle Jeunesse" (Beautiful Youth), which was never realized. During this same period, Debord attempted suicide by asphyxiation. The instability of his personal life, as well as his ideological ambivalence, is registered by a quote from the conclusion of seventeenth- century historian Jacques-Bénigne Bossuet's "Panegyric of St. Bernard," which makes an appearance in the third section of *Memoires:* "Bernard, Bernard, this green youth won't last forever." Perhaps punning on the names of Debord's half brother and stepbrother, the quote hovers above the photo of a young woman (possibly Bernstein) reading alone at a café, surrounded by a ruggedly florid, Rorschach-like blotch of light blue.

Inscribing a reevaluation of this period in his life from the perspective of the early years of the Situationist International, the third section of the book is resonant with contradictory senses of idealism and resignation, cynicism and celebration of the possibilities of a revolution of everyday life that would never be realizable. The last collage of the book is a simple, yet forceful, design: At the top of the page, a single, small-pitched, fading line, as if generated by a typewriter running out of ink—"I wanted to speak the beautiful language of my century"—angles tentatively above a solid red blotch, out of which streak attenuated gestures.

During this same period (the mid to late 1950s), Debord developed the trademarks of his cinematic style and honed the philosophical tenets of Situationism that guided his future life and works. He experimented with qualities peculiar to the cinematic medium, including the flickering of a projector, various manipulations of the film surface (such as hand marking, coloring, and scratching), and disjunctions of sound and image; unlike the Abstract Expressionists' explorations of the materiality of paint during the same period, Debord was concerned not with emotional density but with calling attention to the motion picture as a medium, as an organization of formal elements producing a representational illusion in the service of specular culture. The goal of Debord's filmic experiments was not just to provide a new experience of the medium but to challenge cultural conventions—the way people see and live. By the time Debord founded the Situationist International in 1957, he had developed the major theories necessary to realize his social and aesthetic agenda: unitary urbanism, the creation of situations, *detournement* (detouring), *dé'rive* (drift), and psychogeography. These concepts laid the foundation for Debord's deployment of text, cinema, and events in his private life to critique a passive, object-fixated, socially and personally prefabricated ("spectacular") culture.

As the name of the group indicates, the Situationists advocated people taking control of their own lives, creating the situations and circumstances in which they lived and hence their own history rather than passively accepting the range of more or less alienated (and alienating) roles, work, and leisure activities offered by consumer culture; choosing among such social products gives one an illusory sense of freedom, since they are merely different brands of essentially the same limited set of stances "officially" recognized by the dominant ideology. The Situationists also stressed making art part of one's everyday life, transforming an economy of profit into one of pleasure. For Debord, a "democracy" based on entrepreneurial capitalism is simply another form of totalitarianism, disguised by a pseudodiversity; individuals must redefine their needs against those manufactured for them according to the mandates of market economy. The ideal society, according to Situationist theory, free of class divisions, private property, and state control, would allow each individual to realize his or her own potential and participate fully in the circumstances of his or her life.

On the activist side, the Situationists preferred everyday "situations" as sites of critical inquiry (playing an active role, for example, in developing the ideological contours and determining the direction of the 1968 student and worker uprisings in Paris). Though calling for a destruction of the manufactured spectacle and the undermining of state authority through both direct and covert operations, the Situationists tempered their anarchist tendencies by stressing the importance of praxis, of theoretically informed action in both life and art. The life of a committed Situationist should be a performance of cultural criticism.

Situationism emphasizes the importance of recognizing how all cultural productions–from advertising to philosophy (even cultural theory itself)–manipulate people and of attempting to turn manipulation back against the manipulator. The praxis of *detournement* involves stripping an idea, image, or historical event of its self-justifying context by putting it in dialogue with images, ideas, and events that challenge its ideological base. Similar to earlier theater theorists and practitioners such as Bertolt Brecht, contemporary ones such as Augusto Boal, and earlier cultural theorists such as Mikhail Bakhtin, Debord developed a mode of cultural criticism that was both theoretical and performative. Two other forms of critical praxis, the *dérive* and psychogeography, offer means to achieve a more immediate–unmediated–sensual relation with the environment, to empty oneself of preconceptions and brochure-like images of a milieu by moving meditatively through it, absorbing its materiality and experiencing its actual texture. Such exercises in perceiving, thinking, and experiencing–being at "play" in the world–would enable people, the Situationists believed, to see the "spectacle" for the sham that it was, leading them to an enlightened, unitary urbanism, a sense of who they are and what they really want in the world, empowering them to rebel against the Machiavellian mechanizations of consumer capitalism.

As examples of Situationist praxis thoroughly informed by Situationist International theory, the movies *Sur le passage de quelques personnes à travers une assez courtre unité de temps* (On the Passage of a Few Persons through a Rather Brief Unit of Time, 1959) and *Critique de la Separation* (Critique of Separation, 1961) collage imagery and sound in a dialogical, contrapuntal mode of composition that encourages critical awareness rather than passive reception. Perhaps alluding to Henri Bergson's notion of time as "real duration" rather than chronometric abstraction, *Sur le passage de quelques personnes à travers une assez courtre unité de temps* is a mock-lyrical sketch (à la Alain Resnais) of young Situationists creatively passing time in their Paris environs; images of Japan and revolutionary Algeria, clips from advertising shorts, and filmic reimaginings of Andre Mrugalski's photographs in a pseudodocumentary style are juxtaposed with shots of Debord and friends in their Paris environs, along with disembodied tracking shots through Parisian neighborhoods. Utilizing a mise-en-scène similar to *Sur le passage de quelques personnes à travers une assez courtre unité de temps, Critique de la Separation* is a more general criticism of culture–specifically movies, which "present a false, isolated coherence"–and a call for social-political action. In one scene, as images of Anglo-European history and current events abut shots of unrest in Africa, the voice-over comments on the disjunction between everyday life and a broader historical field encountered as spectacle: "But it's always far away. . . . We remain outside of it. . . . separated from it by our own non-intervention."

Perhaps influenced by Marxist philosopher Henri Lefebvre's *Critique de la vie quotidienne* (Critique of Everyday Life, 1958), which calls for a restructuring of daily experience to remedy the alienating effects of consumer capitalism, both *Critique de la Separation* and *Sur le passage de quelques personnes à travers une assez courtre unité de temps* criticize separation and distance–between persons, between people and their surroundings, between global and local points of view; they challenge conventions of *not* seeing (passive seeing), unthinking acceptance of cultural givens, and modes of the unlived life. Attacking prescribed responses to a ready-made culture and spectacular voyeurism, the motion pictures themselves offer a counterstrategy, creating an engaged (and engaging) cinematic experience, or "situation," through the creative detouring of found cultural material.

Debord's cinematic and "real-life" experiments in critical cultural praxis eventually captured the imagination of the Paris avant-garde. Though the Situationist International held several "international" conferences, or "congresses," the French section, centered around Debord and his theories, eventually dominated, renaming itself the SI Central Council and briefly merging with Lefebvre's Group for Research on Everyday Life; by 1963, for all practical and theoretical purposes, *SI* came to designate Debord and his circle in Paris.

Partially because of inadequate distribution of his movies, Debord is perhaps best known for his radical work of cultural criticism, *La Société du spectacle* (1967; translated as *The Society of the Spectacle,* 1970). According to Bracken, editors at the Buchet-Chastel publishing house were afraid the French public might mistake the book as a display of celebrity lifestyles, since *spectacle* in French designates a show. The book was published the same month as the pamphlet *De la misère en milieu étudiant* (translated as *On the Poverty of Student Life,* 1967), which Debord and the Situationists deployed, along with other tracts, to incite unrest on campuses around the country. *La Société du spectacle* consists of nine chapters and 221 numbered theses. The first 34 theses (comprising chapter 1, "La Séparation achevée" [Separation Per-

Debord's first wife, novelist Michele Bernstein (from Len Bracken,
Guy Debord: Revolutionary, *1997; Thomas Cooper*
Library, University of South Carolina)

fecte], published separately in issue 11 of *Internationale Situationniste,* October 1967) lay out the basic concept of spectacular society. The first line of the book parallels the opening of volume one of Karl Marx's *Das Kapital* (1867) while veering away from it. The final word in Marx's "all life in societies under the reign of modern conditions of production displays itself as an immense accumulation of capital" is changed to *spectacle.* Hence, Debord acknowledges his precursors while making strategic use of them to articulate his own theory. Social control is effected not merely through monetary maneuvers and economic abstraction, but through manipulating the material presence (the signs) of social life itself. Thesis 1 concludes with a postmodern tag to Marx's perspective: "All that once was directly lived has become mere representation." That is, social life has become mediated through a vocabulary of representations; whoever controls these representations influences patterns of thought and behavior and hence the flow of cultural as well as monetary capital (the latter merely a subset of the former). Of course, the producers, rather than the consumers, of the spectacle benefit most from it.

The bulk of the book historically contextualizes spectacular society. In successive chapters, Debord examines the development of revolutionary politics (especially the "proletarian revolution") in Russia and Europe and critiques its failures. He describes the three main forms in the evolution of the spectacle: "concentrated" (delusions and illusions promulgated by the state, a form associated with Stalinist Russia), "diffuse" (a function of consumerism, the modern American version), and "integrated" (a combination of the two, permeating all reality—a globalized, postmodern adaptation). He also discusses the relationship of the spectacle to postmodern forms of production and labor, its sustained growth through advertising and the media, and the way people's sense of history and concepts of time itself have been distorted by spectacular culture.

Debord's broad goal is to initiate an enlightened resistance among the "proletariat class," which he expands beyond traditional Marxist boundaries to include white-collar as well as blue-collar workers—anyone whose labor is co-opted to serve the spectacle. Debord's self-admittedly nearly impossible task is to mobilize society against an "enemy" that has subtly interwoven itself into the fabric of social life—in everything from the food people eat to the way they conduct their personal relationships to the way they see themselves represented in the media. The operation of spectacular society is much more insidious than previous forms of totalitarianism, according to Debord, because it lacks a human dimension; it desires only to perpetuate itself through the marshaling of representations and globalized self-reproduction. Everywhere asserting the "predominance of appearances" and that "all human life is mere appearance," the spectacle displaces lived experience with pseudolife (a "negation of life"), according to thesis 10, eventually creating a false consciousness in the individual that makes this antilife acceptable and even desirable. The repressive, alienating effects of the spectacle, then, in conjunction with modern forms of production and specialization that separate people from others, from their environment, and even their own lives and true desires, are actually sustained by those it represses. Debord wants everyone to become cognizant of this apparent yet mostly invisible (hence highly seductive) form of reified ideology, to completely see the hall of mirrors one is trapped within, in order to escape and realize oneself as (diverting Lefebvre's phrase) "total [wo]/man."

In the final chapter of *La Société du spectacle,* Debord provides an overview of the subtle and not so subtle materializations of ideology in consumer culture and closes with a plea for theoretically informed, historically grounded action: "Emancipation in our time," he counsels, "is emancipation from the material bases of an inverted truth" but cannot be realized "until dialogue has taken up arms to impose its own conditions upon the world." The monolithically dissimulative modes and mores of spectacular life must be melted down by an alert, agile critical consciousness, trained to recognize and expose the spectacle on its ever-broadening fronts.

In his *Préface à la quatrième édition Italienne de "La Société du Spectacle"* (1979; translated as *Preface to the Fourth Italian Edition of "The Society of the Spectacle,"* 1983), Debord recalls that he wrote the book so that Situationist theory could serve future subversive activities, the historical function of the group having drawn close to completion by the late 1960s. Though in 1967 *La Société du spectacle* was harshly received–a critic for *Le Monde* accused Debord of rhetorical bravado and being out of touch with the reality of events–by 1968 the book was being hailed as the new *Das Kapital,* a sourcebook for evolving revolutionary thought and action.

In 1968, Debord and the Paris-based Situationist International participated in the May revolution at the barricades and the student occupation of the Sorbonne, issuing several pamphlets calling for a countrywide workers' occupation of all factories. Though the Situationist International was constituted on a dual aesthetic and political platform–Situationist artists believing that changing one's worldview through experimental art was a fundamental first step to revolutionary action–by 1973, Debord's increasingly radical activist political stance left little room for purely aesthetic activity. Despite his earlier experiments with art books, during the 1960s (influenced by Lefebvre's neo-Marxist sociology) Debord became disillusioned about the potential of art to serve a revolutionary agenda; at the fifth Situationist International conference in the fall of 1961, artistic activity was officially eliminated from the revolutionary program. Thenceforth, any members who continued to produce art were required to label such work "anti-Situationist art." Several artists either left the group voluntarily or were expelled, including Jorn, who resigned in 1961. Through the late 1970s, however, Debord continued to assault the status quo ("bourgeois" society), theoretically and cinematically, along lines he had laid out at the inception of the movement.

As in all of Debord's work, theory is valid only in praxis; one way to defeat the spectacle is to divert its cultural products. In chapter 8 of *La Société du spectacle,* "La négation et la consommation dans la cultura" (Negation and Consumption in the Cultural Sphere), Debord discusses the process of *detournement:* the deployment of the tools and media–both textual and graphic–of the spectacle against itself (a guerrilla aesthetic that includes the alteration of billboards, replacing ad copy with revolutionary slogans). The point of

such subversive play, according to Debord, is to "take effective possession of the community of dialogue" in order to advance revolutionary agendas. Debord's cinematic version of *La Société du spectacle* (1973) is a masterpiece of *detournement.*

Since Debord's reputation as a moviemaker and theorist had become well established by the early 1970s, Gérard Lebovici's Simar Films, which produced *La Société du spectacle* and Debord's next two movies, granted him complete artistic freedom. Like Debord's previous cinematic experiments, the mise-en-scène of *La Société du spectacle* consists of found imagery, music, and quotations from various sources collaged with autobiographical material. The imagery includes clips from advertisements and fashion shows; news coverage of local, national, and international events (such as the Vietnam War and the 1968 Paris uprisings), along with other documentary footage; sequences from classic motion pictures by Sergei Eisenstein and Orson Welles, Hollywood westerns, industrial training movies, and autobiographical sequences featuring Debord's second wife, Alice Becker-Ho (to whom *La Société du spectacle* is dedicated). The images, forming a dialogue with theoretical excerpts from Debord's book and briefs from the Committee of Occupation of the Sorbonne, along with citations from the works of Niccolò Machiavelli, Marx, and seventeenth-century German military strategist Carl von Clausewitz, enact both a parody and compelling critique of an image-obsessed culture. Tonally, Debord tempers the pop and kitsch aspects of the imagery through his vapidly elegiac reading of the text and the formalized somberness of Michel Corrette's cello and harpsichord sonatas, as well as the harshness of some of the documentary footage.

Initially, the text of the movie follows chapter 1 of *La Société du spectacle* closely, quoting in order from half the theses, then leaps ahead to chapter 8, works backward through the previous chapters and concludes with thesis 123 from the end of chapter 4, ultimately citing about half of the theses in the book. The effect for a viewer who knows Debord's work (as most of its contemporary viewers would have) is of the theory working the imagery back through itself, encompassing or encamping it, a particularly apt structural strategy since the book helped generate events that were later featured in the movie (in other words, the Situationists' intervention in the 1968 uprisings is partly responsible for the character of the footage documenting those events). In the motion picture, images counter other images, as text and imagery comment on each other; the juxtaposition and interaction of the various elements–image, text, and music–create an ongoing dialogue that leaves no cultural stone unturned critically.

Front page of a Lettrist journal to which Debord frequently contributed in the late 1950s (from Len Bracken,
Guy Debord: Revolutionary, *1997; Thomas Cooper Library, University of South Carolina)*

After Debord reads the final sentence of thesis 123—"Revolutionary theory is now the enemy of all revolutionary ideology, and knows it"—*La Société du spectacle* concludes with a newsreel montage of proletarian and race riots juxtaposed with shots of calvary charges from a Hollywood rendition of the American Civil War and a final title-board style quotation (à la silent movies) from Clausewitz about the importance, in military campaigns, of putting theory into practice. All of these elements suggest that though revolutionary agendas, too, have become part of the spectacle, the skillful use of *detournement* as a praxis of critical consciousness can keep people just this side of capitulation.

The reviews of *La Société du spectacle* were mixed. Seeing a larger issue in the critical reception, Debord made another movie, in the same style as *La Société du spectacle,* that condemns both the negative and the positive reviews of the previous motion picture. In keeping with the Situationist method of operations (staging the movie is an engaged critical act confronting yet another outcropping of false consciousness), Debord's *Réfutation de tous les jugements, tant elogieux qu'hostiles, qui ont été portes sur le film "La Société du Spectacle"* (In Refutation of All Judgments, Whether for or against, Which Have Been Brought to Date on the Film "The Society of the Spectacle," 1975) argues that contemporary critics' involvement with the spectacle has destroyed their ability to perceive the objects of their criticism clearly and directly, disqualifying them to judge experimental art accurately. In effect, Debord puts his own art above all criticism, but only because, in his view, criticism itself has been devalued by the spectacle, having lost the means to achieve "direct and profound knowledge, a complete praxis and authentic taste."

Produced in 1978, Debord's sixth cinematic feature, *In girum imus nocte et consumimur igni*—titled after a medieval palindrome—was not shown publicly until 1981 because no theater would run it. The movie continues to critique the spectacle and its deceitful manifestations but also eulogizes Debord's life in Paris, including the people, places, movies, books, and music that he loves. *In girum imus nocte et consumimur igni* received mixed reviews and has a recollective and estranged feel, as of one's life and personal history inevitably, irretrievably receding: in one lyric sequence, illustrative of the Situationist concept of the *dérive,* a disembodied camera moves through Paris streets to the fluid rhythms of Art Blakey's "Whisper Not."

During the 1980s and 1990s, perhaps goaded by the mystery surrounding the 1984 assassination of his publisher, Gérard Lebovici (within weeks of Lebovici's publication of the autobiography of notorious French criminal and political radical Jacques Mesrine), and the ensuing libel suits he filed against police allegations of his involvement in the murder, Debord became increasingly suspicious, if not paranoid, of secret agencies serving the dominant order and infiltrating all facets of society to suppress and diffuse revolutionary thought and activity. In protest over police investigations into the Lebovici incident and the handling of the affair by the media, Debord refused to let any of his motion pictures be shown in public; he published a slim volume, *Considérations sur l'assassinat de Gérard Lebovici* (1985; translated as *Considerations on the Assassination of Gerard Lebovici,* 2001), in which he defends his innocence, expresses his embitterment over the affair, and chastises the French press. In the years following Lebovici's death, increasingly reclusive and disillusioned about the feasibility of a proletarian revolution capable of overthrowing the well-entrenched, all-powerful society of the spectacle, Debord restaged revolutionary theory as a board game, *Le "Jeu de la Guerre": Relevé des positions successives de toutes les forces au cours d'une partie* (1987; translated as "The Game of War," 1997), designed in collaboration with Becker-Ho.

Debord had been perfecting the *Kriegspiel,* as he called the game, since the 1950s. The final product (published by Lebovici's firm) includes rules of play and a section outlining principles "On the Conduct of War" (the translation of *Le "Jeu de la Guerre"* published in Bracken's *Guy Debord: Revolutionary* includes a diagram of the board and a table of the pieces, allowing the reader to manufacture the actual game). The sections "Rules of Play" and especially "On the Conduct of War" suggest that "Jeu de la Guerre" is a metaphor for the game of life, à la Situationism. Players must always be on the alert and strategically engaged, thinking on their feet in a field of play, since the game "tends to impose at each instant, considerations of contradictory necessities." Operating under constraints of time and space in a hostile territory, one can never be sure of the success of a strategy; defensive maneuvers cannot remain "static," and an offensive strategy is often forced, by an opponent's "counter-maneuvers," to turn

defensive. Also, though one can make many "bad" maneuvers in the game, even a "good" maneuver is never "assured of being good." As Debord puts it later in *Commentaires sur la société du spectacle* (1988; translated as *Comments on the Society of the Spectacle,* 1990), in a world where the spectacle has infiltrated all aspects of life and it is no longer clear "who is observing whom," one can never be sure that he or she is not being manipulated, but neither can the manipulator be sure that his or her manipulations will achieve the intended result. Finally, the game stresses the importance of coordinated group action: a "detached corps should remain so for the shortest possible time," evoking the Situationists' fundamental role in orchestrating the events of 1968.

In the closing section outlining the rules of the game ("Absent or Under-represented Factors"), Debord admits that certain factors of real war are absent: the role of chance, environmental and climatic factors, lack of knowledge of an opponent's actual position and activities, and psychological factors such as troop morale. The game is a somewhat idealized exercise in strategic thinking, reproducing the essential "dialectic of all conflicts" while emphasizing the distinction between theory and praxis and the inherent instability of the former, which at any moment is subject to change in its tactical engagements with material culture.

Debord's last major work of cultural theory, *Commentaires sur la société du spectacle,* analyzes trends in the development of the spectacle during the twenty years since the publication of *La Société du spectacle.* The book concentrates on the "integrated" spectacle, which, according to Debord, permeates all cultural life, reconstructing reality in the process of describing it. The book goes on to indict recent economic and political developments for having helped globalize the spectacle, effectively unifying the world in its image to the point that it is no longer possible to distinguish "true" from "false" representations. A confusion of overlapping secret networks in government and business perpetuate the spectacle; people's lives have become thoroughly mediated, supplanting direct, individual observation of the world with the image construct of the dominant ideology. This dense culture of image noise, in which, in collusion with various news and commercial media, "thousands of plots in favor of established order clash everywhere," effectively disempowers and controls people by eliminating the contexts of events. The following year Debord published *Panégyrique, Tome premier,* an autobiographical pastiche à la Laurence Sterne's *Tristram Shandy* (1759–1767) that briefly narrates Debord's life as a more or less believable series of adventures and debaucheries, an un- or antieconomic, antiproductive exploitation and celebration of excess in dialectic opposition to the exploitation of labor of commodity culture.

Cover for Fin de Copenhague *(End of Copenhagen, 1957),
the first of the two art books Debord created in collaboration
with painter Asger Jorn (from Len Bracken,* Guy Debord:
Revolutionary, *1997; Thomas Cooper Library,
University of South Carolina)*

Other than these two slim volumes (both well under 100 pages), Debord produced little significant new work during the late 1980s and 1990s (a critical edition of *In girum imus nocte et consumimur igni* appeared in 1999; *Memoires* was reprinted in 1993). He spent his days preparing dinners for a few close friends, provoking debates in cafés and bars, wandering the streets of Paris with an acquaintance while delivering critical commentary on the surroundings, and drinking to excess, though rarely appearing drunk. According to Merci Jolivet, a painter who befriended Debord in his last days, he was a "warm, refined aristocrat," never vulgar or trivial, and always "extremely precise, never banal" (quoted in *Guy Debord: Revolutionary*) in his conversation and observations.

While suffering the painful late stages of an alcohol-related, degenerative nerve disease (he had been diagnosed in 1990 with peripheral neuritis), Debord collab-

orated with Cornand on his seventh and final cinematic project, *GuyDebord: Son Art et Son Temps*. Like his previous motion pictures, *GuyDebord* collages autobiographical and found footage. Debord suggested the project to Cornand after seeing her 1994 movie *The Situation Must Change,* which incorporated excerpts from Situationist motion pictures by Wolman and René Vienet, as well as text from Debord's *In girum imus nocte et consumimur igni.* As the title suggests, *GuyDebord: Son Art et Son Temps* is divided into two sections. In "Son Art," the first, shorter segment, Cornand reviews Debord's previous work, including stills from *In girum imus nocte et consumimur igni* and *Hurlements en Faveur de Sade.* In the second section, in characteristic Situationist style, the personal (photos of friends), the political (protests and violent repression in Tiananmen Square), and the pop-cultural (female Japanese wrestlers) dialogically interact, though textual references to disease and greater emphasis on scenes of sociopolitical turmoil make the tone darker than that of previous motion pictures. Overall, the movie suggests that one's personal history cannot be separated from one's interventions into the often irrational flux and accumulation of images that are one's "time." *GuyDebord,* produced by French avant-garde television Channel +, was first broadcast on 9 January 1995, though Debord did not live to see the premiere. On Wednesday, 30 November 1994, he shot himself through the heart in Champor, Upper Loire.

Guy Debord may best be remembered as a provocative experimental moviemaker and trenchant cultural critic, but what distinguishes him from more-academic thinkers is that, to a large extent, he succeeded in evading and making tropes of what he felt was a repressive ideological and economic system. Though he never "worked" in the conventional sense (effectively denying the society of the spectacle his labor power) and though he never obtained a university degree, he has had an international impact on sociopolitical theory as well as the art of cinema. Perhaps more importantly, he lived his theories. Debord's example of staging active intervention into the circumstances of his life is perhaps his most significant legacy to future revolutions, both in art and sociopolitical life.

Letters:

Correspondance, 2 volumes, edited by Patrick Mosconi (Paris: Fayard, 1999).

Biographies:

Len Bracken, *Guy Debord: Revolutionary* (Venice, Cal.: Feral House, 1997);

Christophe Bourseiller, *Vie et Mort de Guy Debord* (Paris: Plon, 1999).

References:

A. H. S. Boy, "Biding Spectacular Time," *Postmodern Culture,* 6, no. 2 (January 1996) <http://muse.jhu. edu/journals/postmodern_culture/toc/pmc6.2.html>;

Len Bracken, *Guy Debord: Revolutionary* (Venice, Cal.: Feral House, 1997);

Bracken, "The Spectacle of Secrecy," *CTHEORY* (May 1994) <http://www.ctheory.net/text_file. asp?pick=275>;

Joshua Glenn, "The Death of a Situationist," *Utne Reader* (September–October 1995): 16–17;

J. P. Issenhuth, "The Tomb of Guy Debord—Another Look at the Writer's Work after 25 Years of Neglect," *Liberté,* 37, no. 6 (December 1995): 104–107;

Vincent Kaufmann, "Angels of Purity," *October,* 79 (Winter 1997): 49–68;

Ken Knabb, ed., *Situationist International Anthology* (Berkeley, Cal.: Bureau of Public Secrets, 1981);

Myriam D. Maayan, "From Aesthetic to Political Vanguard: The Situationist International, 1957–1968," *Arts Magazine,* 65 (January 1989): 49–53;

Peter Marshall, "Situationism," in *Demanding the Impossible: A History of Anarchism* (London: HarperCollins, 1992), pp. 549–555;

S. McLemee, "Prophet of Extremity: The Shrouded Life of an Intellectual Provocateur," *Lingua Franca,* 5, no. 3 (March–April 1995): 61–65;

Christopher Phillips, "The Invisible Films of Guy Debord," *Art in America,* 77 (October 1989): 190;

Sadie Plant, *The Most Radical Gesture: The Situationist International in a Postmodern Age* (London & New York: Routledge, 1992);

Brian Price, "Plagiarizing the Plagiarist: Godard Meets the Situationists," *Film Comment,* 33 (November–December 1997): 66–69;

Elisabeth Sussman, ed., *On the Passage of a Few People through a Rather Brief Moment in Time: The Situationist International, 1957–1972* (Cambridge, Mass.: MIT Press, 1989);

Milo Sweedler, "Representation Today: Subjectivity and Historicity," *Tacho: Zeitschrift für Perspektivenwechsel,* 4, no. 1 (1994): 89–98;

P. Taminiaux, "The Show Must Not Go On," *Text: Revue de critique et de théorie littéraire,* 17, 18 (1995): 59–77;

C. Vidal, "Drift as Liberty, Liberty as Drift (The Song Goes On)," *Coloquio-Artes,* 105 (April–June 1995): 27–38.

Gilles Deleuze

(18 January 1925 – 4 November 1995)

Jennifer A. Rich
Manhattanville College

BOOKS: *David Hume: Sa vie, son oeuvre. Avec un exposé de sa philosophie,* by Deleuze and André Cresson (Paris: Presses Universitaires de France, 1952);

Empirisme et subjectivité: Essai sur la nature humaine selon Hume (Paris: Presses Universitaires de France, 1953); translated, with an introduction, by Constantin V. Boundas as *Empiricism and Subjectivity: An Essay on Hume's Theory of Human Nature* (New York: Columbia University Press, 1991);

Nietzsche et la Philosophie (Paris: Presses Universitaires de France, 1962); translated by Hugh Tomlinson as *Nietzsche and Philosophy* (New York: Columbia University Press, 1983);

La Philosophie critique de Kant: Doctrines de facultés (Paris: Presses Universitaires de France, 1963); translated by Tomlinson and Barbara Habberjam as *Kant's Critical Philosophy: The Doctrine of Faculties* (Minneapolis: University of Minnesota Press, 1984; London: Athlone, 1984);

Proust et les signes (Paris: Presses Universitaires de France, 1964); translated by Richard Howard as *Proust and Signs* (New York: Braziller, 1972; London: Lane, 1972);

Nietzsche: Sa vie, son oeuvre. Avec un exposé de sa philosophie (Paris: Presses Universitaires de France, 1965);

Le Bergsonisme (Paris: Presses Universitaires de France, 1966); translated by Tomlinson and Habberjam as *Bergsonism* (New York: Zone Books, 1988);

Présentation de Sacher-Masoch, le froid et le cruel. Avec le texte intégral de la Vénus a la fourrure, by Deleuze and Leopold von Sacher-Masoch (Paris: Editions de Minuit, 1967); translated by Jean McNeil as *Masochism: An Interpretation of Coldness and Cruelty. Together with the Entire Text of Venus in Furs* (New York: Braziller, 1971); republished as *Sacher-Masoch: An Interpretation* (London: Faber & Faber, 1971);

L'Idée d'expression dans la philosophie de Spinoza (Paris: Editions de Minuit, 1968);

Différence et répétition (Paris: Presses Universitaires de France, 1968); translated by Paul Patton as *Differ-*

Gilles Deleuze (photograph by Helene Bamberger; from the cover for Pourparlers 1972–1990, *1990; Memphis University Library)*

ence and Repetition (New York: Columbia University Press, 1994);

Spinoza et le problème de l'expression (Paris: Editions de Minuit, 1968); translated by Martin Joughin as *Expressionism in Philosophy: Spinoza* (New York: Zone Books / Cambridge, Mass.: MIT Press, 1990);

Logique du sens (Paris: Editions de Minuit, 1969); translated by Mark Lester and Charles Stivale as *The Logic of Sense,* edited by Boundas (New York: Columbia University Press, 1990);

Spinoza (Paris: Editions de Minuit, 1970); revised and enlarged as *Spinoza: Philosophie pratique* (Paris: Edi-*

tions de Minuit, 1981); translated by Robert Hurley as *Spinoza: Practical Philosophy* (San Francisco: City Lights Books, 1988);

Un nouvel archiviste (Montpellier: Fata Morgana, 1972);

Capitalisme et schizophrénie, by Deleuze and Félix Guattari (Paris: Editions de Minuit, 1972); revised and enlarged as *Capitalisme et schizophrénie: L'anti-Oedipe* (Paris: Editions de Minuit, 1975); translated by Hurley, Mark Seem, and Helen R. Lane as *Anti-Oedipus: Capitalism and Schizophrenia* (New York: Viking, 1977);

Fromanger: Le peintre et le modele, by Deleuze and Gérard Fromanger (Paris: Baudard Alvarez, 1973);

Le XXe siècle, by Deleuze and others (Paris: Hachette-Littérature, 1973);

Kafka: Pour une littérature mineure, by Deleuze and Guattari (Paris: Editions de Minuit, 1975); translated by Dana Polan as *Kafka: Toward a Minor Literature* (Minneapolis: University of Minnesota Press, 1986);

Rhizome: Introduction, by Deleuze and Guattari (Paris: Editions de Minuit, 1976); translated by John Johnston in *On the Line* (New York: Semiotext(e), 1983);

Dialogues, by Deleuze and Claire Parnet (Paris: Flammarion, 1977); translated by Tomlinson and Habberjam (New York: Columbia University Press, 1987; London: Athlone, 1987);

Capitalisme et schizophrénie: Mille Plateaux, by Deleuze and Guattari (Paris: Editions de Minuit, 1980); translated by Brian Massumi as *A Thousand Plateaus: Capitalism and Schizophrenia* (Minneapolis: University of Minnesota Press, 1987; London: Athlone, 1988);

Francis Bacon: Logique de la Sensation, 2 volumes (Paris: Editions de la Différence, 1981);

Cinéma I: L'Image-mouvement (Paris: Editions de Minuit, 1983); translated by Tomlinson and Habberjam as *Cinema I: The Movement-Image* (Minneapolis: University of Minnesota Press, 1986; London: Athlone, 1986);

Cinéma 2: L'Image-temps (Paris: Editions de Minuit, 1985); translated by Tomlinson and Robert Galeta as *Cinema 2: The Time-Image* (Minneapolis: University of Minnesota Press, 1989; London: Athlone, 1989);

Foucault (Paris: Editions de Minuit, 1986); translated by Seán Hand (Minneapolis: University of Minnesota Press, 1988);

Le Pli: Liebniz et le Baroque (Paris: Editions de Minuit, 1988); translated by Tom Conley as *The Fold: Leibniz and the Baroque* (Minneapolis: University of Minnesota Press, 1993);

Péricles et Verdi: La Philosphie de François Châtelet (Paris: Editions de Minuit, 1988);

Pourparlers 1972–1990 (Paris: Editions de Minuit, 1990); translated by Joughin as *Negotiations, 1972–1990* (New York: Columbia University Press, 1995);

Qu'est-ce que la Philosophie? by Deleuze and Guattari (Paris: Editions de Minuit, 1991); translated by Tomlinson and Graham Burchell as *What Is Philosophy?* (New York: Columbia University Press, 1994);

Critique et clinique (Paris: Editions de Minuit, 1993); translated by Daniel W. Smith and Michael A. Greco as *Essays Critical and Clinical* (Minneapolis: University of Minnesota Press, 1997);

L'Ile déserte et autres textes: Textes et entretiens 1953–1974, edited by David Lapoujade (Paris: Editions de Minuit, 2002); translated by Mike Taormina as *Desert Islands and Other Texts (1953–1974)* (Cambridge, Mass. & London: Semiotext(e), 2003);

Deux régimes de fous: Textes et entretiens 1975–1995, edited by Lapoujade (Paris: Editions de Minuit, 2003).

Editions in English: *The Deleuze Reader,* edited by Constantin V. Boundas (New York: Columbia University Press, 1993);

Gilles Deleuze: Minor Works, edited by Sylvère Lotringer (Cambridge, Mass. & London: MIT Press, 2001);

Pure Immanence: Essays on a Life, by Deleuze and Anne Boyman (New York: Zone Books / Cambridge, Mass.: MIT Press, 2001).

Intellectual historian Michel Foucault remarked in an introduction to Gilles Deleuze and Félix Guattari's *Capitalisme et schizophrénie: L'anti-Oedipe* (1975; translated as *Anti-Oedipus: Capitalism and Schizophrenia,* 1977) that the twentieth century may at some point be known as "Deleuzian." Foucault believed that Deleuze's challenge to traditional epistemologies of thought and his consequent creation of a new, subject-free epistemology would influence the thought patterns of an entire generation. Battling the Enlightenment legacy of the all-knowing subject—the cogito—and the privileging of singularity over multiplicity, Deleuze inaugurated a philosophy that celebrated an antihumanist, anti-Enlightenment understanding of the subject, history, psychology, and the natural and social world. To read Deleuze is to undergo a different thought process—to experience an alternative epistemology that subjects the old certainties of identity, logic, and meaning to profound interrogation.

Any consideration of Deleuze's life is hampered by the subject's resistance to talking about his own "life-story." In a series of interviews with Claire Parnet (published in English as *Dialogues*), Deleuze gives the most

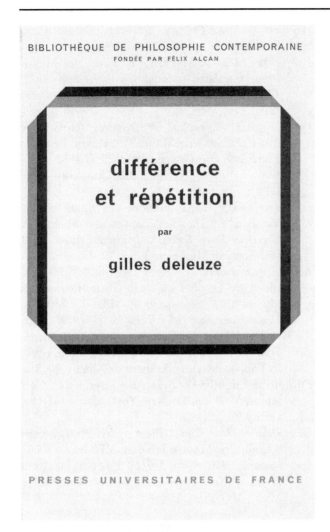

BIBLIOTHÈQUE DE PHILOSOPHIE CONTEMPORAINE
FONDÉE PAR FÉLIX ALCAN

différence et répétition

par

gilles deleuze

PRESSES UNIVERSITAIRES DE FRANCE

Paperback cover for Deleuze's 1968 work (translated as Difference and Repetition, *1994), in which he expands on the philosophy of Friedrich Nietzsche (Jean and Alexander Heard Library, Vanderbilt University)*

bourgeoisie to the social advances" made under Blum's government–such as the reduction of the workweek.

In his youth Deleuze was a mediocre student. Before the German invasion, however, he and his brother were enrolled in a lycée in Deauville, created to accommodate émigrés from Paris. Here, in his early teens, he came under the tutelage of a teacher, Pierre Halwachs, who introduced him to such writers as Anatole France and André Gide, instantiating a lifelong love of writing in the young student. Soon after, Deleuze returned to Paris and attended the Lycée Carnot. As he recalls in an interview with Parnet, he was again fascinated by the political atmosphere in the school, since there was a clear division in the student body between Nazi sympathizers and those who supported the French resistance.

After the lycée, Deleuze studied at the Sorbonne in the 1940s, receiving his *agrégation* in philosophy in 1948. At the Sorbonne his principal teachers were George Canguilhem, author of *Essai sur quelques problèmes concernant le normal et le pathologique* (1943; translated as *On the Normal and the Pathological,* 1978) and Foucault's mentor, and Ferdinand Aliquié, a specialist in René Descartes.

After graduation Deleuze taught in several lycées. In the late 1950s he began teaching at the university–delivering a famous series of lectures on the history of philosophy at the Sorbonne. In 1956 Deleuze married Denise "Fanny" Grandjouan, a translator specializing in D. H. Lawrence. Together, they had two children, Julien and Emilie. Emilie works as a documentary filmmaker. From 1960 to 1964 Deleuze worked as a researcher with the Centre Nationale de Recherche Scientifique (National Center for Scientific Research). Finally, in 1969, he was appointed to his lifelong post as professor of philosophy at Vincennes, part of the University of Paris system. He retired from this post in 1987.

In 1962 Deleuze published *Nietzsche et la Philosophie* (translated as *Nietzsche and Philosophy,* 1983). *Nietzsche et la Philosophie* is an important introduction to Deleuze's work. His reading of Friedrich Nietzsche clearly expresses his own philosophical ethics and provides an important preview of the key themes expounded in such texts as *Logique du sens* (1969; translated as *The Logic of Sense,* 1990), *Capitalisme et schizophrénie* (1972), and *Capitalisme et schizophrénie: Mille Plateaux* (1980; translated as *A Thousand Plateaus: Capitalism and Schizophrenia,* 1987).

Deleuze's attention to Nietzsche signaled a significant departure from his own philosophical education in the French university system. While the French academy of the 1940s and 1950s–the time when Deleuze was a student–was immersed in the dialectical materialism of Georg Wilhelm Friedrich Hegel, the new intel-

in-depth summary of what he sees as the important moments in his development as a philosopher. Even in discussing his childhood, however, he resists assigning a singularity to his life. He was, as he comments to Parnet, formed by his interactions with the collectivity that surrounded him at the time. Gilles Deleuze was born on 18 January 1925 to a conservative French family living in Paris. Deleuze's father was especially conservative; he despised the socialist government of Léon Blum of the 1930s both because of Blum's Jewishness and because of his politics. In an interview Deleuze recalled the tension that characterized French life after the Wall Street crash and before the Nazi invasion in 1940. In his book *Gilles Deleuze: Vitalism and Multiplicity* (1998), John Marks notes that at this time "Deleuze began to understand the world in what broadly might be called 'political' terms, becoming aware of a deep seated anti-Semitism in French society . . . and the antipathy of the

lectual movements of the early 1960s were increasingly moving toward a renewed interest in such nondialectical thinkers as Nietzsche and Benedict de Spinoza. Foucault, for example, and Jean-François Lyotard, the "father" of postmodernist thought, were gradually moving the center of French philosophical thinking from the Hegelian dialectic to what Allan D. Schrift has called the "masters of suspicion," namely, Nietzsche, Sigmund Freud, and Karl Marx. While Marx and especially Freud did not sit easily with Deleuze, Nietzsche was important to Deleuze's own formulation of a philosophy of "becoming" and an ethics of multiplicity and difference as opposed to what he calls the "arborescent," or rooted, thinking of traditional Western philosophy. "What I detested more than anything else was Hegelianism and the Dialectic," Deleuze notes in his article-letter "Cher Michel, je na'i rien a avouer" (Dear Michel, I Have Nothing to Admit), first published in *La Quinzaine Litteraire* in 1973. For Deleuze, Nietzsche expressed the new epistemology of the present post-Hegelian moment, what some call the "post-structuralist" ethics of the modern world; as Deleuze explains in his self-reflective text, *Pourparlers 1972–1990* (1990; translated as *Negotiations, 1972–1990,* 1995), Nietzsche allowed him to escape from the fetters of Hegelianism: "It was Nietzsche who I read only later who extricated me from all this. Because you just can't deal with him in the same sort of way. He gets up to all sorts of things behind your back. He gives you a perverse taste . . . for saying simple things in your own way, in affects, intensities, experiences, experiments."

Deleuze felt that Nietzsche freed philosophy from the repressive hypotheses of Hegel and others. One crucial distinction that separates Nietzsche from Hegel is the affirmative nature of his philosophy. While Hegel was concerned to understand the goal of philosophy as what he called "the negation of the negation," the erasure of negativity that characterizes the dialectic, Nietzsche refused the terms of this dialectic. Unlike Hegel, Nietzsche did not understand history or human existence as trapped within a dialectic—a constant seesaw of identity and contradiction (or identity and its negation) moving toward a unified synthesis of the social world, or what Hegel names "the Absolute." According to Hegel, history inexorably moves toward this synthesis, and it is philosophy's task to anatomize the dialectic and its resolution.

Nietzsche refuses the possibility of such a synthesis, and, even more radically, rejects the desire for it, what he might understand as the death of "becoming." For Nietzsche difference, even contradiction, are not to be overcome, but to be understood and celebrated. The unitary self is not a desirable goal for Nietzsche; rather, Nietzsche understands such a construct as an obfuscating fiction, a result of the confusing and arbitrary nature of language. Because of the tricky nature of language, what is understood as "truth" may be nothing more than "congealed metaphors"–a metaphor that has been struck down in the midst of its play of signification. Truth, for Nietzsche, is nothing but this play of language, a "mobile army of metaphors, metonymies, and anthropomorphisms," as Deleuze says in *Nietzsche et la Philosophie*. Nietzsche's reliance on the aphorism as his favored mode of philosophical expression is an indicator of his understanding of language and signification as something always in movement and ever changing.

Deleuze understood Nietzsche's philosophy as a genealogy of thought. Rather than understanding the world as comprising solid identities and categories of thought, Deleuze saw Nietzsche as positing an alternative model: a genealogy of forces, or the dynamic movement of the noumena that make up historical and social reality. This particular understanding of the nature of forces is bound up with an understanding of how thought itself proceeds–how, in other words, epistemology is constituted by the forces it both produces (thinks) and of which it is the object.

For Deleuze, a consideration of Nietzschean thought is inevitably also a consideration of Nietzsche's other key theme: the will, especially the will to power. He relates Nietzsche's concept of the will to power to the genealogy of forces that is the focus of Nietzsche's philosophy. Deleuze is careful to clarify this concept: the will to power is not, as has been routinely interpreted, the desire for power; rather, it is "the genealogical element of force, both differential and genetic. *The will to power is the element from which derives both the quantitative difference of related forces and the quality that devolves into each force in this relation.* The will to power here reveals its nature as the principle of the synthesis of forces." The will to power is not a psychological investigation into the unconscious will to dominate. It is simply the "genetic element of force"–the psychological and ontological ability to be affected by force.

For Deleuze, this notion of a nonstatic, revolutionary, dynamic, chaotic ontology of the social and natural world was the answer to the Hegelian philosophies against which he and others in the poststructuralist movement of the 1960s were rebelling. Nietzsche's philosophy and its privileging of dynamism over stasis provided the building ground for Deleuze's later philosophical work. The concept of a dynamic philosophy—an ethics of philosophy based on the celebration of difference, plurality, vitalism, and affirmation—presents itself in all of Deleuze's significant work.

While the first period of Deleuze's career may be understood as a rereading and reformulation of key philosophers (Nietzsche and Spinoza) to recuperate them, in part, from their misreadings by European intellectuals of the early twentieth century, his later work reads more like a philosophical manifesto influenced by the works of these key thinkers. In *Différence et répétition* (1968; translated as *Difference and Repetition*, 1994) and *Logique du sens* Deleuze expands on Nietzsche's work. In *Logique du sens* he writes what he describes as a "logical and psychoanalytic novel" divided into thirty-four sections, named in the text as "series." Written in 1969, this playful work examines the writings of Lewis Carroll, particularly *Alice's Adventures in Wonderland* (1865) and *Through the Looking-Glass* (1871), in their promotion of an understanding of sense divorced from traditional conceptions of representational logic. Each series analyzes a paradox and attempts to instantiate a new notion of "logic and sense" that frees these concepts from situated meanings. One of the tasks of this work—as well as the two volumes of *Capitalisme et schizophrénie*—is to deterritorialize signification from its usual embeddedness or territorialization in the relation of signifier (word) to signified (meaning).

Deleuze begins this work by attacking the Platonic celebration of ontological fixity—the celebration of the essence over its appearance-in-the-world, otherwise understood as distorting simulations (simulacra). He rejects the primacy of fixity and instead locates meaning—sense—within the flux and dynamics of "becoming," a becoming of time, of identity, and of the event: "Plato invites us to distinguish between two dimensions: (1) that of limited and measured things, of fixed qualities, permanent or temporary which always presuppose pauses and rests, the fixing of presents, and the assignation of subjects (for example, a particular subject having a particular largeness or a particular smallness at a particular moment); and (2) a pure becoming without measure, a veritable becoming-mad, which never rests." Like *Capitalisme et schizophrénie*, *Logique du sens* bears the marks of the history of its composition. In itself, it is what Deleuze would call an event—"an impassive result . . . [an] infinitive" that came about within the complex interstices of late 1960s French politics, in particular, May 1968 and the Indochinese struggle that provided the political horizon against which these works were written.

The concern of *Logique du sens* is not only a celebration of indeterminacy, but also a new understanding of "states of affairs"—the dynamic contexts in which production (of texts, of bodies, of wars) takes place. Against Plato, Deleuze cites the Stoics, who rejected the Platonic dualism between essence and appearance or model and copy: "It is not longer a question of simulacra that elude the ground and insinuate themselves everywhere, but rather a question of effects that manifest themselves and act in their place. These are effects in the causal sense, but also sonorous, optical or linguistic 'effects'—and even less or more since they are no longer corporeal entities, but rather form the entire Idea." This concentration on surface effects—the work of the Stoics against the Ideality of Plato—is what Deleuze argues that Carroll takes up in *Alice's Adventures in Wonderland* and *Through the Looking-Glass*. Both of these texts are exemplars for Deleuze of the Stoic philosophy of surface effects, sense, events, and becoming: "One could say that the old depth having been spread out became width. The becoming unlimited is maintained entirely within this inverted width. 'Depth' is no longer a complement. . . . This is the case—even more so—in *Through the Looking-Glass*. Here events differing radically from things are no longer sought in the depths but at the surface, in the faint incorporeal mist, a film without volume which envelops them, a mirror which reflects them . . . Paul Valéry had a profound idea: what is most deep is the skin."

With this notion of an incorporeal mist, Deleuze enters into a detailed consideration and critique of the nature of the proposition. The nature of the proposition—the relation of language to truth—has been a key struggle in philosophical thinking from Plato to the present. Deleuze identifies four key elements of the proposition, the fourth of which is important for its presentation of the logic of signification. Deleuze argues that this fourth proposition is ignored in traditional thought about signification. Yet, it is what allows propositions to *mean* or *to make sense* in linguistic and social communities and to escape their presumed predication in certain conceptual and linguistic "conditioning"—what may be understood as the conditions of possibility for the "truth" to be true. The condition of truth "ought to have *something unconditioned* capable of assuring a real genesis of denotation and of the other dimensions of the proposition. Thus the condition of truth would be defined no longer as the form of conceptual possibility, but rather as ideational material or 'stratum,' that is to say no longer as signification, but rather as sense."

Deleuze offers a straightforward explanation of what this "something" is that can ensure that the condition of truth be freed of its own conceptual conditioning; yet, it is nevertheless difficult to conceptualize concretely. This avoidance of concreteness—the deferral of meaning—allows readers to experience epistemologically the fourth proposition in all of its refusal of denotation. The "something" is simply and not so simply *sense*—what Deleuze defines as the "expressible or the expressed of the proposition, and the attribute of the state of affairs. It is exactly the boundary between propositions and things. . . . As an attribute of states of affairs, sense is extra-being. It is not being; it is an *aliquid* which is appropriate to non-being. As that which is expressed by the proposition, sense does not exist, but inheres or subsists in the proposition."

Deleuze further clarifies the sense of the *aliquid* through a consideration of Carroll's neologisms: "The circulating word is of a different nature or principle, it is the empty square, the empty shelf, the blank word. . . . This word therefore is called by names which indicate evanescences and displacements: the Snark is invisible, and the Phlizz is almost an onomatopoeia for something vanishing. Or again, the word is called by names which are quite indeterminate: *aliquid* it, that thing, gadget, or 'whatchamacallit.'"

Although it might seem to resist such a comparison, Deleuze's logic of sense can be understood as a radical empiricism—but one that takes the knowing subject out of his or her usually central position in this methodology. The concept of the event clearly illustrates the subjectively decentered empiricism of this text. Like the notion of sense, which exists not in things but in the midst of states of affairs and things, the event happens not only to people and things but exists also within an impersonal dimension in which the subject does not exist: "With every event, there is indeed the present moment of actualization, . . . the moment we designate by saying '*here,* the moment has come.' . . . But, on the other hand, there is the future and the past of the event considered in itself, sidestepping each present, being free of the limitations of the state of affairs, impersonal and pre-individual, neutral neither general nor particular, *eventum tantum.*" For Deleuze, death is a good example of an event because it is grounded in the subject but also transcends the subject: the one dying, the subject of death, is always secondary to it.

Many of the themes discussed in *Nietzsche et la Philosophie* and *Logique du sens* have their fullest fruition in the two books of *Capitalisme et schizophrénie: L'anti-Oedipe* and *Mille Plateaux.* Written with Guattari, an experimental materialist psychoanalyst, these texts are a series devoted to the study of capitalism and schizophrenia—what Deleuze and Guattari describe as a "genealogy of capitalism." Both works are a result of the political upheavals of the late 1960s; *L'anti-Oedipe,* first published as *Capitalisme et schizophénie* in 1972, quickly became a manifesto for social, sexual, and political liberation. *Mille Plateaux* was published in 1980 within radically different political circumstances, with the almost universal push to the right after the perceived social excesses of the 1960s. After the publication of both works, Deleuze and Guattari were accused of promoting an ethical anarchism, an accusation that caused Foucault to defend their work and characterize *L'anti-Oedipe* in particular as a new ethics for the late twentieth century.

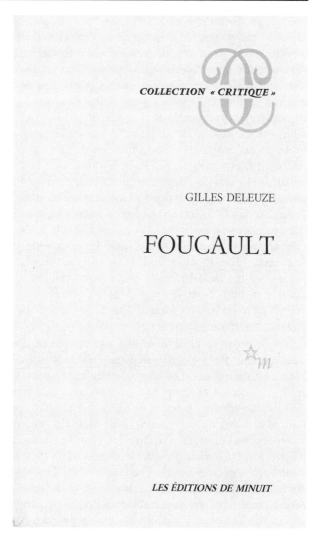

COLLECTION « CRITIQUE »

GILLES DELEUZE

FOUCAULT

LES ÉDITIONS DE MINUIT

Paperback cover for Deleuze's examination of his fellow French culture theorist Michel Foucault, published in 1986 (Thomas Cooper Library, University of South Carolina)

L'anti-Oedipe and *Mille Plateaux,* then, are not so much philosophical analyses but critiques of the roles played by psychoanalysis in capitalist society. The central thesis of both books is that psychoanalysis "territorializes" or confines desire within the realm of the family, what the authors somewhat humorously call the "mommy-daddy-me" triad. Psychoanalysis and capitalism work hand in hand although at somewhat opposite purposes. While capitalism, according to Deleuze and Guattari, liberates or deterritorializes desire through its processes of production and commodification, psychoanalysis reterritorializes desire within the accepted forms of the cultural system: the nuclear family, religion, class structure, and work relationships. The relationship between psychoanalysis and capitalism should not, however, be understood as one of opposition. Through its focus on production and economic relations of production–worker and boss, for example, or capitalist and proletariat–capitalism also works to territorialize desire even as it deterritorializes it through its commodification of social relationships. Thus, capitalism spawns deterritorialized fragments, subverting traditional social relationships, while at the same time it works with psychoanalysis to reterritorialize those desires that evade social coding: "What we are really trying to say is that capitalism, through the process of production, produces an awesome schizophrenic accumulation of energy or charge, against which it brings all its vast powers of repression to bear, but which nonetheless continues to act as capitalism's limit. For capitalism constantly counteracts, constantly inhibits this inherent tendency while at the same time allowing it free rein." For Deleuze and Guattari, the "schizophrenic" is the model of embodied deterritorialization, figuring in both *L'anti-Oedipe* and *Mille Plateaux* as the heroic entity who has evaded the social codes that attempt to contain him or her.

In order to understand the significance of the schizophrenic for Deleuze and Guattari's program of liberation, their concept of "desire" must first be considered. The notion of desire and its repression underlie the psychoanalytic projects of Freud and Jacques Lacan. In differing ways, both these thinkers understand desire as an unruly "child" that must be directed toward its appropriate expression–ideally through the model of the nuclear family. The theory of the Oedipus complex is a narrative of this rechanneling of the desire of the child from an incestuous focus on the mother and/or the father to a socially acceptable desire for a spouse and child. Deleuze and Guattari reject this programmatic notion of desire and especially disavow the Oedipal project. They describe the attempt to control (territorialize) desire as fascist, and through their work they hope to instantiate a psychological methodology– what they call schizoanalysis–that will reveal the fascist underpinnings of instruments of sexual and social control, such as the psychoanalytic reliance on the Oedipal triumvirate of "mommy-daddy-me." As Foucault explains in his introduction to *L'anti-Oedipe:* "I would say that *L'anti-Oedipe* . . . is a book of ethics, the first book of ethics to be written in France in quite a long time. . . . How does one keep from being fascist, even when (especially) one believes oneself to be a revolutionary militant? How do we rid our speech and our acts, our hearts and our pleasures, of fascism? How do we ferret out the fascism that is ingrained in our behavior?"

Like Deleuze and Guattari, Foucault is here using fascism not to refer to the historical experience of Italy and Germany in the twentieth century (although *Mille Plateaux* does discuss the importance of desire and its manipulation to Adolf Hitler's ascendancy in Germany), but to the predominantly Western impulse to control and direct desire in order to maintain certain relations of hegemony and repression in the social world. Deleuze and Guattari wish to liberate desire from its entrapment in certain social codes. The first paragraph of *L'anti-Oedipe* reconceptualizes desire as an irrepressible machine, proliferating and constantly evading the social structures that wish to control it. In a section titled "Desiring-Production" Deleuze and Guattari reconceptualize social and familial relationships as relations between desiring-machines: "It is at work everywhere, functioning smoothly at times, at other times in fits and starts. It breathes, it heats, it eats. . . . What a mistake to have ever said *the* id. Everywhere *it* is machines–real ones, not figurative ones; machines driving other machines, machines being driven by other machines with all the necessary couplings and connections. An organ-machine is plugged into an energy-source-machine; the one produces a flow that the other interrupts. A breast is a machine that produces milk, and the mouth a machine coupled to it." Such a conception of desire is a profound challenge to the traditional psychoanalytic understanding of desire. In psychoanalysis all desire is, according to Deleuze and Guattari, "structuralized" and "personalized." Their understanding of desire rejects this attempted structuralization. As they describe it, desire is *anoedipal:* rather than a "mommy-daddy-me" conception of desire, they propose a schizophrenic understanding. In this "model," desire is no longer oedipally based but machine-like: "Wouldn't it be better to schizophrenize– to schizophrenize the domain of unconscious as well as the sociohistorical domain, so as to shatter the collar of Oedipus and rediscover everywhere the force of desiring-production."

This reconceptualization of desire entails a similar rethinking of social and historical relationships. In *L'anti-Oedipe* Deleuze and Guattari understand history as a dizzying succession of territorializations, deterritorializations, and reterritorializations of desiring "flows." They advance a "molecular" theory of history, where microflows evolve and interact in unpredictable relationships of contingencies, ruptures, and limits: "First of all, universal history is the history of contingencies, and not the history of necessities." In this work the molar is identified with overdetermination and territorialization; the Oedipal construct is molar, while desiring-machines work through the molecular, even when they lead to historical forms that would seem to destroy this molecularity. Writing about the rise of fascism in Germany and Italy, Deleuze and Guattari decry a molecular basis to the eventual consolidation of fascism: "fascism is inseparable from a proliferation of molecular forces in interaction, which skip from point to point, *before* beginning to resonate together in the National Socialist State."

This passage is from Deleuze and Guattari's second book in their study of capitalism and schizophrenia, *Mille Plateaux,* which presents a more in-depth system of historical methodology. In this work Deleuze and Guattari advance a planar and rhizomatic (as opposed to aborescent) conception of historical and social processes. Arguing against philosophical traditions that rely upon an arborescent system of thought, they write: "the Tree or Root as an image endlessly develops the law of the One that becomes two. . . . Binary logic is the spiritual reality of the root-tree. Even a discipline as 'advanced' as linguistics retains the root-tree as its fundamental image, and thus remains wedded to classical reflection."

Against this image of the rooted tree, Deleuze and Guattari articulate an alternative epistemology, based upon the rootless root, or the rhizome. The rhizome may be understood as the philosophical mascot of Deleuze and Guattari's celebration of multiplicity as opposed to binary structure. Rootless and nomadic, the rhizome "ceaselessly establishes connections between semiotic chains, organizations of power and circumstances relative to the arts, sciences and social struggles." The rhizome is the key symbol of deterritorialization. Its ontology resists territorialization. Viewing history rhizomatically conjures a picture of society as constituted by random assemblages of multiplicities operating across a social landscape that continually attempts to territorialize them.

In its form, *Mille Plateaux* models the planar, non-hierarchical system—or more accurately, refusal of system—that defines the schizoanalysis of Deleuze and Guattari. The book is composed of random chapters or plateaus that may be read in any order—these plateaus treat a dizzying array of subjects in a tone that is consistently politicized and perspectival. Describing his writing process in *Pourparlers,* Deleuze remarks: "I'm interested in the way a page of writing flies off in all directions and at the same time closes right up on itself like an egg. And in the reticences, the resonances, the lurches, and all the larvae you can find in a book."

Rejecting argumentation, Deleuze and Guattari make diverse connections between their philosophy and prominent (and not so prominent) figures in philosophy, literature, and art in order to exemplify their rhizomatic philosophy. Locating minifascisms in art and music, Deleuze and Guattari celebrate those artists who resist territorialization in their fields; among their favorites are Franz Kafka, Virginia Woolf, and Ludwig van Beethoven. All of these artists enact a planar, rhizomatic aesthetics; in one of Woolf's novels, *The Waves*

Paperback cover for the U.S. edition (1987) of the English translation of Mille Plateaux, *the second and final volume of Deleuze's* Capitalisme et schizophrénie *(1972, 1980), co-authored with the psychoanalyst Félix Guattari (Thomas Cooper Library, University of South Carolina)*

(1931), for example, the characters resist "oneness" and instead "designate a multiplicity." A character in *The Waves* is not just himself or herself but is ontologically tied to whatever surrounds him or her. "Each is simultaneously in this multiplicity and at its edge, and crosses over into others." In this way, Woolf's characters mirror the complex becomings and deterritorializations that Deleuze and Guattari believe typify the natural and social world. As they note, "each individual is an infinite multiplicity, and the whole of nature is a multiplicity of perfectly individuated multiplicities." Within this epistemology, subjectivity does not exist as it is commonly understood in traditional philosophy. Rather than the "one" of the cogito, for example, Deleuze and Guattari propose a subjectivity of the pack, of (borrowing a metaphor from Antonin Artaud) the "body without organs"—bereft of subjectivity, decentralized, multiple, and endlessly proliferating: "The body without organs is not an empty body stripped of organs, but a body upon which that which served as organs (wolves, wolf eyes, wolf jaws?) is distributed according to crowd phenomena . . . in the form of molecular multiplicities."

Along with subjectivity, Deleuze and Guattari argue that power, politics, and history must be reconceptualized in their functioning. Arguing against a *grand récit* version of history, where history is apprehended as a synthetic narrative, Deleuze and Guattari propose a rhizomatic conception. In their thinking, the historian must work within a model of flows, deterritorializations, and reterritorializations operating across shifting planar surfaces, understanding history as subsisting within a complex network of molar and molecular flows: "one distinguishes between the molecular aspect and the molar aspect: on the one hand, *masses or flows,* with their mutations, quanta of deterritorialization, connections and accelerations; on the other hand, *classes or segments* with their binary organization, resonance, conjunction or accumulation, and line of overcoding favoring one line over the others."

Deleuze and Guattari's critique of Marxism focuses on its inability to appreciate the molecular dynamic of historical shift and movement. Marxism rests within an almost obsessive consideration of macroflows of historical change, particularly those within the segmentation of capitalism and its labor relationships. According to Deleuze and Guattari, it ignores the important molecular flows that may disrupt the overdeterminations of hegemonic capital: "Mass movements accelerate and feed into one another . . . but jump from one class to another, undergo mutation, emanate or emit new quanta that then modify class relations, bring their overcoding . . . into question, and run new lines of flight in new directions." As such, any apprehension of a single class—such as the proletariat or the bourgeoisie—acting as a seamless entity is profoundly misguided, in Deleuze and Guattari's reading. The Marxian insistence on the inevitability of proletarian revolution within a capitalist economic context particularly misses the subtle and complex molecular flows that compro-

mise any understanding of a class or segment as immune to such microeffects.

Deleuze and Guattari's last collaborative work was published in 1991. *Qu'est-ce que la Philosophie?* (translated as *What Is Philosophy?,* 1994) is a meditation on the task of the philosopher and, as such, is a fitting end to their collaboration. Deleuze and Guattari write the following about the role of the philosopher in modern society and his or her relationship to the "concept": "The philosopher is the concept's friend; he is potentiality of the concept. That is, philosophy is not the simple art of forming, inventing, or fabricating concepts, because concepts are not necessarily forms, discoveries or concepts. More rigorously the philosophy is the discipline that involves creating concepts." In its understanding of the philosopher's task, *Qu'est-ce que la Philosophie?* extolls the creative aspect of thinking and writing philosophically. As the translator's introduction notes, an appropriate slogan for the text might be "Philosophers of the world, Create!"

Deleuze committed suicide on 4 November 1995 after a protracted respiratory illness. He continues, however, to exert a powerful hold over the minds and imaginations of those who read his works: his conceptual creations have profoundly influenced new thought in a variety of contexts—from motion pictures and literature to historical analysis. These analyses adopt what is called a Deleuzian epistemology, wherein they interrogate received systems of thought and methodology: in so doing, they attempt to heed Deleuze's final injunction that the task of philosophy is not simply analysis but conceptual creation.

References:

Alain Badiou, *Deleuze: The Clamor of Being,* translated by Louise Burchill (Minneapolis: University of Minnesota Press, 2000);

Steven Best and Douglas Kellner, *Postmodern Theory: Critical Interrogations* (New York: Guilford Press, 1991);

John Marks, *Gilles Deleuze: Vitalism and Multiplicity* (London & Sterling, Va.: Pluto Press, 1998);

Paul Patton, ed., *Deleuze: A Critical Reader* (Oxford & Cambridge, Mass.: Blackwell, 1996).

Frantz Fanon
(20 July 1925 – 6 December 1961)

Guillemette Johnston
De Paul University, Chicago

BOOKS: *Peau noire, masques blancs* (Paris: Seuil, 1952); translated by Charles Lam Markmann as *Black Skin, White Masks: The Experiences of a Black Man in a White World* (New York: Grove, 1967);

L'An V de la Révolution algérienne (Paris: Maspero, 1959); translated by Haakon Chevalier, with an introduction by Adolfo Gilly, as *Studies in a Dying Colonialism* (New York: Monthly Review Press, 1965); translation republished as *A Dying Colonialism* (New York: Grove, 1967);

Les Damnés de la terre, with a preface by Jean-Paul Sartre (Paris: Maspero, 1961); translated by Constance Farrington as *The Wretched of the Earth* (New York: Grove, 1963; London: MacGibbon & Kee, 1963);

Pour la révolution africaine: Ecrits politiques (Paris: Maspero, 1964); translated by Chevalier as *For the African Revolution* (New York: Monthly Review Press, 1967); translation republished as *Toward the African Revolution* (New York: Grove, 1967).

Edition in English: *The Fanon Reader,* edited, with an introduction, by Azzedine Haddour (London & Sterling, Va.: Pluto, 2002).

OTHER: *Tam Tam,* edited by Fanon (21 February 1948);

"Sur quelques cas traités par la méthode de Bini" (by Fanon and François Tosquelles), "Sur un essai de réadaptation chez une malade avec épilépsie morphéique et troubles de caractère graves" (by Fanon and Tosquelles), "Indications de la thérapeutique de Bini dans le cadre des thérapeutiques institutionnelles" (by Fanon and Tosquelles), and "Note sur les techniques de cure de sommeil avec conditionnement et contrôle électro-encéphalographique" (by Fanon, Maurice Despinoy, and W. Zenner), in *Congrès des médecins aliénistes et neurologues de France et des pays de langue française* (Pau, 1953), pp. 363, 539–544, 545, 616;

"Conduites d'aveu en Afrique du nord," by Fanon and R. Lacaton, in *Congrès des médecins aliénistes et neuro-*

Frantz Fanon (photograph by Seuil/Olivier Fanon; from Patrick Ehlen, Frantz Fanon: A Spiritual Biography, *2000; Thomas Cooper Library, University of South Carolina)*

logues de France et des pays de langue française (Nice, 1955), pp. 657–660;

"Le TAT chez la femme musulmane: sociologie de la perception et de l'imagination," by Fanon and Charles Geronimi, *Congrès des médecins aliénistes et neurologues de France et des pays de langue française* (Bordeaux, 1956), pp. 364–368;

"Rencontre de le société et de la psychiatrie (Notes de cours, Tunis, 1959–1960)," in *Etudes et recherches sur la psychologie en Algérie* (Oran: CRIDSSH, 1984).

SELECTED PERIODICAL PUBLICATIONS–
UNCOLLECTED: "A Propos d'un cas de syndrôme de Cotard avec balancement psychosomatique," by Fanon and Maurice Despinoy, *Annales médico-psychologiques,* 2 (June 1952): 381;

"La Socialthérapie dans un service d'hommes musulmans: difficultés méthodologiques," by Fanon and Jacques Azoulay, *Information psychiatrique,* 30 (1954): 349–361;

"Aspects actuels de l'assistance mentale en Afrique du nord," by Fanon and others, *Information psychiatrique,* 31 (1955): 11–18;

"Considérations éthno-psychiatriques," anonymous, *Consciences maghrébines* [Roneotype], 5 (Summer 1955): A4+;

"Attitude du musulman maghrébin devant la folie," by Fanon and François Sanchez, *Revue pratique de psychologie de la vie sociale et d'hygiène sociale,* 1 (1956): 24–27;

"Le Phénomène de l'agitation en milieu psychiatrique: Considérations générales, signification psychopathologique," by Fanon and S. Assehah, *Maroc médical,* 36 (1957): 21–24;

"A Propos d'un cas de spasme de torsion," by Fanon and Lucien Lévy, *La Tunisie médicale,* 36 (1958): 506–523;

"Premiers essais de méprobamate injectable dans les états hypochondriaques," by Fanon and Lévy, *La Tunisie médicale,* 37 (1959): 175–191;

"L'Hospitalisations de jour en psychiatrie: valeur et limites," *La Tunisie médicale,* 37 (1959): 689–732;

"'Anticolonialistes et non racistes' déclare le délégué algérien à Accra [Intervention à la Conférence pour la paix et la sécurité en Afrique]," *El Moudjahid,* 63, "D'Accra à Conakry" section (23 April 1960): 7, 12;

"A Conakry, il déclare: 'La paix mondiale passe par l'indépendance nationale' [Intervention en qualité du représentant de l'Algérie à la Conférence Afro-asiatique de Conakry]," *El Moudjahid,* 63, "D'Accra à Conakry" section (23 April 1960): 7;

"The Stooges of Imperialism," *Mission in Ghana Information Service,* 1, no. 6 (14 December 1960);

"Le Trouble mental et le trouble neurologique," *Information psychiatrique,* 59 (1975).

Frantz Fanon's literary and philosophical odyssey started with a personal, existential confrontation linked to his blackness in a white world and led him to the war of liberation of his adopted home, Algeria. In the process he developed a revolutionary theory that seemed applicable to Africa, if not to all the Third World, and so influenced liberation politics among colonized nations. From his youth in Martinique, he moved on to fight in World War II, became a working psychiatrist whose studies have formed part of the basis for a transcultural psychiatric practice, and then, as his involvement in the Algerian revolution increased, became a writer, propagandist, spokesperson, and diplomat for the Front de Libération National (FLN), as well as a theorist of anticolonial revolution. After his death at age thirty-six his writing, especially his book *Les Damnés de la terre* (1961; translated as *The Wretched of the Earth,* 1963), had a strong impact on Third World politics. Fanon also became a seminal figure for the Black Power movement in the United States during the 1960s and, later, largely because of his book *Peau noire, masques blancs* (1952; translated as *Black Skin, White Masks: The Experiences of a Black Man in a White World,* 1967), in theoretical discourses on identity politics and postcolonial theory.

To understand the impact of Fanon's work, one must examine the forces associated with his formation. From a French perspective, one can see in Fanon's education the product of a curriculum developed to make French culture uniform, a tradition established centuries earlier after the wars of religion and the cultural divisions in France. From another angle, the implanted cultures of the French West Indies and the many political, sociological, and racial strands that make up such places as Martinique played an important role in defining the angst that exposure to such a blatantly divided world could provoke. Finally, Fanon's pursuit of an education off his native island in both the traditional background of a provincial though established French city (Lyon) and at a more marginalized hospital at Saint-Alban added to the formation of a character whose writings reflect the complexity of these diverse influences. Additionally, the political climate of the early and mid twentieth century ensured that following the era of colonization, a predominantly white culture would try to maintain its position in the world. Blatant racism revealed itself in Europe through the dictatorships of Adolf Hitler and Benito Mussolini. Combined with the socialist fervor that emerged in the aftermath of the Russian Revolution, a virulent political ferment came into being that strongly influenced Fanon's worldview.

Born in Fort-de-France, Martinique, on 20 July 1925, the fifth of eight children born to Félix Casimir Fanon, a customs service inspector, and Eléanore Médélice, the owner of a hardware and drapery shop,

Fanon came from a fairly well-off, middle-class family. His great-grandfather on his father's side had been a slave, and the family lived within the racialized atmosphere of French West Indian society. Fanon's mother, believed to be half Alsatian, was the dominant force in the family, while his father remained distant from daily household life. Fanon resented his father's aloofness. Biographers have alternately presented Fanon's mother as "difficult" and favoring the girls of the family and as a strong-willed, intellectual woman with ambitions for all her children.

Fanon's childhood involved an attraction for football and other activities, but he also spent his early teens reading French classic literature at the Bibliothèque Schoelcher. He started studies at the Lycée Schoelcher, but it closed with the outbreak of World War II. Martinique came under Vichy command, and the sudden presence of Vichy French sailors blockaded in Fort-de-France by Allied forces caused racial tensions to flare. These experiences began to change Fanon's vision of Europeans and of race relations. In November 1939 his mother sent him for two years to Le François, Martinique, to attend the school where his uncle Edouard Fanon taught. When he returned to Fort-de-France and the Lycée Schoelcher in 1941, Fanon studied under Aimé Césaire, the great poet of *Négritude*–the Francophone celebration of the power and dignity of black African and diaspora culture. Fanon writes of Césaire in "Antilles et Africains" (West Indians and Africans), an essay in *Pour la révolution africaine: Ecrits politiques* (1964; translated as *For the African Revolution*, 1967), that he was the first person in a respectable position to tell West Indians that it is "beau est bon d'être nègre" (fine and good to be a Negro). Fanon's education had led him to think of himself as more closely linked to France and Europe than to his racial and cultural roots in Africa. Césaire's assertion provided Fanon with a key insight into his racial identity, though ultimately Fanon rejected the essentialist *Négritude* vision of blackness, coming to see blackness as a creation of experience rather than as a category of being.

The war prevented Fanon from completing his orals for the *baccalauréat,* though he did finish his written exams. Fanon's sympathies were with the Free French forces, and in 1943, at age seventeen, he ran off to Dominica to join them; but after the Vichy government of Martinique collapsed he was returned home because he was too young to enlist. He reentered school, but when he turned eighteen he left to join the Free French. In 1944 and 1945, after having been stationed in Morocco and Algeria, Fanon participated in the campaign in Europe. He was cited for bravery in the battle for Alsace, in which he was wounded, but his experience of racism throughout the war made him lose faith in the Allied cause. He came to see World War II as a white man's war and resented his treatment as a second-class citizen. He returned to Martinique disillusioned with everything he had fought for so bravely. His concern with his identity as a black man rather than as a European developed at this time. He finished the orals for his *baccalauréat* while in Martinique and assisted in Césaire's campaign to become Communist mayor of Fort-de-France; yet, in late 1946 Fanon returned to France to take advantage of his veterans' benefits and enroll in university.

At first Fanon planned to study in Paris, but he soon moved to the University of Lyon. He started in dentistry and general medicine, then switched to psychiatry. His social life, however, seems to have been shaped as much by experiences outside the university as by his studies. He was involved in political demonstrations; had an illegitimate child, Mireille, in 1948 by a woman whom biographer David Macey, in his *Frantz Fanon* (2000), identifies as "Michelle B."; and in 1949 met Marie-Josephe Dublé, or "Josie," whom he married in 1952 and with whom he had another child, Olivier, in 1955. His interactions in the intellectual community around the university, as well as his readings in contemporary literature and existentialist philosophy, also influenced him. In 1948 he edited and possibly wrote the contents to a review called *Tam Tam* (Tom Tom), which seems not to have survived, and in 1949–1950 he wrote at least three plays, none of which were published or performed and none of which seem to have survived. These endeavors recall on one hand the philosophical theater of Jean-Paul Sartre–the title of Fanon's play *Les Mains parallèles* (Parallel Hands) echoes that of Sartre's *Les Mains sales* (Dirty Hands, 1948)–and on the other a link to the *Négritude* movement popularized with the publication of Léopold Sédar Senghor's *Anthologie de la nouvelle poésie nègre et malgache de langue française* (Anthology of New Negro and Malagasy Poets in French, 1948), which included works by Césaire as well as an introduction by Sartre, "Orphée noir" (Black Orpheus), that ultimately had a profound effect on Fanon's view of *Négritude*. In May 1951 Fanon debuted as a published writer when "L'expérience vécue du noir" (The Lived Experience of the Black), a chapter from *Peau noire, masque blancs,* appeared in the journal *Esprit*. Works cited in this chapter and throughout *Peau noire, masque blancs* point to familiarity with African American novels, particularly works by Richard Wright and Chester Himes. Fanon additionally read contemporary but marginal psychiatric studies, including early works by Jacques Lacan, who had yet to achieve prominence in psychiatric circles. These last readings were separate from his university preparations.

Regarding his medical training, while following his rounds, Fanon encountered "the North African syndrome," a manifestation of symptoms among poverty-stricken, socially ostracized Algerian and Moroccan immigrants that doctors often regarded as psychosomatic. Fanon also confronted the incongruity of his adopting the European practice of "talking down" to Arab and North African patients. These concerns led him to write "Le 'Syndrome nord africain'" (The "North African Syndrome"), which appeared in *Esprit* in February 1952 and was republished in *Pour la révolution africaine*. Here Fanon posits "theses" concerning the preconditioned responses of French doctors, whose prejudices often make them skeptical regarding the diseases of North African patients. The "diagnostic de situation" (situational diagnosis) of the North Africans' condition locates the "syndrome" in the European attitude toward the North African, whom the European dehumanizes.

Peau noire, masques blancs, one of the seminal texts in postcolonial studies and arguably Fanon's most influential work, also appeared in 1952. The power of this book lies in its inquiry into the black man's experience of blackness. Fanon establishes "blackness" as an internalized effect of "expérience vécue" (lived experience). A key passage in the book describes an encounter with a white European child who cries, "Maman, regarde le nègre, j'ai peur!" (Mama, see the Negro! I'm frightened!). This moment re-creates for Fanon a social mythos surrounding blackness (recognition of the category of black and association of fear with it) and simultaneously determines a condition of otherness from whites that both generates and defines other dualities.

Fanon starts by warning readers why he wrote the book, exposing a predicament that has reached crisis levels for persons of color. He wants to surpass simple denunciations of abuse by analyzing the complex repercussions of racial attitudes. Stating right away that "le Noir n'est pas un homme" (the Black is not a man), Fanon immediately delineates the message white culture sends and blacks try to deny. The reader understands that Fanon means not to be taken literally, but from a social perspective the statement exposes something everyone knows but no one dares mention. Racism against blacks stems from economic processes that blacks have internalized as an inferiority complex linked to history and skin color. Fanon does not pretend that racist black or white attitudes are givens or universal, but suggests that they occur frequently enough to need clinical study.

The first chapter emphasizes the impact of language on black identity. One can sense Sartre's influence on Fanon's approach to identity when Fanon underlines "la dimension *pour autrui*" (the dimension of the other) at work in the man of color: "parler, c'est exister absolument pour l'autre" (to speak is to exist absolutely for the other). Before studying specific black behaviors, Fanon describes the significance of language from a subordinate position, when knowing a language does not reflect one's original culture but rather linguistic mastery of a dominating culture. Language confers power, and for black West Indians, mastering French means inclusion in the world that has appropriated them. Through reverse appropriation blacks can acquire an *imposed* authenticity, since the colonizers' destruction of colonized culture forces the colonized to situate themselves in relation to the colonizing culture, thereby obfuscating native culture and favoring development of an inferiority complex.

Fanon describes a series of attitudes displayed by West Indians in relation to French as well as to Creole, the "slave" language. A hierarchy of relations determines the favoring of one language over the other, as when the West Indian bourgeoisie uses Creole with servants. When a French West Indian leaves the island to embrace metropolitan culture, he desires even before leaving to return as a "prodigal" who can spread his knowledge, erasing his past by identifying completely with the French European. By obfuscating an original culture embodied in the propensity to speak with an accent, the traveler means to forget having ever used Creole. Studying the scenarios that the traveler and those who welcome him play out, Fanon outlines a series of subtle responses surrounding the desire to adopt a "superior" culture. The returning Martiniquan benefits from his audience of fellow islanders since he now "knows everything," but he may also be put back in place for pretending to be what he is not. Ambiguous attitudes of approval and rejection develop around his pretense and inauthenticity. Fanon realizes that this phenomenon is not exclusively French West Indian; similar behaviors appear in Frenchmen who leave the "province" to go to Paris, then come back only to speak of and "exist" for Paris. From the black perspective, however, Fanon can connect an obsession with French to cultural access, for speaking French opens opportunities once unavailable to blacks.

The chapter "La femme de couleur et le blanc" (The Woman of Color and the White Man) highlights the unhealthy behaviors of black women when their intimate relationships with white men stem from motivations linked to race. Such associations generally develop because of a black desire to gain the social advantages that come with being white or having lighter skin. Fanon explores this narcissistic drama by examining Mayotte Capécia's autobiographical novel *Je suis Martiniquaise* (I Am Martiniquan, 1948). Mayotte loves her white man because he is pale and has blond hair and blue eyes. She is willing to put up with such humiliations as being excluded from the society of her lover's rich white friends as long as she can be with a white man. Mayotte also feels proud of having a white grandmother, since such ancestry carries romantic overtones in Martinique, suggesting, in the colonial context, a love relationship rather than rape. If Mayotte's case is extreme, one can note definite inclinations among Martiniquans to choose lighter-skinned partners. In other words, an insidious racism is perpetuated in blacks who desire to reconstruct the self through qualities associated with whiteness. There is only one way out for blacks, and that is into the white world. Besides the fact that blacks have been made to assimilate white values by force, their condition is exacerbated by their eagerness to erase their blackness. Hence, for Fanon, blacks have become obsessed with both receiving acknowledgment from and acquiring the powers of whites. Fanon complements his study through examples of black women who want to marry lighter-skinned partners and mulattos who want to avoid regression into blackness. He also discusses "psychotic" desires to re-create the attitude of the black in white people, thus reversing the hierarchy as a means of compensation, by telling of a black man who joined the army so he could force whites to adopt the attitude of fear and respect he had internalized.

The third chapter, "L'Homme de couleur et la blanche" (The Man of Color and the White Woman), concentrates mainly on a neurosis Fanon calls *l'abandonnique* (abandonment neurotic) while putting a racialized twist to it. Jean Veneuse, the hero of René Maran's autobiographical novel *Un homme pareil aux autres* (A Man like the Others, 1947), fears he will be abandoned following a childhood trauma. He shapes his character around an intellectual ideal, allowing him to compensate for feelings of inadequacy by using his blackness as an excuse for not getting involved with a white woman. Fanon concludes that Veneuse's story points to a neurosis in a black man that is complicated by his environment.

Next, Fanon approaches "Du prétendu complexe de dépendance du colonisé" (The So-Called Dependency Complex of Colonized Peoples) by examining Dominique O. Mannoni's *Psychologie de la colonisation* (1950; translated as *Prospero and Caliban: The Psychology of Colonization,* 1956). Fanon acknowledges some value to Mannoni's study, since Mannoni tries to explain colonization within the frameworks of both personal history and objective historical conditions as manifested in human attitudes. Yet, Fanon expresses strong reservations concerning Mannoni's view that inferiority complexes found in colonized countries result from the propensity of colonized people toward feelings of inferi-

Poet Aimé Césaire, whose Négritude *movement was a great influence on Fanon (photograph © Bettmann/CORBIS; from Patrick Ehlen,* Frantz Fanon: A Spiritual Biography, *2000; Thomas Cooper Library, University of South Carolina)*

ority. Mannoni's book suggests that colonialism arises from the coexistence of civilized and primitive peoples. But, Fanon asks, if the situation creates the problem, why see the inferiority complex associated with it as a priori? In fact, Fanon postulates a correlation between racism and economic infrastructure. While Mannoni sees racism as manifesting the prejudices of classes that have difficulties succeeding, Fanon sees a fundamental economic cause that surpasses any social segment. Racism can be retraced to the ideology of colonizing countries. What Mannoni sees as snobbery among poor South Africans is for Fanon a displacement of aggressiveness within the white proletariat onto the black proletariat, thereby proving that racism is economic in origin. Political systems reinforce racist values. As for the theory that some peoples have a need to be colonized, since not all do get colonized and since (Mannoni suggests) some countries express unconscious desires for white rule, Fanon disregards this notion as white misunderstanding. The Madagascan myth of the long-awaited white man whom everybody welcomes should not be viewed as an innate desire to be ruled but as an example (as Césaire pointed out) of courteous, civilized behavior. Fanon ends by analyzing Madagascan dreams that suggest the assimilation of white values and demonstrate internalized suspicions toward blacks. He interprets these dreams sociologically, embracing Pierre Naville's view that dreams not only express individual concerns or sexuality but also depend for content upon economic, cultural, social, and class conditions.

The chapter "L'expérience vécue du noir," rendered in the English translation of *Peau noire, masques blancs* as "The Fact of Blackness," addresses many themes linked to the tragedy of being black in a white world. The black condition, the perception of the black in relation to myths about blackness, the frustration caused by feeling like an object in the eyes of the white man, and marginality: all represent difficulties blacks face every day in trying to feel like normal human beings. According to Fanon, a chief tragedy is that blacks constantly balance between two referential systems: their own and that of whites. In fact, Fanon thinks there is no such thing as an ontology, a proper identity, in a colonized society. Black self-knowledge exists in the third person, since black people constantly feel like evaluated objects in white eyes. Fanon's pun on "third person" intensifies this sense of depersonalization; reporting an event on a train when a child identifies him as exotic as well as a curiosity–"Tiens, un nègre!" (Look, a Negro!)–and sensing the distance this experience imposes on him both physically (since people leave several seats between him and them) and emotionally, Fanon calls himself a "triple" or "third" person since he paradoxically feels he is both too much and too little: an exemplar of his race, with all the prejudices that come with it, and a symbol of nothingness, an alien among humans. In this context Fanon expresses both shame and a simple desire to be "un homme parmi d'autres hommes" (a man among other men). Most painful is the insidious racism of well-meaning people, as when someone calls a Senegalese friend refined, as if this quality were exceptional. Fanon sees rebellion as a way out of his predicament. Reacting against such double-edged statements lets him be somebody, erasing his objectification.

Fanon's painful analysis tackles other aspects of racism, as for instance the type reserved for Jews, as explored by Sartre in *Réflexions sur la question juive* (1946; translated as *Portrait of the Anti-semite*, 1948). Yet, in the last resort, Fanon concludes that racism toward blacks is more blatant than that toward Jews, since the Jew can escape recognition, while the Black is defined by appearance. Indeed, Fanon maintains, whites tell him that if he is loved, it is despite his color, and if he is hated, it is not for his color. For Fanon, such irrational white behavior is frustrating. Escaping from this prejudice via *Négritude* is problematic, however, since *Négritude* belongs to a primitive world of black magic. Using poetry by Césaire, Senghor, and others, Fanon praises the black world of sensitivity, sensuality, and emotions, but his appreciation of *Négritude* is hampered by Sartre's argument in "Orphée noir" that it is a means to acceptance, not an end in itself, and so is transitory. To reconstruct his identity, Fanon needs to lose himself in what he calls the night of the absolute, for he cannot live *Négritude* without a Negro past or a Negro future. If, along with frustration at the refusal of a Negro past, Fanon expresses disappointment with Sartre's analysis, one must note that later he reached the same conclusion as Sartre.

"Le Nègre et la psychopathologie" (The Negro and Psychopathology) looks at social structures that acquaint children with cultural values. The paradox for the West Indian child is that values coming from the family differ from those embraced by society and perpetuated by media. Fanon comments on the subtle conditioning that children experience when they read, for instance, cartoons that glorify white values over the savage. Often, evil or negative values are represented by blacks. Studying this conditioning from both sides of the spectrum, Fanon notes from the white perspective a feeling of guilt that is compensated by stories of self-defense. Whites only attack to prevent attacks by savages. From the black West Indian perspective, a sense of wariness and mistrust toward whites appears. Fanon thinks of the repressed collective memory of slavery in the back of each black person's mind. More paradoxical, however, is the predicament of young black West Indians, who develop a propensity to think and see like whites. Unlike black Africans, every day the black West Indian lives a white truth. Only in going to the metropolis can he become a foreigner like the African. While Fanon admits that the black predicament is similar to that of the Jews, since both become scapegoats, blacks have to put up with what Fanon calls the "cycle du *biologique*" (cycle of the *biological*), since from the white point of view the black is defined by sexual potency. Fanon explores white male and above all white female interpretations of black sexuality, examining the white woman's passion for the black man and pointing toward covert desires for pain in which the black man serves as a predestined symbolic representation of aggressiveness.

A common point between myths about blacks and Jews is that both groups represent evil. More painful and complex is Fanon's interpretation of black self-hate, which stems from the black cultural background and reveals another dimension to the title of Fanon's study. Blacks live in an extraordinarily neurotic ambiguity. If French black West Indians have not inherited white anti-Semitism–there being few Jews in the French West Indies–they have inherited white negrophobia, since blacks learn gradually to associate blackness with immorality and evil. Consequently, Fanon says, black people have to fight against a negative self-image. Fanon again mentions Césaire's poetry, which acknowledges the poet's cowardly desire not to identify with his race, yet also emphasizes his need to rehabilitate blackness in his poetry once he recognizes his own self-loathing in the other. Expressing his frustration with the burdensome myths associated with blackness, Fanon asks what, as a Frenchman, he has to do with these notions. He concludes by discussing the myth of the cannibal and a case of psychoneurosis rooted in a fear of black people.

The title of the chapter "Le Nègre et la reconnaissance" (The Negro and Recognition) puns on two meanings of the French word *reconnaissance:* being recognized and being thankful. Tying the painful odyssey of the French West Indian to Adlerian psychology, Fanon talks of the Martiniquan's complex of superiority as compensation for an inferiority complex. Self-centeredness results from a past that leads one to valorize oneself in order to "see" a satisfactory and pleasing self-image in the eyes of the other. This complex stems not only from slavery but also from black West Indian emancipation. Because the French granted black West Indians their freedom, they do not even have the pride of earning their own liberty, as do black Americans. Fanon obviously feels ambivalent about his position as a black Frenchman in white French culture, suspended between a color-blind, universalist point of view and the position of a black man confronting the legacy of capitalist and colonialist abuse. Being thankful for freedom makes the establishment of black identity difficult, since identity as a "black" person who is different from the "white" person is a creation of a white culture that universalizes its values, including the value of "identity," while viewing the "black" as the "other." Fanon ends with an optimistic wish that his body always make him ready to question. As a person of color, he should not try to find out whether his race is superior or inferior to another. There should be no Negro mission or white man's burden, but only human beings looking to the future. Thus, though Fanon defines the category "black" as "other" to whiteness, his intent is to abnegate "color" as a category; as he puts it, "Le nègre n'est pas. Pas plus que le Blanc" (The Negro is not. Any more than the white man).

Peau noire, masques blancs represents an important step in Fanon's development, but some see it as an aberrant thrust in the context of his other writings. His confrontation with black identity may have forced him to move away from individual experience toward the sociogenesis of "blackness" in imperialism and colonialism, a move that is clearly already developing in *Peau noire, masques blancs.* Alternatively, life itself may have forced his attention elsewhere. Whatever the case, his later work deals less with the personal, psychological, and existential and more with the sociological and political.

Fanon's attempt to submit *Peau noire, masques blancs* as his dissertation failed, evidently because of its literary orientation. He quickly composed and submitted a technical study of a case of Friedrich's disease and completed his oral defense of this work, which he later dismissed as unimportant, on 29 November 1951. Around this time, though, he started moving in a direction that undoubtedly influenced his clinical practice more than did his conservative, organically based studies at Lyon. Through a colleague he started working at the hospital in Saint-Alban, where he met another doctor, François Tosquelles. The experiments in group therapy, work therapy, and "environmental" therapy Tosquelles was conducting at Saint-Alban strongly influenced Fanon's psychiatric practice–most likely by reinforcing the linkage between mental problems and society that he was moving toward in "Le 'Syndrome nord africain'" and *Peau noire, masques blancs.* His work with Tosquelles emphasized the idea that treatment of mental illness must occur within a social setting. In the Saint-Alban psychiatric ward every effort was made to establish an atmosphere of trust and community among patients–a far cry from standard contemporary practices of drugging or isolation. Fanon's later efforts to establish similar atmospheres of trust among his patients in Algeria, as well as his research into Algerian and Arabic views of mental illness in order to work within the cultural context of his patients, show the influence of Tosquelles. The two co-authored three clinical papers while Fanon was at Saint-Alban; all were presented to the *Congrès des médecins aliénistes et neurologues de France et des pays de langue française* (Congress of French and Francophone Mental Specialist Doctors and Neurologists) and published in proceedings of this conference in June 1953. That same month he passed an examination to become *médecin des hôpitaux psychiatriques* (doctor of psychiatric hospitals) and qualify as *médecin-chef* (chief physician). Once he completed his examinations he took a post at Pontseron, Normandy-Brittany, for little more than a month before accepting a position as *médecin-chef* in the hospital at Blida-Joinville, Algeria.

After arriving at Blida-Joinville in November 1953, Fanon attempted to introduce therapeutic strategies similar to those developed by Tosquelles. He soon

The psychiatric hospital in Blida-Joinville, Algeria, where Fanon
served as chief resident from 1953 until 1956 (from Patrick
Ehlen, Frantz Fanon: A Spiritual Biography, 2000;
Thomas Cooper Library, University of South Carolina)

concluded that European approaches were inappropriate for Arabic or Islamic patients, however. The assumption that indigenous Algerians were developmentally inferior to their European counterparts, as described in the colonial psychology of Antoine Porot and others, was standard. Fanon's concern for his patients and efforts to reform clinical practice at the hospital alienated him from other members of the hospital staff, who either cared little about the well-being of native patients or had a limited understanding of Algerian mentality, reflecting the attitudes Fanon had exposed in "Le 'Syndrome nord africain.'" Fanon soon began investigating Mahgrebian culture to create environments and activities that would more closely mirror traditional Algerian life. Many clinical papers he wrote or co-authored between 1954 and 1956 reflect an increased attention to ethnopsychiatry, research into Algerian attitudes toward and cures for mental illness, and efforts to reform clinical practice at Blida-Joinville.

Soon, Fanon's work at hospital exposed him to more-sinister sides of Algerian life. On 31 October 1954, the FLN started its campaign to liberate Algeria. French attempts to repress the rebellion swiftly caused violence on both sides to escalate. French forces system-

atically used torture to obtain information, and Algerian reprisals were harsh. Patients traumatized by torture, sometimes to the point of psychosis, started appearing in psychiatric wards, as did the torturers whose work unbalanced them. Case histories from this period appear in the final chapter of *Les Damnés de la terre*.

While impartially treating patients from both sides of the conflict, Fanon, already disillusioned by his experiences with French racism, found himself immersed in the Algerian cause. Since publishing *Peau noire, masques blancs,* his work in psychiatry had led him to concentrate on writing clinical articles for professional journals, but in February 1955 "Antilles et Africains" appeared in *Esprit.* This work illustrates Fanon's rejection of the emphasis of *Négritude* on black essence by stressing differences between black Africans and black Martiniquans while pointing to changes in Martiniquan society during World War II that led to increased acceptance of *Négritude* ideology on the island. Before the war, Fanon claims, social divisions in Martinique focused more on class than on race, and Martiniquans identified with European rather than with African culture. Martiniquan perceptions of racial identity changed, however, with the return of Césaire, who pointed out to his compatriots that being black was both acceptable and good. Shortly after Césaire's arrival came the initial defeat of France in the war, which Fanon compares to the "meurtre du père" (murder of the father). When de Gaulle organized the Free French movement, the view arose that France had been betrayed from within, and consequently that the white, racist Vichy French sailors blockaded on the island were enemy agents. Opposition to the white sailors became identified with blackness, and then blackness was valorized in all its aspects, including "le noir fiction, le noir-idéal, le noir dans l'absolu, le noir-primitif, le nègre" (black fiction, ideal black, black in the absolute, primitive black, the Negro). The liberation of the island in 1943 coincided with the emergence of a black proletariat that refocused cultural identification from Europe to Africa. Fanon concludes that after having lived "la grande erreur blanche" (the great white error), the Martiniquans were now living "le grand mirage noir" (the great black mirage).

Despite his criticisms of *Négritude,* Fanon attended the first Congrès des Ecrivains et Artistes Noirs (World Congress of Black Writers and Artists) in Paris in September 1956. Here he delivered his paper "Racisme et culture" (Racism and Culture), later published in *Pour la révolution africaine,* which outlines a theoretical interpretation of the interplay between cultural perception and racism. Tracing the egocentric and sociocentric concepts that support certain standardized, "universal-ized" cultural values, this essay explores how these values shift from the view that some humans exist without culture through belief in cultural hierarchy to a recognition of cultural relativity. An initial biological racism advances such positions as the theory that colonized people lack cortical integration. This crude "biological" racism quickly gives way to cultural racism, which privileges Western values. This shift, however, reveals that racism is actually only a function of an oppressive system that seeks to fossilize colonized cultures and stultify individual thought, generating apathy among the colonized. "Respect" for native culture among the colonizers actually involves its confinement or objectification. For instance, the construction of the dominated culture as "exotic" or as an object of study places it outside the cultural norm, objectifying the native. In turn, members of the colonized culture try to assimilate to the dominant culture, leading to alienation, guilt, and a sense of inferiority. At this stage colonizers normally hold racist views, since this shows alignment between economic realities and ideology. Attacks on racism address an effect of imperialism rather than its cause. Once oppressed peoples recognize this fact, they often return to their original, oppressed culture, valorizing tradition in defense against colonialism but also often paradoxically supporting outdated institutions. Nevertheless, this return to native culture ultimately leads to efforts toward cultural liberation, whereupon "race" as an issue disappears, replaced by conflicts that center in liberation from colonization. Hence, cultural reciprocity replaces the hierarchy inherent in colonialism, completing the movement from nonrecognition of cultures to cultural relativity.

By late 1956 Fanon was no longer able to accept his impartial role as a psychiatrist working for French colonialists. He was also at some risk because of his clandestine support for the Algerians. His "Lettre à un Français" (Letter to a Frenchman), first published in *Pour la révolution africaine,* poetically and disturbingly evokes his criticism of those who flee the violence in Algeria rather than becoming involved. This letter, unaddressed and undated, appears never to have been posted. He also wrote a harsh "Lettre au Ministre Résident" (Letter to the Resident Minister), reproduced in *Pour la révolution africaine,* resigning his post at Blida-Joinville and making clear his disgust with the social and political situation. Fanon; his wife, Josie; and their son, Olivier, were rapidly expelled from Algeria.

The events of Fanon's life after 1956 become harder to trace, because as a supporter of the Algerian revolution he was possibly engaged in covert activities. In exile in Tunis, where he arrived on 28 January 1957, Fanon resumed his psychiatric practice at the Clinique Manouba, under the name Fares, and soon started work at the Hôpital Charles-Nicolle, where he established the first psychiatric day clinic in Africa. In the latter institution he continued experiments in socially directed treatment, recording a high rate of success with patient cures compared to other institutions. His views of psychiatric difficulties, as lecture notes and other sources suggest, concentrated increasingly on the role of social relationships in mental illness. As Macey points out in *Frantz Fanon,* Fanon came to view "mental illness as a loss of individual freedom that results in the social exclusion and alienation of the sufferer." Fanon's continuing psychiatric publications in *Maroc médical* (Medical Morocco) and *La Tunisie médicale* (Medical Tunisia) point to his interest in these areas, as well as documenting drug trials and traditional psychiatric treatments.

While practicing psychiatry in Tunisia, Fanon started writing regularly for *El Moudjahid* (The Freedom Fighter), the foremost journal of the FLN, publishing his first piece, "Déceptions et illusions du colonialisme français" (Disappointments and Illusions of French Colonialism), in September 1957. This work identifies strategies the French used to subvert the revolution–using collaborators, addressing economic and social issues to make the war appear as a revolt, playing minority groups against each other, and isolating "foreign influences"–to suggest that the tactics adopted by colonizing countries to retain their colonies follow stereotypical patterns. This essay, and the others Fanon wrote for *El Moudjahid,* were published anonymously and subject to editorial control. The pieces Fanon authored were collected after his death by Josie Fanon and published in *Pour la révolution africaine.*

All were written between 1957 and 1960, and all aim at furthering the Algerian cause. Sometimes propagandistic in tone, these essays boost the position of the FLN while decrying French efforts to quell the opposition. Yet, often they strike important chords that anticipate *Les Damnés de la terre.* In "L'Algérie face aux tortionnaires français" (Algeria Face to Face with the French Torturers), published in the September 1957 issue of *El Moudjahid,* Fanon describes the poursuivie de façon rationelle" (rationally pursued) strategies of organized racism, police domination, and dehumanization that colonizers use. He states that when struggles of national liberation occur, they are presented as expressions of contradictions within the colonizing country. He also calls torture a modality of the relation between occupying force and occupied population, mentioning the increase in insanity among police as a corollary of torture (featured later in *Les Damnés de la terre*).

The essays Fanon wrote for *El Moudjahid* include a three-part criticism of the French Left, "Les Intellectuels et les démocrates français devant la révolution algérienne" (French Democrats and Intellectuals and the Algerian Revolution), published throughout December 1957 and republished in part in *France-Observateur* in December 1957 and January 1958. Fanon's call for French leftists to oppose French aggression in Algeria rests on his argument that a community of interest exists between the working class of the colonizing country and all classes in the colonized country, since all colonized people perceive foreign domination as an undifferentiated oppositional front. He then defines *colonialism* as a term created by oppressing powers to generate confusion between nationalistic and psychological issues. For Fanon, "democrats" link opposition to colonialism not to the right of the colony to self-determination, but to a need to develop liberal, antiracist behaviors at the individual level. Fanon argues that colonialism is not a matter of individual relations but one of conquest and oppression.

Thirteen essays by Fanon appeared in *El Moudjahid* in 1958, all republished in *Pour la révolution africaine*. These range from commentaries on political developments to more sweeping considerations of the implications of colonial liberation. In "Le Sang maghrebin ne coulera pas en vain" (Maghreb Blood Shall Not Flow in Vain, February 1958), Fanon advises the United States that it must assume communistic attitudes if it wishes to fight communist advancement in the underdeveloped world, and in "La farce qui change de camp" (The Farce That Changes Sides, April 1958) he criticizes Anglo-American "blackmail" revealed in the warnings against communist influences during the crisis created by French action against Algerian revolutionaries in Tunisia, including the seizure of a Tunisian naval base and the assassination of Sakiet Sidi Youssef. In "Décolonisation et indépendance" (Decolonization and Independence, April 1958), he links the Algerian insistence on independence with individual liberation, claiming that while the colonized person often can only choose either to retract his being or to identify fully with the colonizing power, in Algeria a new type of personality has appeared, one based on a recognition that it incarnates "un moment décisif de la conscience nationale" (a decisive moment of the national consciousness). Fanon maintains that individual liberation leads to national liberation and describes the Algerian revolution as the first step in an historic process of national sovereignty across sub-Saharan Africa and in the Caribbean that must be achieved through the efforts of oppressed peoples.

"Une Crise continuée" (A Continued Crisis, May 1958) introduces an international perspective by looking at European and American reactions to French actions in the Algerian War, linking European perspectives to Continental power struggles and the American perspective to the larger struggle of the Cold War.

"Lettre à la jeunesse Africaine" (Letter to the Youth of Africa, May 1958) identifies the collapse of colonialism and the emergence of new states, driven by contradictions within capitalism and the will of oppressed national groups, as the distinguishing feature of the postwar period. "Vérités premières à propos du problème colonial" (First Truths on the Colonial Problem, July 1958) describes the "dialectic" of forces influencing and obstructing the establishment of independence in colonized countries. These include "Neo-colonialism," a system geared toward the intellectual and middle-class sectors of colonial societies that grants independence while establishing economic dependence on the colonizing power. Other counteracting factors include economic "zones of influence" established by the colonizer and other developed countries and the larger, world-dominating competition between the United States and the Soviet Union. Here Fanon raises the spectacle of a possible "third bloc" of nonaligned underdeveloped nations that remains neutral in international conflicts since it must concentrate on economic development and feeding its populations. This third force, Fanon suggests, represents the only hope for a "nouvel humanisme" (new humanism). He links proletarian class struggles in colonizing countries to wars of independence in "La guerre d'Algérie et la libération des hommes" (The Algerian War and Man's Liberation, November 1958), pointing out that racism and hatred in the working class of colonizing countries reflects the economic crisis inflicted by the withdrawal of the imperialist country, an effect first felt by the proletariat. He also describes Algeria as a "guide territory" for all liberation struggles, since the Algerian struggle has profoundly upset the balance of colonial power in Africa.

Fanon first became an international spokesperson for the FLN in 1958. Using the pseudonym Omar Ibrahim Fanon and claiming to be a native of Tunisia, he visited Rome in September 1958 and returned there in December, this time in transit to Accra, Ghana, as part of the FLN delegation to the All-African People's Congress. At the congress Fanon met several African nationalists and expressed views that echo comments on violence later presented in *Les Damnés de la terre*. Audience response was enthusiastic. He returned to Tunisia after a stop in Portugal and reported on the conference in *El Moudjahid* in two articles published on 24 December 1958, "L'Algérie à Accra" (Algeria in Accra) and "Accra: l'Afrique affirme son unité et définit sa stratégie" (Accra: Africa Affirms Its Unity and Defines Its Strategy). Here he describes the "solidarité 'biologique'" ("biological" solidarity) of the African people and mentions as central topics of the conference the debate over the role of violence in struggles for independence and the extent to which former colonies should collaborate with their colonizers. Both articles were republished in *Pour la révolution africaine*. From 26 March to 1 April 1959, Fanon attended the Second Congress of Black Writers and Artists in Rome, delivering a speech, "Fondements réciproques de la culture nationale et des luttes de libération" (The Reciprocal Foundation of National Culture and Liberation Struggles), that was later published, with minor revisions, in *Les Damnés de la terre*. A little more than a month later he traveled to Morocco to work on reorganizing medical services for revolutionary forces in Algeria. He was apparently at this time working on *L'An V de la Révolution algérienne* (1959; translated as *Studies in a Dying Colonialism,* 1965). Fanon's service in Morocco suddenly ended when he was injured in an incident variously described as an assassination attempt, a land-mine explosion, and an automobile accident. The back injury he sustained necessitated removal to a hospital in Oudja, where it was determined that he required treatment in Europe. Fanon flew to Rome as Omar Ibrahim Fanon with a Libyan passport on 5 July 1959. The day he arrived, the person meant to pick him up narrowly escaped assassination. Fanon was given an armed guard at the hospital, but when he learned of local press coverage of the assassination attempt, he insisted on changing rooms, thereby escaping assassination when gunmen, apparently from an underground right-wing terrorist organization called the Red Hand, broke into his original room.

After several weeks of treatment, Fanon returned to Tunis in August 1959 to attend a policy meeting of the FLN. The recognition by the FLN of the seminal role of the peasantry in the revolutionary effort following this meeting matches Fanon's insistence in *Les Damnés de la terre* on the importance of the peasant to the revolution, implying his participation in policy discussions. That fall *L'An V de la Révolution algérienne* appeared. This work offers direct analysis of specific forces Fanon saw as both shaping and being shaped by the Algerian War, including both a new society and a "new humanity" created by the development of national consciousness. Fanon points out that this development of national consciousness before national existence reverses the standard pattern, wherein national existence informs national consciousness. In short, for Fanon in 1959, Algeria represents a reassertion of humanity's ability to progress, and the Algerian War gains its significance from the radical change it created among Algerians.

One social factor Fanon sees as clearly affected by the revolution concerns women, as his chapter "L'Algérie se dévoile" (Algeria Unveiled) demonstrates. Identifying the veil, or *haîk,* as a marker of Arab culture and

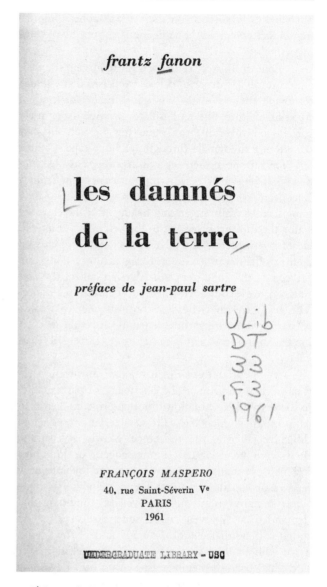

Title page for Fanon's most influential work, which is regarded as "the Bible of Third Worldism" (Thomas Cooper Library, University of South Carolina)

clothing in general as the most apparent cultural symbol, Fanon describes how the colonizer's standardized reaction to the veil makes it a sign of the belittled status of women in Algerian society. This perspective posits a hidden matriarchal structure behind the visible patriarchy of Arabian culture and therefore targets the condition of women as a way of conquering the colonized society. Indeed, French society has emphasized women's education and Europeanization, including discarding the veil and involving women in social events (as when European employers invite Arab employees to a party but insist they bring their wives).

Such strategies, which on the surface appear liberating, in fact denigrate the indigenous culture by devaluing its values.

Beneath this concentration on removing the veil, Fanon traces a European cult of exoticism that equates removing the veil with possessing the woman. If, in Algerian culture, the veil isolates women from male society, for the European removing the veil suggests conquering the female through symbolic rape. Culturally, for European men the veil also suggests possibilities of surrender or even nymphomania, while from a European woman's perspective the veil serves to hide imperfection while suggesting beauty. But the elevated status the European accords to the veil makes it a vehicle of resistance for the Algerian, since the oppressed culture offers resistance according to the actions and projects of the colonizers. An Algerian cult of the *haïk* thus ensures continued Algerian cultural resistance. The veil accordingly becomes an instrument of "cold" warfare, emphasizing coexistence. As a result, in colonized Algeria women became more cloistered than ever.

With the outbreak of hostilities, however, Algerian women confronted the possibility of participating in the revolution, though without any role models such as Western women had. Thus, Algerian women had difficulty entering the resistance. Slowly but surely, they were incorporated as messengers or lookouts. Women eventually carried weapons for revolutionary leaders or suicide attackers. These adaptations sometimes required removing the veil, a condition that demanded a "nouvelle dialectique du corps et du monde" (new dialectic of the body and of the world) since without the *haïk* the woman often felt as if her body had been dismembered or cast adrift. Beginning in 1957, the veil was readapted, but now for camouflage as women carried weapons. Thus, the veil became an object of manipulation and so part of an historic dynamic, even as the Algerian woman has imposed the restriction of the home upon herself as a revolutionary gesture.

Fanon also considered the role that radio played in the revolution. Before the revolution, Fanon writes in another chapter in *L'An V de la Révolution algérienne*, "'Ici la voix de l'Algérie . . .'" ("This Is the Voice of Algeria . . ."), radio existed outside the sign system of Algerians, who perceived radio programming as "Des Français parlent aux Français" (Frenchmen speaking to Frenchmen) or as offensive to family taste and protocol. With the establishment of Arabian states after World War II, radio ownership started increasing. The revolution brought a need for news dissemination, and as the situation intensified, the native Algerian press was censored and purchasing European newspapers cast suspi-

cion upon one's loyalties. The Algerian press was boycotted to attack colonial interests, and so the popularity of radio increased. Fanon discusses jamming strategies and their effect on the fabrication of news among the indigenous peasant populations, who had to choose between the deliberate lies of the colonizing power and the lie of "the people," which suddenly gained a dimension of truthfulness. Fanon concludes with observations on the psychopathology associated with radios; hallucinated radio voices heard by mental patients shifted from provoking negative affect to evoking more-positive responses as radio became a tool of revolution.

The revolution's effect on the Algerian family, analyzed in "La famille algérienne" (The Algerian Family), involved total rupture and ultimately, in Fanon's view, liberation as traditional family roles collapsed. Because of the war, children often became radicalized, and the authority of the father gave way before revolutionary values. Women assumed a new authority as they shifted from being daughters and wives into revolutionary activity. In couples and in marriage, ruptures led to the adaptation of social and revolutionary values. Couples often became more closely knit by the revolution.

Fanon points out in "Médecine et colonialisme" (Medicine and Colonialism) that colonialism generates a system of resentment among the colonized. Regarding medicine, this resentment translates into a profound ambivalence toward the colonial medical establishment. Distrust of colonial doctors fosters a return to traditional medicine, which the colonized person follows for social, psychological, and political reasons. Abandoning native healing practices appears to validate Western technique, which is why the native doctor who adopts Western medicine feels psychologically driven to prove his involvement in the rational universe he has entered. In its reversed aspect, rejection of native tradition compels the native who turns to Western medicine to go to a European doctor, who is perceived as naturally better versed in European practice. Further complicating issues, the European doctor in the colonies generally adopts colonial values, rejecting medical ethics. Finally, with medical supplies cut off by the French, the native doctor has become the doctor of the revolution.

The final chapter of *L'An V de la Révolution algérienne*, "La minorité européenne d'Algérie" (Algeria's European Minority), published separately in *Les Temps modernes* in May through June 1959, describes the endeavors of activists who have broken with France. Though Fanon feels the Left has done nothing for Algeria, he does suggest that it has prevented some things. The European presence in Algeria consists of democratic supporters of the revolution, war criminals from other colonies, and people who view the colony as a sort of "chasse gardée" (private preserve). Fanon points out that the native Algerian Jewish population supports the revolution and describes how its European supporters avoid casting suspicion on their sympathies.

Of all the sections of this book, "L'Algérie se dévoile" has been the most popular. Though *L'An V de la Révolution algérienne* was not successful, it had a significant impact on what Macey, in *Frantz Fanon,* calls French Third Worldism, in which disaffected youth turned from the policies of the old Left to countries such as Algeria and Cuba as emerging humanitarian or socialist states that offered the true next step in revolution. It encouraged an idealistic view of the revolution, especially as regards the emancipation of women and the restructuring of the family. One source Macey cites describes this effect as involving "a romantic and almost mystical vision . . . that the salvation of the world would perhaps come from the Third World"—an attitude that became known as "Fanonism."

In February 1960 Fanon became the permanent representative of the Gouvernement Provisoire de la République Algérienne (Provisional Government of the Algerian Republic, or GPRA) in Accra, recognized as the Algerian ambassador by the Ghanan government though he did not have diplomatic status and was identified as Libyan on his passport. He met several leading figures in African independence movements and promoted the cause of Algerian independence among sub-Saharan African nations. He continued to write for *El Moudjahid,* including articles on developments in Martinique and the French West Indies. Fanon's efforts included attempts to establish an "African Legion," a sub-Saharan force that would support the Algerian War. He also spoke passionately on pan-African solidarity at the Conference of African Peoples in Tunis (January 1960); the Afro-Asiatic Solidarity Conference in Conakry, Guinea (April 1960); the Conference on Positive Action in Accra (April 1960); the Conference of Independent African States in Addis Ababa (June 1960); and the Pan-African Congress in Léopoldville (September 1960), gaining moral support for his causes if little else. His speeches from this period only survive as secondary reportage. On his way to this last conference, Fanon narrowly escaped capture by the French. His flight from Monrovia to Conakry was full. He refused both accommodations and a seat on the next day's flight. This second flight was diverted and searched by French forces.

On 12 September 1960, after the conference in Léopoldville, Fanon undertook an expedition to find potential supply routes to Algeria through Mali and the Sahara. His notes from this trip were published in *Pour la révolution africaine* as "Cette Afrique à venir" (This Africa to Come). The expedition involved extensive

travel through rough terrain and potentially dangerous situations. Fanon was back in Ghana in late October. The extent of his exhaustion after this journey convinced Fanon that he might have a serious ailment, and in Tunis later that year he was diagnosed with leukemia. In spring 1961 he received treatments in the Soviet Union, returning to Tunis by early April.

Throughout spring and summer 1961 Fanon dictated to his wife *Les Damnés de la terre,* which has become known as the "Bible of Third Worldism"; he supplemented the new material that makes up half of the book with previous work, including a speech he had given at a conference sponsored by the journal and publishing house *Présence africaine* in Rome during Easter 1959, case notes from Blida and Tunis from 1954 to 1959, material related to his 1952 essay "Le 'Syndrome nord africain,'" and a contribution to *Consciences maghrébines.* The first chapter appeared in *Les Temps modernes* in May 1961 but was later revised, so that the full text of the book was complete in July 1961 when Fanon met Sartre and Simone de Beauvoir in Rome. A short time later Sartre agreed to write the preface to *Les Damnés de la terre.* Fanon's book went beyond events in Algeria to present what Sartre felt was a voice from the Third World.

Fanon here departs from FLN positions to provide an historical and theoretical basis for violent colonial revolution. He states immediately in the most controversial chapter of this book, "De la violence" (Concerning Violence), that decolonization is always violent and involves the sudden and complete "remplacement d'une 'espèce' d'hommes par une autre 'espèce' d'hommes" (replacing of a certain "species" of men by another "species" of men). Decolonization is a program of absolute disorder. As a willed involvement in an historical process, it necessitates total reconsideration of the situation created by the colonizer. Fanon describes the colonial world as a Manichean world of "exclusion réciproque" (reciprocal exclusivity) in which the colonizer possesses all; the police or military serve as go-betweens; and the colonized live in perpetual envy. No superstructure or prevailing function exists in colonial society other than the enrichment of the colonizing country at the expense of the colony.

Fanon criticizes the colonized intelligentsia, whose opportunism often collides with the interests of the rebels. These intellectuals often have benefited from colonial culture and fraternize with the colonial elite. Similarly, the native colonial bourgeoisie, which is invested in maintaining the established order, seeks compromise with the colonizers. Though the bourgeoisie functions well in negotiation and compromise, it can fulfill this role only because of its complicity with the colonial powers that established it. In the colonial situation, therefore, the peasants are the true revolutionary force, for they have gained nothing from colonialism. According to Fanon, only drastic, violent measures suffice to abolish the colonial regime, since whatever benefits the colonizer harms the colonized. All colonial systems are violent, so the only solution is greater violence. As Fanon puts it, "Le colonisé est un persécuté qui rêve en permanence de devenir persécuteur" (The native is an oppressed person whose permanent dream is to become the persecutor).

In colonized societies before decolonization, the urge to violence often manifests itself as criminality and violence within the native community. The native uses self-destructive behaviors to release tensions generated by the colonial situation. Fatalism and reliance on magic serve similar functions. If, among the peasantry, unconscious compensation expresses itself through magic, which Fanon sees as internalized violence, fighting for liberation brings a noticeable change in attitudes as new generations become more attuned to reality.

Fanon speaks of the many subtleties that revolutionary movements must address to create a successful revolution. Crucial to the initiation of rebellion is a leader who becomes central to the momentum of the movement. Fanon points out that often violence becomes the central focus of a political party whose leaders call the people to revolt and asks why the masses sometimes come to see violence as their only recourse. He identifies among the colonized an awareness that, in the contemporary world, military force is overstretched by the possibility of global conflict. Thus, violence becomes central to decolonization, but violent decolonization does not necessarily lead to social justice. For many people in the liberated country, liberation brings no immediate change in lifestyle, and so violence continues after liberation, especially when forces of capitalism and socialism compete for hegemony in the newly liberated nation. Nevertheless, Fanon maintains, violence unifies colonized peoples and works as a cleansing force at the individual level, since it frees the native from his inferiority complex, despair, and inaction.

At the international level, Fanon argues in the chapter titled "De la violence dans le contexte international" (Violence in the International Context), violent decolonization unveils the true nature of colonialism and illuminates the contrast between developed and underdeveloped countries, showing the extent to which the wealth of the developed world has been extracted from the underdeveloped world and redistributed.

Once revolution has freed the colonized country and the colonizing bourgeoisie has left, the national bourgeoisie takes over. This development occurs because the national political parties are centered in the towns and are dominated by middle-class factions that deeply distrust the peasantry. In "Grandeur et faiblesses de la spontanéité" (Spontaneity: Its Strength and Weakness), Fanon criticizes the inadequacy of this unimaginative class, which selfishly imitates the occidental bourgeoisie it replaces. Before decolonization, the colonial bourgeoisie exploited the land in sectorial fashion, leaving disparities of wealth between districts. Once the country is liberated, this unequal distribution contributes to new abuses and to competition within the liberated country, often resulting in tribal intolerance and chaos. Another discouraging factor is that in order to control the people, the national bourgeoisie often manages to rally the old leader as well as the party that led the revolution. Using the aura of the past, the former revolutionary leader and his party cultivate influence, sometimes centralizing power in dictatorial fashion. In another twist, Fanon explains, prior to decolonization the nationalist parties combine the desire to end colonialism with a wish to establish accord with the colonizing forces. Any reconciliation to the advantage of the bourgeoisie can lead to counterrevolutions in which the disenchanted intelligentsia link with the peasantry and spread rebellion. Such peasant revolts need to be redirected to the purpose of the nationalist party, since these "spontaneous" uprisings lack ideological solidarity and can deteriorate into tribal discontent, brutality, and anarchy.

Fanon continues his exploration of the challenges that face the new nation in "Mésaventures de la conscience nationale" (The Pitfalls of National Consciousness). Here he attacks the narcissistic belief of the national middle class that it can replace the colonial bourgeoisie and so gain advantage in the new state. Fanon contrasts this belief with the horrible, antinational behavior that the business-minded bourgeoisie actually adopts. The native bourgeoisie in fact sees nationalization as a chance to transfer the unfair advantages of the colonial period into native hands. Continued abuse within the decolonized nations leads to aggression against nonnationals and foreigners, undermining any efforts toward African unity, which Fanon believes can only be achieved by the people's will in defiance of bourgeois interests. He argues for establishing conditions that limit or eliminate the role of the bourgeoisie and improve general living conditions and education. Because a newly freed country does not yet have homogeneous material well-being and educational opportunity, Fanon believes that retaining an infrastructure like that of First World countries is an error. He suggests that the jobless youth of African countries be given a strong education and be directed toward useful work to make them more aware of the needs of their countries. Fanon advocates establishing a national government that governs for and with the people by establishing national politics on the will of the masses.

In the chapter "Sur la culture nationale" (On National Culture) Fanon analyzes the legitimacy of the claim to national identity of a decolonized nation by exploring cultural expression. To counteract colonial brainwashing, the intellectual component of the colonized community has found it necessary to rediscover a culture that valorizes the African. Indeed, one strategy of control developed by the colonizers is to persuade the colonized that without the colonizer the colony would fall back into barbarism. If rediscovery of an African cultural identity can help reestablish dignity, this trend can also create problems at the practical level, since it does not represent current economic, political, or cultural realities or take into account the role of history in forming national and individual character. Cultures that felt ashamed of their exploitation by European cultures are now remote from their cultural roots and in some cases cannot reconnect to them because the necessary infrastructures no longer exist. Fanon gives the example of Arabic cultures that now have more in common with Mediterranean cultures than with other Arabic or Islamic nations. He describes three steps that colonized intellectuals go through in establishing national as opposed to racial culture: a period of assimilation of European culture leads to a return to roots that is somewhat artificial, since it strangulates itself in exoticism based on memories. Finally, a period of rebellion emerges in which the literary intellectual becomes the mouthpiece of a new, active, politicized reality. This shift accompanies a shift in the audience addressed by the work, from the colonizer to the native. Fanon ends the book with a chapter on "Guerre coloniale et troubles mentaux" (Colonial Wars and Mental Disorders), using case studies to show that colonial oppression and violence are directly implicated in the development of mental pathologies.

A few weeks before *Les Damnés de la terre* was published, Fanon suffered a serious relapse of his leukemia. Arrangements were made to take him to the United States for treatment, though Fanon initially opposed the idea. He arrived in Washington, D.C., on 3 October 1961, but rather than being directly admitted to a hospital was kept in a hotel until 10 October. After admission to the National Institute of Health in Bethesda, Maryland, Fanon underwent treatment but died of complications arising from pneumonia on 6 December 1961. His body was returned to Tunisia and buried across the battle lines on the Algerian frontier. His anonymous articles from *El Moudjahid* and other works were assembled with the help of his wife, Josie, and published by Maspero as *Pour la révolution africaine* in 1964, while some of his psychiatric publications were

Monument to Fanon at the entrance to the University of the Antilles in Schoelcher, Martinique (photograph by Patrick Ehlen; from his Frantz Fanon: A Spiritual Biography, *2000; Thomas Cooper Library, University of South Carolina)*

gathered in a 1975 issue of *Information psychiatrique* (Psychiatric Information).

Fanon's legacy remains complex, and his works invite manifold interpretations. The depth and intensity of his character is reflected in the multidirectional quality of his writing, which touches on such diverse spheres as psychology, sociology, literary criticism, economics, and politics. This diversity of interests has made his work available for use by scholars in disciplines as varied as postcolonialism, feminism, and gender criticism, sometimes in ways that appear distant from Fanon's original intentions. Yet, despite the fact that his work crosses boundaries, one can isolate recurrent themes in his contributions. Foremost among these is the passionate exploration of the interplay between racism and social justice, which appears in his first introspective analyses of human behavior and remains prevalent in his later investigations of the interweaving of politics and economics in the division between colonizer and colonized, developed and underdeveloped worlds. From this angle, what most determines Fanon's charismatic status is his deep, personal involvement in two revolutions. The first is an intimate, inner-directed struggle of discovery, reflecting his growing awareness that race is a social construct that profoundly influences psychological development. The other revolution involves an exploration of the economic and political construction of race and of how the forces of capital shape human behaviors. This last stance especially contributed to his decision to fight for the liberation of Algeria and all colonized countries. Perhaps the clearest testimony to his power appears in his prayer at the end of *Peau noire, masques blancs* that he continue his quest after knowledge and truth: "O mon corps, fais de moi toujours un homme qui interroge!" (O my body, make of me always a man who questions!).

Bibliographies:

Emmanuel Hansen, "Frantz Fanon: A Bibliographical Essay," *Pan-African Journal,* 5 (Winter 1972): 387–405;

Alice Cherki, *Frantz Fanon: Portrait* (Paris: Seuil, 2000);

Joan Nordquist, *Frantz Fanon: A Bibliography* (Santa Cruz, Cal.: Reference and Research Service, 2002).

Biographies:

David Caute, *Frantz Fanon* (New York: Viking, 1970);

Pierre Bouvier, *Fanon* (Paris: Editions universitaires, 1971);

Peter Geismar, *Fanon* (New York: Dial, 1971);

Irene L. Gendzier, *Frantz Fanon: A Critical Study* (New York: Pantheon, 1973);

Joby Fanon, "Pour Frantz, pour notre mère," *Sans frontière* (February 1982): 5–11;

B. Marie Perinbam, *Holy Violence: The Revolutionary Thought of Frantz Fanon: An Intellectual Biography* (Washington, D.C.: Three Continents Press, 1982);

D. B. Wyrick, *Fanon for Beginners* (New York: Writers and Readers, 1998);

David Macey, *Frantz Fanon: A Biography* (London: Granta Books, 2000; New York: Picador, 2001);

Patrick Ehlen, *Frantz Fanon: A Spiritual Biography* (New York: Crossroad, 2000).

References:

Lionel Abel, "Seven Heroes of the New Left," in *Molders of Modern Thought,* edited by Ben B. Seligman (Chicago: Quadrangle Books, 1970), pp. 334–349;

Christiane Achour, ed., *Journée d'hommage à Frantz Fanon: 25 septembre 1982 à l'Université d'Alger* (Oran: Kalim CRIDSSH, 1982);

H. M. Adam, "Frantz Fanon as a Democratic Theorist," *African Affairs,* 92 (1993): 499–518;

Paul L. Adams, "The Social Psychiatry of Frantz Fanon," *American Journal of Psychiatry,* 127, no. 6 (December 1970): 109–114;

Anthony C. Alessandrini, ed., *Frantz Fanon: Critical Perspectives* (London & New York: Routledge, 1999);

Hannah Arendt, *On Violence* (New York: Harcourt, Brace & World, 1970), pp. 59–87;

A. K. Armah, "African Socialism: Utopian or Scientific?" *Présence africaine,* 64, no. 4 (1967): 6–30;

Alessandro Aruffo, *Frantz Fanon, o, L'eversione anticoloniale* (Rome: Erre emme, 1994);

Aruffo and Giovanni Pirelli, *Fanon, o l'eversione anticoloniale* (Rome: Erre emme, 1994);

Paul A. Beckett, "Algeria versus Fanon: The Theory of Revolutionary Decolonization and the African Experience," *Western Political Quarterly,* 26, no. 1 (March 1973): 5–27;

A. Ben Bella, "La Mémoire de Frantz Fanon," *Le Monde,* 27 December 1972, p. 4;

Gwen Bergner, "Who Is That Masked Woman? Or, The Role of Gender in Fanon's *Black Skin, White Masks,*" *PMLA,* 110, no. 1 (January 1995): 75–88;

Robert Bernasconi, "Sartre's Gaze Returned: The Transforming of the Phenomenology of Racism," *Graduate Faculty Philosophy Journal,* 18, no. 2 (1995): 201–221;

Jacques Berque and others, "Hommages à Frantz Fanon," *Présence africaine,* 60 (1962): 118–141;

Homi K. Bhabha, "Interrogating Identity: The Postcolonial Prerogative," in *Anatomy of Racism,* edited by David Theo Goldberg (Minneapolis: University of Minnesota Press, 1990);

Robert Blackey, "Fanon and Cabral: A Contrast in Theories of Revolution for Africa," *Journal of Modern African Studies,* 12 (June 1974): 191–209;

M. Boucebci, "Aspects actuels de la psychiatrie en Algérie," *Information psychiatrique,* 10, no. 66 (December 1990): p. 951;

Antoine Bouillon, *Madagascar, le colonisé et son âme: Essai sur le discours psychologique colonial* (Paris: L'Harmattan, 1981), pp. 195–232;

Hussein Abdilahi Bulhan, "Black Psyches in Captivity and Crises," *Race and Class,* 20, no. 3 (1979): 243–261;

Bulhan, "Dynamics of Cultural In-Betweenity: An Empirical Study," *International Journal of Psychology,* 15 (1980): 105–121;

Bulhan, "Frantz Fanon: The Revolutionary Psychiatrist," *Race and Class,* 21, no. 3 (1980): 252–271;

Bulhan, *Frantz Fanon and the Psychology of Oppression* (New York: Plenum, 1985);

Bulhan, "Psychological Research in Africa: Genesis and Function," *Race and Class,* 23, no. 1 (1981): 25–41;

Bulhan, "The Revolutionary Psychology of Frantz Fanon and Notes on His Theory of Violence," *Fanon Center Journal,* 1, no. 1 (1980): 51–71;

Mohamed Cherif, "Frantz Fanon: La Science au service de la révolution," *Jeune Afrique,* 295 (4 September 1966): 24;

Pietro Clemente, *Frantz Fanon tra esistenzialismo e rivoluzione* (Bari: Laterza, 1971);

Comité Frantz Fanon, *Memorial international Frantz Fanon* (Paris: Présence Africaine, 1984);

Elo Dacy, ed., *L'Actualité de Frantz Fanon: Actes du Colloque de Brazzaville, 12–16 décembre 1984* (Paris: Karthala, 1986);

Horace B. Davis, *Toward a Marxist Theory of Nationalism* (New York: Monthly Review Press, 1978), pp. 202–239;

J. L. Decker, "Terrorism (Un)veiled, Frantz Fanon and the Women of Algeria," *Cultural Critique,* 17 (1990): 177–198;

Halford F. Fairchild, "Frantz Fanon's *Wretched of the Earth* in Contemporary Perspective," *Journal of Black Studies,* 25, no. 2 (December 1994): 191–199;

Carlos A. Fernández Pardo, *Frantz Fanon* (Buenos Aires: Editorial Galerna, 1971);

Chester J. Fontenot Jr., *Frantz Fanon: Language as the God Gone Astray in the Flesh* (Lincoln: University of Nebraska Press, 1979);

Diane Fuss, "Interior Colonies: Frantz Fanon and the Politics of Identification," *Diacritics,* 24, nos. 2–3 (1974): 215–227;

Henry Louis Gates Jr., "Critical Fanonism," *Critical Inquiry,* 17 (Spring 1991): 457–478;

Nigel C. Gibson, *Fanon: The Postcolonial Imagination* (Cambridge: Polity Press, 2003);

Gibson, ed., *Rethinking Fanon: The Continuing Dialogue* (Amherst, N.Y.: Humanity Books, 1999);

Lewis R. Gordon, *Fanon and the Crisis of European Man: An Essay on Philosophy and the Human Sciences* (New York: Routledge, 1995);

Gordon, ed., *Existence in Black: An Anthology of Black Existential Philosophy* (New York: Routledge, 1996), pp. 11–36, 263–272;

Gordon, T. Denean Sharpley-Whiting, and Renée T. White, eds., *Fanon: A Critical Reader* (Oxford & Cambridge, Mass.: Blackwell, 1996);

Emmanuel Hansen, "Frantz Fanon: Portrait of a Revolutionary Intellectual," *Transition,* 46 (October–December 1974): 25–36;

Hansen, *Frantz Fanon: Social and Political Thought* (Columbus: Ohio State University Press, 1977);

Mohammed Harbi, *Le FLN: Mirage et réalité* (Alger: NAQD-ENAL, 1993), pp. 237–253;

John Hopton, "The Application of the Ideas of Frantz Fanon to the Practice of Mental Health Nursing," *Journal of Advanced Nursing,* 21, no. 4 (1995): 723–728;

Paulin J. Hountondji, *African Philosophy: Myth and Reality,* translated by Henri Evans and Jonathan Rée (Bloomington: Indiana University Press, 1983), pp. 23–25;

F. A. Irele, *Literature and Ideology in Martinique: René Maran, Aimé Césaire, Frantz Fanon* (Buffalo: Council on International Studies, State University of New York, 1971);

B. K. Jha, "Fanon's Theory of Violence: A Critique," *Indian Journal of Political Science,* 49, no. 3 (1988): 359–369;

L. Adele Jinadu, *Fanon: In Search of the African Revolution* (Enugu, Nigeria: Fourth Dimension, 1980);

Philippe Lucas, *Sociologie de Frantz Fanon: Contribution à une anthropologie de la libération* (Algiers: SNED, 1971);

Christiane Makward, *Mayotte Capécia, ou L'Aliénation selon Fanon* (Paris: Karthala, 1999);

Manuel Maldonado-Denis, *Marti y Fanon* (Mexico City: Universidad Nacional Autónoma de México, 1978);

Marcel Manville, "Hommage à Frantz Fanon," *Sans Frontière* (February 1982): 35–37;

Guy Martin, "Fanon's Relevance to Contemporary African Political Thought," *Ufahamu,* 4 (Winter 1974): 11–34;

Tony Martin, "Rescuing Fanon from the Critics," *African Studies Review,* 13 (December 1970): 381–399;

Clément Mbom, *Frantz Fanon aujourd'hui et demain: Refléxions sur le tiers monde* (Paris: Nathan, 1985);

Jock McCulloch, *Black Soul, White Artifact: Fanon's Clinical Psychology and Social Theory* (Cambridge & New York: Cambridge University Press, 1983);

Albert Memmi, "La Vie impossible de Frantz Fanon," *Esprit,* no. 406 (September 1971): 248–273;

M. Neill, "Guerrillas and Gangs: Frantz Fanon and V. S. Naipaul," *Ariel: A Review of International English Literature,* 13, no. 4 (October 1982): 21–62;

Nguyen Nghe, "Frantz Fanon et les problèmes de l'indépendance," *La Pensée,* 107 (January–February 1963): 23–36;

P. Nursey-Bray, "Marxism and Existentialism in the Thought of Frantz Fanon," *Political Studies,* 20 (1972): 152–168;

Richard C. Onwuanibe, *A Critique of Revolutionary Humanism: Frantz Fanon* (St. Louis: W. H. Green, 1983);

B. Marie Perinbam, "Fanon and the Revolutionary Peasantry—The Algerian Case," *Journal of Modern African Studies,* 11, no. 3 (1973): 440–442;

C. Razanjao and Jacques Postel, "La Vie et l'œuvre psychiatrique de Frantz Fanon," *Information psychiatrique,* 51, no. 10 (December 1975): 1053–1073;

Alan Read, ed., *The Fact of Blackness: Frantz Fanon and Visual Representation* (London: Institute of Contemporary Arts and Institute of International Visual Arts / Seattle: Bay Press, 1995);

Cedric Robinson, "The Appropriation of Frantz Fanon," *Race and Class,* 35, no. 1 (July–September 1993): 79–91;

Darieck Scott, "Jungle Fever? Black Gay Identity Politics, White Dick, and the Utopian Bedroom," *GLQ,* 1 (1994): 299–321;

Ato Sekyi-Otu, *Fanon's Dialectic of Experience* (Cambridge, Mass.: Harvard University Press, 1996);

T. Denean Sharpley-Whiting, *Frantz Fanon: Conflicts and Feminisms* (Lanham, Md.: Rowman & Littlefield, 1998);

Martin Staniland, "Frantz Fanon and the African Political Class," *African Affairs,* 68, no. 270 (1969): 4–25;

Charles Sugnet, *"Nervous Conditions:* Dangarembga's Feminist Reinvention of Fanon," in *The Politics of (M)othering: Womanhood, Identity, and Resistance in African Literature,* edited by Obioma Nnaemeka (London: Routledge, 1997), pp. 33–49;

François Tosquelles, "Fanon à Saint-Alban," *Information psychiatrique,* 51, no. 10 (1975);

Lou Turner, "Frantz Fanon's Journey into Hegel's 'Night of the Absolute,'" *Quarterly Journal of Ideology,* 13, no. 4 (1989): 47–63;

Turner, "The Marxist Humanist Legacy of Frantz Fanon," *News and Letters,* 38, no. 10 (1991): 47–63;

Turner and John Alan, eds., *Frantz Fanon, Soweto, and American Black Thought,* expanded edition (Chicago: News and Letters, 1986);

Françoise Vergès, "Creole Skin, Black Masks: Fanon and Disavowal," *Critical Inquiry,* 23 (Spring 1997): 578–595;

I. M. Wallerstein, "Frantz Fanon: Reason and Violence," *Berkeley Journal of Sociology,* 15 (1970): 222–231;

Michael Wayne, "The Critical Practice and Dialectics of Third Cinema," in *The Third Text Reader on Art, Cultures and Theory,* edited by Rasheed Araeen, Sean Cubitt, and Ziauddin Sarder (London: Continuum, 2002), pp. 211–225;

Patrick Williams and Laura Chrisman, eds., *Colonial Discourse and Post-Colonial Theory: A Reader* (New York: Columbia University Press, 1994), pp. 36–52, 112–123;

Jack Woddis, *New Theories of Revolution: A Commentary on the Views of Frantz Fanon, Régis Debray and Herbert Marcuse* (New York: International Publishers, 1972);

Derek Wright, "Fanon and Africa: A Retrospect," *Journal of Modern African Studies,* 24, no. 4 (December 1986): 679–689;

Renate Zahar, *Frantz Fanon: Colonialism and Alienation: Concerning Frantz Fanon's Political Theory,* translated by W. F. Freuser (New York: Monthly Review Press, 1974);

Aristide R. Zolberg, "Frantz Fanon," *The New Left: Six Critical Essays,* edited by Maurice Cranston (New York: Library Press, 1971), pp. 119–136;

Zolberg and Vera Zolberg, "The Americanization of Frantz Fanon," *Public Interest,* 9 (1966): 49–63.

Sigmund Freud
(6 May 1856 – 23 September 1939)

Elizabeth Losh
University of California at Irvine

BOOKS: *Studien über Hysterie,* by Freud and Josef
Breuer (Leipzig & Vienna: Deuticke, 1895); trans-
lated by A. A. Brill as "Studies in Hysteria," in
Selected Papers on Hysteria and Other Psychoneuroses
(New York: Journal of Nervous and Mental Dis-
eases Publishing, 1909);

Die Traumdeutung (Leipzig & Vienna: Deuticke, 1900
[i.e., 1899]); translated by Brill as *The Interpretation
of Dreams* (London: Allen & Unwin / New York:
Macmillan, 1913);

Über den Traum (Wiesbaden: Bergmann, 1901); translated by M. D. Eder as *On Dreams* (London:
Heinemann, 1914; New York: Rebman, 1914);

*Zur Psychopathologie des Alltagslebens (Über Vergessen, Ver-
sprechen, Vergreifen, Aberglaube und Irrtum)* (Berlin:
Karger, 1904); translated by Brill as *The Psychopathology of Everyday Life* (London: Fisher/Unwin,
1914; New York: Macmillan, 1914);

Der Witz und seine Beziehung zum Unbewussten (Leipzig &
Vienna: Deuticke, 1905); translated by Brill as
Wit and Its Relation to the Unconscious (London:
Kegan Paul, Trench, Trübner, 1916; New York:
Moffat, Yard, 1916);

Drei Abhandlungen zur Sexualtheorie (Leipzig & Vienna:
Deuticke, 1905); translated by Brill as *Three Con-
tributions to the Sexual Theory* (New York: Journal of
Nervous and Mental Diseases Publishing, 1910);

Der Wahn und die Träume in W. Jensens "Gradiva" (Leipzig
& Vienna: Heller, 1907); translated by H. M.
Downey as *Delusion and Dream: An Interpretation in
Light of Psychoanalysis of Gradiva, a Novel, by Wilhelm
Jensen* (New York: Moffat, Yard, 1917);

*Über Psychoanalyse: Fünf Volesungen gehalten zur zwanzigjähri-
gen Gründungsfeier der Clark University in Worcester,
Mass., Sept. 1909* (Leipzig & Vienna: Deuticke,
1910);

Eine Kindheitserinnerung des Leonardo da Vinci (Leipzig &
Vienna: Deuticke, 1910); translated by Brill as
*Leonardo da Vinci: A Psychosexual Study of Infantile
Reminiscence* (New York: Moffat, Yard, 1916; Lon-
don: Kegan Paul, Trench, Trübner, 1922);

Sigmund Freud (Bettman Archive; from Paul Roazen, Brother
Animal: The Story of Freud and Tausk, *1969;
Thomas Cooper Library, University
of South Carolina)*

*Totem und Tabu: Einige Übereinstimmungen im Seelenleben der
Wilden under der Neurotiker* (Leipzig & Vienna:
Heller, 1913); translated by Brill as *Totem and
Taboo: Resemblances between the Lives of Savages and
Neurotics* (New York: Moffat, Yard, 1918; Lon-
don: Routledge, 1919);

Vorlesungen zur Einführung in die Psychoanalyse, 3 volumes
(Leipzig & Vienna: Heller, 1916, 1917); translated
by Joan Riviere as *Introductory Lectures on Psycho-
Analysis* (London: Allen & Unwin, 1922); repub-

lished as *A General Introduction to Psychoanalysis* (New York: Boni & Liveright, 1927);

The History of the Psychoanalytic Movement, translated by Brill (New York: Journal of Nervous and Mental Diseases Publishing, 1917); original German version published as *Zur Geschichte der psychoanalytischen Bewegung* (Vienna, Leipzig & Zurich: Internationaler Psychoanalytischer Verlag, 1924);

Reflections on War and Death, translated by Brill and Alfred B. Kuttner (New York: Moffat, Yard, 1918); original German version published as *Zeitgemässes über Krieg und Tod* (Leipzig: Internationaler Psychoanalytischer Verlag, 1924);

Jenseits des Lustprinzips (Vienna, Leipzig & Zurich: Internationaler Psychoanalytischer Verlag, 1920); translated by C. J. M. Hubback as *Beyond the Pleasure Principle* (London & Vienna: International Psychoanalytical Press, 1922; New York: Boni & Liveright, 1922);

Massenpsychologie und Ich-Analyse (Vienna, Leipzig & Zurich: Internationaler Psychoanalytischer Verlag, 1921); translated by James Strachey as *Group Psychology and the Analysis of the Ego* (London & Vienna: International Psychoanalytical Press, 1922; New York: Boni & Liveright, 1922);

Das Ich und das Es (Vienna, Leipzig & Zurich: Internationaler Psychoanalytischer Verlag, 1923); translated by Riviere as *The Ego and the Id* (London: Hogarth Press/Institute of Psychoanalysis, 1927);

Aus der Geschichte einer infantilen Neurose (Leipzig: Internationaler Psychoanalytischer Verlag, 1924);

Beträge zur Psychologie des Liebeslebens (Vienna: Internationaler Psychoanalyticsher Verlag, 1924);

Hemmung, Symptom und Angst (Vienna, Leipzig & Zurich: Internationaler Psychoanalytischer Verlag, 1926); translated by L. P. Clark as *Inhibitions, Symptoms, and Anxiety* (Stamford, Conn.: Psychoanalytic Institute, 1927);

Die Frage der Laienanalyse: Unterredungen mit einem Unparteiischen (Vienna, Leipzig & Zurich: Internationaler Psychoanalytischer Verlag, 1926); translated by A. P. Maerker-Brandon as *The Problem of Lay-Analyses* (New York: Brentano's, 1927);

Die Zukunft einer Illusion (Vienna, Leipzig & Zurich: Internationaler Psychoanalytischer Verlag, 1927); translated by W. D. Robson-Scott as *The Future of an Illusion* (New York: Liveright, 1928);

Das Unbehagen in der Kultur (Vienna: Internationaler Psychoanalytischer Verlag, 1930); translated by Riviere as *Civilization and Its Discontents* (London: Hogarth Press, 1930; New York: Cape & Smith, 1930);

Neue Folge der Vorlesungen zur Einführung in die Psychoanalyse (Vienna: Internationaler Psychoanalytischer Ver-

lag, 1933); translated by W. J. H. Sprott as *New Introductory Lectures on Psycho-analysis* (London: Hogarth Press/Institute of Psychoanalysis, 1933; New York: Norton, 1933);

Warum Krieg? by Freud and Albert Einstein (Paris: Internationales Institut für geistige Zusammenarbeit, 1933); translated by Stuart Gilbert as *Why War?* (Paris: International Institute of Intellectual Cooperation, 1933);

Der Mann Moses und die monotheistische Religion: Drei Abhandlungen (Amsterdam: Verlag Allert de Lange, 1939); translated by Katherine Jones as *Moses and Monotheism* (London: Hogarth Press/Institute of Psychoanalysis, 1939);

An Outline of Psycho-Analysis, translated by James Strachey (London: Hogarth Press, 1949; New York: Norton, 1949; revised, 1969).

Collections: *Sammlung kleiner Schriften zur Neurosenlehre,* 5 volumes (Leipzig & Vienna: Deuticke, 1906–1922); translated by Joan Riviere as *Collected Papers,* 5 volumes, edited by Riviere (London: Hogarth Press/Institute of Psychoanalysis, 1924–1950; New York: Basic Books, 1959);

Gesammelte Schriften, 12 volumes, edited by Anna Freud (Leipzig, Vienna & Zurich: Internationaler Psychoanalytischer Verlag, 1924–1934);

Gesammelte Werke, 18 volumes, edited by Anna Freud (London: Imago, 1940–1953).

Editions in English: *Selected Papers on Hysteria and Other Psychoneuroses,* edited and translated by A. A. Brill (New York: Journal of Nervous and Mental Diseases Publishing, 1909; enlarged, 1912; enlarged again, 1920);

The Standard Edition of the Complete Psychological Works of Sigmund Freud, 24 volumes, translated under the general editorship of James Strachey in collaboration with Anna Freud, assisted by Alix Strachey and Alan Tyson (London: Hogarth Press, 1953–1974)—comprises volume 1, *Pre-psycho-analytic Publications and Unpublished Drafts (1886–1899);* volume 2, *Studies on Hysteria (1893–1895);* volume 3, *Early Psycho-analytic Publications (1893–1899);* volume 4, *The Interpretation of Dreams (First Part) (1900);* volume 5, *The Interpretation of Dreams (Second Part) and On Dreams (1900–1901);* volume 6, *The Psychopathology of Everyday Life (1901);* volume 7, *A Case of Hysteria, Three Essays on Sexuality, and Other Works (1901–1905);* volume 8, *Jokes and Their Relation to the Unconscious (1905);* volume 9, *Jensen's "Gradiva" and Other Works (1906–1908);* volume 10, *Two Case Histories ("Little Hans" and the "Rat Man") (1909);* volume 11, *Five Lectures on Psycho-analysis, Leonardo da Vinci and Other Works (1910);* volume 12, *Case History of Schreber, Papers on Tech-*

nique and Other Works (1911–1913); volume 13, *Totem and Taboo and Other Works (1913–1914);* volume 14, *On the History of the Psycho-analytic Movement, Papers on Metapsychology and Other Works (1914–1916);* volume 15, *Introductory Lectures on Psychoanalysis (Parts One and Two) (1915–1916);* volume 16, *Introductory Lectures on Psycho-analysis (Part Three) (1916–1917);* volume 17, *An Infantile Neurosis and Other Works (1917–1919);* volume 18, *Beyond the Pleasure Principle, Group Psychology and Other Works (1920–1922);* volume 19, *The Ego and the Id and Other Works (1923–1925);* volume 20, *An Autobiographical Study, Inhibitions, Symptoms and Anxiety, The Question of Lay Analysis and Other Works (1925–1926);* volume 21, *The Future of an Illusion, Civilization and Its Discontents and Other Works (1927–1931);* volume 22, *New Introductory Lectures on Psycho-analysis and Other Works (1933–1936);* volume 23, *Moses and Monotheism, An Outline of Psycho-analysis and Other Works (1937–1939);* and volume 24, *Indexes and Bibliographies,* compiled by Angela Richards.

OTHER: "Selbstdarstellung," in *Die Medizin der Gegenwart in Selbstdarstellungen,* edited by L. R. Grote (Leipzig: Meiner, 1925), IV: 1–52; translated as "An Autobiographical Study," in *The Problem of Lay-Analyses* (New York: Brentano's, 1927), pp. 189–316.

In a 1935 postscript to his "Selbstdarstellung" (1925; translated as "An Autobiographical Study," 1927), founder of psychoanalysis Sigmund Freud wrote about the intimate connection between "the story of my life" and "the history of psychoanalysis," while denying the possibility that "personal experiences of mine are of any interest in comparison to my relations with that science." Despite his protestations to the contrary, however, Freud clearly brought much of his life experience not only to his analysis of the individual human psyche but to his contributions to many fields of cultural study: sociology, aesthetics, semiotics, anthropology, philosophy, and even theology.

Sigismund Schlomo Freud was born on 6 May 1856 in Freiberg, a small town in Moravia, which is now Pøíbor in the Czech Republic. He was the son of Jakob Freud, a Jewish wool merchant, and his considerably younger second or third wife, Amalia Nathansohn, a Polish Jew. Although the elder Freud was raised in the Hasidic tradition, he was married to Amalia in a Reform service. During a ten-year period Jakob and Amalia Freud had eight children: Sigismund, Anna, Julius, Rosa, Marie, Adolfine, Pauline, and Alexander. Throughout Freud's childhood the family struggled

financially. Seeking opportunity, the Freuds moved to Leipzig in 1859, and the following year they moved to Vienna. Freud's own version of his family history in "Selbstdarstellung" focuses much more on the migrations of previous generations: "I have reason to believe that my father's family was settled for a long time on the Rhine (at Cologne), that, as a result of a persecution of the Jews during the fourteenth or fifteenth century, they fled eastwards, and that, in the course of the nineteenth century, they migrated back from Lithuania through Galicia into German Austria."

According to *The Life and Work of Sigmund Freud* (1953–1957), by Freud's English disciple Ernest Jones, many of the seminal childhood experiences that Freud analyzes in depth were part of his own private autobiography: aggressive feelings toward a younger sibling rival (at the birth of Julius, who ultimately died in infancy); excited ambivalence at the encounter with his mother's nude body (at age four in a train compartment); a traumatic entry into the parents' bedroom, which Freud later dubbed the "primal scene" (at age seven or eight, when he also urinated in their presence); and other such quintessentially Freudian developmental experiences of sexuality and aggression. Freud also encountered virulent Viennese anti-Semitism in his youth, which profoundly shaped his pessimism about religion and politics as motivating forces in social life.

Biographers know less about the personal details of Freud's adolescence than his childhood. Despite his position of relative financial and ethnic disadvantage, Freud excelled at gymnasium: "I was first in my class for seven years," he wrote in his "Selbstdarstellung." According to Jones, he read Latin, Greek, French, and English, and he taught himself Italian and Spanish to supplement his native German. At age sixteen, in 1872, when visiting his hometown of Freiberg, Freud experienced his first feelings of love, for Gisela Fluss, the sister of a school companion, but the relationship was not a lasting one. He graduated summa cum laude from Sperl Gymnasium in June 1873.

Freud began his studies at the University of Vienna, where he was aware of the heightened anti-Semitism that had followed the collapse of the stock market. As he writes of that time in "Selbstdarstellung," "I have never been able to see why I should feel ashamed of my descent or, as people were beginning to say, of my 'race.'" Freud credits his "independence of judgment" at the university to this hostile environment. In retrospect Freud, in his 1926 essay *Die Frage der Laienanalyse: Unterredungen mit einem Unparteiischen* (translated as *The Problem of Lay-Analyses,* 1927), also describes considerable ambivalence about his choice of a career in medicine:

Freud with his mother, Amalia, and sisters Rosa and Adolfine around 1864 (Omri David Marle; from Ernst Freud, Lucie Freud, and Ilse Grubrich-Simitis, eds., Sigmund Freud: His Life in Pictures and Words, *1978; Thomas Cooper Library, University of South Carolina)*

After forty-one years of medical activity, my self-knowledge tells me that I have never really been a doctor in the proper sense. I became a doctor through being compelled to deviate from my original purpose; and the triumph of my life lies in my having, after a long and roundabout journey, found my way back to my earliest path. I have no knowledge of having had any craving in my early childhood to help suffering humanity. My innate sadistic disposition was not a very strong one, so that I had no need to develop this one of its derivatives. Nor did I ever play the "doctor game"; my infantile curiosity evidently chose other paths. In my youth I felt an overpowering need to understand something of the riddles of the world in which we live and perhaps contribute something to their solution. The most hopeful means of achieving this end seemed to be to enroll myself in the medical faculty; but even after that I experimented–unsuccessfully–with zoology and chemistry.

Stimulated by an interest in Darwinian theory, Freud began his medical research working on evolutionary structures, with a focus on sexual organs and neural structures. He published his first scientific papers, written between 1877 and 1883, on the anatomy of marine animals such as eels and crayfish. Freud credited renowned physiologist Ernst Brücke with dis-

suading him from the unprofitable life of "theoretical interests," while also training Freud in experimental science and laboratory methods. From 1880 to 1881 Freud fulfilled his compulsory military service, which he spent in relative boredom working as a staff physician in peacetime. During this period he translated essays by John Stuart Mill for a German-language edition of Mill's complete works (1869–1880). Despite passing his exams early in his university training, Freud did not receive his medical degree until the spring of 1881.

In April 1882 Freud met Martha Bernays, a young woman from a distinguished Orthodox Jewish family from Bremen. Two months later they were engaged. During the extended engagement that followed, Freud carried on a voluminous and passionate correspondence with his fiancée, from which biographers have learned much about his three years at the General Hospital of Vienna, where he worked in several departments while he nursed his ambitions for greater things. During this period, one so-called opportunity for fame that Freud felt was missed was the discovery of the anesthetic properties of cocaine. Freud first obtained the then-obscure alkaloid in 1884 and authored the paper "Ueber Coca" (On Coca) that same year. Into the mid 1890s he used the drug himself. He claimed to have deduced the properties of the drug as a local anesthetic but said that he failed to publicize his results in his haste to rejoin Bernays. Of the cocaine episode Freud writes in "Selbstdarstellung" that although "it was the fault of my *fiancée* that I was not already famous at that youthful age . . . I bore my *fiancée* no grudge for the interruption."

In spring 1885 Freud was appointed a *dozent* (lecturer) in neuropathology and received a stipend for travel to study clinical hysteria at the Salpêtrière Hospital in Paris, where specialist Jean Martin Charcot gave lectures and dramatic demonstrations with hysterical patients who manifested bizarre symptoms such as paralysis and blindness. Charcot had realized, unlike most of his contemporaries, that the disorder affected men as well as women, despite the traditional association of hysteria with the uterus. Charcot also had discovered that hysteria could respond to treatment by hypnotic suggestion. Freud was impressed by his experiences in France. He translated Charcot's *Leçons sur les maladies du système nerveux, faites a la Salpêtrière* (Lectures on the Diseases of the Nervous System: Delivered at Salpêtrière, 1872) in 1886 and a treatise of Charcot's follower Hippolyte Bernheim, *De la suggestion et de ses applications à la thérapeutique* (On Suggestion and Its Applications to Therapy, 1886), in 1888. After his extended visit to Paris, Freud spent a few weeks in Berlin, where he studied childhood neurological disorders.

Freud produced several monographs on cerebral palsies as a result of this visit, although his first significant publication was his research on hysteria.

In autumn 1886 Freud at last married Bernays. They had six children: Mathilde (1887), Martin (1889), Oliver (1891), Ernst (1892), Sophie (1893), and Anna (1895). His wife ran the household and managed the domestic world of Berggasse 19, the address in Vienna where the Freuds lived from 1891 to 1938. By many accounts Freud was an involved and progressive parent. His correspondence indicates a preoccupation with the childhood illnesses of his offspring and admiration for their precocious wit. Jones's biography includes several anecdotes about Freud's compassionate and good-humored parenting.

Although his home life had been solidly established, the other part of Freud's bourgeois existence, his career, continued to suffer. Colleagues expressed contempt for the revolutionary new ideas about hysteria Freud brought back from study with Charcot. With the help of another important mentor, Josef Breuer, Freud set up his first clinical practice. He quickly abandoned the reigning "electrotherapy" treatment of neurotic patients as ineffective. As Freud writes in his autobiography, "The realization that the work of the greatest name in German neuropathology had no more relation to reality than some 'Egyptian' dream-book, such as is sold in cheap book shops, was painful, but it helped to rid me of another shred of the innocent faith in authority from which I was not yet free." The other method for treating neurotic patients, hypnosis, had certain limitations as well. Freud found a significant number of patients who were entirely resistant to hypnosis, and the remainder could only reach a superficial state. In the summer of 1889 Freud traveled to Nancy, France, in an effort to improve his hypnotic technique, but he only became more discouraged. The hypnotic method seemed to him impractical for private practice and short-lived in its results.

Working with Breuer, Freud discovered another avenue for treatment, which was actually suggested by one of Breuer's patients, "Anna O," a pseudonym for Bertha Pappenheim, who in later life became an important feminist and social reformer. At the time of treatment, the creative and intelligent young woman had become almost totally debilitated by an illness now labeled "somatoform disorder." Her hysterical symptoms included visual impairment, partial paralysis, loss of sensation, and even an inability to speak her own language, German. She experienced a particularly dramatic period of hallucination during 1882, when she hallucinated memories from 1881. To deal with these symptoms, Anna O had devised a system of unrestricted narration with Breuer, what she called "chim-

ney sweeping" and what he called "the talking cure." This uncensored flow of words from what Anna O called "her private theatre" came to be known as "free association" in Freudian theory. Freud praised this method for using hypnotic suggestion while also capitalizing on the articulate activity of the patient's waking state.

Freud further refined free association with his own patients. He described his method as searching for "isolated key-words" that the therapist could "work into sentences" after their appearance in "oracular fashion" from his free-associating subject. Freud argued that the therapist could reconstruct a meaningful psychic narrative, despite the initial "disconnectedness" and "irrelevance" of the patient's vocabulary. Freud had also begun to record his patients' dreams in his diaries of hypnotic sessions, as he did with Frau Emmy Von N., who was analyzed during May 1889. Although *Studien über Hysterie* (1895; translated as "Studies in Hysteria," 1909) introduces dream interpretation in an early footnote, Freud explored the analogy between dreams and mental illness much further in *Die Traumdeutung* (1900; translated as *The Interpretation of Dreams*, 1913).

Despite their pioneering work in free association, Freud and Breuer's *Studien über Hysterie* is a remarkably self-censored final work. According to Freud, the actual reason for terminating Anna O's treatment was her paternity accusation aimed at Breuer after she began to manifest symptoms of a hysterical pregnancy. What Freud later described in a 2 June 1932 letter to Stefan Zweig as Anna O writhing in pain and declaring "Now Dr. B's child is coming!" is significantly omitted in *Studien über Hysterie*. The phenomenon of the patient who falls in love with the analyst proved to be essential in Freud's later theory of transference, but Breuer apparently worried about the effect on his reputation from reporting such an impropriety.

In the accounts of other patients, sexual details are either removed or altered, as Freud's notes to a later edition of *Studien über Hysterie* show. Breuer and Freud present an argument that there is a relationship between "precipitating trauma" and its "idiopathic products" in hysterical patients but censor information. Although many of the women had symptoms related to the trauma of mourning the illness and death of a father after having played sick nurse to him, like Breuer's patient Anna O and Freud's patient Fräulein Elisabeth von R., many others indicated that sexual trauma was central to the etiology of their illness. These patients reported specific incidents of sexual abuse to Breuer and Freud, but their accounts were subject to significant revision before publication. For example, two patients reported sexual advances by fathers, but in the 1895 edition Freud and Breuer present the encounters as

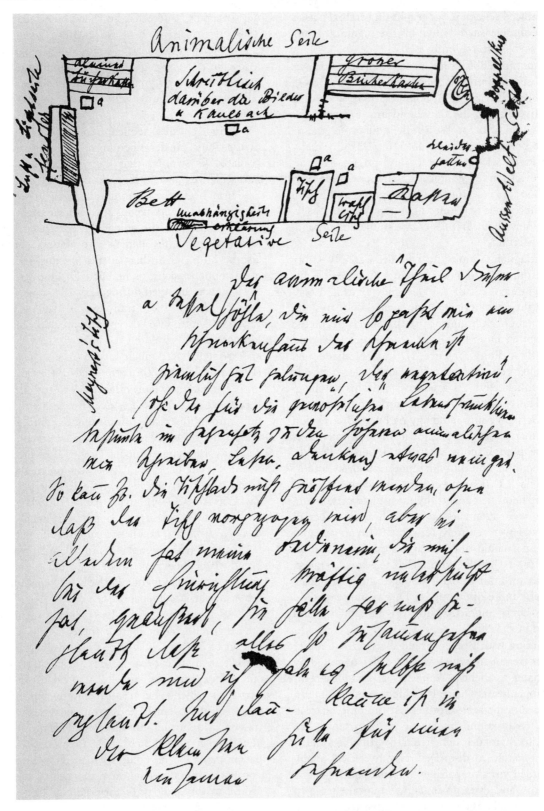

Freud's sketch of his room at the General Hospital of Vienna, where he worked for three years in the 1880s (Sigmund Freud Collection, Manuscript Division, Library of Congress; from Ernst Freud, Lucie Freud, and Ilse Grubrich-Simitis, eds., Sigmund Freud: His Life in Pictures and Words, *1978; Thomas Cooper Library, University of South Carolina)*

though the offenders were uncles to make the incest more remote and less offensive to Victorian readers. According to Jones, Freud claimed to find collaborating with Breuer frustrating, because they were only able to offer a descriptive account of hysterical symptoms and courses of treatment. Freud believed that the book lacked the necessary level of interpretation appropriate to a major theoretical work. Nonetheless, Breuer's part of *Studien über Hysterie* appears to develop many key Freudian concepts: unconscious ideas, hysterical conversion, and the splitting of the psyche in response to trauma.

Freud and Breuer's partnership had already been effectively dissolved in 1894, the year before they published *Studien über Hysterie.* Freud had a new colleague by this time, an eccentric personality that swayed him from the conservatism of Breuer. In 1887 Freud had met Wilhelm Fliess, a Berlin rhinologist, and began an extensive and intimate correspondence from which biographers have learned much. Like Freud, Fliess's interests were wide-ranging. Fliess claimed expertise far beyond his ear, nose, and throat specialty. He was particularly concerned with elaborate schemes for charting biorhythmic human cycles. Fliess was an avid audience for Freud's ideas and made some considerable contributions to Freud's thinking, particularly about the natural bisexuality of all human beings, in which Fliess was a great believer. It proved to be a stormy friendship, however, particularly after 1904, when Fliess accused Freud of stealing his bisexuality theory without due credit. By 1906 Fliess publicly denounced Freud. Freud characterized the relationship as one of mutual homosexual attraction and was wary of intimate friendships with his colleagues afterward.

In April 1896 Freud gave a lecture to the local Society for Psychology and Neurology on "Zur Ätiologie der Hysterie" (The Etiology of Hysteria) and further committed himself to the seduction theory. In the lecture Freud is insistent about the connection between illness and event: "I therefore put forward the thesis that at bottom of every case of hysteria there are *one or more occurrences of premature sexual experience,* occurrences which belong to the earliest years of childhood but which can be reproduced through the work of psychoanalysis in spite of the intervening decades." He had already developed the concept of "overdetermination" the previous year in "A Reply to Criticisms of My Paper on Anxiety Neurosis." In "Zur Ätiologie der Hysterie" he argues that both dreams and hysterical symptoms have multiple causes. Freud still believed at the time that hysteria was primarily caused by sexual trauma, although soon he came to believe that the incestuous encounters described by his hysterical

patients were fantasies invented to express forbidden wishes.

Freud's initial explanation proved important in helping him lay the groundwork of psychoanalysis. He asserted that incidents in the distant past, especially those essential in shaping a patient's sexuality, could disrupt normal functioning by manifesting themselves as symptoms. In short, the hysteric experienced symptoms in the way that normal people experienced memories, Freud and Breuer argued. In the words of *Studien über Hysterie,* "Hysterics suffer mainly from reminiscences." But by September 1897, in a letter to Fliess, Freud was already doubting his female patients' veracity on grounds that "it was hardly credible that perverted acts against children were so general." Later, Freud called these supposedly inaccurate memories of seduction "screen memories" and discussed this phenomenon in an 1899 paper of the same name.

At this point in his life Freud began his famous "self-analysis," which reached its height in 1897 and provided much of the material for his *Die Traumdeutung.* The death of Freud's father, Jakob Freud, in October 1896 was a particularly important event in this process. Through rigorous personal examination and autobiographical review, Freud came to believe that the same forces of desire and repression that operated in his neurotic patients operated in everyone. This process of analyzing the analyst became central to the new discipline of *psychoanalysis,* a term Freud coined in 1896. Freud theorized that although unconscious wishes might not manifest themselves through symptoms in "normal" subjects, these wishes were apparent in a variety of universally experienced phenomena: dreams, jokes, forgetting, and accidental slips of the tongue.

In 1899 Freud published the groundbreaking *Die Traumdeutung.* The book, which was misprinted with a 1900 publication date, sold few copies, received scattered reviews, and did little to help Freud's career, which seemed stalled. Freud had been a *privatdozent* (lecturer) since 1885, despite attempts by many, including noted sexologist Richard von Krafft-Ebing, to acquire a professorship for him.

In spite of its initial reception, *Die Traumdeutung* remains one of Freud's major works in its exploration of the unconscious and the mechanisms of repression that operate upon it. Freud opens the book with a critical review of the scientific literature on dreaming, a contemporary view largely dominated by a focus on internal or external factors that might impact the physiology of the sleeper. Freud critiques these causal hypotheses as reductionist for underestimating the human psyche. He also finds fault with the basic logic of even the most assiduous keepers of dream data. For example, Freud points out that his fellow scientists are

Freud and Martha Bernays the year before their marriage in 1886 (from Ronald W. Clark, Freud: The Man and the Cause, *1980; Thomas Cooper Library, University of South Carolina)*

unable to explain the occurrence of multiple dreams in response to the same single physiological stimulus. Although Freud grants these stimuli some role in dream formation, he relegates them to a minor position. More significant, he claims, are the "day's residues" in dream content: memories about people and events the dreamer has encountered recently. Even these "residues" of the events of the previous day, however, seem to dictate only a portion of scenes that play out in the distorted imagery of dream life.

After reviewing the theories of other scientists, Freud presents an analysis of one of his own dreams, the dream of "Irma's Injection." Freud had treated "Irma" in 1895 before his intense period of self-analysis. In *Die Traumdeutung* he candidly describes his considerable anxiety about providing therapy to someone in his own social circle and his disappointment over the persistence of Irma's symptoms despite his best efforts. In

the dream Irma is in a crowd of medical men. His older mentor Breuer is there, as is Freud's nonconformist contemporary Fliess. In the dream Irma complains of various ailments, and Freud examines her throat, which appears to be grossly diseased. The culprit in the dream is an injection from one of Freud's friends, the pediatrician Oscar Rie. The names of the chemical in the syringe are nonsensical, and the needle is dubbed unclean. The dream, Freud argues, is a wish fulfillment that presents him as "innocent" of Irma's illness.

Dreaming, Freud notes, is a time in which the unconscious has free play without the restrictions of waking rationality. Dreams perform a function for the psyche in allowing the unconscious to express itself. Unlike those who view dreaming as a passive, neutral state, Freud sees the tasks undertaken in the act of dreaming as "dream-work," full of affect and intellectual activity. Freud theorizes that much of the material for dreams actually comes from psychic forces and conflicts experienced much earlier in life and more basic to the dreamer's constitution than the more obvious material from the "day's residues." These unconscious desires are not manifested in easily decodable ways, because even while the dreamer is asleep, repression operates on dream content. In this book Freud first formulates an early version of his well-known equation, expressed in "Selbstdarstellung": "a dream is the (disguised) fulfillment of a (repressed) wish." The terms in parentheses are important for Freud in that, unlike more simplistic approaches to dream analysis, his rebuts the notion that there is a simple one-to-one correspondence between symbol and meaning. Dreams are always overdetermined. For example, Freud argues the presence of a dead person in a dream can have many meanings: a haunting criticism of the sleeper's actions from beyond the grave, a manifestation of the sleeper's previously repressed death wish toward the departed, or even an expression of the sleeper's emotional ambivalence toward the deceased.

Before Freud presents the taxonomy of dreams and corresponding theory of representation that compose the second half of *Die Traumdeutung,* he theorizes that three operations take place in dream-work: "condensation," "displacement," and "secondary revision." Freud uses these processes to explain the relationship between the "manifest" content of the dream that the dreamer experiences while asleep and the "latent" dream content of unconscious wishes. Later in his career Freud revised his interpretations of some types of dreams that had been difficult to analyze with his initial schema. In other words, before Freud had developed theories of the superego or the death drive, it was difficult to locate the wish that would produce a nightmare. For example, in *Die Traumdeutung* Freud presents the category of dreams about failing academic examinations and theorizes that they represent a wish for punishment. He further hypothesizes that many anxiety dreams may be caused by repression in that the sleeper comes too close to the truth in the manifest dream context and must be woken up or frightened away.

The expansive work of *Die Traumdeutung* was greatly abridged in his subsequent 1901 "brochure" *Über den Traum* (translated as *On Dreams*, 1914). The prose style of *Über den Traum* is also quite different: much of it is written in first person, with many informal anecdotes. Freud omits opening with a review of the prevailing literature; instead he explores the dual meaning of the significance of dreams: "It enquires in the first place as to the psychical significance of dreaming, as to the relation of dreams to other mental processes, and as to any biological function they may have; in the second place it seeks to discover whether dreams can be interpreted, whether the content of individual dreams has a 'meaning,' such as we are accustomed to find in other psychical structures." Freud makes the surprising claim that the "popular" view of dreams is actually more accurate than either the "philosophical" view that treats them as transcendental states of awareness or the "medical" view that treats them as somatic functions without psychic significance. To emphasize the transparency of the function of dreams as wish fulfillment, he uses examples from children's dreams about food. He then moves into adult dreams. To explain the mechanisms of displacement, Freud continues with a culinary example from one of his own dreams. In the dream, spinach is being served at the table, and one of his dinner companions, Frau E.L., with whom, Freud says, he was not on intimate terms in real life, places her hand on his knee and admires his eyes. Freud keeps coming back to the dream, which is full of both wish fulfillment and repression, to explain its manifest features. He describes a structure of "condensation, displacement and pictorial arrangement of the psychical materials . . . in such a way that they form an approximately connected whole, a dream-composition."

In February 1902 Freud was finally made a professor under the decree of Emperor Franz Josef, but this event occurred only after he had enlisted powerful friends to appeal to the Austrian bureaucratic administration, which apparently responded only to those with connections. Significantly, this year was also when Freud's long period of isolation came to an end. In the autumn of 1902, according to Jones's biography, Freud addressed a postcard to four men–Alfred Adler, Max Kahane, Rudolf Reitler, and Wilhelm Stekel–suggesting a meeting at his residence to discuss his work and its implications. In this way he began the Vienna Psychoanalytical Society, which was inaugurated as the "Psychological Wednesday Society" in Freud's waiting room. Discussions were reported in the Sunday edition of the *Neues Wiener Tagblatt* (New Viennese Daily).

For many years the group remained small, with Adler as a key member. In 1906 a young Otto Rank, who became well known for his myth analysis, joined the group. That same year, on the occasion of Freud's fiftieth birthday, the Vienna circle presented Freud with a medallion inscribed with a line from Sophocles, commemorating his work with the Riddle of the Sphinx. In 1907 important visiting members came from the prestigious Burghölzli Hospital near Zurich: Freud's initial heir apparent, the Swiss Carl Jung, and German Karl Abraham, who subsequently opened a practice in Berlin. Englishman Ernest Jones, Hungarian Sandor Ferenczi, and American A. A. Brill joined the circle as visiting members the following year.

The years following *Die Traumdeutung* were productive ones for Freud, especially compared to his output of published papers during the previous decade. In these years Freud also began to travel more widely. He considered these voyages as important to his analytic work, particularly the trips between 1901 and 1905 to Greece and Rome, where he went with his brother Alexander and sister-in-law Minna Bernays. His interest in classical antiquities was also heightened by his lifelong friendship with Emanuel Löwy, a professor of archaeology in Rome.

After writing *Die Traumdeutung*, Freud expanded his analysis of phenomena indicating both unconscious wishes and simultaneous repression in more areas of "non-neurotic" life. In 1904 he published *Zur Psychopathologie des Alltagslebens (Über Vergessen, Verspechen, Vergreifen, Aberglaube und Irrtum)* (translated as *The Psychopathology of Everyday Life*, 1914) and in 1905 *Der Witz und seine Beziehung zum Unbewussten* (translated as *Wit and Its Relation to the Unconscious*, 1916), two books that continued his work in this vein. *Zur Psychopathologie des Alltagslebens* is organized with a heading for each of the following "normal" dysfunctions: "Vergessen von Eigennamen" (The Forgetting of Proper Names), "Vergessen von fremdsprachigen Worten" (The Forgetting of Foreign Words), "Vergessen von Namen und Wortfolgen" (The Forgetting of Names and Sets of Words), (Über Kindheits- und Deckerinnerungen" (On Childhood Memories and Screen Memories), "Das Versprechen" (Slips of the Tongue), "Verlesen und Verschreiben" (Misreadings and Slips of the Pen), "Vergessen von Eindrückken und Vorsätzen" (The Forgetting of Impressions and Intentions), "Das Vergreifen" (Bungled Actions), "Symtom- und Zufallshandlungen" (Symptomatic and Chance Actions), "Irrtümer" (Errors), and "Kombinierte Gesichtespunkte" (Combined Paraphraxes). Much of the human fallibility that

STUDIEN

ÜBER

HYSTERIE

VON

Dr. JOS. BREUER und Dr. SIGM. FREUD

IN WIEN.

———————•———————

LEIPZIG UND WIEN.

FRANZ DEUTICKE.

1895.

Title page for Freud and Josef Breuer's early work (translated as "Studies in Hysteria," 1909) that develops key Freudian concepts such as unconscious ideas, hysterical conversions, and the splitting of the psyche (Sigmund Freud Collection, Manuscript Division, Library of Congress; from Ernst Freud, Lucie Freud, and Ilse Grubrich-Simitis, eds., Sigmund Freud: His Life in Pictures and Words, *1978; Thomas Cooper Library, University of South Carolina)*

Freud describes is derived from his own experiences: being unable to recall the name of an artist, forgetting the name of a small country, scrambling the name of a railway station, altering the name of a doorkeeper in a misremembered quotation. The book closes with the chapter "Determinismus, Zufalls- und Aberglauben, Gesichtespunkte" (Determinism, Belief in Chance, and Superstition), in which Freud lays the groundwork for his later attacks on religious belief and occult thinking: "Conscious ignorance and unconscious knowledge of the motivation of accidental psychical events is one of the psychical roots of superstition." Freud insists that "incompletely suppressed psychical material," rather than supernatural forces, is to blame for otherwise mysterious events.

Der Witz und seine Beziehung zum Unbewussten, like *Die Traumdeutung,* opens with a review of the existing literature. From previous writers on the topic of humor, Freud presents a catalogue of features that characterize jokes: "activity, relation to the content of our thoughts, the characteristic of playful judgment, the coupling of dissimilar things, contrasting ideas, 'sense in nonsense,' the succession of bewilderment and enlightenment, the bringing forward of what is hidden, and the peculiar brevity of wit." Jokes, he argues, manifest a similar structure of condensation, displacement, and representation to that of dreams. After detailing "the technique of jokes" in the second part of the book, Freud progresses to "the purposes of jokes," explaining how "the methods of joke-work are able to excite pleasure." Jokes, Freud argues, can be characterized as either "hostile jokes" for the purposes of aggression or "obscene jokes" for the purposes of exposure. Jokes thereby serve as "psychical reliefs" and can, like dreams, give pleasure. Unlike dreams, jokes often express more proximate egoistic, jealous, or hostile impulses and are less closely related to infantile wish fulfillment. Jokes serve social purposes as well by liberating psychic energy and facilitating "discharge." As part of a social process, jokes mediate between both a "first person" and a "third person" to create a "Janus-like two-way-facing character."

Freud wrote his book on humor simultaneously with *Drei Abhandlungen zur Sexualtheorie* (translated as *Three Contributions to the Sexual Theory,* 1910), which also appeared in 1905. Unlike *Die Traumdeutung, Drei Abhandlungen zur Sexualtheorie* received considerable public notice at its initial printing. Jones describes widespread consternation as the result of Freud's published "assertion that children are born with sexual urges, which undergo a complicated development before they attain the familiar adult form, and that their first sexual objects are their parents." Furthermore, in this work Freud shows little care for the distinction between "normal" and "perverse" sexuality that was essential to the work of contemporaries such as Krafft-Ebing.

Drei Abhandlungen zur Sexualtheorie is divided into three sections: "Die sexuellen Abirrungen" (The Sexual Aberrations), "Die infantile Sexualität" (Infantile Sexuality), and "Die Umgestaltungen der Pubertät" (The Transformations of Puberty). In treating the subject of sexual aberration Freud distinguishes between deviations in "sexual object" (relating to specific persons and things) and deviations in "sexual aim" (relating to the gratification sought by the sexual instinct). In the former group, he discusses the "sexual inversions" of homosexuals and bisexuals in what contemporary audiences might see as relatively nonjudgmental language, since Freud depicts homosexuals as individuals who may be "quite sound in other respects." In contrast, those whose sexual objects are children or animals suffer from a "cheapening" of the sexual object that is much more clearly pathological, although Freud asserts the importance of including their activities in the work to emphasize the variety of sexual objects in human beings. The part of the essay that addresses deviancy of sexual aim describes perversions that involve gratification other than genital satisfaction. Freud discusses oral, anal, and visual fixations, as well as those that involve aggressive drives rather than sexual ones, such as sadism and masochism.

In his essay "Infantile Sexuality" Freud stresses how sexual variety in both aim and object is an innate human characteristic. Although he describes childhood as a period of "sexual latency," it is clearly not exclusively presexual. Thumb sucking and autoeroticism point to the importance of "erotogenic zones" and the corresponding sexual aim to achieve satisfaction through stimulation. Masturbatory activity, Freud asserts, can often be associated with normal anal and urinary activities. Moreover, Freud does not present sexual development as a clear pattern of constant progress toward adult sexuality; rather, he argues that sexual development moves in phases that are characterized by regression and amnesia. Freud also explores the logic of children's own theories about sexuality and reproduction. In fact, as a general rule in Freud's writing, the nonscientific thinking of children is often presented as more "logical" than similar attitudes manifested by religious adults.

At the end of the section on infantile sexuality, Freud presents the myth of the Riddle of the Sphinx and begins to sketch out the parameters of his new theory of the Oedipus complex, which by then had supplanted the seduction theory of his earlier work in hysteria. Freud sketches out very different developmental profiles for boys and girls as infantile sexuality draws to a close: boys experience a "castration complex," while girls experience "penis envy." Although both sexes go through the first "oral phase" (or "cannibalistic phase") and the second "anal-sadistic phase," the sexes are distinguished during the third "phallic phase," based on their relationship to the male member. Even after the most successful transitions to adulthood, however, Freud claims that the choice of object and aim in mature sexuality is not reached without "ambivalence."

In the final essay, "The Transformations of Puberty," Freud develops the idea of "fore-pleasure," in which sexual tension and associations with preludes to sexual stimuli can have negative consequences if fixations are formed that inhibit development. Although Freud gives space to anatomical and chemical theories of human sexuality, his focus is on the "libido theory" of sexuality, in which psychical mechanisms control the interaction of ego and object. "This ego-libido is, however, only conveniently accessible to analytic study when it has been put to the use of cathecting sexual objects, that is, when it has become object-libido."

For Freud, sexual development is always critical to the social development of individuals. In these essays he theorizes that object-love in infancy, which pursues an incestuous object, must be overcome in puberty through repression. In particular, boys must overcome their Oedipal attachments to their mothers and experience anxiety about castration. At the same time they must preserve their competitive feelings about their fathers to prevent their sexuality from "inverting" toward homosexual relations. Relatively little is said about female sexual identity and femininity, a topic that Freud picks up again in later works, the essay "Über die weibliche Sexualität" (Female Sexuality, 1931) and the lecture "Über Weiblichkeit" (Femininity, 1933).

In 1901 Freud wrote the paper "Dreams and Hysteria," which indicated substantial changes in his thinking about the role of seduction in hysterical illness. The larger case study with which he was working was not published until 1905, when it appeared in an issue of *Monatsschriften für Psychiatrie und Neurologie* (Monthly Reviews of Psychiatry and Neurology) as "Bruchstück einer Hysterie-Analyse" (Fragment of an Analysis of a Case of Hysteria) with a preface that explains its delay in publication as an attempt to protect his patient's privacy. In this case history Freud analyzes an eighteen-year-old patient, "Dora," who suffers from a hysterical cough, along with many more debilitating symptoms. In therapy Freud's investigations reveal multiple love triangles in Dora's domestic arrangements: Dora's father has been having an affair with Frau K., to whom Dora has felt some homosexual attraction, while the woman's husband, Herr K., has made sexual advances toward Dora.

Freud's analysis consists of close work with two dreams. In one dream Dora's house is on fire and her mother and father are arguing about whether or not to save her mother's jewel case. In the other dream Dora must get home for the funeral of her father, and the relationship between the words *bahnhoft* (train station) and *friedhof* (cemetery) is of central importance. In his analysis Freud draws Dora's attention to the sexual slang associated with key terms in the dreams: jewel case, train station, and cemetery, which in German all relate to the female genitalia. He also presupposes her masturbatory activity and her knowledge of oral sexual gratification, to which he theorizes her hysterical cough is related.

With his earlier hysterical patients, Freud had considered the sexual overture of an older male to a young

DIE

TRAUMDEUTUNG

VON

DR. SIGM. FREUD.

FLECTERE SI NEQUEO SUPEROS, ACHERONTA MOVEBO.

LEIPZIG UND WIEN.
FRANZ DEUTICKE.
1900.

Title page for Freud's study (translated as The Interpretation of
Dreams, *1913) based on material derived from a rigorous
process of "self-analysis" (Sigmund Freud Copyrights, Ltd.,
London; from Ernst Freud, Lucie Freud, and Ilse
Grubrich-Simitis, eds.,* Sigmund Freud:
His Life in Pictures and Words,
*1978; Thomas Cooper Library,
University of South Carolina)*

female patient to be a traumatic event. In his recounting of the Dora case, however, Freud seems to argue that Dora should have seriously considered Herr K.'s merits as a prospective sexual partner, because he deems it unhealthy for Dora to repress her natural arousal and her understandable displacement of Oedipal attachments. Freud acknowledges the domestic sexual hypocrisy against which Dora revolts, but at the same time he encourages her to accept her assigned lot. Given Freud's advice, Dora abruptly terminated therapy.

The case is also significant in that Freud has to explain Dora's decision to abort therapy without diminishing his authority as an analyst. Therefore, "Bruchstück einer Hysterie-Analyse" also presents Freud's most fully developed thinking about a patient's "resistance" in the analytical situation. Feelings toward the therapist, Freud claims, are always ambivalent and can be expressed by either hostile resistance or loving transference. Moreover, in this fragment Freud is forced to critically examine his own role in Dora's decision to abort therapy, which he refuses to attribute to any misinterpretations or faulty advice. By examining the workings of the analyst's unconscious feelings in particular, part of a phenomenon that he came to call "countertransference," both successes and failures in the analytic situation could be better understood.

In contrast to his work with Dora, Freud's case histories of male patients report decisive analytical successes. In October 1907 he began treatment of an obsessive patient, whose analysis grew into the case history of "The Rat Man" or "Bemerkungen über einen Fall von Zwangsneurose" (Notes upon a Case of Obsessional Neurosis), which first appeared in the *Jahrbuch für psychoanalytische und psychopathologische Forschungen* (Yearbook for Psychoanalytic and Psychopathological Research) in 1909. During the account of his free association, this rat-fixated army officer admits to a nexus of obsessions in which the rat serves as a symbol of sexual disease, sexual organs, money, and even himself. In this case history Freud delineates between "obsession" and "compulsion" while arguing that they are part of the same disorder. The case is also important in that Freud yet again makes an explicit connection between normal function and mental illness: "Obsessional ideas, as is well known, have an appearance of being either without motive or without meaning, just as dreams do." Although the Rat Man's neurosis represents a form of "regression," his symptoms can be logically explained as the intrusion of the young man's father complex as he courts prospective women for marriage. Freud is even able to break through the Rat Man's superstitious associations by presenting rational, cause-and-effect psychoanalytic explanations, so that the Rat Man can see wish fulfillment in operation rather than imagined supernatural factors.

In 1908 Freud began treatment of five-year-old "Little Hans," the son of musicologist and personal friend Max Graf and one of Freud's former female patients. This case history was published in the *Jahrbuch für psychoanalytische und psychopathologische Forschungen* in 1909 as "Analyse der Phobie eines fünfjährigen Knaben" (Analysis of a Phobia in a Five-Year-Old Boy). In the beginning of the case history Little Hans suffers from an intense phobia about horses, which has not been solved despite his father's analytical interventions. Freud rarely worked with children, but he also believed such cases had great theoretical import. In children, Freud theorized, general principles of wish fulfillment and repression should be more easily observed by the analyst. The case would also provide "proof" to respond to critics of *Drei Abhandlungen zur Sexualtheorie.* As Freud writes, "My impression is that the picture of a child's sexual life presented in this observation of little Hans agrees very well with the account I gave of it (basing my views upon psychoanalytic examinations of adults) in my *Three Essays.*" In the case of Hans, Freud quickly identifies Hans's sexual desire for his mother, hostility toward his father, and Hans's own autoerotic preoccupations. In his discussion of the case history, Freud defends the work against two anticipated objections: the argument that his patient is biologically predisposed to neuroses so that family dynamics play no role in his illness, and the charge that his analysis lacks objectivity because the involvement of the father inserts Freudian suggestion in his son's "free" association. After disposing of these objections Freud moves into a larger defense of the patient's central role in psychoanalysis, regardless of age or even the initial credibility of the testimony offered:

The arbitrary has no existence in mental life. The untrustworthiness of the assertions of children is due to the predominance of their imagination, just as the untrustworthiness of the assertions of grown-up people is due to the predominance of their prejudices. For the rest, even children do not lie without a reason, and on the whole they are more inclined to a love of truth than are their elders. If we were to reject little Hans's statements root and branch we should certainly be doing him a grave injustice.

During the years he was working on these case histories, Freud also published papers on applied psychoanalysis: "Zwangshandlungen und Religionsübungen" (Obsessive Acts and Religious Practices, 1907), first published in *Zeitschrift für Religionspsychologie* (Journal for the Psychology of Religion), in which neurosis serves as a "private religious system" and religion serves as a "universal obsessional neurosis"; "Charakter und Analerotik" (Character and Anal Eroticism), published in *Psychiatrisch-neurologische Wochenschrift* (Psychiatric-Neurological Weekly Revue) in 1908, in which he details the features of the anal-retentive personality; and "Der Dichter und das Phantasieren" (The Relation of the Poet to Daydreaming), published in the *Neue Revue* (10 March 1908), in which he argues that though creative works represent displacements of the artist's private fantasies, these works give an audience more pleasure than straightforward representation of personal fantasies because the audience experiences "fore-pleasure" in appreciation of the author's artistic technique.

Freud also expanded his work on cultural criticism during this period. In "Die 'kulturelle' Sexualmoral und die moderne Nervosität" ("Civilized" Sexual Morality

First page of Freud's case history of Dora in the Monatsschriften für Psychiatrie und Neurologie *(1905), in which he uses dream analysis to alleviate an eighteen-year-old woman's hysterical symptoms (Sigmund Freud Collection, Manuscript Division, Library of Congress; from Ernst Freud, Lucie Freud, and Ilse Grubrich-Simitis, eds.,* Sigmund Freud: His Life in Pictures and Words, *1978; Thomas Cooper Library, University of South Carolina)*

and Modern Nervousness), published in *Sexual-Probleme: Zeitschrift für sexualwissenschaft und sexualpolitik* (Sexual Disorders: Journal of Sexual Science and Sexual Politics) in 1908, he sets the stage for his extended argument of two decades later, *Das Unbehagen in der Kultur* (1930; translated as *Civilization and Its Discontents,* 1930). In "Die 'kulturelle' Sexualmoral und die moderne Nervosität" what Freud calls "the glorification of monogamy" works against both the natural operations of Darwinian natural selection and the values of objective truth by creating a "double morality" for those who cannot abide by repressive sexual regulation. The stimulating conditions of modern life with its urban living, consumer culture, and mass communication only exacerbate these tensions. He rejects arguments from other sexologists that focus on a lack of "sexual hygiene" as a culprit and who link the prevalence of neurosis to inherited disease. He also challenges the view that sexual aims are naturally linked to procreation rather than pleasure. Civilization, he argues, is founded on the suppression of instincts and therefore is the logical causal agent in modern neurotic disorders.

Freud's first critical works on specific pieces of art and literature began to appear as part of his interest in applied psychoanalysis during this period. In 1907 he published *Der Wahn und die Träume in W. Jensens "Gradiva"* (translated as *Delusion and Dream: An Interpretation in Light of Psychoanalysis of Gradiva, a Novel, by Wilhelm Jensen,* 1917), a literary analysis of a popular 1903 novel about Pompeii, in which an archaeologist falls in love with the excavated image of a young and beautiful girl. Freud examines the role of dreams, delusions, ambiguous speeches, and a character who seems to play the role of analyst in this fictional text. He also criticizes Jensen as an author who "quite arbitrarily tacked a love story onto his archeological fantasy." In fact, in *Der Wahn und die Träume in W. Jensens "Gradiva"* Freud argues that the author is expressing his own subconscious wishes for unity with a lost love object. Freud corresponded with Jensen and was gratified to learn some of the history of an early infatuation that fit his hypothesis, but was generally frustrated by his attempts to psychoanalyze such a remote patient. In a 1912 postscript Freud describes the author as one who "refused his cooperation" in research.

In this same vein, Freud's 1910 work on Leonardo da Vinci, *Eine Kindheitserinnerung des Leonardo da Vinci* (translated as *Leonardo da Vinci: A Psychosexual Study of Infantile Reminiscence,* 1916), explores how art that represents sexual ambivalence could be created by da Vinci's unusual family situation as an illegitimate child. Freud sees the artist expressing this ambivalence in two famous paintings of the baby Jesus in which two mothers are depicted on the same canvas. Although it is conventional in religious art to show the infant Jesus with the Virgin Mary and another female saint, Freud argues these paintings express a particular idealization of a family organization with two loving and yet interchangeable mothers. Freud also discusses the androgyny of the figures in da Vinci's artwork, da Vinci's scientific interests in bisexuality as they were expressed in drawings about the reproductive organs, the artist's obsessional accounting, and an entry in Leonardo's notebooks about a childhood recollection of an oral encounter with a vulture's tail to develop Freud's hypothesis about the particular character of da Vinci's homosexuality. According to James Strachey's editorial notes, this essay revisits Freud's debates

about bisexuality with Fliess but rebuts many of his former friend's ideas.

In September 1909 Freud traveled to the United States with an international group of psychoanalysts and gave a series of lectures at Clark University in Worcester, Massachusetts, where he received an honorary doctorate. The trip included a visit with William James, the Harvard philosopher-psychologist, who was nearing the end of his life. Franz Boas and Adolf Meyer were also in the audience. The Clark lectures were largely improvised; each morning before, they were rehearsed on a stroll with Ferenczi. They were subsequently published as *Über Psychoanalyse: Fünf Volesungen gehalten zur zwanzigjährigen Gründungsfeier der Clark University in Worcester, Mass., Sept. 1909* (1910; translated as *Five Lectures on Psycho-Analysis, Leonardo da Vinci and Other Works* in volume 11 of *The Standard Edition of the Complete Psychological Works of Sigmund Freud,* 1957), a collection that showcases Freud's mastery of analogy as a rhetorical technique. For example, he draws a comparison between the commemorative function of medieval Charing Cross or the monument to the 1666 Great Fire of London and the illnesses suffered by hysterical patients:

> These monuments, then, resemble hysterical symptoms in being mnemic symbols; up to that point the comparison seems justifiable. But what should we think of a Londoner who paused to-day in deep melancholy before the memorial of Queen Eleanor's funeral instead of going about his business in the hurry that modern working conditions demand or instead of feeling joy over the youthful queen of his own heart? Or again what should we think of a Londoner who shed tears before the Monument that commemorates the reduction of his beloved metropolis to ashes although it has long since risen again in far greater brilliance? Yet every single hysteric and neurotic behaves like these two unpractical Londoners.

The American lectures cover the trajectory of Freud's published writings. They open with a tribute to the legacy of Breuer, move through the essential concepts of psychoanalysis (such as study of dream-work, repression, and resistance), develop the case for infantile sexuality, and close with discussion of applied psychoanalysis and cultural criticism. Jung and the Zurich school are mentioned approvingly, although–in retrospect–Freud saw the American trip as the beginning of the end of his close association with Jung. Freud had fainted in Jung's presence in Bremen, just before they boarded the ship for the United States. Freud later ominously associated this fainting spell with an episode of fainting in front of Jung that took place in November 1912.

Freud was already conscious that psychoanalytic vocabulary and techniques were being misapplied as the process of popularization continued. "Über 'wilde' Psychoanalyse" (Concerning "Wild" Psychoanalysis), published in the *Zentralblatt für Psychoanalyse* (Central Newsletter for Psychoanalysis) in 1910, presents the comic situation of a divorced woman who comes to Freud's practice because she has been advised by her young physician that she must either return to her husband, take a lover, or undertake a regime of masturbation; meanwhile, the prospective patient's elderly female companion points out her respectable and non-neurotic widowhood as proof counter to the physician's recommendation. Freud contends that this dilemma shows how a new generation of pseudopractitioners have been applying the terms of psychoanalysis too broadly, while at the same time imagining human sexuality itself too narrowly.

In the years before World War I, the psychoanalytic community grew from two major centers: Vienna and Zurich. After a congress of "friends of psychoanalysis" on 26 April 1908 in Salzburg, the first psychoanalytic periodical, *Jahrbuch für psychoanalytische und psychopathologische Forschungen*, began publication. The Second International Psycho-Analytical Congress took place at Nuremberg on 30–31 March 1910. To counter the influence of Swiss non-Jews, who now held top positions in the new International Psycho-Analytical Association, Stekel and Adler founded the Viennese *Zentralblatt für Psychoanalyse*, the first number of which appeared in October 1910. The following year Rank and Hanns Sachs founded another Viennese journal, *Imago*, which was devoted to the application of psychoanalysis to the cultural sciences. Freud's essays on art, literature, and myth often first appeared in *Imago*.

In September 1911 the Weimar congress was held, and a significant number of female analysts attended. One of the women, who played a major role in Freud's later life, was the writer Lou Andreas-Salomé, who had counted among her other illustrious friends Ivan Turgenev, Leo Tolstoy, August Strindberg, Auguste Rodin, Rainer Maria Rilke, Arthur Schnitzler, and Friedrich Nietzsche. At this point in the history of psychoanalysis, Freud had encountered little criticism from female analysts in the young movement. His saying "Anatomy is destiny," which is credited to Napoleon in Freud's 1912 essay "Über die allgemeinste Erniedrigung des Liebeslebens" (On the Universal Tendency to Debasement in the Sphere of Love; first published in the *Jahrbuch für psychoanalytische und psychopathologische Forschungen*), is not used as an affirmation of traditional gender roles but as a critique of the attempts of civilization to control the natural impulses of the human animal.

In the 1911 *Jahrbuch für psychoanalytische und psychopathologische Forschungen* Freud published "Formulierun-

Title page for Freud's study (translated as Three Contributions to the Sexual Theory, *1910) that created outrage by asserting that children have sexual urges (Sigmund Freud Copyrights, Ltd., London; from Ernst Freud, Lucie Freud, and Ilse Grubrich-Simitis, eds.,* Sigmund Freud: His Life in Pictures and Words, *1978; Thomas Cooper Library, University of South Carolina)*

gen über die Zwei Prensipien des psychischen Geschehens" (Formulations Regarding Two Principles of Mental Functioning), which laid the initial groundwork of his metapsychology. In this essay he characterizes two principles in mental life: "the pleasure principle," which involves the seeking of pleasure, and "the reality principle," which involves the avoidance of pain. Freud lists a range of strategies for balancing the interests of the two principles in the essay: the institution of attention with a system of notation known as memory; the preservation of daydreaming as the continuation of earlier fantasy-making, in accordance with the economic principle of conserving pleasure; the association of sexual instincts with fantasy and ego instincts with consciousness; the renunciation of pleasure either incompletely through religion or more effectively through science; education as the substitution of the principle of reality for pleasure; art as a reconciliation of the two principles; the transformation of the pleasure-ego to the reality-ego in stages from original autoeroticism to "object-love in the service of procreation"; and the analytical situation of therapy itself, in which Freud argues "one is bound to employ the currency that prevails in the country one is exploring."

Freud also published another case history in the 1911 *Jahrbuch für psychoanalytische und psychopathologische Forschungen,* "Psychoanalytische Berkungen über einen autobiographich beschriebenen Fall von Paranoia (Dementia Paranoides)" (Psychoanalytic Notes upon an Autobiographical Case of Paranoia [Dementia Paranoides]). Like his work on da Vinci, this case history was done without ever actually having met the patient; it was based on reading the 1903 autobiography of Daniel Paul Schreber, *Denkwürdigkeiten eines Nervenkranken* (translated as *Memoirs of My Nervous Illness,* 1955), in which the once well-respected jurist and former candidate for the Reichstag records his grandiose delusions while hospitalized for insanity in the Leipzig Psychiatric Hospital. Schreber suffered from four separate bouts of mental illness during his life but could be a lucid author during the intervening periods. The delusions he describes in his narrative include bouts of persecution by his physician or "soul murderer," the presence of "nerve contacts" in his body that could receive divine messages, and the belief that he could fulfill his mission to redeem the world if he were first transformed into a woman. Schreber's full-blown delusional state is characterized by hallucinations about being the wife of God. It is worth noting that Schreber also describes some obsessive symptoms involving evacuation and feces. This case history is unique for Freud in presenting a psychotic rather than a neurotic patient, although—as in his other case histories of male patients—Freud locates a father complex in Schreber and the structure of wish fulfillment in his delusional fantasies. In examining Schreber's mix of religious and transsexual fantasies, Freud sees the judge's fantasies of submission being played out. Freud also takes the opportunity to point out the feminine character of religious belief in general. In the case of Schreber, Freud also begins to move beyond his earlier case histories by attempting to elucidate the psychic structures and instinctual functions at work in clinical paranoia. By presenting a scenario in which the "normal" relationship of the ego to the "real" world has utterly deteriorated, Freud is beginning to articulate his views about the ego as a provisional structure under threat.

During this time Freud was working on his most ambitious work of anthropology, *Totem und Tabu: Einige Übereinstimmungen im Seelenleben der Wilden under der Neurotiker* (translated as *Totem and Taboo: Resemblances between the Lives of Savages and Neurotics,* 1918), which did not appear until 1913. Some related speculative papers about the horrors of incest had appeared earlier in *Imago,* but *Totem und Tabu* fully develops a revolutionary theory about the origins of human society that critic Peter Gay has compared to that of Jean-Jacques Rousseau in its philosophical scope. Although Freud uses the work of James George Frazer on totemism as a reference point in the essay, biographer Jones points out that as far back as the case of Little Hans and his phobia about horses Freud had been concerned with "the unconscious significance of animals and the totemistic equation between them and the idea of a father." The book begins with taboos and ends with totems. In *Totem und Tabu* Freud recounts a prehistory of mankind in which Oedipal aggression is actually enacted rather than fantasized. Freud uses the Darwinian image of the primal horde that is controlled by a powerful male who has appropriated all the females. This primal father is a tyrant, who is killed by his sons in an act of originary violence. The power of the father is not vanquished, however, in that the cultural institutions, which are founded after the death of this father, originate in guilt and perpetuate the father's dominance through law. Like later French structuralists, such as the anthropologist Claude Lévi-Strauss, Freud also argues that totemism and exogamy were closely related. After the publication of *Totem und Tabu,* Freud was subject to much criticism, particularly since the book alludes to Lamarckian evolutionary ideas about inheriting acquired traits, which had already been discredited. The book received negative reviews from British anthropologists, who dismissed it as a "just-so" story by a nonprofessional.

The same year, Freud delivered a paper that capitalized on his aesthetic interests in English literature, by working with the plays of another one of his favorite creative writers, William Shakespeare. "Das Motiv der Kätschenwahl" (The Theme of the Three Caskets), published in *Imago* in 1913, discusses *The Merchant of Venice* (circa 1596–1597), in which suitors of the heroine, Portia, are asked to choose between three caskets of gold, silver, and lead in order to win her hand; her last, and favored, suitor, Bassanio, chooses the lead casket, which—despite its unpromising appearance—contains the treasure he is seeking, thus making matrimony possible for the two of them. Freud points out that in myth and folklore the choice among three objects is usually presented as a man choosing among three women, as it is for King Lear or Paris. Although he notes the fact that these three elements have astral analogues with the sun, moon, and stars, Freud resists an interpretation that depends on a transcendental archetype. Freud points out, "we do not share the belief of many investi-

Freud (seated at left) at Clark University in Worcester, Massachusetts, where he gave a series of lectures in 1909, with (seated) G. Stanley
Hall, Carl Gustav Jung, (standing) A. A. Brill, Ernest Jones, and Sandor Ferenczi (from Wayne Gilbert Rollins,
Jung and the Bible, 1983; Thomas Cooper Library, University of South Carolina)

gators that myths were read off direct from the heavens; we are more inclined to judge with Otto Rank that they were projected on the heavens after having arisen quite otherwise under purely human conditions." The leaden casket of Bassanio, like the dumb Aphrodite or the uncommunicative Cordelia, represents the choice of death, Freud claims. This choice of death is the ultimate example of what Freud calls "reaction-formation," in which mental life fosters replacement of something by its opposite.

By this point in his career, Freud had survived a series of schisms with former followers and correspondents: he broke with Adler in 1911, Stekel in 1912, and Jung in 1913. Within the international psychoanalytic movement, much of the same language that had been used to describe patients' pathologies was turned on colleagues. Analysts in competing circles accused each other of paranoia, narcissism, Oedipal hostilities, and homosexual attachments. At the time Freud also believed Jung was diluting his theory of the libido and denying its specific association with sexual aims and objects by describing it as a more general instinctual

force. At the Munich conference in 1913, divisions between the Swiss and the Viennese became insuperable. Two-fifths of the attendees abstained from reelecting Jung. The following April, Jung resigned the presidency of the International Psycho-Analytical Association. Freud became sole director of the *Jahrbuch*, and Jung was removed from his editorial position.

Jung withdrew from the association entirely after Freud published *Zur Geschichte der psychoanalytischen Bewegung* (translated as *The History of the Psychoanalytic Movement*, 1917) in the *Jahrbuch der Psychoanalyse* (Yearbook of Psychoanalysis) in 1914. The German-language version of the essay was published in book form in 1924. In this essay Freud distances himself from his former mentor Breuer and his early "cathartic procedures," while also attacking the recent work of former disciples such as Adler and Jung. Freud opens the book by asserting that psychoanalysis is his personal creation and claims, "I consider myself justified in maintaining that even to-day no one can know better than I do what psychoanalysis is." Repression, Freud maintains, is a "premise," not a "finding," of psychoanalysis. Moreover, he accuses his

Freud and his daughter Anna in the Dolomite Mountains, 1913
(from Ronald W. Clark, Freud: The Man and the Cause,
1980; Thomas Cooper Library, University of South Carolina)

former colleagues of denying the sexual character of neuroses and even the libido itself. He maintains that their dilution of his theories consequently weakens the theoretical force of the movement: "Men are strong as long as they represent a strong idea; they will become powerless when they oppose it. Psycho-analysis will survive this loss and gain new adherents in place of these."

About the same time that Freud was reaching conclusions about his own ambivalence toward his followers, he examined the relationship of Moses to the Israelites in a paper that was initially published anonymously in *Imago*. Like his essay on da Vinci, "Der Moses des Michelangelo" (The Moses of Michelangelo, 1914) analyzes a specific work of art by a homosexual Italian Renaissance artist. In this essay, however, Freud's attention is on the subject represented in the artwork rather than the artist himself. From the position of layman rather than art historian, he focuses more on his own reactions to the aesthetic object rather than the

motivations of the artist. After presenting a range of contradictory interpretations from art historians, Freud presents his own reading of the sculpture. He argues Moses is both eager to share with his followers and angry with them for their infidelity. Moses is depicted in a moment of transition between bringing the tablets to his people and reacting to the spectacle of their celebration of the golden calf. Although Freud does not present his own motivations for his attraction to the statue, critics have argued that Freud was a similarly conflicted leader. He returned again to the ambivalence of the figure of Moses late in his career in the controversial *Der Mann Moses und die monotheistische Religion: Drei Abhandlungen* (1939; translated as *Moses and Monotheism,* 1939).

Freud also devoted attention to metapsychology. His initial opposition of the "pleasure principle" and the "reality principle" was first significantly revised in 1914 in his paper "Zur Einführung des Narzissmus" (On Narcissism: An Introduction), published in the *Jahrbuch für psychoanalytische und psychopathologische Forschungen* for that year, in which he argues that the libidinal drive could merely be considered a variant of the drive for self-preservation. He also uses this essay to rebut Jung's monism by returning to the Schreber case. Freud posits the existence of an "ego ideal" that develops in response to criticism. In pathological development this ego ideal becomes the delusion of "being watched," as in the Schreber case, but in normal development the guardian of the ego ideal, the conscience, serves this purpose.

Revision of the model of the two principles continued in "Triebe und Triebschicksale" (Instincts and Their Vicissitudes), which appeared in the *Zentralblatt für Psychoanalyse* in 1915. "Triebe und Triebschicksale" attempts to develop the scientific structure of psychoanalysis while also acknowledging its limits as a young science. In the essay Freud grapples with a definition of *instinct*. Simple physiological reflexes that respond to stimuli are considerably complicated by instinct, which appears as a "borderland concept between the mental and the physical." Like physics, Freud presents psychoanalysis as a science of conflicting forces. In "Triebe und Triebschicksale" he defines *impetus, aim, object,* and *source* in terms of instinct. The two major "primal instincts" are self-preservative or ego instincts and sexual instincts. He also details the vicissitudes to which instincts are subject: "reversal into its opposite," "turning round upon the subject," "repression," and "sublimation." The first category resolves itself into two different processes: a change of active and passive and a reversal of content. As examples, Freud points to pairings of sadism and masochism, and of scopophilia and exhibitionism. The second category, reaction-formation, can also operate in this scheme, as in the case of the relation of pity to sadism. The presence of the final category, sublimation, shows how much Freud has expanded upon his earlier theories, which only presented repression as a simple force for negation. Sublimation describes a category of activities in which unacceptable impulses can be channeled into socially acceptable products. In this more complicated version of the earlier model, three polarities operate: subject-object, pleasure-pain, and active-passive. Freud closes the essay with an exploration of ambivalence and the close relationship between love and hate. He uses metaphors of both economics and physics. Like "Formulierungen über die Zwei Prensipien des psychischen Geschehens," "Triebe und Triebschicksale" presents conservation of energy as a key law to these psychic transformations.

In 1915 Freud also published *Zeitgemässes über Krieg und Tod* (translated as *Reflections on War and Death*, 1918; German-language version published in book form in 1924), which reflects his growing pessimism about the global conflict that was raging in Europe. World War I destroyed, at enormous human cost, the remnants of the Hapsburg Austro-Hungarian Empire in which Freud lived. Freud became unconvinced that any outcome, even one founded on rational liberal democracy, could somehow save men from their own innate aggression. Freud began the war with jingoistic patriotism, but the financial and personal privations that resulted from the war soon wore on him, and in July 1915 his daughter Anna found herself trapped in England on the wrong side of enemy lines. Freud's three sons survived combat, as did his friend and colleague Ferenczi, who served in the Hungarian army, but many other young men died or were mutilated. Among them, one of Freud's best-known patients, the Rat Man, died. The war also divided the psychoanalytical community yet again into different geographical camps.

In a way, however, Freud ultimately benefited from the war because of increased attention paid to the fledgling field of psychoanalysis, since only psychoanalysts seemed to have promising treatments for otherwise incurable war neuroses. Shell-shocked soldiers manifested many of the same symptoms as hysterical patients, so Freud found himself returning again to the subject of trauma. "Traued und Melancholie" (Mourning and Melancholia), published in the *Zentralblatt für Psychoanalyse* in 1917, focuses on the link between normal and neurotic manifestations of grief in civilian patients. In his introduction to *Zur Psychoanalyse der Kriegsneurosen* (Toward a Psychoanalysis of War Neuroses, 1919), the publication of the fifth congress of the International Psycho-analytical Association, held in Budapest in 1918, Freud argues that conflicts within the ego are to

blame for neurotic conditions in soldiers who face battle.

During the war Freud also gave a series of lectures that began in 1915, which were published in 1916–1917 as *Vorlesungen zur Einführung in die Psychoanalyse* (translated as *Introductory Lectures on Psycho-Analysis,* 1922). The lectures were widely translated and reprinted. *Vorlesungen zur Einführung in die Psychoanalyse* was second in circulation only to *Zur Psychopathologie des Alltagslebens*. In these lectures Freud serves as both a theorist and a popularizer of psychoanalysis. In printed form they appear in three parts: paraphraxes, dreams, and a general theory of neurosis. The first two parts, which were delivered in the winter of 1915–1916, are devoted to mechanisms of the unconscious in normal, nonneurotic life. The first part covers a wide range of phenomena, from slips of the tongue to accidental self-injury. The second part focuses on dreams and includes analysis of negative unconscious wishes such as death wishes or incestuous wishes. Freud concludes this section by admitting the limitations of dream theory, particularly the drawbacks of linguistic analogies to hieroglyphic writing. The final part of *Vorlesungen zur Einführung in die Psychoanalyse* was delivered in the winter of 1916–1917 and was described by Jones as significantly more didactic in presenting the breadth and depth of pychoneurosis. Most of these lectures are devoted to mental functions and malfunctions. In his final lecture Freud grapples with the difficulties that his young scientific field still faces, such as the problem of whether to interpret elements presented in analysis literally or symbolically and the variance between individual analysts in interpreting the same elements from the same patient.

In 1918, in volume four of his *Sammlung kleiner Schriften zur Neurosenlehre,* Freud published *Aus der Geschichte einer infantilen Neurose* (From the History of an Infantile Neurose; published in book form, 1924), a case history of "The Wolf Man," a wealthy Russian émigré who was almost completely incapacitated by mental illness. Freud had actually begun treating this patient in 1914 and had written the case history at the time of therapy but had delayed publication for fear of identifying his patient. Like Little Hans, the Wolf Man had a debilitating animal phobia, which Freud tied directly to his powerful but unconscious fear of his father. In *Aus der Geschichte einer infantilen Neurose* Freud analyzes his patient's dream about six or seven large white wolves sitting on a walnut tree outside his bedroom. Through free association, Freud's patient tells him about witnessing the primal scene of his parents engaged in sexual intercourse and explains his associations with wolves in fairy tales and his grandfather's story about a tailor and a wolf from the same period. After a digression about his patient's anal retentiveness

TOTEM UND TABU

Einige Übereinstimmungen im
Seelenleben der Wilden und der Neurotiker.

Von

Prof. Dr. Sigm. Freud

1913
HUGO HELLER & CIE.
LEIPZIG UND WIEN, I. BAUERNMARKT 3

Title page for the book (translated as Totem and Taboo: Resemblances between the Lives of Savages and Neurotics, *1918) in which Freud applies his Oedipal theory to prehistoric cultures (Sigmund Freud Collection, Library of Congress; from Ernst Freud, Lucie Freud, and Ilse Grubrich-Simitis, eds.,* Sigmund Freud: His Life in Pictures and Words, *1978; Thomas Cooper Library, University of South Carolina)*

in his pecuniary relations with his mother, Freud gets to the "solution" of the Wolf Man case and his patient's substitution of fear of his father with fear of a wolf. Freud also explicitly attacks Jung again for underestimating the sexual character of the libido.

Experiences of unreality became increasingly important subject matter in Freud's writings from this period, as he explored the boundary between perceptions of the real and the imaginary in voyeuristic situations. "Ein Kind wir geschlagen" (A Child Is Being Beaten, 1919) presents a common fantasy in neurotic patients, one in which the distinction between sadism and masochism collapses as patients identify with both the abuser and the abused. Freud argues for the auto-erotic character of these fantasies, the imagined participation of a parent in the activity (even in individuals who grew up without corporal punishment), and the differences between the sexes in how they experience

each phase of apprehension in the fantasy. Unlike in the later "Das Ökonomische Problem des Masochismus" (The Economic Problem of Masochism; *Zentralblatt für Psychoanalyse,* 1924), the death drive does not play a major role. Also in 1919, in *Imago,* Freud published another essay about the position of spectatorship, "Das 'Unheimlich'" (The Uncanny). The German word *unheimlich* has more-ambiguous associations because it means both "un-homelike" and "un-concealed." To exemplify the uncanny, Freud discusses encounters with an automaton or a dead body in which the viewer registers the qualities of both a living and a nonliving thing. He reads E. T. A. Hoffmann's short story "Der Sandmann" (The Sandman, 1817) closely to discuss the uncanny in aesthetic experiences. He also explores the theme of the double, with a narrative about his own encounter with his mirror image and references to the theories of Rank.

In 1920 Freud's daughter Sophie Halberstadt died from influenza and pneumonia during her third pregnancy. She left two young sons behind, and Freud was profoundly shaken by the event and his subsequent mourning. That same year he published *Jenseits des Lustprinzips* (translated as *Beyond the Pleasure Principle,* 1922), which was actually written in 1919, so its pessimism is likely unrelated to his daughter's death. *Jenseits des Lustprinzips* is characterized by a preoccupation with destructive forces and often uses examples of war neuroses as illustrations. Freud makes a critical distinction in the work between an "instinct" and a "drive" that places a drive on the frontier between the somatic and the mental. To illustrate the interplay of attraction and renunciation in human beings in general, Freud tells the story of a little boy who plays a game in which he hurls his toys away and then reels them back. Freud extends this metaphor of the "fort/da game," from the German for the boy's alternating exclamations of "fort" (gone) and "da" (there), as follows:

This, then, was the complete game—disappearance and return. As a rule one only witnessed its first act, which was repeated untiringly as a game in itself, though there is no doubt that the greater pleasure was attached to the second act. The interpretation of the game then became obvious. It was related to the child's great cultural achievement—the instinctual renunciation (that is, the renunciation of instinctual satisfaction) which he had made in allowing his mother to go away without protesting.

The "compulsion to repeat" is a theme throughout *Jenseits des Lustprinzips.*

Jenseits des Lustprinzips is important as a significant departure from Freud's earlier work. In this essay he considers the central psychic opposition not to be "conscious" versus "unconscious," as it was at the beginning of his career, but rather "ego" versus "repressed." In addition, he notes that much of the ego is also repressed. As a revision of Freud's theory of drives, *Jenseits des Lustprinzips* is quite different from "Instincts and Their Vicissitudes," which focuses merely on the interactions between the reality principle and the pleasure principle. In *Jenseits des Lustprinzips* Freud develops his theory of the death drive, which many of his followers came to call *thanatos* in opposition to *eros* or the drive for self-preservation. Freud dubs this fundamental need for rest from the psychic and biological conflict of living the "Nirvana principle," a term he borrows from Barbara Low. Freud points to truisms such as "the aim of all life is death" to demonstrate this principle. Furthermore, he argues, this revision is consistent with his overall philosophy: "Our views have from the very first been *dualistic,* now that we are able to describe the opposition as being, not between the ego instincts and sexual instincts but between life instincts and death instincts. Jung's libido theory is on the contrary *monistic.*"

Freud's pessimism extended to his work in cultural studies. He expressed his distrust of the democratic ideals of liberal rationalism in *Massenpsychologie und Ich-Analyse* (translated as *Group Psychology and the Analysis of the Ego,* 1922), which appeared in 1921. *Massenpsychologie und Ich-Analyse* examines crowd psychology as a natural regression to the primal horde. Although Freud begins with the concept of a "group mind" from Gustave Le Bon, he rejects any Jungian connotations to the term. Instead, Freud reasons that the libidinal drives of individuals are fulfilled by their connection to an authoritarian group leader through the mechanism of identification. *Massenpsychologie und Ich-Analyse* is a major essay that explores fundamental questions about political philosophy such as "why do individuals deny desires to live together?" and "why do people follow leaders?" In retrospect, many readers have seen Freud foreshadowing the coming of totalitarianism in this essay.

In 1923 Freud published *Das Ich und das Es* (translated as *The Ego and the Id,* 1927), which was his first comprehensive attempt to present his new model of the psyche in which "the repressed" and "the unconscious" were not necessarily synonymous. In this book the unconscious is a larger and more dynamic category, one that even includes parts of the ego itself. If his early work presents a psyche divided into unconscious, preconscious, and conscious states, *Das Ich und das Es* elaborates on a different structure: the id, the ego, and the superego. The id is the primitive urge to seek pleasure without concern for boundaries. The infant experiences frustration of these urges and consequently develops the ego, which must abide by the reality principle. The

ego can never entirely displace the id, however. The ego is constantly under attack and so must undertake "defense mechanisms." Furthermore, the id is not the only adversary of the ego. The superego, which develops in individuals from conflicts around castration anxiety and identification and in societies in response to a prehistoric crime against the father, functions as an internal father substitute that judges and even punishes the ego.

The year 1923 was difficult for Freud for many reasons. His pregnant and unmarried twenty-three-year-old niece, Caecilie Graf, committed suicide. In June his grandson Heinele Halberstadt, the son of his daughter Sophie, died at the age of four from tuberculosis. In September, Freud was diagnosed with cancer, developed from his lifelong habit of smoking cigars. Until his death his daughter Anna nursed him through multiple surgeries and a succession of prostheses that Freud found interfered with his speech and comfort.

As he struggled with self-described depression, Freud developed his work on the death instinct. In "Das Ökonomische Problem des Masochismus" the pleasure principle is represented by the metaphor of the "watchman." Unlike in Freud's early work on the drives, pleasure is presented as a fundamentally conservative principle. Freud presents three kinds of masochism in the essay: erotogenic, moral, and feminine. Assuming feminine masochism to be the most accessible to analysis, Freud argues that fantasies of passivity relate to both childish regression and the drama of castration. Freud claims moral masochism, or excessive inhibition, is actually a form of sadism. Erotogenic masochism is most mysterious to Freud.

He returns to the theme of interpretation in the essay "Das Verneinung" (Negation), published in *Imago* in 1925. Surprisingly, given Freud's other writings, negation is presented in simple terms as a clear relationship of denial to repression. Unlike dream-work or joke-work—which involve multiple transformations from the processes of condensation, displacement, and secondary revision—situations of verbal negation are comparatively easy for the analyst to interpret:

> The manner in which our patients bring forward their associations during the work of analysis gives us an opportunity for making some interesting observations. "Now you'll think I mean to say something insulting, but really I've no such intention." We see at once that this is a repudiation, by means of projection, of an association that has just emerged. Or again: "You ask who this person in the dream can have been. It was *not* my mother." We emend this: so it *was* his mother. In our interpretation we take the liberty of disregarding the negation and simply picking out the subject-matter of the association.

*Freud with his sons Ernst and Martin in 1916 (Sigmund Freud Copyrights, Ltd., London; from Ernst Freud, Lucie Freud,
and Ilse Grubrich-Simitis, eds.,* Sigmund Freud: His Life in Pictures and Words, *1978;
Thomas Cooper Library, University of South Carolina)*

In short, Freud's position on negation assumes a complete inversion of meaning and the adversarial role of the analyst with his free-associating patient.

Soon after publishing "Selbstdarstellung" in 1925, Freud produced a summary work in 1926, *Hemmung, Symptom und Angst* (translated as *Inhibitions, Symptoms, and Anxiety,* 1927), which presents the ego as an even less secure psychic construction than it is in *Das Ich und das Es.* Freud contends that the ego is an "organization" whose defensive character is twofold, as an entity that must adapt to both external and internal worlds. Under siege from the superego, the id, and the outside world, the ego must respond to multiple threats. In *Hemmung, Symptom und Angst* Freud also amends his earlier views of repression, anxiety, and mourning to reflect his postwar theoretical modifications. Most significantly, he elevates anxiety as a mental process and points to similarities between its neurotic and normal manifestations, in that

anxiety both records past traumas and signals future ones. He also criticizes the work of his straying followers, particularly Rank, whose new elevation of the birth trauma as a major psychic event is explicitly criticized. In April 1926 Rank had finally said farewell to Freud. Long after the others in the original Vienna circle had turned against Rank, however, Freud had been reluctant to publicly criticize his former protégé.

The second phase of breaks from former colleagues occurred during the 1920s and was harder for Freud to assign to a single factor, as he had done in *Zur Geschichte der psychoanalytischen Bewegung.* Many of the new renegades were associated with psychiatric circles from Berlin, where the Berlin Psychiatric Institute had instituted a rigorous program of training different from the Vienna model. The debate between Melanie Klein and Anna Freud exacerbated conflicts in the movement. From 1925 to 1928 Anna Freud, a published child psychologist in her own right, served as chair of the Vienna Psycho-Analytic Society, and in that capacity she codified Freudian dogma. She viewed children's play only as an adaptation to reality, not as a vehicle for unconscious conflicts. Klein had developed a radically different analytical model for working with children, play therapy, and was theorizing that infants had an even more powerful destructive drive and experienced the Oedipus complex and the rise of the superego sooner than either Sigmund or Anna Freud believed. Ferenczi and Abraham defended Klein against more-traditional Freudians, and Freud accused Jones of also being an ally of the Kleinians.

Freud's attitudes toward gender roles also came under attack during this period. In 1922 Karen Horney questioned the doctrine that penis envy created femininity; she vehemently argued that such envy was an expression of femininity, not its point of origin. During the 1920s and the 1930s Horney went on to attack the male bias of psychoanalysis more generally, and Jones defended her. She asserted that the dominant culture played a greater role in the development of the psyche than the instincts. As late as 1925, however, Freud cites Horney's work approvingly, as he does in "Einige psychische Folgen des anatomischen Geschlectsunterschieds" (Some Psychological Consequences of the Anatomical Distinctions between the Sexes, published in the *Zentralblatt für Psychoanalyse,* 1925).

There were still other battles, however, such as the battle over lay analysis with American practitioners who wanted to professionalize the field, which demanded much of Freud's attention. In 1926 Freud published *Die Frage der Laienanalyse,* an essay that did considerably more than merely take a position on the contemporary debate about whether those without medical degrees should be allowed to practice psychoanalysis. In this essay Freud imagines an elaborate dialogue between himself and an "Impartial Person," who is presented with the problems of the analytical situation. To acquaint his imagined hearer with the polymorphous character of mental illnesses, Freud begins the essay with a survey of different types of disorders—"neurasthenia, psychasthenia, phobias, obsessional neurosis, hysteria"—and questions whether these illnesses can be treated by focusing on individual symptoms and the organs that seem to produce them. Freud defends verbal therapy as more effective than medicine.

When his interlocutor points out that words seem a harmless method of treatment, Freud maintains that words are the most powerful tool in human society. When his audience suggests that this operation is like magic, Freud wryly says it is slower. When the "Impartial Person" claims that what analysis does is solicit confessions, just as the Catholic Church does, Freud

differentiates psychoanalysis from religion by pointing out that analysis asks patients to tell more than they know. Freud then explains the thinking of psychoanalytic circles and the descriptive function of psychoanalysis, which necessarily functions by making analogies. He also explains the structures of the psyche and the function of the ego and the id. Then Freud moves into the more contentious subject of infantile sexuality and the developmental process. He discusses the drawbacks of societies in which infant sexuality is given free rein, because they suffer from a corresponding lack of intellectual and creative achievements, which are necessarily generated by sublimation of sexual instincts. He explains this conflict between societal models with the analogy of Scylla and Charybdis, which appears several times in Freud's other works to represent the danger of both "civilized" and "primitive" modes. After devoting most of his space to an overview of psychoanalysis, Freud turns to the problems of the analytical situation, with the concepts of resistance and transference presented in particularly colloquial language. He finishes the essay with a comparison of the "quackery" of the medical profession with that of the psychoanalytic profession, with a clear critique of the former in mind.

In a 25 November 1928 letter to his friend clergyman Oskar Pfister, Freud points out the connection between *Die Frage der Laienanalyse* and the book that followed it in 1927, *Die Zukunft einer Illusion* (translated as *The Future of an Illusion,* 1928): "I do not know if you have guessed the secret link between *Lay Analysis* and *Illusion.* In the former I wish to protect analysis from the doctors and in the latter from the priests." Freud's lifelong atheism was manifest in many of his works, but this essay is his most militant statement of opposition. In *Die Zukunft einer Illusion* Freud represents religion as an attempt to provide impossible comfort and satisfaction in a hostile world. Religion also expresses the ambivalent feelings of both love and fear for a father figure.

Das Unbehagen in der Kultur, published in 1930, expanded Freud's pessimistic analysis of contemporary society. He opens the book with an inquiry about religion in which he questions the origins of a friend's "oceanic" feeling. The friend describes a feeling of connection with something beyond himself, which the friend associates with spiritual experience. As a good empiricist who has never felt this feeling, Freud is skeptical and wonders how this sensation relates to normal ego-feeling. According to his own developmental model, the early ego is inclusive but the later ego separates from the external world. In mental life, Freud argues, nothing ever perishes. Then he presents his well-known metaphor of an imaginary version of the city of Rome in which ancient Rome and Catholic Rome could coexist with all their buildings from all his-

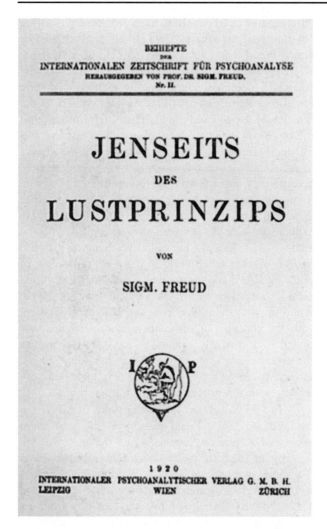

BEIHEFTE
DER
INTERNATIONALEN ZEITSCHRIFT FÜR PSYCHOANALYSE
HERAUSGEGEBEN VON PROF. DR. SIGM. FREUD.
Nr. II.

JENSEITS

DES

LUSTPRINZIPS

VON

SIGM. FREUD

1920
INTERNATIONALER PSYCHOANALYTISCHER VERLAG G. M. B. H.
LEIPZIG   WIEN   ZÜRICH

Title page for Freud's study (translated as Beyond the Pleasure
Principle, *1922) of destructive psychological forces, particularly
the "death drive" (Sigmund Freud Collection, Library of
Congress; from Ernst Freud, Lucie Freud, and Ilse
Grubrich-Simitis, eds.,* Sigmund Freud:
His Life in Pictures and Words,
*1978; Thomas Cooper Library,
University of South Carolina)*

torical periods simultaneously extant. The image is one in which nothing in mental life ever is demolished, from the earliest times of psychic origin to the most recent.

Freud follows this introductory material, much of which reviews ideas in *Die Zukunft einer Illusion,* with a discussion of what human beings want, which he identifies as "happiness," defined by the avoidance of pain and the acquisition of pleasure. Yet, Freud claims, humans seem unable to attain happiness. As they face threats from the decay of their own bodies, the power of forces in the outside world, and the danger of human conflicts, unhappiness seems a more likely outcome. He characterizes the many strategies that human beings use in order to achieve and extend periods of happiness and rejects them all as futile. The doomed strategies include chemical intoxication, extinction of instinctual drives through disciplines such as yoga, sublimation of the instincts through intellectual work, fantasizing through the appreciation of art, withdrawal from reality, and the channeling of sexual love into religious activities.

As *Das Unbehagen in der Kultur* brings its focus onto its subject matter, Freud points out that the cause for this misery is civilization, which forces people to renounce their instincts. Even the supposed benefits conferred upon modern people by modern transportation, technology, and medicine ultimately lead to other miseries and alienation. Like human individuals, civilizations also go through a developmental process during the course of history as they move from "primitive" forms of social organization to contemporary ones. First the fallible human body needs to be improved, as natural forces and materials are harnessed through technology. Then human beings must secure cleanliness (or distance from filth and feces), order, and aesthetic beauty. The next step involves the treatment of intellectual, scientific, and artistic achievements with esteem. Finally, social relationships must be regulated so that the power of the individual is replaced by the power of the community, particularly by the institution of justice.

Although love and necessity, *eros* and *ananke,* are "the parents of civilization," Freud also claims that love threatens civilization and consequently must be regulated. Another threat to civilization is posed by women, who must be severely restricted. To bind individuals together libidinously, society commands them to "Love thy neighbor as thyself," which Freud considers to be an untenable demand, like the even more impossible order to "Love thine enemies." Civilization is designed to restrict aggression, which Freud feels long predates the institution of private property, but he points out that civilization has its own aggressive force as well. This point leads Freud into more discussion of the death drive and the two opposing physical forces: one "to preserve living substance and to join it into ever larger units" and the other "to dissolve those units and bring them back to their primaeval, inorganic state."

Freud closes the book with a discussion of the development of the superego and the institution of guilt as a process of internalization. He again rehearses the prehistory of man that he presents in *Totem und Tabu.* Like people, communities also evolve superegos. Civilized institutions, however, do little to further the education of young people to understand their basic drives. As Freud writes, "In sending young people out into life with such a false psychological orientation, education is behaving as though one were to equip people starting on a Polar expedition with summer clothing and maps of the Italian Lakes." He ends profoundly ambivalent about the value of civilization.

The Nobel Prize eluded Freud throughout his lifetime, despite a variety of luminaries who nominated him. Well-orchestrated campaigns in 1928 and again in 1930 were not successful despite a petition with signatories from the philosopher Bertrand Russell to the novelist Alfred Döblin. Most of the people in Freud's original intellectual circle had died. Abraham, known for his theories of child sexuality, died from cancer in 1925. By the late 1920s most of his other long-term friends, with whom he had played the card game tarok on Saturday nights for decades, had died as well. In September 1930 his mother, Amalie, died at the age of ninety-five.

In 1931 Freud returned to the thorny topic of female sexuality. In "Über die weibliche Sexualität" he attempts to explain two shifts that occur in women: the movement from the mother as love-object to the father, and the transfer of autoerotic attention from the clitoris to the vagina. Given his postulate that both sexes consider the mother the original love-object, he devotes more attention in this essay to the pre-Oedipal phase in female sexual development. Unlike his earlier work that treated the father as the essential actor in neurotic etiology, in "Über die weibliche Sexualität" Freud links the figure of the mother to the origin of both hysteria and paranoia in female patients. Freud rejects the "Electra complex" as a false analogy of equivalence between the sexes. He also argues that the earlier clitoral phase of female sexual development is masculine, while the latter, which centers on the vagina, is feminine. Female subjects respond to their own feelings of castration in one of three ways: rejection of sexuality, masculine sexuality with a homosexual object choice, or the "very circuitous path" to normal feminine sexuality via the feminine form of the Oedipus complex. For Freud, male subjects encounter the Oedipus complex first and then the castration complex, while female subjects experience castration first and then the Oedipal relation, which Freud claims has consequences for women, who therefore lack the moral sense associated with castration.

Freud's final set of lectures, *Neue Folge der Vorlesungen zur Einführung in die Psychoanalyse* (translated as *New Introductory Lectures on Psycho-analysis*, 1933), was published in 1933. Although there are many appeals to "Ladies and Gentlemen" in his audience, the lectures were never actually delivered: surgical operations on his jaw to treat the encroaching cancer had made public speaking impossible. Freud opens the lectures by returning to the subject of dreams. He acknowledges contributions from "philology, folklore, mythology, and ritual" to psychoanalysis for explaining how particular symbols have particular meanings but criticizes Jung for neglecting the importance of childhood and Rank for

Freud in 1929 (Sigmund Freud Copyrights, Ltd., London; from Ernst Freud, Lucie Freud, and Ilse Grubrich-Simitis, eds., Sigmund Freud: His Life in Pictures and Words, 1978; Thomas Cooper Library, University of South Carolina)

overvaluing the importance of birth experience. In these lectures he also develops his argument that psychoanalysis is a science and sharpens his critiques of religion and occultism. The concluding lecture, "Über eine Weltanschauung" (The Question of a Weltanschauung), discusses the weltanschauung, or worldview, of science and explains how psychoanalysis represents the scientific worldview. Freud contrasts the scientific worldview with that of religion and politics, with the latter critique bisected between arguments against anarchism and those against Marxism.

In his lecture "Über Weiblichkeit" from the same collection, Freud examines how a child with a naturally bisexual disposition becomes a woman, particularly when both sexes pass through the early stages of libidinal development in the same manner. As Freud writes, "the little girl is a little man." Girls even appear to be as aggressive as boys, Freud notes, building on the work of female analysts such as his daughter Anna. Without

DAS UNBEHAGEN
IN DER
KULTUR

VON

SIGM. FREUD

1.—12. Tausend

1930
INTERNATIONALER
PSYCHOANALYTISCHER VERLAG
WIEN

Title page for Freud's pessimistic analysis (translated as Civilization
and Its Discontents, *1930) of humans' futile attempts to find
happiness in modern society (Sigmund Freud Collection,
Library of Congress; from Ernst Freud, Lucie Freud,
and Ilse Grubrich-Simitis, eds.,* Sigmund Freud:
His Life in Pictures and Words, *1978;
Thomas Cooper Library, University
of South Carolina)*

going through the castration complex, however, girls are unable to fully surmount the Oedipus complex, and Freud reiterates his claim that women therefore never fully develop a strong and independent superego. He credits this "pre-history of women" to the work of female analysts such as Ruth Mack Brunswick, Jeanne Lamp-de-Groot, and Helene Deutsch. Despite the differences that are the focus of the essay, he also asserts: "There is only one libido, which serves both the masculine and feminine sexual functions."

As an avid reader of newspapers and a correspondent on current events, Freud turned his attention to politics during this period. He and Albert Einstein had exchanged open letters. In this correspondence Freud's pessimism about human aggression and destructiveness is in marked contrast to Einstein's scientific positivism. For many years Freud had considered physics as the natural analogue to psychoanalysis as a science and had followed twentieth-century revolutions in physics from a lay perspective. A book emerged from the Freud-

Einstein correspondence, *Warum Krieg?* (1933; translated as *Why War?,* 1933), in which Einstein presents a central opposition between might and right but Freud proposes that "violence" is a more useful construct. Furthermore, Freud questions whether communities can actually shield their members from violent conflict by creating a structure of rights-based liberal law, or if cultures merely reinscribe violence in the more civilized and sublimated form of law.

The political situation had begun to deteriorate in Europe with the rise of fascism and organized anti-Semitism. Psychoanalysis, as an international intellectual movement founded by Jews that constantly interrogated the motivations of naive nationalism, was under threat. On 10 March 1933 the Nazis publicly burned Freud's books in several German cities. In the 1930s pro-Nazi politicians also made significant inroads as Austria suffered through a string of economic and electoral crises.

On 12 March 1938 the new Austrian prime minister invited German troops to cross the border. Jones came to Freud on 15 March to convince him to leave Vienna and to impress upon him the dire situations of acquaintances who had been in concentration camps in Germany, but Freud still expressed unwillingness to go. Throughout the 1930s his medical condition had greatly worsened; a bombardment of radiation treatments and surgeries had failed, which was undoubtedly a factor in his reluctance to emigrate. While British and American diplomatic channels at the highest levels were working to secure exit visas for the Freud family, Anna Freud was arrested on 22 March and spent the day in custody. Under the protection of powerful friends, such as his benefactor and colleague Princess Marie Bonaparte, who had known Freud since the 1920s, the Freuds were finally allowed to leave the country in June, but only after a final interview with the Gestapo. The property of the Vienna Psycho-Analytic Society was confiscated by the Nazis, and Freud was compelled to sign a paper attesting that he had not been mistreated. "I can most highly recommend the Gestapo to everyone," Freud is said to have responded. His sisters stayed behind and ultimately died in the concentration camps.

Freud soon antagonized his fellow Jews with the publication of *Der Mann Moses und die monotheistische Religion* in 1939, in which he argued that Moses was an Egyptian, not a Jew. He connects Moses to the figure of Pharaoh Akhenaton and argues that Jewish monotheism was derived from the earlier Egyptian form. Freud claims that the Israelites' original deity, in contrast, is a bloodthirsty demon whose religion is based on sacrifice, not law. Freud also includes accounts about a mythical murder of Moses to argue for a model of primal crime, parallel to the prehistory of *Totem und Tabu*, in which the Jews inherit similar guilt. The book roused a storm of theological controversy in both Jewish and Christian circles.

As the cancer worsened, Freud retreated entirely into a life limited by his London home in Marefield Gardens. His close companion, sister-in-law Minna Bernays, was now bedridden in a nursing home. As a celebrity Freud avoided well-wishers and gave little public comment. Close to the end of his life, however, in a statement for the BBC, his voice was still intelligible and his opinions still combative. He continued to work on "Abriss der Psycho-analyse" (1940; translated as *An Outline of Psycho-Analysis*, 1969), which appeared in the *Internationale Zeitschrift für Psycho-analyse und Imago* (International Magazine for Psychoanalysis and Imago) after his death, in which he elaborates further on the relationship between the "external world" and the "internal world." The pain of his disease grew greater. Freud found himself miserable from the stench of his septic flesh, which repelled even his beloved chow dogs. He became disfigured and was unable to eat. He decided to follow through with a previously arranged plan with his physician to end his life and asked for a fatal dose of morphine. The next day, on 23 September 1939, he died.

The legacy of Freud in twentieth-century cultural theory is so large that it is difficult to summarize. His immediate circle of followers made many important contributions to psychoanalytic theory, even those who departed from the circle on hostile terms. Adler used Freud's work on instinctual drives to launch his theories of power and aggression and argue that what he termed an "inferiority complex" can stifle human potential. Jung appropriated much Freudian language in his analysis of the "archetypes" of myths and symbols from world cultures and in his theories of the "collective unconscious" and the relationship of psychology to religion. Rank wrote *Der Mythus von der Geburt des Helden* (1909; translated as *The Myth of the Birth of the Hero*, 1914) and contributed much to the developing field of folklore and mythology. Wilhelm Reich, who broke with Freud in 1926 after challenging Freud's libido theory with his own "orgasm theory," developed Reichian depth psychology and a system of character analysis. Freud's daughter and champion of his principles, Anna, whom Freud came to call "My Antigone," was also a major figure in psychoanalysis, as was her rival Klein.

Freud certainly also influenced the intellectuals and writers who came to him for analysis, such as the American imagist poet H.D. (Hilda Doolittle). Other important writers and artists, from Thomas Mann to Salvador Dali, credited Freud's ideas as stimuli to cre-

Freud in the garden of his home in Vienna in 1938, shortly before he left Austria to escape the Nazis (Sigmund Freud Copyrights, Ltd., London; from Ernst Freud, Lucie Freud, and Ilse Grubrich-Simitis, eds., Sigmund Freud: His Life in Pictures, *1978; Thomas Cooper Library, University of South Carolina)*

ative work, particularly about the unconscious. Poets Dylan Thomas and W. H. Auden eulogized him. Freudian analysis even came to be important in literary criticism, as it was to Harold Bloom's *The Anxiety of Influence* (1973), in which the father complex is applied to the situation of a writer working in the shadow of a great literary forebear. Freudian themes have appeared in novels, plays, musicals, and movies that dramatize the unconscious, the incestuous dynamics of Freud's "family romance," the explanatory powers of dreams and illness, and the dangers of civilized sexual repression. In the mid 1920s studio magnate Samuel Goldwyn tried to lure Freud to Hollywood. Movie directors such as Alfred Hitchcock and Roman Polanski displayed their knowledge of Freud's ideas on screen. Dozens of new words and phrases entered the modern vocabulary.

Even those who disagreed with Freud on basic philosophical grounds were interested in preserving his legacy. For example, in 1958 the existentialist philosopher Jean-Paul Sartre wrote a movie script loosely based on Freud's life for director John Huston. The script pre-

Freud in 1939, the year of his death (Sigmund Freud Copyrights, Ltd., London; from Ernst Freud, Lucie Freud, and Ilse Grubrich-Simitis, eds., Sigmund Freud: His Life in Pictures and Words, *1978; Thomas Cooper Library, University of South Carolina)*

ture of the Freudian developmental model was accepted, many rejected Freud's empirical scientism. For example, critic and psychoanalyst Julia Kristeva focused on the pre-Oedipal phase in her early work on semiotics and wrote about its synthetic rather than analytic character. Others openly rebutted Freud's family narrative as hegemonic, as Gilles Deleuze and Félix Guattari do in the two volumes of their *Capitalisme et schizophrénie* (Capitalism and Schizophrenia): *L'anti-Oedipe* (1975; translated as *Anti-Oedipus,* 1977) and *Mille Plateaux* (1980; translated as *A Thousand Plateaus,* 1987).

Continuing into the twenty-first century, several schools of Freudian thought still flourish. Lacanian psychoanalysis, founded by French analyst Jacques Lacan in the years after World War II, represents a combination of French poststructuralism and linguistics with Freud's ideas. For Lacanians the relationship of the psychoanalytic subject to the phallus is a linguistic rather than a literal one, in which the "signifier" takes a central place and "the unconscious is structured like a language." In Lacan's model, human development is characterized by three stages: the Real, the Imaginary, and the Symbolic, although access to the Real is always mediated. While some schools of feminism reacted against Freud's theories, other feminist critics argue for the continuity of feminism with Freudian ideas about bisexuality and symbolic thinking. Marxist thinkers have tried to synthesize elements of Marxism and Freudianism, despite the irony of this endeavor, given Freud's lifelong aversion to Marxism. Critics of late capitalism adopt elements of the psychoanalytic model, as the title of Fredric Jameson's work *The Political Unconscious* (1981) indicates, or explicitly equate mechanisms of political repression with psychic repression, as Slavoj Žižek does in his anticapitalist critiques.

Although highly critical of Freud, French philosopher Jacques Derrida has argued that Freud laid the groundwork for deconstruction. Derrida reads Freud's texts closely and sees in them a fundamental revision of the traditional Cartesian model of the self-conscious subject aware of its own mental functioning. Freud himself, Derrida asserts, could not see all the way through to the logical consequences of his critique, because he was caught in a philosophical construct of "phallologocentrism."

Both of Sigmund Freud's homes are now museums. The Library of Congress, the largest repository of his work, holds approximately eighty thousand Freud-related items. In 1998 the Library of Congress opened a major exhibition on Freud's life and legacy, "Sigmund Freud: Conflict and Culture." The exhibition itself was not without controversy. The show was nearly canceled in 1995 amid protests by feminists, religious critics, and psychoanalysts from rival schools. The

sented a hero's monumental struggle toward great discovery and against a succession of controlling father figures such as Breuer. Sartre also depicted Freud's marriage with Martha Bernays with many more storms and sexual frustrations than Jones's idyllic matrimonial picture. Philosopher Ludwig Wittgenstein admired Freud's work, even if he disputed it, and returned to consider Freud several times in his aphorisms.

Post-Freudian psychoanalysis often fundamentally altered Freud's models, however. For example, if the Freudian developmental model posited that the ego formed as it separated from the outside world—with a sequence based on separation from breast, feces, and phallus—object-relations theorists from the British School, such as D. W. Winnicott, argued that it was the connection with the outside world, established first through transitional objects such as children's toys, that constituted the individual. And even if the basic struc-

opening date of this major retrospective was postponed for two years while the difficult process of developing a balanced curatorial strategy was negotiated between warring factions, some who thought Freud's work had been discredited by modern experimental psychology and others who argued his intellectual legacy could not be ignored.

Letters:

Aus den Anfängen der Psychoanalyse: Briefe an Wilhelm Fliess, Abhandlungen und Notizen aus den Jahren 1887–1902 (London: Imago, 1950); translated by Eric Mosbacher and James Strachey as *The Origins of Psycho-Analysis: Letters to Wilhelm Fliess, Drafts and Notes, 1887–1902,* edited by Marie Bonaparte, Anna Freud, and Ernst Kris (New York: Basic Books, 1954);

Briefe: 1873–1939, edited by Ernst L. Freud (Frankfurt am Main: Fischer, 1960); translated by Tania Stern and James Stern as *Letters of Sigmund Freud* (New York: Basic Books, 1960);

Psychoanalysis and Faith: The Letters of Sigmund Freud and Oskar Pfister, edited by Heinrich Meng and Ernst L. Freud, translated by Mosbacher (New York: Basic Books, 1963).

Bibliography:

Alexander Grinstein, comp., *Sigmund Freud's Writings: A Comprehensive Bibliography* (New York: International Universities Press, 1977).

Biographies:

Ernest Jones, *The Life and Work of Sigmund Freud,* 3 volumes (New York: Basic Books, 1953–1957);

Paul Roazen, *Brother Animal: The Story of Freud and Tausk* (New York: Knopf, 1969);

Richard Wollheim, *Sigmund Freud* (New York: Viking, 1971);

Roazen, *Freud and His Followers* (New York: Knopf, 1975);

Ronald W. Clark, *Freud: The Man and the Cause* (New York: Random House, 1980);

Peter Gay, *Freud: A Life for Our Time* (New York: Norton, 1988).

References:

Harold Bloom, *The Anxiety of Influence: A Theory of Poetry* (New York: Oxford University Press, 1973);

Gilles Deleuze and Félix Guattari, *Anti-Oedipus: Capitalism and Schizophrenia,* translated by Robert Hurley, Mark Seem, and Helen R. Lane (New York: Viking, 1997);

Deleuze and Guattari, *A Thousand Plateaus: Capitalism and Schizophrenia,* translated by Brian Massumi (Minneapolis: University of Minnesota Press, 1987; London: Athlone, 1988);

Jacques Derrida, "Freud and the Scene of Writing," in *Writing and Difference,* translated by Alan Bass (Chicago: University of Chicago Press, 1978), pp. 196–231;

Derrida, *Resistances of Psychoanalysis,* translated by Peggy Kamuf, Pascale-Anne Brault, and Michael Naas (Stanford, Cal.: Stanford University Press, 1999);

Derrida, "To Speculate on 'Freud'," in his *The Post Card: From Socrates to Freud and Beyond,* translated by Bass (Chicago: University of Chicago Press, 1987), pp. 256–409;

Julia Kristeva, *Revolution in Poetic Language,* translated by Margaret Waller (New York: Columbia University Press, 1984);

Jacques Lacan, *The Seminar of Jacques Lacan,* 4 volumes, edited by Jacques-Alain Miller (New York: Norton, 1988);

Ludwig Wittgenstein, *Culture and Value,* edited by George H. Von Wright, translated by Peter Winch (Chicago: University of Chicago Press, 1984);

Slavoj Žižek, *Enjoy Your Symptom! Jacques Lacan in Hollywood and Out* (New York: Routledge, 1992);

Žižek, *The Sublime Object of Ideology* (London & New York: Verso, 1989).

Papers:

The largest collection of Sigmund Freud's papers is located at the Library of Congress in Washington, D.C.

Erich Fromm

(23 March 1900 – 18 March 1980)

Craig B. Matarrese
Minnesota State University, Mankato

BOOKS: *Die Entwicklung des Christusdogmas: Eine psycho-analytische Studie zur sozialpsychologischen Funktion der Religion* (Vienna: Internationaler Psychoanalytischer Verlag, 1931); translated by James Luther Adams as "The Dogma of Christ," in *The Dogma of Christ and Other Essays on Religion, Psychology, and Culture* (New York: Holt, Rinehart & Winston, 1963), pp. 1–70;

Escape from Freedom (New York: Farrar & Rinehart, 1941); republished as *The Fear of Freedom* (London: Kegan Paul, Trench, Trübner, 1942);

Man for Himself: An Inquiry into the Psychology of Ethics (New York: Rinehart, 1947);

Psychoanalysis and Religion (New Haven: Yale University Press, 1950);

The Forgotten Language: An Introduction to the Understanding of Dreams, Fairy Tales and Myths (New York: Rinehart, 1951);

The Sane Society (New York: Rinehart, 1955);

The Art of Loving, World Perspectives, no. 9 (New York & Evanston, Ill.: Harper, 1956);

Sigmund Freud's Mission: An Analysis of His Personality and Influence, World Perspectives, no. 21 (New York: Harper, 1959);

Let Man Prevail: A Socialist Manifesto and Program (New York: Call Association, 1960);

May Man Prevail? An Inquiry into the Facts and Fictions of Foreign Policy (Garden City, N.Y.: Doubleday, 1961);

Beyond the Chains of Illusion: My Encounter with Marx and Freud, Credo Perspectives Series (New York: Simon & Schuster, 1962);

War within Man: A Psychological Inquiry into the Roots of Destructiveness. A Study and Commentary (Philadelphia: American Friends' Service Committee, 1963);

The Heart of Man: Its Genius for Good and Evil, Religious Perspectives, no. 12 (New York & London: Harper & Row, 1964);

Erich Fromm (from Rainer Funk, Erich Fromm: His Life and Ideas. An Illustrated Biography, *2000; Thomas Cooper Library, University of South Carolina)*

You Shall Be as Gods: A Radical Interpretation of the Old Testament and Its Tradition (New York: Holt, Rinehart & Winston, 1966);

The Revolution of Hope: Toward a Humanized Technology, World Perspectives, no. 38 (New York: Harper & Row, 1968);

Social Character in a Mexican Village: A Sociopsychoanalytic Study, by Fromm and Michael Maccoby (Englewood Cliffs, N.J.: Prentice-Hall, 1970);

The Anatomy of Human Destructiveness (New York: Holt, Rinehart & Winston, 1973);

To Have or to Be? World Perspectives, no. 30 (New York: Harper & Row, 1976);

The Greatness and Limitations of Freud's Thought (New York: Harper & Row, 1980);

Arbeiter und Angestellte am Vorabend des dritten Reiches: Eine sozialpsychologische Untersuchung, edited by Wolfgang Bonss (Stuttgart: Deutsche Verlags-Anstalt, 1980); translated by Barbara Weinberger as *The Working Class in Weimar Germany* (Leamington Spa, Warwickshire: Berg, 1984);

Gesamtausgabe, 12 volumes, edited by Rainer Funk (Stuttgart: Deutsche Verlags-Anstalt, 1980–1999);

On Disobedience and Other Essays (New York: Seabury, 1981; London: Routledge & Kegan Paul, 1984);

For the Love of Life, translated by Robert Kimber and Rita Kimber, edited by Hans Jürgen Schultz (New York: Free Press, 1986);

Das jüdische Gesetz: Zur Sociologie des Diaspora-Judentums: Dissertation von 1922, edited by Funk and Bernd Sahler (Weinheim: Beltz, 1989);

The Art of Being, foreword by Funk (New York: Continuum, 1993).

Editions and Collections: *The Dogma of Christ and Other Essays on Religion, Psychology, and Culture* (New York: Holt, Rinehart & Winston, 1963);

The Crisis of Psychoanalysis: Essays on Freud, Marx, and Social Psychology (New York: Holt, Rinehart & Winston, 1970);

The Revision of Psychoanalysis, edited by Rainer Funk (Boulder, Colo.: Westview Press, 1992);

The Art of Listening, edited by Funk (New York: Continuum, 1994);

The Erich Fromm Reader, edited by Funk (New Jersey: Humanities Press, 1994);

On Being Human, foreword by Funk (New York: Continuum, 1994);

The Essential Fromm: Life between Having and Being, edited by Funk, portions translated by Lance W. Garmer (London: Constable, 1995; New York: Continuum, 1995);

Love, Sexuality, and Matriarchy: About Gender, edited by Funk (New York: Fromm International, 1997).

OTHER: "Sozialpsychologischer Teil," "Geschichte und Methoden der Erhebung," and "Die Arbeiter- und Angestellten-Erhebung," in *Studien über Autorität und Familie: Forschungsberichte aus dem Institut für Sozialforschung,* volume 5 of *Schriften des Insti-*

tuts für Sozialforschung, edited by Max Horkheimer (Paris: Alcan, 1936), pp. 71–135, 231–238;

Edward Bellamy, *Looking Backward (2000–1887),* foreword by Fromm (New York: New American Library, 1960);

"Psychoanalysis and Zen Buddhism," in *Zen Buddhism and Psychoanalysis,* edited by D. T. Suzuki, Fromm, and Richard De Martino (New York: Harper, 1960);

"Marx's Concept of Man," in *Marx's Concept of Man,* edited by Fromm (New York: Ungar, 1961), pp. 1–83;

George Orwell, *Nineteen Eighty-Four,* afterword by Fromm (New York: New American Library, 1961);

"Sane Thinking in Foreign Policy," in *Sane Comment,* edited by Fromm and others (New York: National Committee for a Sane Nuclear Policy, 1961);

"The Application of Humanist Psychoanalysis to Marx's Theory," in *Socialist Humanism: An International Symposium,* edited by Fromm (Garden City, N.Y.: Doubleday, 1965), pp. 207–222;

The Nature of Man, edited by Fromm and Ramón Xirau (New York: Macmillan, 1968; London: Collier-Macmillan, 1968);

"Psychoanalysis and Sociology" and "Politics and Psychoanalysis," in *Critical Theory and Society: A Reader,* edited by Stephen Eric Bronner and Douglas MacKay Kellner (New York: Routledge, 1989), pp. 37–39, 213–218;

"The State as Educator: On the Psychology of Criminal Justice" and "On the Psychology of the Criminal and Punitive Society," translated by Heinze D. Osterle and Kevin Anderson, in *Erich Fromm and Critical Criminology,* edited by Anderson and Richard Quinney (Urbana & Chicago: University of Illinois Press, 2000), IV: 123–156.

SELECTED PERIODICAL PUBLICATIONS–
UNCOLLECTED: "Zum Gefühl der Ohnmacht," *Zeitschrift für Sozialforschung* (1937): 95–119;

"The Psychology of Normalcy," *Dissent,* 1 (Spring 1954): 139–143.

Because of the interdisciplinary nature of his work and because he acquired a large and diverse audience for his writings, Erich Fromm is known under various guises. Philosophers typically know him through his affiliation with the so-called Frankfurt School, which is credited for developing twentieth-century critical theory, as the author of *Escape from Freedom* (1941), as the person who brought Karl Marx's early "Paris Manuscripts" to the American readership, and as someone who helped lay the founda-

Fromm with his parents, Naphtali and Rosa (née Krause), in Bad Homburg von der Hohe, 1913 (from Rainer Funk,
Erich Fromm: His Life and Ideas. An Illustrated Biography, *2000;*
Thomas Cooper Library, University of South Carolina)

tions for contemporary political communitarianism. Psychologists know Fromm as one who criticized, revised, and developed Sigmund Freud's psychoanalytic theory, who pioneered research investigating the authoritarian personality and fascism, who developed a taxonomy of character types in contemporary capitalist society, and who was an innovative and influential practicing psychoanalyst who late in his career integrated the insights of Zen Buddhism into his work. Sociologists know Fromm for his research on the social, political, and economic determination of individual character development and as one who championed the position that psychology must ultimately become social psychology if it is to accurately understand its subject matter. Socialists and peace activists are familiar with Fromm's political activity in support of the international peace movement, as well as his writings on Marx, socialism, technology, and nuclear disarmament. Finally, a large audience of readers around the world know Fromm's books *The Art of Loving* (1956), *To Have or to Be?* (1976), and many of his other writings about humanism, religion, and modes of living.

In the context of twentieth-century European cultural theory, most commentators would argue that Fromm's main contribution is his broad theory of social psychology, which represents the first attempt to compre-

hensively synthesize Marx and Freud. Fromm characterized his work as "radical-humanistic-psychoanalysis," and his description of his view as a kind of humanism is significant, for humanism is perhaps the only rubric sufficiently broad to capture the interdisciplinary nature of his work. Indeed, it is Fromm's humanistic perspective, his emphasis on human creativity, expressiveness, and integrity, that allows him to stress both the determining influence of social forces and the importance of a critical and individual point of view; Fromm is at pains to avoid reducing individuals to mere manifestations of social forces, and he consistently argues that human needs and human interests must ultimately shape political projects. Fromm thought that modern society had become a Procrustean bed on which humankind is forced to lie, a bed not adequately proportioned to meet human needs; though most powerful contemporary social forces compel and coerce people to accept this bed, a situation in which they are alienated from themselves, from others, and from nature, it was Fromm's optimistic project to offer a humanistic alternative.

Erich Seligmann (Pinchas) Fromm was born in Frankfurt am Main, Germany, on 23 March 1900, the only child of Orthodox Jewish parents, Naphtali Fromm and Rosa Krause. He was raised in Frankfurt and remained there until he was nineteen years old, during which time he studied the Talmud seriously and considered making such studies a lifelong project, which would have continued the rabbinical tradition of his father's family. Fromm's own recollections of his early intellectual interests while he was growing up in Frankfurt centered on the influence of his parents, whom he described in a March 1980 interview with Guide Ferrari for Swiss television as "very neurotic and anxious," and his general interest in understanding why people do what they do, especially when they do things that seem outrageous or highly irrational. When Fromm was twelve years old, he struggled to understand the suicide of a close family friend, a woman who killed herself at the age of twenty-six, ostensibly so that she could join her beloved and recently deceased father. Similarly, as a young student at the Wöhlerschule in Lessingstrasse, he was struck by the irrationalities generated by World War I, especially the extreme anti-English sentiment among his peers. By the age of eighteen Fromm was deeply preoccupied, even obsessed, with the reasons why people become involved with war and with the seemingly pathological psychology that lies behind human behavior in times of war.

Weighing in against these troubling forces, however, were those individuals Fromm admired for defending enlightened and genuinely humanistic ideals. The young Fromm was impressed by the prophets of the Old Testament, because they seemed to him not only to defend laudable ideals but also to embody and express these ideals in their lives and actions. Fromm never abandoned his early interest in the biblical prophets but later generalized his admiration for them to include many of the other great teachers in history, such as Confucius, Buddha, and Socrates. His mature view was that all of these teachers were in general agreement about basic normative principles and about what makes for a fully flourishing human life.

After passing his final examinations at the Wöhlerschule in 1918, Fromm studied jurisprudence for two semesters at Frankfurt University and then moved to Heidelberg, where he earned his doctorate in sociology. For his doctoral studies, he worked primarily with the sociologist Alfred Weber, Max Weber's brother, but also with Karl Jaspers and Salman Rabinkov, a Hasidic scholar of the Talmud and a socialist. His dissertation, *Das jüdische Gesetz: Zur Soziologie des Diaspora-Judentums* (Jewish Law: On the Sociology of the Jewish Diaspora; published in 1989), was completed in 1922 and prefigures his lifelong interest in working at the intersection of sociology, psychology, and philosophy. During the time that Fromm was studying in Heidelberg, he was also traveling to Frankfurt and teaching at the Freies Jüdisches Lehrhaus (Free

Jewish Teaching Institute) alongside such notable figures as Martin Buber.

In Heidelberg in the mid 1920s, Fromm opened up a psychoanalytic practice (a "therapeuticum") with Frieda Reichmann, a Jewish psychoanalyst who had practiced in Frankfurt years earlier, that was aimed explicitly at Jewish patients and was focused on unmasking and working through their repressions. Fromm married Reichmann on 16 June 1926, around the same time that he was turning away from Orthodox Judaism. In fact, both Reichmann and Fromm published articles in 1927 that reflected their rejection of Orthodox Judaism by way of psychoanalytic explanations of religious practices.

In the late 1920s and early 1930s, Fromm was studying and practicing psychoanalysis in Berlin, teaching at the Frankfurt Institute of Psychoanalysis, and starting to develop his ideas about synthesizing Marx's theory of class and Freud's theory of instinctual drives. At the opening of the Institute of Psychoanalysis in February 1929, Fromm gave a lecture titled "The Application of Psychoanalysis to Sociology and Religious Studies," in which he argues that both psychology and sociology must be brought to bear on contemporary problems, and that one must try to discern the relations between the ego formation of the individual and the broad sociological forces in which the individual exists. Fromm was also at this time developing his interpretation of Marxist humanism, and in this lecture he makes reference to Marx and Friedrich Engels's *Die heilige Familie* (1845; translated as *The Holy Family,* 1956), emphasizing how a genuine humanism must focus on the concrete relations between human beings; an adequate theory, in his view, must deflate any fetishistic claims that suggest that social forces are somehow detached from human individuals (the same sort of criticism Marx and Engels used against Georg Wilhelm Friedrich Hegel and others).

Fromm's first extensive study was *Die Entwicklung des Christusdogmas: Eine psychoanalytische Studie zur sozialpsychologischen Funktion der Religion* (The Development of the Dogma of Christ: A Psychoanalytic Study on the Social-Psychological Function of Religion), published in the psychoanalytic journal *Imago* in 1930 and then in book form in 1931; *Die Entwicklung des Christusdogmas* first characterized his work as a kind of radical Marxist social psychology. His arguments in this essay flow from the methodology he outlined in his lecture at the opening of the Institute of Psychoanalysis and are tailored to respond to the psychoanalytic treatment of religion defended by Theodor Reik, one of Fromm's teachers at the Psychoanalytic Institute in Berlin and the author of *Dogma und Zwangsidee* (Dogma and Compulsion, 1927). Fromm's criticisms of Reik here mirror

Fromm as a student at the University of Heidelberg, where he completed his dissertation in 1922 (from Rainer Funk, Erich Fromm: His Life and Ideas. An Illustrated Biography, *2000; Thomas Cooper Library, University of South Carolina)*

Marx and Engels's criticisms of their idealistic predecessors: one cannot understand people merely as instantiations of ideologies, but must rather understand the concrete individuals who create and believe in ideologies. Whereas both Fromm and Reik agree that Christian dogma is an expression of hostility toward a father figure, only Reik assumes that the psychological subject under investigation is a homogeneous group of religious believers, whereas Fromm argues that psychic and social interests subdivide the group and are conditioned by divergent political interests. Though Fromm later described himself as a "strict Freudian" in the early 1930s, his work at this time extends beyond the claim that religious persons are reduced to an infantile state; indeed, he explains that whereas psychoanalysis studies neurotic or sick individuals, social psychology studies normal individuals, and that in the latter case, social and political forces have a much greater influence. With this distinction in mind, he argues that a similar psychological dynamic is at work in class-divided society, where the ruling class serves as the father figure.

Around the same time as the publication of *Die Entwicklung des Christusdogmas,* Fromm became a member of the Institut für Sozialforschung in Frankfurt (Institute for Social Research, the so-called Frankfurt School)

working in social psychology. Though some commentators characterize Fromm as a minor player in the early years of the institute, many others argue that his contribution to the Frankfurt School, as well as his importance for the development of critical theory, has been greatly underestimated. His main contribution was without doubt his work on synthesizing Marx and Freud, combining psychoanalysis and historical materialism, but he also conducted research on the German working class in collaboration with others at the institute. On the theoretical side of his concerns, Fromm's most important contribution to the program of the early Frankfurt School was his 1932 article "Über Methode und Aufgabe einer Analytischen Sozialpsychologie: Bemerkungen über Psychoanalyse und historischen Materialismus" (The Method and Function of an Analytical Social Psychology: Remarks on Psychoanalysis and Historical Materialism), published in the first edition of the journal of the institute, the *Zeitschrift für Sozialforschung* (Magazine for Social Research). The empirical research he carried out at this time focused mainly on the administration and interpretation of more than six hundred questionnaires given to German workers regarding their political views. Working from this data, Fromm attempted to discern the contradictions and conflicts between the workers' unconscious attitudes and conscious political views.

In response to the growing influence of National Socialism, the Institut für Sozialforschung moved first to Switzerland in 1932 and then to Columbia University in New York City in 1934. Fromm continued to work for the institute through both moves, first in Switzerland, where he convalesced from having tuberculosis, and then in New York after his emigration from Germany on 25 May 1934 (he acquired American citizenship in 1944). Fromm had already traveled to the United States in 1933 to give lectures at the Psychoanalytical Institute in Chicago, upon the invitation of the German psychoanalyst Karen Horney (initiating a friendship that lasted until 1943), and had made various plans with Max Horkheimer, the director of the Institut für Sozialforschung, about continuing the group's research with the support of Columbia University. Also during this period of illness and relocation, Fromm separated from Frieda Fromm-Reichmann.

From 1934 to 1939 Fromm worked at the Institute for Social Research, taught as a visiting professor at Columbia University, and conducted research mainly on the authoritarian character and the various contemporary manifestations of masochism and sadism. In this period, he published essays in Horkheimer's *Studien über Autorität und Familie: Forschungsberichte aus dem Institut für Sozialforschung* (Studies on Authority and Family: Research Reports from the Institute for Social

*Fromm's first wife, Frieda Reichmann, with whom he opened a psychoanalytic practice for Jewish patients in the mid 1920s
(from Rainer Funk,* Erich Fromm: His Life and Ideas. An Illustrated Biography, *2000;
Thomas Cooper Library, University of South Carolina)*

Research, 1936). During these years, however, Fromm was plagued with illness, both relapses of tuberculosis and kidney problems, and so he traveled extensively with Horney, seeking out optimal locations for recuperation, alternating between mountain and sea climates. Fromm's health seemed to stabilize by 1939, most likely a result of new pharmaceutical innovations.

In 1939 Fromm left the Institute for Social Research, ostensibly because it was unable to support him in light of financial limitations, but it seems clear that there were other additional reasons. First of all, Horkheimer, the leading member of the group, was less than fully supportive of Fromm's research on German workers. Fromm reported at the time that Horkheimer had accused him of being a conformist and had taken the position that Fromm's psychological methodology was no longer useful for the social sciences. Compounding this chilled enthusiasm was the arrival in 1937 of Theodor Adorno, another German social theorist and philosopher, who was also reluctant to support Fromm's work. Fromm's persistent absence from New York as a result of his illnesses and traveling may have also been a contributing factor. The main reason for Fromm's departure, however, was most likely his theo-

retical disagreements with the other members regarding orthodox and revisionist Freudianism.

Fromm's complex appropriation and revision of Freud preoccupied him during this period and continued to be of concern for the rest of his career; he returns to issues of Freudian theory in almost every book, each time addressing and criticizing Freud's ideas in new contexts. The basic disagreement that Fromm had with Freud concerned the latter's theory of instincts or drives. Freud had argued that most social behaviors and pathologies could be reduced to a set of basic natural drives or instincts, and that these were genetic and inherited. Fromm argued that instincts are always already adapted to social conditions and, therefore, that the attempt to reduce behaviors to biologically based instinct would yield distorted explanations: he had taken a step in the direction of seeing instincts as being mediated and socially constructed instead of being simply natural. Of course, Fromm did not deny that all human beings have basic natural desires and instincts to secure food, water, and sex; he argued that the different ways that particular individuals express these instincts can only be understood as products of specific social processes, that what must be understood is the dialectic between natural and historical forces. Historical forces include modes of economic production and class structures, and these forces give rise to different character structures in individuals. Fromm was also at this time starting to develop his ideas about those existential features of the human situation that are completely irreducible to physiology, though these ideas did not become fully expressed until years later. Fromm was starting to defend the view, connected with his inchoate sense of the human existential situation, that the fundamental problem of psychology has to do with the ways human individuals are related to each other and the world, and not the problem of whether or not physiologically reducible drives or instincts are being satisfied. Horkheimer and Adorno (also Herbert Marcuse and Leo Löwenthal) were more interested in defending orthodox Freudianism, however, which they took to be a better interpretation of historical materialism. In their view, psychic phenomena were rooted in physiological processes, and so the Freudian picture of modern society as a set of institutions that impose restrictions on primal drives (mainly the instinct to life and the instinct to death) was correct.

The conflict between Freud's and Fromm's views might also be characterized as one between a generally pessimistic and a generally optimistic picture of contemporary society, and it would be fair to say that this same conflict is at work between Horkheimer and Adorno's view and Fromm's. The orthodox Freudian view is that civilization is essentially at odds with human nature and that the relationship between humans and society is static, which yields a rather pessimistic view since it suggests that humans will be more frustrated (and more likely to fall into neuroses) as they become more civilized. Fromm wanted to leave this pessimistic struggle behind and consider whether the causes of destructive human behavior might be particular social and historical conditions instead of society in general. In Fromm's view, humanity has the potential for loving and positive behavior, and this potential could be expressed given the right historical conditions. Fromm's critics seized upon this optimism, arguing that it is not justified by the rejection of Freud's instinct theory by itself, for it may well be that social conditions will inevitably do the work that Freud attributed to instincts. Indeed, as Fromm's critics point out, there needs to be another argument that shows that such optimism is actually warranted so that Fromm's view does not degenerate into messianic utopianism.

After breaking from the Institute for Social Research, Fromm cultivated connections with a new circle of researchers, among them Harry Stack Sullivan, an American psychiatrist who had invited Fromm to lecture at the Washington School of Psychiatry in the late 1930s and whose work on the psychology of interpersonal relations had influenced Fromm. He also strengthened his relationship with Horney, whose books *The Neurotic Personality of Our Time* (1937) and *New Ways in Psychoanalysis* (1939) were hugely successful at the time. In 1941 Fromm published *Escape from Freedom* (his first book written in English, since he stopped writing in German in 1938), started teaching at the New School for Social Research in New York City, and in 1942 began teaching at Bennington College in Vermont as well.

Escape from Freedom was the culmination of Fromm's research from 1936 to 1940, and its publication secured for him a broad readership and new level of fame. One reason for the impact of the book is that it offered an explanation for why the German and Italian bourgeoisie fell into fascism, an issue that weighed heavily on the American readership, and he grounded this explanation in a general theory of how and why people tend to flee from their own freedom, why they tend toward escape into structures of submission and domination. Although most of Fromm's work had grown out of the research program of the Institute for Social Research, he published *Escape from Freedom* outside of the auspices of the institute and failed to mention any of the collaboration with his former colleagues (aside from a single footnote to one of Horkheimer's essays). Even with this lack of acknowledgment, the journal of the institute, *Zeitschrift für Sozialforschung* (Journal for Social Research), printed a positive review of the book, possibly as an attempt to avoid alienating the newly famous Fromm.

The historical argument of *Escape from Freedom* shows how history has been a process of individuation, how humans have gradually taken themselves to be individuals who stand against nature and external authorities. Modern humanity, however, finds itself in a precarious position, Fromm argues, because although modern individualistic freedoms are typically considered an advance over premodern and traditional societies, these freedoms are also a curse: detached from traditional schemes of value and ways of interpreting the world, people are left uneasy, insecure, anxious, and isolated in a disenchanted world. Fromm argues that there are two ways to go: either embrace particularly modern freedoms and attempt to develop human intellectual and emotional potentials, or retreat in fear of freedom back to various dependencies.

Although Fromm claimed to have read only Jean-Paul Sartre's *Les Mouches* (1943; translated as "The Flies," 1946) and *L'Existentialisme est un humanisme* (1946; translated as *Existentialism,* 1947) at the time he was revising *Man for Himself: An Inquiry into the Psychology of Ethics* (1947), his ideas in the 1940s have a rather striking similarity to those of the existentialists. Indeed, his claims that humans live in existential disequilibrium, and that this predicament underlies most neuroses, ties his position to existentialism and increases the distance between his view and Freud's. Fromm argues, along with the existentialists writing in the early and mid twentieth century (for example, Martin Heidegger, Albert Camus, and Sartre), that although people say that what they want is freedom, there is a sense in which they are at the same time terrified of freedom, because it carries with it enormous responsibility, which leads to existential anxiety. Fromm quotes Fyodor Dostoevsky, a nineteenth-century precursor to existentialism, from the "Grand Inquisitor" chapter in his novel *Brat'ia Karamazovy* (The Brothers Karamazov, 1881), regarding how people are quick to give up their freedom as soon as it has been granted to them. This existential strain of Fromm's thinking also informs his willingness to defend a universal human situation instead of a universally shared determinate human nature: all human individuals find themselves in the same existential predicament but develop in different ways as they cope with this existential disequilibrium by way of dynamic adaptation to social and historical conditions.

Fromm's explanation of the psychology of fascism hinges on the human tendency to try to go back on the historical process of individuation, the individual's attempt to disburden himself or herself of this existential anxiety and aloneness by denying freedom, by fleeing into pathologies of denial. Such an escape would give the illusion of recapturing the unity with others and with nature that was lost through history. Fromm calls this irreversibly lost union "symbiosis" and argues that it is what both the sadist and the masochist are after: sadism and masochism are both escapes from aloneness, attempts to fuse with another person, to recapture the lost sense of unity. The sadist tries to join with another person by making him or her fully dependent, by robbing the other person of integrity and individuality; the masochist, on the other hand, tries to join with another person by becoming completely submissive and dependent on them. In both cases, the sadist and the masochist are trying to get rid of their selves, to forget themselves, and so disburden themselves of freedom.

A few features of Fromm's analysis of sadism and masochism in *Escape from Freedom* should be emphasized. First, there is nothing necessarily sexual about sadism or masochism; they are not expressions of sexual instincts, though they may sometimes be expressed in sexual ways. In fact it is more common to find sadism and masochism expressed in the nonsexual contexts of nationalism, religion, conformism, and destructiveness.

Fromm's psychoanalyst colleague Karen Horney, with whom he traveled extensively in the United States during the 1930s (Collection of Marianne Horney; from Rainer Funk, Erich Fromm: His Life and Ideas. An Illustrated Biography, *2000; Thomas Cooper Library, University of South Carolina)*

Second, sadism and masochism are not expressions of physiological instincts at all: contrary to Freud, Fromm argues that human beings are driven to avoid aloneness and to cope with existential anxiety, and that since human beings always find themselves in webs of interconnected relations with others, they will seek out strategies within these webs. Both the sadist and the masochist desperately need the other person to whom they are relating. Finally, Fromm thinks that the social conditions for producing what he calls the "authoritarian character," a person in whom both sadistic and masochistic tendencies exist, are just as ripe in the contemporary United States as they were in Germany and Italy during the rise of fascism. All human beings experience existential insecurity, and all people are prone either toward the submission to some authority or other or toward the sadistic destruction of others; whether societies produce authoritarian characters or turn toward an embrace of freedom, toward love and productive work, is a matter of how social, political, and economic forces are arranged.

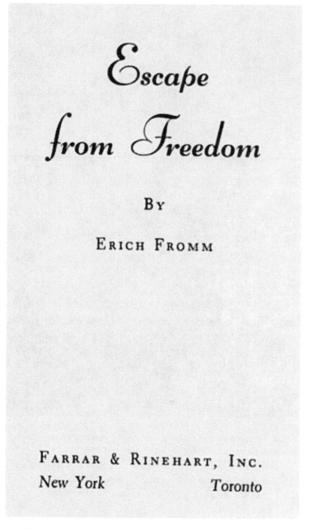

Escape from Freedom

By

Erich Fromm

Farrar & Rinehart, Inc.
New York   Toronto

Title page for Fromm's 1941 book, in which he presents his theory of why fascism appealed to the German and Italian middle classes (from Rainer Funk, Erich Fromm: His Life and Ideas. An Illustrated Biography, *2000; Thomas Cooper Library, University of South Carolina)*

During the 1940s, after the publication of *Escape from Freedom,* Fromm was dividing his teaching energies between the University of Michigan, Yale University, Bennington College, and New York University. In 1944 he married Henny Gurland, who had left France in 1940 to escape the Nazis (and was witness to Walter Benjamin's suicide in Spain during her escape), and in 1945 he founded the William Alanson White Institute of Psychiatry, Psychoanalysis, and Psychology (along with Sullivan). His most significant work during the 1940s, though, following *Escape from Freedom* and largely as a development of the ideas in that book, was *Man for Himself.*

Fromm's view that psychology cannot be separated from philosophy and ethics becomes clear in *Man for Himself,* along with his more general claim that psy-chology, philosophy, and sociology are comprehensively wrapped up in normatively grounded humanism. Fromm's view is that a healthy and productive sense of self-identity entails the embrace of a rationalistic and humanistic ethics. He defends the roughly Aristotelian view that human nature is fully expressed in an ethical way of life and that questions of ethics rest on both the science of human nature and the study of human psychology. In *Escape from Freedom* Fromm had tried to capture this Aristotelian model of human development with the notion of "spontaneity," but in *Man for Himself* he begins to employ the notion of the "productive character," which is a mode of openness and relatedness to the world and other persons. Fromm distinguishes between productive and nonproductive character orientations, where the former is expressive of human capacities and the latter is destructive of them. These character types are not organizations of libido, as Freud would have it, but ways that a person can be related to the world and others.

The most important type of nonproductive character orientation is what Fromm calls the "marketing character," and his discussion of this character type has been the most enduring contribution of *Man for Himself.* This character orientation is particular to modern society and capitalist market economies and results in the reduction of diverse human values to exchange value. In its most exaggerated form, this character orientation leads to an individual's experiencing him- or herself as a commodity, as a thing with an assignable exchange value. The person of this character type eventually begins to commodify his or her own personality and becomes alienated from his or her human capacities, since these capacities are being bundled and sold for a price. Fromm argues that contemporary capitalist society celebrates and successfully promotes this character orientation because people have become indifferent about their own selves; this indifference opens one up to manipulation, alienation, and nonproductivity.

By the late 1940s Henny Fromm was suffering from a mysterious and seemingly untreatable illness that resembled lead poisoning and that left her with excessively painful arthritis; Fromm canceled the majority of his lecturing engagements in 1948–1949 to assist her. They discovered, however, that the radioactive springs in San José Purua, Mexico, effectively treated her pain, so they moved to Mexico City in June 1950. For the first two years in Mexico, Fromm stopped teaching at Bennington and the New School and stopped lecturing in New York generally; but after his wife's death in June 1952, he began teaching again annually at the White Institute and at the New School. Fromm continued to live in Mexico until 1973, during which time he started lecturing in Spanish at the University of Mexico, trained psychoanalysts (psychoanalytic theory was not well known in Mexico at the time), and taught at the National Autonomous University in Mexico City (from 1957 to 1965), lecturing on psychoanalysis and Freud. From 1957 to 1961 he also gave seminars twice a year at Michigan State University and lectured extensively around the United States in 1961 and 1962. On 18 December 1953, Fromm married Annis Freeman, his third wife, to whom he remained married until his death.

Also during this period Fromm had a growing interest in religious mysticism, which developed into his book *Psychoanalysis and Religion* (1950), and began the serious study of Zen Buddhism, quickly integrating Buddhist ideas into his psychoanalytic practice. This influence was mainly the result of Fromm's relationship with Daisetz T. Suzuki, the widely known teacher of Zen Buddhism, a relationship that began in the 1940s and intensified in the 1950s. Suzuki visited Mexico in 1957 to hold a week-long seminar at which Fromm presented a paper titled "Psychoanalysis and Zen Buddhism," which was later published under the same title in the journal *Psychologia* in 1959. Fromm was particularly attracted to Buddhism because its practice did not entail that individuals submit to an irrational authority; that is, it does not share the regressive and infantilizing tendencies of Christianity. He also thought that the principles of Zen Buddhism could be used in the investigation of the unconscious and toward the integration of one's ego into the world, and to this end he committed to a daily mediation practice; indeed, he argued, the analyst-patient relationship could be enhanced if the analyst could cultivate his or her powers of concentration through Zen meditation.

Though Fromm had supported socialism since his student days, as he characterized it, he had never participated in a socialist party until the 1950s, when he joined the American Socialist Party. He also became involved in the peace movement and in 1957 cofounded SANE (National Committee for a Sane Nuclear Policy), which turned out to have an important role in the movement. Indeed, his activism was significant enough to draw the attention of the Federal Bureau of Investigation, which had a large file on him (more than six hundred pages). Fromm himself always held the belief that he simply did not have the personality or abilities required for political activity; but he felt it would be morally reprehensible to remain passive in light of the dangers in the world, so he became involved despite his own self-assessment. He also felt that the increasing insanity of the world drove people, himself included, into cooperative political association of necessity, as a means for preserving their humanity. With these issues in mind, in 1961 Fromm wrote his

book *May Man Prevail? An Inquiry into the Facts and Fictions of Foreign Policy,* which is an analysis of Cold War antagonisms.

In *Das Unbehagen in der Kultur* (1930; translated as *Civilization and Its Discontents,* 1930) Freud considers the possibility that an entire society could be sick and argues that, in his view, the conflict between natural human instincts and the institutional demands of society makes this communal sickness an actuality. Freud is careful, however, in that work to note that the main difficulty with diagnosing a collective neurosis is that the notion of "normality" utterly dissolves, because there is no standard to compare the sick individual with, and so it is difficult to avoid a paralyzing relativism. Fromm addresses precisely this problem in *The Sane Society* (1955), based in large part on the ideas he developed in his lectures at the New School in New York in 1953 regarding the "pathology of normalcy." In addition to venturing the diagnosis that contemporary capitalist society is quite alienated from itself–indeed, pathologically insane–he attempts to ground this analysis on a theory of human nature. *The Sane Society* is an important work in Fromm's career because it restates and develops the key ideas he had been working on in *Escape from Freedom* and *Man for Himself,* especially the idea of social character; moreover, in this book he returns to his existential view of human nature and has more to say about the concrete contemporary political situation and what specific changes must occur if society is to better express human potentials.

Fromm's restatement of his existential theory of human nature here is helpful because, while describing it now as a "normative humanism," he differentiates his view from the existentialist view defended by Sartre. In a lecture delivered in 1945 (later published as *L'Existentialisme est un humanisme*), Sartre argues that existentialism is a kind of humanism because it values highly individual freedom, which is the source of human dignity; but the criticism that plagued Sartre and other existentialists was that this sort of existentialist humanism is an empty formalism, that it does not have the resources to recommend one way of life over another. This problem is the one that worried Freud in *Das Unbehagen in der Kultur.* With his "normative humanism" Fromm tries to acknowledge that the human existential situation does not by itself escape relativism and yet argue that there are nonetheless satisfactory and unsatisfactory ways to go about responding to this situation. The most fundamental human drive, according to Fromm, is to figure out answers to the fundamental existential problem of being human, to recapture some sort of unity with nature and with other human beings. Fromm thought that the drive to respond to the existential situation could be directed either toward freedom and life or

Fromm with his second wife, Henny Gurland, whom he married in 1944 (from Rainer Funk, Erich Fromm: His Life and Ideas. An Illustrated Biography, *2000; Thomas Cooper Library, University of South Carolina)*

toward escape and destruction, and he saw this conflict as being functionally analogous to Freud's positing of the life and death instincts but with the difference that, in his view, the drive to freedom and life is stronger than its counterpart. Fromm tried to relate this basic choice between life and death to a variety of contrasting evaluative pairs: relatedness versus narcissism, transcendence (creativeness) versus destructiveness, rootedness (brotherliness) versus incest, sense of identity (individuality) versus conformity, and reason versus irrationality.

Fromm, however, argues that if society is to promote the instinct to life instead of to death, it must conform to genuine human needs. One must look at how political, economic, and ideological forces shape the formation of social character and ask whether these forces are a recipe for producing healthy or sick people. In accordance with the question—"Are we sane?"—with which Fromm opens the book, one must consider what society specifies as "normality" and "health" and ask whether, when examined from the perspective of normative humanism, these states are not actually insanity. Fromm argues that contemporary capitalist society has sketched out a model of the healthy person as one who

is cooperative and tolerant yet competitive, aggressive, and ambitious; but if this so-called healthy person is seen as alienated and as one who pursues answers to the existential problematic of the human situation in self-frustrating ways, then some alternative form of society is required. In *The Sane Society* Fromm specifically recommends universal, guaranteed subsistence income and generally endorses socialism as the only economic arrangement that can genuinely address human needs.

The Art of Loving, first published in 1956, is Fromm's best-selling work. It has sold more than twenty-five million copies and been translated into more than fifty languages. In this work Fromm argues that the basic problem of human existence, that all humans find themselves looking for wholeness and unity and trying to overcome their persistent sense of separateness, has only one sane and satisfactory answer: love. The more-common ways that humans attempt to overcome their experience of separateness, though, typically fail for one reason or another. Some individuals, for example practitioners of primitive religions, try to experience unity through orgiastic activities, which offer only a transitory and fleeting satisfaction. Others, for example those participating in more recent organized religions, reach for wholeness through conformity, which also is not a genuine unity. Some individuals attempt to overcome separateness through creative and artistic pursuits, but these pursuits, Fromm argues, are not sufficiently interpersonal to constitute a genuine unity. Love, Fromm thinks, is a genuine overcoming of separateness, but only if understood properly, as the transcending of what he calls "symbiotic union," which is the union between mother and fetus. Masochism and sadism are attempts to overcome separation that reduce to merely symbiotic union and so are fusions without integrity: the former is a passive form of fusion by submission, and the latter is an active form of fusion by control. Genuine love must be the experience of unity that nonetheless preserves individual integrity.

The Art of Loving is for Fromm yet another attempt to come to terms with Freud's theory, and in this work Fromm clarifies his disagreements more effectively than in previous works. He describes Freud's view here as a kind of "physiological materialism" that takes the sexual instinct to be primary and the varieties of love as mere manifestations of that more fundamental urge. Fromm argues, though, that the primary human desire is for unity, for the overcoming of separateness, and that love and sex are just manifestations of this more basic desire. One difficulty that Fromm finds with Freud's view is that it is not clear why individuals seek out loving interpersonal relationships over autoeroticism, since there is no necessity on the Freudian model that sexual pleasure and release be experienced with another person as opposed to alone. Equally problematic is the implication of Freud's view of love as merely the expression of a biological instinct and thus essentially irrational; Fromm argues that the more convincing view is that love is actually a kind of rational judgment and commitment. Another problem Fromm finds with Freud's view is that its physiological materialism is narrowly masculine: Freud models the sexual instinct on specifically male sexual behavior, but Fromm argues that this premise misses the point that both masculine and feminine viewpoints are partial, viewpoints that must be overcome through the genuine unity that love provides.

Fromm's view of love is deeply connected with his humanism, because for him it is a general attitude and orientation of character, not merely a set of feelings, and it must culminate in reason and humility. For Fromm, the extent to which one cultivates a humanistic attitude and character orientation is the extent to which one can experience loving relations with others. Indeed, he argues that the primary task in practicing the art of loving is learning how to overcome narcissism, which is tantamount to cultivating objectivity and taking up the view of humanity as a whole. Fromm argues, though, that the currently fashionable models of love as "mutual sexual satisfaction" and love as "teamwork" fail to live up to the humanistic ideal. He also argues in this book that while genuine love and capitalism seem contradictory, they are actually only incompatible in principle, that some people will be able to experience genuine love despite the fact that contemporary capitalist society trains people to take up degenerating forms of love.

Between 1959 and 1962 Fromm published three books that developed and clarified his complex appropriation of both Freud and Marx, the two most important influences on his intellectual development. These books were *Sigmund Freud's Mission: An Analysis of His Personality and Influence* (1959), *Marx's Concept of Man* (1961), and *Beyond the Chains of Illusion: My Encounter with Marx and Freud* (1962). In one sense, these books sum up and consolidate ideas Fromm had been working on since *Die Entwicklung des Christusdogmas,* but they also deepen the central claims of the main view he was developing, especially regarding his notion of social character and his distinction between productive and nonproductive character orientations. Fromm also reveals important autobiographical insights in *Beyond the Chains of Illusion* and makes clear the importance of Marx's theory of alienation for his position in *Marx's Concept of Man.*

Though parts of Marx's economic and philosophical manuscripts of 1844 (also known as "The Paris Manuscripts") were available in translation in Raya Dunayevskaya's book *Marxism and Freedom: From 1776 until Today* in 1958, and an English translation from Russia was available in England in 1959, Fromm's *Marx's Concept of Man* made a much more complete translation of Marx's work available to an English-speaking audience in the United States when it was published in 1961 (Fromm recruited Tom B. Bottomore to provide translation). The importance of this translation and Fromm's essay for the reception of Marx in the United States is difficult to overestimate, for this work makes it clear that in addition to being a radical economic theorist, Marx was also a philosopher, humanist, and theorist of alienation. Indeed, Marx was misunderstood by those unfamiliar with his humanist concerns and also, as Fromm explains, by those who are blinded by ignorance and hysteria. At the time Fromm was writing, many people associated Marx's theory with the political states of affairs in the Soviet Union and China, but Fromm clarifies in his essay that Marx is defending an ideal that is wholly unrealized in those countries. Against such common distortions and falsifications, he argues that Marx is properly understood as standing squarely in the Western humanist tradition, that his main interest is in the sort of political and economic system that best realizes human capacities and potentials.

Two features of Marx's theory that Fromm explains in *Marx's Concept of Man,* and that are of particular importance for Fromm's own view, are his theory of human nature and his theory of alienation. Fromm explains that Marx does in fact defend a conception of human nature, but he argues that it is one that must always be expressed through human self-development and human activity. That is to say, even if one accepts that the basic need for food is biologically given, that need will always be expressed in some particular fashion or other, and it is expressed through human action in conditions that have been produced by human efforts. Looked at this way, the expression of human need and human essence will always already be part of human self-realization and creative expression, part of the process by which people are actively defining what it means to satisfy basic needs in human as opposed to merely animalistic ways. Marx's notion of expressive "self-activity" is a parallel concept to Fromm's productivity, and Fromm shows in his essay that the contrasting evaluative pairs he used in *The Sane Society* can be traced back to Marx's basic distinction between the human and the nonhuman.

Fromm also explains Marx's theory of alienation in capitalist society, arguing that the theory identifies different kinds of alienation: alienation of the product of labor, alienation of the activity of labor itself, alienation of humans from their species, and alienation of humans

Fromm with his third wife, Annis Freeman, and his mother, Rosa, at Fromm and Freeman's wedding reception on 18 December 1953 (from Rainer Funk, Erich Fromm: His Life and Ideas. An Illustrated Biography, *2000; Thomas Cooper Library, University of South Carolina)*

from themselves. For Marx, the alienation of the product from the laborer is not a simple externalization but a separation in which the product returns as a "hostile" force. This hostility consists in the fact that after the worker has created a product, it is owned by someone else; it was never really the laborer's product. Moreover, the owner of the product (the employer) stands in a hostile and alien relationship to the laborer. The worker's labor itself is also alienated because it is forced and exploitative. Especially important for Fromm's view is the third aspect of Marxian alienation: alienation from one's species. This type of alienation takes the form of egoism, individualism, atomism, or any other general estrangement from all other individuals. Marx (and Fromm) feels that under capitalism, individuals are forced to view others as means and potential obstacles to their ends. For the worker, every other worker must be viewed as a competitor for jobs; for the capitalist, every other capitalist must be seen as a competitor for profit. In both cases, it becomes rational to

cheer at the failure of one's competitors. Speaking of the alienation of one's self is a way of summing up all the other senses of alienation, and Fromm takes up this meaning in his notion of the "marketing character" that he addressed especially in *Man for Himself*. Marx argues that when a product that one has worked on is sent down the assembly line, it is in a real sense part of one's self and one's activity, because one's life is one's labor. When one loses touch with one's productive activity and one's relations to others, one has become alienated from one's self.

Just a year after publishing *Marx's Concept of Man*, Fromm published *Beyond the Chains of Illusion*, which highlights the general sense in which Marx and Freud develop critical theories of the individual and society, how they both aim at debunking myths and dispelling illusions that are generated by social relations but that prevent individuals in modern society from attaining any sort of healthy self-realization. Looking back over his sixty-two years of life, Fromm also in this book gives his readers some insights into his personal encounter with these two thinkers. He observes that both thinkers defended a critical attitude that requires the self-scrutiny of one's thoughts, feelings, and intuitions, especially where these were wrapped up in common political ideology. The cultivation of this critical attitude is precisely the project Fromm takes to animate his intellectual biography.

Also in *Beyond the Chains of Illusion* Fromm presents his clearest statement of humanism and how it is offered as a solution to alienation. The final chapter of the book is titled "Credo" and states in programmatic form the key tenets of Fromm's humanism: that human beings are part nature and part transcendence; that they have an ascertainable essence; that they can respond to their existential disequilibrium by personally and individually choosing either life or death; that society has the power both to further and to inhibit human development; that the only force that can save them from themselves is reason, which is a matter of character and not intelligence; and that they must rid themselves of illusion and alienation if they expect to utilize reason in their striving toward human perfectibility.

Fromm spent his last years, roughly from 1965 to 1980, preoccupied with the effects of technology on individuals, especially where technology has led to the threat of nuclear war, discussed in, for example, *The Revolution of Hope: Toward a Humanized Technology* (1968); he was also preoccupied with what he took to be a general culture of declining and decaying human life. His research on these issues is comprehensively addressed in his *The Anatomy of Human Destructiveness* (1973). Fromm also continued his political involvement through his support of Senator Eugene McCarthy in 1968, with speeches and appearances in support of his nomination for president by the Democratic Party. McCarthy did not win the nomination, and Richard Nixon went on to become president; consequently, Fromm withdrew from political activity to some extent, but he was nonetheless able to channel his experience in the campaign toward a productive end by writing about it in *The Revolution of Hope*.

In 1970, Fromm published his book *Social Character in a Mexican Village: A Sociopsychoanalytic Study,* which was based on the research he had conducted in Mexico throughout the 1960s with his collaborator, Michael Maccoby. It studies the dependence of character formation on class and other socio-economic factors, especially with respect to how these forces led to harmful behaviors such as alcoholism. In this sociopsychological field-research project Fromm and Maccoby studied roughly eight hundred Mexican farmers in Chiconcuac, primarily through the use of questionnaires; it was designed to show the way social character functioned, especially the way it tends to be shaped by class status. Fromm and Maccoby found that the class-determined features of social character are reliably expressed in economic behavior. Notably, Fromm and his associate discussed their findings with the farmers themselves as a form of group therapy, which was directed at treating alcoholism and other class-related social problems.

The study of the Mexican village was important for the reception of Fromm's work because it decisively answered a common complaint that had been directed at his work over the years: that it was speculatively breezy, overly philosophical, and lacking sufficiently hard data to support his claims. Since *Social Character in a Mexican Village* was supported by five years of field research, it could hardly be criticized as too speculative. In any case, Fromm always maintained the position that every theoretical and speculative claim he made was supported by his psychoanalytic practice, his therapeutic dealings with actual patients. Fromm's incorporation of philosophical ideas into his work was also quite deliberate, and he could always answer such criticisms by turning the tables and accusing his critics of arguing from excessively positivistic premises.

After completing his work on the Mexican village, Fromm returned to his work on aggression and published *The Anatomy of Human Destructiveness,* which represents the culmination of his lifelong preoccupation with the authoritarian personality and destructive and aggressive tendencies. Here again, he develops a point of contention between himself and Freud. The latter argued that human beings have both a drive to life and a drive to death and that both of these drives are natural and equal in strength; but Fromm argued that the drive to death is not natural but pathological. Indeed, in Fromm's view, there is only a drive to life, an instinct to flourishing and development, but often socio-economic conditions thwart this drive, and that circumstance is when destructive tendencies arise. Destructive tendencies, then, represent failures to live well.

In *The Anatomy of Human Destructiveness* Fromm develops his ideas about necrophilia (ideas that he had originally introduced in *The Heart of Man: Its Genius for Good and Evil* in 1964), now considering it to be another common form of destructive behavior alongside sadism and masochism. The necrophiliac character is one who is attracted to things that are dead or decayed, who wants to transform the living into the dead, who enjoys destruction, and who is fascinated by the technological and mechanical. Importantly, there is nothing necessarily sexual about the necrophiliac character, though the most documented cases prior to Fromm's work concerned the purely sexual practices of necrophilia. Fromm uses case studies as well as his own psychoanalytic research to enumerate the various personality traits, habits, and language of the necrophiliac character, from the tendency toward lifelessness in conversation to the obsession with the mechanical ability to reduce living persons to corpses and the general perspective on the world that is preoccupied with lifeless artifacts and dead objects. Earlier, in *Escape from Freedom*, Fromm had argued that Adolf Hitler was the perfect example of the "authoritarian character," of someone in whom both sadistic and masochistic tendencies exist; here, Fromm develops an "analytic psychobiographical study" of Hitler as a clinical case of necrophilia. Fromm scrutinizes Hitler from his childhood to his adult life, his personality, habits, neuroses, and relations to women and others to show that Hitler manifests an extreme form of alienation and hatred of life.

Fromm's last two major works, *To Have or to Be?* and *The Art of Being* (published posthumously in 1993), represent his attempt to explore the contrary orientation to necrophilia, which he called "biophilia," or love of life, the sort of productive, open, loving, and humanistic life he comes to defend repeatedly in his writings. In *To Have or to Be?* Fromm concentrates mainly on the basic character orientations of selfishness and altruism, but the book also diagnoses contemporary society as a whole as being in crisis and so offers suggestions for a solution, thus serving as an extension of his arguments in *Man for Himself, The Sane Society,* and *The Revolution of Hope.* Fromm argues in *To Have or to Be?* that contemporary society suffers from a chronic low-grade schizophrenia and alienation that are concentrated in the "marketing character" or "marketing orientation" that he had described in earlier works. The kind of work Fromm is doing in *To Have or to Be?* might be characterized as the application of Marx's theory of alienation to contemporary culture, but with special sensitivity to the way alienation can be widespread in a society that is stable and prosperous, and suffered acutely by those individuals who are wealthy, healthy, and seemingly happy. The contemporary version of Marx's alienated person is one who may have much but who has not learned to be much. Fromm argues that the tendency toward a declining mode of living is correlated with a dependence on outside things and values instead of internal powers and capacities, which are productive of an ascending mode of living. People want to "have" things to compensate for their own lack of being. So, for example, a person who lives outwardly, who develops a sense of identity based on having possessions, will be crushed if these possessions are taken away, because that person will no longer have a self. Importantly, Fromm is not arguing against any outward relations at all; he is just arguing that one should not be so dependent on outward relations that one's self is totally destroyed by the loss of those things. In other words, a person can exist in the mode of being and still have many possessions; those possessions are not constitutive of the person's self-identity, however.

From 1974 to 1980 Fromm lived in Switzerland with his wife, Annis Freeman, but during this period his health began to fail him. He had already suffered a heart attack in 1966, when he was visiting New York City to give a speech in Madison Square Garden expressing his criticisms of the war in Vietnam, and he had three more between 1977 and 1980, the last of which caused his death. He died in Switzerland on 18 March 1980.

In considering the major innovations and achievements of twentieth-century European cultural theory, Fromm's importance can hardly be contested. Apart from his influence as an interpreter of Freud and of Marx, as an early influence on the development of critical theory, and as a creative psychoanalytic theoretician and practitioner, Fromm's studies of social character, character types, sadism, masochism, and necrophilia are serious contributions to understanding the problematic relationship between the individual and society. Contemporary commentators will disagree about whether Fromm's humanism should ultimately be characterized as naive optimism or as an inspiring synthesis, but at least his view must be acknowledged as a distinctive, forceful, and articulate engagement with the central concerns and questions of social theory in the middle twentieth century.

Biography:

Rainer Funk, *Erich Fromm: His Life and Ideas. An Illustrated Biography,* translated by Ian Portman and Manuela Kunkel (New York: Continuum, 2000).

References:

Douglas Kellner, *Critical Theory, Marxism and Modernity* (Baltimore: Johns Hopkins University Press, 1989), pp. 36–43, 154–157, 161–162, 251–252;

Bernard Landis and Edward S. Tauber, *In the Name of Life: Essays in Honor of Erich Fromm* (New York: Holt, Rinehart & Winston, 1971);

Rolf Wiggershaus, *The Frankfurt School: Its History, Theories, and Political Significance,* translated by Michael Robertson (Cambridge, Mass.: MIT Press, 1994), pp. 52–60, 117–120, 150–155, 265–273.

Papers:

Erich Fromm's papers are held at the Erich Fromm Archives, Tübingen, Germany, and the Instituto Mexicano de Psicoanálisis in Mexico City.

Hans-Georg Gadamer
(11 February 1900 – 14 March 2002)

Matthew Beedham
Malaspina University-College

BOOKS: *Platos dialektische Ethik: Phänomenologische Interpretationen zum "Philebos"* (Leipzig: Meiner, 1931); revised as *Platos dialektische Ethik und andere Studien zur platonischen Philosophie* (Hamburg: Meiner, 1968); translated by Robert M. Wallace as *Plato's Dialectical Ethics: Phenomenological Interpretations Relating to the "Philebus"* (New Haven & London: Yale University Press, 1991);

Plato und die Dichter (Frankfurt: Klostermann, 1934);

Volk und Geschichte im Denken Herders (Frankfurt am Main: Klostermann, 1942);

Bach und Weimar (Weimar: Böhlau, 1946);

Goethe und die Philosophie (Leipzig: Volk & Buch, 1947);

Über die Ursprünglichkeit der Wissenschaft (Leipzig: Barth, 1947);

Über die Ursprünglichkeit der Philosophie: Zwei Vorträge (Berlin: Chronos, 1948);

Vom geistigen Lauf des Menschen: Studien zu unvollendeten Dichtungen Goethes (Godesberg: Küpper, 1949);

Gedächtnisrede auf Oskar Schürer (Darmstadt: Neue Darmstädter Verlagsanstalt, 1952);

Wahrheit und Methode: Grundzüge einer philosophischen Hermeneutik (Tübingen: Mohr, 1960; revised, 1965; revised again, 1972; revised again, 1975; revised again, 2 volumes, 1986; revised again, 1990); translated by William Glen-Doepel as *Truth and Method,* edited by Garrett Barden and John Cumming (New York: Seabury Press, 1975; London: Sheed & Ward, 1975); translation revised by Joel Weinsheimer and Donald G. Marshall (New York: Crossroad, 1989; London: Sheed & Ward, 1989);

Le problème de la conscience historique (Louvain & Paris: Béatrice-Nauwelaets, 1963); translated as "The Problem of Historical Consciousness," *Graduate Faculty Philosophy Journal* (New School for Social Research), 5 (1975): 1–52;

Dialektik und Sophistik im siebenten platonischen Brief (Heidelberg: Winter, 1964);

Kleine Schriften, 4 volumes (Tübingen: Mohr, 1967–1972);

Hans-Georg Gadamer (from Philosophische Lehrjahre: Eine Rückschau, *1977; Thomas Cooper Library, University of South Carolina)*

Werner Scholz (Recklinghausen: Bongers, 1968);

Die Begriffsgeschichte und die Sprache der Philosophie (Opladen: Westdeutscher Verlag, 1971); translated as "The History of Concepts and the Language of Philosophy," *International Studies of Philosophy,* 18, no. 3 (1986): 1–16;

Hegels Dialektik: Fünf hermeneutische Studien (Tübingen: Mohr, 1971); translated by Smith as *Hegel's Dialec-*

tic: Five Hermeneutical Studies (New Haven & London: Yale University Press, 1976);

Über die Naturanlage des Menschen zur Philosophie (Pforzheim: Stadt Pforzheim, 1971);

Wer bin Ich und wer bist Du?: Ein Kommentar zu Paul Celans Gedichtfolge Atemkristall (Frankfurt am Main: Suhrkamp, 1973); translated by Richard Heinemann and Bruce Krajewski as *Gadamer on Celan: "Who Am I and Who Are You?" and Other Essays,* edited by Heinemann and Krajewski (Albany: State University of New York Press, 1997), pp. 67–126;

Idee und Wirklichkeit in Platos Timaios (Heidelberg: Winter, 1974);

Rhetorik und Hermeneutik (Göttingen: Vandenhoeck & Ruprecht, 1976);

Vernunft im Zeitalter der Wissenschaft: Aufsätze (Frankfurt am Main: Suhrkamp, 1976);

Die Aktualität des Schönen: Kunst als Spiel, Symbol, und Fest (Stuttgart: Reclam, 1977); translated by Nicholas Walker as *The Relevance of the Beautiful and Other Essays,* edited by Robert Bernasconi (Cambridge & New York: Cambridge University Press, 1986);

Philosophische Lehrjahre: Eine Rückschau (Frankfurt am Main: Klostermann, 1977); translated by Robert R. Sullivan as *Philosophical Apprenticeships* (Cambridge, Mass.: MIT Press, 1985);

Poetica: Ausgewählte Essays (Frankfurt am Main: Insel-Verlag, 1977); revised and expanded in *Gedicht und Gespräch* (Frankfurt: Insel, 1990);

Die Idee des Guten zwischen Plato und Aristoteles (Heidelberg: Winter, 1978); translated by Smith as *The Idea of the Good in Platonic-Aristotelian Philosophy* (New Haven & London: Yale University Press, 1986);

Lectures on Philosophical Hermeneutics (Pretoria: Universiteit van Pretoria, 1982);

Heideggers Wege: Studien zum Spätwerk (Tübingen: Mohr, 1983); translated by John W. Stanley as *Heidegger's Ways* (Albany: State University of New York Press, 1994);

Lob der Theorie: Reden und Aufsätze (Frankfurt am Main: Suhrkamp, 1983); translated by Chris Dawson as *Praise of Theory: Speeches and Essays* (New Haven: Yale University Press, 1998);

Die Vielfalt Europas: Erbe und Zukunft (Stuttgart: Robert Bosch Stiftung, 1985);

Gesammelte Werke, 10 volumes (Tübingen: Mohr, 1985–1995);

Die Universität Heidelberg und die Geburt der modernen Wissenschaft (Berlin & New York: Springer-Verlag, 1986); translated by Lawrence Schmidt and Reuss as "The University of Heidelberg and the Birth of Modern Science," in *Hans-Georg Gadamer on Education, Poetry, and History: Applied Hermeneutics,* pp. 37–46;

Platon als Porträtist (Munich: Freunde und Förderer der Glyptothek und der Antikensammlungen München, 1988);

Das Erbe Europas: Beiträge (Frankfurt am Main: Suhrkamp, 1989);

Sprache und Ethik im technologischen Zeitalter: Bamberger Hegelwoche 1990, by Gadamer and others (Bamberg: Fränkischer Tag, 1991);

Über die Verborgenheit der Gesundheit: Aufsätze und Vorträge (Frankfurt am Main: Suhrkamp, 1993); translated by Jason Gaiger and Nicholas Walker as *The Enigma of Health: The Art of Healing in a Scientific Age* (Oxford: Polity Press, 1996; Stanford, Cal.: Stanford University Press, 1996);

L'Inizio della filosofia occidentale: Lezioni raccolte da Vittorio De Cesare (Milan: Guerini, 1993); translated by Joachim Schulte as *Der Anfang der Philosophie* (Stuttgart: Reclam, 1996); translated by Rod Coltham as *The Beginning of Philosophy* (New York: Continuum, 1998);

Die Moderne und die Grenze der Vergegenständlichung, by Gadamer and others, edited by Bernd Klüser (Munich: Klüser, 1996).

Editions in English: *Philosophical Hermeneutics,* edited and translated by David E. Linge (Berkeley: University of California Press, 1976);

Dialogue and Dialectic: Eight Hermeneutical Studies on Plato, edited and translated by P. Christopher Smith (New Haven & London: Yale University Press, 1980)–includes "Plato and the Poets" *[Plato und die Dichter],* pp. 39–72; "Plato's Educational State" *[Platos Staat der Erziehung],* pp. 73–92; "Dialectic and Sophism in Plato's *Seventh Letter*" *[Dialektik und Sophistik im siebenten platonischen Brief],* pp. 93–122; "Idea and Reality in Plato's *Timaeus*" *[Idee und Wirklichkeit in Platos Timaios],* pp. 156–192;

Reason in the Age of Science, translated by Frederick G. Lawrence (Cambridge, Mass.: MIT Press, 1981)–includes "On the Natural Inclination of Human Beings toward Philosophy" *[Über die Naturanlage des Menschen zur Philosophie],* pp. 139–150;

The Relevance of the Beautiful and Other Essays, translated by Nicholas Walker, edited by Robert Bernasconi (Cambridge & New York: Cambridge University Press, 1986)–includes "The Relevance of the Beautiful: Art as Play, Symbol, and Festival" *[Die Aktualität des Schönen: Kunst als Spiel, Symbol, und Fest],* pp. 1–56;

Hans-Georg Gadamer on Education, Poetry, and History: Applied Hermeneutics, translated by Lawrence

Schmidt and Monica Reuss, edited by Dieter Misgeld and Graeme Nicholson (Albany: State University of New York Press, 1992)–includes "On the Primordiality of Science: A Rectoral Address" [Über die Ursprünglichkeit der Wissenschaft], pp. 15–22; "The Diversity of Europe: Inheritance and Future" [Die Vielfalt Europas: Erbe und Zukunft], pp. 221–236; "The University of Heidelberg and the Birth of Modern Science" [Die Universität Heidelberg und die Geburt der modernen Wissenschaft], pp. 37–46;

Literature and Philosophy in Dialogue: Essays in German Literary Theory, translated by Robert H. Paslick (Albany: State University of New York Press, 1994)–includes "Goethe and Philosophy" [Goethe und die Philosophie], pp. 21–30; "On the Course of Human Spiritual Development: Studies of Goethe's Unfinished Writings" [Vom geistigen Lauf des Menschen: Studien zu unvollendeten Dichtungen Goethes], pp. 31–66; "Bach and Weimar" [Bach und Weimar], pp. 109–118;

The Philosophy of Hans-Georg Gadamer, edited by Lewis Hahn (Chicago: Open Court, 1997).

OTHER: "Zur Systemidee in der Philosophie," in *Festschrift für Paul Natorp zum siebzigsten Geburtstage* (Berlin: De Gruyter, 1924), pp. 55–75;

"Zu Kants Begründung der Ästhetik und dem Sinn der Kunst," in *Festschrift Richard Hamann zum sechzigsten Geburtstage 29. Mai 1939, überreicht von seinen Schülern* (Burg bei Magdeburg: Hopfer, 1939), pp. 31–39;

Aristotle, *Metaphysik XII,* edited by Gadamer (Frankfurt am Main: Klostermann, 1948);

Wilhelm Dilthey, *Gundriss der allgemeinen Geschichte der Philosophie,* edited by Gadamer (Frankfurt am Main: Klostermann, 1949);

"Bemerkungen über den Barock," in *Retorica e barocco,* edited by Enrico Castelli (Rome: Fratelli Bocca, 1955), pp. 61–63;

"Einleitung," in *Denken: Eine Autobiographie,* translated by H.-J. Finkeldei, edited by R. G. Collingwood (Stuttgart: Koehler, 1955), pp. v–xiv;

"Denken," "Geisteswissenschaften," "Geschichte und Geschichtsauffassung," and "Geschichtlichkeit," in *Die Religion in Geschichte und Gegenwart,* third edition, volume 2, edited by Kurt Galling (Tübingen: Mohr, 1958), cols. 84–85, 1304–1308, 1488–1496, 1496–1998;

"Historismus," in *Die Religion in Geschichte und Gegenwart,* third edition, volume 3, edited by Galling (Tübingen: Mohr, 1959), cols. 369–371;

"Sprache, II. Philosophisch," "Tradition, I. Phanomenologisch," and "Verstehen," in *Die Religion in*

Geschichte und Gegenwart, third edition, volume 6, edited by Galling (Tübingen: Mohr, 1962);

"Hegel: Vollendung der abendländischen Metaphysik?" in *Hegel, Holderlin, Heidegger,* edited by Hans Gehrig (Karlsruhe: Badenia, 1971), pp. 11–23;

"Historicité," in *Encyclopaedia universalis* (Paris: Encyclopaedia Universalis, 1971), VIII: 452–455;

"Einführung," in *Seminar: Philosophische Hermeneutik,* edited by Gadamer and Gottfried Boehm (Frankfurt: Suhrkamp, 1976), pp. 7–40;

"Die Kunst des Feierns," in *Was der Mensch braucht,* edited by Hans Jürgen Schultz (Stuttgart & Berlin: Kreuz, 1977), pp. 61–70;

"Religious and Poetical Speaking," in *Myth, Symbol, and Reality,* edited by A. M. Olson (Notre Dame, Ind.: University of Notre Dame Press, 1980), pp. 86–98;

"A Classical Text–A Hermeneutic Challenge," translated by Fred Lawrence, in *Contemporary Literary Hermeneutics and Interpretation of Classical Texts,* edited by Stephanus Kresic (Ottawa: University of Ottawa Press, 1981), pp. 327–332;

"Die Kultur und das Wort," in *Kultur als christlicher Auftrag heute,* edited by Ansgar Paus (Graz: Styria, 1981), pp. 11–23; translated by Dennis J. Schmidt as "Culture and Words," in *Hermeneutics and the Poetic Motion,* edited by Schmidt (Binghamton: Center for Research in Translation, State University of New York at Binghamton, 1990), pp. 11–23;

"Discussion" (by Gadamer and Paul Ricoeur) and "The Conflict of Interpretations," in *Phenomenology: Dialogues and Bridges,* edited by Ronald Bruzina and Bruce Wilshire (Albany: State University of New York Press, 1982), pp. 299–304, 213–230;

"Articulating Transcendence," in *The Beginning and the Beyond: Papers from the Gadamer and Voegelin Conferences,* edited by Lawrence (Chico, Cal.: Scholars Press, 1984), pp. 1–12;

"The Hermeneutics of Suspicion," in *Hermeneutics: Questions and Prospects,* edited by Gary Shapiro and Alan Sica (Amherst: University of Massachusetts Press, 1984), pp. 54–65;

"Die gemeinschaftsbildende Kraft der Kultur: Ein Beitrag zur Umformung deutschen Geisteslebens," in *Die Deutschen und die deutsche Frage 1945–1955: Darstellung und Dokumente,* edited by Manfred Overesch (Dusseldorf: Droste, 1985), pp. 89–91;

"Der Kunstbegriff im Wandel," in *Künste unserer Zeit,* edited by the University of Heidelberg (Heidelberg: Heidelberger Verlagsanstalt und Druckerei, 1985), pp. 7–19;

"Einleitung in den philosophischen Teil," in *Karl Jaspers: Philosoph, Arzt, politischer Denker,* edited by Jeanne Hersch, Jan Milic Lochmen, and Reiner Wiehl (Munich: Piper, 1986), pp. 200–206;

"Tradition und Autorität," in *Was halten sie von Thomas Mann? Achtzehn Autoren antworten,* edited by Marcel Reich-Ranicki (Frankfurt am Main: Fischer, 1986), pp. 85–88;

"Bild-Gedicht-Gespräch," in *Dieter Stöver 1922–1984,* edited by Gadamer (Bod Tölz: Kunstverein Bad Tölz, 1987), pp. 2–10;

"*Sein und Zeit,*" in *Die Heidegger Kontroverse,* edited by Jürg Altwegg (Frankfurt am Main: Athenäum, 1988), pp. 11–13;

"Oberflächlichkeit und Unkenntnis: Zur Veröffentlichung von Victor Farias," in *Antwort: Martin Heidegger im Gespräch,* edited by Günther Neske and Emil Kettering (Pfullingen: Neske, 1988), pp. 152–156; translated by John McCumber as "'Back from Syracuse?'" *Critical Inquiry,* 15, no. 2 (1989): 427–430;

"Anfang und Ende der Philosophie," in *Heideggers These vom Ende der Philosophie: Verhandlungen des Leidener Heidegger-Symposiums April 1984,* edited by Marcel F. Fresco, Rob J. A. van Dijk, and H. W. Peter Vijgeboom (Bonn: Bouvier, 1989), pp. 7–19; translated as "The Beginning and the End of Philosophy," in *Martin Heidegger: Critical Assessments,* 4 volumes, edited by Christopher Macann (London & New York: Routledge, 1989), I: 16–28;

"Kultur und Medien," in *Kultur und Medien,* edited by Gadamer and G. Pflug (Hamburg: Freie Akademie der Künste, 1989), pp. 4–19; translated by Barbara Fultner as "Culture and Media," in *Cultural-Political Interventions in the Unfinished Project of Enlightenment,* edited by Axel Honneth and others (Cambridge, Mass.: MIT Press, 1992), pp. 172–199;

"Der Mensch als Naturwesen und als Kulturträger," in *Mensch und Natur: Auf der Suche nach der verlorenen Einheit,* edited by Gotthard Fuchs (Frankfurt am Main: Knecht, 1989), pp. 9–30;

"Text and Interpretation," "Letter to Dallmayr," and "Hermeneutics and Logocentrism," in *Dialogue and Deconstruction: The Gadamer-Derrida Encounter,* edited and translated by Diane P. Michelfelder and Richard E. Palmer (Albany: State University of New York Press, 1989), pp. 21–50, 93–101, 114–128;

"Humanismus heute?" in *Die Wissenschaft und das Gewissen: Vorträge und Beiträge als Grundlage für Deutung und Bewältigung heutiger Probleme* (Stuttgart: Württembergischer Verein zur Förderung der humanistischen Bildung, 1992), pp. 57–70;

"Philosophizing in Opposition: Strauss and Voegelin on Communication and Science," in *Faith and Political Philosophy: The Correspondence between Leo Strauss and Eric Voegelin, 1934–1964,* edited and translated by Peter Emberley and Barry Cooper (University Park: Pennsylvania State University Press, 1993), pp. 249–259;

"Der Kunstbegriff im Wandel," in *Kunst ohne Geschichte? Ansichten zu Kunst und Kunstgeschichte heute,* edited by Anne-Marie Bonnet and Gabrielle Kopp-Schmidt (Munich: Beck, 1995), pp. 88–103;

"Hermeneutik–Theorie und Praxis," in *Psychoanalyse heute und vor 70 Jahren,* edited by Heinz Weiss and Hermann Lang (Tübingen: Diskord, 1996), pp. 359–368.

SELECTED PERIODICAL PUBLICATIONS–
UNCOLLECTED: "Metaphysik der Erkenntnis: Zu clem gleichnamigen Buch von Nicolai Hartmann," *Logos,* 12, no. 3 (1923/1924): 340–359;

"Wissenschaft als Bernf: Uber den Ruf und Bernf der Wissenschaft in unserer Zeit," *Leipziger Neueste Nachrichten und Handels-Zeitung,* 270 (27 September 1943): 3;

"Was ist der Mensch?" *Der europäischen Mensch,* special issue of *Illustrierte Zeitung Leipzig* (1944): 31–34;

"Universität in ungerer Zeit: Der Leipziger Rektor über den gesellschaftlichen Auftrag der Wissenschaft," *Göttinger Universiäits-Zeitung,* no. 11 (9 May 1947): 10–11;

"Die Philosophie in den letzten dreissig Jahren," *Ruperto-Carola* (Heidelberg), 5 (December 1951): 33–34;

"Die Mythologie der Griechen: Zu dem Pastellwerk von Werner Scholz," *FAZ,* 130 (7 June 1955): 8;

"Aristophanes in Schwetzingen," *Die Gegenwart,* 13, no. 12 (14 June 1958): 372;

"Das Faktum der Wissenschaft," *Sitzungsberichte der Wissenschaftlichen Gesellschaft zu Marburg,* 88, no. 1 (1967): 11–20;

"Metaphysik im Zeitalter der Wissenschaft," *Akten des Internationalen Leibniz-Kongresses* (Hanover), 1 (1968): 1–12;

"Die Gegenwartsbedeutung der Griechischen Philosophie," *Praktika tis Akadimias Athinon* (Athens, Greece), 47 (7 November 1972): 243–265;

"Hermeneutics and Social Science," *Cultural Hermeneutics,* 2, no. 2 (1975): 307–316;

"L'herméneutique philosophique," *Sciences religieuses: Revue canadienne,* 5, no. 1 (Summer 1976): 3–13;

"Wissenschaft und Öffenlichkeit," *Diagnostik,* 10, no. 4 (October 1977): 770–774; translated as "Science and the Public," *Universitas,* 23, no. 3 (1981): 161–168;

"Die Ausdruckskraft der Sprache," *Jahrbuch der Deutschen Akademie für Sprache und Dichtung* (1979): 45–55; translated as "The Expressive Power of Language," *PMLA,* 107, no. 2 (March 1992): 345–352;

"Practical Philosophy as a Model of the Human Sciences," *Research in Phenomenology,* 9 (1980): 74–85;

"Was ist Geschichte? Anmerkungen zu ihrer Bestimmung," *Neue Deutsche Hefte,* 27, no. 3 (1980): 451–456;

"Die Aufgabe der Philosophie," *Neue Zürcher Zeitung,* 204, no. 30 (5/6 February 1983): 65–66;

"Die dreifache Auflärung," *Neue Deutsche Hefte,* 33, no. 2 (1986): 227–233;

"Heideggers 'theologische' Jugendschrift," *Dilthey Jahrbuch für Philosophie und Geschichte der Geisteswissenschaften,* 6 (1989): 228–234;

"Erinnerung," *Jahrbuch der Deutschen Schillergesellschaft,* 34 (1990): 464–468;

"Wahrheit und Methode: Der Anfang der Urfassung [ca. 1956]," edited by Jean Grondin and Hans-Ulrich Lessing, *Dilthey Jahrbuch für Philosophie und Geschichte der Geisteswissenschaften,* 8 (1992–1993): 131–142;

"Arbeiterstudium und Universität," *Kultur und Kritik: Leipziger philosophische Zeitschrift,* 6 (March 1994): 112–122.

Hans-Georg Gadamer was one of the leading figures of postwar German culture. His vast writings—collected in the ten-volume *Gesammelte Werke* (Collected Works, 1985–1995), with previously uncollected writings continuing to be published in book form—have significantly influenced not only philosophical discourse but other disciplines, including history, art history, and literature. While Greek philosophy and hermeneutics were the two main foci of his work, it is for his magnum opus, *Wahrheit und Methode: Grundzüge einer philosophischen Hermeneutik* (1960; translated as *Truth and Method,* 1975), that he is known as the creator of modern hermeneutics. Written from his base at the University of Heidelberg, *Wahrheit und Methode* has been a center of discussion and critique both within Germany and in the wider world since its publication in 1960.

Hans-Georg Gadamer was born in Marburg an der Lahn on 11 February 1900 to Johanna and Johannes Gadamer. His father, a university professor in the natural sciences, had an excellent knowledge of Horace but was basically averse to all book knowledge. In fact, throughout Gadamer's young life his father had tried to interest him in the natural sciences but was continually disappointed by his lack of success. He eventually let Gadamer have his way in choosing his discipline but clearly was unhappy about his choice of studies.

Gadamer's parents, Johanna (née Gewiese) and Johannes Gadamer (from Jean Grondin, Hans-Georg Gadamer: A Biography, *translated by Joel Weinsheimer, 2003; Thomas Cooper Library, University of South Carolina)*

Gadamer graduated from Holy Spirit Gymnasium in Breslau in 1918. During his final year of high school, Thomas Mann's *Betrachtungen eines Unpolitischen* (1918; translated as *Reflections of a Nonpolitical Man,* 1983) gave him his first introduction to critical thinking. Similarly, he had been enchanted by the melancholy tone of Herman Hesse's early novels. When he enrolled at Breslau University, however, he had no idea that this literary path would lead to philosophy. In fact, Gadamer was enticed by a whole range of academic disciplines, but his interest in philosophy finally asserted itself over his genuine interests in literature, history, and art history. In his essay "Reflections on My Philosophical Journey," published in *The Philosophy of Hans-Georg Gadamer* (1997), he refers to the choice as "really less a turning away from one of these and towards the others so much as it was a gradual pressing further and further on into the discipline of scholarly work as such."

The Holy Spirit Gymnasium in Breslau, Poland, from which Gadamer graduated in 1918 (from Jean Grondin,
Hans-Georg Gadamer: A Biography, *translated by Joel Weinsheimer, 2003;*
Thomas Cooper Library, University of South Carolina)

He started at the university as World War I was in its last year, and the confusion that reigned in Germany at the time served as an impetus to philosophical questioning. Specifically, in the grisliness of the war he perceived the defeat of Neo-Kantianism. It was no longer possible, he felt, simply to join a surviving tradition. A mood of catastrophe was spreading, along with continuing pressure on the old traditions, as described in Paul Ernst's *Der Zusammenbruch des deutschen Idealismus* (The Collapse of German Idealism, 1918). Similarly, Theodor Lessing's *Europa und Asien* (Europe and Asia, 1918), a work based on Eastern wisdom, questioned the totality of European accomplishment-oriented thinking. The book had a profound effect on young Gadamer, relativizing all the ideas that he had grown up with and leading him to think.

Expressionism, the dominant mode in art and life at the time, fueled his search, along with that of many other young scholars, for a new orientation. His first introduction to conceptual thinking came from Richard Hönigswald. Gadamer meticulously took down his lecture course "Basic Questions in the Theory of Knowledge" (the two notebooks from this course are in the Hönigswald Archive in Würzburg). The lectures offered Gadamer a good introduction to transcendental

philosophy, so when he arrived in Marburg in 1919 he already had some preparation in this field.

Marburg offered new academic experiences. The critique of historical theology, later called "dialectical theology," that followed from Karl Barth's *Der Römerbrief* (1919; translated as *The Epistle to the Romans,* 1933) was beginning in Marburg, and Edmund Husserl's art of phenomenological description, offering a counterpoint to the "methodologism" of the Neo-Kantians, was similarly highly regarded. It was the "life philosophy" supported by Friedrich Nietzsche, however, and the problem of historical relativism found in the work of Wilhelm Dilthey and Ernst Troeltsch that garnered the attention of many of the young students. The atmosphere was set for a strong critique of academic culture.

Gadamer was sure that the experience of art had something to do with philosophy. One of his most important artistic influences at the time was the poet Stefan George. In "Reflections on My Philosophical Journey," Gadamer recalls the enchantment of George's poetry and its role in his studies: "The fact that a poet like George could, with the magical sound of his verse and the force of his person, exercise such a powerful formative effect on human beings remained a nagging question for many thoughtful persons, represented a never completely forgotten corrective to the play with concepts I was encountering in my philosophical study." Other artistic influences at the time include Vincent van Gogh, especially his letters, and Søren Kierkegaard, beginning with *Enten-eller* (Either/Or, 1843). Following the new reception of Kierkegaard in Germany at that time, the claim to truth was proposed in "existentialism." Newer ground was being broken, however, in the "Marburg School" of philosophy, which boasted scholars such as Paul Natorp, Max Scheler, and Nicolai Hartmann, who all played important roles in Gadamer's dissertation on Plato, for which he received his doctorate in 1922. Gadamer's first article, published in 1923, was, in fact, on Hartmann's *Grundzüge einer Metaphysik der Erkenntnis* (Basics of a Metaphysics of Knowledge, 1921). Later, after attending the philological seminar of Paul Friedländer, Gadamer published "Der aristotelische *Protreptikos* und die entwicklungsgeschichtliche Betrachtung der aristotelischen Ethik" (The Aristotelian *Protreptikos* and Aristotelian Ethics from the Standpoint of Their Developmental History), a critique of Werner Jaeger, in *Hermes: Zeitschrift für klassische Philologie* (Hermes: Journal of Classical Philology) in 1928. Despite the fact that Gadamer was a student of Martin Heidegger at the time, the article brought him some acclaim in philological circles.

During the summer of 1923 Gadamer went to Freiburg, where he studied Book 6 of Aristotle's *Nicomachean Ethics* with Heidegger. Gadamer once claimed that he owed everything to Heidegger, and the tribute was not exaggerated. From Heidegger, Gadamer learned to bring historical thinking into the recovery of his own questions. Especially important was Heidegger's evocation of Greek philosophy. Gadamer realized that the philosophy of Greece could only be fetched back once self-consciousness had been forfeited. This idea led to his early essay "Zur Systemidee in der Philosophie" (On the Idea of System in Philosophy, 1924), in which he attempted to refute the new idea that philosophy could be reduced to basic experiences and explained without historical understanding.

After passing a rigorous state examination in classical philology in 1927 and his *habilitation* in 1928, Gadamer entered a new phase of his career. In 1928 Heidegger had left Marburg and returned to Freiburg, and with this departure Gadamer's apprenticeship ended and the beginning of his own teaching activities in Marburg began. Eight years later, Heidegger gave three lectures in Frankfurt, known as *Der Ursprung des Kunstwerkes* (The Origin of Artwork). Gadamer went to Frankfurt to hear them and found that the lectures so closely addressed his own questions and experience of the proximity of art and philosophy that they awakened an immediate response in him.

Discovering Heidegger's use of the term "historically affected consciousness," Gadamer realized the need to recognize the limitation placed on consciousness by history having its effect. This experience provided Gadamer with his first introduction to the universality of hermeneutics, and quite suddenly he realized that all of his studies up to that point were of no use in grappling with the challenge that Heidegger's interpretations had forced upon him. Guided by Friedländer, he began a systematic study of classical philology, reading Friedrich Hölderlin's translation of Pindar, the Greek philosophers, and ancient rhetoric. "Antike Atomtheorie" (Ancient Atomic Theory), which appeared in *Zeitschrift für die gesamte Naturwissen* (Journal of Universal Natural Science) in 1935, is the only piece published from that time. Given these scholarly interests, at this time Gadamer also became interested in Georg Wilhelm Friedrich Hegel.

Plato was at the center of Gadamer's studies. In fact, his first book about Plato, *Platos dialektische Ethik: Phänomenologische Interpretationen zum "Philebos"* (1931; translated as *Plato's Dialectical Ethics: Phenomenological Interpretations Relating to the "Philebus,"* 1991), was based on his *habilitation* thesis. It was originally a book on Aristotle's two treatises on pleasure in the *Nicomachean Ethics* (Book H: 10–13 and Book K: 1–5), but to tackle the subject in a phenomenological way he had to relate the treatises to the Platonic *Philebus,* so he undertook a phenomenological interpretation of this dialogue. His two aims were to understand the function of Platonic dialectic from a phenomenology of the dialogue and to explain the teaching about pleasure and its forms of appearance from a phenomenological analysis of real phenomena found in life. The book had relative success and received some recognition.

Gadamer then undertook more than ten years of mathematics-oriented studies. He was assisted in the area of mathematics and number theory by working with Jakob Klein, who wrote the treatise "Greek Logistics and the Rise of Algebra" (1936). Given the turbulence of events at that time, Gadamer abandoned a larger study of the Sophistic and Platonic doctrines of the state, publishing only two parts: *Plato und die Dichter* (1934; translated as "Plato and the Poets," 1980) and *Platos Staat der Erziehung* (translated as "Plato's Education State" in *Dialogue and Dialectic: Eight Hermeneutical Studies on Plato,* 1980), published in volume one (1942) of the journal *Das neue Bild der Antike* (The New Picture of Antiquity). The law of self-preservation dictated that one strenuously avoid politically relevant themes. Gadamer's only book published during the Third Reich was *Volk und Geschichte im Denken Herders* (People

Gadamer in his apartment in Marburg in the early 1920s (from Jean Grondin, Hans-Georg Gadamer: A Biography, *translated by Joel Weinsheimer, 2003; Thomas Cooper Library, University of South Carolina)*

and History in the Thinking of Herder, 1942), in which he attempts to work out the role of the concept of power in Johann Gottfried Herder's historical thinking. He strictly avoided any hint of relevance to the present, although some were still offended.

Having managed to continue publishing without offending the Nazi regime too much, in the spring of 1937 Gadamer was finally able to move from the position of *dozent* (a position akin to that of adjunct in the United States), which he had held for ten years in Marburg, to the position of professor. In rapid succession, he was then offered the chair in classical philology at Halle and then the position of philosophical *ordinariate* in Leipzig. At the end of the war, Gadamer, now as the first postwar rector of the University of Leipzig in the new communist state of East Germany, had administrative tasks that disrupted the continuation of his philosophical work. He wrote the majority of the interpretations of poetry that appear in his four-volume *Kleine Schriften* (Small Writings, 1967–1972) on weekends.

In the fall of 1947, after two years as rector in Leipzig, he moved to Frankfurt am Main in West Germany, where he was able to return entirely to teaching and research. Alongside his attempts to rectify the distressed situation of students at the time through intensive teaching hours, he edited two new editions: Aristotle's *Metaphysik XII* (Metaphysics: Book XII, 1948) and Dilthey's *Gundriss der allgemeinen Geschichte der Philosophie* (Outline of the History of Philosophy, 1949). While he had clearly begun a successful academic career, the call he received in 1949 to succeed Karl Jasper's chair in Heidelberg marked the beginning for Gadamer of true accomplishment in the academic world. The next year he married Kaete Lekebusch. The Gadamers had one child–a daughter, Andrea–from the marriage. He taught at Heidelberg for forty years, and despite the task of rebuilding, he managed to avoid politics and work toward the publication, in 1960, of *Wahrheit und Methode*.

At its root, *Wahrheit und Methode* is a result of Gadamer's dedication to teaching. He had always been a teacher who offered his students intensive contact, and

Gadamer (left) and the philosopher Martin Heidegger in August 1923, shortly after Gadamer arrived at the University of Freiburg to study Aristotle's Nicomachean Ethics *under Heidegger (from* Philosophical Apprenticeships, *translated by Robert R. Sullivan, 1985; Thomas Cooper Library, University of South Carolina)*

teaching helped him work out his ideas, because he was able to teach in line with his research plans. "Hermeneutical philosophy" arose, in fact, from his effort to be theoretically accountable for the style of his studies and teaching. On the other hand, his teaching perhaps prevented the book from being published sooner: the writing of the book always had to wait for his vacations, and consequently, it took ten years to complete.

In *Wahrheit und Methode* Gadamer establishes his own branch of philosophical, or dialectical, hermeneutics. The term *hermeneutics* is the ancient Greek word for *interpret* or *interpretive understanding*. In Greek mythology, Hermes was Zeus's messenger and, as such, was responsible for coming down to Earth to tell humans what Zeus had said. Although one can understand utterances, texts, people, works of art, and historical events, hermeneutics is the art of interpreting such enti-

ties. Despite this ancient root, *hermeneutics* did not take on its modern meaning—a way of interpreting—until the period of the Protestant Reformation. At this time, when the Bible became available to a much larger readership, arguments about what it said became increasingly frequent, and hermeneutics emerged as the way to interpret the Bible. Later, people started to use it to interpret law and literature, and by the 1800s it was used as a method of interpretation across the humanities. Prior to Gadamer, hermeneutics was the attempt to refine a methodology for the proper interpretation of such entities.

In *Wahrheit und Methode* Gadamer attempts to demonstrate that the truths of history cannot be discerned by scientific observation because these truths are only revealed through a kind of dialogue. He begins this study using Heidegger's "hermeneutic of facticity" to critique German idealism and its Romantic traditions. Specifically, he starts with Dilthey's attempt to establish the methodological foundations of the humanities (*Geisteswissenschaften*) and then critically contrasts Dilthey's work with his own philosophical hermeneutics. Noting the bias whereby only methods appropriate to natural sciences were being prescribed in hermeneutics, Gadamer attempts to show that truths arrived at in the human sciences are legitimate even though they are established through methods quite different from those employed in the natural sciences. He does not intend to prescribe a specific methodology for the human sciences; rather, he wants to establish how understanding can be procured. His attempt, therefore, is in part to clarify the phenomenon of *Verstehen* (understanding) in contrast with *Erklären* (explanation), the characteristic mode of the natural sciences. Alongside this concern, he also wants to correct the misrepresentations of the human sciences Dilthey and Friedrich Schleiermacher propagated. He feels that Dilthey and Schleiermacher's insistence on the necessity of adopting the point of view of the author of a text or historical event requires a kind of objectivity that is not possible.

In seeking to develop a philosophical hermeneutics, disciplines based on "understanding" form an obvious starting point, but Gadamer adds the experience of art, a topic that he returns to in several of his later essays, such as those in *Die Aktualität des Schönen: Kunst als Spiel, Symbol, und Fest* (1977; translated as *The Relevance of the Beautiful and Other Essays,* 1986). He perceives that both art and historical disciplines present ways of experiencing in which the understanding of experience is brought into play, but he begins with art because he sees it as involved in undermining the confidence in the methodologies of the hermeneutic disciplines, a phenomenon he views largely as the unintentional consequence of Immanuel Kant's work in *Kritik der Urtheilskraft* (Critique of Judgment, 1790). Once Kant conceived taste as a subjective judgment concerning the pleasure or dissatisfaction aroused by the formal properties of a thing, no room was left for the idea of taste as a special sensitivity to the uniqueness of particular situations: a sensitivity that facilitates sound interpretive judgments. Instead, knowledge, after Kant, is acquired in accordance with strict principles of reason, not through subtle discriminations that lack objective justifications. Gadamer attempts to reverse this development in the understanding of the human sciences, and he begins with the recognition that art cannot be correctly understood as an extension of natural beauty. He educes that art is created not only for the sake of providing aesthetic pleasure but also for the sake of sharing insights and discoveries, and thus, it allows a fuller understanding of the world because it provides a possible world in which people can see themselves. That is, any artwork is a human creation, and thus there is always a continuity of meaning linking the work of art with the existing world. Because of this continuity of meaning, the audience is able to understand and appreciate the work of art.

Truth, then, in the interpretation of a work of art is not the exclusive reserve of science. Rather than methodological judgments about art or the intentions and genius of the artist, Gadamer's central concern is the experience of art, and this experience he tries to describe as accurately as possible. To experience a work of art does not mean to reconstruct the circumstances of its original moment but to take part in a living relationship. A work of art created in the past still speaks to modern audiences. In fact, the work of art can only speak to a modern audience. Their world is their perspective, their vantage point, from which they view what happens and from which they try to make out the past. To explain this relationship, Gadamer refers to "worlds" as horizons. One can see only so far over the horizon into the past. When earlier proponents of hermeneutics attempted to refine a methodology for the proper interpretation of some entity, they failed to grasp that their own understanding of an object—the methodological principles they devised—were historically conditioned. The interpreter of a text from a past culture belongs to and is conditioned by his own different culture, so he is, to use a term that Gadamer borrows from Heidegger, a *wirkungsgeschichtliches bewusstsein* (historically affected consciousness) who views the past and its remnants from a particular horizon, involving a particular "pre-understanding." Self-understanding comes up against limits: the "historically affected consciousness," which is "more being than consciousness." People inherit forms of consciousness through their education, but these are only alienated forms of their true historical being. The originary experiences provided by art and history cannot be grasped by these forms because they insert a distance that prevents an audience from taking account of how much of themselves must come into play when they encounter art or studies of history.

Gadamer therefore sought a hermeneutics that would overcome the primacy of self-consciousness and the prejudices of idealism rooted in consciousness. To make this jump, he refers to the mode of *Spiel* (game or play). He positions at the pivot of experience not the audience but the artwork, and working with this positioning, he determines *Spiel* a suitable term to describe art: it is a game that "tends to master its players." In playing a game, the game itself is never a mere object. The game exists in those who play it and for those who play or even participate as spectators. Not only inter-

Gadamer (right) and Jürgen Habermas, with whom he carried on a long-running intellectual debate
(photograph by Silvana Condemi; from Jean Grondin, Hans-Georg Gadamer: A Biography,
translated by Joel Weinsheimer, 2003; Thomas Cooper Library, University of South Carolina)

pretations of art, then, but also the artwork itself makes a claim to truth. Works of art are not isolated from the world, and the experience of art "does not leave him who has it unchanged."

Gadamer's understanding of history thus involves an interplay between past and present—a "fusion of horizons." Culture changes over history: to restate Gadamer's example, *classical* has a different meaning for a citizen of Athens in the fifth century than it does for an eighteenth-century German historian, which is different again from its meaning, for a twenty-first-century American philosopher. One cannot decide which of these interpretations is correct since any verdict is historically conditioned and liable to a revision by a later age. At best an interpretation can be authentic, making the best possible reflective use of the preunderstanding or prejudice from which one inevitably begins. This interpretative limit raises the issue of accountability. Gadamer asks, "In how far is method a guarantor of truth? It is the role of philosophy to make us aware that scholarship and method have a limited place within the whole of human *Existenz* and its rationality." Thus one needs to explore one's own preunderstanding and all the relations to the world and to

history that it involves. An understanding of the past and its remains not only depends on, but also promotes, one's self-understanding.

Gadamer's idea of the "hermeneutic circle" is a useful tool for moving toward self-understanding. The reader of a sentence needs to know the words of which it is composed, but often to know those words the reader has to understand the sentence: the words need a context in order to mean something. The reader moves forward by making tentative guesses at the meaning of the words and revising those guesses until she has read enough of the sentence to know for sure whether she has guessed correctly. So every time one reads there is a process of moving back and forth between words and sentences, between the particulars and the whole. This recursion occurs not just in the attempt to understand words and sentences, but whenever one attempts to understand something. Such is Gadamer's hermeneutic circle: the dialectical movement between the parts and the whole that leads to understanding.

The inspiration for the hermeneutic circle can be traced back to Gadamer's classical Greek studies of the 1920s. Based on this work, he developed a strong inter-

Gadamer and his wife, Kaete Lekebusch-Gadamer, at a 2000 ceremony at the University of Heidelberg celebrating
Gadamer's one hundredth birthday (photograph by Udo Worffel; from Jean Grondin, Hans-Georg
Gadamer: A Biography, translated by Joel Weinsheimer, 2003;
Thomas Cooper Library, University of South Carolina)

est in rhetoric, both as the art of speaking and as theory. He finds the rationality of the rhetorical way of arguing a far greater consequence for society than the excellence of science. Although rhetoric attempts to bring emotions into play, it also highlights arguments and probabilities, and thus in *Wahrheit und Methode* he relates himself to rhetoric. He sees one task of hermeneutics as the integrating of the monologic quality of science into the communicative consciousness, a problem that has existed, he determines, since Plato. Gadamer insists that one accesses the world through language: that language is universal. Totality is never an object but rather a world-horizon that encloses everyone. Dialectic is the art of having a conversation, including a conversation with oneself—perhaps seeking an understanding of oneself.

Gadamer compares understanding to a conversation. Not only is the dialectical movement of a conver-

sation like the hermeneutic circle, but a conversation is also a fusion of horizons between oneself and someone else. The conversation is also a useful model for the way audiences think about art. For example, the stimulus to respond to what one reads is the same as that in a conversation. The text asks one to think about things in a new or different way, and by responding one makes one's responses clearer to oneself. Just as conversations with people prompt new thoughts, one can also have conversations with paintings, music, and sculpture.

Aristotle and Plato have perhaps been even more important to Gadamer's thinking than the great thinkers of German idealism. Taking Aristotle's idea of "practical philosophy," which is more than a methodological model (more of a substantive foundation) for the "hermeneutic" discipline, Gadamer finds that the Hegelian dialectic renews many of the truths of a practical philosophy. Plato must, Gadamer cautions, be read mimetically, however. The hermeneutical effort to think of the nature of language in terms of dialogue ultimately signified that every formulation one might make was in principle surpassable in the process of conversation. The rigid fixing of things in terminology, which is appropriate for modern science in its effort to put knowledge into the hands of its anonymous society of investigators, is suspect in relation to the realm of motion called philosophical thought.

Recognizing "historically affected consciousness" was not Gadamer's only goal. There is also a "hermeneutical problem" in the natural sciences, as has been discussed by Thomas S. Kuhn. Kuhn describes how the reigning paradigm is decisive in terms of which questions research proposes and what data is considered. So in order to have a fusion of horizons and broader horizons, one must stay open to whatever experience one is having. The hermeneutic process takes place by putting an experience into words and thereby into the common consciousness. One way to initiate this process is to ask questions, because asking questions requires being open to the experience. When good questions are asked, new knowledge can be produced. Gadamer envisions hermeneutic philosophy not as an absolute position but as a path of experiencing. Aware of the need to resist the arbitrariness of constructed definitions and the illusion that philosophical speaking can be standardized into obligatory forms, in the years following the publication of *Wahrheit und Methode* Gadamer and Helmut Kuhn launched *Philosophische Rundschau* (Philosophical Panorama), a journal dedicated to critique. Gadamer's wife, Kaete Lekebusch-Gadamer, managed the journal for twenty-three years.

After formally retiring from Heidelberg in 1968, Gadamer was able to present his ideas on hermeneutics in other countries and became a traveling scholar. Free from the demands of teaching, he ventured to the United States and Canada for a series of lectures. Although fluent in French, his English was initially limited; regardless, he strived to lecture in English and, notably, without a prepared text in the attempt to give expression to his own style of thinking. During his time in the United States and Canada, and later in Europe, he linked his teaching to his research by focusing on the role of Greek philosophy in Western culture. As his English improved, so too did his knowledge of American philosophy, and he noted the possibility of a bridge between analytic philosophy and hermeneutics. Theology, with its roots in Greek and Latin, provided another link. In fact, the "hermeneutical approach" is a part of several fields, and Gadamer connected with several departments outside of philosophy. Departments related to language and literature, especially comparative literature, offered fruitful associations. He was also embroiled in a somewhat friendly debate with another scholar, Jürgen Habermas, who injected the therapeutic situation of psychoanalysis into the program of critique of ideology, a step that Gadamer rejected. (This debate with Habermas is well documented in the 1971 volume *Hermeneutik und Ideologiekritik.*)

More than thirty years after publishing *Wahrheit und Methode,* Gadamer looked back to his major work to reconsider his argument. At the end of "Reflections on My Philosophical Journey" he points out how the debate with Habermas has prompted him to go more deeply into rhetoric and its role in the history of hermeneutics: a direction that leads him to practical philosophy. Only after completing the path that led to *Wahrheit und Methode* did he have time to study the later work of Ludwig Wittgenstein, and only much later did he conclude that he had not yet defined with enough precision the necessary difference between the game of language and the game of art. He does, however, point out that the relationship between language and art is nowhere so apparent as it is in the case of literature, which is both speech and writing.

Another attack on his ideas came from historians. In *Wahrheit und Methode* Gadamer starts with the presupposition that historical research is in its final sense interpretation, and thus a performance and a fulfillment of meaning. The resistance of historians to his arguments in *Wahrheit und Methode* made him realize the different senses of text and what understanding the text means. "The whole of the past" is not a text as the individual textual structure is a text for the philologist; as he writes in "Reflections on My Philosophical Journey," "For the philologist, the text, especially a poetic text, is there in front of its interpreter like a fixed given that precedes every new interpretation. The historian, on the other hand, has first to reconstruct his basic text, namely history itself." When he came back to *Wahrheit und Methode* to prepare it for publication as the first volume in his collected works, he did not attempt to rework it but rather attempted to supplement it with a volume of essays, the second volume of *Gesammelte Werke.* This volume brings together several different investigations from several perspectives. It includes two essays from the 1980s related to the literary text: in "Text und Interpretation" (Text and Interpretation) he analyzes the various forms of texts with which hermeneutics deals and attempts to draw together several of his ideas on the literary text; "Destruktion und Dekonstruktion" (Destruction and Deconstruction), on the other hand, deals with the debate over poststructuralism. He attempted to weld the essays in this volume into a philosophic statement.

Interest in Hans-Georg Gadamer's work, based on these two foci, Greek philosophy and modern hermeneutics, has perhaps dimmed amid the wake of postmodernism. His conceptualization of the hermeneutic circle and its attending ideas related to conversation and questioning remain of great importance, however. His long life and career, marked by continuous publishing and lecturing, came to an end when he died in Heidelberg on 14 March 2002.

Interviews:

Roy Boyne, "Interview with Hans-Georg Gadamer," *Theory, Culture, and Society,* 5 (1988): 25–34;

Hermeneutik, Ästhetik, Praktische Philosophie: Hans-Georg Gadamer im Gespräch, edited by Carsten Dutt (Heidelberg: Universitätsverlag C. Winter, 1993);

"Hans-Georg Gadamer: Interview with Christiane Gehron and Jonathan Rée," *Radical Philosophy,* 69 (January/February 1995): 27–35;

Alfons Grieder, "A Conversation with Hans-Georg Gadamer," *Journal of the British Society for Phenomenology,* 26, no. 2 (May 1995): 116–126.

Bibliographies:

Etsuro Makita, *Gadamer-Bibliographie (1922–1994)* (Frankfurt am Main & New York: Peter Lang, 1995);

Joan Nordquist, comp., *Hans-Georg Gadamer: A Bibliography* (Santa Cruz, Cal.: Reference and Research Services, 1998).

Biography:

Jean Grondin, *Hans-Georg Gadamer: Eine Biographie* (Tübingen: Mohr Siebeck, 1999); translated by Joel Weinsheimer as *Hans-Georg Gadamer: A Biography* (New Haven: Yale University Press, 2003).

References:

Richard J. Bernstein, *Beyond Objectivism and Relativism: Science, Hermeneutics, and Praxis* (Philadelphia: University of Pennsylvania Press, 1983);

Josef Bleicher, *Contemporary Hermeneutics: Hermeneutics as Method, Philosophy, and Critique* (London & Boston: Routledge & Kegan Paul, 1980);

Shaun Gallagher, *Hermeneutics and Education* (Albany: State University of New York Press, 1994);

Jean Grondin, *Introduction to Philosophical Hermeneutics* (New Haven & London: Yale University Press, 1994);

E. D. Hirsch Jr., *Validity in Interpretation* (New Haven & London: Yale University Press, 1967);

David Couzens Hoy, *The Critical Circle: Literature, History, and Philosophical Hermeneutics* (Berkeley: University of California Press, 1978);

Gary B. Madison, *The Hermeneutics of Postmodernity: Figures and Themes* (Bloomington: Indiana University Press, 1988);

Richard E. Palmer, *Hermeneutics: Interpretation Theory in Schleiermacher, Dilthey, Heidegger, and Gadamer* (Evanston, Ill.: Northwestern University Press, 1969);

Paul Ricoeur, *Hermeneutics and the Human Sciences: Essays on Language, Action, and Interpretation,* translated and edited by John B. Thompson (New York: Cambridge University Press, 1981);

Lawrence K. Schmidt, *The Epistemology of Hans-Georg Gadamer: An Analysis of the Legitimization of Vorurteile* (Frankfurt am Main & New York: Peter Lang, 1985);

P. Christopher Smith, *Hermeneutics and Human Finitude: Toward a Theory of Ethical Understanding* (New York: Fordham University Press, 1991);

Robert R. Sullivan, *Political Hermeneutics: The Early Thinking of Hans-Georg Gadamer* (University Park: Pennsylvania State University Press, 1989);

Georgia Warnke, *Gadamer: Hermeneutics, Tradition, and Reason* (Stanford, Cal.: Stanford University Press, 1987);

Joel Weinsheimer, *Gadamer's Hermeneutics: A Reading of "Truth and Method"* (New Haven & London: Yale University Press, 1985).

Antonio Gramsci

(22 January 1891 – 27 April 1937)

Brad E. Lucas
Texas Christian University

BOOKS: *Lettere dal carcere,* Opere di Antonio Gramsci, volume 1 (Turin: Einaudi, 1947; revised, 1952; revised and enlarged, edited by Sergio Caprioglio and Elsa Fubini, 1965);

Il materialismo storico e la filosofia di Benedetto Croce, Opere di Antonio Gramsci, volume 2 (Turin: Einaudi, 1948);

L'albero del riccio, edited by Giuseppe Ravegnani (Milan: Milano-Sera, 1948);

Gli intellettuali e l'organizzazione della cultura, Opere di Antonio Gramsci, volume 3 (Turin: Einaudi, 1949);

Il Risorgimento, Opere di Antonio Gramsci, volume 4 (Turin: Einaudi, 1949);

Note sul Machiavelli, sulla politica e sullo Stato moderno, Opere di Antonio Gramsci, volume 5 (Turin: Einaudi, 1949);

Americanismo e fordismo, edited by Felice Platone (Milan: Universale economica, 1950);

Letteratura e vita nazionale, Opere di Antonio Gramsci, volume 6 (Turin: Einaudi, 1950);

Passato e presente, Opere di Antonio Gramsci, volume 7 (Turin: Einaudi, 1951);

La questione meridionale, Piccola biblioteca marxista, no. 30 (Rome: Rinascita, 1951); translated by Pasquale Verdicchio as *The Southern Question* (West Lafayette, Ind.: Bordighera, 1995);

L'Ordine Nuovo: 1919–1920, Opere di Antonio Gramsci, volume 9 (Turin: Einaudi, 1954);

Antologia poplare degli scritti e delle lettere (Rome: Riuniti, 1957); revised as *Antologia degli scritti,* edited by Carlo Salinari and Mario Spinella (Rome: Riuniti, 1963);

Scritti giovanili: 1914–1918, Opere di Antonio Gramsci, volume 8 (Turin: Einaudi, 1958);

Sotto la Mole: 1916–1920, Opere di Antonio Gramsci, volume 10 (Turin: Einaudi, 1960);

Il Vaticano e l'Italia, edited by Fubini (Rome: Riuniti, 1961);

Il Pensiero di Gramsci, edited by Salinari and Spinella (Rome: Riuniti, 1963);

Antonio Gramsci (from Robert S. Dombroski, Antonio Gramsci, *1989; Thomas Cooper Library, University of South Carolina)*

Elementi di politica, edited by Spinella (Rome: Riuniti, 1964);

2000 pagine di Gramsci, 2 volumes, edited by Giansiro Ferrata and Niccolò Gallo (Milan: Il Saggiatore, 1964);

Socialismo e fascismo: L'Ordine Nuovo, 1921–1922, Opere di Antonio Gramsci, volume 11 (Turin: Einaudi, 1966);

La formazione dell'uomo: Scritti di pedagogia, edited by Giovanni Urbani (Rome: Riuniti, 1967);

Scritti politici, 3 volumes, edited by Paolo Spriano (Rome: Riuniti, 1967);

Antonio Gramsci, Amadeo Bordiga: Dibattito sui consigli di fabbrica, by Gramsci and Amadeo Bordiga (Rome: La nuova sinistra, 1971);

La costruzione del Partito comunista: 1923–1926, edited by Fubini, Opere di Antonio Gramsci, volume 12 (Turin: Einaudi, 1971);

I consigli e la critica operaia alla produzione (Milan: Servire il popolo, 1972);

Sul fascismo, edited by Enzo Santarelli (Rome: Riuniti, 1973);

Per la verità: Scritti 1913–1926, edited, with an introduction, by Renzo Martinelli (Rome: Riuniti, 1974);

Quaderni del carcere, 4 volumes, edited by Valentino Gerratana, Edizione critica dell'Istituto Gramsci (Turin: Einaudi, 1975); translated by Joseph A. Buttigieg and Antonio Callari as *Prison Notebooks,* 2 volumes, edited, with an introduction, by Buttigieg (New York: Columbia University Press, 1992, 1996);

Arte folclore, edited by Giuseppe Prestipino, Paperbacks marxisti, no. 40 (Rome: Newton Compton, 1976);

Scritti 1915–1921: Inediti dal Grido del popolo e dall'Avanti! edited by Caprioglio (Milan: Moizzi/Contemporanea, 1976);

Cronache torinesi, 1913–1917, edited by Caprioglio (Turin: Einaudi, 1980);

Favole di libertà, edited by Fubini and Mimma Paulesu (Florence: Vallecchi, 1980);

La città futura, 1917–1918, edited by Caprioglio (Turin: Einaudi, 1982);

Il nostro Marx, 1918–1919, edited by Caprioglio (Turin: Einaudi, 1984);

Croce e Gentile (Rome: Riuniti, 1992);

Dante e Manzoni (Rome: Riuniti, 1992);

Il Lorianismo (Rome: Riuniti, 1992);

Pirandello, Ibsen e il teatro (Rome: Riuniti, 1992);

Gramsci a Roma, Togliatti a Mosca: Il carteggio del 1926, edited by Chiara Daniele (Turin: Einaudi, 1999).

Editions and Collections: *Lettere dal carcere,* edited by Paolo Spriano (Turin: Einaudi, 1971);

L'alternativa pedagogica: Antologia, edited by Mario A. Manacorda, Educatori antichi e moderni, no. 270 (Florence: La Nuova Italia, 1972);

Lettere dal carcere, edited by Sebastiano Vassalli (Turin: Einaudi, 1977).

Editions in English: *The Modern Prince and Other Writings,* translated, with an introduction, by Louis Marks (London: Lawrence & Wishart, 1957; New York: International Publishers, 1957);

Selections from the Prison Notebooks of Antonio Gramsci, translated and edited by Quintin Hoare and Geoffrey Nowell-Smith (New York: International Publishers, 1971; London: Lawrence & Wishart, 1971);

Letters from Prison, selected and translated, with an introduction, by Lynne Lawner (New York: Harper & Row, 1973; London: Cape, 1975);

History, Philosophy and Culture in the Young Gramsci, translated by Pierluigi Molajoni and others, edited, with an introduction, by Pedro Cavalcanti and Paul Piccone (St. Louis: Telos, 1975);

Letters from Prison, Political History and Conference Papers: The Collected Edition of Three Special Issues of New Edinburgh Review, edited by Hamish Henderson (Edinburgh: Edinburgh University Student Publications, 1975);

Antonio Gramsci: Selections from Political Writings (1910–1920): With Additional Texts by Bordiga and Tasca, translated by John Mathews, edited by Hoare (New York: International Publishers, 1977; London: Lawrence & Wishart, 1977);

Antonio Gramsci: Selections from Political Writings (1921–1926): With Additional Texts by Other Italian Communist Leaders, translated and edited by Hoare (New York: International Publishers, 1978; London: Lawrence & Wishart, 1978);

Selections from Cultural Writings, translated by William Boelhower, edited, with an introduction, by David Forgacs and Nowell-Smith (Cambridge, Mass.: Harvard University Press, 1985; London: Lawrence & Wishart, 1985);

An Antonio Gramsci Reader: Selected Writings, 1916–1935, edited by Forgacs (London: Lawrence & Wishart, 1988; New York: Schocken, 1988);

Letters from Prison, 2 volumes, translated by Raymond Rosenthal, edited, with an introduction, by Frank Rosengarten (New York: Columbia University Press, 1994);

Pre-Prison Writings, translated by Virginia Cox, edited, with an introduction, by Richard Bellamy (Cambridge & New York: Cambridge University Press, 1994);

Further Selections from the Prison Notebooks, translated and edited by Derek Boothman (Minneapolis: University of Minnesota Press, 1995; London: Lawrence & Wishart, 1995).

Antonio Gramsci's work is pivotal for addressing history, politics, sociology, literature, and the larger field of cultural studies that draws from these and related disciplines. Gramsci's ideas have been taken up across disciplinary boundaries and national borders, and while he is most easily classified as a Marxist thinker, Gramsci's ideas of hegemony, organic intellectuals, and the subaltern classes have become an integral part of cultural theory and critical discourse. Interpretations of his work continue to reveal a more complex and rich way of looking at the dynamics of power and privilege manifested in contemporary life.

The youngest of four children, Antonio Gramsci was born in Ales, Cagliari (a rural province of Sardinia), on 22 January 1891 to parents Francesco Gramsci, a middle-class bureaucrat from Ghilarza, and Peppina Marcias, a literate woman from a well-respected family. Contrary to widely held beliefs, Antonio did not come from a peasant background; he did know hardship at an early age, however, when his father was sentenced to prison in 1900 for a minor embezzlement charge that was politically motivated. Francesco spent roughly six years away from his family, disrupting their comfortable life and putting pressures on Antonio (Nino) that weighed heavily on his future work and studies. His family circumstances were not the only misfortunes he faced, for Antonio did not fully develop physically: he stood at roughly four and a half feet, afflicted with a hunched back and chronic illnesses for his entire life.

According to biographer Giuseppe Fiori in his *Vita di Antonio Gramsci* (1966; translated as *Antonio Gramsci: Life of a Revolutionary,* 1970), Gramsci was an insatiable reader as a child, taking in whatever was available; his studies were cut short after completing primary school, however, when his father was taken to prison. He continued his schooling sporadically until 1905, when he began secondary school in the Sardinian city of Santulussurgiu, but his education was at the hands of ill-trained and underpaid instructors. At this time Sardinia was troubled by unrest among the masses of people who were starving, resentful of industrial machinery, and facing decreasing wages among mining and agricultural workers (the majority of the population). This unrest continued, and labor protests emerged, culminating in a strike in Cagliari that brought thousands of police and military troops in May 1906. Gramsci continued his schooling from 1908 to 1911 at the Dettòri Lycée in Cagliari, a city still politically volatile at that time.

Gramsci began study under Raffa Garzìa, a new Italian master at the lycée, who took a liking to the highly literate eighteen-year-old, and this friendship enabled Gramsci to begin writing newspaper articles for *L'Unione sarda* (The Sardinian Union). He began this work in 1910, relocating to serve as the correspondent from Aidomaggiore, a village near Ghilarza. Grown accustomed to the urban environment at Cagliari, Gramsci began to attend the theater, developing his own political perspectives about the oppression of the working class. Even at this time, his optimism for politi-

SELECTIONS FROM THE

PRISON NOTEBOOKS

OF

ANTONIO GRAMSCI

edited and translated by
QUINTIN HOARE
and
GEOFFREY NOWELL SMITH

1971

LAWRENCE AND WISHART

LONDON

Title page for the 1971 English translation of Gramsci's writings during his incarceration in Turin from 1928 until 1937 (Carol M. Newman Library, Virginia Polytechnic Institute and State University)

cal change was clear. In one of his essays from the Dettòri school, reprinted in *Antonio Gramsci: Selections from Political Writings (1910–1920)* (1977), he contends that "social privileges and difference, being products of society and not of nature, can be overcome." In 1911 he began schooling at the University of Turin, coming into contact with fellow Sardinian Palmiro Togliatti, who later became an Italian communist leader. This period marks the emergence of Gramsci's adult intellectual growth, when he developed a keen sense of research methodology and intellectual discipline. His first university exams began in 1912, when he was helping a linguistics professor, Matteo Bartoli, study the Sardinian language. The 1913 elections in Sardinia were also an intellectual turning point for Gramsci, showing him that the southern populace was suffering from the oppression of the southern ruling class and that the industrialists were responsible for the social impoverishment over the previous several years. The outcome of these elections made Gramsci a socialist, shaping the development of his idea that intellectuals should play a central role in the process of revolution.

Never abandoning his rural past, Gramsci continued to hone his political views, and this tension between his country upbringing and his city-based education emerged as a theme throughout his works: namely, the interrogation and explanation of the political dynamics between the peasantry and the urban working class. Gramsci's view of history as primarily an intellectual activity derived from Italian philosopher Benedetto Croce, a figure whose liberal idealism inspired much of Gramsci's intellectual development. As biographer James Joll, in *Antonio Gramsci* (1977), explains, "What Gramsci learned from Croce was a belief in history as an intellectual activity which dominated and embraced all others—morals, politics, art— and as the way of relating the past to the present and the present to the future." Admiring Croce's identification of philosophy with historical judgment, Gramsci also faulted Croce's criticisms of Karl Marx and his adherence to speculation without political action. Later, writing from prison, Gramsci further questioned Crocean idealism for neglecting the interplay between theoretical and active engagement with the world; he also interrogated the dynamics of Crocean literary aesthetics and criticism. In Fiori's account, Annibale Pastore, a professor of theoretical philosophy at Turin, recalled that Gramsci

had been a Crocean originally, but was now very restless, without knowing how or why he had to break away. . . . He wanted to understand how culture developed, for revolutionary reasons: the ultimate practical significance of theoretical life. He wanted to find out how thinking can lead to actions (the technique of propaganda), how a thought can make peoples' hands move, and how and in what sense ideas themselves may be actions. . . . In short, like the outstanding pragmatist he was, Gramsci was concerned above all else at this time to understand *how ideas became practical forces*.

Gramsci's isolation and sickness began his cycle of neurosis; yet, he took his third-year examination in Italian literature in April 1915. By this point, World War I had been underway for almost nine months and the socialist Second International (founded in 1889) had collapsed. When Italy entered the war in May, Gramsci's physical and mental health began to improve, and after his three brothers entered the war, he began to envision the potentials of revolution at home. Gramsci began publishing pieces on a wide

range of subjects—ranging from theater reviews to political satire—in *Il Grido del Popolo* (The Cry of the People) and the Turin edition of the socialist paper *Avanti!* (Forward!) on a regular basis, although rarely appending his name to the essays and articles. On 26 August 1916 one of his articles in *Avanti!*, collected in *Selections from Cultural Writings* (1985), featured a scathing critique of the theater industry in light of the increasingly popular cinema:

The reason for the success of the cinema and its absorption of former theatre audiences is purely economic. The cinema offers exactly the same sensations as the popular theatre, but under better conditions, without the choreographic contrivances of a false intellectualism, without promising too much while delivering little. The most commonly staged productions are nothing but cinema. The most commonly staged productions are nothing but fabrics of external facts, lacking any human content, in which talking puppets move about variously, without ever drawing out a psychological truth, without ever managing to impose on the listener's creative imagination a character or passions that are truly felt and adequately expressed.

Regardless of the subject matter, these articles were mostly directed toward preparing workers for revolution, urging readers to link ideas among them to further one continuing argument. Gramsci's question-and-answer process focused on the interrelation between theory and fact, between politics and culture, and his distinctive emphasis on culture allowed him to seek answers in sources other than economic forces. Gramsci continued to discuss culture and politics in *Il Grido del Popolo*. For example, in January 1916 he published "Socialismo e cultura" (Socialism and Culture), collected in *Antonio Gramsci: Selections from Political Writings (1910–1920)*, warning of the dangers of "seeing culture as encyclopaedic knowledge, and men as mere receptacles to be stuffed full of empirical data and a mass of unconnected raw facts." He envisioned culture as a means for self-awareness, albeit one that had to be rooted in historical consciousness:

It is organization, discipline of one's inner self, a coming to terms with one's own personality; it is the attainment of a higher awareness, with the aid of which one succeeds in understanding one's own historical value, one's own function in life, one's own rights and obligations. . . . Above all, man is mind, i.e. he is a product of history, not nature. . . . only by degrees, one stage at a time, has humanity acquired consciousness of its own value and won for itself the right to throw off the patterns of organization imposed on it by minorities at a previous period in history. . . . every revolution has been preceded by an intense labor of criticism, by the diffusion of culture and the spread of ideas amongst masses of men who are at first resistant, and think only of solving their own immediate economic and political problems for themselves, who have no ties with others in the same condition.

For Gramsci, criticism was an empowering force that was no less striking than military maneuvers. In "Socialism and Culture" he identifies historical evidence supporting the importance of culture in the French Revolution and the Enlightenment, claiming that publishing paved the way for Napoleon and his armies.

With news of the February 1917 revolution in Russia, widespread unrest in Italy had found an outlet: the populace was disenchanted with the war and frustrated with the military discipline present at the factories. On 23 August mob revolution began in Turin, resulting in more than fifty dead and two hundred wounded by military troops. The activity ended within eight days of fighting, and Gramsci was appointed to a provisional committee of twelve representing the socialist movement. By 14 November, the Russian Revolution was complete: the Bolshevik party had taken power. For Gramsci, however, the turbulence of revolution was not a signal for unhindered success. In "La revoluzione contro il *Capitale*" (The Revolution against 'Capital'), an essay published in *Avanti!* in December 1917 and collected in *Antonio Gramsci: Selections from Political Writings (1910–1920)*, Gramsci warns of the looming problems in Russia: "The revolutionaries themselves will create the conditions needed for the total achievement of their goal. . . . It will first be a collectivism of poverty and suffering." Gramsci argues that "even in absolute, human terms, socialism can *now* be justified in Russia. The hardships that await them after the peace will be bearable only if the proletarians feel they have things under their own control and know that by their efforts they can reduce these hardships in the shortest possible time." He was most concerned with the historical moments of transition from one social arrangement to another, but Gramsci did not wholly embrace Marx's historical materialism.

As the philosophy of Marxist-Leninist history, historical materialism has its origins in the materialism of Ludwig Feuerbach and the deterministic philosophy of history espoused by Georg Wilhelm Friedrich Hegel. Although the materialist conception of history provides the foundation for Marxism, Gramsci found fault with it. Because he recognized that class rule was not dependent on economic or material forces alone, he contended that persuasion enabled one class to rule over another: the ruled class, if persuaded to accept the belief system of the ruling class, would willingly share its cultural and moral values. This conceptualization of "hege-

mony" is Gramsci's most enduring legacy to Western thought. Gramsci later described the revolution in Russia as a "war of manoeuver," a direct assault on the state that was possible because the state did not depend on the consensus of the masses. In western European countries, however, this approach was not possible: a "war of position" was needed, wherein the proletariat would try to achieve hegemony in society before the capture of state power.

Gramsci developed a discussion circle for revolutionaries and became the editor of *Il Grido del Popolo* in 1916, later publishing translations of Russian Bolshevik texts and stimulating thoughts of the role of Italy in both a national and a global revolution. The war ended in November 1918, and by March 1919 the Third Communist International (Comintern) was founded. Emerging from the work of Gramsci, Togliatti, Angelo Tasca, and Umberto Terracini, *L'Ordine Nuovo: Rassegna Settimanale di Cultura Socialista* (The New Order: A Weekly Review of Socialist Culture) debuted in May 1919. Within a few years it became the preeminent Marxist revolutionary newspaper in Italy. Gramsci was listed as "editorial secretary" and began to develop his theories of the "factory councils" that were based on the Russian organizing councils known as soviets, which were to run all facets of production and reclaim worker control of everyday life. These councils were quite a departure from the earlier councils, which simply acted as representative bargaining groups. The first factory council emerged in the Fiat factory in September, and others appeared throughout the following months. By March 1920 the industrialists began to retaliate against one of the Fiat strikes; an eleven-day general strike throughout Piedmont ensued, but Gramsci recognized that a unified socialist party was not a reality: the movement was divided by ignorant optimism, action without intellect, and excessive quibbling over perspectives. On 8 May 1920 he published "Per un rinnovamento del Partito socialista" (Towards a Renewal of the Socialist Party), a report presented to the national council meeting of the Partito Socialista Italiano (Italian Socialist Party, or PSI) in Milan, in *L'Ordine Nuovo*. In the report, collected in *Antonio Gramsci: Selections from Political Writings (1910–1920)*, he predicts the backlash against the movement in the form of industrialist-fueled fascism:

> The present phase of the class struggle in Italy is the phase that precedes: either the conquest of political power on the part of the revolutionary proletariat and the transition to new modes of production and distribution that will set the stage for a recovery in productivity—or a tremendous reaction on the part of the propertied classes and governing caste. No violence will be spared in subjecting the industrial and agricultural

ANTONIO GRAMSCI
QUADERNI
DEL CARCERE

I

Edizione critica dell'Istituto Gramsci
A cura di Valentino Gerratana

EINAUDI EDITORE

Paperback cover for the first volume of the standard edition (1975) of Gramsci's prison notebooks (Howard-Tilton Memorial Library, Tulane University)

proletariat to servile labour: there will be a bid to smash once and for all the working class's organ of political struggle (the Socialist Party) and to incorporate its organs of economic resistance (the trade unions and cooperatives) into the machinery of the bourgeois state.

Despite the meetings, disputes among the party continued through the summer, splitting loyalties among the *L'Ordine Nuovo* group (Gramsci broke with Tasca, Togliatti, and Terracini). By October the workers had lost their battle and returned to work; the factory-council movement was over, and Gramsci and his circle had failed to effect change on the decisions of the larger socialist movement outside of Turin.

Gramsci became the editor of the daily *L'Ordine Nuovo* in December 1920 and served on the central committee of the Italian Communist Party (PCI) in 1921, which was dominated by Amadeo Bordiga, who disagreed with the policies of the Comintern. Gramsci's

prediction of fascism materialized in 1919–1922, culminating in the 28 October 1922 march on Rome that enabled Benito Mussolini to form a new government. The leadership of the Communist International called for a united front of socialist and communist parties. As the Italian representative at the Comintern, Gramsci lived in Moscow during these months. There he met Julca "Giulia" Schucht, the woman who became his wife and mother of his two sons, Delio (born in 1924) and Giuliano (born in 1926). The recommendations from the International were not implemented, and after the arrests of several Italian communist leaders in November 1923, Gramsci moved to Vienna to lead the PCI, returning to Italy in May 1924 to serve as parliamentary deputy. From 1921 to 1926 Gramsci was not only directing his energies toward the Communist Party in Italy but also was highly active in the Comintern.

In the summer of 1924 the murder of Giacomo Matteotti, a reformist socialist, shook the foundations of Mussolini's power—men loyal to him were responsible. Parliamentary opposition parties abstained from proceedings, but the government was preparing a law that enabled any antifascist organization to be disciplined by Mussolini's forces. On 16 May 1925 Gramsci delivered his only speech to parliament, attacking the law, which was purportedly aimed only at the Freemasons and denouncing the fascist rise to power as a simple administrative change, rather than a revolution. (His speech was no charismatic oration: his delivery was weak, and constant interruptions broke his train of thought.)

Gramsci's intellectual strength is evident in his writings, particularly the series of documents, now called the "Lyons Theses," prepared for the January 1926 congress of the Italian Communist Party, in which he clearly signals his allegiance to the International. It was originally published in five separate sets of articles in *L'Unitá* (Unity) during October and November 1925 and subsequently published in pamphlet form as "La situazione italiana e i compiti del P.C.I." (The Italian Situation and the Tasks of the PCI), later collected in *Antonio Gramsci: Selections from Political Writings (1921–1926)* (1978). In the Lyons Theses he stresses the importance of a united working-class front directed not by partisan or intellectual leaders but by the workers themselves. He calls for the necessary resistance against fascism in a production-based organizational form of "cells," essentially proposing newly reformed councils based on the factory-council movement. Gramsci articulates the principles he had been developing for years, including an analysis of the Italian social structure and the claims that Italy was particularly suited for revolution. His revamped Soviet model in tandem with a worker-based leadership is one of his distinctive contributions to Marxist thought.

In the autumn Gramsci began writing an essay, "Alcuni temi della questione meridonale" (translated as "Some Considerations on the Southern Question" in the second volume of *Selections from Political Writings*), that was not completed because of his arrest in 1926. First published in *Lo Stato operaio* (The State Laborer) in January 1930, the essay explores the relationship between the urban centers and the countryside, examining thirty years of Italian political development through a Marxist lens. Drawing from his experiences in Sardinia, he asserts that the so-called Southern Question could not be addressed without placing it in the larger framework of a national perspective. Gramsci argues that remnants of conflict inspired by bourgeois propaganda must be overcome by uniting urban and rural proletariat forces.

In "Alcuni temi della questione meridonale" Gramsci makes clear distinctions about the intellectuals who are mainly smaller landowners who extract the maximum profit from their lands by exploiting the peasant laborers, for whom they have a blend of aversion and fear. The southern peasants that compose the agrarian bloc are tied to the large landowners through the intellectual bloc, which also serves to prevent any peasant movements from gaining widespread support. The proletariat, Gramsci argues, "will destroy the southern agrarian *bloc* to the extent to which, through its Party, it succeeds in organizing ever larger masses of peasants in autonomous and independent formations; but it will exceed to a more or less large extent in this obligatory task according to its capacity to break up the intellectual *bloc* which forms the flexible but very resistant armour of the agrarian *bloc*." Gramsci's interest in the Catholic Church is also present in this document, for he envisioned the Communist Party as an entity less authoritarian than, and comparable to the structure, propaganda, and organization of the Church: a new intellectual class to replace the priests as social mediators and facilitators of political power.

Gramsci was arrested on 8 November 1926 after being added to a list of secessionist deputies ordered arrested by Mussolini; the rules of parliamentary immunity should have protected him, but they were ignored. He was sent to the island of Ustica with other political prisoners and then to the San Vittore prison in Milan. He spent two years in prison before facing trial. In May and June 1928, Gramsci went before Mussolini's Special Tribunal for the Defense of the State, a "show trial" that sentenced Gramsci to slightly more than twenty years in prison. He arrived at the prison in Turin on 19 July 1928 and was denied writing materials for roughly six months. When he was allowed to write, he was heavily scrutinized by a censor, a mediating figure that makes interpretation of his writings problematic at best.

While in prison Gramsci began work on the series of writings that are known as *Quaderni del carcere* (Prison Notebooks, 1975). During his incarceration he composed more than thirty notebooks that were eventually smuggled out of the country and preserved by his wife's sister, Tatiana Schucht, who was Gramsci's frequent visitor and source of emotional support while he was in prison. Suffering from insomnia and bouts of severe illness, he spent the last years of his life in prison, filling his notebooks with nearly three thousand pages exploring the realms of theory and the material reality of Italy as well as the larger global community. Gramsci continued his politics through writing, never ceasing his concerns with the future of class injustice and sociocultural oppression. A committee was formed in mid 1933 to fight for Gramsci's release. For medical reasons he was moved to clinics in Formia in 1934 and then Rome in 1935. His prison sentence expired on 21 April 1937, but within days he suffered a cerebral hemorrhage and died on 27 April at the age of forty-six.

Gramsci's notebooks were first published between 1948 and 1951 as volumes two through seven of the twelve-volume Opere di Antonio Gramsci (Works of Antonio Gramsci, 1947–1971). Many later editions and selections exist; the standard Italian edition is the four-volume *Quaderni del carcere* (1975), edited by Valentino Gerratana under the auspices of the Istituto Gramsci. Joseph Buttigieg's two-volume translation, *Prison Notebooks* (1992, 1996), is based on this edition. These writings include translations from German texts; essays on Marxist philosophy, Italian history, grammar and linguistics, popular literature, and political strategy; journalism; and theoretical works on historiography. In the notebooks he contemplated the works of many authors, including Dante Alighieri, Honoré de Balzac, Emile Zola, Luigi Capuana, Sinclair Lewis, Leo Tolstoy, and Alessandro Manzoni. Gramsci is known primarily as a political figure, but his role as a literary critic merits similar attention and has gained increasing notice. While much scholarly attention is directed toward Gramsci's heritage as a critical theorist, his own scholarly criticism is valuable evidence of his cultural engagement, for in Gramsci's eyes the multiple forms of literature act as sites of sociocultural expression and contestation.

Gramsci's notebooks provide an extension of the ideas posited in "Alcuni temi della questione meridonale": namely, how to extract the peasantry from the historical bloc wherein the intellectual minority serves the interests of the bourgeoisie. Gramsci's struggle with Marxism—what he refers to throughout his writings as "the philosophy of praxis"—was an ongoing attempt to reconfigure the deterministic, authoritarian elements of Marxism that emphasized discipline from above; he sought out ways that achieved political goals through the use of persuasion and acknowledged the individual role of human consciousness. Gramsci realized that before revolution, the leaders of the proletariat and the proletarian masses had to be united in a representative relationship that shared power.

A recurring theme in the prison notebooks is the conception of the "historical bloc," often related to the structure-superstructure relations of Marxism but also characterized as a site for joining concrete applications and theoretical concepts. Gramsci believed that both structures and superstructures constituted an historic bloc, but he also argued that the economic base of Marxism did not determine the superstructure; rather, he understood that the superstructure was restrained by the economic base. Thus, in multiple ways the populace constitutes the superstructure through its action and ideologies, and hegemony holds the historic bloc together.

It is important to realize that Gramsci never treated his concept of hegemony systematically in the notebooks. Gramsci believed that bourgeois rule over the proletariat was made possible not through brute force or threat, but in the acceptance by the ruled class of bourgeois ideology as its own. Gramsci opposed economic factors and forces as the sole means through which power was exercised, turning his attention to the role of the political in civil society and the state itself. Gramsci saw the state as consisting of the coercive elements of the army, police, and other political forces imposing will backed by force. What also played a central role in the struggle for hegemony was the means of establishing leadership through various institutions: education, religion, trade unions, and various mass-circulated media. Through these collective forces, the ruling class was able to maintain power, even after it was deposed or otherwise replaced.

For the establishment of cultural hegemony and a new society to emerge, it is necessary for the "traditional intellectuals" (autonomous, independent, class-removed intellectuals such as the clergy) to be won over to socialism. In his notebooks from 1933, translated and published as the title essay of *The Modern Prince and Other Writings* (1957), Gramsci also called for a "collective intellectual," one embodied as the "Modern Prince," a concept discussed in terms of Niccolò Machiavelli's *Il principe* (The Prince, 1532):

> The modern prince, the myth-prince, cannot be a real person, a concrete individual; it can only be an organism; a complex element of society in which the cementing of a collective will, recognized and partially asserted in action, has already begun. This organism is already provided by historical development and it is the political party: the first cell containing the germs of collective will which are striving to become universal and total. . . .

It is necessary to define collective will and political will in general in the modern sense; will as working consciousness of historical necessity, as protagonist of a real and effective historical drama. . . .

The "collective intellectual" would strive for a total cultural and intellectual revolution among the lay persons of society, one that "takes the place, in the conscience, of the divinity or of the categorical imperative, and becomes the basis of a modern laicism, of a complete laicisation of the whole of life and of all customary relations." Thus, the revolution would not only change the state, but the foundations of consciousness and systems of belief (and perhaps even faith)—all for the benefit of the socialist party.

In the prison notebooks Gramsci takes up the discussion of the social role of intellectuals he began in "Alcuni temi della questione meridionale." Contrary to the prevalent conception of intellectuals as an elite group of thinkers superior in intelligence, reason, and moral judgment, Gramsci argues for a redefinition of "intellectuals" to include all people. Despite the redefinition of terms, Gramsci maintains that not everyone necessarily holds a functional social role as an intellectual. Of the range of intellectuals in a given society, Gramsci argues for "organic intellectuals," those who identify with and share the interests of the proletariat. He first identifies the organic intellectuals whose work is essential to reproducing capitalist society:

> Every social group, coming into existence on the original terrain of an essential function in the world of economic production, creates together with itself, organically, one or more strata of intellectuals which give it homogeneity and an awareness of its own function not only in the economic but also in the social and political fields. The capitalist entrepreneur creates alongside himself the industrial technician, the specialist in political economy, the organisers of a new culture, of a new legal system, etc. . . . It can be observed that the "organic" intellectuals which every new class creates alongside itself and elaborates in the course of its development, are for the most part "specialisations" of partial aspects of the primitive activity of the new social type which the new class has brought into prominence.

The social group, in addition, selects other "specialized" workers outside of the business enterprise to "be an organizer of society in general, including all its complex organism of services, right up to the state organism, because of the need to create the conditions most favorable to the expansion of their own class." For Gramsci, intellectuals comprise the masses of individuals who hold roles in the organizational structures of society. Although Gramsci's notion of the organic intellectual has been applied—and often misused and distorted—in many other contexts, he was aiming for an intellectual class based on technical skill and concrete practice, rather than one trained in the discourses of philosophy or belles lettres.

For these perspectives on traditional intellectualism, Gramsci was particularly appealing for the project sponsored by the Centre for Contemporary Cultural Studies (CCCS) at the University of Birmingham in 1964, the locus for the field of inquiry and practice now known as "cultural studies." Fomented by the work of Richard Hoggart, Raymond Williams, E. P. Thompson, and Stuart Hall, cultural studies developed out of class politics persisting in Britain following World War II. Arguably, Hoggart, Williams, and Thompson were "organic intellectuals" themselves, coming from working-class backgrounds and sharing a common experience working in adult-education universities. They were largely concerned with the "practice" and "production" of culture. Cultural studies is indebted to the New Left, which developed out of a collective response to the 1956 invasion of Hungary by the Soviet Union, and although the CCCS and the New Left were deeply concerned with the power dynamics of culture and politics, the field of cultural studies traces its lineage to literary studies. The *New Left Review,* the leading periodical for British Marxists, was also responsible for many translations of socialist and Marxist writings, making the work of Gramsci and others available for the first time to the English-speaking world.

Williams, in his *Marxism and Literature* (1977), calls Gramsci's work "one of the major turning-points in Marxist cultural theory." Williams later celebrated the use of "hegemony" as a conceptual analytic tool, particularly if it was understood as dynamic and transformative. He writes, "A lived hegemony is always a process.... it does not just passively exist as a form of dominance. It has to be renewed, recreated, defended, and modified. It is also continually resisted, limited, altered, challenged by pressures not at all its own." While finding Gramsci's ideas useful for cultural inquiry, Williams's use of Gramsci for literary criticism has enabled culture-based readings of texts to take on new and useful forms. The larger project of cultural studies (in all of its emergent forms that migrated from Britain in the 1980s and after) did extend Gramsci's ideas beyond class to issues pertaining to gender, race, and mass culture, performing its critical interpretive work on increasingly political levels, shifting focus not just away from class issues but also away from the mainstream to the margins of society.

Although Marxism and cultural studies use Gramsci in various ways, many of them literary, they were by no means mutually agreeable or consistent. In a paper

ANTONIO GRAMSCI

SELECTIONS FROM

POLITICAL WRITINGS

(1921–1926)

with additional texts by other Italian Communist leaders

translated and edited by
QUINTIN HOARE

LAWRENCE AND WISHART
LONDON

Title page for the 1977 anthology of Gramsci's essays for leftist periodicals. It includes his "Lyons Theses" (1925), in which he calls for a united working-class front against fascism (Clemson University Library).

presented at the 1990 University of Illinois conference on cultural studies, published as "Cultural Studies and Its Theoretical Legacies" in *Cultural Studies* (1992), Stuart Hall recalled what cultural studies in Britain learned from Gramsci: "immense amounts about the nature of culture itself, about the discipline of the conjunctural, about the importance of historical specificity, about the enormously productive metaphor of hegemony, about the way in which one can think questions of class relations only by using the displaced notion of ensemble and blocs." Furthermore, the legacy of cultural studies includes the emergence of postcolonial theory and its impact on literary and discourse studies. In his *Orientalism* (1978), Edward Said describes "a created theory and practice" that made Orientalism "a system of knowledge about the Orient," and he asserts that Gramsci's notion of hegemony and "the result of cultural hegemony at work" gives Orientalism the strength and durability that enables it to persist. Gramsci's notions of "hegemony" and "the subaltern" (a collective term for subjugated groups lacking in class consciousness) continue to be essential for studies of colonial discourse and postcolonial theory, wherein scholars such as Gayatri Chakravorty Spivak invoke his "Alcuni temi della questione meridonale" as a means of interrogating Indian colonial historiography.

The extent to which Gramsci's work affected late-twentieth-century critical discourse is difficult to determine because he has been appropriated for virtually every discipline, directly or indirectly, and scholarship on his work continues to expand. In the decades following his death, thousands of publications have been composed about Gramsci and his work. Scholarship on Gramsci is tracked in the *Bibliografia gramsciana*, a research bibliography of more than eleven thousand items published by the Fondazione Istituto Gramsci in Rome (and offered on-line at Queens College–CUNY). The work of such organizations and the International Gramsci Society signals that Gramsci's impact on the study of culture is just beginning to be acknowledged.

Letters:

Nuove lettere di Antonio Gramsci: Con altre lettere di Piero Sraffa, edited by Antonio A. Santucci (Rome: Riuniti, 1986);

Forse rimarrai lontana: Lettere a Iulca, 1922–1937, edited by Mimma Paulesu Quercioli (Rome: Albatros/Riuniti, 1987);

Lettere, 1908–1926, edited by Santucci (Turin: Einaudi, 1992);

Vita attraverso le lettere 1908–1937, edited by Giuseppe Fiori (Turin: Einaudi, 1994);

Lettere: 1926–1935, edited by Aldo Natoli and Chiara Daniele (Turin: Einaudi, 1997).

Bibliography:

John M. Cammett, ed., *Bibliografia gramsciana, 1922–1988* (Rome: Riuniti, 1991).

Biographies:

Giuseppe Fiori, *Vita di Antonio Gramsci* (Bari: Laterza, 1966); translated by Tom Nairn as *Antonio Gramsci: Life of a Revolutionary* (London: New Left Books, 1970; New York: Dutton, 1971);

Piero Spriano, *Gramsci, la vita, le idée, il sacrificio* (Rome: Stabilimento Grafico Fratelli Spada, 1967);

Alastair Davidson, *Antonio Gramsci: Towards an Intellectual Biography* (London: Merlin Press, 1977; Atlantic Highlands, N.J.: Humanities Press, 1977);

James Joll, *Antonio Gramsci* (Harmondsworth, U.K. & New York: Penguin, 1977);

Paweł Śpiewak, *Gramsci* (Warsaw: Wiedza Powszechna, 1977);

Giuseppe Tamburrano, *Antonio Gramsci* (Milan: SugarCo, 1977);

Santo Mandolfo, *Antonio Gramsci* (Catania: CUECM, 1987);

Emilio Russo, *Antonio Gramsci* (Rimini: Luisè, 1990);

Aurelio Lepre, *Il prigioniero: Vita di Antonio Gramsci* (Rome & Bari: Laterza, 1998).

References:

Carl Boggs, *Gramsci's Marxism* (London: Pluto, 1976);

Robert S. Dombroski, *Antonio Gramsci* (Boston: Twayne, 1989);

Stuart Hall, "Cultural Studies and Its Theoretical Legacies," in *Cultural Studies,* edited by Lawrence Grossberg, Cary Nelson, and Paula Treichler (New York & London: Routledge, 1992), pp. 277–294;

Edward Said, *Orientalism* (New York: Pantheon, 1978; London: Routledge & Kegan Paul, 1978), pp. 6–11, 25–26, 329–330;

Gayatri Chakravorty Spivak, "Can the Subaltern Speak?" in *Marxism and the Interpretation of Culture,* edited by Nelson and Grossberg (Basingstoke, U.K.: Macmillan, 1988; Urbana: University of Illinois Press, 1988), pp. 271–313;

Raymond Williams, *Marxism and Literature* (Oxford: Oxford University Press, 1977), pp. 108–112.

Papers:

The papers and other archival materials of Antonio Gramsci are held at the Gramsci Foundation Institute (Fondazione Istituto Gramsci) in Rome, Italy.

Martin Heidegger

(26 September 1889 – 26 May 1976)

John Phillips
National University of Singapore

BOOKS: *Die Kategorien- und Bedeutungslehre des Duns Scotus* (Tübingen: Mohr, 1916);

Sein und Zeit: Erste Hälfte (Halle: Niemeyer, 1927); translated by John MacQuarrie and Edward Robinson as *Being and Time* (London: SCM Press, 1962; New York: Harper, 1962);

Was ist Metaphysik? (Bonn: Cohen, 1929);

Kant und das Problem der Metaphysik (Bonn: Cohen, 1929); translated by James S. Churchill as *Kant and the Problem of Metaphysics* (Bloomington: Indiana University Press, 1962);

Vom Wesen des Grundes (Halle: Niemeyer, 1929); edited and translated by Terrence Malick as *The Essence of Reasons* (Evanston, Ill.: Northwestern University Press, 1969);

Die Selbstbehauptung der deutschen Universität (Breslau: Korn, 1934); translated by Karsten Harries as "The Self-Assertion of the German University," *Review of Metaphysics,* 38 (1985): 467–481;

Erläuterungen zu Hölderlin's Dichtung (Frankfurt am Main: Klostermann, 1944; enlarged, 1951; enlarged again, 1971); translated by Keith Hoeller as *Elucidations of Hölderlin's Poetry* (Amherst, N.Y.: Humanity Books, 2000);

Platons Lehre von der Wahrheit: Mit einem Brief über den "Humanismus" (Bern: Francke, 1947); translated by John Barlow and Edgar Lohner as "Plato's Doctrine of Truth: Letter on Humanism," in *Philosophy in the Twentieth Century: An Anthology,* 4 volumes, edited by William Barrett and Henry David Aiken (New York: Random House, 1962), III: 271–302;

Holzwege (Frankfurt am Main: Klostermann, 1950)—includes "Der Ursprung des Kunstwerks," translated by Albert Hofstädter as "The Origin of the Work of Art," in *Philosophies of Art and Beauty: Selected Readings in Aesthetics from Plato to Heidegger,* edited by Hofstädter and Richard Kuhns (New York: Modern Library, 1964), pp. 647–701; "Die Zeit des Weltbildes," translated by Marjorie Grene as "The Age of the World View," *Measure,*

Martin Heidegger (Vittorio Klostermann Verlag, Frankfurt am Main; from Arland Ussher, Journey through Dread: A Study of Kierkegaard, Heidegger, and Sartre, *1955; Thomas Cooper Library, University of South Carolina)*

2 (1951): 269–284; "Hegels Begriff der Erfahrung," translated by J. Glenn Gray and Fred D. Wieck as *Hegel's Concept of Experience* (New York: Harper & Row, 1970); "Nietzsches Wort 'Gott ist Tot'"; "Wozu Dichter?"; "Der Spruch der Anaximander," translated by David Farrell Krell as

177

"Martin Heidegger: The Anaximander Fragment," *Arion: A Journal of Humanities and Classics,* new series 1 (Winter 1974): 576–626; and *Holzwege,* edited and translated by Julian Young and Kenneth Haynes as *Off the Beaten Track* (Cambridge & New York: Cambridge University Press, 2002);

Einführung in die Metaphysik (Tübingen: Niemeyer, 1953); translated by Ralph Manheim as *Introduction to Metaphysics* (New Haven: Yale University Press, 1959);

Aus der Erfahrung des Denkens (Pfullingen: Neske, 1954);

Vorträge und Aufsätze (Pfullingen: Neske, 1954)—includes "Die Frage Nach der Technik"; "Wissenschaft und Besinnung"; "Überwindung der Metaphysik"; "Wer ist Nietzsches Zarathustra?" translated as "Who Is Nietzsche's Zarathustra?" *Review of Metaphysics,* 20 (1966/1967): 411–431; "Bauen Wohnen Denken"; ". . . Dichterisch wohnet der Mensch . . ."; "Logos"; "Moira"; and "Aletheia";

Was heisst Denken? (Tübingen: Niemeyer, 1954); translated by Gray as *What Is Called Thinking?* (New York: Harper & Row, 1968);

Was ist Das—die Philosophie? (Pfullingen: Neske, 1956); translated by William Kluback and Jean T. Wilde as *What Is Philosophy?* (London: Vision, 1956; New Haven, Conn.: College and University Press, 1956);

Zur Seinsfrage (Frankfurt am Main: Klostermann, 1956); translated by Kluback and Wilde as *The Question of Being* (New York: Twayne, 1958);

Der Satz vom Grund (Pfullingen: Neske, 1957); translated by Reginald Lilly as *The Principle of Reason* (Bloomington: Indiana University Press, 1991);

Identität und Differenz (Pfullingen: Neske, 1957); translated by Kurt F. Leidecker as *Essays in Metaphysics: Identity and Difference* (New York: Philosophical Library, 1960);

Gelassenheit (Pfullingen: Neske, 1959); translated by John M. Anderson and E. Hans Freund as *Discourse on Thinking* (New York: Harper & Row, 1969);

Unterwegs zur Sprache (Pfullingen: Neske, 1959); translated by Peter Hertz and Joan Stambaugh as *On the Way to Language* (New York: Harper & Row, 1971);

Nietzsche, 2 volumes (Pfullingen: Neske, 1961); translated by Krell, Frank A. Capuzzi, and Stambaugh as *Nietzsche,* 4 volumes (New York: Harper & Row, 1979–1987);

Die Frage nach dem Ding: Zu Kants Lehre von den transzendentalen Grundsätzen (Tübingen: Niemeyer, 1962); translated by W. B. Barton Jr. and Vera Deutsch as *What Is a Thing?* (Chicago: Regnery, 1967);

Die Technik und die Kehre (Pfullingen: Neske, 1962)—includes "Die Kehre";

Kants These über Sein (Frankfurt am Main: Klostermann, 1963); translated by Ted E. Klein and William E. Pohl as "Kant's Thesis about Being," *Southwestern Journal of Philosophy,* 4 (1973): 7–33;

Wegmarken (Frankfurt am Main: Klostermann, 1967); edited and translated by William A. McNeill as *Pathmarks* (Cambridge & New York: Cambridge University Press, 1998);

Zur Sache des Denkens (Tübingen: Niemeyer, 1969); translated by Stambaugh as *On Time and Being* (New York: Harper & Row, 1972);

Phänomenologie und Theologie (Frankfurt am Main: Klostermann, 1970);

Schellings Abhandlung Über das Wesen der menschlichen Freiheit, edited by Hildegard Feieck (Tübingen: Niemeyer, 1971); translated by Stambaugh as *Schelling's Treatise on the Essence of Human Freedom* (Athens: Ohio University Press, 1985);

Frühe Schriften, edited by Friedrich-Wilhelm von Herrmann (Frankfurt am Main: Klostermann, 1972);

Die Grundprobleme der Phänomenologie, edited by Herrmann (Frankfurt am Main: Klostermann, 1975); translated by Hofstädter as *The Basic Problems of Phenomenology* (Bloomington: Indiana University Press, 1982);

Gesamtausgabe, 62 volumes to date (Frankfurt am Main: Klostermann, 1975–   );

Der Begriff der Zeit: Vortrag vor der Marburger Theologenschaft, Juli 1924 (Tübingen: Niemeyer, 1989); translated by McNeill as *The Concept of Time* (Oxford & Cambridge, Mass.: Blackwell, 1992);

Beiträge zur Philosophie: Vom Ereignis, edited by Herrmann (Frankfurt am Main: Klostermann, 1989); translated by Parvis Emad and Kenneth Maly as *Contributions to Philosophy: From Enowning* (Bloomington: Indiana University Press, 1999).

Editions in English: *Existence and Being,* edited by Werner Brock (Chicago: Regnery, 1949; London: Vision, 1949)—includes "Remembrance of the Poet," translated by Douglas Scott; "Hölderlin and the Essence of Poetry" ["Hölderlin und das Wesen der Dichtung"], translated by Scott; "On the Essence of Truth," translated by R. F. C. Hull and A. Crick; and "What Is Metaphysics?" *[Was ist Metaphysik?],* translated by Hull and Crick;

Poetry, Language, Thought, edited and translated by Albert Hofstädter (New York: Harper & Row, 1971)—includes "The Thinker as Poet *[Aus der Erfahrung des Denkens],* "What Are Poets For?" ["Wozu Dichter?"], "Building, Dwelling, Thinking" ["Bauen Wohnen Denken"], and ". . . Poetically Man Dwells . . ." [". . . Dichterisch wohnet der Mensch . . ."];

The End of Philosophy, translated by Joan Stambaugh (New York: Harper & Row, 1973)–includes "Overcoming Metaphysics" ["Überwindung der Metaphysik"];

Early Greek Thinking, translated by David Farrell Krell and Frank A. Capuzzi (New York: Harper & Row, 1975)–comprises "The Anaximander Fragment," "Logos (Heraclitus, Fragment B 50)," "Moira (Parmenides VIII, 34–41)," and "Aletheia (Heraclitus, Fragment B 16)";

The Piety of Thinking: Essays, edited and translated by James Hart and John Maraldo (Bloomington: Indiana University Press, 1976)–includes "Phenomenology and Theology" *[Phänomenologie und Theologie]*;

The Question Concerning Technology and Other Essays, edited and translated by William Lovitt (New York: Harper & Row, 1977)–includes "The Question Concerning Technology" ["Die Frage Nach der Technik"], "The Turning" ["Die Kehre"], "The Word of Nietzsche: God Is Dead" ["Nietzsches Wort 'Gott ist Tot'"], "The Age of the World Picture" ["Die Zeit des Weltbildes"], and "Science and Reflection" ["Wissenschaft und Besinnung"];

Basic Writings: From Being and Time (1927) to The Task of Thinking (1964), edited by Krell (New York: Harper & Row, 1977; London: Routledge & Kegan Paul, 1978; revised and expanded edition, San Francisco: HarperSanFrancisco, 1993).

Martin Heidegger's 1927 publication, *Sein und Zeit: Erste Hälfte* (translated as *Being and Time,* 1962), can plausibly be considered the most influential philosophical text of the twentieth century. Its main focus had been announced at least fifteen years earlier when Heidegger was still in his early twenties, and it remained his lifelong topic until his death in 1976. He treated this subject matter in several ways, beginning with concepts of phenomenology, such as life, world, historicity, and facticity, which were illuminated by what he called the question of being. Later he developed this topic as *das Ereignis,* "the event of appropriation," which designates the singular unfolding of being. The topic, in short, concerns how human beings are situated historically in a world that from the beginning has some meaning for them, both making possible and setting limits to their future. *Sein und Zeit* emerged as a seamless amalgamation of relatively independent drafts written during the years after World War I and should be regarded as just one of the stages in Heidegger's long philosophical life. It emerged after an intense period of philosophical struggle and breakthrough and was

incomplete on its publication. Heidegger's roots lie in deeply conservative rural Southern Germany. His lifelong suspicion of modernity, machinery, democracy, liberalism, and the commoditized styles found, for instance, in journalism and mass culture contributed to his radical critiques of the productivity and efficiency that are valorized by forms of modern life, its bland cosmopolitanism and its perpetually seductive novelty. Alongside this, Heidegger's untiring philosophical questing was able to disclose a deep complicity between the tradition he was committed to preserve (in other words, Western metaphysics) and the conditions he despised. An acknowledged and powerful alternative to predicative logic, Heidegger's thought opens with the way beings are revealed through the question of being, which he formulates as follows: why are there beings at all, rather than nothing? The "why" in this case would not be a question about the *cause* of beings but something more like a commemoration of the sense of wonder that anything exists at all, thus revealing beings in hitherto unthinkable ways, for instance, by opening experience up to the essential and constitutive indeterminacy of its future. Heidegger's critique of Western metaphysics lies in his discovery that these constitutive aspects of experience have been systematically excluded by the metaphysical tradition, which reaches its completion as technological rationality.

Heidegger was born to a cellarer and a church sexton, Friedrich and Johanna (née Kempf) Heidegger, in Messkirch, a small rural town in Baden, southwest Germany, on 26 September 1889. His sister, Marie, was born three years later and his brother, Fritz, two years after that. In 1903 Heidegger won a scholarship to the Jesuit gymnasium in Konstanz and stayed, with other scholarship children from similarly poor Catholic families, in a local Catholic boardinghouse. Here he prepared for a clerical career. In 1906 he transferred to Bertholds gymnasium in Freiburg, boarding at the archiepiscopal seminary of St. Georg, where the church gave him free board and lodging.

While there he received a copy of Franz Brentano's *Von der mannigfachen Bedeutung des Seienden nach Aristoteles* (On the Manifold Meaning of Being According to Aristotle, 1862) from a paternal friend. Heidegger later claimed that his interest in philosophy was first aroused on studying Brentano's book, which then led him to Carl Braig's *Vom Sein: Abriss der Ontologie* (On Being: An Outline of Ontology, 1896). There he discovered excerpts from Aristotle and commentaries from Thomas Aquinas and other Scholastic thinkers. In 1909 he became a novice of the Society of Jesus at Tisis near Feldkirch in Austria, but on 13 October, at the end of two weeks of candidature, he left, having been turned down for health reasons and possibly for doubts

*Heidegger's parents, Johanna Heidegger (née Kempf) and
Friedrich Heidegger (from Walter Biemel,* Martin
Heidegger: An Illustrated Study, *translated by
J. L. Mehta, 1976; Thomas Cooper Library,
University of South Carolina)*

about his spiritual vocation. In the winter semester he
began studying for the priesthood at the Albert-Ludwig
University in Freiburg, where he focused on philosophy
and moral and natural sciences. His introduction to
contemporary philosophy came when he read Edmund
Husserl's *Logische Untersuchungen* (Logical Investigations,
1900–1901). Husserl later became a key influence in
the development of *Sein und Zeit.*

In 1910 Heidegger gave his first lecture, on the
seventeenth-century court preacher Abraham a Santa
Clara, in Hausen im Tal near Messkirch. He again lectured on Abraham at the unveiling of a monument in
Kreenheinstetten, the town of the preacher's birth. The
lecture is one of the earliest works in Heidegger's
Gesamtausgabe (Complete Works), the first volume of
which appeared in 1975. Here his philosophical interests are couched in language that ties the young Heidegger to a conservative, antimodernist tradition, which at
that time favored the tough self-assurance of the educated peasant classes against the fashionable bourgeoisie of modern urban life. Abraham had been adopted as
a role model by those with an increasingly polemical
attitude toward various liberal tendencies in the Catho-

lic Church. At this time Heidegger began to publish
articles, reviews, and poems in *Der Akademiker* (The
Graduate), the journal of the German Association of
Catholic Graduates.

In 1911 he spent the summer semester at home
because of asthma and heart problems and abandoned
the theological seminary on the advice of his superiors.
Heidegger changed his studies to mathematics and philosophy, now concentrating on problems of logic in the
history of metaphysics. He continued to publish
reviews and poems. In 1912 he published his last articles in *Der Akademiker* and wrote two articles for philosophy journals, which have since been published in
revised versions as part of the *Frühe Schriften* (Early
Writings, 1972): "Das Realitätsproblem in der modernen Philosophie" (The Problem of Reality in Modern
Philosophy) and "Neuere Forschungen über Logik"
(New Investigations of Logic).

Heidegger graduated on 26 July 1913 after his
doctoral examination and was awarded a Ph.D. summa
cum laude on the basis of his dissertation, *Die Lehre vom
Urteil im Psychologismus* (The Doctrine of Judgment in
Psychologism). Here the influence of Husserl is evident
in Heidegger's criticism of attempts to analyze the logical notion of judgment from the perspective of human
psychology. He focuses on aspects of everyday experience as well as on history and metaphysics, and his
main claim is that logic cannot be reduced to psychological processes. This claim was an early formulation of
Heidegger's notion of the everyday and resulted two
years later in what is now recognized as a step on the
way to the philosophy presented in *Sein und Zeit.* By
1913 his intention to "articulate the whole region of
'being' in its various modes of reality" had been made
clear, and he harnessed the combined resources of
Scholasticism, phenomenology, and neo-Kantianism
toward this end.

In 1915 he completed his habilitation dissertation,
Die Kategorien- und Bedeutungslehre des Duns Scotus (The
Doctrine of Categories and Signification in Duns Scotus, published in 1916), which earned him the license to
teach philosophy at the Philosophical Faculty at
Freiburg. He began by lecturing theology students in
philosophy. In his habilitation lecture, "Der Zeitbegriff
in der Geschichtswissenschaft" (The Doctrine of Time
in the Science of History), Heidegger distinguishes
between the notion of time as understood by modern
physics and the nonuniform and qualitatively differentiated periodic time of historians, which is not reconcilable with calculable duration. Heidegger's focus on
metaphysics is complicated by the dense fusion of Scholastic philosophy, neo-Kantianism, and Husserlian phenomenology. His inquiries are already directed to what
is more fully developed in *Sein und Zeit* as a schematic

interpretation of facticity. Facticity denotes the conditions according to which one's possibilities are determined and limited by one's circumstances, one's "In-der-Welt-Sein" (being-in-the-world). His interest in Scholasticism focuses on categories of language that have no correspondence with objects in the world, such as marks of privation and negation and categories for nonexistent entities such as "Nothing." Brentano's book on Aristotle is influential at this stage. Categorical extremes of signification such as univocality and equivocality indicate why there must be a role for a category that rescues the univocal ideal from the inevitable consequences of equivocal language use (in other words, the use of words in more than one sense–for the Scholastics the paradigm was the word *god*). In the Scholastic texts, following Aristotle, the analogy of being mediates between such extremes. So the empty word *being* figures at the heart of questions about the generation of sense in everyday human experience.

At this stage the problem of what Heidegger calls "the hermeneutics of facticity" lies in the self-reflexive puzzle according to which facticity must be considered, already, as a kind of hermeneutics. Everyday experience already articulates and interprets its world, so that any attempt to interpret facticity would be an attempt to interpret interpretation. Husserl's account of the natural or pretheoretical attitude, which is intensified rather than exposed by theoretical procedures, indicates a way forward in the attempt to resist the philosophical tendency to objectify experience. So by 1915 Heidegger had been able to move beyond the neo-Kantian account of facticity, which posits a chaotic flux at the origin of sensation, by drawing out from the phenomenology of categorical intuition the conclusion that humans live from the first in a context, a world, that is already meaningful and that they already know interpretively.

World War I interrupted Heidegger's academic career. He published nothing between this time and 1927, but the period is marked by intense study and, after 1919, a series of reportedly compelling lectures. Courses on German idealism, on Aristotle's logic, and on basic questions of logic were announced for the 1915–1916 academic year, but in 1915 Heidegger was conscripted. Because he was regarded as unsuitable for combat, he was assigned to the postal and meteorological services as military censor at the Freiburg post office.

In 1915 he had met Elfride Petri, a student of political economy, and on 21 March 1917 they were married. Because Martin was a Catholic and Elfride a Lutheran, they were remarried a week later in a Protestant ceremony with her parents. By Elfride's account, she was never to find her faith and he shortly lost his.

In 1919 their son Jörg was born, and in 1920 a second son, Hermann, was born.

On 2 August 1917 Heidegger gave a talk on Friedrich Schleiermacher, the key figure in the German hermeneutic tradition and an important forerunner of Wilhelm Dilthey, whose attempt to establish the conditions of possibility for the study of history had become a crucial reference point for Heidegger's account of historicity. He lectured on Georg Wilhelm Freidrich Hegel in the summer semester and on Plato in the winter semester. On 17 January 1918 Heidegger, a private in the territorial reserve, reported to barracks for basic training and was then sent to the front to serve at a meteorological station. He was promoted to lance corporal on 5 November and was discharged eleven days later. He was never involved in any military action. In the meantime, he had broken with what he saw as the dogmatic system of Catholicism. Heidegger continued to lecture and met with Karl Jaspers in Freiburg, where Husserl had become professor of philosophy in 1916.

On his return from the front, Heidegger became Husserl's unsalaried lecturer and assistant at Freiburg, where he taught courses on phenomenology, the foundations of logic, the history of metaphysics, and the nature of the university. His teaching during the so-called Kriegnotsemester (war-emergency semester) of 1919 advocated a kind of phenomenology that was set apart from all hitherto existing theoretical science. The new science does not have an object as such because its topic is the process of life itself, within which one is already caught up in meaningful ways. Before Heidegger, this subject occupied the domain traditionally regarded–in the language of neo-Kantianism–as the transcendental, which is traditionally opposed to the empirical domain of human experience. Strictly, then, Heidegger was proposing a science of the nonobjectifiable, unspeakable grounds of experience. The human being is not to be understood any longer as being derived from some extratemporal transcendental source but is to be derived from the categories of its own facticity as a finite, situated historical being grounded toward death. His fame as a teacher spread rapidly on the basis of his exposition of the nature of the world of everyday experience and the human being. His studies of Max Scheler's philosophical anthropology were added to his unusual adoption of Husserl's phenomenology, Dilthey's hermeneutics, and the Christian texts of St. Paul, St. Augustine, and Martin Luther. The role of the Scholastic texts becomes clearer too, showing how they contributed to Heidegger's compelling alternative to contemporary versions of ontology and epistemology still rooted in the standard readings of Greek thought. The hermeneutics of facticity–of life before theory–thus merges with the

Albert-Ludwig University in Freiburg, where Heidegger studied for the priesthood from 1909 to 1911
(from Alfred Denker, Historical Dictionary of Heidegger's Philosophy, *2000;*
Thomas Cooper Library, University of South Carolina)

phenomenology of religious experience to provide a radical phenomenology of the everyday context or world of human experience.

In 1922 Elfride, as a present, had a small wooden cabin built in Todtnauberg, where Heidegger could work in solitude. It is possible to date the early stages of the development of the first draft of *Sein und Zeit* from this period. He did not publish the book until 1927, and then only under considerable pressure for him to do so, but during this time he continued to write and to lecture. A letter from Husserl to Paul Natorp at the University of Marburg from 1922 describes the young Heidegger as a highly original personality but one not ready to publish. Heidegger himself sent Natorp an article planned as an introduction to a projected book on Aristotle, which secured him a position at Marburg in 1923. The article, "Phänomenologische Interpretationem zu Aristoteles: Einfürung in die Phänomenologische Forschung" (Phenomenological Interpretations with Respect to Aristotle: Indication of the Hermeneutical Situation), reveals something of the laborious shaping that Husserl describes. The vocabulary of phenomenology, the attempt to bring systematic think-

ing to bear on problems of philosophy, and historical considerations of philosophy are interconnected in a critical account of the human condition. "Phänomenologische Interpretationem zu Aristoteles" is the first of Heidegger's extant works to introduce the distinction between authentic and inauthentic existence. He also announces the project of destruction, sometimes translated as *deconstruction,* of metaphysical tradition.

In the summer of 1923 he taught a final course at Freiberg, with the title "Ontologie (Hermeneutik der Faktizität)" (Ontology [Hermeneutics of Facticity]), which is one of the core strands of *Sein und Zeit*. The focus was on *Dasein,* the existing human being in its aspect as someone who is placed somewhere and lives in a particular time. By the end of the course the notion of facticity had developed into the notion of In-der-Welt-Sein, which allowed Heidegger to focus on the being, the *Sein* of that which discloses or interprets being, *Dasein*. As the subtitle of the course indicates, Heidegger had intensified his radical revision of the long tradition of exegesis and commentary called hermeneutics. The process of disclosing one's facticity would operate only on the assumption that for *Dasein* this process is already an operative function of facticity. One would be disclosing the event of disclosure itself, from the intelligible structure of *Dasein*'s own being.

Heidegger's time at Freiberg came to an end in July when with Natorp's help he moved to the University of Marburg to take up the post of associate professor. Here he met the newly enrolled, eighteen-year-old Hannah Arendt. In February 1924 they became lovers in an affair that lasted until 1933. Their friendship, which they resumed after World War II, lasted Heidegger's lifetime. In July the lecture presented to a society of Marburg theologians, *Der Begriff der Zeit* (The Concept of Time), recalls the theme of his habilitation lecture and also provides an introduction to one of the central distinctions of *Sein und Zeit* between temporality in everyday human experience and time as it is conceived by the physical sciences. *Dasein* is now conceived, in its most radical possibility of being, as time itself rather than a being in time. Time, however, must be understood as essentially futural, which means that the essential moment in the experience of time must be considered not as the present but as the undetermined future. The tradition has always understood time as presence. To say that one has "no time" is to cast time into the bad present of the everyday. It is the time one is yet to have, however, that gives one an experience of the present, because it allows the past to be repeated as life. Time, therefore, will now be regarded as "the possibility of repetition," which, as Heidegger points out at the conclusion of the lecture, is historicity. The possibility of repetition connects two essential concepts, in the German *die Möglichkeit,* meaning possibility, and *Wiederholen,* meaning repetition, though an adequate translation would need to acknowledge the sense of revision that is also implied. The phrase "possibility of repetition" is similar in formulation to the phrase "hermeneutics of facticity." The *of* in each case serves as a double genitive because it can signify in two ways. The attempt to interpret facticity yields to the realization that interpretation already belongs to facticity. In the same way, if *Dasein* is time, and if the fundamental phenomenon of time is the future, *Dasein* would not be separable from its future possibilities, that is, the possibilities available in repeating the past. The possibility of repetition, then, already simply is possibility.

Heidegger's father died in December 1924 at age seventy-three. His mother died less than three years later, in 1927, at the age of sixty-nine, shortly after the publication of *Sein und Zeit*. In 1925 faculty members at Marburg proposed Heidegger as the replacement for Nicolai Hartmann in the philosophy chair, as a tenured full professor. But in January 1926 Berlin authorities rejected the proposal on the grounds of Heidegger's lack of publications. Heidegger then, in March, worked

intensely to produce a substantial draft of the work he was planning at the time, completing the first and most of the second division of the first part of what was supposed to have been a work in two parts with three divisions each. Heidegger presented the manuscript to Husserl at his sixty-seventh birthday party in Todtnauberg on 8 April. With the work less than half finished Heidegger found himself under increasing pressure to publish something. In June the university again proposed to appoint Heidegger to tenured professor, and again in November, Berlin refused on the same grounds as before. The completed sections of *Sein und Zeit* went to press and were published in April 1927, in the *Jahrbuch für Philosophie und phänomenologische Forschung* (Yearbook for Philosophy and Phenomenological Research), edited by Husserl, and at the same time as a separate work.

In the summer semester Heidegger taught the course *Die Grundprobleme der Phänomenologie* (translated as *The Basic Problems of Phenomenology,* 1982), which is close in subject matter to *Sein und Zeit* and helps to fill in some of what is missing there, although the published version did not appear until 1975. Heidegger examines the philosophical history of ontology, with an emphasis on Immanuel Kant in the first half, and then examines time as temporality and its relation to being. The material covered may have been intended as part of the third division of the first part of *Sein und Zeit* and perhaps even looks forward to the second part. The published version does not in fact add anything new philosophically to *Sein und Zeit,* but it does help to clarify and deepen one's understanding of it. The Kantian context reveals the extent to which Heidegger's thinking had developed during the writing of *Sein und Zeit* by way of a critical reading of Kant that becomes yet more explicit during the lecture courses of 1928 and 1929. In fact the notion of critical reading itself undergoes a powerful transformation here, as it takes the form of the destruction of metaphysics that is promised in *Sein und Zeit* but which in fact constitutes *Sein und Zeit* in its manifestation as part of Heidegger's *Wiederholen*–repetition/revision–of the tradition. For this reason, the texts that lead up to the publication of *Sein und Zeit* and the lecture courses that immediately follow provide indispensable supplements to it.

Sein und Zeit aims to address the question of the meaning of being. The introduction to the treatise sets out its design. The response to the question involves first an interpretation of the entity for whom being is a question, *Dasein,* and second an interpretation of historicity, because *Dasein* is an historical entity. Heidegger explains that since the treatment of the question of being branches out into these two distinct tasks, the treatise itself must have two parts. The first part is concerned with the interpretation of *Dasein* in terms of temporality and explicates time as the transcendental horizon of the question. It was to have three divisions: a preparatory analysis of *Dasein;* the analysis of *Dasein* and *Zeitlichkeit* (temporality, in the sense of transitoriness); and an exposition of the relation between time and being. The third division never appeared. Part 2 was supposed to have addressed the basic features of a phenomenological destruction (or deconstruction) of the history of ontology, with *Temporalität* (the problematic of temporality) as a guide. It was also supposed to have three divisions: one dealing with Kant's doctrine of schematism and time; one with the ontological foundations of René Descartes's cogito and medieval ontology; and one with Aristotle's essay on time, providing a way of examining the limits of ancient ontology. None of part 2 ever appeared, but the plan is clear enough in outline. The destruction would work backward as a way of disclosing the repetitive nature of the problematic of temporality and ontology, working first from Kantian ontology, then back through the repetition of medieval ontology represented by Descartes, which itself would be revealed as a repetition of ancient ontology and the limits imposed by the phenomenal basis found in Aristotle. Indeed the groundwork of *Sein und Zeit* can be traced back to Heidegger's critique of Aristotle's concept of time.

What Heidegger published fulfills the design for the first two divisions. The book starts with an analysis of *Dasein* as the being for whom being is a question. In order to address the meaning of being in general, the being that poses the question must first look into its own way of being. The use of the term *Dasein* (which is accordingly rarely translated) remains one of Heidegger's most striking innovations. An ordinary German word, which in most philosophical contexts means something like the English *existence,* takes on a forceful character in Heidegger's use, in which the etymological root–*Da-Sein*–is emphasized. Heidegger makes several other innovative terminological distinctions early in *Sein und Zeit* that help to distinguish *Dasein* and its peculiar way of being. The most important of these is the distinction between the ontological and the ontical. Paragraph 4 addresses the "ontical priority" of the question of being. The ontical denotes whatever pertains to the factual world, the world conventionally explored by the sciences. In this world a peculiar fact emerges concerning the being that Heidegger calls *Dasein.* It is distinguished from all other beings by the fact that, for *Dasein* alone, being is an issue for it. Neither rocks nor vegetables, nor even other animals, concern themselves with the question of the meaning of being. So, ontically speaking, *Dasein* is distinguished by being ontological, which means that it has a relation to being. This quality

does not mean it has developed an ontology, however. Heidegger reserves this term for the theoretical inquiry into being. *Dasein,* then, is ontically distinguished from other beings, insofar as it has an understanding of being, but for the most part it remains "pre-ontological" because it has yet to work out its ontology.

Heidegger adds to this distinction between the ontological and the ontical a further, surprising one, which seems to recall the contemporary and fashionable versions of existentialism that Heidegger despised. The ability to make decisions about the future characterizes the existence of *Dasein.* So Heidegger uses the terms *existenziell* and *existenzial* to distinguish between the everyday decisions made by the particular *Dasein* and the a priori structures and modes of existence itself. Ontology must begin with the preontological understanding of being because this understanding is the definitive characteristic of *Dasein. Dasein* operates in the everyday world and must deal with other entities in practical ways. To that extent *Dasein* is *existenziell,* which means practical competence and an understanding of human existence that remains implicit. On the basis of this implicit understanding it should be possible to develop an explicit ontology, so that the question of being would concern the a priori conditions of possibility for all sciences.

Having defined *Dasein* in terms of existence, Heidegger develops the implications, which effectively overturn several metaphysical doctrines. *Dasein* cannot be considered as a particular type (belonging to the genus *Homo,* for instance). Rather, as an entity considered as its own possibility, *Dasein* is in each case its own being. Its possibility or existence thus always overflows or outstrips its actuality. This possibility implies two alternative conditions: *Eigentlichkeit* (authenticity) or *Uneigentlichkeit* (usually translated as *inauthenticity,* though not without controversy). The latter condition should be regarded as the normal condition for *Dasein* most of the time. It implies that in this modality *Dasein* is not properly its own being. To be authentic is to be one's own self rather than to belong to some other–a social group, family, friend, or institution. Heidegger's term for these others, *das Man,* can be translated as "the one" or "the they," and it implies a condition according to which *Dasein* exists without making its own decisions, conforming instead to habits, customs, and practices that determine relative cultural conditions. The authentic condition, on the contrary, implies resoluteness in assuming the ability to make one's own decisions.

The authentic and inauthentic ways of being that are grounded in the existence of *Dasein* correspond to the "existentialia" that characterize its everydayness. By *existentialia* Heidegger means the a priori conditions of possibility for being in the world. Because the world, in this sense, is a world only for *Dasein* (there is no world independent of *Dasein,* although there are certainly beings that are), the other kinds of entity that populate it must be considered in terms of how *Dasein* engages with them. The world of *Dasein* is populated not only by others but also by tools and equipment, which are not simply *vorhanden* (present-at-hand), inert and without practical significance, but are *zuhanden* (ready-to-hand), available for work or leisure and without the need to deliberate unduly about them.

	Dasein can also be characterized in terms of the moods it finds itself in—its throwness. Throwness designates the fact that *Dasein*'s possibilities belong in a world that is already determined in some ways, particularly in relation to other beings. Through mood the world is revealed to *Dasein* colored by joy, boredom, or sadness, and through mood *Dasein* can take up its own possibilities itself. *Befindlichkeit* (the state one finds oneself in) can be grasped as a kind of attunement. Heidegger's examples, angst and boredom, illustrate what is meant by moods: they are conditions of being that, if one is responsive to them, disclose the world in its ontological dimension. Neither angst (anxiety over nothing in particular) nor boredom can be said to have a specific object or external cause. Rather they are moods capable of disclosing the world in its everyday ordinariness.

	Dasein is constantly dealing with entities whose meanings are implicitly understood in the way *Dasein* makes use of them and in the way they are related to each other. This everyday concern, which Heidegger characterizes in terms of the way the craftsman operates in his work space, can also be made into the topic of philosophical reflection, so that the mode of being of entities in the world is shown to be special to the mode of being of *Dasein,* revealing the a priori nature of the world of *Dasein* as a "for the sake of which," grounded in *Dasein*'s own existentiality—possibility itself. Similarly, *Dasein*'s understanding of the world is disclosed as an active interpretation, projecting an a priori condition, *Dasein*'s own possibility, onto the entities that populate its world. The significance of the tools or equipment that *Dasein* habitually uses turns out to be a projection of its mode of existence. *Dasein* understands its environment in terms of possibilities offered and is therefore always active, always meddling in some way. These considerations of mood, understanding, and interpretation emphasize the active role of being-in, the verbal aspect of being-in-the-world. They also indicate why Heidegger privileges temporality. *Dasein*'s throwness, revealed through moods like angst and boredom, show that its existence involves both having been and being to come. *Dasein* can either exist in an inauthentic way, governed by *das Man* and the fashionable currency of the everyday, or it can exist in an authentic way, project-

Heidegger in 1914, the year after he completed his Ph.D. at the University of Freiburg (Vittorio Klostermann Verlag, Frankfurt am Main; from Jean-Pierre Cotten, Heidegger, 1974; Thomas Cooper Library, University of South Carolina)

ing its own possibilities into a future that it can have a say in determining for itself. Through the experience of anxiety *Dasein* learns about its facticity, that it is thrown in a world that is already marked by significance. It also learns that the character of this throwness is possibility and, therefore, that its existence is its own. Finally, it learns that it is fallen among other beings whose being is *not* its own. The fundamental unifying structure that supports these related dimensions is *Sorge* (usually translated as *care*). *Sorge* must use time and must reckon with time. The "time" that *Dasein* experiences, however, is the phenomenal aspect of temporality—the proximal experience of the present. This experience, Heidegger argues, is not only what arises as the everyday understanding of time, but also what has evolved into the traditional ontological understanding of time, according to which being is determined as presence. Having derived the ontological meaning of care, according to which temporality involves both running ahead and reaching back, Heidegger moves on to division 2 of *Sein und Ziet*.

Division 2 begins by acknowledging that the "Preparatory Fundamental Analysis" of division 1 has only dealt with being-in-the-world in a partial way. The structure of care has revealed a depth and complexity that demands a different approach. If being in the world involves reaching back into the past and running ahead into the future, then division 1 has only managed to bring into view the everyday happenings between birth and death. The structural roles of the end and the beginning remain obscure. Furthermore, the character of "mine-ness," which forms the ground of both authentic and inauthentic existence, has been brought into view only in terms of the inauthentic, average way of being. It will thus be the task of division 2 to reveal in the structure of care the deepest ground of the whole of *Dasein*'s being. Division 2 begins, accordingly, with the questions of how *Dasein* can be a whole and how *Dasein* can wholly be.

For this reason, Heidegger argues, the analysis must engage with the most extreme possibilities of *Dasein*'s existence, the possibilities of birth and death (the ends of being) and the possibility of authentic existence, in which *Dasein* can be wholly its own. The first problem emerges with the terms of the question itself: in what sense can a being, who is to be understood in terms of its finitude and freedom, also be considered as a whole? The essence of *Dasein*'s care is its active interpreting, which follows from an essential constitutional structure of *Dasein,* the temporal phenomenon of the future, the ahead-of-itself, according to which there is "eine ständige Unabgeschlossenheit" (constantly something to be settled). So *Dasein* cannot be considered a finished whole in the conventional sense, a sum of attributes or a living thing. If *Dasein* is to be considered as a whole, then this eventuality will be through an interpretation by *Dasein* that can disclose the whole of its own being. The first serious problem thus emerges. The two extremes of life—birth and death—remain outside the temporal structure of *Dasein*'s throwness. *Dasein* can never reach back behind its thrown facticity to the moment of birth nor run ahead so far as to experience its death before ceasing to be. This problem rules out the method operational in division 1, where the ontical and *existenziell* aspects of existence served as an essential starting point for approaching the ontological and existential problem. Here, Heidegger points out, the problem of not being able to eradicate the "ahead-of-itself" as an essential structural aspect of care need only be regarded as insurmountable from a perspective that posits *Dasein* as a present-to-hand just waiting for a not-yet-present-to-hand to be added onto it. Rather, if it is

going to be possible to make *Dasein* accessible in its wholeness, it must be disclosed (as it must disclose itself) in an existential and ontological way.

Heidegger accomplishes this disclosure through an extended and detailed series of analyses, which link the problems of death, guilt, and history to the meaning of care as time; and he concludes by arguing that *Dasein*'s being is always and from the beginning being-toward-an-end. The fore-structure, or a priori givenness, of the end of its existence forces *Dasein* to relate to this end in definite, authentic or inauthentic, ways.

Shortly after the publication of *Sein und Zeit* Heidegger's fame as a philosopher spread internationally, and consequently he was promoted to full professor at Marburg on 19 October 1927. In 1928 he was offered the chair of philosophy at Freiberg, which had been vacated by its founder, the retired Husserl. The post represented the highest honor possible in the field of phenomenological philosophy. Heidegger accepted the invitation and took up the position for the winter semester.

In 1929 he published *Kant und das Problem der Metaphysik* (translated as *Kant and the Problem of Metaphysics,* 1962), which explicitly sets out how the futural dimension makes interpretation both possible and necessary. In *Sein und Zeit* Heidegger had argued that the historicity of *Dasein* implies a legacy that one inherits. And as *Sein und Zeit* teaches, the aim of locating and understanding conditions cannot necessarily be achieved by simply studying the phenomena (historical events) that they make possible. In other words Heidegger is interested in the connection that Aristotle had suggested between what is necessary and what is possible (but not always necessary). In a strange reversal the necessary turns out to be possibility, the possibility of repetition, which overflows all the ways in which possibilities can be actualized. The consequence for Heidegger is that the best way forward, in any of the dimensions that humans operate in, implies types of *response* to the traditions, legacies, and histories that make people what they are. Whatever form it takes, the response always implies a responsibility to what is *unthought* (or as yet not thought).

Heidegger's inaugural lecture at Freiburg, *Was ist Metaphysik?* (translated as "What Is Metaphysics?" in *Existence and Being,* 1949), on its publication in the same year, attracted considerable attention among those in the Anglo-American analytic tradition, for whom it confirmed the suspicion that Heidegger, and by extension other fashionable Continental philosophers, were hopelessly unclear and muddled. This suspicion hardened into prejudice in the years that followed and led to almost wholesale scorn toward Heidegger's thought among the English-speaking philosophical community.

At the same time the lecture attracted hyperbolic praise among existentialist philosophers and led to a long-term association of Heidegger's thought with French existentialism. The lecture can be read as a challenge to philosophize. It takes up issues familiar from *Sein und Zeit*, particularly the analysis of anxiety and nothingness, but presents them in a new and provocative way. Heidegger's language seemed to some to be contorted and unwieldy. The notorious phrase from the lecture, "the nothing noths," draws attention to a characteristic that had long been a part of Heidegger's style—the active verbalizing of noun phrases. Just as being is (re)verbalized in its context in *Sein und Zeit* as *Da-Sein*, the active be-ing of being-in-the-world, so too the nothing is put to work as an activity constitutive also of *Dasein*'s world. The nothing helps to disclose being in its previously concealed strangeness, showing how the transcendence of *Dasein* is held out over the nothing from the strictly finite and limited vantage of being, which can now be revealed in contrast as temporarily meaningful but bounded by meaninglessness.

Heidegger's rise to fame between the end of World War I through the years immediately after the publication of *Sein und Zeit* coincided with the period of the Weimar Republic, a period of turbulent political activity, economic depression, and cultural vibrancy. By September 1930, Adolf Hitler's National Socialist German Workers Party (NSDAP, or the Nazi Party) had become one of the most powerful and popular political organizations in Germany. Heidegger's political leanings had been unfocused and largely localized in his youth and had not been evident at all during the years leading up to *Sein und Zeit*. Nevertheless, during the early 1930s, he became sympathetic to Nazism. He had read Hitler's *Mein Kampf* (My Struggle, 1925) and, along with many of his generation, had sought in the political world an answer to the global problems caused by what he had started to describe as the fulfillment of metaphysics in technology. On 30 January 1933 Hitler was appointed chancellor of the winning coalition of right-wing parties and, after 27 February, absolute power was conferred on the NSDAP. Heidegger's enthusiasm for the new regime led, in a series of swiftly changing circumstances, to his appointment as rector of the University of Freiburg on 22 April, and on 1 May he became an official member of NSDAP.

On 27 May, Heidegger gave his rectoral address, *Die Selbstbehauptung der deutschen Universität* (translated as "The Self-Assertion of the German University," 1985), which provoked ironic responses from some commentators of the time, who suggested substituting *Selbstenthauptung* (Self-Beheading) for *Selbstbehauptung,* having observed that self-assertion, in Heidegger's view, meant adherence to National Socialism. In a move that is actu-ally entirely in line with his long-term philosophical preoccupations, he condemns contemporary versions of academic freedom as arbitrary and lacking constraint. He sees the occasion as an opportunity to establish a firm ground at last for knowledge, which would spell the end for the looseness of the various ungrounded empirical sciences and the prevalence of relativism among the disciplines. Despite his clear alignment with the party, however, his sense of what this opportunity would mean has less to do with concrete Nazi politics—there is no discussion of racial superiority or of global domination—but more with his own philosophy, such that the confrontation with being would act as a ground and unifying force for the German university in its role in the destiny of the German *Volk* (people) and in what he calls its spiritual mission. Students will henceforth fulfill their mission in three ways: in labor, in the military, and in knowledge. Furthermore, Heidegger sees this mission as one that will restore to the West its spiritual strength before what he calls the "moribund pseudocivilization" collapses into itself. On 11 November he gave a radio broadcast supporting Hitler's withdrawal of Germany from the League of Nations, revealing both an idealism regarding international relations and apparent ignorance about the nature of National Socialism itself.

During 1933 some of the Jewish people most closely associated with Heidegger were forced to leave the country. His former lover, Arendt, and his lifelong correspondent Elisabeth Blochmann both renewed relations with Heidegger after the war, but for the moment their contacts were broken off. Heidegger's contacts with Husserl also ceased at this time. Relations between the two had become strained anyway when Husserl had digested the extent to which *Sien und Zeit* departed from his own project of phenomenological science. Their break during this time contributed to the unfounded rumor that Heidegger had banned his friend and former teacher from the university, however. While Heidegger did little or nothing to discourage the official dissociation of Jewish colleagues and students from the university during his time as rector, there remains scant evidence of any overt anti-Semitism. Heidegger's relations with the party were neither comfortable nor mutually supportive, despite his consistently expressed enthusiasm for the opportunities the regime seemed to him to offer for his ideals. Conflicts with party officials as well as with students and faculty led him to resign as rector on 21 April 1934, after which he played no further part in political affairs, though he continued to engage with contemporary issues on an increasingly more developed political level. In June, Hitler had several of his rivals murdered, including Ernst Röhm's Storm Troopers and several

Heidegger and his fiancée, Elfride Petri, the year before their marriage in 1917 (from Walter Biemel,
Martin Heidegger: An Illustrated Study, *translated by J. L. Mehta, 1976;*
Thomas Cooper Library, University of South Carolina)

party members whose politics were not sharply focused on opposition to Jews and to communism. The so-called Röhm putsch turned out to be a thinly veiled pre-text for clearing the party of potential rivals, and on 1 August, Hitler became "Fürher of the German Reich." Heidegger later claimed that he became disillusioned with National Socialism after the Röhm putsch, but there exist both witnesses and documents suggesting that Heidegger's support of Nazism continued at least until 1936.

Heidegger did not publish much during the remainder of the war, though he continued to lecture. In 1934 he began a series of lectures on Friedrich Hölderlin, the enigmatic German poet and contemporary of Hegel, which occupied him until the early 1940s. Hölderlin's poetry emerges in Heidegger's discussions as a resource for his radically alternative exposition of the place of human beings in the world.

In 1935 he lectured on "Der Ursprung des Kunstwerks" (published in *Holzwege* [Wrong Paths], 1950; translated as "The Origin of the Work of Art" in *Philosophies of Art and Beauty: Selected Readings in Aesthetics from Plato to Heidegger,* 1964). The article works through

three different kinds of artworks using the key distinction between *world* and *earth*. His reading of Vincent van Gogh's painting *Shoes* shows that art can be regarded neither as merely an aesthetic object designed to give pleasure or to portray beauty, nor as a kind of thing with the addition of aesthetic beauty. Rather, art discloses the nature of things. Equipment, unlike art, disguises its status as a thing. Its material nature is absorbed in its function. The artwork, however, draws attention to the materials from which it was formed. The artwork thus draws attention to the struggle between form and matter. Van Gogh's painting of shoes shows what would not normally be evident. The involvement of the shoes in the world of the peasant disappears from view while they are being worn; but put into view, as in van Gogh's painting, the shoes reveal the world itself and the relation of that world to the earth.

The painting also provokes a question about the earth. The shoes in the van Gogh example do the work of explication not because of the naturalistic or evocative qualities of the painting. Rather, the role of the shoes as equipment is revealed in an artwork that takes as its topic the medium between the world of the peasant and the earth on which the peasant treads. Meyer Schapiro's "The Still Life as Personal Object: A Note on Heidegger and van Gogh" (collected in his *Theory and Philosophy in Art: Style, Artist, and Society,* 1994) takes Heidegger to task rather pedantically by pointing out that the shoes in van Gogh's painting were actually his own. To avoid this kind of misreading, Heidegger shifts his attention to a Greek temple, underlining the fact that his reading of artworks is not based on a model of representation. The temple shows how a work of art not only opens up a world but also unifies and structures the world of an historical people. In doing so it contextualizes the earth upon which it stands, instituting a particular interpretation of the relationship between the cultural contrivances of *Dasein* and the natural world with which those contrivances are engaged.

Finally, Heidegger turns to what he calls *Dichtung,* which in its etymological sense means *invention.* The ordinary and the everyday is made strange in art, revealing the struggle between the newness of art and the state of things out of which it must have emerged. The meaning of *Dichtung* in the normal sense is poetry. Because the matter or earth of poetry is language and because language is what gives *Dasein* names for beings, then poetry has the power of addressing the possibility of human communications and relations. The relationship between world and earth, when it takes the form of linguistic innovation, reveals the tortuous ways in which the relations between concepts and words are formed and form each other. Poetry can thus be grasped as the most essential kind of artwork because it performs an absolutely singular intervention that is also a form of disclosing. Poetry reveals the conditions on which not only artworks but all other kinds of communicating and all other kinds of thing are possible at all. For this reason Heidegger increasingly privileges *Dichtung* in his works of this period and later. The disclosing of being—if it is to be achieved in any way that eludes the classifying, calculating procedures of modernity—must be an evidently singular event each time.

The changes in focus that Heidegger's philosophy passes through during this time have been described as a *Kehre* (turn), though the nature and implications of this *Kehre* have since been a topic of dispute and debate and remain undecided. When Heidegger uses the term himself, he tends to refer to a stage or procedure that allows the passage from division 2 of *Sein und Zeit* to division 3 (which did not appear). In 1935 Heidegger's thought was still dominated by the distinction between everydayness and what had become "creative self-assertion," a version of the distinction in *Sein und Zeit* between inauthentic and authentic existence. If *Die Selbstbehauptung der deutschen Universität* had

transferred the topic of fundamental ontology from individual *Dasein* to a people or a state, then the resoluteness of one's being becomes the creative self-assertion of a people's spirit. By implication, inauthentic everyday distraction by the present should be overcome in the authentic disclosure of being as historical destiny. The lecture course on Hölderlin makes this point explicit. The task is to learn how to listen to the poet. The approach is similar to that which begins *Sein und Zeit,* insofar as it begins with the need to clear away the obstacles to asking the question, "Who is *Dasein?*" In the Hölderlin lectures, the everyday world and its distracting forms must be discarded before *Dasein* can be disclosed as the authentic gathering of individuals in a community. The argument suggests that Heidegger was locked in a struggle both with himself and with the politics of the German nation. The critical, arguably moral, attitude toward the everyday—which is not evident in *Sein und Zeit*—relates explicitly to the everyday life of the Nazi regime, which Heidegger found himself in the midst of: the political subordination of thought, art, history, and writing to the urgency of everyday political interests; the busy cultural activities; the explicit biologism of racist dogma; and the ubiquity of bureaucratic procedures and hierarchies. Heidegger thus sought to transcend this everyday Nazism in an authentic version that would disclose the innermost historicity of a people. An authentic historicity would be the domain of only a few creative individuals, poets, thinkers, and founders of states (thus evoking the triumvirate Hölderlin, Heidegger, and Hitler). The poet institutes the truth of a people's *Dasein.* The thinker explicates the poet's disclosure of being. The creator of states can manage the state in such a way as to adjust it to the essence revealed and explicated by the poet and thinker respectively.

Einführung in die Metaphysik (published in 1953; translated as *Introduction to Metaphysics,* 1959), from the lecture course given in the summer of 1935, reveals beneath Heidegger's compromising adherence to a spurious kind of geopolitical propriety, a degree of insight that ultimately renders his political ideals untenable. He gives an account of Europe, "in its unholy blindness," as always on the point of cutting its own throat. In the pincers between Russia on the one side and the United States on the other, Europe struggles against the mundane technologization it has spawned as the outcome of its metaphysics. Russia and the United States, Heidegger explains, are the same metaphysically insofar as they are dominated by uncontrolled technological development and loss of historical responsibility. Europe—with Germany at its core—suffers from its inability to see its own essence as the heir of the historicity of metaphysics, which completes itself in technol-

Philosopher Hannah Arendt, Heidegger's lover from 1924 until 1933 (Ullstein Bilderdienst, Berlin; from Walter Biemel, Martin Heidegger: An Illustrated Study, *translated by J. L. Mehta, 1976; Thomas Cooper Library, University of South Carolina)*

bal urbanism, mass communications, and the rapid expansion of military powers.

In 1936 Heidegger went to Rome to lecture on Hölderlin. He met his former pupil Karl Lowith there, who later insisted that Heidegger's adherence to Nazism was then still evident. In that year Heidegger also began his series of lectures on Friedrich Nietzsche, which ran until 1942 and which was eventually published in 1961 in two volumes. The first volume covers the years 1936 to 1939. It interprets Nietzsche approvingly as foreshadowing Heidegger's analytic of *Dasein* and is consistent with Heidegger's other writings of the mid 1930s. The second volume departs both in style and content from the first, however, in that it is marked by a polemic directed against Nietzsche that characterizes him as the fulfillment of the tradition. The lectures present an account of Western metaphysics that finally does the work of destruction advertised in *Sein und Zeit*.

The argument is foreshadowed by the book-length work that Heidegger wrote between 1936 and 1938, probably for his private use, and which he did not publish in his lifetime, *Beiträge zur Philosophie: Vom Ereignis* (1989; translated as *Contributions to Philosophy: From Enowning,* 1999). It includes a horrified account of the abandonment of being in modernity and suggests how Heidegger's thought was undergoing some alterations in emphasis. Being is not anything that *is*. So being withdraws in granting to beings their presence. Everything that exists does so because *Dasein* stands in a relation to being. Being will be discovered, however, in its most essential form, time and time again—and in this repetition—as *nothing*. The statement is enacted in the enunciation of increasingly empty phrases and achieved through this recitative mode, which springs from the various "moods"—such as deep awe, wonder, boredom—that disclose beings in relation to their being. Heidegger's philosophical project manifests here as the desire to empty all ontic statements of their content in order to open up the relationship between the beings that appear and their secret and thus unthematizable emergence.

This emergence is explicated by the phrase "Being essentially unfolds as appropriation," or *Ereignis*. The subtitle, "Vom Ereignis," offers a deliberate and, Heidegger says, proper alternative to the conventional academic banality of the main title. *Ereignis* is difficult to translate into English. The translators of *Beiträge zur Philosophie* coin a new word, *enowning,* in an attempt to convey how it works in Heidegger's German, stressing both the active, verbal aspect as well as the sense of appropriating that it suggests etymologically. Elsewhere the phrase "event of appropriation" and the catachresis "event of *propering*" (this phrase with some irony) are both used. The word, in its conventional sense, might

ogy. The "darkening of the world" implies the fulfillment of the metaphysics of Europe in Josef Stalin's Russia and in the capitalist United States, now returning as the ends of the pincers and surrounding their own source. The geographical distinction represents three ways in which spirit is reduced to the mere instrument of intelligence: the arranging of material relations (Stalinism); the ordering and explanation of the present-to-hand (positivism); and management of vital resources and race (everyday National Socialism). So *spirit* relates to the dimension in which the gods might again become thinkable, that is, to the holy. The emphasis on *das Heiligen* (the holy) and its cognate *Heilen* or "healing" (resonating at once with notions of salvation, well-being, and wholeness) suggests a connection between Heidegger's theological heritage and his absorption of ethics into fundamental ontology. The loss of the holy provokes a kind of questioning through which the truth of being becomes a distress. Questions such as "what for?—where to?—and what then?" echo the question of being but respond more explicitly to glo-

have been faithfully transposed as *event*. Heidegger claims that, like the Greek *Logos* or the Chinese *Tao,* his use of it cannot be translated. It does not mean a happening or occurrence in the ordinary sense, but it must retain the sense that what happens does so uniquely. This resistance to translation thus remains faithful to the sense of the term itself. It supposedly resists much more than simple translation. The singular unfolding of being as *Ereignis* would hardly come into experience at all if the forms of representation, predication, classification, calculation, and conceptualization, which characterize modernity from Plato to Nietzsche in an intensification of the obliviousness to the unfolding of being, now dominate, as Heidegger claims they do. The difficulty is not simply a matter of forgetfulness. It is a structural condition, according to which the singular event always and immediately drops out of sight and withholds itself in what it gives.

The fact that this withholding can only be experienced as a lack leads Heidegger to describe technology as the perpetual organization of this lack. Technology disguises the emptiness of being beneath an insistent functionality. In his "Überwindung der Metaphysik" (published in *Vorträge und Aufsätze,* 1954, but based on notes made during the 1936–1940 Nietzsche lectures; translated as "Overcoming Metaphysics" in *The End of Philosophy,* 1973) he suggests that the animal (or subhuman) instinct has become indistinguishable from calculating rationality. Heidegger's reflections turn to the phenomenon of armament, which for him fulfills technology as the inevitable consequence of the ordered use of beings. The escalating consumption of beings conceals the fact that technology is itself purely aimless. In this way the groundlessness of an ethical ground shows that self-guaranteeing armament seems designed to remove the power of decision and responsibility entirely from the human sphere. *Das Man* has been captured by the machination of a technics that they fail to grasp in its historicity. This failure would nevertheless still be found as the historicity—or emergence—of technology itself, and it inevitably imposes a powerful deconstruction on Heidegger's adherence to the spirit of the German *Volk* still inherent in his arguments of the mid to late 1930s. Accordingly, Heidegger's philosophy begins increasingly to emphasize the enigmatic withdrawal of that which grants presence. Rather than maintain the strict division between the authentic and the inauthentic in terms of the voluntarism that marks the Hölderlin lectures and *Einführung in die Metaphysik,* according to which *Dasein* discloses its own truth, Heidegger increasingly characterizes truth as a mode of unconcealment to which humans are exposed and to which they belong.

Whether this characterization is what one should understand by *Kehre* remains debatable. The difference is more like a refinement. Heidegger's philosophy develops through what is most characteristic in his style as well as in his subject matter, the repetition/revision that characterizes the work of deconstruction. The entity that in *Sein und Zeit* anticipates the end of its existence and is thus capable of freely taking over its own being now belongs together with being on the basis of an unfolding that withholds itself. In each case the relationship between *Dasein* and being eludes the conceptualizations that dominate metaphysics.

The Nietzsche lectures have been read as a covert criticism of the appropriation by the Nazi regime of Nietzsche in support of its racist practices, especially the second volume, which includes the lectures given during the early years of World War II. Heidegger was under Gestapo surveillance at this time, according to the confession of an official infiltrator who claimed that he rejected Nazism on the strength of Heidegger's way of thinking. The arguments of the period make regular references to the political situation leading up to and after the breaking out of war, connecting it to the metaphysical foundations of technology and the forgetting of being. It is not the self-assertion of individuals, dictators, or authoritarian states that leads to the emergence of powerful imperialist movements (a clear if still covert reference to the Nazi regime), but rather "the metaphysical essence of modernity," or, echoing Nietzsche, the will to power over nature. Nietzsche's doctrines of the will to power and the eternal return of the same are now read as the culmination (rather than the overcoming) of Western metaphysics in nihilism.

Heidegger returns to the earliest sources of philosophy, the pre-Socratics, whose term *alçtheia* is normally translated as *truth.* In Heidegger's reading it designates a process in which beings appear; yet, what grants them presence withholds itself in what it gives. Heidegger argues that this process indicates an experience of being in which withdrawal or withholding is experienced simultaneously with what appears. For the earliest philosophers, then, thinking was a matter of remaining receptive to the withholding of being. In Plato's philosophy, however, the mere effects of the process—the appearing of things, which are regarded as the manifestation of ideas—then get abstracted from the process of unconcealment and set apart as clarity and light. Thus, for Heidegger, the essence of truth as idea in Plato signals the beginning of metaphysics and ontotheology and can be grasped as the first stage in the forgetting of being and the obliteration of *alçtheia.* Truth now means conformity of the mind to essence. A further step in the forgetting of being occurs with the Scholastic philosophy of the Middle Ages, in which truth as *adequatio* (adequacy of the mind to the thing) is grounded in the concept of divine (the mind of God). At the beginning of the so-called modern age a further step in the oblivion of being occurs with the establishment of the human subject and the rationality championed by Descartes and Galileo. In Descartes the cogito sets itself up as the basis on which objects reveal themselves. Heidegger traces the term *hupokeimenon* (the Greek for *basis*) through its translation into the Latin *subiectum* to the institution of the human *cogito* as subject of philosophy and the one true basis upon which things can appear.

So, according to Heidegger, at the beginning of the modern era a technological interpretation of the world was instituted in which the whole of nature was regarded mechanically. Heidegger traces Nietzsche's notion of will to power back to this beginning, insisting that Descartes and those who followed had already anticipated it. Nietzsche's philosophy, which claims to break from past philosophy, actually brings it to its climax as the ultimate accomplishment of onto-theology. The relation between subject and object discovered in Descartes has been pushed to its extremes in the notion of will to power. The will regards everything as an object to be stored and manipulated and, in an extreme form of subjectivity, reduces everything to the values it projects upon them in its drive for power over them. The meaning of being is now as far from the ancients' conception as it could be. Being has become as nothing.

By the 1940s Heidegger had began to suspect that the route taken by *Sein und Zeit* had been in danger of unintentionally repeating the intensification of the subjective turn of modern philosophy. Since *Beiträge zur Philosophie* he had been using the term *Ereignis* in opposition to the term *Ge-stell* (framework), which implies a process of assembling and ordering. *Ge-stell* designates activities of framing that subordinate beings to the interminable conceptualizing, evaluating, storing, manipulating, and calculating of the technological era. In the Nietzsche lectures, the discussion of *Ereignis* recapitulates the work of *Beiträge zur Philosophie*. *Ereignis* designates that which thinking can meditate upon in resistance to nihilism, in which thinking has been replaced by calculation and instrumentality. The notion of the frame plays a crucial role in Heidegger's discussions because it allows him to show how the technological era has long been anticipated by metaphysics. It was now necessary to meditate on the emergence of the frame itself. Framing has taken specific forms, as the Nietzsche lectures teach, but each time the determination of being as presence divides the transcendental from the empirical, giving priority to the modes of framing by which philosophy designates its subject matter. In *Ereignis* the possibility arises that it might over-

come the dominant character of the frame and transform it into the *Ereignis*, the singular unfolding that gives rise to the belonging together of mind and being. In other words, the possibility arises of meddling with the transcendental. It will be a matter of repeating the *Ereignis* in a way that is each time singular. The special character of *Wiederholen* is once more activated, as a repetition that is at the same time something new.

Toward the end of the war, late in 1944, Heidegger was drafted into the Volkssturm, the people's army, as one of the "least indispensable" members of the university, to join a labor force whose work was to dig trenches by the Rhine. The following year, as Germany approached collapse, he managed to return to Messkirch to put his manuscripts in order and to arrange their security. A manuscript dated May 1945, but rediscovered long after Heidegger had died, indicates how Heidegger felt about Germany and its collapse. "Abendgespräch in einem Kriegsgefangenenlager in Rusland zwischen einem Jüngeran und einem Älteren" (Evening Dialogue in a Prisoner of War Camp in Russia between a Younger and an Older Man), published in *Feldweg-Gespräche (1944/5)*, a 1995 volume in Heidegger's *Gesamtausgabe*, uses the dialogue to express the conclusion that the Nazi regime had been a catastrophe for Germany (both his sons were at that time in Russian camps). It goes on to suggest that Germany in defeat should not be made responsible for the evils of war but should be seen as a victim of the global devastation consequent on the metaphysical oblivion of being. In June, after the capitulation of Germany, he was forced to attend a hearing on his political activities by a university "denazification" committee in French-occupied Freiburg, to his documented indignation. The hearing considered testimony from several important figures. Some implicated him, while others defended his actions. One of the most decisive testimonies came from Jaspers, who volunteered instances of Heidegger's active support of National Socialism during the years of 1933–1934. Jaspers suggested that German students after years of growing up in an authoritarian state were not ready for critical responses toward a teaching that had been associated with Nazism. In 1946 the hearing concluded that Heidegger should be banned from teaching. He was, however, allowed to keep his library and was granted the title of professor emeritus.

Shortly thereafter, experiencing emotional crisis, Heidegger sought psychiatric help from Medard Boss, who not only helped him regain his emotional stability but came to admire and to be influenced by his patient's way of thinking. Heidegger held regular seminars for Boss's circle, made up primarily of professionals trained in the sciences and social sciences. Boss, with Ludwig

Heidegger (left) and Jean Beaufret, to whom Heidegger's 1947 essay "Brief über den Humanismus" (translated as
"Plato's Doctrine of Truth: Letter on Humanism," 1962) is addressed (from Heinrich Wiegand Petzet,
Encounters and Dialogues with Martin Heidegger 1929–1976, translated by Parvis Emad
and Kenneth Maly, 1993; Thomas Cooper Library, University of South Carolina)

Binswanger, went on to develop an influential branch of existential psychiatry.

During his time in French-occupied Freiburg, Heidegger had been introduced to the French intellectual Jean Beaufret, and they became friends. Beaufret helped to raise awareness of and interest in Heidegger's thought in France, where a new generation of academics turned to Heidegger despite official disapproval. The global successes of the 1920s were then repeated in a second wave, which coincided with the revival of Heidegger's publishing and lecturing career. In 1946 he spoke at an occasion commemorating the twentieth anniversary of Rainer Maria Rilke's death. And in 1947 he published what turned out to be one of his most influential articles, "Brief über den Humanismus" (translated as "Plato's Doctrine of Truth: Letter on Humanism," in *Philosophy of the Twentieth Century: An Overview*, 1962), an "open letter" that responds to questions that Beaufret had posed to Heidegger regarding Jean-Paul Sartre's brief but renowned statement of existentialism, *L'existentialisme est un humanisme* (1946; translated as *Existentialism*, 1947). True to the genre, Heidegger's anecdotal and meandering meditation

nonetheless refuses to accept an alignment of his own thought with either existentialism or humanism and asserts that no ethics would need to be added to a philosophy that begins with the question concerning the truth of being.

In December 1949 Heidegger lectured to the Bremen Club. The ban on his teaching was lifted, and he resumed correspondence with both Arendt and Jaspers. In 1950 the first of a series of major publications appeared: *Holzwege*, which collects revised versions of some of his most important lectures and seminars on art, technology, and language. Throughout the 1950s he continued to publish what were for the most part revised versions of older works, largely related to his teaching. In 1951 he taught a lecture series, *Was heisst Denken?* (published in 1954; translated as *What Is Called Thinking?*, 1968). This course was the first he had been allowed to teach since 1944 and his last before retiring from the university. He revisits previous engagements with Parmenides, Plato, and Kant as well as Hölderlin and Nietzsche in his pursuit of that which gives thought its topic by withdrawing, a withdrawal that by absenting itself is both more present than everything present and yet infinitely exceeds the actuality of everything actual. He observes that the possibility of thinking is given by what is not yet thought.

In 1955–1956 he returned as professor emeritus for a series of lectures, which were published in 1957 as *Der Satz vom Grund* (translated as *The Principle of Reason,* 1991). These lectures were followed by a series on Hegel's *Wissenschaft der Logik* (Science of Logic, 1812–1816). These lecture series are closely linked to a short text, "Der Satz der Identität" (The Principle of Identity), which he presented on Faculty Day, 27 June 1957, for the five-hundredth anniversary of the University of Freiburg. The current milieu is now characterized as "the atomic age" and described with Heidegger's usual grim humor as the "mushrooming" of instrumental rationality. *Der Satz vom Grund* culminates in an address that condenses the readings of the thirteen lectures into a thesis outlining the conditions and the destiny of modernity in terms of its paradoxical grounds, indicated by the phrase Gottfried Wilhelm Leibniz coins for the principle of reason, "nihil est sine ratione" (nothing is without reason).

Here Heidegger's emphasis moves away from the category of being to what he calls its *Geschick,* its destination or its sending-forth. What saves this *Geschick* (a destiny that all philosophical determinations of being share) from the chaotic dissemination it appears to have in its history is what is not determined in it each time, which alone captures its sameness and simplicity. The critique of the metaphysics of presence that always animates Heidegger's works leads him to evoke the constancy of being's *Geschick* in terms of presencing, lingering, and light. Being means different things for different philosophers in different epochs, to the extent that one epoch *can* be distinguished from another, in which case these heterogeneous determinations of being might be a helpful historiographical guide. What is significant is the sameness that lies hidden beneath these determinations. He points out that this sameness does not run between the epochs like a band linking them. The legacy comes each time from what is concealed in the *Geschick.* One must talk of absencing as well as presencing. The difference, repeating the ontical-ontological difference of *Sein und Zeit,* gives a vision of the ontological as that which is nowhere. The being-nowhere animates beings wherever they are (everywhere).

Taking the phrase "nihil est sine ratione," Heidegger proceeds to uncover the hidden grounds of the principle itself–the principle of the principle. The two negatives (*nihil,* "nothing" and *sine,* "without") cancel each other out to give a positive, the belonging together of being *(est)* and reason *(ratione)* as in "reason to be" or raison d'être. The principle of this belonging together is identified in terms of a kind of sounding. Heidegger focuses on the German word *Klang,* which draws attention to the musical belonging together of the two terms *est* and *ratione.* The effect is to give being an equal status with reason in a construction where they "ring" in unison. With this altered emphasis the principle of reason now says that the relation between ground and reason belongs to being. In the unfolding of this logic of the ring, the repetition of reason in ground renders them equivalent but, in order to save their sense in this equivocation, a further ground (and reason) is posited beneath them, their being, to which they belong. This belonging has a further ground (the belonging that being is) in the *Klang,* however, the ringing that one must hear while seeing. In this sense being (in this case the belonging together of ground and reason) has no ground, reason, or even being, because it is what grounds, gives reasons to, and allows beings to be beings. Being is thus not a ground beneath the various forms of determination that metaphysics variously privileges. Rather, by occupying a place alongside these other terms, being reveals itself and all such terms to be grounded only in the indeterminate *Klang* of their belonging together as *Geschick.* Being cannot thus be represented.

There is nothing here that departs from the pattern that all metaphysical concepts fall into. Their various means of representation inevitably fall short of representation strictly speaking, for their supersensible status must remain infinitely outside the spatial and temporal conditions of representation, outside experience. The reason why being cannot be represented at all has nothing to do with any atemporal status that might be supposed of it as a metaphysical concept, however; rather, being cannot be represented because the meaning of "being" is simply the possibility of representation. It cannot be determined because it is what gives itself to determination. It has no reason itself because it gives reasons. So the ground of reason is not a ground but a kind of grounding potential, something in the determination that is not given but nonetheless gives itself to possible determinations as *Geschick*–the sending forth that makes it possible to respond to a legacy.

The argument performs the *Wiederholen* that was described as early as 1915 and that took a more developed form in *Sein und Zeit,* according to which a legacy or tradition can be read in terms of its *Geschick.* The concept of the *same* in Heidegger's text turns out to be a quite precise *Wiederholen* of a problem that persists in Hegel's *Wissenschaft der Logik.* Distinguishing the *same* from the empty repetition of identities, Heidegger, like Hegel, is led to a notion of identity that maintains the contradiction of difference within it. What is *(est)* the same–not itself a being–holds what belong together in

*Heidegger at the commemoration of the five hundredth anniversary of the University of Freiburg, 27 June 1957,
where he presented a lecture on the principle of identity (from Heinrich Wiegand Petzet,* Encounters
and Dialogues with Martin Heidegger 1929–1976, *translated by Parvis Emad and
Kenneth Maly, 1993; Thomas Cooper Library, University of South Carolina)*

a kind of radical difference. What is the same is their radical difference. Heidegger affirms Hegel's *Logic,* which returns rather forcefully in these pages as the text in which *verhältnis* (relation) most purely comes to be thought as "what is *to be* thought." This relation, or holding together, of radical differences is *yet* to be thought—it is a *not yet.* This, then, is what *Geschick* sends forth in the legacy of metaphysical thinking, the un-*thought*—the thought of the *un-,* or *not,* that gives itself to be thought, handing down what is not determined for an event of appropriation, that is, a singular determination.

In the 1960s and 1970s Heidegger's work activities became less intense. Most of his time was spent at his home in Freiburg or at the solitary mountain cottage in Todtnauberg. In 1966 he recorded an interview with *Der Spiegel,* on the condition that it would be published only after he had died. Heidegger died on 26 May 1976. His last word was "Thanks." He had made plans for the publication of all his writings in 1972, a huge undertaking that began in 1974, with around one hundred volumes projected. The project is expected to go on through the first decades of the twenty-first century.

The *Gesamtausgabe* is a complete edition "in the last hand" and so includes only Heidegger's final revisions, which he prefaced with the motto "Ways not works." Heidegger's publishers have taken his request literally, to publish the works with no scholarly apparatuses whatsoever. The motto has with unintentional irony been reversed. It is more difficult than ever to assess his works as "ways," because readers only have access to the final versions, many of which include revisions made to the earlier manuscripts that are not reflected in the published texts. For this reason the *Gesamtausgabe* cannot be regarded as the definitive edition for Heidegger scholarship.

The *Spiegel* interview was published in May 1976 with the title "Nur noch ein Gott kann uns retten" (translated as "Only a God Can Save Us," 1976), which echoes a line from Hölderlin. In it Heidegger responds to questions about his involvement with the Nazis in 1933–1934. Those who were looking for stronger expressions of regret than Heidegger had hitherto offered were disappointed. Their disappointment contributed to misleading debates about Heidegger's silence on the matter. The most disturbing aspect of

Heidegger's involvement has been less a matter of what he did not say and more a matter of the little he *did* say. Nazism was, for Heidegger, one more creation of modern metaphysics, no worse than the hydrogen bomb, mechanized agriculture, or automated kitchens. He admitted during the postwar years that he had been wrong in his support of the Nazis, but he never accepted that the Holocaust was more horrific than other events. He defended his attitude by drawing attention to the victimization of East Germans, who were, he said, victims no less than Jews. He minimized the extent of his involvement in Nazi politics, emphasizing instead the covert resistance of his lectures. Debates about the connections between Heidegger's philosophy and his involvement with Nazism continued throughout the remainder of the twentieth century. Works by Victor Farías and Hugo Ott during the 1980s revealed the extent of Heidegger's involvement and his later misrepresentation of it. Research and scholarship during the final decade of the twentieth century has considerably clarified the question of the connection between his political involvement and his philosophy.

Heidegger was one of the greatest philosophers of the twentieth century. The impact of his writing not only in Europe and the United States but also in Asia is hardly calculable. He has been described as the hidden master of modern thought and as a man tormented both by philosophy and by his ambiguous relationship to his faith. His impact has been felt not only in philosophy but also in literary theory, psychology, psychiatry, psychoanalysis, theology, and ecology. A growing interest in Continental philosophy in the United States has led to a wider understanding and appreciation of his work, highlighting his role in the development of hermeneutics and deconstruction and his influence on theorists such as Hans-Georg Gadamer and Jürgen Habermas as well as on French thinkers such as Jacques Derrida, Michel Foucault, Gilles Deleuze, and Pierre Bourdieu.

Martin Heidegger's philosophy has led to significant developments, especially in the analysis of modernity, historicity, and technology. It is also the case that he developed his mode of thinking independently of several contemporary thinkers who by radically different routes achieve positions with comparable implications for critical and cultural thought. For instance, Foucault's notion of discourse owes as much to Ferdinand de Saussure's distinction between the language system and the speech event as it does to Heidegger's notion of *alçtheia*, though his mode of radical revision is reminiscent of Heidegger's destruction. Here it is no longer possible to distinguish between direct influence and independent thought. The notion of destruction, or deconstruction, implies at once the repetition and the revision of the thought of a prior thinker. The hinge between repetition and revision implies a potential for singular decisions. If Heidegger never expressed this thought as such, his philosophy nevertheless leads in this direction. The historicity of modern thought implies that beyond its systematic calculations there remains the undecidable. It is only on the basis of the undecidable that decisions can be made. Otherwise thought would be following the preprogrammed plan of an autotelic universe.

Letters:

Martin Heidegger, Erhart Kästner: Briefwechsel, 1953–1974, edited by Heinrich Wiegand Petzet (Frankfurt am Main: Insel, 1986);

Martin Heidegger, Elisabeth Blochmann: Briefwechsel, 1918–1969, edited by Joachim W. Storck (Marbach am Neckar: Deutsche Schillergesellschaft, 1989);

Heidegger and Karl Jaspers, *Briefwechsel 1920–1963,* edited by Walter Biemel and Hans Saner (Frankfurt am Main: Klostermann / Munich: Piper, 1990); translated by Gary E. Aylesworth as *The Heidegger-Jaspers Correspondence (1920–1963)* (Amherst, N.Y.: Humanity Books, 2003).

Interview:

Rudolph Augstein and George Folff, "Nur noch ein Gott kann uns retten" [interview recorded 23 September 1966], *Der Spiegel,* 30, no. 23 (31 May 1976): 193–219; translated by Maria P. Alter and John D. Caputo as "Only a God Can Save Us," *Philosophy Today,* 20, no. 4 (1976): 267–285.

Bibliographies:

Hermann Lübbe, *Bibliographie der Heidegger-Literatur, 1917–1955* (Meisenheim am Glan: Hain, 1957);

Winfried Franzen, *Martin Heidegger* (Stuttgart: Metzler, 1976);

Thomas Sheehan, "Bibliographies," in *Heidegger: The Man and the Thinker,* edited by Sheehan (Chicago: Precedent, 1981), pp. 275–347;

Hans-Martin Sass, *Martin Heidegger: Bibliography and Glossary* (Bowling Green: Philosophy Documentation Center, Bowling Green State University, 1982);

Joan Nordquist, comp., *Martin Heidegger: A Bibliography* (Santa Cruz, Cal.: Reference and Research Service, 1990).

Biographies:

Heinrich Wiegand Petzet, *Auf einen Stern zugehen: Begegnungen und Gespräche mit Martin Heidegger, 1929–1976* (Frankfurt am Main: Societäts-Verlag, 1983); translated by Parvis Emad and Kenneth

Maly as *Encounters and Dialogues with Martin Heidegger 1929–1976* (Chicago: University of Chicago Press, 1993);

Hugo Ott, *Martin Heidegger: A Political Life,* translated by Allan Blunden (London: HarperCollins / New York: Basic Books, 1993);

Rüdiger Safranski, *Ein Meister Aus Deutschland: Heidegger und seine Zeit* (Munich: Hanser, 1994); translated by Ewald Osers as *Martin Heidegger: Between Good and Evil* (Cambridge, Mass.: Harvard University Press, 1998).

References:

Hannah Arendt, *The Life of the Mind,* 2 volumes (New York: Harcourt Brace Jovanovich, 1977, 1978);

Jeffrey Andrew Barash, *Martin Heidegger and the Problem of Historical Meaning* (Dordrecht & Boston: Nijhoff, 1988);

Jean Beaufret, *Dialogue avec Heidegger,* 4 volumes (Paris: Minuit, 1973–1985);

Robert Bernasconi, "Descartes in the History of Being: Another Bad Novel?" *Research in Phenomenology,* 17 (1987): 95–114;

Bernasconi, "'The Double Concept of Philosophy' and the Place of Ethics in *Being and Time,*" *Research in Phenomenology,* 18 (1988): 41–57;

Bernasconi, *The Question of Language in Heidegger's History of Being* (Atlantic Highlands, N.J.: Humanities Press / London: Macmillan, 1985);

Walter Biemel, *Martin Heidegger: An Illustrated Study,* translated by J. L. Mehta (New York: Harcourt Brace Jovanovich, 1976);

Henri Birault, *Heidegger et l'expérience de la pensée* (Paris: Gallimard, 1978);

Mark Blitz, *Heidegger's* Being and Time *and the Possibility of Political Philosophy* (Ithaca, N.Y.: Cornell University Press, 1981);

Pierre Bourdieu, *The Political Ontology of Martin Heidegger,* translated by Peter Collier (Stanford, Cal.: Stanford University Press, 1981);

Marcus Brainard, David Jacobs, and Rick Lee, eds., *Heidegger and the Political,* special issue of *Graduate Faculty of Philosophy Journal,* 14–15 (1991);

John D. Caputo, *Demythologizing Heidegger* (Bloomington: Indiana University Press, 1993);

Jay A. Ciaffa, "Toward an Understanding of Heidegger's Conception of the Inter-Relation between Authentic and Inauthentic Existence," *Journal of the British Society for Phenomenology,* 18 (1987): 49–59;

Timothy Clark, *Martin Heidegger* (London & New York: Routledge, 2002);

David Cooper, *Heidegger* (London: Claridge, 1996);

Jean-Pierre Cotten, *Heidegger,* Ecrivains de toujours, no. 95 (Paris: Seuil, 1974);

Fred Dallmayr, *Between Freiburg and Frankfurt: Toward a Critical Ontology* (Amherst: University of Massachusetts Press, 1991);

Dallmayr, "Heidegger and Marxism," *Praxis International,* 7 (October 1987): 207–224;

Dallmayr, "Heidegger, Hölderlin and Politics," *Heidegger Studies,* 2 (1986): 81–95;

Dallmayr, "Ontology of Freedom: Heidegger and Political Philosophy," *Political Theory,* 12 (May 1984): 204–234;

Françoise Dastur, *Heidegger et la question du temps* (Paris: Presses Universitaires de France, 1990);

John N. Deely, *The Tradition via Heidegger: An Essay on the Meaning of Being in the Philosophy of Martin Heidegger* (The Hague: Nijhoff, 1971);

J. M. Demske, *Being, Man and Death: A Key to Heidegger* (Lexington: University Press of Kentucky, 1970);

Alfred Denker, *Historical Dictionary of Heidegger's Philosophy* (Lanham, Md.: Scarecrow Press, 2000);

Jacques Derrida, *De l'esprit: Heidegger et la question* (Paris: Galilée, 1987); translated by Geoffrey Bennington and Rachel Bowlby as *Of Spirit: Heidegger and the Question* (Chicago: University of Chicago Press, 1989);

Hubert L. Dreyfus, *Being-in-the-World: A Commentary on Heidegger's* Being and Time, *Division I* (Cambridge, Mass.: MIT Press, 1991);

Dreyfus and Harrison Hall, eds., *Heidegger: A Critical Reader* (Oxford & Cambridge, Mass.: Blackwell, 1992);

Parvis Emad, *Heidegger and the Phenomenology of Values: His Critique of Intentionality* (Glen Ellyn, Ill.: Torey, 1981);

Emad, "The Place of Hegel in Heidegger's *Being and Time,*" *Research in Phenomenology,* 13 (1983): 159–173;

Victor Farías, *Heidegger and Nazism,* edited by Joseph Margolis and Tom Rockmore, translated by Paul Burrell (Philadelphia: Temple University Press, 1989);

Dagfinn Føllesdal, "Husserl and Heidegger on the Role of Actions in the Constitution of the World," in *Essays in Honour of Jaakko Hintikka,* edited by Esa Saarinen and others (Dordrecht & Boston: Reidel, 1979), pp. 365–378;

Christopher Fynsk, *Heidegger, Thought and Historicity* (Ithaca, N.Y.: Cornell University Press, 1986);

Hans-Georg Gadamer, *Heidegger's Ways,* translated by J. W. Stanley (Albany: State University of New York Press, 1994);

Charles Guignon, *Heidegger and the Problem of Knowledge* (Indianapolis: Hackett, 1983);

Giugnon, ed., *The Cambridge Companion to Heidegger* (Cambridge & New York: Cambridge University Press, 1993);

Michael Inwood, *Heidegger* (Oxford & New York: Oxford University Press, 1997);

Inwood, *A Heidegger Dictionary* (Oxford & Malden, Mass.: Blackwell, 1999);

Theodor Kisiel, "En Route to *Sein und Zeit*," *Research in Phenomenology,* 10 (1980): 307–327;

Kisiel, "The Genesis of *Being and Time:* The Primal Leap," in *Phenomenology, Interpretation, and Community,* edited by Lenore Langsdorf and Stephen H. Watson with E. Marya Bower (Albany: State University of New York Press, 1996), pp. 29–50;

Kisiel, "On the Way to *Being and Time:* Introduction to the Translation of Heidegger's 'Prolegomena zur Geschichte des Zeitbegriffes,'" *Research in Phenomenology,* 15 (1985): 193–226;

Kisiel, "Why the First Draft of *Being and Time* Was Never Published," *Journal of the British Society for Phenomenology,* 20 (1989): 3–22;

Philippe Lacoue-Labarthe, *Heidegger, Art and Politics: The Fiction of the Political,* translated by Chris Turner (Oxford & Cambridge, Mass.: Blackwell, 1990);

Christopher Macann, ed., *Critical Heidegger* (London & New York: Routledge, 1996);

Reinhard May, *Heidegger's Hidden Sources: East Asian Influences on His Work* (London & New York: Routledge, 1996);

Allan Megill, *Prophets of Extremity: Nietzsche, Heidegger, Foucault, Derrida* (Berkeley: University of California Press, 1985);

Robert Mugerauer, *Heidegger's Language and Thinking* (Atlantic Highlands, N.J.: Humanities Press, 1988);

Mugerauer, *Interpreting Environments: Tradition, Deconstruction, Hermeneutics* (Austin: University of Texas Press, 1995);

Günther Neske and Emil Kettering, eds., *Antwort: Martin Heidegger im Gespräch* (Pfullingen: Neske, 1988); translated by Lisa Harries and Joachim Neugroschel as *Martin Heidegger and National Socialism: Questions and Answers* (New York: Paragon, 1990);

Graeme Nicholson, "The Politics of Heidegger's Rectoral Address," *Man and World,* 20 (1987): 171–187;

Carlos G. Noreña, "Heidegger on Suárez: The 1927 Marburg Lectures," *International Philosophical Quarterly,* 23 (December 1983): 407–424;

Herman Philipse, *Heidegger's Philosophy of Being: A Critical Interpretation* (Princeton: Princeton University Press, 1998);

John Phillips, "The Enigma in Question: Ethics after Heidegger," in *Postmodern Surroundings,* edited by Steven Earnshaw (Amsterdam & Atlanta: Rodopi, 1994), pp. 203–213;

Otto Pöggeler, *Martin Heidegger's Path of Thinking,* translated by Daniel Magurshak and Sigmund Barber (Atlantic Highlands, N.J.: Humanities Press, 1987);

Richard Polt, *Heidegger: An Introduction* (Ithaca, N.Y.: Cornell University Press, 1999);

Jonathan Rée, *Heidegger* (London: Phoenix, 1998);

William J. Richardson, *Heidegger: Through Phenomenology to Thought,* third edition (The Hague: Nijhoff, 1974);

John Sallis, "Echoes: Philosophy and Non-Philosophy after Heidegger," in *Philosophy and Non-Philosophy since Merleau-Ponty,* edited by Hugh J. Silverman (New York & London: Routledge, 1988), pp. 84–105;

Meyer Schapiro, "The Still Life as Personal Object: A Note on Heidegger and van Gogh," in *Theory and Philosophy of Art: Style, Artist, and Society* (New York: Braziller, 1994);

Silverman, "Heidegger," in *Derrida and Deconstruction,* edited by Silverman (New York & London: Routledge, 1989), pp. 154–169;

William V. Spanos, *Heidegger and Criticism: Retrieving the Cultural Politics of Destruction* (Minneapolis: University of Minnesota Press, 1993);

Spanos, ed., *Martin Heidegger and the Question of Literature: Toward a Postmodern Literary Hermeneutics* (Bloomington: Indiana University Press, 1976);

George Steiner, *Martin Heidegger,* revised edition (Chicago: Chicago University Press, 1991);

Arland Ussher, *Journey through Dread: A Study of Kierkegaard, Heidegger, and Sartre* (New York: Devin-Adair, 1955);

Richard Wolin, ed., *The Heidegger Controversy: A Critical Reader* (Cambridge, Mass.: MIT Press, 1993);

Julian Young, *Heidegger, Philosophy, Nazism* (Cambridge & New York: Cambridge University Press, 1997);

Young, *Heidegger's Later Philosophy* (Cambridge & New York: Cambridge University Press, 2002);

Krzysztof Ziarek, "The Reception of Heidegger's Thought in American Literary Criticism," *Diacritics,* 19 (1989): 114–126;

Michael E. Zimmerman, *Heidegger's Confrontation with Modernity: Technology, Politics, and Art* (Bloomington: Indiana University Press, 1990).

Papers:

Martin Heidegger's papers are deposited mainly in the Martin Heidegger Archive in the Deutsches Literaturarchiv in Marbach am Neckar, but some are also retained in the private possession of the Heidegger family.

Eric Hobsbawm
(Francis Newton)
(9 June 1917 –)

Adam Muller
University of Manitoba

BOOKS: *What Democracy Means for Us: A Report by E. J. Hobsbawm, Student Committee, British Youth Peace Assembly* (Paris: Third International Conference of the World Student Association, 1939);

Primitive Rebels: Studies in Archaic Forms of Social Movement in the Nineteenth and Twentieth Centuries (Manchester: Manchester University Press, 1959); republished as *Social Bandits and Primitive Rebels* (Glencoe, Ill.: Free Press, 1960); revised and enlarged as *Primitive Rebels: Studies in Archaic Forms of Social Movement in the Nineteenth and Twentieth Centuries* (Manchester: Manchester University Press, 1971);

The Jazz Scene, as Francis Newton (London: MacGibbon & Kee, 1959; New York: Monthly Review Press, 1960; revised edition, Harmondsworth, U.K.: Penguin, 1961; revised and enlarged edition, New York: Pantheon, 1993);

The Age of Revolution: Europe, 1789–1848 (London: Weidenfeld & Nicolson, 1962); republished as *The Age of Revolution, 1789–1848* (Cleveland: World, 1962);

Labouring Men: Studies in the History of Labour (London: Weidenfeld & Nicolson, 1964; New York: Praeger, 1969);

Industry and Empire: An Economic History of Britain since 1750 (London: Weidenfeld & Nicolson, 1968; New York: Pantheon, 1968);

Captain Swing, by Hobsbawm and George Rudé (New York: Pantheon, 1968; London: Lawrence & Wishart, 1969; revised edition, Harmondsworth, U.K.: Penguin, 1973);

Bandits (London: Weidenfeld & Nicolson, 1969; New York: Delacorte, 1969; revised and enlarged edition, Harmondsworth, U.K.: Penguin, 1972; revised and enlarged edition, New York: Pantheon, 1981);

Eric Hobsbawm (photograph by Jerry Bauer; from The Age of Empire, 1875–1914, *1987; Richland County Public Library, Columbia, South Carolina)*

Revolutionary Perspectives: A Discussion of Alternative Strategies (London: London Central Students Branch of the Communist Party/Birkbeck College Socialist Society, 1974);

The Age of Capital, 1848–1875 (London: Weidenfeld & Nicolson, 1975; New York: Scribners, 1975);

The Crisis and the Outlook (London: London Central Students Branch of the Communist Party/Birkbeck College Socialist Society, 1975);

Revolutionary Advances (Swansea, U.K.: Swansea Broad Left, 1976);

Worlds of Labour: Further Studies in the History of Labour (London: Weidenfeld & Nicolson, 1984); republished as *Workers: Worlds of Labor* (New York: Pantheon, 1984);

The Age of Empire, 1875–1914 (London: Weidenfeld & Nicolson, 1987; New York: Pantheon, 1987);

Echoes of the Marseillaise: Two Centuries Look Back on the French Revolution (London: Verso, 1990; New Brunswick, N.J.: Rutgers University Press, 1990);

Nations and Nationalism since 1780: Programme, Myth, Reality (Cambridge & New York: Cambridge University Press, 1990; revised and enlarged, 1992);

Birth of a Holiday: The First of May (London: Queen Mary and Westfield College, University of London, 1991);

The Age of Extremes: The Short Twentieth Century, 1914–1991 (London: Joseph, 1994); republished as *The Age of Extremes: A History of the World, 1914–1991* (New York: Pantheon, 1994);

On History (London: Weidenfeld & Nicolson, 1997; New York: New Press, 1997);

Behind the Times: The Decline and Fall of the Twentieth-Century Avant-Gardes (London: Thames & Hudson, 1998; New York: Thames & Hudson, 1999);

Uncommon People: Resistance, Rebellion, and Jazz (London: Weidenfeld & Nicolson, 1998; New York: New Press, 1999);

Interesting Times: A Twentieth-Century Life (London: Allen Lane, 2002; New York: Pantheon, 2002).

Editions and Collections: *Revolutionaries: Contemporary Essays* (London: Weidenfeld & Nicolson, 1973; New York: Pantheon, 1973);

Politics for a Rational Left: Political Writing, 1977–1988 (London & New York: Verso, 1989).

OTHER: *Labour's Turning Point, 1880–1900: Extracts from Contemporary Sources,* edited by Hobsbawm (London: Lawrence & Wishart, 1948; revised and enlarged edition, Brighton, U.K.: Harvester, 1974; Rutherford, N.J.: Fairleigh Dickinson University Press, 1974);

"Jazz Concerts," as Francis Newton, in *This Is Jazz,* edited by Ken Williamson (London: Newnes, 1960), pp. 11–16;

Karl Marx, *Pre-Capitalist Economic Formations,* translated by Jack Cohen, edited, with an introduction, by Hobsbawm (London: Lawrence & Wishart, 1964);

"The Nineteenth Century London Labour Market," in *London: Aspects of Change,* edited by Ruth Glass (London: MacGibbon & Kee, 1964), pp. 3–28;

"The Crisis of the Seventeenth Century," in *Crisis in Europe, 1560–1660,* edited by T. H. Aston (London: Routledge & Kegan Paul, 1965; Garden City, N.Y.: Anchor, 1967), pp. 5–58;

"Peasants and Rural Migrants in Politics," in *The Politics of Conformity in Latin America,* edited by Claudio Veliz (London: Oxford University Press, 1967; London & New York: Oxford University Press, 1970), pp. 43–65;

Friedrich Engels, *The Condition of the Working Class in England: From Personal Observation and Authentic Sources,* introduction by Hobsbawm (London & New York: Granada, 1969; revised edition, Chicago: Academy Chicago, 1994);

"Class Consciousness in History," in *Aspects of History and Class Consciousness,* edited by István Mészaros (London: Routledge & Kegan Paul, 1971), pp. 5–21;

"The Lesser Fabians," in *The Luddites, and Other Essays,* edited by L. M. Munby (London: Katanka, 1971), pp. 231–244;

"Some Reflections on Nationalism," in *Imagination and Precision in the Social Sciences: Essays in Memory of Peter Nettl,* edited by T. J. Nossiter, A. H. Hanson, and Stein Rokkan (London: Faber & Faber, 1972), pp. 385–406;

"Whatever Happened to Equality? Equality in the Past," in *Whatever Happened to Equality?* edited by John Vaizey (London: British Broadcasting Corporation, 1975), pp. 31–46;

Feudalism, Capitalism, and Absolutist State: Reviews of Perry Anderson, edited by Hobsbawm and Douglas Bourn (London: History Group of the Communist Party, 1976)–includes contribution by Hobsbawm, pp. 3–13;

The Italian Road to Socialism: An Interview by Eric Hobsbawm with Giorgio Napolitano of the Italian Communist Party, translated by John Cammett and Victoria DeGrazia (Westport, Conn.: Hill, 1977; London: Journeyman, 1977);

"The Historians' Group of the Communist Party," in *Rebels and Their Causes: Essays in Honour of A. L. Morton,* edited by Maurice Cornforth (London: Lawrence & Wishart, 1978), pp. 21–47;

"Pre-Political Movements in Modern Politics," in *Powers, Possessions, and Freedom: Essays in Honour of C. B. Macpherson,* edited by Alkis Kontos (Toronto & Buffalo: University of Toronto Press, 1979), pp. 89–106;

Peasants in History: Essays in Honour of Daniel Thorner, edited by Hobsbawm, Ignacy Sachs, and Ashok Mitra (Calcutta & New York: Oxford University Press, 1980);

"The Forward March of Labour Halted?" in *The Forward March of Labour Halted?* edited by Martin Jacques and Francis Mulhern (London: New Left Books, 1981), pp. 1–19;

Marxism in Marx's Day, edited by Hobsbawm, volume 1 of *The History of Marxism* (Brighton, U.K.: Harvester, 1982; Bloomington: Indiana University Press, 1982);

"Mass Producing Traditions: Europe, 1870–1914," in *The Invention of Tradition,* edited by Hobsbawm and Terence O. Ranger, introduction by Hobsbawm (Cambridge & New York: Cambridge University Press, 1983), pp. 263–307;

Georges Haupt, *Aspects of International Socialism 1871–1914,* translated by Peter Fawcett, preface by Hobsbawm (Cambridge & New York: Cambridge University Press, 1986);

Antonio Gramsci, *The Antonio Gramsci Reader: Selected Writings, 1916–1935,* edited by David Forgacs, introduction by Hobsbawm (London: Lawrence & Wishart, 1988; New York: Schocken, 1988);

Harvey J. Kaye, *The British Marxist Historians,* revised edition, foreword by Hobsbawm (New York & London: Palgrave Macmillan, 1995);

"L'année improbable," in *1968: Magnum throughout the World,* edited by Hobsbawm and Marc Weitzmann (Paris: Hazan, 1998), pp. 8–10;

Marx and Engels, *The Communist Manifesto: A Modern Edition,* introduction by Hobsbawm (London & New York: Verso, 1998), pp. 1–30;

J. D. Bernal: A Life in Science and Politics, edited by Brenda Swann and Francis Aprahamian, preface by Hobsbawm (London & New York: Verso, 1999).

SELECTED PERIODICAL PUBLICATIONS–
UNCOLLECTED: "The Taming of Parliamentary Democracy in Britain," *Modern Quarterly,* new series 6 (1951): 319–339;

"The Political Theory of Auschwitz," *Cambridge Journal,* 5 (1952): 455–467;

"The British Communist Party," *Political Quarterly,* 25 (1954): 30–43;

"The Economics of the Gangster," *Quarterly Review,* 604 (1955): 243–256;

"Where Are British Historians Going?" *Marxist Quarterly,* 2, no. 1 (1955): 14–26;

"The British Standard of Living, 1798–1850," *Economic History Review,* 10, no. 1 (1957): 46–68;

"The Seventeenth Century in the Development of Capitalism," *Science and Society,* 24, no. 2 (1960): 97–112;

"Progress in History," *Marxism Today,* 6, no. 2 (1962): 44–48;

"From Feudalism to Capitalism," *Marxism Today,* 6, no. 8 (1962): 253–256;

"The Revolutionary Situation in Colombia," *World Today,* 19, no. 6 (1963): 248–258;

"The Standard of Living during the Industrial Revolution: A Discussion," by Hobsbawm and R. M. Hartwell, *Economic History Review,* 16, no. 1 (1963): 119–134;

"The End of European World Domination," *Afro-Asian and World Affairs,* 2 (1964): 93–99;

"Karl Marx's Contribution to Historiography," *Diogenes,* 64 (1968): 37–56;

"A Case of Neo-Feudalism: La Convención, Peru," *Journal of Latin American Studies,* 1 (1969): 31–50;

"Confronting Defeat: The German Communist Party," *New Left Review,* 61 (1970): 83–92;

"The Social Function of the Past: Some Questions," *Past and Present,* 55 (1972): 3–17;

"Peasants and Politics," *Journal of Peasant Studies,* 1, no. 1 (1973): 3–22;

"Labour History and Ideology," *Journal of Social History,* 7, no. 4 (1974): 371–381;

"Peasant Land Occupations," *Past and Present,* 62 (1974): 120–152;

"The Crisis of Capitalism in Historical Perspective," *Marxism Today,* 19, no. 10 (1975): 300–308;

"Gramsci and Political Theory," *Marxism Today,* 21, no. 7 (1977): 205–213;

"Some Reflections on 'The Break-up of Britain,'" *New Left Review,* 105 (1977): 3–23;

"Man and Woman in Socialist Iconography," *History Workshop,* 6 (1978): 121–138;

"Peasant Movements in Colombia," *Cahiers Internationaux d'Histoire Economique et Sociale,* 8 (1978): 166–186;

"Religion and the Rise of Socialism," *Marxist Perspectives,* 1, no. 1 (1978): 14–33;

"Development of the World Economy," *Cambridge Journal of Economics,* 3, no. 3 (1979): 305–318;

"Intellectuals and the Labour Movement," *Marxism Today,* 23, no. 7 (1979): 212–220;

"Socialism and the Avant-Garde in the Period of the Second International," *Mouvement Social,* 111 (1980): 189–199;

"The Contribution of History to Social Science," *International Social Science Journal*, 33, no. 4 (1981): 624–640;

"Looking Forward: History and the Future," *New Left Review*, 125 (1981): 3–19;

"*Past and Present:* Origins and Early Years," by Hobsbawm, Christopher Hill, and R. H. Hilton, *Past and Present*, 100 (1983): 3–14;

"Artisan or Labour Aristocrat?" *Economic History Review*, 37, no. 3 (1984): 355–372;

"Marx and History," *New Left Review*, 143 (1984): 39–50;

"Labour in the Great City," *New Left Review*, 166 (1987): 39–51;

"Offering a Good Society," *New Statesman*, 113 (1987): 11–13;

"The Making of a 'Bourgeois Revolution,'" *Social Research*, 56, no. 1 (1989): 5–31;

"Lost Horizons: Socialists Have Repudiated Their Utopian Longings and Beliefs at the Very Time They Are Most Needed," *New Statesman and Society*, 3 (1990): 6–18;

"The Crisis of Today's Ideologies," *Left Review*, 192 (1992): 55–64;

"The Time of My Life," *New Statesman and Society*, 70 (1994): 12–16;

"Edward Palmer Thompson, 1924–1993," *Proceedings of the British Academy*, 90 (1996): 521–539;

"History and Illusion," *New Left Review*, 220 (1996): 116–125;

"Identity Politics and the Left," *New Left Review*, 217 (1996): 38–47;

"Language, Culture, and National Identity," *Social Research*, 63, no. 4 (1996): 1065–1080;

"Democracy Can Be Bad for You," *New Statesman and Society*, 130 (1996): 25–27;

"Is History Dangerous?" *Historian*, 62 (1999): 4–5.

Eric Hobsbawm remains one of the great figures of twentieth-century cultural and economic history, a thinker distinguished less by his articulation and defense of a distinctive historiographical style or method than by his exceedingly broad conceptual and thematic ranges of reference, and by the originality, topicality, and suppleness of his Marxist cultural-critical analyses. The incisiveness of his meditations on a diverse array of phenomena, all of enduring intellectual and political import—including nineteenth-century and contemporary working-class cultures, modern jazz, nationalism, globalization, avant-gardism, and banditry—distinguish Hobsbawm as perhaps the preeminent intellectual cosmopolitan of his generation, a reputation secured over the course of a distinguished academic career spanning more than fifty years.

Eric John Ernest Hobsbawm was born in Alexandria, Egypt, on 9 June 1917 to Leopold Hobsbawm and Nelly (née Grün), the son of a Russian Jewish immigrant to the East End of London and his Viennese wife. Taken by his parents to Vienna in 1919, Hobsbawm spent his childhood and early adolescence ensconced in one of the liveliest middle-class Jewish communities in Central Europe, in a city desperately attempting to come to terms with the socio-economic and political legacies of World War I. During his twelve years in Vienna, Hobsbawm first encountered politics, not as a philosophical abstraction but as something alive, resonating in the people around him and particularly real to other Jews gradually becoming aware that they were living on borrowed time. In the midst of this ferment, and in no small way because of it, Hobsbawm began to edge toward the Marxism that in a more refined form indelibly marked his adult worldview.

Following the deaths of his parents in 1931, Hobsbawm relocated to Berlin to live with his uncle, who worked in Germany for an American movie company. Much later in life Hobsbawm remembered the city as one of the most dynamic places on earth. Even more than in Vienna, in Berlin Hobsbawm felt deeply implicated in history: not the inheritor of some static culture or traditions, but someone living and making history through acts basic to everyday life. In his struggle to understand what was going on around him, Hobsbawm found himself increasingly attracted to communism, and at the suggestion of an interested teacher, who encouraged him to read Karl Marx and Friedrich Engels, he formally entered into the most rewarding intellectual relationship of his life. Through Marx, Hobsbawm came to know history.

Unlike other Jews in the early 1930s, Hobsbawm and his family were spared the more grotesque anti-Semitic humiliations plaguing Germany. His classmates thought of him as "the Englishman" and not as "the Jew," teasing him only on account of the Treaty of Versailles. The onset of the Depression, however, coupled with tough new antiforeigner laws in Germany, put Hobsbawm's uncle's employment at risk. With considerable reluctance, Hobsbawm and the rest of his family moved to London in 1933, the same year Adolf Hitler came to power in Germany.

Hobsbawm found himself depressed by his English surroundings. He entered his third high school in three years, St. Marylebone Grammar School in London, and began working for the first time primarily in English in an environment he found comparatively dull. After Berlin, London seemed parochial, and Hobsbawm was regularly frustrated by the tendency of the British to avoid ideological discussions of any sort. He found naive their belief that if left alone the problems of the world would naturally resolve themselves, and he was sustained socially and intellectually by what he had brought with him from abroad, most notably his Marxism. As his secondary education and his teen years neared their end, Hobsbawm won a scholarship to King's College, Cambridge, and he began looking forward to remaking himself in an environment in which he hoped to continue many of the conversations in which he had participated in Berlin.

Hobsbawm entered Cambridge in 1936 and was presented with the choice of studying history, modern languages, or literature. Largely by virtue of his interest in Marx he chose history, and he soon found himself surrounded by an enthusiastic and accomplished student cohort actively wrestling with the problems of the day. Even in the company of such talented peers Hobsbawm soon distinguished himself, and he was recognized as an undergraduate with singular gifts extending beyond history to include popular culture, English literature, and the languages and cultures of France and Germany. Hobsbawm proved a popular student, especially in the company of other talented undergraduates, many of whom were, like him, members of the Communist Party.

In his first term at college Hobsbawm approached the editors of the literary magazine *Granta* and asked for a job, and between 1936 and his graduation in 1939 he wrote regularly for the periodical, producing movie and book reviews and op-ed pieces published under the headings "Cambridge Cameos" and "E.J.H. Observes." In 1939 Hobsbawm became the last pre–World War II editor of *Granta,* a short-lived post abbreviated by the wartime hibernation of the magazine and by Hobsbawm's own graduation, immediately following which Cambridge offered him a research studentship to study the agrarian problem in French North Africa. Three months later, however, war broke out, and this project was abandoned as, for the moment, infeasible.

Hobsbawm, like many of his fellow students, was drafted soon after the outbreak of hostilities in September 1939. Unlike many other middle Europeans, however, whose proficiency with foreign languages found ready use in the British War Office and Intelligence Services, Hobsbawm, whose reputation as an active communist was by now widely known, was made a sapper in a largely working-class unit assigned to build coastal defenses in East Anglia before he was assigned to the Education Corps. These army experiences proved revelatory, most notably in virtue of Hobsbawm's coming to recognize a potent and implacably conservative streak within the British working class, one that inflected their aspirations as well as their self-understanding as a class. This conservatism contrasted dramatically with Hobsbawm's own Marxist view of

Hobsbawm speaking at a conference on Antonio Gramsci in Rome, 1958 (from Interesting Times: A Twentieth-Century Life, *2002; Thomas Cooper Library, University of South Carolina)*

labor as inherently desiring to unite and overthrow the bourgeoisie, thereby sharing in the means of production, and the realization fueled in him a desire to make sense of the working class holistically, in all its messy complexity.

In 1943 Hobsbawm married Muriel Seaman, a communist educated at the London School of Economics; the couple had no children. He was demobilized early in 1946; he returned to Cambridge and began doctoral research into the early history of the Fabian Society, his plans for studying French North Africa now permanently shelved owing largely to the time he felt his primary research would take him away from his wife. In 1947 he was appointed a lecturer in history at Birkbeck College of the University of London, thus initiating his connection with a school that remained his primary professional affiliation until his retirement in 1982. In many ways Hobsbawm considered himself fortunate to obtain his position when he did, since a year later, following the Berlin Airlift of 1948, his reputation as a communist would have made it much more difficult to secure permanent work. As it stands, there is almost no question that being a communist at the height of the Cold War severely retarded Hobsbawm's rise through the academic ranks, resulting over the years in the rejection of his applications for positions at several leading universities and delaying his advancement at Birkbeck, where he was belatedly promoted to the position of professor of economic and social history in 1970.

As he taught and worked toward the completion of his dissertation, "Fabianism and the Fabians, 1884–1914," which he finally submitted in 1950, Hobsbawm became involved with a group of politically like-minded historians–including E. P. Thompson, Rodney Hilton, Christopher Hill, John Saville, Victor Kiernan, Raphael Samuel, Dona Torr, and Royden Harrison–who banded together to form the "Historians Group" of the Communist Party of Great Britain (CPGB). Reacting to a paucity of Marxist historical studies in Britain, and particularly to historiographical neglect of the working class as such, the Historians Group helped to initiate the influential and ongoing project of "history from below," or popular history, in the spirit (if not the letter) of the French Annales school. Their activities served to reorient historical analysis away from the Disraelian notion of history as the "biography of great men" and toward what Hobsbawm famously termed "grass roots" history.

Hobsbawm's period of greatest involvement with the Historians Group occurred between 1946 and 1956, during which time he, along with Hilton, Hill, and Kiernan, oversaw the expansion of the group beyond its headquarters in London in a bid to popularize the research perspective they were collectively developing. The main focus of the group remained on pre-twentieth-century British labor history, and in addition to generating many individual publications, it also planned several collaborative projects, the most significant of which was the publication under the general editorship of Torr of a series of historical documents covering different periods of British history titled *History in the Making*. The third volume of this series, *Labour's Turning Point, 1880–1900: Extracts from Contemporary Sources* (1948), covered the years 1880 to 1900 and was edited by Hobsbawm.

A related Historians Group project, a collection of essays in honor of Torr, appeared in 1954 and included one of the most influential of Hobsbawm's early essays, "The Labour Aristocracy in Nineteenth-Century Britain," later a chapter in his *Labouring Men: Studies in the History of Labour* (1964), and a topic profitably revisited in his subsequent study of labor history *Worlds of Labour: Further Studies in the History of Labour* (1984) alongside work on labor rituals, human rights, and 1970s syndicalism. *Labouring Men* remains noteworthy, however, not just as a collection of Hobsbawm's most important work of the late 1940s, 1950s, and early 1960s, but because it includes his provocative article "The British Standard Of Living: 1790–1850," in which he challenges the orthodox view of the Industrial Revolution as resulting in a substantial improvement in the

real incomes of the laboring poor in Britain in the first period of industrialization. So compelling was his challenge to historical orthodoxy that Hobsbawm's essay, along with his postscript to the so-called standard of living debate it engendered (which also appears in *Labouring Men*), was reprinted along with work by seven other historians in Arthur Taylor's collection *The Standard of Living in Britain in the Industrial Revolution* (1975).

In addition to these early projects, several members of the Historians Group, who along with Hobsbawm self-consciously refused to isolate themselves from non-Marxist historians, founded the journal *Past and Present* in 1952 to encourage discussion between academics sharing common interests and sympathies. *Past and Present* was not published by the Historians Group, nor was it intended solely to reflect Marxist concerns (its editorial board has always included non-Marxist historians and historical social scientists), and Hobsbawm, in addition to having been its editor, has remained involved in the ongoing operations of the periodical in an executive capacity.

The 1950s were difficult years for Hobsbawm, both because as a Communist he attracted the negative attention of many of his professional colleagues whose political sympathies lay elsewhere, and because the middle 1950s saw a damaging rift emerge in the CPGB itself, with thousands of its members, including Hobsbawm's friends Thompson, Hilton, and Hill, renouncing their memberships in the wake of the Soviet invasion of Hungary in 1956 and the failure of the CPGB to oppose it. Although damaged by these experiences, Hobsbawm remained an active member of the party throughout the Cold War, and in 1959 he published the first two of his many monographs, as well as accepting a promotion at Birkbeck to the position of reader.

Primitive Rebels: Studies in Archaic Forms of Social Movement in the Nineteenth and Twentieth Centuries (1959) was Hobsbawm's first sustained analytical foray into the world of political and social dissent, a topic he revisited later in such studies as *Bandits* (1969) and, with George Rudé, *Captain Swing* (1968), an account of the farm laborers' riots in southeast England in the autumn of 1830 to protest inadequate wages and working conditions, as well as the insufficiencies of the Poor Laws. In *Primitive Rebels,* however, Hobsbawm's focus remains fixed on nineteenth- and twentieth-century rural protest in Europe (mostly in Spain and Italy) as he develops the thesis that social bandits–a category encompassing rural secret societies, millenarian peasant revolutionary movements, and preindustrial urban mobs–must be viewed as popular attempts to adapt to the modernization of precapitalist societies. Against historians who tended to view bandits as political aberrations, or "odd

Hobsbawm and his second wife, Marlene (née Schwarz), in 1971 (photograph by Enzo Crea; from Interesting Times: A Twentieth-Century Life, *2002; Thomas Cooper Library, University of South Carolina)*

survivals," and more particularly in response to Marxist labor historians who understood banditry as merely the crude forerunner of modern trade unions and cooperative political organizations, Hobsbawm contends that banditry is a primitive form of organized social protest, one noteworthy for its uniformity and standardization across all substantially agrarian nations and marked by intense popular respect and support. For Hobsbawm, as a prepolitical phenomenon the bandit is created and called upon for protection by the peasantry at precisely the moment when he is least able to help it, for in order to successfully champion the peasants' cause the bandit must cease to operate outside the law. Thus, Hobsbawm shows that banditry could never be "a lasting form of organization for revolutionary peasants. It could at best be a temporary auxiliary for otherwise unorganized ones."

Like *Primitive Rebels, The Jazz Scene* (1959), which was published under the pseudonym "Francis Newton," testifies to Hobsbawm's enduring fascination with popular expressions of resistance and dissent. The book also demonstrates Hobsbawm's longtime admiration for jazz as an art form, the point of origin of which he traces back to the thrill he felt seeing Duke Ellington

play in Streatham in 1933. During the 1950s, in response to the decision by the *Observer* to hire an ill-equipped Kingsley Amis to write on jazz, Hobsbawm approached the *New Statesman and Nation* and talked his way into a job as its regular jazz columnist. His first column appeared in June 1956, and thereafter he contributed regularly (for example, fourteen articles in 1957) until 1962. From 1962 on, his columns continued to be published, but less frequently, with the last of them appearing in 1966, a decline largely attributable to the demands of Hobsbawm's increasingly complex family life. Divorced in 1950 in circumstances that, as he guardedly puts it in his autobiography, "left me wounded and for some time acutely unhappy," he was married a second time, to the Viennese-born Marlene Schwarz, in 1962. By the mid 1960s Hobsbawm found himself the father of two children with Marlene, Julia and her younger brother, Andy, as well as responsible for an illegitimate son named Joshua, the by-product of an earlier affair that took place when he was still single, with a married woman who refused to leave her husband. These domestic developments combined to render his late-night jazz club-hopping finally impossible.

Dust jacket for the U.S. edition (1987) of the third of the four volumes of Hobsbawm's history of the world from 1789 to 1991 (Richland County Public Library, Columbia, South Carolina)

As with many other scholars of his generation, Hobsbawm opted for a nom de plume when publishing ostensibly nonacademic work, but it would be a mistake to view his articles for the *New Statesman,* as well as *The Jazz Scene* itself, which contains several chapters drawn from Hobsbawm's journalistic writings, as thoroughly divorced from the politics marking the rest of his oeuvre. For Marxism crucially informs Hobsbawm's view of jazz as a social production and thus as understandable not simply in aesthetic terms but also variously as working-class music, as a form expressive of certain aspects of the African American experience, as players' music (and thus as symptomatic of a traditionalistic devotion to craft), and, finally, as revolutionary music. This last attribute is the most profound of jazz, since it reveals the music and its performance as organized around the essentially anticommercial, though nonetheless incomplete, rejection of traditions, conventions, and—as with the blues—the vicissitudes of an overpowering fate.

Hobsbawm's next major study was published in 1962 and proved to be the first of an ambitious four-volume study of world history from the late eighteenth to the late twentieth century, a massive and virtuosic accomplishment by which Hobsbawm's contribution to historiography has been measured. *The Age of Revolution: Europe, 1789–1848,* along with *The Age of Capital, 1848–1875* (1975), *The Age of Empire, 1875–1914* (1987), and *The Age of Extremes: The Short Twentieth Century, 1914–1991* (1994), collectively chart the bourgeois-capitalist transformation of the world in the wake of what he terms the "dual revolution": the French Revolution of 1789 and the Industrial Revolution begun in, and largely confined to, Britain. These four texts collectively and self-consciously constitute what Hobsbawm refers to as an interpretive work of "haute vulgarisation" in that they are intended to be read by educated general readers concerned with determining how the world has come to be what it is, and they have gained for Hobsbawm his largest and most varied audience.

In *The Age of Revolution* Hobsbawm shows that the most profound consequence of the upheavals initiated by the dual revolution was the complete military and political domination of the world by Europe and her white settler communities abroad. The dual revolution, that is, made European expansion both inevitable and irresistible, although it simultaneously provided non-Europeans with the means and motive for radically reconfiguring the terms of their oppression. At the same time Hobsbawm contends that the "great revolution of 1789–1848 was the triumph not of 'industry' as such, but of *capitalist* industry; not of liberty and equality in general but of *middle class* or '*bourgeois*' *liberal* society; not of 'the modern economy' or 'the modern state,' but of the economies and states in a particular geographical region of the world."

The theme of the global triumph of capitalism structures and is extended in *The Age of Capital,* in which Hobsbawm marks the advance not just of the capitalist world economy but also of the bourgeois social order it represented and the beliefs and ideas—including liberalism, reason, science, and progress—required for its sustenance from 1848 to 1875. This bourgeois revolution, in Hobsbawm's view, remained significantly incomplete, at least insofar as the reluctance of the bourgeoisie to commit itself to a system of public political rule was concerned. This incompleteness was because the European middle classes could not quite manage to conceive of themselves sharing power with workers and peasants, and they viewed "democracy" as the inevitable precursor to "socialism." Between the revolution of 1848 and the onset of the so-called Great Depression in 1873, thanks largely to the apparently boundless expansion of the world economy, political alternatives to revolution emerged in the "advanced" countries that effectively suppressed, if only temporarily, larger working-class ambitions and demands for equality and justice. The age of capital is thus marked for Hobsbawm by economic and technological—and not social or political—advancement.

In *The Age of Empire* Hobsbawm explores the contradictions accompanying the further globalization of capital between 1875 and 1914, the basic pattern of which "is of the society and world of bourgeois liberalism advancing towards what has been called its 'strange death' as it reaches its apogee, victim of the very contradictions inherent in its advance." Among these contradictions may be counted great political stability, at least at the center of empires, accompanied by unrest and revolt at their margins; the advent of massive organization by wage earners, but in economies that were flourishing and expanding and within which the working classes were reaping the political benefits of bourgeois liberalism as never before; and, partly as a result of this democratizing shift in the locus of power, the beginning of the collapse of the bourgeoisie under the weight of its own accumulations of wealth and related perquisites. The period from 1875 to 1914 is thus understood by Hobsbawm to be an age of tension and flux as revolutionary avant-gardes (political and cultural) prepared to transcend their moment even as they remained ineluctably defined by it.

Their opportunity for transcendence came in 1914 with the onset of World War I, a conflict that initiated another revolutionary age and that Hobsbawm terms an undeniable "natural break" in history, one concluding the "long" nineteenth century. Hobsbawm therefore takes 1914 as the starting point for his *The Age of Extremes,* which was published in 1994 in the wake of the turbulent dismantling of the communist dictatorships of Europe. *The Age of Extremes* is subtitled *The Short Twentieth Century,* a phrase that Hobsbawm borrows from Ivan Berend and uses to capture the distinctive structure and (intermittent) coherence of the period. This structure is mirrored in Hobsbawm's subdivision of the century into "The Age of Catastrophe" (1914–1950), "The Golden Age" (1950–1975), and "The Landslide" (1975–1991), which he offers as a way of signaling disjunctions in the larger meanings of those cultural and political triumphs and tragedies composing the recent past. The twentieth century for Hobsbawm is "extreme" precisely insofar as over its course capitalism came to operate more or less unchecked, the failure of socialism to sustain itself as an ideological option marking a profound rejection of the role of the state in the management of human affairs. He goes on to argue that, in the absence of compelling alternatives to liberal-individualist ideologies, massive environmental and

social degradation has occurred and hope for justice and equality has faded. His concerns with the liberal hegemony have found expression in *The New Century* (2000), a collection of Antonio Polito's interviews with Hobsbawm in which, amid a more general set of reflections on neoliberalism and its discontents, he again makes the point that "the globalized economy struck at the foundations of the social-democratic Left, because it undermined its ability to defend its social constituency within national borders through a redistributive fiscal policy, welfare, and macro-economic stimulation of full employment."

More so perhaps than in the first two volumes of his tetralogy, which remain significant largely by virtue of the quality of his socio-economic analyses, in *The Age of Empire* and *The Age of Extremes* Hobsbawm aims at providing "total" history, a synthetic amalgamation of complex causes and effects encompassing all aspects of the human experience, including politics, economics, science, technology, and the arts. This holism defines Hobsbawm's distinctive brand of nonpartisan Marxism, which rejects reductive readings of causal links between the social, the economic, the cultural, and the political even as it affirms the essential legitimacy of the base-superstructure model. The benefits of this approach, particularly the enrichment of awareness and understanding of the complex, top-down and bottom-up initiatives and networks of routine and convention out of which national pasts are invented and remembered, are clearly evident in *The Invention of Tradition* (1983), Hobsbawm's collection of essays edited with the Africanist Terence O. Ranger, and in his subsequent monograph *Nations and Nationalism since 1780: Programme, Myth, Reality* (1990).

Hobsbawm retired from Birkbeck in 1982, a departure that was met with not one but two festschriften: *Culture, Ideology, and Politics* (1982), edited by Raphael Samuel and Gareth Stedman Jones; and *The Power of the Past* (1984), edited by Pat Thane, Geoffrey Crossick, and Roderick Floud. During the 1980s, in addition to his academic work, Hobsbawm became what some have termed the unofficial philosopher and intellectual conscience of the British Labour Party, a role he assumed following the publication of his immensely influential article "The Forward March of Labour Halted?" and one that he has subsequently maintained. Originally the text of Birkbeck's 1978 Marx Memorial Lecture, "The Forward March of Labour Halted?" was first published in *Marxism Today* (a journal with which Hobsbawm had a lengthy association) and then later reprinted alongside responses in a 1981 essay collection edited by Martin Jacques and Francis Mulhern. The essay, which acknowledges the crisis-ridden state of the British labor movement, rejects

Hobsbawm lecturing in the Assembly Hall of the University of Guadalajara in Jalisco, Mexico, in 1997 (from Interesting Times: A Twentieth-Century Life, *2002; Thomas Cooper Library, University of South Carolina)*

the prevailing metaphor that the bird of labor can fly on one wing and instead urges a broadening of the appeal of the Labour Party beyond its traditional working-class constituency. The deep resonance of this message caused the essay to become an early catalyst for New Labour, although Hobsbawm has since publicly criticized the leadership and policies of party leader Tony Blair. Nevertheless, in "The Forward March of Labour Halted?" Hobsbawm urges an expansion of the political frame of reference of Labour, a demand entirely consistent with his overarching intellectual aims and ambitions. Hobsbawm's entire corpus can be viewed as a series of attempts to enlarge the meaning of the term *political,* thereby rescuing the bandit, the peasant, the jazz musician, and the illiterate factory worker from the condescension of scholars on the Left and the Right alike.

Eric Hobsbawm is currently Emeritus Professor of Economic and Social History at Birkbeck College and University Professor Emeritus of Political Science at the New School for Social Research in New York. He lives with his wife in Hampstead, England.

Interviews:

Steve Paulson, "The Age of Extremes: An Interview with Eric Hobsbawm," *Queen's Quarterly,* 102, no. 2 (1995): 269–281;

Daniel Snowman, "Eric Hobsbawm," *History Today,* 49, no. 1 (1999): 16–19;

Antonio Polito, *The New Century,* translated by Allan Cameron (London: Little, Brown, 2000); republished as *On the Edge of the New Century* (New York: New Press, 2000);

Nicholas Wroe, "To Criticise the Future," *Guardian* (Manchester), 23 December 2000, p. 11;

Tim Adams, "The Lion of the Left," *Observer,* 21 January 2001, p. 27.

Bibliography:

Keith McClelland, "Bibliography of the Writings of Eric Hobsbawm," in *Culture, Ideology, and Politics: Essays for Eric Hobsbawm,* edited by Raphael Samuel and Gareth Stedman Jones (London & Boston: Routledge & Kegan Paul, 1982), pp. 332–363.

Biographies:

Pieter Keunemann, "Eric Hobsbawm: A Cambridge Profile, 1939," *Culture, Ideology, and Politics: Essays for Eric Hobsbawm,* edited by Raphael Samuel and Gareth Stedman Jones (London & Boston: Routledge & Kegan Paul, 1982), pp. 366–368;

John Lloyd, "Profile: Eric Hobsbawm," *New Statesman,* 126 (1997): 28–32.

References:

Tony Coe, "Hobsbawm and Jazz," in *Culture, Ideology, and Politics: Essays for Eric Hobsbawm,* edited by Raphael Samuel and Gareth Stedman Jones (London & Boston: Routledge & Kegan Paul, 1982), pp. 149–157;

Eugene D. Genovese, "The Politics of Class Struggle in the History of Society: An Appraisal of the Work of Eric Hobsbawm," in *The Power of the Past: Essays for Eric Hobsbawm,* edited by Pat Thane, Geoffrey Crossick, and Roderick Floud (Cambridge & New York: Cambridge University Press, 1984), pp. 13–36;

Paul Hollander, "Further Explorations in the Theories and Practices of Socialism," *Partisan Review,* 52, no. 2 (1985): 120–132;

Harvey J. Kaye, *The British Marxist Historians: An Introductory Analysis* (Cambridge: Polity Press, 1984), pp. 131–166;

Samuel, "British Marxist Historians, 1880–1980, Part One," *New Left Review,* 120 (1980): 21–96.

Max Horkheimer
(14 February 1895 – 7 July 1973)

Christopher C. Brittain
Atlantic School of Theology

and

Kenneth G. MacKendrick
University of Manitoba

BOOKS: *Über Kants Kritik der Urteilskraft als Bindeglied zwischen theoretischer und praktischer Philosophie* (Stuttgart: Kohlhammer, 1925);

Anfänge der Bürgerlichen Geschichtsphilosophie (Stuttgart: Kohlhammer, 1930);

Die gegenwärtige Lage der Sozialphilosophie und die Aufgaben eines Instituts für Sozialforschung, Frankfurter Universitätsreden, no. 37 (Frankfurt am Main: Englert & Schlosser, 1931);

Dämmerung: Notizen in Deutschland, as Heinrich Regius (Zurich: Oprecht & Helbling, 1934); translated by Michael Shaw in *Dawn and Decline: Notes 1926–1931 and 1950–1969* (New York: Seabury Press, 1978);

Dialektik der Aufklärung: Philosophische Fragmente, by Horkheimer and Theodor W. Adorno (Amsterdam: Querido, 1947); translated by John Cumming as *Dialectic of Enlightenment* (New York: Herder & Herder, 1972);

Eclipse of Reason (New York: Oxford University Press, 1947);

Survey of the Social Sciences in Western Germany: A Report on Recent Developments (Washington, D.C.: Library of Congress, 1952);

Zum Begriff der Vernunft, Frankfurter Universitätsreden, no. 7 (Frankfurt am Main: Klostermann, 1952);

Gegenwärtige Probleme der Universität: Drei Universitätsreden, Frankfurter Universitätsreden, no. 8 (Frankfurt am Main: Klostermann, 1953);

Über die deutschen Juden (Cologne: DuMont Schauberg, 1961);

Sociologica II: Reden und Vorträge, by Horkheimer and Adorno, Frankfurter Beiträge zur Soziologie, no. 10 (Frankfurt am Main: Europäische Verlagsanstalt, 1962);

Um die Freiheit (Frankfurt am Main: Europäische Verlagsanstalt, 1962);

Über das Vorurtell (Cologne: Westdeutscher Verlag, 1963);

Zur Kritik der instrumentellen Vernunft: Aus den Vorträgen und Aufzeichnungen seit Kriegsende, edited by Alfred Schmidt (Frankfurt am Main: Fischer, 1967); translated by Matthew J. O'Connell and others as *Critique of Instrumental Reason: Lectures and Essays since the End of World War II* (New York: Seabury Press, 1974);

Kritische Theorie: Eine Dokumentation, 2 volumes, edited by Schmidt (Frankfurt am Main: Fischer, 1968); translated by O'Connell and others as *Critical Theory: Selected Essays* (New York: Herder & Herder, 1972);

Vernunft und Selbsterhaltung (Frankfurt am Main: Fischer, 1970);

Sozialphilosophische Studien: Aufsätze, Reden und Vorträge 1930–1972, edited by Werner Brede (Frankfurt am Main: Athenäum-Fischer, 1972);

Gesellschaft im Übergang: Aufsätze, Reden und Vorträge 1942–1970, edited by Brede (Frankfurt am Main: Athenäum-Fischer, 1972);

Aus der Pubertät: Novellen und Tagebuchblätter (Munich: Kösel, 1974);

Notizen 1950 bis 1969 und Dämmerung: Notizen in Deutschland, edited by Brede, introduction by Schmidt (Frankfurt am Main: Fischer, 1974); translated by Michael Shaw in *Dawn and Decline: Notes 1926–1931 and 1950–1969* (New York: Seabury Press, 1978);

Gesammelte Schriften, 19 volumes, edited by Schmidt and Gunzelin Schmid Noerr (Frankfurt am Main: Fischer Taschenbuch, 1985–1996);

Horkheimer und Italien: Dokumente, Texte, Interviews, edited by Gerd van de Moetter (Frankfurt am Main & New York: Lang, 1990).

Editions in English: *Between Philosophy and Social Science: Selected Early Writings,* translated by G. Frederick Hunter, Matthew S. Kramer, and John Torpey (Cambridge, Mass.: MIT Press, 1993)–includes "The Beginnings of the Bourgeois Philosophy of History" *[Anfänge der Bürgerlichen Geschichtsphilosophie];* "A New Concept of Ideology?" ["Ein neuer Ideologiebegriff?"]; and "The Present Situation of Social Philosophy and the Tasks of an Institute for Social Research" *[Die gegenwärtige Lage der Sozialphilosophie und die Aufgaben eines Instituts für Sozialforschung];*

Dialectic of Enlightenment: Philosophical Fragments, edited by Gunzelin Schmid Noerr, translated by Edmund Jephcott (Stanford, Cal.: Stanford University, 2002).

OTHER: *Studien über Autorität und Familie,* edited, with a foreword, by Horkheimer (Paris: Alcan, 1936);

"Sociological Background of the Psychoanalytic Approach," in *Anti-Semitism: A Social Disease,* edited by Ernst Simmel (New York: International Universities Press, 1946), pp. 1–10;

"Authoritarianism and the Family Today," in *The Family: Its Function and Destiny,* edited by Ruth Nanda Anshen (New York: Harper, 1949), pp. 359–374;

"The Lessons of Fascism," in *Tensions That Cause Wars,* edited by Hadley Cantril (Urbana: University of Illinois Press, 1950), pp. 209–242;

"On Schopenhauer Today," translated by Robert Kolben, in *The Critical Spirit: Essays in Honor of Herbert Marcuse,* edited by Kurt H. Wolff and Barrington Moore Jr. (Boston: Beacon, 1967), pp. 55–71;

"The End of Reason," "The Authoritarian State," and "On the Problem of Truth," in *The Essential Frankfurt School Reader,* edited by Andrew Arato and Eike Gebhardt (New York: Urizen, 1978), pp. 26–48, 95–117, 406–443;

"The Jews of Europe," in *Critical Theory and Society: A Reader,* edited by Stephen Eric Bonner and Douglas MacKay Kellner (New York: Routledge, 1989).

SELECTED PERIODICAL PUBLICATION–UNCOLLECTED: "Ernst Simmel and Freudian Philosophy," *International Journal of Psychoanalysis,* 29 (1948): 110–113.

Max Horkheimer was a social philosopher and one of the founders of the Institut für Sozialforschung (Institute for Social Research), commonly known as the Frankfurt School. He was the director of the institute from 1930 until 1959, during which time the institute was successively located in Frankfurt am Main, Geneva, New York, and Los Angeles. His leadership and influence spanned the social and political backdrop of the Weimar Republic, the Nazi seizure of power, the New Deal, World War II, the McCarthy era in the United States, the restoration of democracy in Germany, and various periods of student protest and reform in West Germany. Although at no time could the Frankfurt School be understood as a "school" in a formal sense, its members began to produce a coherent body of literature in the 1960s, represented by Theodor W. Adorno and Jürgen Habermas in Germany, Herbert Marcuse in the United States, and the earlier, radical, social-critical Freudian-Marxist writings published under Horkheimer's direction.

The combined efforts of the membership of the institute produced an unparalleled body of cross-disciplinary literature traversing fields including aesthetics, economics, law, philosophy, psychology, and sociology. The primary achievement of the institute was the way in which its members integrated a diverse array of theoretical reflections with empirical research. Horkheimer's single most notable accomplishment is successfully combining the roles of programmatic social theorist, manager of collective social scientific projects, editor of a journal, and mediator and charismatic facilitator of a talented group of nonconformist intellectuals. Although the membership of the institute fluctuated, its "inner circle" prior to Horkheimer's return to Germany after World War II included Friedrich Pollock, Leo Löwenthal, Erich Fromm, Marcuse, and Adorno. Other notable associates of the institute included Henryk Grossmann, Karl August Wittfogel, Franz Neumann, Otto Kirchheimer, and Walter Benjamin.

As one of the principal architects of "critical theory," the main label used by the theoreticians of the institute to describe themselves, Horkheimer was responsible for setting the agenda for the institute and maintaining its stability and continuity. He was the social and theoretical conscience of the group, constantly urging that their common task was to produce a theory of society whose subject would be human beings as makers of history, but also as produced and alienated by social life. All of Horkheimer's writings deal with this theme in one way or another. His best-known works include *Dialektik der Aufklärung: Philosophische Fragmente* (1947; translated as *Dialectic of Enlightenment*, 1972), which he co-authored with Adorno; *Eclipse of Reason* (1947); *Zur Kritik der instrumentellen Vernunft: Aus den Vorträgen und Aufzeichnungen seit Kriegsende* (1967; translated as *Critique of Instrumental Reason: Lectures and Essays since the End of World War II*, 1974); and the anthology *Kritische Theorie: Eine Dokumentation* (1968; translated as *Critical Theory: Selected Essays*, 1972). As the director of the institute he was also responsible for the publication of the *Zeitschrift für Sozialforschung* (Journal for Social Research) from 1932 to 1941 and for coordinating the research published in the series Studies in Prejudice, published by Harper and Brothers in 1949–1950.

Max Horkheimer was born in Stuttgart on 14 February 1895, the only son of Moses Horkheimer; his mother's name is unknown. His father was the owner of several textile factories in Zuffenhausen, near Stuttgart. Both his parents were Jewish and lived in a conservative but not orthodox manner. In his youth Horkheimer was trained in the commercial aspects of his father's business, and his apprenticeship, lasting from 1910 until 1917, took him out of secondary school a year before completing his degree. This training gave Horkheimer a financial shrewdness that served the Frankfurt Institute well throughout periods of financial crisis. This experience also fueled Horkheimer's outrage at the sufferings of workers for whom he had direct responsibility during his apprenticeship.

Horkheimer in 1930, the year he became the director of the Institut für Sozialforschung in Frankfurt am Main—popularly known as the Frankfurt School (from <www.ifs.uni-frankfurt.de/institut/ geschichte3.htm>)

During the eighteen months prior to World War I, Horkheimer spent time with Pollock in Brussels and London as part of his apprenticeship. Pollock, whom he met in 1911, and Horkheimer established close bonds emotionally and intellectually, so much so that they even signed a contract of mutual solidarity about how to resolve differences between them. Their friendship lasted a lifetime, taking second place in Horkheimer's life only to his loving relationship with his wife, Rose (Maidon) Rieker, which began in 1916. She was a Christian, eight years older than he, and his father's secretary. Consequently, his relationship with his parents was strained, although the rift was eventually reconciled (Horkheimer's parents were more concerned that Horkheimer was involved with a Gentile than with his becoming a revolutionary).

Pollock introduced Horkheimer to philosophy in 1913 when he gave him a book by Arthur Schopenhauer, a philosopher to whom Horkheimer returned again and again throughout his career and late in life. Together they read the writings of Benedict de Spinoza, Immanuel Kant, and various works of literary naturalism and social protest.

When World War I began, Horkheimer returned to Germany. He was conscripted into the military in 1916 and released for medical reasons in 1918. The war years were formative for Horkheimer's political and philosophical development, especially with regard to the indignation he felt at the injustices perpetrated on those who were exploited and humiliated. His earliest political sympathies were aligned with Rosa Luxemburg. After she was murdered in 1919, he never found another socialist leader to champion.

Horkheimer's earliest writing consists of novellas and diary entries composed during the war and published posthumously as *Aus der Pubertät: Novellen und Tagebuchblätter* (From My Adolescence: Novellas and Diaries, 1974). These early stories and plays question the relationship between morality and material success, such as one narrative that describes the struggle of two young men against the hollow existence of their parents. These sentimental writings celebrate the potential of love and beauty to break down social barriers and uphold the importance of living according to one's individual convictions. Horkheimer's heroes in his stories are those who help others in need, resist violence, and are prepared to sacrifice in the name of the higher moral virtues of love and compassion. These notes express the moral core of what became one of the hallmarks of critical theory: a protest against social injustice and a utopian desire for a better world.

In 1919 Horkheimer began his studies in Munich, focusing primarily on psychology, philosophy, and economics. After one semester he transferred to the new university in Frankfurt am Main (opened in 1914). He moved into a residential house with Pollock in Kronberg, not far from Frankfurt, and made the decision to break away from his father's business to pursue a career as an academic and philosopher. At Frankfurt University the professors that influenced Horkheimer the most were Friedrich Schumann (a Gestalt psychologist) and Hans Cornelius (a philosopher). He also had the opportunity to meet Adorno at one of Cornelius's lectures on Husserl, and Martin Heidegger, whom he was duly impressed by but suspected that he could not agree with on the level of basic principles.

During his studies, Horkheimer worked as Cornelius's assistant from 1922 until 1925. He was awarded his doctorate in 1922 and was encouraged to take up a postdoctorate in philosophy on Kant's *Kritik der Urteilskraft* (1790; translated as *Critique of Judgement*, 1892). He took his *habilitation* (postdoctorate) in 1925 on Kant with a primary emphasis on practical and theoretical reason.

While Horkheimer was just starting his *habilitation,* Felix J. Weil was in the process of establishing the Institute of Social Research. Weil was an entrepreneur, scholar, and artist, most noted for being a patron of the Left. Weil conceived the idea of a Marxist institute, loosely modeled on the Moscow Marx-Engels Institute, after the "First Marxist Work Week," a weeklong discussion group held in the summer of 1922 in Ilemenau. Participants in these discussions included many of the luminaries of the Left, including György Lukács and Karl Korsch.

Horkheimer and Pollock both supported the idea of an institute. Financial arrangements were made, and Kurt Albert Gerlach was scheduled to be the its first director. When Gerlach died in October 1922, Carl Grünberg, a professor at Vienna (the "father of Austro-Marxism"), was then named as his replacement. Affiliated with Frankfurt University, the institute formally opened on 22 June 1924, and Grünberg announced an interdisciplinary research program with a materialist emphasis. Although Horkheimer was not directly involved in the institute in its early years, he regularly attended seminars along with Adorno, Löwenthal, and Pollock.

After his postdoctorate, Horkheimer worked as a *privatdozent* (lecturer) at Frankfurt University from 1926 until 1930. During this time he developed an interest in psychoanalysis and went into therapy in 1928 with Karl Landauer. Landauer was one of the founders of the Frankfurt Psychoanalytic Institute, which opened in the same building as the institute in 1929.

When Grünberg suffered a stroke in 1928, forcing him into early retirement, Pollock assumed interim leadership of the institute. In 1929 a chair in social philosophy was established in the faculty of philosophy at Frankfurt University, which was to incorporate the directorship of the institute. Paul Tillich sponsored Horkheimer for the position. He was appointed to this post at the end of July 1930, two months before being appointed director of the institute. Horkheimer was chosen in part because Pollock was prepared to withdraw from consideration in favor of his friend. Although not the most obvious choice for the position, it was thought that Grossmann's and Pollock's political past might endanger the reputation of the institute. During Horkheimer's directorship, owing much to the force of his personality and the range of his intellect, his charismatic leadership of the institute was virtually unquestioned.

Two of the essays that served as his credentials for the position were *Anfänge der Bürgerlichen Geschichtsphilosophie* (1930; translated as "The Beginnings of the Bourgeois Philosophy of History" in *Between Philosophy and Social Science: Selected Early Writings,* 1993) and "Ein neuer Ideologiebegriff?" (1930; translated as "A New Concept of Ideology?" in *Between Philosophy and Social Science*). The former analyzes major "bourgeois" theorists (Niccolò Machiavelli, Thomas Hobbes, and Spinoza) in order to demonstrate the ways in which their theories justify the existing society. From Horkheimer's perspective, the bourgeoisie freed itself from the aristocracy only to subject the lower classes to its will. He insists that the historical consequences of the ideas of these philosophers were often at odds with their actual intentions. Machiavelli, for example, challenged unconditional obedience to the Church only to imply unquestioned obedience to the sovereign of the state. After criticizing these earlier authors, Horkheimer concludes this essay with a discussion of the Italian philosopher Giambattista Vico, since Vico's search for "history's hidden laws" appealed to him. Having identified the contradictions existing between the ideals of bourgeois society and the actuality of social injustices, Horkheimer sought to uncover the true nature of social reality behind its surface contradictions.

In the essay "Ein neuer Ideologiebegriff?" Horkheimer outlines the theoretical approach he takes to uncover forces at work beneath the surface of society that support unjust conditions. He does so in opposition to Karl Mannheim's "sociology of knowledge." In his book *Ideologie und Utopie* (1929; translated as *Ideology and Utopia,* 1936), Mannheim states that cognitive structures are directly related to social structures. He understands this "situational determinism" to allow sociology to achieve a new understanding of the concept of "ideology." Mannheim argues that "particular" notions of ideology tend to be reduced to labeling the views of one's opponents to be false concepts that merely serve their self-interest. This position intends to seek out a broader "total concept" of ideology, one that acknowledges that all worldviews represent ideological perspectives on society.

Horkheimer finds this shift toward a more neutral perspective on ideology deeply disturbing. In his opinion, Mannheim's claim that forms of knowledge simply correspond to the situation of certain social groups effectively undermines the Marxist understanding of "false consciousness." It suggests that there can be no nonideological perspective from which to criticize ideology, so that one must adopt a relativistic approach to truth. Horkheimer, by contrast, is concerned to defend a more Marxian understanding of ideology, so that social injustices and contradictions can be criticized from a perspective that is not regarded as merely one ideology among others.

After being appointed as director of the Institute for Social Research and to the chair of social philosophy, Horkheimer gave his inaugural lecture, *Die gegenwärtige Lage der Sozialphilosophie und die Aufgaben eines Instituts für Sozialforschung* (1931; translated as "The Present Situation of Social Philosophy and the Tasks of

an Institute for Social Research" in *Between Philosophy and Social Science*). His address set out a series of aims for the institute and the basic tenets of his philosophical position.

One of the primary concerns of Horkheimer's program was the question of how knowledge about society is possible. Horkheimer maintains that the present state of knowledge requires a continuing fusion of philosophy and the various branches of science. As he wrote in *Die gegenwärtige Lage der Sozialphilosophie und die Aufgaben eines Instituts für sozialforschung,* he believed that this approach should center on the question "of the connection between the economic life of society, the psychical development of the individuals, and the changes in the realm of culture in the narrower sense (to which belong not only the so-called intellectual elements, such as science, art, and religion, but also law, customs, fashion, public opinion, sports, leisure activity, lifestyle, etc.)." This agenda implies a focus on the "superstructure" of society–those aspects external to the economic structure itself, but which are influenced by it.

Horkheimer's approach to the various disciplines was to be grounded in a general theory of society in order to overcome the fragmentation of knowledge caused by increasing specialization. The linkage sought between the partial results of different disciplines was to be achieved through a research strategy consisting of three elements: social philosophy, social research, and a theory of history. Thus, Horkheimer advocates an approach to social theory that begins with some general assumptions about society, which are then tested by methodologies from particular disciplines such as economics, social psychology, and the human sciences. In effect, he was connecting Lukács's and Korsch's recovery of the philosophical elements of Marxism with Max Scheler's incorporation of the abundance of empirical knowledge into philosophy. Under Horkheimer's directorship the theorists of the institute were steered toward reflecting on the philosophical ground of Marxism, looking in particular at the gap between the individual and society, far more than their predecessors.

The first issue of the *Zeitschrift für Sozialforschung* appeared in 1932, replacing Grünberg's journal *Archiv für die Geschichte des Sozialismus und der Arbeiterbewegung* (Archive for the History of Socialism and the Workers' Movement), which had focused almost exclusively on economic concerns and social history. The new journal was distinguished from its predecessor by its broader concern with social theory. The journal was published regularly for a decade and was the principal organ of the institute. The first issue centered on a defense of a materialist conception of history, a brief sketch of his-

*Horkheimer with Friedrich Pollock, his close friend and fellow
founding member of the Institute for Social Research (from
<www.stub.uni-frankfurt.de/archive/hork.htm>)*

torical materialism, and the way in which consciousness
is determined by social existence.

In Horkheimer's contribution to the first issue,
"Bemerkungen über Wissenschaft und Krise" (collected
in *Kritische Theorie: Eine Dokumentation* and translated as
"Notes on Science and the Crisis" in *Critical Theory:
Selected Essays*), he criticizes the ideological assumptions
within science, often rooted in the economic class structure. Similarly, in his essay "Geschichte und Psychologie" (1932; translated as "History and Psychology" in
Between Philosophy and Social Science), he argues that psychic life is conditioned by the economy, and with the
quickening of economic development, changes occur in
the modes of human response and the capacity for
human rationality.

Like many of his colleagues at the institute,
Horkheimer had little sympathy for the authoritarian
nature of many of the leftist political parties, and he was
deeply disturbed by events in Russia. Furthermore, his
assessment of the political potential of the labor movement in Germany was not optimistic. The first research
project undertaken by the institute was a study of the
German working class. It focused on the social-
psychological structures of society under the Weimar
Republic and how far the working class could be relied

upon to stand by their left-wing views in crisis situations. As one of Horkheimer's reflections in *Dämmerung:
Notizen in Deutschland* (1934; translated in *Dawn and
Decline: Notes 1926–1931 and 1950–1969,* 1978) demonstrates, he had little confidence in the revolutionary
potential of the working class: "Unlike the prewar proletariat, these unemployed who are most directly interested in revolution lack the capacities for education and
organization, the class consciousness and dependability
of those who are more or less integrated into the capitalist enterprise." He continues, "The impatience of the
unemployed finds theoretical expression in the mere
repetition of the slogans of the Communist Party." In
his estimation the lower classes were too internally
divided to form a politically unified proletariat. The
interests of employed workers were often in conflict
with those of the unemployed, and these conflicts were
further complicated by issues of class, region, and gender. For this reason, Horkheimer and the other members of the institute opposed the dogmatism of the
German socialists, the Sozialdemokratische Partei Deutschlands (SPD, German Social Democratic Party) and
communists, the Kommunistische Partei Deutschlands
(KPD, German Communist Party). They argued that a
thorough reexamination of historical materialism must
be undertaken and began to incorporate social psychology (especially through Fromm's work) into the scope
of social analysis.

When the Nazis became the second largest party
in the Reichstag in the elections of September 1930,
Horkheimer, Pollock, Weil, and Löwenthal decided to
make preparations in case a withdrawal by the institute
became necessary. A branch office was set up in
Geneva, and the endowment of the institute was
invested in the Netherlands. On the same day that
Adolf Hitler was appointed chancellor of Germany (30
January 1933), the house in which Horkheimer and
Pollock lived in Kronberg was occupied by the SA (Nazi
storm troops) and converted into a barracks. Since
Horkheimer and his wife had been warned, they were
already living in a hotel near the railway station in
Frankfurt. In February, the institute, along with
Horkheimer, Marcuse, Pollock, and Lowenthal, relo-
cated to Geneva. On 13 March the former facility of the
institute was searched by the police and, deemed hostile
to the state, was closed in May. Publication of the
Zeitschrift für Sozialforschung resumed in Paris.

During this troubled period the institute began an
empirical study of authority and the family. A question-
naire was initiated in France among urban families,
white-collar or skilled workers unemployed for at least
six months, and experts in several European countries.
According to Horkheimer's foreword to *Studien über
Autorität und Familie* (1936), "Autorität und Familie"

(translated as "Authority and the Family" in *Critical Theory: Selected Essays*), this research was intended to characterize current attitudes toward authority in the state and in society and to analyze the breakdown of authority in the family that was produced by the ongoing political crisis. Horkheimer further suggests that the aspects of family life that stand in an antagonistic relationship with bourgeois society include an anti-authoritarian element.

In 1934 the central members of the institute immigrated to the United States and established themselves at Columbia University in New York. Horkheimer maintained his contacts with colleagues and scholars still in Europe, often supporting émigré academics financially so that they might leave Europe (130 people were given individual grants between 1933 and 1942). He traveled to France in 1937 to meet with Benjamin and in 1938 arranged for Adorno to come to New York.

Horkheimer sought to integrate the results of empirical inquiries within various scientific disciplines into a theory of how society as a whole functioned. He maintained a loose connection between empirical work and theory in order not to restrict theory, with the result being that many of the findings of the institute were not published. For although Horkheimer was interested in developing an interdisciplinary program, which included an occasional focus upon methodology, other tendencies in his thought resisted this emphasis on procedure, particularly in relation to the importance he continued to place (carried on from his early writings) on issues of morality and ethics. As outlined in "Bemerkungen über Wissenschaft und Krise," he became increasingly impatient with scientific methodology that he understood to display an uncritical acceptance of existing social conditions. This attitude toward "positivism" was not solely the epistemological concern that "usefulness" does not equal truth; he also intended to criticize science for evading its responsibility to society.

This moralistic concern is developed more fully in essays such as "Materialismus und Metaphysik" (1933; translated as "Materialism and Metaphysics" in *Critical Theory: Selected Essays*) and "Der neueste Angriff auf die Metaphysik" (1937; translated as "The Latest Attack on Metaphysics" in *Critical Theory: Selected Essays*), both of which were collected in *Kritische Theorie: Eine Dokumentation*. In both of these works Horkheimer links positivism, metaphysics, and the rising fascism of the day. Scientific knowledge is customarily viewed to be objective and accurate, and yet its assumptions and biases, rooted in social structures and norms, go unrecognized, and so in Horkheimer's opinion they function no differently than metaphysical beliefs. The unques-

tioned authority of a knowledge-producing procedure, focused on the instrumental control of nature, encourages the same authoritarian mentality that contributes to the rise of fascism. Surrendering science and knowledge to such a condition, continues Horkheimer, amounts to a resignation in the face of unjust social conditions and threatens to undermine the individual subject that is valued so highly in Western culture. Horkheimer intends to counter this narrow and dehumanizing trend by insisting that "right thinking" is linked to "right willing." Without a concern for a more humane world, the increasing specialization and instrumentalization of science threatens to become a tool of domination and oppression, rather than a humanizing process of enlightenment.

Horkheimer's most direct summation of this view appears in his essay from 1937, "Traditionelle und kritische Theorie" (included in *Kritische Theorie: Eine Dokumentation* and translated as "Traditional and Cultural Theory" in *Critical Theory: Selected Essays*). He argues that "traditional theory," or the perspective of the logical positivists, fails to acknowledge the social location of its assumptions. He locates their understanding of science in the context of a bourgeois society dominated by techniques of industrial production. Traditional theory fails to acknowledge that facts and theories can "be understood only in the context of real social processes." This perspective demands that, unlike the position of the Vienna Circle of logical positivists including Rudolph Carnap and Otto Neurath, a radical reconsideration of the knowing individual is required, along with an analysis of how social conditions influence the production of knowledge. The program of a critical theory of society, Horkheimer argues, "is a theory dominated at every turn by a concern for reasonable conditions of life."

To Horkheimer, this conclusion implies a theoretical position that resists keeping the subject and object of thought strictly separate and demands that theory be linked with practice. Unlike the positivists, therefore, critical theory does not demand absolute value neutrality. This circumstance did not suggest to Horkheimer a relativistic or irrational position, nor a simplistic reduction of science to social consensus. Rather, he sought to establish an interdisciplinary approach to social research that would bring philosophy and the scientific method together, so that both the rational concept of society and empirical reality could be unified.

The events of the war, and the flight to the United States, had an impact upon the tone of Horkheimer's subsequent writing. From his perspective it appeared that the bourgeoisie of Europe had rejected the liberal values of the Enlightenment and that this weakness of Western culture resulted from flaws inher-

MAX HORKHEIMER
UND THEODOR W. ADORNO

DIALEKTIK
DER
AUFKLÄRUNG

PHILOSOPHISCHE FRAGMENTE

QUERIDO VERLAG N.V.
AMSTERDAM
1947

Title page for the work (translated as Dialectic of Enlightenment,
*1972) in which Horkheimer and his Frankfurt School colleague
Theodor W. Adorno assert that social progress is illusory
and that civilization remains barbaric (Olin
Memorial Library, Wesleyan University)*

ent to the Enlightenment project itself. This perspective emerged as Horkheimer's earlier, more optimistic understanding of human action and a planned economy was challenged by his developing analysis of capitalism. In this period Horkheimer outlined what he called a "theory of rackets," as he attempted to come to terms with the possibility that authoritarian political and economic structures might have a good chance of success.

In "Die Juden und Europa" (1939–1940), which was collected in volume four (1988) of *Gesammelte Schriften* (Collected Writings, 1985–1996) and translated as "The Jews of Europe" in *Critical Theory and Society: A Reader* (1989), he describes how the world was being divided up into large economic power blocs, or "rackets," which regard their industrial workers as part of their military power. The nations, therefore, were increasingly interested in disciplining this industrial

army, so that political domination was becoming closely associated with economic domination. Horkheimer compares the fascist with a businessman, arguing that both desire power and control in the midst of the unpredictable forces of the capitalist economy. This understanding of rackets was intended to explain how Western society functioned after it ceased to correspond to the bourgeois ideal. Horkheimer argues that the new rackets seek to develop group loyalties in the midst of fragmentation, and he compares them to gangsters and a criminal mob. Rather than offering services to clients, they instead extort payment by way of threats and intimidation.

These alarming trends led Horkheimer to conclude that the fundamental ideals supporting Western civilization were in decay. The Enlightenment was betraying itself as it was consumed from within. In "The End of Reason," which was published in volume nine of *Studies in Philosophy and Social Science* (1941), he recalls much of his earlier critique of the positivist view of human rationality but is less confident about what resources are available to resist this development. Reason has been reduced simply to mirroring the demands of competitive society, whereas, in the humanistic tradition of philosophy, reason was understood as being aimed at a balance between what is good for the individual and good for the whole.

This essay also recalls themes from Horkheimer's "Autorität und Familie." The social changes he identifies, and the shifts in science and knowledge, are also understood to have direct impact on the most intimate of human relations. Along with reason and individuality, morality also disappears, for all depend upon some universal ideals independent of the merely given. In an environment dominated by instrumentalization and the economic bottom line, not even the family or intimate human relations are able to mediate a more humane existence, because everything becomes objectified. Procreation becomes a form of service to the state (as under National Socialism), and sexual freedom is reduced to a scorn for love and commitment. This vision was, in Horkheimer's mind, coming to fruition within Western culture in the 1930s and 1940s.

These issues are also discussed in the 1942 essay "Autoritärer Staat" (collected in *Gesellschaft im Übergang: Aufsätze, Reden und Vorträge 1942–1970* [Society in Transition: Essays, Speeches, and Lectures 1942–1970, 1972] and translated as "The Authoritarian State" in *The Essential Frankfurt School Reader,* 1978). Horkheimer argues, again, that the authoritarian state, mediated by liberalism, is a regime of gangsters ruling through violence, guided solely by the principle of pure profit. Horkheimer argues that state capitalism is not a form of economic regression but an intensification of forces and a parody of a classless society. He argues, then, that the end of exploitation is not a further acceleration of progress but a qualitative leap out of the dimension of progress altogether.

Horkheimer and Adorno had long respected one another's work, and their mutual appreciation led to significant parallels in their theoretical writing. Horkheimer's critique of self-preserving reason bore a strong resemblance to Adorno's view of music, which focused on the attempt to bring nature into submission. What Adorno denounced as the self-glorification of mind dominating nature, Horkheimer termed the self-refinement of reason resulting from the exclusion of critical thought and morality. When Adorno made the unrestricted and nonidentical the measure of his critique, Horkheimer referred to ideas that point beyond given reality. Their collaboration produced *Dialektik der Aufklärung,* one of the most influential texts of the Frankfurt School.

Dialektik der Aufklärung deals with the protohistory of Western culture. The book places Horkheimer's critique of positivism and bourgeois anthropology in a broader context, pursuing the implications of his critique of the repression of metaphysical and religious problems into the sphere of Western culture in general. Throughout, Horkheimer and Adorno demonstrate the ambiguity of the Enlightenment, rendering this ambivalence palpable with two themes: the view of Western civilization as a process of rationalization and disenchantment, as Weber had diagnosed; and the triumphant hostility of human beings toward nature, a thesis also examined in the work of Ludwig Klages.

The book is composed of three sections (on the concept of enlightenment, the culture industry, and anti-Semitism), two excursuses (on myth and enlightenment and on enlightenment and morality), and a series of notes and sketches. Its basic intention is to show that progress is an illusion and that civilization has emerged as a new form of barbarism. Written in a highly dialectical style, Horkheimer and Adorno elucidate the concept of enlightenment equivocally: they both critique the notion of rationality and defend rationalism; they demonstrate the Enlightenment to be a "disaster triumphant" and also seek to vindicate its ideals. The book was originally intended to be supplemented by a second volume, a positive idea of enlightenment, but it was never written.

Following the completion of *Dialektik der Aufklärung,* and as the war came to a close, Horkheimer was immersed in the vast anti-Semitism project. He had become an American citizen, and the project gave him and the other institute members the chance to make a name for themselves in American social studies by combining European ideas with American research methods. Horkheimer combined this effort with a series of lectures at the University of Chicago in 1947, published as *Eclipse of Reason.* As in *Dialektik der Aufklärung,* he describes the situation facing philosophy in modern society as being at an impasse. He repeats his criticism of purposive instrumental reason and defends the notion of a more substantive form of rationality, without identifying how such thinking can be developed under existing social conditions. The focus of philosophy, therefore, becomes simply to keep the possibility of critique open, searching for potentialities within the social order for a more just world while unmasking the forces of domination at work below the surface of Western culture and society.

In 1948 Horkheimer traveled to Europe to determine if a return to Frankfurt was possible. His strategy was twofold. On the one hand he wanted to establish the "splendid isolation" he desired to facilitate his theoretical work; on the other, he sought the security, influence, and recognition granted by academic institutions. He held lectures and seminars in Frankfurt, Munich, Stuttgart, Marburg, and Darmstadt, not once refusing a request to lecture and persisting in his strategy of maintaining the goodwill and support of the American authorities. Upon taking up a guest professorship at Frankfurt University in 1948, Horkheimer noted that the rector, deans, and other officials of the institution that had expelled him before the war now greeted him warmly but with an awkward embarrassment. Shortly afterward, he was reappointed to the chair of social philosophy, along with agreements welcoming the return of the Institute for Social Research.

In 1950 the institute was reopened, and Horkheimer became rector of the university. Only Horkheimer, Pollock, and Adorno returned to Germany. Of the three, only Adorno remained theoretically productive, as Horkheimer became involved in demanding administrative positions. To secure additional finances for the institute, he was prepared to emphasize its participation in postwar reconstruction and reeducation. Funds were eventually received from the Allied High Commission for rebuilding, with the assurances that the Frankfurt Institute would contribute to the promotion of democracy.

To enhance the reputation of the institute, Horkheimer was also prepared to state that social research was not restricted to the field of education and information, but also made it possible to decide where and how a factory should be correctly set up for its workers and how to achieve the highest productivity. Such lobbying secured a research project on German political awareness for the institute, which investigated the attitudes of the German population toward foreign countries, the occupying powers, the Third Reich and the question of responsibility for its crimes, democracy, and the place of Germany in the world. A pilot study was carried out in the winter of 1950–1951. Later, Horkheimer accepted a controversial contract with the Mannesmann corporation. Although the members of the institute had no experience with industrial sociology and were skeptical about this kind of research from the outset, the contract was accepted for various financial and strategic reasons.

In the years that followed, Horkheimer gave a series of lectures and speeches and was much in demand. In many respects, he took on a ceremonial and diplomatic role, attempting to preserve the institute and do what was possible to promote democratic thinking within the context of a restorative project. Despite his relative popularity, Horkheimer worried about the possible demise of the institute and saw publications as the best possible solution. At that time, Studies in Prejudice was not yet prepared for publication in German, nor was the study on West German political consciousness. He took up the idea of restarting the Zeitschrift für Sozialforschung but was frustrated by the lack of available time and talent. The plan fell through at the end of 1954, largely because there was no one available to represent the continuity of critical theory from the 1930s and 1940s. When Horkheimer suggested that perhaps he should withdraw from the institute to work on the journal, a conflict flared up between him and Adorno, who was adamant that they remain involved in its administration and functioning. Under a steady workload, Horkheimer eventually showed the senate of Frankfurt University his cardiogram to demonstrate the stress he was under and received permission to appoint a deputy director of the institute to replace him until Adorno returned from the United States in 1953.

During the 1950s and 1960s Horkheimer was living ambiguously. He was highly critical of contemporary society, although more secretly than in his earlier years, but also active in advertising liberal-bourgeois cultural traditions as part of the German restoration. The tensions between his criticism of Western society and the political and institutional demands of postwar West Germany were difficult to balance or reconcile. In this context both Adorno and Horkheimer sought to provide nuance to some of the more radical tones of their earlier work; yet, it was precisely these writings that became celebrated by the emerging student movement in Germany. The student movement adopted slogans from the early work of the institute, largely from pirated copies, demanding that critical thought must lead to social transformation. In the late 1960s Horkheimer also spoke out against the dangers of fascism in the antinuclear movements and worried about the anti-American sentiment expressed in the anti-Vietnam protests, taking up more of a securing and restorative pub-

lic position with regard to German democracy and culture. The conservatism often attributed to Horkheimer also emerged after Adorno took over as director of the institute and hired Habermas as a research assistant. Horkheimer strongly disapproved of the overtly political and abstract tenor of Habermas's writings. Eventually he urged that Habermas be removed from the institute, forcing him to complete his habilitation in Marburg with Wolfgang Abendroth.

Horkheimer retired in 1958 and moved to Montagnola in Italy (near Lugano), living next door to Pollock. He continued to be a sought-after speaker and was frequently interviewed and honored with prestigious awards: the freedom of the City of Frankfurt (1960) and the Lessing Prize of the City of Hamburg (1971). In 1969 he mourned the death of his wife, along with that of Adorno.

Horkheimer's postwar writings wrestled with how to continue to speak about justice and freedom in a world he considered to be manipulated and controlled by capitalist exchange and authoritarian political structures. His notes from this period (published as Notizen 1950 bis 1969 in 1974 and translated in Dawn and Decline) lament the state of many of the highest ideals of Western society: love, truth, morality, and individual autonomy. If reason had become predominantly instrumental, then what resources could individuals draw upon that might embody more substantive forms of rationality? Faced with this question, Horkheimer tended to turn to two sources in his attempt to answer it: the philosophy of Schopenhauer and Western religion.

Horkheimer was interested in Schopenhauer's response to Kantian philosophy. Schopenhauer had accepted Kant's epistemological understanding of the world of appearances, agreeing that human knowledge was restricted to the relative manifestations of objects and events as they are conditioned by human activity. He did not, however, accept Kant's claim to be unable to discern what might be found behind these phenomena. For Kant, the thing-in-itself (as opposed to the thing as it appears to people) remains unknowable. Schopenhauer argued that behind appearances is found the will. The "inner being" of nature is comprised of the constant motion of the will. That he offered this argument without glorifying the will or sanctioning its uninhibited expression is what Horkheimer appreciates in "Die Aktualität Schopenhauers" (published in Sociologica II: Reden und Vorträge [Sociologica II: Readings and Lectures, 1962] and translated as "On Schopenhauer Today" in The Critical Spirit: Essays in Honor of Herbert Marcuse, 1967).

Horkheimer sees in Schopenhauer's work a refusal to allow the world-in-itself to be collapsed into the world-for-us. In other words, he refuses to allow the classical idealist dualism to be discarded and reduced to an acceptance of the world as it is given, for to do so amounts to a resignation to an unjust society. At the same time, Schopenhauer did not succumb to deifying some pure vision of the world behind appearances but remained content to criticize absolute claims about the world without proposing one of his own. This process is supported in his work by his understanding of the will, which, remaining unappeasable, encourages endless striving and struggle. In the face of what he considered to be utter hopelessness, Horkheimer found in this idea a glimmer of hope.

Horkheimer's response to the tragedies of the war and the Holocaust, as well as to the consumerism of Western capitalism, was therefore focused on two projects: to preserve as much freedom as possible through critical analysis and practical activity, and to nurture a longing for a more humane world, so that the existing order could not make people forget that things could be otherwise. This latter concern was related to Horkheimer's interest in religion, which remained constant throughout his career. Even in his early notes in *Dämmerung,* religion figures prominently. Although he certainly criticizes Christianity for its ideological support of the nation-state and for encouraging people to bear passively injustice in the hope of attaining reward in the afterlife, Horkheimer also appreciates how religion maintains a vision that life could be better, and that it often refuses to accept that the status quo is all there is. In *Eclipse of Reason,* while commenting on the relationship that religion has to philosophy, Horkheimer states that what is often lost when religion is left behind is its relationship to truth. Although religion often fetishizes its quest for truth, Horkheimer maintains that it is also intimately related to the desire for truth.

This perspective on religion is summarized in essays such as "Gedanke zur Religion" (1935; collected in *Kritische Theorie: Eine Dokumentation* and translated as "Thought on Religion" in *Critical Theory: Selected Essays)* and especially "Theismus–Atheismus" from *Zur Kritik der instrumentellen Vernunft* (translated as "Theism and Atheism" in *Critique of Instrumental Reason).* In the latter, Horkheimer by no means adopts a sentimental view of Christianity, pointing out the collusion of dogmatic theology with power, the jealous defense by the Church of its own authority, and its temptation to provide an empty world-denying consolation. At the same time, however, he intends to warn the atheist against a naive response to the faults of religion. To be an atheist at the height of the power of the Church was one thing—for, in Horkheimer's view, to do so meant identifying with the commandment to love one's neighbor in a more profound way than the Christian. In the contemporary world, however, to profess to be an atheist in a society

Max Horkheimer

Kritische Theorie
Eine Dokumentation

Herausgegeben von Alfred Schmidt

Band I

S. Fischer Verlag

Title page for the first volume of Horkheimer's 1968 collection of articles (translated in 1972 as Critical Theory: Selected Essays) *he had published throughout his career (Thomas Cooper Library, University of South Carolina)*

that holds nothing sacred is another matter entirely. Such a stance often fails to resist unjust social conditions, so that atheism becomes the attitude of those who follow whatever power structures happen to be dominant.

In his last notes in *Notizen 1950 bis 1969,* and in essays such as "Pessimismus heute" (Pessimism Today), which was published in 1972 in *Gesellschaft im Übergang,* Horkheimer struggles with how to articulate any sense of hope for a better world. He compares the state of critical theory at this stage with the Jewish prohibition against portraying God—one can identify what is evil (like the Jewish criticism of idolatry), but one cannot define what is in fact good (one cannot make images of the divine or name the "Holy of Holies"). Critical theory could criticize social injustice and domination, but it could not provide a blueprint for a better world. It was left with a concept of negativity, which, to its critics, appeared to signal a resigned pessimism.

Horkheimer in particular was criticized in this way, especially because his interest in religion seemed to suggest to some of his opponents that he had adopted a melancholy theology. In 1970 he was interviewed for an article published as the pamphlet *Die Sehnsucht nach dem ganz Anderen* (Longing for the Wholly Other); it was later included in volume seven (1985) of Horkheimer's *Gesammelte schriften*. In this discussion Horkheimer maintains that a critical theory of society is to be a determined negative dialectical method in pursuit of a just society. He then proceeds to add that in this pursuit "the role of faith becomes central" and speaks favorably about theology. What he means by *theology*, however, is not a return to a dogmatic claim about the true nature of ultimate reality but an awareness that the world of appearances does not represent absolute truth. Yet, at this stage of his life, this perspective had become crucial for his understanding of critical theory, for he had come to believe that one could no longer strive for unconditional meaning without employing the word *God*. Some sense of a better world—of a "wholly other"—was required in order to support critical thought and action.

Horkheimer's *Gesammelte Schriften* comprises nineteen volumes and, overall, is indicative of the way in which he thought not only in terms of rigorous internal consistency but also aporetically, constructing frameworks that open up complementary contradictions to productive reflection. The legacy of Horkheimer's programmatic critical theory remains intact and vibrant today. After his death on 7 July 1973, a second generation of critical theorists remained committed to his original program in a variety of new and innovative ways. Thinkers including Habermas, Albrecht Wellmer, Claus Offe, Alexander Kluge, and Oskar Negt have all followed in the footsteps of the Frankfurt School, and since then critical theory has proliferated into third and fourth generations, including prominent theorists such as Seyla Benhabib, Thomas McCarthy, and Axel Honneth.

Letters:

Horkheimer and Theodor W. Adorno, *Briefweschel, 1927–1969,* edited by Christophe Gödde and Henri Lonitz (Frankfurt am Main: Suhrkamp, 2003).

Interviews:

Helmut Gumnior, *Die Sehnsucht nach dem ganz Anderen* (Hamburg: Furche, 1970);

Otmar Hersche, *Verwaltete Welt* (Zurich: De Arche, 1970);

Hugo Staudinger, *Humanität und Religion: Briefweschel und Gespräch* (Würzburg: Naumann, 1974).

Bibliography:

Gunzelin Schmid Noerr, "Bibliographie der Erstveröffentlichungen Max Horkheimers," in *Max Horkheimer heute: Werk und Wirkung,* edited by Alfred Schmidt and Norbert Altwicker (Frankfurt am Main: Fischer, 1986), pp. 372–383.

Biographies:

Helmut Gumnior and Rudolf Ringguth, *Max Horkheimer in Selbstzeugnissen und Bilddokumenten* (Reinbek bei Hamburg: Rowohlt, 1973);

Anselm Skuhra, *Max Horkheimer: Eine Einführung in sein Denken* (Stuttgart: Kohlhammer, 1974);

Rolf Wiggershaus, *Max Horkheimer: Zur Einführung* (Hamburg: Junius, 1998).

References:

Seyla Benhabib, Wolfgang Bonß, and John McCole, eds., *On Max Horkheimer: New Perspectives* (Cambridge, Mass.: MIT Press, 1993);

Susan Buck-Morss, *The Origin of Negative Dialectics: Theodor W. Adorno, Walter Benjamin and the Frankfurt Institute* (New York: Free Press, 1977; Hassocks, U.K.: Harvester, 1977);

David Held, *Introduction to Critical Theory: Horkheimer to Habermas* (Berkeley: University of California Press, 1980), pp. 29–246;

Marsha A. Hewitt, *Critical Theory of Religion: A Feminist Analysis* (Minneapolis: Fortress, 1995), pp. 1–112;

Martin Jay, *The Dialectical Imagination: A History of the Frankfurt School and the Institute for Social Research, 1923–1950* (Boston: Little, Brown, 1973);

Jay, *Permanent Exiles: Essays on the Intellectual Migration from Germany to America* (New York: Columbia University Press, 1986), pp. 3–137;

Martin Beck Matuštík, *Jürgen Habermas: A Philosophical-Political Profile* (Lanham, Md.: Rowman & Littlefield, 2001), pp. 1–63;

Peter M. R. Stirk, *Max Horkheimer: A New Interpretation* (Hemel Hempstead: Harvester Wheatsheaf / Lanham, Md.: Barnes & Noble, 1992);

Rolf Wiggershaus, *The Frankfurt School: Its History, Theories, and Political Significance,* translated by Michael Robertson (Cambridge: Polity Press, 1944; Cambridge, Mass.: MIT Press, 1994).

Papers:

Max Horkheimer's papers are held at the Horkheimer-Pollock Archive at the university library of the University of Frankfurt am Main.

Edmund Husserl

(8 April 1859 – 27 April 1938)

Peter R. Costello
Saint Peter's College

BOOKS: *Über den Begriff der Zahl: Psychologische Analysen* (Halle: Heynemann, 1887); translated by Dallas Willard as "On the Concept of Number: Psychological Analyses," *Philosophica Mathematica,* 9 (1972): 44–52; 10 (1973): 37–87;

Philosophie der Arithmetik: Psychologische und logische Untersuchungen, Erster Band (Halle: Pfeffer, 1891);

Logische Untersuchungen, 2 volumes (Halle: Niemeyer, 1900, 1901; revised, 1913, 1921); translated by J. N. Findlay as *Logical Investigations,* 2 volumes (London: Routledge & Kegan Paul / New York: Humanities Press, 1970);

Méditations cartésiennes: Introduction à la phénoménologie, French translation by Gabrielle Peiffer and Emmanuel Lévinas (Paris: Colin, 1931); translated by Dorion Cairns as *Cartesian Meditations: An Introduction to Phenomenology* (The Hague: Nijhoff, 1960);

Ideas: General Introduction to Pure Phenomenology, translated by W. R. Boyce Gibson (London: Allen & Unwin / New York: Macmillan, 1931); original German version published as *Ideen zu einer reinen Phänomenologie und phänomenologischen Philosophie,* 3 volumes, edited by Walter Biemel and Marly Biemel, volumes 3–5 of *Husserliana* (The Hague: Nijhoff, 1950–1952; volume 3 revised, edited by Karl Schuhman, 1976);

Cartesianische Meditationen und Pariser Vorträge, edited by Stephan Strasser, volume 1 of *Husserliana* (The Hague: Nijhoff, 1950);

Die Idee der Phänomenologie: Fünf Vorlesungen, edited by Walter Biemel, volume 2 of *Husserliana* (The Hague: Nijhoff, 1950; revised and expanded, 1973); translated by William P. Alston and George Nakhnikian as *The Idea of Phenomenology* (The Hague: Nijhoff, 1964);

Die Krisis der europäischen Wissenschaften und die transzendentale Phänomenologie: Eine Einleitung in die phänomenologische Philosophie, edited by Walter Biemel, volume 6 of *Husserliana* (The Hague: Nijhoff, 1954); translated by David Carr as *The Crisis of European Sci-*

Edmund Husserl (from Maurice Natanson, Edmund Husserl: Philosopher of Infinite Tasks, *1973; Thomas Cooper Library, University of South Carolina)*

ences and Transcendental Phenomenology: An Introduction to Phenomenological Philosophy (Evanston, Ill.: Northwestern University Press, 1970);

Erste Philosophie (1923/24), 2 volumes, edited by Rudolf Boehm, volumes 7–8 of *Husserliana* (The Hague: Nijhoff, 1956, 1959);

Phänomenologische Psychologie: Vorlesungen Sommersemester 1925, edited by Walter Biemel, volume 9 of *Hus-*

serliana (The Hague: Nijhoff, 1962); translated by John Scanlon as *Phenomenological Psychology: Lectures, Summer Semester, 1925* (The Hague: Nijhoff, 1977);

The Phenomenology of Internal Time-Consciousness, edited by Martin Heidegger, translated by James S. Churchill (The Hague: Nijhoff, 1964); original German version published as *Zur Phänomenologie des inneren Zeitbewusstseins (1893–1917),* edited by Boehm, volume 10 of *Husserliana* (The Hague: Nijhoff, 1966);

Analysen zur passiven Synthesis: Aus Vorlesungs- und Forschungsmanuskripten (1918–1926), volume 11 of *Husserliana,* edited by Margot Fleischer (The Hague: Nijhoff, 1966);

Philosophie der Arithmetik: Mit ergänzenden Texten (1890–1901), edited by Lothar Eley, volume 12 of *Husserliana* (The Hague: Nijhoff, 1970); translated by Dallas Willard as *Philosophy of Arithmetic: Psychological and Logical Investigations—with Supplementary Texts from 1887–1901* (Dordrecht & Boston: Kluwer, 2003);

Zur Phänomenologie der Intersubjektivität: Texte aus dem Nachlass, 3 volumes, edited by Iso Kern, volumes 13–15 of *Husserliana* (The Hague: Nijhoff, 1973);

Ding und Raum: Vorlesungen 1907, edited by Ulrich Claesges, volume 16 of *Husserliana* (The Hague: Nijhoff, 1973);

Formale und transzendentale Logik: Versuch einer Kritik der logischen Vernunft, edited by Paul Janssen, volume 17 of *Husserliana* (The Hague: Nijhoff, 1974);

Logische Untersuchungen, 2 volumes, edited by Ursula Panzer, volumes 18–19 of *Husserliana* (The Hague: Nijhoff, 1975);

Aufsätze und Rezensionen, 1890–1910, edited by Bernhard Rang, volume 22 of *Husserliana* (The Hague & Boston: Nijhoff, 1979);

Phantasie, Bildbewusstsein, Erinnerung: Zur Phänomenologie der anschaulichen Vergegenwärtigungen. Texte aus dem Nachlass, 1898–1925, edited by Eduard Marbach, volume 23 of *Husserliana* (The Hague & Boston: Nijhoff, 1980);

Studien zur Arithmetik und Geometrie: Texte aus dem Nachlass (1886–1901), edited by Ingeborg Strohmeyer, volume 21 of *Husserliana* (The Hague & Boston: Nijhoff, 1981);

Einleitung in die Logik und Erkenntnistheorie: Vorlesungen 1906/07, edited by Melle, volume 24 of *Husserliana* (Dordrecht & Boston: Nijhoff, 1984);

Aufsätze und Vorträge (1911–1921), edited by Thomas Nenon and Hans-Rainer Sepp, volume 25 of *Husserliana* (Dordrecht & Boston: Nijhoff, 1986);

Vorlesungen über Bedeutungslehre: Sommersemester 1908, edited by Panzer, volume 26 of *Husserliana* (Dordrecht & Boston: Nijhoff, 1987);

Vorlesungen über Ethik und Wertlehre, 1908–1914, edited by Melle, volume 28 of *Husserliana* (Dordrecht & Boston: Kluwer, 1988);

VI. cartesianische Meditation: Texte aus dem Nachlass Eugen Finks (1932) mit Anmerkungen und Beilungen aus dem Nachlass Edmund Husserls, 2 volumes, edited by Hans Ebeling, Jann Holl, and Guy van Kerckhoven, introduction by Ronald Bruzina (Dordrecht & Boston: Kluwer, 1988);

Aufsätze und Vorträge (1922–1937), edited by Nenon and Sepp, volume 27 of *Husserliana* (Dordrecht & Boston: Kluwer, 1989);

Die Krisis der europäischen Wissenschaften und die transzendentale Phänomenologie. Ergänzungsband: Texte aus dem Nachlass 1934–1937, edited by Reinhold N. Smid, volume 29 of *Husserliana* (Dordrecht & Boston: Kluwer, 1993);

Logik und allgemeine Wissenschaftstheorie: Vorlesungen 1917/18, mit ergänzenden Texten aus der ersten Fassung 1910/11, edited by Panzer, volume 30 of *Husserliana* (Dordrecht & Boston: Kluwer, 1996);

Aktive Synthesen: Aus der Vorlesung "Transzendentale Logik" 1920/21: Ergänzungsband zu "Analysen zur passiven Synthesis," edited by Roland Breeur, volume 31 of *Husserliana* (Dordrecht & Boston: Kluwer, 2000);

Natur und Geist: Vorlesungen, Sommersemester 1927, edited by Michael Weiler, volume 32 of *Husserliana* (Dordrecht & Boston: Kluwer, 2001);

Die "Bernauer Manuskripte" über das Zeitbewusstsein (1917/18), edited by Rudolf Bernet and Dieter Lohmar, volume 33 of *Husserliana* (Dordrecht & Boston: Kluwer, 2001);

Logik: Vorlesung 1896, edited by Elisabeth Schuhmann, volume 1 of *Husserliana Materialienbände* (Boston: Kluwer, 2001);

Logik: Vorlesung 1902/03, edited by Schuhmann, volume 2 of *Husserliana Materialienbände* (Dordrecht & Boston: Kluwer, 2001);

Allgemeine Erkenntnistheorie: Vorlesung 1902/03, edited by Schuhmann, volume 3 of *Husserliana Materialienbände* (Dordrecht & Boston: Kluwer, 2001);

Logische Untersuchungen. Ergänzungsband zur Umarbeitung der VI. Untersuchung: Texte aus dem Nachlass (1911–1917), edited by Ulrich Melle, volume 20 of *Husserliana* (The Hague: Nijhoff, 2002);

Zur phänomenologischen Reduktion: Texte aus dem Nachlass (1926–1935), edited by Sebastian Luft, volume 34 of *Husserliana* (Dordrecht & Boston: Kluwer, 2002);

Einleitung in die Philosophie: Vorlesungen 1922/23, edited by Berndt Goossens, volume 35 of *Husserliana* (Dordrecht & Boston: Kluwer, 2002);

Natur und Geist: Vorlesungen, Sommersemester 1919, edited by Weiler, volume 4 of *Husserliana Materialienbände* (Dordrecht & Boston: Kluwer, 2002);

Urteilstheorie: Vorlesung 1905, edited by Schuhmann, volume 5 of *Husserliana Materialienbände* (Dordrecht & Boston: Kluwer, 2002).

Editions in English: *Ideas: General Introduction to Pure Phenomenology,* translated by W. R. Boyce Gibson (London: Allen & Unwin / New York: Macmillan, 1931);

The Paris Lectures, translated, with an introduction, by Peter Koestenbaum (The Hague: Nijhoff, 1964);

Formal and Transcendental Logic, translated by Dorion Cairns (The Hague: Nijhoff, 1969);

Experience and Judgment: Investigations in a Genealogy of Logic, revised and edited by Ludwig Landgrebe, translated by James S. Churchill and Karl Ameriks (Evanston, Ill.: Northwestern University Press, 1973; London: Routledge & Kegan Paul, 1973);

Introduction to the Logical Investigations: A Draft of a Preface to the Logical Investigations (1913), edited by Eugen Fink, translated, with an introduction, by Philip J. Bossert and Curtis H. Peters (The Hague: Nijhoff, 1975);

Ideas pertaining to a Pure Phenomenology and to a Phenomenological Philosophy, 3 volumes, translated by F. Kersten and others (The Hague & Boston: Nijhoff, 1980–1989);

Husserl: Shorter Works, edited by Peter McCormick and Frederick A. Elliston (Notre Dame, Ind.: University of Notre Dame Press / Brighton, U.K.: Harvester, 1981);

Early Writings in the Philosophy of Logic and Mathematics, translated by Dallas Willard (Dordrecht & Boston: Kluwer, 1994);

Psychological and Transcendental Phenomenology and the Confrontation with Heidegger (1927–1931): The Encyclopaedia Britannica Article, the Amsterdam Lectures, "Phenomenology and Anthropology," and Husserl's Marginal Notes in Being and Time and Kant and the Problem of Metaphysics, translated by Thomas Sheehan and Richard E. Palmer (Dordrecht & Boston: Kluwer, 1997);

Thing and Space: Lectures of 1907, translated by Richard Rojcewicz (Dordrecht & Boston: Kluwer, 1997);

The Idea of Phenomenology, translated and introduced by Lee Hardy (Dordrecht & Boston: Kluwer, 1999);

The Essential Husserl: Basic Writings in Transcendental Philosophy, edited by Donn Welton (Bloomington: Indiana University Press, 1999);

Analyses Concerning Passive and Active Synthesis: Lectures on Transcendental Logic, translated by Anthony J. Steinbeck (Dordrecht & Boston: Kluwer, 2001).

SELECTED PERIODICAL PUBLICATION–UNCOLLECTED: "Philosophie als strenge Wissenschaft," *Logos,* 1 (1911) 289–341; translated by Quentin Lauer as "Philosophy as Rigorous Science," in *Edmund Husserl: Phenomenology and the Crisis of Philosophy* (New York: Harper & Row, 1965), pp. 71–147.

Edmund Husserl is a philosopher whose work has been involved in the genesis of several philosophical movements—phenomenology, existentialism, and deconstructionism are among the most notable. In fact, many twentieth-century philosophers and theorists have begun their careers with critical or interpretative works on Husserl. Early philosophical works of Theodor W. Adorno, Jacques Derrida, Martin Heidegger, Emmanuel Lévinas, Herbert Marcuse, Maurice Merleau-Ponty, Jean-Paul Sartre, and Edith Stein all deal explicitly or implicitly either with Husserl's method of philosophical description, which he named phenomenology, with his general descriptions of the acts and objects of consciousness, or with his more specific descriptions of internal time-consciousness, perception, and intersubjectivity.

In addition to philosophy, the social sciences have also developed paths of analysis and description that originate to a large extent with Husserl. Alfred Schutz, who develops the anthropological implications of Husserl's notion of the *Lebenswelt* (life-world), the sphere of meaning and objects that predates and makes possible explicit theoretical cognition, and R. D. Laing, who does phenomenological work in the psychology of interpersonal perception and family disorders, are among the most notable. This important scientific outgrowth of Husserl's work is appropriate, since his texts consistently attempt to cast philosophy as a productive, rigorous, and disciplined science—in other words, to show that philosophy is a science that can serve to ground and stimulate the other sciences in the evident foundation, intuition, and interconnection of essences and concepts.

In addition to his impact on twentieth-century philosophy and the social sciences, Husserl maintains an influence, albeit perhaps a limited one, in the humanities, especially in literature and theology. Pieces of phenomenological literary criticism, particularly on modernist authors, continue to appear even into the twenty-first century. This growth happens despite the perception that most recent literary criticism has followed the later theoretical work of Michel Foucault and

Husserl in 1920 (Collection of Anna-Maria Husserl; from Donn Welton,
The Other Husserl: The Horizons of Transcendental
Phenomenology, *2000; Thomas Cooper Library,*
University of South Carolina)

Derrida and their explicit (or attributed) arguments that phenomenology is a totalizing and therefore violent method of description. Similarly, in theology, writers such as Rudolph Otto and Paul Tillich, who carry out a kind of phenomenological description of the holy, remain recognizable figures.

In current philosophical circles, Husserl's work remains compelling for several contemporary Continental and analytic theorists. Analytic philosophers, such as John R. Searle and Hubert Dreyfus, and Continental philosophers, such as Donn Welton and Dan Zahavi, continue to deal with the issues surrounding Husserl's notions of logic, intentionality (or the correlation experienced between consciousness and objects), and intersubjectivity. The largest testament to Husserl's influence is the fact that the volume of secondary literature in philosophy on his work has made it, as J. N. Mohanty asserts in "The Development of Husserl's Thought," an essay included in *The Cambridge Companion to Husserl* (1995), nearly impossible to survey.

There are two main reasons why the Husserlian literature is so massive. First, there is the fact that Husserl wrote so much in his lifetime. The massive, forty-thousand-page *Nachlass* (Legacy) comprising Husserl's letters, lecture notes, versions of manuscripts, and partially completed explorations has been moving through the editorial process and emerging as the *Husserliana* series since 1950. This procedure is complicated by the fact that Husserl wrote his notes and manuscripts in a particular, and particularly abbreviated, Gabelsberg shorthand. Second, the changing themes and contents of Husserl's works (even just the published or translated ones) seem to make a single narrative of his thought and development a difficult undertaking.

Most commentators, including Mohanty and Marianne Sawicki, agree that a discussion of Husserl's work should be divided according to the periods of his academic affiliations: from 1886 to 1900, the period when he was a student and *Privatdozent* (lecturer) at Halle; from 1901 to 1916, when he was a professor at Göttingen; from 1916 to 1928, when he was a professor at Freiburg; and from 1929 to 1938, when he was an emeritus professor, also at Freiburg. The shifts in Husserl's thought between these periods at first appear quite radical. Since his second major published work emerged in 1913, commentators have argued about the significance of his "transcendental turn," that is, how his work went from descriptions of mathematics, logical structures, and logical objects to a description of pure subjectivity, which he called the transcendental ego. Furthermore, commentators have disagreed over whether Husserl's post-1913 concerns with the genetic and historical structures of the social life-world and of one's own bodily perceptions could be reconciled with his claim that phenomenology needs to be done within a kind of methodological thought experiment that he called the *phenomenological reduction,* which attempts to reduce all meanings to the present experience of an absolute consciousness and which appears to limit phenomenology to a static description of the essential elements of that experience. Many philosophers have tried to interpret all of Husserl's work as occurring solely on behalf of one period or another, to argue that he was in fact always transcendental or always empirical, that he is a realist who believes in the existence of objects outside of consciousness or an idealist who reduces all objects to one's consciousness of them.

Instead of attempting to take one side or another, it is preferable to follow the thesis put forward by scholars such as Mohanty, Sawicki, and Welton, that Husserl's work is a careful development and redevelopment of the proper manner of description of both the genesis and ongoing structural life of consciousness and its organized multiplicity of interrelations to its objects.

Husserl himself, in a conversation with phenomenologists Dorion Cairns and Eugen Fink in 1931, describes his project of phenomenology as remaining "a zig-zag," that is, "one starts out, goes a certain distance, then goes back to the beginning, and what one has learned applies to the beginning." Husserl's works support this autobiographical remark in two important ways. First, he never separates the object from consciousness but describes experience as a kind of implication, a zig-zag back and forth from ego to object. Second, his entire career is visible to a large extent within each work since many of his own technical terms and themes run throughout much of his *Nachlass*. For example, central to the description of not only pure logic but also internal time-consciousness, bodily perception, intersubjectivity, and passivity is the description of how consciousness constitutes (that is, responds to and recognizes) identities through the correlation between, on the one hand, its acts of *Deckung* (overlaying) and *Übergang* (transitioning) between one experience and another and, on the other hand, the way in which the *Abschattungen* (profiles) or object-appearances in view correspond to those active motions of consciousness in the sedimentation or the passive *Überschiebung* (overlapping) of one profile onto another.

Even in his final published works, Husserl remains interested in the layers of consciousness and the ways in which any description of the subject or of its objects necessarily involves the recognition that there is not a simple independence of one from the other. In fact, given this penchant for describing consciousness as a unification and interpenetration of layers, the most consistent metaphor applicable to Husserl might be that of a geologist of consciousness. For the phenomenologist, according to Husserl, is a scientist who has the patience to perform the slow reconstruction of processes that map out just how consciousness transcends itself (statically and genetically) toward God, others, and even itself in the working out of the sense of its objects and the manners of their appearance.

Edmund Husserl was born on 8 April 1859, in the town of Prossnitz, Moravia, which is now part of the Czech Republic, to Adolf Abraham Husserl, a milliner, and his wife, Julie (née Selinger). He was the second of four children, with an older brother, Heinrich, and younger sister and brother, Helene and Emil. As Sawicki and others note, the fact that Husserl and his family were Jewish was to become of great importance in the final stages of his career, when German National Socialism made it increasingly difficult for him to function professionally. Husserl's own relation to Judaism, however, is not one of orthodoxy. On the one hand, he married Malvine Steinschneider in 1887, also a Jewish resident of Prossnitz. On the other hand, however, both

he and his wife converted to Protestant Christianity and were baptized before their wedding.

Husserl attended university at Leipzig, Berlin, and Vienna, where he studied mainly mathematics along with some astronomy and philosophy. In Berlin, he was in the tutelage of the mathematician Karl Weierstrass and served as his personal assistant. Husserl received his doctorate in January 1883 after the acceptance of his dissertation, "Beiträge zur Theorie der Variationsrechnung" (Contributions Toward a Theory of Variation Calculus), in October 1882 at the University of Vienna.

After receiving his dissertation and performing military service, Husserl returned to Vienna to study with the philosopher Franz Brentano from 1884 to 1886. Brentano introduced Husserl to the field of empirical psychology and its potential status as a kind of universal science. Brentano also taught Husserl about intentionality, the recognition that the acts or phenomena of one's psyche or mind refer to and contain objects. As scholars, for example Robin Rollinger, point out, Husserl later revised Brentano's conception of intentionality quite significantly, insofar as Husserl finds some cases where a psychical act has and contains no object. Husserl also later disputed Brentano's conception of psychology, since Husserl argued in *Logische Untersuchungen* (1900, 1901; translated as *Logical Investigations,* 1970), contrary to Brentano, that there was a pure logic that did not derive its rules from the particular makeup or functioning of the human psyche. His relations with Brentano and with the circle of students around him, however, most notably Kazimierz Twardowski and Alexius Meinong, remained of continued importance for Husserl, and Husserl's ongoing discussions of the relationship between phenomenology and psychology attest to the careful way in which his early work with Brentano is never simply put behind him.

At the recommendation of Brentano, who was a *privatdozent* at Vienna and so could not direct Husserl's *habilitationsschrift,* Husserl went to study with Carl Stumpf at Halle. While at Halle, Husserl studied mainly formal mathematics and formal logic. In 1887 Husserl finished and printed his *Habilitationsschrift,* titled *Über den Begriff der Zahl: Psychologische Analysen* (translated as "On the Concept of Number: Psychological Analyses," 1972). Also in 1887, Husserl became a *privatdozent* at Halle. In his lectures at Halle, Husserl often taught René Descartes, David Hume, and Immanuel Kant, figures that he continued to emphasize at Göttingen and Freiburg as being of immense importance to the development of phenomenology. In 1891 Husserl published his first manuscript, *Philosophie der Arithmetik: Psychologische und logische Untersuchungen* (Philosophy of Arithmetic: Psychological and Logical Researches). After this

Husserl (left) and his best-known student, Martin Heidegger, in St. Margen, Germany, 1921 (Husserl-Archief te Leuven; from Donn Welton, The Other Husserl: The Horizons of Transcendental Phenomenology, *2000; Thomas Cooper Library, University of South Carolina)*

publication, Husserl's views on Brentano's work and the role of psychology and intentionality changed, perhaps partly because of Gottlob Frege's criticism of the book as arguing for psychologism, the doctrine that philosophical problems and logical laws were reducible to empirical psychological processes and events.

Between 1892 and 1895, Husserl and his wife, Malvine, had three children. Their daughter, Elisabeth, was born on 2 June 1892; their son Gerhart was born on 22 December 1893; and their younger son, Wolfgang, was born on 18 October 1895. Husserl cared a great deal about his children, and when his sons were later sent to perform military service and even to the front in World War I, he went to visit them.

Husserl's first successful philosophical work, *Logische Untersuchungen,* appeared in two volumes in the years 1900 and 1901, with its first volume devoted

largely to arguing first against psychologism and the danger of relativism that psychologism posed and then toward a pure logic, one whose concepts were immediately graspable or "intuitable" as ideal, unchanging, and absolute. The rest of the two volumes is taken up with six investigations into the structural relation of expressions to meaning, the nature of ideal objects, the identification of the part-whole relations, the distinction between independent and dependent meanings, the proper conception of consciousness and its relation to its intentional acts and objects, and the description of knowledge as a kind of synthesis of an act of intending with further intuitive acts of fulfillment. These investigations launched Husserl's career and brought phenomenology to the fore of European philosophy. It was also a problematic work, however. According to Marvin Farber in *The Foundation of Phenomenology: Edmund Husserl and the Quest for a Rigorous Science of Philosophy* (1943), *Logische Untersuchungen* was not read carefully by Husserl's contemporaries, and he labored to revise for many years. The eventual second edition, the final part of which did not appear until 1921, was not complete, nor was it entirely satisfactory to Husserl. He emphasizes much more strongly in the second edition, however, the fact that phenomenology, the new method of philosophy as a rigorous science that he had developed in the years since the first edition, is not merely a kind of descriptive psychology and that it deals with the fact that consciousness intuits essences, general objects, and categorical relations (such as those between different kinds of parts and the wholes) directly, according to a priori laws and relationships. The outcome of *Logische Untersuchungen* is the terminological and thematic basis for the whole of Husserl's phenomenology.

In 1901, having had success with the publication of *Logische Untersuchungen,* Husserl received an appointment to the University at Göttingen, where he remained for approximately sixteen years. At Göttingen, several students who were studying in Munich with Theodor Lipps came to study with Husserl and endeavored to further his phenomenological method. Phenomenology, as Husserl formulated it, is the way "to the things themselves." Phenomenology makes explicit what is already implicit in experience through careful investigations that limit presuppositions and metaphysical excesses. In other words, phenomenology begins with the recognition that all consciousness is consciousness *of* something and then works to uncover the ways in which consciousness is united with (or fulfills its experience of) its objects.

From 1905 to 1913, Husserl was active in teaching and writing. His lectures on time-consciousness in 1904, 1905, and 1910 formed the basis of his *Vorlesungen zur Phänomenologie des inneren Zeitbewusstseins* (translated as *The*

Phenomenology of Internal Time-Consciousness, 1964), but the lectures remained unpublished until Stein and Martin Heidegger edited and published them in 1928 in the *Jahrbuch für Philosophie und phänomenologische Forschung* (Yearbook for Philosophy and Phenomenological Research), a periodical Husserl founded with Heidegger and a few other colleagues in 1912. In 1911 Husserl published "Philosophie als strenge Wissenschaft" (translated as "Philosophy as Rigorous Science" in *Edmund Husserl: Phenomenology and the Crisis of Philosophy,* 1965) in the periodical *Logos,* of which he agreed to be an editor in 1910. In 1913 his next major and immensely successful work, *Ideen zu einer reinen Phänomenologie und phänomenologischen Philosophie* (translated as *Ideas: General Introduction to Pure Phenomenology,* 1931), was published in the first volume of the *Jahrbuch für Philosophie und phänomenologische Forschung.* This work launched phenomenology as a radical and transcendental method, which required "a new style of attitude . . . which is entirely altered in contrast to the natural attitude," as Husserl wrote in his introduction. It is most often called *Ideen I* by scholars, since Husserl planned two other companion volumes to this work, which he did not publish but which were edited and prepared for publication by others.

The second volume, or *Ideen II,* subtitled *Phänomenologische Untersuchungen zu Konstitution* (Studies in the Phenomenology of Constitution; translated in volume two of *Ideas Pertaining to a Pure Phenomenology and to a Phenomenological Philosophy,* 1989), was edited and prepared for more than forty years by his students Stein and Ludwig Landgrebe and finally published in volume four of the *Husserliana* in 1952, even though Husserl had written a good deal of the work by 1913. One of the reasons it was not published earlier is that Husserl appears to have been dissatisfied with it, as Sawicki notes. *Ideen II* describes the structures of the experiences of materiality, animality, and culture. Husserl's description of these experiences and of the way consciousness constitutes or implicates itself with them cause a great deal of controversy among commentators as they try to reconcile them with the discussions in the earlier volume, which is less rooted in the lived body of consciousness.

Published in 1952 as volume five of the *Husserliana,* the third book, or *Ideen III,* subtitled *Die Phänomenologie und die Fundamente der Wissenschaften* (Phenomenology and the Foundations of the Sciences; translated in volume three of *Ideas Pertaining to a Pure Phenomenology and to a Phenomenological Philosophy,* 1980), deals with the relation of phenomenology to ontology. According to commentators such as Welton, the second and third volumes of the *Ideen* suggest that Husserl's concern starts to shift from static phenomenology, which describes a restricted grasp of essential meanings in the narrowness of what he calls the "living present," to genetic phenomenology,

which describes what is involved in the fact that consciousness builds its recognition of objects over time. The shadow of the transcendental phenomenology of the first volume, however, combined with the fact that Husserl does not adequately discuss temporality in any of the volumes, means that his descriptions in the later volumes do not really signify as great a shift in orientation as Husserl's last published work suggests. *Ideen I* remains the touchstone for Husserlian thought from 1912 to 1931.

Within the three volumes (and particularly the first) of *Ideen zu einer reinen Phänomenologie und phänomenologischen Philosophie* Husserl notes that, in order to formulate the new transcendental phenomenology as a science of essences, he needs the notion of the transcendental *epoche,* the bracketing of the belief in and judgment of an experienced object's existence. After this *epoche* is performed, Husserl asserts that what is left is the sense of the object in its manners of appearing, that is, the most original presentation or intuition of the object within the limits of its manner of appearance or givenness. In performing this *epoche,* one does not lose or annihilate objects and the world as experienced in the ordinary, natural attitude, but one gains the potential to discover the structures of consciousness that allows objects to be integrated into experience in just these ways—that is, that allow objects as existents to appear in the first place. One gains these potential discoveries because while one is able to bracket belief in the spatiotemporal actuality of the world, one is not able to bracket those beliefs about consciousness itself. Consciousness has absolute being; the being of the experienced world can be "reduced" after the *epoche* to a *sense,* however, which appears as contingent upon the acts of consciousness. This "transcendental reduction" of being to sense is a process of making explicit the self-evident and eidetic (essential) structures of experience. Particular facts, tables, and chairs, and people perceived as existing here and now, could not appear as such to consciousness without evident, actual processes of the intuition of essences and of the correlation of structures of objectivity and subjectivity to one another. Transcendental phenomenology makes clear those intuitions and those structures.

Transcendental reduction promotes a particular kind of reflection that is not a mere articulation outside of experience of what must be the case in consciousness, however; rather, this transcendental reduction produces self-consciousness of intentional acts and objects in such a way that any structure or relation discovered is also able to be experienced. As a phenomenologist, one "swims along" with oneself in the transcendental reduction and one grasps the a priori structures of consciousness in their activity, in their coming into view and

Jahrbuch für Philosophie und
phänomenologische Forschung

In Gemeinschaft mit

M. GEIGER-Göttingen, M. HEIDEGGER-Marburg,
A. PFÄNDER-München, M. SCHELER-Köln

herausgegeben von

EDMUND HUSSERL

Achter Band

Halle a. d. S.
Max Niemeyer Verlag
1927

Title page for the eighth volume of the annual of which Husserl was one of the cofounders in 1912 (BN/Seuil; from Jean-Pierre Cotten, Heidegger, *1974; Thomas Cooper Library, University of South Carolina)*

passing into concealment or memory—in other words, a transcendental-phenomenological reflection grasps acts of consciousness (and even consciousness as a whole) with all of the limitations imposed on such a reflection by the fact that one grasps them *in act,* that is, in relation to and distinction from other processes that are also coming to notice or becoming concealed.

The internal references of consciousness to itself (and between consciousnesses) are extraordinarily (infinitely) complicated. Therefore, phenomenology is not finished after a few months of work. For although one grasps each act and the unity in outline of consciousness as a whole in absolutely valid givenness, there is always the need for more supplementation—for making more explicit the parts of each act, the relation of each act to other acts, and the relation of each act to the whole. Some of the more important clusters of the self-relations

of subjectivity explored in *Ideen zu einer reinen Phänomenologie und phänomenologischen Philosophie* include the correlation of each conscious act (which Husserl calls *noesis*) to its object in consciousness (which Husserl calls *noema*), the relation of the horizons of sense and activity to their foregrounded objects, and the relation of perception to other modes of intuition such as imagination.

In 1916 Husserl received an appointment (ordinarius professor) at Freiburg. In that same year his son Wolfgang was killed in World War I, at the battle of Verdun. In 1917 Husserl's other son, Gerhart, was wounded in the war and was in the hospital at Speyer. Partially because of his sons' casualties, Husserl published sparingly in the years before 1929. He published some memories on Brentano in a memorial anthology in 1919 and some articles in 1923 and 1924 in a Japanese journal, *Kaizo.* These articles stimulated an interest in phenomenology in Japan, an interest that is still prominent. In 1927 Husserl's gifted student Heidegger published his *Sein und Zeit* (translated as *Being and Time,* 1962), which he officially dedicated to Husserl. Husserl read this work closely, as evidenced from his notes in his copy of *Sein und Zeit,* but he was disappointed by Heidegger's unorthodox phenomenological descriptions. Husserl and Heidegger did work together in 1927 and 1928, however, on the article Husserl published on phenomenology in *Encyclopaedia Britannica.* In 1928, when Husserl became an emeritus professor at Freiburg, Husserl's time-consciousness lectures were finally published with Heidegger's help in volume nine of the *Jahrbuch für Philosophie und phänomenologische Forschung.*

In 1928 Husserl gave a series of lectures in Amsterdam on the relation between transcendental phenomenology and psychology. These lectures, published in *Phänomenologische Psychologie: Vorlesungen Sommersemester 1925* (1962; translated as *Phenomenological Psychology: Lectures, Summer Semester, 1925,* 1977), provide another route into transcendental phenomenology other than the transcendental reduction outlined in *Ideen I.* Also in 1928, Husserl wrote another major work on logic, *Formale und transzendentale Logik: Versuch einer Kritik der logischen Vernunft* (translated as *Formal and Transcendental Logic,* 1969), which he completed in a few months and published in volume ten of the *Jahrbuch für Philosophie und phänomenologische Forschung* in July 1929. Also in 1929 Husserl gave a series of important lectures in Paris, where he met Lévinas. Out of the success of those lectures, Husserl revised his Paris lectures and sent them for publication in French, hoping to publish them in German as well in that same year. The French translation of those lectures, *Méditations cartésiennes: Introduction a la phénoménologie* (published in English as *Cartesian Meditations: An Introduction to Phenomenology,* 1960), was published in 1931 with Lévinas having acted as one of the translators. The German edition of the meditations, *Cartesianische Meditationen und Pariser Vorträge* (1950), published as volume one of *Husserliana,* did not appear in Husserl's lifetime. This fact is probably because, as Ronald Bruzina notes in his introduction to *VI. cartesianische Meditation* (Sixth Cartesian Meditation, 1988), of Husserl's belief that the meditations needed to be revised to confront Heidegger's methodological unorthodoxy. In any case, the *Méditations cartésiennes* show Husserl's continual exploration of some of the themes that others emphasized in order to criticize his method, including the supposed solipsism and ahistorical nature of the transcendental ego.

Of the five meditations, the fifth is the longest and most crucial for understanding the further developments in Husserlian thought. There, Husserl refutes the charge of solipsism by noting that one always already has an immanent experience of the alien other persons and that the immanent experience of alien others makes an absolute existential claim, pushing one's consciousness to transcend its own limits toward (and recognize its unity with) those others who are already implicated in its own perceptions, cognition, and activities. Husserl's response to the supposed problem of solipsism, in other words, is that the problem of producing intersubjectively valid cognitions is not a problem to which transcendental phenomenology is susceptible, since the transcendental ego is, from the beginning, between subjects or intersubjectivity. In a description within the fifth meditation that links the *Méditations cartésiennes* to *Ideen II,* Husserl implies that it is in the fact that consciousness must be a body, and the fact that this body experiences itself caught in a network of other bodies that pair with it and contest it, that the absolute purity of consciousness is produced as a possibility for all.

There has been significant critical debate over whether this description of Husserl's is accurate and whether it is a sufficient response to the charge of solipsism. The predominant thought at one point was that Husserl had failed to show the validity of transcendental intersubjectivity as an inherent structure of consciousness. More-recent Husserlian commentators, however, are beginning to reexamine and defend Husserl's descriptions of other people and transcendental intersubjectivity as themselves valid and as holding valid insights for ethical and epistemological problems. Whatever the critical reception of transcendental intersubjectivity, however, the fact remains that Husserl worked in the 1920s and 1930s on this description of intersubjectivity a great deal, and his notes on this subject compose three large volumes of the *Husserliana* series.

In the years after 1931, even though Husserl had converted to Christianity and even though his son had died at Verdun, his Jewish heritage became an issue for the Nazis as they began to forbid him access to the university and to suppress his writings and influence. Husserl was devastated by these events, and he was depressed even more by Heidegger's increasing participation in the Nazi Party and his refusal to acknowledge Husserl. Husserl published one last work before his death in 1938, however, that directly criticizes the lack of foundation in the sciences in the twentieth century as leading to the potential annihilation of what is most distinctively human. In other words, Husserl once more maintains the possibility of radical, consistent, and productive reflection. This last work, "Die Krisis der europäischen Wissenschaften und die transzentale Phänomenologie: Eine Einleitung in die phänomenologische Philosophie" (translated as *The Crisis of European Sciences and Transcendental Phenomenology: An Introduction to Phenomenological Philosophy,* 1970), is the result of several lectures in 1935 and was published in 1936 in the first issue of a new journal, *Philosophia,* in Belgrade. This work institutes a theme that has not been present in Husserl's work so far—that of the historically layered *Lebenswelt.* In discussing the *Lebenswelt,* Husserl details a third way into transcendental phenomenology from the critique of the way each epoch of science sediments itself into the history of knowledge, a history that is then presupposed without adequate evidence in order to perform further practical work at a fast pace. In clarifying presuppositions, in acknowledging the lack of foundations in the practice of a science, Husserl can move toward the need for transcendental reflection, toward the justification of the transcendental *epoche* and reduction.

When Edmund Husserl died on 27 April 1938, his *Nachlass* had been completely organized by his students Fink and Ludwig Landgrebe; it became an impossibility to secure and publish them in Germany, however. The *Nachlass* was then clandestinely brought to Louvain, Belgium, by a Franciscan priest, H. L. Van Breda, where it has remained in the Husserl Archives.

Husserl's work did not simply remain archived, however. Instead, it motivated the production of an enormous set of works from those he lectured to and taught during his lifetime. His researches had opened a new door to describing experience, to the relevance and task of philosophy. The strength of his presence in his writings and the memory of his rigorous and painstaking researches into consciousness provoked others to come to the archives and research or to comment on what he had already published.

Significantly, many of his students and listeners began by debating Husserl. The clarity and emphasis that he placed on the transcendental ego in particular shook them, and they immediately attempted to redirect his phenomenological method toward notions of existentialism, otherness, and particularity. Essences, on which Husserl focused a great deal of his attention describing, were too close to the notion of essentialism, to notions of totalitarianism that had been imposed during World War II. In the hands of philosophers such as Sartre and Merleau-Ponty, Husserlian descriptions of consciousness had to be adapted to the recognition that meaning was a tense locus of negotiation between oneself and others.

These apparent differences aside, however, there is a notable continuity from Edmund Husserl to someone such as Derrida. For those who practice phenomenology in the shadow of Husserl, to interpret a piece of literature, a person's psyche, or the culture of a country is still to engage not merely in a flight of metaphysical speculation or in a labor of logical deduction. Rather, interpretation requires an *epoche* of presuppositions. Husserl's gift to the social sciences is the recognition that an accurate description of a situation requires that one begin with the terms of that situation itself, from inside it, according to it.

Letters:
Briefwechsel, 10 volumes, edited by K. Schuhmann (The Hague: Kluwer, 1994).

Interviews:
Dorion Cairns, *Conversations with Husserl and Fink* (The Hague: Nijhoff, 1976).

References:
Jean-Pierre Cotten, *Heidegger,* Ecrivains de toujours, no. 95 (Paris: Editions du Seuil, 1974);

Marvin Farber, *The Foundation of Phenomenology: Edmund Husserl and the Quest for a Rigorous Science of Philosophy* (Cambridge, Mass.: Harvard University Press, 1943);

Joseph J. Kockelmans, *Edmund Husserl's Phenomenology* (West Lafayette, Ind.: Purdue University Press, 1994);

Maurice Natanson, *Edmund Husserl: Philosopher of Infinite Tasks* (Evanston, Ill.: Northwestern University Press, 1973);

Robin Rollinger, *Husserl's Position in the School of Brentano* (Dordrecht & Boston: Nijhoff, 1999);

Marianne Sawicki, "Edmund Husserl (1859–1938)," *Internet Encyclopedia of Philosophy* <www.iep.utm.edu/h/husserl.htm> [accessed 19 March 2004];

Barry Smith and David Woodruff Smith, eds., *The Cambridge Companion to Husserl* (Cambridge & New York: Cambridge University Press, 1995);

Donn Welton, *The Other Husserl: The Horizons of Transcendental Phenomenology* (Bloomington: Indiana University Press, 2000).

Papers:

The papers of Edmund Husserl are preserved at the Catholic University of Louvain (Husserl Archives) in Belgium. Copies of these archives are also held currently in the Universities of Köln and Freiburg, in the Ecole Normale Superieure in Paris, and, in the United States, at the New School for Social Research in New York City and at Duquesne University in Pittsburgh.

Carl Gustav Jung

(26 July 1875 – 6 June 1961)

Stacy Mulder
Ball State University

BOOKS: *Zur Psychologie und Pathologie sogenannter occulter Phänome: Eine psychiatrische Studie* (Leipzig: Mutze, 1902);

Über die Psychologie der Dementia praecox (Halle: Marhold, 1907); translated by Frederick W. Peterson and A. A. Brill as *The Psychology of Dementia Praecox* (New York: Journal of Nervous and Mental Disease Publishing, 1909);

Wandlungen und Symbole der Libido: Beiträge zur Entwicklungsgeschichte des Denkens (Leipzig: Deuticke, 1912); translated by Beatrice M. Hinkle as *Psychology of the Unconscious: A Study of the Transformation and Symbolisms of the Libido. A Contribution to the History of the Evaluation of Thought* (New York: Moffat, Yard, 1916; London: Kegan Paul, Trench, Trübner, 1917); revised and expanded as *Symbols of Transformation: An Analysis of the Prelude to a Case of Schizophrenia* (London: Routledge & Kegan Paul, 1951);

Versuch einer Darstellung der psychoanalytischen Theorie (Leipzig: Deuticke, 1913); translated by M. D. Eder, Edith Eder, and Mary Moltzer as *The Theory of Psychoanalysis* (New York: Journal of Nervous and Mental Disease Publishing, 1915);

Collected Papers on Analytical Psychology, edited by Constance E. Long (New York: Moffat, Yard, 1916; London: Ballière, Tindall & Cox, 1916; enlarged, 1917);

VII Sermones ad Mortuos: Die sieben Belehrungen der Tuten (Zurich: Privately printed, 1916); translated by H. G. Baynes as *VII Sermones ad Mortuos: The Seven Sermons to the Dead Written by Basilides in Alexandria, the City Where the East Toucheth the West* (London: Stuart & Watkins, 1967);

Psychologische Typen (Zurich: Rascher, 1921); translated by H. G. Baynes as *Psychological Types, or, The Psychology of Individuation* (New York: Harcourt, Brace / London: Kegan Paul, Trench, Trübner, 1923);

Two Essays on Analytical Psychology, translated by H. G. Baynes and Cary F. Baynes (New York: Dodd, Mead, 1928; London: Ballière, Tindall & Cox, 1928);

From Gerhard Wehr, Carl Gustav Jung: Leben, Werk, Wirkung, *1985; Thomas Cooper Library, University of South Carolina*

Contributions to Analytical Psychology, translated by H. G. Baynes and Cary F. Baynes (New York: Harcourt, Brace / London: Kegan Paul, Trench, Trübner, 1928);

Modern Man in Search of a Soul, translated by W. S. Dell and Cary F. Baynes (New York: Harcourt, Brace / London: Kegan Paul, Trench, Trübner, 1933);

Psychology and Religion (New Haven: Yale University Press / London: Oxford University Press, 1938);

The Integration of the Personality, translated by Stanley M. Dell (New York: Farrar & Rinehart, 1939; London: Kegan Paul, Trench, Trübner, 1940);

Einführung in das Wesen der Mythologie, by Jung and Karl Kerényi (Amsterdam & Leipzig: Akademische Verlagsanstalt Pantheon, 1941); translated by R. F. C. Hull as *Essays on a Science of Mythology: The Myth of the Divine Child and the Mysteries of Eleusis* (New York: Pantheon, 1949); republished as *Introduction to a Science of Mythology: The Myth of the Divine Child and the Mysteries of Eleusis* (London: Routledge & Kegan Paul, 1951);

Psychologie und Alchemie (Zurich: Rascher, 1944); translated by Hull as *Psychology and Alchemy,* in *The Collected Works of C. G. Jung,* volume 12 (New York: Pantheon/Bollingen, 1953; London: Routledge & Kegan Paul, 1954);

Aufsätze zur Zeitgeschichte (Zurich: Rascher, 1946); translated by Elizabeth Welsh, Barbara Hannah, and Mary Briner as *Essays on Contemporary Events* (London: Kegan Paul, Trench, Trübner, 1947);

On the Psychology of the Spirit, translated by Hildegard Nagel (New York: Analytical Psychology Club, 1948);

Über psychische Energetik und das Wesen der Träume (Zurich: Rasher, 1948);

Symbolik des Geistes, by Jung and Riwkah Schärf (Zurich: Rascher, 1948); translated by Nagel and Gladys Phelan as *The Spirit Mercury* (New York: Analytical Psychology Club, 1953);

Antwort auf Hiob (Zurich: Rascher, 1952); translated by Hull as *Answer to Job* (New York: Pantheon, 1954; London: Routledge & Kegan Paul, 1954);

Naturerklärung und Psyche: Synchronizität als ein Prinzip akausaler Zusammenhänge, by Jung and Wolfgang Pauli (Zurich: Rascher, 1952); translated by Hull and Priscilla Silz as *The Interpretation of Nature and the Psyche* (New York: Pantheon, 1955; London: Routledge & Kegan Paul, 1955);

The Collected Works of C. G. Jung, 20 volumes and one supplemental volume, edited by Herbert Read, Michael Fordham, Gerhard Adler, and William McGuire (volumes 1–17, New York: Pantheon/ Bollingen, 1953–1966; London: Routledge & Kegan Paul, 1953–1966; volumes 18–21, Princeton: Princeton University Press, 1966–1983; London: Routledge & Kegan Paul, 1967–1983)— comprises volume 1, *Psychiatric Studies,* translated by Hull (1957); volume 2, *Experimental Researches,* translated by Leopold Stein and Diana Riviere (1973); volume 3, *The Psychogenesis of Mental Disease,* translated by Hull (1960); volume 4, *Freud and Psychoanalysis,* translated by Hull (1961); volume 5, *Symbols of Transformation: An Analysis of the Prelude to a Case of Schizophrenia,* translated by Hull (1956); volume 6, *Psychological Types,* translated by H. G. Baynes and Hull (1971); volume 7, *Two Essays on Analytical Psychology,* translated by Hull (1953); volume 8, *The Structure and Dynamics of the Psyche,* translated by Hull (1960); volume 9, part 1, *The Archetypes and the Collected Unconscious,* translated by Hull (1959); volume 9, part 2, *Aion: Researches into the Phenomenology of the Self,* translated by Hull (1959); volume 10, *Civilization in Transition,* translated by Hull (1964); volume 11, *Psychology and Religion: West and East,* translated by Hull (1958); volume 12, *Psychology and Alchemy,* translated by Hull (1953; revised, 1968); volume 13, *Alchemical Studies,* translated by Hull (1967); volume 14, *Mysterium Coniunctionis: An Inquiry into the Separation and Synthesis of Psychic Opposites in Alchemy,* translated by Hull (1963); volume 15, *The Spirit in Man, Art, and Literature,* translated by Hull (1966); volume 16, *The Practice of Psychotherapy: Essays on the Psychology of the Transference and Other Subjects,* translated by Hull (1954; revised and augmented, 1966); volume 17, *The Development of Personality,* translated by Hull (1954); volume 18, *The Symbolic Life: Miscellaneous Writings,* translated by Hull (1977); volume 19, *General Bibliography,* compiled by Lisa Ress (1979); volume 20, *General Index,* compiled by Barbara Forryan and Janet M. Glover (1979); and volume 21 [supplemental volume A], *The Zofingia Lectures,* translated by Jan van Heurck (1983);

Von den Wurzeln des Bewusstseins. Studien über den Archetypus (Zurich: Rascher, 1954);

Mysterium Coniunctionis (Zurich: Rascher, 1955); translated by Hull, in *The Collected Works of C. G. Jung,* volume 14 (New York: Pantheon / Bollingen, 1963; London: Routledge & Kegan Paul, 1963);

Gegnwart und Zukunft (Zurich: Rascher, 1957); translated by Hull as *The Undiscovered Self* (Boston: Little, Brown, 1957; London: Routledge & Kegan Paul, 1958);

Ein moderner Mythus: Von Dingen, die am Himmel gesehen werden (Zurich: Rascher, 1958); translated by Hull as *Flying Saucers: A Modern Myth of Things Seen in the Skies* (New York: Harcourt, Brace, 1959; London: Routledge & Kegan Paul, 1959);

Erinnerungen, Träume, Gedanken, recorded and edited by Aniela Jaffé (Zurich: Rascher, 1962); translated by Richard Winston and Clara Winston as *Memories, Dreams, Reflections* (New York: Pantheon, 1963;

London: Collins/Routledge & Kegan Paul, 1963; revised edition, New York: Vintage, 1965);

Man and His Symbols, by Jung with Marie-Luise von Franz, Joseph L. Henderson, Jolande Jacobi, and Jaffé (Garden City, N.Y.: Doubleday, 1964; London: Aldus, 1964);

The Visions Seminars: From the Complete Notes of Mary Foote, 2 volumes (Zurich: Spring, 1976);

Dream Analysis: Notes of the Seminar Given in 1928–1930, edited by William McGuire (Princeton: Princeton University Press, 1984; London: Routledge & Kegan Paul, 1984);

Nietzsche's Zarathustra: Notes of the Seminar Given in 1934–1939, 2 volumes, edited by James L. Jarrett (Princeton: Princeton University Press, 1988; London: Routledge, 1989);

Analytical Psychology: Notes of the Seminar Given in 1925 by C. G. Jung, edited by McGuire (Princeton: Princeton University Press, 1989; London: Routledge, 1990);

Seminars, edited by Jarrett (Princeton: Princeton University Press, 1998);

Die Psychologie des Kundalini-Yoga: Nach Aufzeichnungen des Seminars 1932, edited by Sonu Shamdasani (Zurich & Dusseldorf: Walter, 1998).

Collection: *Psychologische Betrachtungen: Eine Auslese aus den Schriften von C. G. Jung,* selected and edited by Jolande Jacobi (Zurich: Rascher, 1945); translated by R. F. C. Hull as *Psychological Reflections: An Anthology of the Writings of C. G. Jung* (New York: Pantheon, 1953; London: Routledge & Kegan Paul, 1953; revised and enlarged edition, Princeton: Princeton University Press, 1970).

Editions in English: *Psyche and Symbol: A Selection from the Writings of C. G. Jung,* translated by Cary F. Baynes and R. F. C. Hull, edited by Violet Staub de Laszlo (Garden City, N.Y.: Doubleday, 1958);

The Basic Writings of C. G. Jung, edited by de Laszlo (New York: Modern Library, 1959);

Analytical Psychology: Its Theory and Practice (New York: Pantheon, 1968; London: Routledge & Kegan Paul, 1968);

The Portable Jung, translated by Hull, edited by Joseph Campbell (New York: Viking, 1971);

The Essential Jung, selected, with an introduction, by Anthony Storr (Princeton: Princeton University Press, 1983); republished as *Jung: Selected Writings* (London: Fontana Pocket Readers/Collins, 1983); revised as *The Essential Jung: Selected Writings* (Princeton & Chichester: Princeton University Press, 1999).

OTHER: *Diagnostische Assoziationsstudien: Beiträge zur experimentellen Psychopathologie,* edited by Jung (Leipzig: Barth, 1906); translated by M. D. Eder as *Studies in Word-Association: Experiments in the Diagnosis of Psychopathological Conditions Carried Out at the Psychiatric Clinic of the University of Zurich, under the Direction of C. G. Jung* (London: Heinemann, 1918; New York: Moffat, Yard, 1919);

Tung-pin Lü, *Das Geheimnis der goldenen Blüte,* translated by Richard Wilhelm, commentary by Jung (Munich: Dorn, 1929); translated by Cary F. Baynes as *The Secret of the Golden Flower: A Chinese Book of Life* (New York: Harcourt, Brace / London: Kegan Paul, Trench, Trübner, 1931).

SELECTED PERIODICAL PUBLICATIONS–
UNCOLLECTED: "On the Psychogenesis of Schizophrenia," *Journal of Mental Science,* 85 (1939): 999–1011;

"Letters to a Friend: Part I," *Psychological Perspectives,* 3 (Spring 1972): 9–18;

"Letters to a Friend: Part II," *Psychological Perspectives,* 3 (Fall 1972): 167–178;

"To Oskar Schmitz (1921–1931)," *Psychological Perspectives,* 6 (Spring 1975): 79–95.

In Küsnacht, Zurich, carved in stone above the entrance to 228 Seestrasse, is a Latin phrase that Erasmus borrowed from the Greeks. The inscription reads, "Vocatus atque non vocatus Deus aderit" (Bidden or not bidden, God is present). These are the words that the Swiss psychiatrist Carl Jung himself selected not only as a greeting to those who entered his home but as a standard for his life and work as well.

Though Jung never attempted to formulate a closed system of thought or to posit any all-inclusive cultural theory, his work has nevertheless been widely influential in the philosophical and cultural disciplines, as well as in his chosen field of psychology. In his work, frequently published first in German and later appearing in translated collections, Jung strove always to relate the individual to the larger society and culture, continually bringing to bear his considerable knowledge of anthropology, mythology, and comparative religion upon a wide range of issues and always remaining open to revision of his own conjectures. As a consequence, a great deal of Jungian thought and a sizable Jungian "vocabulary" now inhabit the lexicon of the average educated individual; terms and concepts such as *archetype, extravert* and *introvert, individuation, personality typology,* and *shadow* hold meaning far beyond the scope of psychology and psychiatry. Jung's ability to forge links among various schools of thought and disciplines iden-

Jung's parents, Johann Paul Achilles and Emilie Jung, née Preiswerk, 1876 (from Wayne Gilbert Rollins,
Jung and the Bible, *1983; Thomas Cooper Library, University of South Carolina)*

tifies him not simply as a well-known psychiatrist but also as a cultural theorist.

Carl Gustav Jung was born 26 July 1875 in Kesswil, Switzerland, in the Canton Thurgau on Lake Constance. He was named after his paternal grandfather, who had moved from Germany in 1822 to serve as a professor of surgery at the University of Basel. Jung's father, Johann Paul Achilles Jung, was a pastor who eventually saw himself as a failure. His mother, née Emilie Preiswerk, was herself a minister's daughter and came from a family long established in Basel.

The financially insecure family moved to Laufen near the Falls of the Rhine when Carl was just six months old. By 1879 the family had relocated again, this time to the small hamlet of Klein-Hüningen near

Basel. In 1884 the Jungs had another child—Carl's sister, Gertrud. Throughout these early years the young Carl often remained at home, suffering from delicate health and ailments that included croup and eczema. Frequently indoors, Jung learned Latin from his father and listened to tales of faraway places read to him by his mother from illustrated children's books. His public primary schooling earned him some notoriety as "the minister's son."

In 1885, when he was ten years old, Carl transferred to the Gymnasium at Basel. Here, among relatively well-to-do classmates, Jung found himself disliked by teachers and students alike; his status as a humble pastor's son won him no favors in this new educational arena. Consequently, Jung had virtually no close friends, learning to entertain himself through solitary activities such as drawing or building towers from wooden blocks. Both of these activities served him well in later life and studies.

At one point it appeared that Jung might never complete his education at all. During his early years of puberty he began experiencing fainting spells that were ostensibly caused by a blow to the head suffered during a fall. Unable to attend school because of the fainting spells, he spent long periods of time at home before recognizing that his lapses in consciousness were more likely related to his fear of school than to physical trauma; he noted that the fainting fits occurred mainly when he tried to read. Refusing to succumb to something over which he felt he had no control, Jung forced himself to read even when doing so brought on faint after faint; in time the spells subsided altogether, and Jung returned to school.

As he neared the end of his high-school years, Jung faced the task of selecting a profession. Certain he did not want to follow his father into the ministry, he considered a variety of fields, including archaeology, history, and philosophy. Finally, however, he entered the natural-sciences program at the University of Basel, and in the spring of 1895 he registered as a medical student. His entry into medical school was followed a year later in 1896 by the death of his father.

During Jung's medical-school years one of his relatives—a teenage girl named Helene Preiswerk—began to exhibit skills as a medium. Fascinated by the mysticism, Jung began to attend her séances, maintaining an involvement with those gatherings for some two years. He abandoned the séances when Helene, feeling that her abilities were diminishing, began to use tricks. Jung did not, however, abandon his interest in parapsychology.

As a medical-school graduate, Jung began his internship in December 1900. He took the post of first assistant physician at the Burghölzli Psychiatric Clinic in Zurich, working under the supervision of Eugen Bleuler. Jung's colleagues at the clinic considered him somewhat standoffish and at times even arrogant; yet, in general, they felt Jung was energetic and full of interesting ideas, not the least of which surfaced with publication of his doctoral dissertation in 1902. *Zur Psychologie und Pathologie sogenannter occulter Phänomene* (On the Psychology and Pathology of So-Called Occult Phenomena) presents a case study of Jung's experiences with Helene Preiswerk, combining his own analyses of her séance activity with reviews of other studies that also deal with altered states of consciousness. Significant here is that several major motifs of Jung's lifework appear already in his first publication; topics such as the protective nature of certain psychic disturbances and the existence of a structuring essence within the human

psyche are more fully elaborated in Jung's later years. Also significant is the fact that because parapsychology was an acceptable area for scientific study at the turn of the twentieth century, Jung's efforts established him as a pioneer in the field.

In addition to his clinical duties Jung began to study theoretical psychopathology with Pierre Janet. In 1903 he worked with Franz Riklin to establish a laboratory for experimental psychology at the Burghölzli Psychiatric Clinic. Also in that year, at the age of twenty-seven, Jung married Emma Rauschenbach, whose friends immediately noted Jung's sensitivity and referred to him as "the prince on the pea." Rauschenbach, at twenty, was the child of a well-to-do manufacturer: the older of two daughters and heir to the family fortune. She and Jung seldom experienced financial difficulties through the years as they raised their five children: four daughters and one son.

At Burghölzli, Riklin and Jung collaborated on a series of word-association tests and investigations. The fruit of their combined labors was published in 1904 in a German psychological journal; two years later the original piece co-authored by Riklin, plus three additional studies by Jung alone, appeared in book form. This text—*Diagnostische Assoziationsstudien: Beiträge zur experimentellen Psychopathologie* (translated as *Studies in Word-Association: Experiments in the Diagnosis of Psychopathological Conditions Carried Out at the Psychiatric Clinic of the University of Zurich, under the Direction of C. G. Jung*, 1918)—helped establish Jung as one of the principals in modern lie detection. Jung's word-association studies describe how individuals react in relatively predictable ways to hearing certain words from "association lists." An abnormal or disturbed reaction to a word generally indicates a negative feeling associated with a specific word or series of words. These feelings tend to cluster around what Jung calls "complexes" and may indicate either the presence of unconscious, suppressed memories or consciously kept secrets. These early investigations in word association not only contributed to the science of criminology but also helped establish Jung's name in American academic circles.

In 1905 Jung assumed added responsibilities. He became the senior physician at the Burghölzli Psychiatric Clinic, and he also was appointed to the post of lecturer in psychiatry at the University of Zurich. In this professional post Jung lectured in both psychotherapy and psychiatry. One notable lecture involved a demonstration that took an unexpected turn. A woman paralyzed in her left leg for seventeen years was invited to Jung's lecture room. After listening to the woman expound upon her story at length, Jung announced to his students that he would hypnotize the woman. Falling immediately into a trance-like state with no hypno-

Jung, age six (Collection of Franz Jung, Kusnacht-Zurich; from Gerhard Wehr, C. G. Jung in Selbstzeugnissen und Bilddokumenten, *1969; Thomas Cooper Library, University of South Carolina)*

sis at all, the woman began to relate a seemingly endless series of dreams. When Jung was finally able to bring the woman out of her trance, she exclaimed that she was cured and promptly proceeded to walk without difficulty. Jung had no idea at that time about exactly what had effected the woman's cure; yet, his fame as a miracle worker immediately began to grow, for the woman repeated the story of her cure to all who would listen.

For several years Jung had been familiar with Sigmund Freud's *Die Traumdeutung* (The Interpretation of Dreams, 1900). Though Jung could not quite accept Freud's argument that repressed memories habitually indicate some sort of sexual affection or disaster, he nevertheless admired Freud well enough to send the Viennese doctor a copy of *Diagnostische Assoziationsstudien.* Freud responded with a brief note of acknowledgment and in March 1907 invited Jung to Vienna. This visit initiated several years of what was mostly an epistolary relationship; outside of trips taken together, face-to-face

talks between the two physicians were actually few. Their first meeting in Vienna resulted in a marathon; the two men began their conversation at one o'clock in the afternoon and concluded some thirteen hours later.

In 1907 Jung sent a copy of his newly published *Über die Psychologie der Dementia praecox* (translated as *The Psychology of Dementia Praecox,* 1909) to Freud. This work begins by reviewing the varying current contemporary views concerning dementia and includes the thoughts of Freud on the subject. The piece also discusses the concept of the "feeling-toned complex," described as a constellation of ideas that surrounds and is associated with a specific feeling. Jung posits that such complexes may be repressed or hidden within the individual unconscious and that such complexes may be touched, tapped, or drawn into the consciousness through means such as word-association tests or dream analysis. Jung also offers a case study as a model of dementia.

After sending Freud a copy of his latest work, Jung was again invited to Vienna, this time taking his wife, Emma, with him. During this second visit, Jung discovered that Freud, while seemingly embarrassed to be seen often in the company of his "elderly" wife, who knew virtually nothing about her husband's work, was rather intimately involved with his sister-in-law, Minna Bernays, a younger woman whose knowledge of Freud's work was considerable and who herself revealed the existence of the relationship to Jung, unbeknownst to Freud. Through succeeding years, Jung found this secret of Freud's to be both a matter of disappointment and a stumbling block to complete honesty in the friendship of the two men.

The First International Congress of Psychoanalysis was held in Vienna in 1908; Jung attended. In 1909 he again visited Freud, who now saw Jung as a protégé and imminent successor. Freud and Jung traveled to the United States together in the fall of that year to receive honorary doctorates from Clark University. They spent a great deal of time analyzing each other's dreams, an activity that Jung found less than edifying because Freud balked at too much self-revelation, fearing his status and authority might be called into question.

Also during this year Jung resigned his position at the Burghölzli Psychiatric Clinic. His private practice had grown to the extent that Jung felt he could no longer do justice to both his private patients and those at the clinic. Additionally, Jung had begun to view Burghölzli as a "secular cloister" that involved an "unending desert of routine, according to Paul Stern in *C. G. Jung: The Haunted Prophet* (1976)." This desert of routine included the clinic patients whose ailments and attitudes were at variance with Jung's private clientele, often referred to as "Jung-Frauen"; the name derives from the fact that most of his patients were female.

Among those female patients who flocked to consult with Jung in ever growing numbers was Toni Wolff. At her mother's insistence, Wolff began speaking with Jung shortly after the death of her father in 1909. Wolff was twenty-one years old, and Jung was thirty-four; the extreme shyness about which Wolff first consulted Jung faded rapidly during their relationship. Indeed, what began in 1909 was more or less a love triangle among Jung, Emma Jung, and Wolff—a triangle that Emma accepted to the extent that she tolerated Jung bringing Wolff to their home regularly for Sunday dinners. The triangular relationship continued for decades, and Wolff eventually published papers dealing with Jungian psychology.

The Second International Congress of Psychoanalysis was held in Nuremberg in 1910. Freud, still convinced that Jung was to be the heir apparent of the Freudian school, lobbied for Jung's permanent presidency of the organization. Freud's politics carried the day, and Jung received the appointment, adding this new responsibility to private practice and investigations that resulted in a series of nine lectures given as an extension course at Fordham University in New York City in September 1912. These lectures, published first in German as *Versuch einer Darstellung der psychoanalytischen Theorie* (1913), then in English in 1915 as *The Theory of Psychoanalysis,* combine Jung's own clinical experiences with current psychoanalytic theories. Among the topics Jung discusses in these lectures—and in those discussions his propositions are occasionally quite at variance with Freud's ideas on the same subjects—are childhood neuroses and their possible causes, the Oedipus complex, and infantile sexuality.

By 1912 Jung had been busy with an in-depth study of mythology for three years. Having noted since childhood an uncanny resemblance among fairy tales worldwide, Jung became convinced that cultural mythologies express certain symbolic values that tend toward universality. The result of Jung's years of myth study was *Wandlungen und Symbole der Libido: Beiträge zur Entwicklungsgeschichte des Denkens* (1912; translated as *Psychology of the Unconscious: A Study of the Transformation and Symbolisms of the Libido. A Contribution to the History of the Evaluation of Thought,* 1916), and though Jung himself faults his own knowledge of Freud's sexual secrets and Freud's inability to relinquish an authoritarian status for the eventual break between the two psychiatrists, *Wandlungen und Symbole der Libido* represents a Jungian philosophy quite divergent from that of Freud and contributed in no small fashion to the two men's discord.

In *Wandlungen und Symbole der Libido,* Jung describes the concept of the symbol as expressing a partially conscious state of the human psyche. Those aspects of the psyche that evade full explanation or analysis often find expression through symbols. Art, therefore, can define a concrete representation of ideas and emotions perhaps only partially recognized by the artist in a conscious condition; art becomes a self-expressive, self-examining, and prophetic activity. Jung thus redeems art from the subservient position it holds in Freudian thought. To Freud, artworks, religion, and dreams are all nothing more than by-products of the angry, irrational, primordial id, one of three divisions into which Freud divides the human psyche. To Freud, the production of art is frequently a neurotic activity; for Jung, art is a gateway to the self.

Wandlungen und Symbole der Libido serves as a milestone in Jung's career. First, the work incorporates Jung's studies in mythology with his clinical work in schizophrenia, explaining the connections between the "stuff of myth" and the mysteries of the mind. Second, within this work Jung provides a firm foundation for a more broadly based psychology than that of Freud, thus offering the psychiatric community a new set of avenues for client treatment and diagnosis. Finally, *Wandlungen und Symbole der Libido* marks the climactic end of the Freud-Jung relationship, transforming Jung's view and methodology from a personal approach toward patient complaints into a more culturally oriented perspective. This larger perspective characterizes Jungian thought from this point onward.

By 1913 the break between Jung and Freud was complete. Jung abandoned the Freudian term *psychoanalysis,* referring to his own methods as "analytic psychology" (later "complex psychology"). Resigning his post at the University of Zurich, he became more and more interested in the imagery produced by the unconscious mind. During the fall months of 1913 Jung was deeply impressed by a series of personal visions. Within these visions he saw images of Europe submerged in blood; he felt certain that impending disaster lay in store for Europe, and World War I erupted not long thereafter.

In attempting to understand his own visions, Jung began to study the spiritual history of Europe. As he studied he began to make personal use of his long-standing reverence for art. Having delighted since childhood in drawing and building, Jung began to produce his own versions of oriental mandalas, or magic meditation circles. Certain that his premonitory visions had foreseen the outbreak of World War I, Jung became more than ever convinced that Freud had erred greatly in assigning sexual foundations as the cause of most psychological aberrations. He therefore resigned the presidency of the International Congress of Psychoanalysis, temporarily alienating most of the psychoanalytic community in Europe.

Alienation did not, however, last long or extend far. In fact, in 1916 Jung's influence took a new turn at

Toni Wolff, who first met Jung as his patient in 1909. She soon became his lover and later published papers on his theories (photograph by Erica Anderson; from C. G. Jung: Letters, *volume 2, edited by Gerhard Adler and Aniela Jaffé, translated by R. F. C. Hull and Jane A. Pratt, 1975; Thomas Cooper Library, University of South Carolina).*

the hands of Edith Rockefeller McCormick, whose husband, Harold, had consulted with Jung in 1908–1909. Impressed with Jung's methods and personality, Edith McCormick helped found the Psychological Club on 26 February 1916. The club, dedicated to Jungian analysts and their patients both past and present, proved a fertile ground for growth in Jungian concepts and helped extend Jung's popularity in the United States even further thanks to the American founders of the club. Emma Jung served as the first president of the club. (When she resigned, she was succeeded by Wolff.)

The first of many collections of Jung's writings and papers appeared in 1916 as *Collected Papers on Analytical Psychology;* the prefaces were probably written in German and then translated into English by Constance Long. These papers, written between 1907 and 1915, address a fairly wide range of topics and reflect Jung's developing psychological perspective. The earliest piece, "The Association Method" (1907), first published in the *American Journal of Psychology* (1910), illustrates the actual word-association test, in which test subjects respond to a list of one hundred stimulus words, which

Jung includes in the paper. Jung describes the four types of associative responses commonly elicited and relates how the method was used in determining a true guilty party from among three suspects in a theft case.

In "Die Bedeutung des Vaters für das Schicksal des Einzelnen" (The Significance of the Father in the Destiny of the Individual), which was first published in *Jahrbuch für psychoanalytische und psychopathologische* (1909), Jung presents four different case histories dealing with children or with the childhood years of adult clients. He explores the effects of the "imago" of the father upon these children, emphasizing that the father figure is a representation of an archetype–a "pre-existent instinctual model," or behavior pattern. The development of a child's psyche is shown to be strongly affected by the influence of the parents and by parental behavior. Further, the child's psychic progress may also be helped or hindered according to the degree of progress achieved by the parental figures.

The essay "Ein Beitrag zur Psychologie des Gerüchtes" (A Contribution to the Psychology of Rumour), first published in *Zentralblatt für Psychoanalyse*

(1910–1911) discusses an instance in which a thirteen-year-old girl suffered expulsion from school as punishment for having circulated a false story about a teacher at the school. The entire episode seems to have derived from a combination of honest misunderstandings and deliberate misstatement, for the young girl's troubles stem from other students and their reports of her dreams. Elaborated upon and in some cases grossly misreported, the dreams involve scenarios such as donning swimsuits in the same dressing room with young boys, going swimming with the teacher, taking part in a wedding, riding on a steamer, and spending the night in a barn. Classmate elaborations upon these dreams describe the girl riding upon her teacher's back while in the water and speak of the participation of two heavyset men in the swimming. Jung's commentary upon these dream sequences explains how the young girl, originally fond of the teacher but extremely upset when that teacher assigned her a poor score, experienced dreams that at first seemed to be expressions of her repressed sexual urges concerning the teacher in an effort to balance the upset she felt over her bad report. The subsequent telling of the dreams to classmates served as a form of payback, as it were, to the teacher.

"The Significance of Number Dreams" (1911) posits that the appearance of numbers or number sequences in dreams often carries an unconscious, universal symbolism and does not necessarily reflect a particular subjective meaning on the part of the dreamer. "On the Importance of the Unconscious in Psychopathology" (1914) describes the compensatory function of the unconscious in relation to the conscious of the normal individual, explaining that dreams are one method used by the unconscious to provide psychic balance.

A final notable essay from this collection is "The Psychology of Dreams." This piece, published for the first time with these collected papers, derives from an undated Jungian manuscript. This brief but powerfully written essay offers much that is considered foundational in Jungian psychological thought. Herein, Jung defines dreams as involuntarily appearing fragments of the psyche, stemming from the unconscious even as they refer to a specific situation from the conscious mind. In eliciting those unconscious roots, dreamers and analysts should make every effort to draw everything out from each dream scenario, establishing as many personal meanings and connections as possible. Dream analysis of this nature tends to become a valuable tool in the diagnosis and treatment of various neuroses; as neuroses often arise as a result of some sort of psychic imbalance, and as one of the many functions of dreams is, according to Jung, that of compensation and an effort to regain psychic equilibrium, then analysis of

a neurotic client's dream life can often uncover the unconscious roots of the presenting neurosis.

Jung also expresses his opinion that dreams serve an important function as aids to the individuation process—the uncovering of the "potential wholeness" of the individual. Some dreams—though not all, Jung is careful to warn—emerge from the collective unconscious. Often these "big" dreams include representations of archetypes or mythological symbols that are recognizable patterns for the human species and that can serve as guides in developing human individuality. Further, Jung describes the dramatic nature of dreams—the active, theatrical aspects of dreaming that often place the dreamer in the position of both participant and audience.

The next year Jung published in German an important work, *Die Psychologie der unbewussten Prozesse* (1917), which was translated by Dora Hecht as *The Psychology of the Unconscious Processes* in the enlarged edition of *Collected Papers on Analytical Psychology* (1917). Several classically "Jungian" concepts are presented in this essay, not the least of which centers around his disagreement with Freud about the nature and contents of the human unconscious. According to Jung, Freud says that the unconscious is full of content that has been repressed; the unconscious exists because content is repressed. Jung, however, notes that there are many occasions when content that has never been repressed at all still comes forth from the individual unconscious. Psychic content simply is, he argues, and it always has been. The unconscious, therefore, has an autonomy that a Freudian view fails to recognize.

There are three other important topics discussed in this piece: neuroses, the collective unconscious, and individualism. In Jung's view a neurosis—a relatively mild psychic disorder—may often exist as an adaptive measure in the human psyche. In other words, Jung posits that unlike the dysfunctional aspect always attributed to a neurosis by psychiatrists such as Freud and Alfred Adler, an adjustive or corrective function may well be the cause of many neuroses. Quite often these types of neuroses are resolved spontaneously, without severe trauma to the individual and without any type of clinical intervention.

Jung next introduces the concept of the collective unconscious. He sees this part of the human psyche as a transpersonal unconscious: a psychic element shared by humanity simply because they are human. Certain DNA structures and genetic combinations automatically "code" for the species *Homo sapiens;* to Jung, there exists a *Homo sapiens* code for the psyche as well. Certain instincts, memories, survival methods, images, tendencies exist in a sort of psychic "stream," equally accessible by everyone and always present.

Jung with his wife, Emma, and their children Franz, Agathe, Marianne, and Gret, 1917 (from Gerhard Wehr, Carl Gustav Jung: Leben, Werk, Wirkung, *1985; Thomas Cooper Library, University of South Carolina)*

Finally, Jung speaks of the process of individuation. Quite often the struggles involved with individuation are evident in dreams. Dream analysis, therefore, becomes an important part of monitoring, and in some ways directing, the individuation process.

In the period immediately following the close of World War I, Jung revised some of his earlier papers and continued to elaborate upon some of his key concepts. In 1920 he visited Algiers and Tunis. He was immediately struck with the perspective on life generated in a society that functioned more or less "outside of time"—without watches or clocks. In his next German publication, "Die psychologischen Grundlagen des Geisterglaubens" (1920; translated as "The Psychological Foundation of Belief in Spirits, 1960). Jung drew upon his experiences among these timeless peoples. He writes that despite humanity's history of belief in the existence of a spirit world, contemporary thought is firmly bastioned in reason and denies the possibility of

an "other" world. Jung expanded on this topic in later texts.

Jung analyzes how visions, disturbances in the psyche, and dreams are related to "autonomous complexes," or projections of the unconscious that have no consistent relationship to the conscious ego. To Jung, the human soul corresponds to projected complexes from the personal unconscious, while spirit manifestations represent projections of the collective unconscious. Jung also touches upon the concept of the archetype as analogous to a crystal lattice emanating from the unconscious.

Some of the terms most widely associated with Jungian thought appear in his 1921 volume *Psychologische Typen* (translated as *Psychological Types, or, The Psychology of Individuation,* 1923); in fact, the last 240 pages of the book comprise a detailed glossary of Jungian terms. Heavily footnoted and referenced, this work first offers some 470 pages of chronologically organized philosophical commentary that ranges in subject matter from the ancient Orient through the Middle Ages and Enlightenment. Jung includes discussions of Gnosticism, Johann Wolfgang von Goethe, Arthur Schopenhauer, and Friedrich Nietzsche. Recognizing the important role of fantasy in fashioning creative art, Jung applauds Goethe and expresses a strong affinity with William James, who along with Jung also displayed a strong curiosity about parapsychology. *Psychologische Typen* includes Jung's exposition of introversion and extraversion, as well as descriptions of psychological functions and the interrelation of all of these personality aspects with the individuation process.

The extravert, according to Jung, exhibits empathy. Stimulated by the external, extraverts tend to be motivated by the objective, seeking fulfillment in the company of others and preferring to make decisions through actively working out the problem at hand. Conversely, the introverted personality feels more comfortable in controlling the object, emphasizing the importance of abstraction and finding excessive external stimulation to be annoying. Introverts, then, often prefer working through problems alone, volunteering suggestions and solutions only after deliberating carefully about all possible alternatives.

People generally tend to favor either the extroverted or introverted attitude, and their methods of approaching life can then be further described according to four psychological functions: sensation, thinking, feeling, and intuition. The sensing function involves a somewhat irrational registering of facts based upon sensory observances. The thinking function seeks to work logically and prizes order. Establishing values according to hierarchical ranking is characteristic of the feeling function, and the intuitive function is concerned with a more unconscious, visceral response to issues and an interest in the future possibilities or consequences of any given action. Later adaptations of Jung's personality type concepts, such as the formulation of the Myers-Briggs Personality Inventory, add two additional methods for approaching life: perception and judgment.

In 1922 Jung purchased a tract of land on upper Lake Zurich at Bollingen. Following the death of his mother the next year, he began a long and unhurried construction project on his estate. Through the ensuing years he built, largely by hand, a stone castle and tower. Equipped with neither electricity nor telephone, the Bollingen residence altered in shape according to Jung's personal whims and moments of enlightenment or revelation, serving as his retreat and eventual retirement haven.

Over the next several years Jung continued the type of travels that had so inspired his work of 1920–1921. Visiting the Taos Pueblo in New Mexico in 1924,

he was fascinated by the Native American philosophy and religion that saw divinity in the mountains, sun, and water. In 1926 he traveled to Kenya and made a trip down the Nile to Egypt. To Jung this excursion represented the "drama of the birth of light," according to Joseph Campbell in *The Portable Jung*. Jung was deeply moved by the fundamental and, he felt, archetypal primitivism in which Africa was immersed; his African journeys impressed him with a sense of having discovered something of an omphalos or spiritual source for the human psyche, as well as an underlying mechanism of psyche balance. Jung's later collaboration with Richard Wilhelm on *Das Geheimnis der goldenen Blüte* (1929; translated as *The Secret of the Golden Flower: A Chinese Book of Life*, 1931) incorporates many of those impressions.

Another collection of Jung's papers appeared in 1928 as *Contributions to Analytical Psychology*. This compilation includes works written between 1919 and 1928, as well as older, undated manuscripts. One of these earlier works, "Seele und Erde" (Mind and Earth) originally published as part of the essay "Die Erdbedingtheit der Psyche" in *Mensch und Erde: Darstadt* (1927), describes the human psyche as an adaptive mechanism governed by the events encountered in day-to-day existence. Archetypes that express ancestral memories are viewed as inherited constellations, connecting the individual psyche with Gaia as earth. The text also discusses the differing views held by Jung and Freud concerning the origins of child neuroses.

One of the undated German manuscripts of this collection is "Analytische Psychologie und Weltanschauung" (Analytic Psychology and *Weltanschauung*), which was published in *Seelenprobleme der Gegenwart* (1931). In this piece Jung argues that one's general view of or attitude toward the world is highly important in the development and assessment of the individual personality. New ideas, new philosophies, and new scientific inroads all have a potential effect upon how one views the world; consequently, all of these new ideas also impact the growing personality and psyche. Generally, Jung posits that the current worldview is one of materialism, a stance that he sees as ineffectual in striking chords deep within the collective unconscious that is replete with archetypes. Through the processes of analytical psychology, humanity can learn to tap into deeply buried imagery, symbolism, and fantasy, enabling a better view of the unconscious and thereby promoting better progress toward individuation. One's ultimate goal is a reconciliation of the current human world experience with all that is ancestral and primordial in humanity's past. To Jung, uncovering the archetypal imagery of the unconscious segment of the human psyche provides liberation from what can be an exceedingly restrictive worldview based upon materialism.

Edith Rockefeller McCormick in 1917. The previous year she had co-founded the Analytical Psychological Club, dedicated to the study and dissemination of Jungian concepts (McCormick–International Harvester Collection, State Historical Society of Wisconsin; from Richard Noll, The Aryan Christ: The Secret Life of Carl Jung, *1997; Thomas Cooper Library, University of South Carolina).*

In "Instinct and the Unconscious," written in 1919, Jung presents definitions of the terms *instinct* and *unconscious*. He also differentiates between the two, offering a variety of historically based opinions about the nature of the human instinct, or indeed, the questionable existence of that instinct as compared to what is commonly accepted as instinctual behavior among the lower animal species. For Jung, instinct involves unconscious processes that are repetitive, more or less uncontrollable, and genetically based in nature. They are action modes that may or may not be associated with conscious motivation. The unconscious, on the other hand, represents the gestalt of psychic phenomena that are not seen as conscious elements. Within this category of the unconscious Jung places the archetypes, deeming them to be modes of perception with a mythological base that may or may not be recognized as such. Ultimately, Jung admits the virtual impossibility of concluding, in all cases, which comes first: the human impulse toward action or the perception and under-

standing of a given situation that prompts or requires an appropriate reaction.

Jung discusses the relationship of art to psychology in "On the Relation of Analytical Psychology to Poetry" (1923). Rather than attempt some universal definition of art, this essay describes the symbolic and emotional aspects of art and of artistic drives. While Jung admits the accuracy of some of Freud's thoughts on the relationship of art and psychology—namely, that the personal life of a poet tends to have a definite influence upon that poet's creative efforts—Jung disagrees here with Freud's assumption that an artist's work can be wholly understood or explained in the light of the artist's personal life experiences. Two types of art are posited. Extraverted art, in which an artist wholly identifies with his or her creation, seems to deindividualize the artist as he becomes almost a part of the supplies needed for the creation of the artwork. In introverted art, the artist projects his conscious goals into the created piece, remaining separate from the work and supposedly more in control of the medium.

"Spirit and Life," written in 1926, derives from a lecture Jung delivered in Augsburg. The piece offers debate upon the somewhat ambiguous nature of "spirit" and its relation to the mind. According to Jung, humanity strives for a balance between the mind and the spirit as each aspect gives life and expression to the other.

One of the latest of the Jungian papers collected in *Contributions to Analytical Psychology,* "Women in Europe," was written in 1927. Here Jung describes contemporary women as participating in a transition that was particularly pronounced in post–World War I women of Europe. Increased numbers of women were entering into fields that had historically been considered to be purely male arenas. The institution of marriage was weakening, in part due to women's demands for freedom. Jung adds that while Eros, as psychic relatedness, and Logos, as objective interest, characterize the female and male psyches respectively, each gendered psyche inherently possesses aspects of the other.

Along with the volume *Contributions to Analytical Psychology,* in 1928 Jung also published *Two Essays on Analytical Psychology.* Of primary importance in this work is the essay "The Relations between the Ego and the Unconscious." Here Jung explains his division of the human psyche into four "processes." First is the ego, which Jung sees as the center of consciousness. The ego comprises the "empirical personality"; yet, it is not the ultimate controller of the psyche. This task Jung delegates to the "Self," which surrounds the ego and from which the ego itself evolves.

Next, Jung discusses the personal unconscious, which contains material never registered in the conscious mind: items that have been repressed or forgotten. Third, Jung describes the cultural unconscious as a repository of material derived from social interactions. Finally, there is the collective unconscious, which Jung views as the origin of archetypes that symbolically show themselves as individual complexes. Jung furthers his explanation by incorporating a discussion of the anima and animus as they relate to the individuation process. The anima is the feminine aspect of a man's soul. The counterpoint of the anima—the animus—is the masculine element of a woman's soul. Jung posits clear differences between the male and female psyches, offering that each gender tends to repress aspects of its opposite in order to develop more fully his or her masculine or feminine personality. According to Jung, individuation is hindered when either gender fails to accept the presence of, and consequently fails in the attempt to integrate, those oppositional gendering elements.

Jung had received, in 1927, a translation of a Taoist treatise, *T'ai i chin hua tsung chih* by the ninth-century alchemist Tung-pin Lü, from friend and scholar Wilhelm. In the ideas expressed within this work, Jung perceived a philosophical balance that he felt was absent in most Western religions. Immensely intrigued by the precepts and methods of alchemy, Jung provided a lengthy commentary on Wilhelm's text, published as *Das Geheimnis der goldenen Blüte*. He reflects upon the differences between Eastern and Western approaches to life, suggesting that a more balanced outlook pervades Eastern philosophy. He explains Taoism as a conscious method of uniting opposites, which includes psychic oppositions. The golden flower itself is a Chinese mandala representing the unified origin of life. Though Jung urges throughout his commentary that Western humanity should by no means seek to deny or abdicate its own philosophical, religious, and cultural heritage, he also highly recommends combining Western thought and Eastern insight.

Jung became vice president of the General Medical Society for Psychotherapy in 1930; in 1932 his accumulated writings earned him the Zurich Literature Prize. He began lecturing at the Eidgenössische Technical High School in Zurich in 1933, and he was appointed president of the General Medical Society for Psychotherapy. Also in 1933 appeared Jung's *Modern Man in Search of a Soul,* a large collection of short papers that Jung wrote between 1930 and 1932.

"Psychology and Literature," written in 1930, delves into reasons and methods for applying psychology to the study of literature. Jung argues that the work of art not only represents the inner aspects of the individual artist but reflects societal needs and cultural symbols as well. Understanding a creative work involves a "participation mystique"—a process of allowing the images of the artist to enter and shape the viewer as they originally did the artist.

In "Stages of Life" (1931), Jung discusses the individual human life as divided into four stages or phases. The first stage, which corresponds to an easterly direction on a circular model, represents the childhood years, in which humans are often problems to others yet do not see themselves as having any problems of their own. Stages two and three bring about conscious awareness of personal challenges and tasks, while the extreme old age of stage four consists of a descent once again into a condition in which, because of frailty, humans again become a problem to others. According to Jung, the midlife years of stages two and three are the moments of "greatest unfolding," for even as one devotes time and energy to family and work, one also experiences a change, a transition from dedication to passion to recognition of duty. There is an involuntary and growing tendency to look backward instead of forward, and in the absence of catastrophe or dysfunction one begins to be cognizant of true motivations for individual actions and to take stock of one's performance and accomplishments in life.

Also written in 1931 were "Archaic Man," "The Spiritual Problem of Modern Man," and "Basic Postulates of Analytical Psychology." In the first of these essays Jung offers comparisons between the conscious perceptivity of contemporary civilization and the "prelogical" condition of the psyche of primitive humanity. Jung feels that in matters of thought, emotion, and perception, primitive humans operated in much the same fashion as do modern humans. The difference between the two groups lies in their methods of explaining events in their lives. Primitive humanity did not find each life event to be easily explained via scientific principles or simple causality, which are the reactive methods of contemporary humans. Rather, primitive society tended to view the mythical or the archetypal as the arbitrary motive force behind events. Additionally, Jung believed that because primitive humanity tended to project their own unconscious psychic contents out into their world, those ancient humans found themselves totally contained by that world—completely immersed both psychically and physically. Because contemporary humanity views itself as separate from and above the events of the natural world, something of humanity's "soul" is lost through conscious denial and repudiation of all that relates to magic or the supernatural.

In "The Spiritual Problem of Modern Man" Jung claims that contemporary humans have denied themselves the ancient forms and structures that expressed the desires of the soul. The result is the crisis of the

Jung on his trip down the Nile River in 1926 (Collection of Franz Jung, Kusnacht-Zurich; from Gerhard Wehr, C. G. Jung in Selbstzeugnissen und Bilddokumenten, *1969; Thomas Cooper Library, University of South Carolina)*

spirit evident after World War I among European peoples, and in Jung's view only a viable, strong religion can offer the form and structure needed to settle, as well as prevent future instances of, this spiritual famine. The hope expressed by Jung is that current developments in medicine and politics, specifically those that indicate a renewed interest in the human body's function and a resurgent nationalism, will eventually lead to renewed contemplation of the human "place" in the natural order and a reevaluation of the worth and importance of things of the soul and spirit.

Jung's "Basic Postulates of Analytical Psychology" again broaches the topic of the materialism of contemporary humanity as an ineffectual system of philosophy that represents an antithetical overreaction to the spiritualism of preceding historical epochs. Jung disagrees with the modern view of the soul of man being nothing more than the result of biological processes; he sees the human soul as existing of and for itself and not as the chance combination of compounds and chemical reactions. The soul, as a set of inherited functions of the psyche, existed a priori of the human conscious thought processes. As an older psychic element, therefore, the unconscious offers a wealth of

knowledge about human nature, behavior, and development—knowledge that should be plumbed and appreciated despite its seemingly paradoxical affect in the light of rationalism. Again, Jung expresses hope that humanity will advance to a stage in which one side or the other of the complete psyche will no longer be rejected or repressed in favor of the opposing influence.

Among the final pieces found in *Modern Man in Search of a Soul* is the essay "Psychotherapists or the Clergy" (1932). Jung begins this piece by providing an outline and sketch of accumulated theories of neurosis. Denying the plausibility of theories proposed by both Freud and Adler, Jung describes a neurotic condition as one that arises when the human soul is unable to discover or achieve its meaning and purpose. Because the clergy seem unable to deal effectively with neuroses, medical doctors are often first asked to contend with essentially mythical and philosophical issues—questions of symbolism and ontology with which they are scarcely equipped to deal. Jung suggests that medical doctors so approached, indeed analysts as well, should attempt to recognize a basic conflict of the archetypes of good and evil in dealing with neurotic clients. To ignore these issues is to leave the neurotic stranded atop a tall building of his own construction without a ladder to safety; the ladder that physicians and analysts can provide involves a willingness to listen, an effort to allow a client to admit and integrate his or her own inner conflicts, and a conscious working toward promoting a balance of the psychic elements presenting in the client.

By now well-known among varied intellectual circles, Jung was instrumental in the development of the annual Eranos Conferences that began in 1933. Initiated by Olga Froebe-Karteyn at Ascona, Switzerland, the Eranos meetings involved a new sort of open-air lecture hall. Here, Jung and representatives of other fields of study met to exchange ideas. Originally centering upon theosophical topics, the Eranos Conferences broadened in scope to embrace an erudite level of humanistic discussion. Jung attended the first gathering in 1933 and continued to attend fairly regularly for the next twenty years.

Jung founded and became the first president of the International General Medical Society for Psychotherapy in 1934; around this time he wrote two important works: "Zur Empirie des Individuationsprozesses" (A Study in the Process of Individuation) and "Über die Archetypen des Kollektiven Unbewussten" (Archetypes of the Collective Unconscious)—both published in the *Eranos-Jahrbuch* (Eranos Yearbook) in 1934 and later translated as part of the collection *The Integration of the Personality* (1939). "Zur Empirie des Individuationsprozesses" traces the individuation process of a fifty-five-year-old woman who began consulting with Jung in 1928. Eleven of the woman's own paintings are displayed and analyzed; emphasis is placed upon fantasies expressed between the conscious and the unconscious. In Jung's view, individuation cannot proceed unless the individual consciously accepts and integrates the dark, less accessible aspects of the unconscious. This goal of assimilating the unconscious with the conscious is a key feature in Jungian methodology in that it represents the union of opposites. Jung writes that any characteristic or action, indulged in to an extreme, can eventually become its opposite; his word for this oppositional shift is "enantiodromia." Ideally, it is a balance between the opposites that one strives to achieve throughout individuation.

In "Über die Archetypen des Kollektiven Unbewussten" Jung compares archetypes to dry riverbeds; though the water has perhaps receded, the bed can be found and filled again at any time. He identifies many archetypes, including the anima and animus, the wise old man, the trickster, the sun and moon, and the persona and the shadow. Jung views the persona as one's conscious adaptation to external life, while the shadow is the adaptation of the unconscious to the persona. The two archetypes are more or less polar opposites; each is everything that the other is not. Often when one views another human with some dislike or distaste, that negative reaction is a function of projection; one has projected one's own hidden undesirable "shadow qualities" onto the other individual. When one can recognize the projected archetype as a part of oneself, progress toward individuation results. Jung adds that as expressions of common human instincts, archetypes in general provide a needed structure upon which humanity builds local, cultural myths. When humanity denies and deserts those myths, pathological imbalances are likely to occur, including both neuroses and psychoses.

Jung received an honorary doctorate from Harvard University in 1936; he also attended that year the Fourth Eranos Conference at Ascona. Deeply involved in alchemical studies since collaborating with Wilhelm on *Das Geheimnis der goldenen Blüte,* Jung began writing on the subject of alchemy. His "Religious Ideas in Alchemy," written in 1936 and later published as part 3 of *Psychologie und Alchemie* (1944; translated as *Psychology and Alchemy,* 1953, volume 12 of *The Collected Works of C. G. Jung*), reviews the basic principles of alchemy and offers reasons for the decline in popularity of the discipline. He notes that alchemy seems to mirror processes of the psyche, expressing itself in what Jung calls a "pseudochemical language." He correlates concepts of psychic opposites with alchemical oppositions; other topics in the essay include the renewal of life, alchemical symbolism in the history of religion, and the chemical

research of alchemists as projections of collective archetypes.

In 1937 Jung composed a series of talks in English known as the Terry Lectures, which were delivered at Yale University as part of the series "Religion in the Light of Science and Philosophy"; the treatises were published in 1938 as *Psychology and Religion.* Viewing the formulation of religion as one of the human mind's earliest activities, Jung feels that psychological practitioners cannot help but confront religion as an enormously significant sociological phenomenon. Additionally, as a Gnostic, Jung sees humanity (the creature) as part of a larger whole (the "pleroma"). As a consequence, killing or harming any part of the natural world invariably affects the human psyche as well. Jung became a member of the Royal Society of Medicine in 1938; in the same year he received another honorary doctorate, this time from Oxford. At the invitation of the British government of India, he traveled to Calcutta for the twenty-fifth anniversary celebration of the Indian Science Conference, contracting amoebic dysentery during his visit.

Despite the outbreak of World War II, the Eranos Conferences in Switzerland continued; Jung attended the Eighth Conference in 1940, and his work received support from two Americans who had been attending his seminars and studying his writings. Mary and Paul Mellon, millionaires in the 1940s, had long talks with Jung about his ideas. The Mellons chartered the Bollingen Foundation in 1940, an organization established to publish Jung's works in English.

Largely because of his repugnance for the actions of the Nazi regime, Jung resigned his post at the Eidgenössische Technical High School in 1942. He became an honorary member of the Swiss Academy of Sciences in 1943; in that same year, he was appointed to the chair of Medical Psychology founded specifically in his name at the University of Basel. Jung also suffered both a broken foot and a coronary embolism during these years, missing both the Eleventh and Twelfth Eranos meetings due to illness.

Jung published *Psychologie und Alchemie* in 1944; the text is based upon papers he presented at the Eranos Conference in 1935–1936. In 1945 he resigned the chair of medical psychology at Basel because of illness, and he received an honorary doctorate (his third) from the University of Geneva in honor of his seventieth birthday. Also in 1945 appeared *Psychologische Betrachtungen: Eine Auslese aus den Schriften von C. G. Jung* (translated as *Psychological Reflections: An Anthology of the Writings of C. G. Jung,* 1953), selected and edited by Jolande Jacobi. Jacobi had met Jung in the late 1920s. She invited him to lecture at the Cultural League of Vienna, for which she was vice president. Topics discussed in

Jung (right) and his mentor Sigmund Freud, with whom he broke in a disagreement over Jung's innovations in analytic psychology (Collection of Franz Jung, Kusnacht-Zurich; from Gerhard Wehr, C. G. Jung in Selbstzeugnissen und Bilddokumenten, *1969; Thomas Cooper Library, University of South Carolina)*

this volume include the path to God, doctor and patient relationships, and issues concerning self-realization.

Having resigned his teaching posts, Jung chose to retreat more and more to his Bollingen Tower beginning in 1946. He spent a great deal of his time over the next several years reworking and revising many of his earlier papers. By 1948 Jacobi was able to found the C. G. Jung Institute in Zurich, a project to which she had given considerable thought since 1939. Hesitant in agreeing to the establishment of the institute for fear it might soon outlive its usefulness, Jung nevertheless described its goals: the conducting of research in the areas of experimental psychology, mythology, dream analysis, and religion. In later years the institute expanded to include the training of analysts in Jungian methods, during which each candidate was required to complete not only a diploma program but also three hundred hours of Jungian analysis.

Illness again prevented Jung's attendance at the Seventeenth and Eighteenth Eranos meetings in 1949 and 1950, but he did attend the nineteenth conference in 1951, presenting a paper titled "On Synchronicity."

Synchronicity is Jung's term for instances of coincidence that connect to each other because of the meaning attributed by the observer or participant. Jung bases his thoughts about synchronicity upon the assumption that matter upon earth appears as an image of the world of spirit or psyche, and vice versa. One event, such as a dream or fantasy, does not cause another event. Instead, two events occur simultaneously and are seen as fortuitous—or disastrous, as the case may be—by the individual and that person's personal interpretation.

In 1952 Jung published the result of many years of thought concerning the Biblical story of Job. *Antwort auf Hiob* (translated as *Answer to Job,* 1954) discusses the paradoxical situation of Job requesting God's assistance in overcoming tribulations that God himself authorized. Jung argues that given the monotheistic stance of Christianity, God as a single deity must embrace or contain both good and evil.

In the spring of 1953 Wolff died of a coronary embolism. Also in that year, Pantheon Books of New York and the Bollingen Foundation began issuing volumes of *The Collected Works of C. G. Jung;* volumes appeared with regularity long after Jung's death. The arrangement of the volumes is both chronological and content based. Because Jung wrote new materials after the original planning stages of *The Collected Works,* and because Jung also revised older works from time to time, the editors tried to structure Jung's volumes in a way that combines chronology and content. Consequently, the first published volume of *The Collected Works* is not the first numbered volume of the collection. The first volume, *Psychology and Alchemy,* comprises the 1935–1936 Eranos papers already published as *Psychologie und Alchemie* in 1944. The second volume published, *Two Essays on Analytical Psychology,* brings together Jung's earlier essays "On the Psychology of the Unconscious" and "The Relations between the Ego and the Unconscious."

Two more volumes of Jung's collected works appeared in 1954. The first, *The Development of Personality,* includes eight essays. Three lectures on the topic of analytical psychology and its relation to education highlight the volume. Jung recommends that any educator who truly wishes to understand his or her students become versed in areas of both dream analysis and analytic psychology. In the first lecture Jung provides case studies in describing what he feels are five primary areas into which psychic upheavals in children often fall. The studies deal with such disturbances as neurosis, shyness, psychopathological conditions, and epilepsy.

Lecture 2 offers Jung's rejections of the theories of both Adler and Freud with respect to self-preservation and the sexual instinct. In illustrating his own theories, Jung examines the relationships between children and their parents, offering reference to religious concepts as well. He also argues that the recommended methods of symptom analysis, association tests, and dream investigation are worthwhile and scientific techniques that are easily applicable to cases of disturbed youth.

In the third lecture of the series Jung reiterates that every neurosis is not a function of infantile sexuality problems and repression. Again, he offers case studies—four histories that support his view that as each case is unique, each case must be treated on the basis of its unique history and characteristics rather than through reduction to a rigid Freudian sexual hypothesis. He also posits that the individual is quite capable of choosing to repress certain unpleasant experiences or ideas, as opposed to a system of psychic repression that leaves the individual as more or less a victim of uncontrollable psychic activity.

Additionally, this volume includes the essays "The Gifted Child," originally presented at an annual meeting of the Basel School Council in December of 1942 and published in volume seventeen of *The Collected Works of C. G. Jung* (1954), and "Marriage as a Psycho-

logical Relationship," which was translated from the original German in 1925 by Theresa Duerr in *The Book of Marriage* (1926) and later included in volume seventeen of *The Collected Works of C. G. Jung.* In the former, Jung recognizes that educational systems, often primarily concerned with the progress of the less talented students, tend to ignore those children whose intellectual capabilities seem above the norm. While Jung feels that the truly gifted child will generally compensate for this lack, drawing upon other sources to fulfill his or her potential, he argues that the tracking of students according to tested or observed levels of ability can seriously harm the academic and emotional development of the talented student. Observation of and participation with "average" students is a much more beneficial arrangement, avoiding potential disturbances that result when the gifted child, who is often skilled in one or two areas yet somewhat deficient in another, is segregated to the degree that inferior areas remain weak and social skills are not fully developed.

"Marriage as a Psychological Relationship," the final essay in the collection, suggests that because humans individuate and progress through definite developmental stages throughout life, quite often there arises a marked change in a marital relationship as a couple approaches the middle years. Jung writes that biological drives and needs tend to be the focus of marriage in the early years. During midlife, however, the more settled and presumably more financially secure partners find themselves more at leisure to investigate personal goals and desires, consequently effecting a change in the roles that each partner has heretofore assumed within the marriage. The likelihood of animosities developing during these transitional years is high; without recognition of these new needs and roles and their importance in human development, couples are prone to blaming each other for the current difficulties and may even decide to end the marriage.

Also published in 1954 was *The Practice of Psychotherapy.* This collection includes twelve works by Jung, most of which focus upon his own clinical experiences with patients as a practicing analyst. Short lectures on general and specific problems of psychotherapy make up the first and second sections of the book; the first part of the text serves as an appendix. In the first section of essays, titled "General Problems of Psychotherapy," Jung defines psychotherapy as a process involving two people in a sort of discussion or dialectic, reminding practitioners that they should not anticipate being able to understand every aspect of a given patient's personality. Further, analysts should never attempt to change a patient's basic personality; instead, analysis should further the patient's course of individuation and focus upon removing hindrances to that individuation.

Jung views psychotherapy as a methodical science, though not in the sense that the same formula should be applied to every case and to every patient. Instead, the methodology that Jung sees is one that is methodically flexible; in other words, the only routine aspect of a course of analytical treatment is to encourage full patient participation, following the various directions that a patient may introduce and avoiding the temptation to influence the client in directions or toward attitudes selected by the therapist.

According to Jung, analytical psychology combines both individual psychology and psychoanalysis, progressing as it combines these two concepts through a series of four stages. These stages—confession, elucidation, education, and transformation—are each described in turn. In the confessional stage the client reveals secrets or repressed emotional states. Stage two involves analysis of whatever fixations are presented by the patient. Stage three stresses attaining a normal adaptive avenue in relation to the displayed fixation. Finally, the fourth stage transforms both patient and analyst as they recognize the degree to which their individual personalities have interacted through the course of analysis, accepting that both parties have engaged in seeking a curative.

In "Specific Problems of Psychotherapy" Jung explains abreaction—the reenacting of traumatic experiences—and its importance in the analytic process. Jung also discusses the concept of the transference, a stage of analysis during which the client's dependence upon the consulting analyst can become pronounced yet ultimately can lead toward the patient feeling more equal with the analyst. He further emphasizes the importance of dream analysis, offering descriptions of several client cases that indicate not only the value of interpreting the dreams in consultation but also the foreshadowing nature of certain dream sequences.

The appendix for this volume, "The Realities of Practical Psychotherapy," serves primarily as a series of admonitions to practicing therapists. Jung reiterates that formulaic methods of therapy can result in further harm and should not be adopted, for even the definitions of conditions such as obsessional neurosis and hysteria are in flux and can be highly individualized. Jung reminds analysts that the possibility always exists of countertransference, the overly close identification of analyst with patient. Jung closes with a restatement of the analyst's primary job: enabling the client to individuate through a process of synthesizing all the experiences of life into an understandable whole.

Jung's wife, Emma, died in 1955. In the same year he was awarded an honorary doctorate from the Eidgenössische Technical High School in honor of his eightieth birthday; he also published his last major psychological work, *Mysterium Coniunctionis* (Secret Union).

This text caps Jung's thirty years of study concerning the connections of alchemy with psychology and describes the alchemical procedure for uniting opposites as representative of the individuation process. Jung felt that *Mysterium Coniunctionis* placed his psychology upon historical foundations and in effect completed his life's work.

Jung subsequently worked mostly at Bollingen, recording experiences from his life with the help of Aniela Jaffé. The resultant work, *Erinnerungen, Träume, Gedanken* (translated as *Memories, Dreams, Reflections,* 1963), was published in 1962 and serves as Jung's autobiography. Within these pages Jung writes of his many dreams, travels, and experiences, presenting his thoughts and recollections chronologically and reaching as far back as his childhood years. Along with memoirs concerning his relationship with Freud, activities at the Bollingen estate, and accumulated visions, the book also includes some letters from Jung to his wife and three letters from Freud to Jung.

Though aging, Jung published two more volumes during his lifetime, and several more were published posthumously. In 1960 appeared *The Psychogenesis of Mental Disease,* volume three of *The Collected Works.* The largest portion of this text consists of a translation of *Über die Psychologie der Dementia praecox;* the text also includes essays on the topics of schizophrenia and psychosis. "On the Psychogenesis of Schizophrenia," for example, offers debate about how the schizophrenic condition originates. While past theories have posited a physical cause for the origin of the disorder, contemporary evidence seems to indicate a psychic causality. Jung compares some of the symptoms that are present in schizophrenia and in neuroses, noting that dysfunctional thought patterns appear more severe among schizophrenics.

In "The Content of the Psychoses" Jung reports that psychoses often appear in conjunction with great and sudden emotional stress. He emphasizes this observation in arguing against a long-held opinion that instances of psychosis result from some biological infirmity or abnormality. As physical evidence in support of Jung's hypothesis are several documented cases in which postmortem brain study of psychotic patients revealed no discernible physical abnormalities.

Jung's next volume, appearing in 1961, is *Freud and Psychoanalysis.* The scope of these collected essays reflects both the collaborative and the divergent stages in the Jung-Freud relationship. Jung outlines Freud's theory of hysteria, offering that the Freudian concepts do indeed seem applicable in a large number of hysterical cases. Next is a discussion of Freudian dream analysis, explaining Freud's terms "manifest content" and "latent content." Jung also includes an article by Morton Prince. Prince had published his analysis of six dreams of one female client; Jung finds the study unscientific, the dreams insufficiently or incorrectly analyzed, and the symbolism of the client's dreams largely ignored.

The final essay of the text is dedicated to contrasts between Jung and Freud. Jung writes that the differing views held by the two physicians arise from basic philosophical disagreements. Freud is accused of abandoning philosophy altogether, refusing to acknowledge the possibility of a psychology based upon anything other than biological, sexual drives. Freud's self-appraisal in fact seems to indicate something of a God complex. Jung, on the other hand, accepts the primacy of both religion and philosophy in evaluating the human psyche, placing value upon the spiritual life of humanity.

Following a brief illness, Jung died at his home in Küsnacht, Zurich, on 6 June 1961. His long record of publications, however, did not cease. *Civilization in Transition* appeared three years later, in 1964. Twenty-four essays are included in this volume, including a lecture dated 1922 and a 1928 piece that discusses a particular student "love" problem. In an essay titled "Wotan," Jung discusses the Nazi movement in Germany as it compares with the psychic forces represented by Wotan, the ancient Germanic myth figure. Jung views Adolf Hitler as Wotan's contemporary agent. In depicting Hitler as an obsessed—or perhaps possessed—individual, Jung places the German people in the role of oppressed instead of oppressors.

Jung also discourses on what he sees as "peculiarities" in the practice of psychology in the United States. Emotionalism and promiscuity appear pronounced in the United States; consequently, the psychic makeup of Americans differs from that of Europeans, and the types of psychic disturbances that appear differ also. Jung looks back upon some twenty-eight years of analysis with American patients that seems to indicate heroism as the ideal of the typical American, and he recalls experiences that led him to conclude that of all the communities of the world, the psychology of the Americans is the most complex.

Volume fifteen of Jung's collected works, *The Spirit in Man, Art, and Literature* (1966), begins with a tribute to the Swiss physician Paracelsus. Jung describes Paracelsus as a "modern materialist" who nevertheless believed in the existence of such mystic creatures as spirits and witches. Like Jung, Paracelsus delved deeply into his own psyche; like Jung, he engaged in studies of superstition. In Jung's view the medieval physician contributed greatly to contemporary medicine and psychology primarily because of his ability to extend his parameters beyond a narrow field of inquiry.

Jung in 1955 at his largely hand-built castle on Lake Zurich (photograph by Dimitri Kessel; from Gerhard Wehr, C. G. Jung in Selbstzeugnissen und Bilddokumenten, 1969; Thomas Cooper Library, University of South Carolina)

Two other essays of note from this 1966 volume are "Ulysses" and "Picasso." In the former, Jung notes certain schizophrenic aspects in James Joyce's *Ulysses* (1922) yet feels the book is no more dysfunctional than is any other piece of contemporary art, and Joyce no more so than any other contemporary artist. Rather, the schizophrenia may be viewed as a "collective manifestation" of the times that Joyce aesthetically and creatively employs in writing his book. The essay "Picasso," though it does not discuss many of the aesthetic qualities of the painter's work, does apply a psychological perspective. Jung views Pablo Picasso's creations as symbolic of inner psychic content, generally deriving from the unconscious. Following a discussion of the harlequin figure as symbol, Jung mentions that this harlequin has appeared clearly and often in some of the latest of Picasso's work; he also notes a similarity between Nietzche's *Zarathustra* and the tale of the harlequin in general.

Volume thirteen of *The Collected Works, Alchemical Studies,* appeared in 1967. Again Paracelsus is a topic, this time described as a "spiritual phenomenon" who managed to balance Catholicism and a fascination with magic. Jung's commentary on Wilhelm's *Das Geheimnis der goldenen Blüte* is reprinted in this volume; also appearing is the essay "The Visions of Zosimos." In keeping with the emphasis placed upon the "mystic" throughout the volume, Jung records and comments upon the dreams of the alchemist Zosimos, a Gnostic whose visions reveal a large number of archetypal symbols that, in Jung's view, mirror both the duality of God and the duality of humanity.

The last volume of Jung's collected works, *The Zofingia Lectures,* appeared in 1983. This collection brings together lectures given by Jung between 1896 and 1899. His fellow students at the Zofingia Club at the University of Basel made up his audience. Among the topics discussed in these lectures are general thoughts about psychology, ideas concerning nature, interpretations on the doctrines of Christianity, and suggested distinctions between exact and abstract sciences.

The C. G. Jung Institute continues, now with a New York site that offers a postgraduate training program for Jungian analysts. The Analytical Psychology Club of New York, the oldest continuing Jungian organization in the United States, offers opportunities for study and discussion of Jungian principles. The New York Association for Analytical Psychology is an organization of professional Jungian analysts, and the C. G. Jung Foundation for Analytical Psychology offers continuing education, workshops, and summer intensive programs related to Jungian psychology.

Carl Gustav Jung's influence, substantial during his life, remains viable in many areas. Behaviorist Abraham Maslow's self-actualization theory, for example, parallels Jungian individuation in emphasizing the unfolding of the individual as a self-determined process. Theorist Jacques Lacan, though primarily a Freudian thinker, nonetheless recognizes that the innate psychic structures described by Jung play an important role in the psychic life of the individual. Elizabeth Kübler-Ross's interest in analyzing the latter portion of the human life span has much in common with the stages of life described by Jung. Additionally, Jungian thought in many ways anticipated several important contemporary interests, such as the question of multiple realities, aspects of spiritual self-awareness, and the need for increasingly multicultural perspectives.

Letters:

Richard I. Evans, *Conversations with Carl Jung and Reactions from Ernest Jones* (Princeton: D. Van Nostrand, 1964);

Miguel Serrano, *C. G. Jung and Hermann Hesse: A Record of Two Friendships,* translated by Frank MacShane (London: Routledge & Kegan Paul, 1966; New York: Schocken, 1966);

C. G. Jung: Briefe, 3 volumes, edited by Gerhard Adler and Aniela Jaffé (Olten, Switzerland: Walter, 1972, 1973); translated by R. F. C. Hull and Jane A. Pratt as *C. G. Jung: Letters,* 2 volumes (Princeton: Princeton University Press, 1973, 1975; London: Routledge & Kegan Paul, 1973, 1976);

The Freud-Jung Letters: The Correspondence between Sigmund Freud and C. G. Jung, edited by William McGuire, translated by Hull and Ralph Manheim (Princeton: Princeton University Press, 1974; London: Hogarth/Routledge & Kegan Paul, 1974);

Edward Foote, *Who Was Mary Foote?* (Zurich: Analytical Psychology Club of New York, 1974), pp. 256–268.

Interviews:

C. G. Jung Speaking: Interviews and Encounters, edited by William McGuire and R. F. C. Hull (Princeton: Princeton University Press, 1977; London: Thames & Hudson, 1978);

Edward A. Bennet, *Meetings with Jung: Conversations Recorded During the Years 1946–1961* (London: Eveline Bennet, 1982);

Richard I. Evans, "Interview with Carl Gustav Jung 1957," *Jung on Film,* selected by Merrill Berger, Public Media Video, 1990.

Bibliographies:

Joseph F. Vincie and Margreta Rathbauer-Vincie, *C. G. Jung and Analytical Psychology: A Comprehensive Bibliography* (New York: Garland, 1977);

Donald R. Dyer, *Cross-Currents of Jungian Thought: An Annotated Bibliography* (Boston: Shambhala, 1991).

Biographies:

Gerhard Wehr, *C. G. Jung in Selbstzeugnissen und Bilddokumenten* (Reinbeck: Rowohlt, 1969);

Marie-Louise von Franz, *C. G. Jung: His Myth in Our Time,* translated by William H. Kennedy (New York: Putnam, 1975);

Paul J. Stern, *C. G. Jung: The Haunted Prophet* (New York: Braziller, 1976);

Barbara Hannah, *Jung, His Life and Work: A Biographical Memoir* (New York: Putnam, 1976; London: Joseph, 1977);

Wehr, *Carl Gustav Jung: Leben, Werk, Wirkung* (Munich: Kösel, 1985); translated by David M. Weeks as *Jung: A Biography* (Boston & London: Shambhala, 1987);

Richard Noll, *The Aryan Christ: The Secret Life of Carl Jung* (New York: Random House, 1997).

References:

Karin Barnaby and Pellegrino D'Acierno, eds., *C. G. Jung and the Humanities: Toward a Hermeneutics of Culture* (Princeton: Princeton University Press, 1990);

Vincent Brome, *Jung: Man and Myth* (New York: Atheneum, 1978; London: Macmillan, 1978);

Edmund D. Cohen, *C. G. Jung and the Scientific Attitude* (New York: Philosophical Library, 1975);

Edward F. Edinger, *Ego and Archetype: Individuation and the Religious Function of the Psyche* (New York: Putnam, 1972);

Brian Feldman, "Jung's Infancy and Childhood and Its Influence upon the Development of Analytical Psychology," *Journal of Analytical Psychology,* 37 (1992): 255–274;

Michael Fordham, ed., *Contact with Jung: Essays on the Influence of His Work and Personality* (London: Tavistock, 1963; Philadelphia: Lippincott, 1963);

Anne Singer Harris, *Living with Paradox: An Introduction to Jungian Psychology* (Albany, N.Y. & London: Brooks/Cole, 1996);

Joseph Henderson, "The Cultural Unconscious," in his *Shadow and Self: Selected Papers in Analytical Psychology* (Wilmette, Ill.: Chiron, 1990), pp. 103–113;

Aniela Jaffé, ed., *C. G. Jung: Word and Image* (Princeton: Princeton University Press, 1979);

James Olney, *Metaphors of Self: A Theory of Autobiography* (Princeton: Princeton University Press, 1972);

Wayne Gilbert Rollins, *Jung and the Bible* (Atlanta: John Knox Press, 1983);

Carrie Lee Rothgeb and Siegfried M. Clemens, eds., *Abstracts of the Collected Works of C. G. Jung* (Rockville, Md.: National Institute of Mental Health, 1978);

Andrew Samuels, Bani Shorter, and Fred Plaut, *A Critical Dictionary of Jungian Analysis* (London & New York: Routledge, 1986);

Stephen Segaller and Merrill Berger, *The Wisdom of the Dream: The World of C. G. Jung* (Boston: Shambhala, 1989);

Richard P. Sugg, ed., *Jungian Literary Criticism* (Evanston, Ill.: Northwestern University Press, 1992);

Laurens van der Post, *Jung and the Story of Our Time* (New York: Pantheon, 1975);

Harry A. Wilmer, *Practical Jung: Nuts and Bolts of Jungian Psychotherapy* (Wilmette, Ill.: Chiron, 1987);

Polly Young-Eisendrath and Terence Dawson, eds., *The Cambridge Companion to Jung* (Cambridge & New York: Cambridge University Press, 1997).

Papers:

The Kristine Mann Library, established in the 1940s by the Analytical Psychology Club of New York, catalogues and houses papers, books, audiovisuals, and other materials by Carl Gustav Jung.

Siegfried Kracauer
(8 February 1889 – 26 November 1966)

Luca Prono

BOOKS: *Die Entwicklung der Schmiedekunst in Berlin, Potsdam und einigen Städten der Mark vom 17. Jahrhundert bis zum Beginn des 19. Jahrhunderts* (Berlin, 1915);

Soziologie als Wissenschaft: Eine erkenntnistheoretische Untersuchung (Dresden: Sibyllen, 1922);

Ginster: Von ihm selbst geschrieben (Berlin: Fischer, 1928; revised, 1963);

Die Angestellten: Aus dem neuesten Deutschland (Frankfurt am Main: Societäts-Verlag, 1930); translated by Quintin Hoare as *The Salaried Masses: Duty and Distraction in Weimar Germany* (London & New York: Verso, 1998);

Jacques Offenbach und das Paris seiner Zeit (Amsterdam: De Lange, 1937); translated by Gwenda David and Eric Mosbacher as *Offenbach and the Paris of His Time* (London: Constable, 1937); republished as *Orpheus in Paris: Offenbach and the Paris of His Time* (New York: Knopf, 1938);

Propaganda and the Nazi War Film (New York: Film Library of the Museum of Modern Art, 1942);

From Caligari to Hitler: A Psychological History of the German Film (Princeton: Princeton University Press, 1947);

Satellite Mentality: Political Attitudes and Propaganda Susceptibilities of Non-Communists in Hungary, Poland and Czechoslovakia, by Kracauer and Paul L. Berkman (New York: Praeger, 1956);

Theory of Film: The Redemption of Physical Reality (New York: Oxford University Press, 1960); republished as *Nature of Film: The Redemption of Physical Reality* (London: Dobson, 1961);

Das Ornament der Masse (Frankfurt am Main: Suhrkamp, 1963); translated and edited, with an introduction, by Thomas Y. Levin as *The Mass Ornament: Weimar Essays* (Cambridge, Mass.: Harvard University Press, 1995);

Strassen in Berlin und aderswo (Frankfurt am Main: Suhrkamp, 1964);

History: The Last Things before the Last (New York: Oxford University Press, 1969);

Siegfried Kracauer (from <home.no.net/wundel/kracauer.htm>)

Über die Freundschaft (Frankfurt am Main: Suhrkamp, 1971);

Schriften, 8 volumes (Frankfurt am Main: Suhrkamp, 1971–1990);

Kino: Essays, Studien, Glossen zum Film, edited by Karsten Witte (Frankfurt am Main: Suhrkamp, 1974);

Berliner Nebeneinander: Ausgewählte Feuilletons 1930–33, edited by Andreas Volk (Zurich: Epoca, 1996);

Frankfurter Tamhäuser: Ausgewählte Feuilletons 1906–30, edited by Volk (Zurich: Epoca, 1997).

Editions: *Georg* (Frankfurt am Main: Suhrkamp, 1977);

Der Detektive-Roman: Ein philosophischer Traktat (Frankfurt am Main: Suhrkamp, 1979).

Editions in English: *History: The Last Things before the Last* (Princeton, N.J.: Marcus Weiner, 1995);

Die Entwicklung der Schmiedekunst in Berlin, Potsdam und einegen Städten der Mark vom 17. Jahrhundert bis zum Beginn des 19. Jahrhunderts, edited by Lorenz Jäger (Berlin: Mann, 1997);

Theory of Film: The Redemption of Physical Reality, edited, with an introduction, by Miriam Bratu Hansen (Princeton: Princeton University Press, 1997);

Jacques Offenbach and the Paris of His Time (New York: Zone Books, 2003).

OTHER: "Leopold Sonnemann (1831–1909)," in *Encyclopedia of the Social Sciences,* 15 volumes, edited by Edwin R. A. Seligman (New York: Macmillan, 1930), pp. 257–258;

"National Types as Hollywood Presents Them," in *Mass Culture: The Popular Arts in America,* edited by Bernard Rosenberg and David Manning White (Glencoe, Ill.: Free Press, 1957), pp. 257–277;

"Jean Vigo," translated by William Melnitz, in *Introduction to the Art of the Movies: An Anthology of Ideas on the Nature of Movie Art,* edited by Lewis Jacobs (New York: Noonday Press, 1960), pp. 223–227;

"The Blue Angel," translated by Jill Dimmock, in *Sternberg,* edited by Peter Baxter (London: BFI, 1980), pp. 21–23.

SELECTED PERIODICAL PUBLICATIONS–
UNCOLLECTED: "Why France Liked Our Films," *National Board of Review Magazine,* 17, no. 5 (May 1942): 15–19;

"The Conquest of Europe on the Screen," *Social Research,* 10, no. 3 (September 1943): 337–357;

"The Hitler Image," *New Republic,* 110, no. 1 (1944): 22;

"Hollywood's Terror Films: Do They Reflect an American Mind?" *Commentary,* 2, no. 2 (August 1945): 132–136;

"The Revolt against Rationality," *Commentary,* 3, no. 6 (June 1947): 586–587;

"Filming the Subconscious," *Theatre Arts,* 32, no. 2 (February 1948): 36–44;

"Psychiatry for Everything and Everybody," *Commentary,* 5, no. 3 (March 1948): 222–228;

"Those Movies with a Message," *Harper's,* 19 (1948): 567–572;

"The Decent German: Film Portrait," *Commentary,* 7, no. 1 (January 1949): 74–77;

"The Mirror up to Nature," *Penguin Film Review,* 9 (1949): 95–99;

"Preston Sturges or Laughter Betrayed," *Films in Review,* 1, no. 1 (1950): 11–13, 43–47;

"How U.S. Films Portray Foreign Types," *Films in Review,* 1, no. 2 (1950): 21–22, 45–47;

"Stage vs. Screen Acting: The Theoretical Differences Are Fundamental," *Films in Review,* 1, no. 9 (December 1950): 7–11;

"Silent Film Comedy," *Sight and Sound,* 21, no. 1 (August–September 1951): 31–32;

"The Challenge of Qualitative Content Analysis," *Public Opinion Quarterly,* 16, no. 4 (Winter 1952–1953): 631–642;

"Opera on Screen," *Film Culture,* 1, no. 2 (March–April 1955): 19–21;

"Attitudes toward Various Communist Types in Hungary, Poland and Czechoslovakia," *Social Problems,* 3, no. 2 (October 1955): 109–114;

"The Found Story and the Episode," *Film Culture,* 2, no. 1 (1956): 1–5.

Throughout his life, Siegfried Kracauer contributed to many different fields of knowledge, disciplines, and genres. His writings range widely from motion-picture theory to cultural criticism, from autobiographical fiction to sociological observations on manifestations of modernity as diverse as operetta, advertising, the circus, and urban life. Accordingly, Kracauer, whose life itself was split between his native Europe and the United States, to which he fled from Nazism, is variously labeled as sociologist, motion-picture theorist, cultural critic, fellow traveler of the Frankfurt School, philosopher, journalist, and novelist. He has come under fire from contemporary motion-picture theorists, who describe his work on cinema as a naive apology for realism, while he has been praised as a central theorist of modernity (together with Georg Simmel and Walter Benjamin) and a sharp observer of new ways of social existence produced by capitalism and the urban experience.

In the often-quoted autobiographical preface to his posthumous volume *History: The Last Things before the Last* (1969), Kracauer discusses his own writings, "so incoherent on the surface," as efforts that really serve a single purpose: "the rehabilitation of objectives and modes of being which still lack a name and hence are overlooked or misjudged," regions of reality "which despite all that has been written about them are still largely *terra incognita.*" In spite of contemporary skepticism of authorial intentions and declarations, Kracauer's oeuvre as a whole does explore areas of social life that had received little attention and consideration during the author's times. For example, he devoted a monograph to the world of white-collar workers in the Berlin of the 1930s, claiming that their lifestyle was still less known than that of the primitive tribes that the same white-collar workers stared at with amazement on cinema screens. As David Frisby has argued in his study *Fragments of Modernity: Theories of Modernity in the*

Work of Simmel, Kracauer, and Benjamin (1985), both Kracauer's essays dating back to his Weimar period and the studies he produced in the United States shed light on a multiplicity of phenomena relating to the advent of modernity. What gives unity to his earlier and his more mature work is the understanding of social trends through cultural phenomena that are usually classified as fleeting and ephemeral.

Siegfried Kracauer was born on 8 February 1889 in Frankfurt, the only child of Rosette and Adolf Kracauer. From his childhood, Kracauer spent a great deal of his time with his uncle Isidor, a history teacher at the Philanthropin, the Jewish high school in Frankfurt, where the young Siegfried himself entered in 1898. In 1904 he moved to the Klinger Upper High, from which he graduated in 1907. In August of the same year, his first article appeared in the arts section of the *Frankfurter Zeitung,* and Kracauer started to study architecture at Darmstadt Polytechnic. He continued his studies in Berlin and Munich Polytechnics, from which he graduated in 1911. Kracauer combined his practical interest in architecture with the study of philosophical and sociological questions that had fascinated him from his student days. After his graduation, he worked briefly for several architectural offices, and from 1911 to 1914 he wrote his Ph.D. thesis, *Die Entwicklung der Schmiedekunst in Berlin, Potsdam und einigen Städten der Mark vom 17. Jahrhundert bis zum Beginn des 19. Jahrhunderts* (On the Development of the Art of Smithery in Berlin, Postdam and Several Towns in the March, from the Seventeenth Century until the Beginning of the Nineteenth Century). The thesis, accepted in Berlin and published in 1915, shows Kracauer's interest in ornaments, which later became apparent in his essay "Das Ornament der Masse" (The Mass Ornament, 1927).

The outbreak of World War I prompted Kracauer to return to Frankfurt, where he started to work for an architect's office. In 1916 he entered and won a competition for a Soldiers' Memorial Cemetery, which he later described in his autobiographical novel *Ginster: Von ihm selbst geschrieben* (Ginster: Written by Himself, 1928) as resembling "a military flow chart," with the monument looking "down on its troops as if stopping to watch them parade; indeed not the slightest irregularity to be seen." Kracauer's writings composed during these years remained mostly unpublished at the time. They anticipate several themes and issues with which he deals in his later works, increasingly concerned with the material reality of little-known aspects of everyday life. The main focus of these war writings is the danger perceived in the development of a materialist society where the single individual cannot feel at home. The individual's essence cannot be fully realized in such a society. Kracauer echoes here Simmel's own writings of

the same period, reproducing the fracture between the objective material culture and the unfulfilled subjective culture of the individual. Material progress is contrasted with the inner sterility of people living according to dated social conventions beyond which the world loses its meaning and is therefore deemed ineffectual to enrich the individual's inner life. Capitalism and science confine the subject to actions and activities that have lost any ultimate end. Henri Bergson's metaphysics, with its emphasis on movement rather than on the purpose of such movement, is, according to Kracauer, the philosophical worldview that best represents the individual's alienated existential condition. Within the reified reality created by capitalism, people are united by vocational interests, but there remains little sense of shared sentiment based on community, friendship, and personal fulfillment. Taking Max Weber's theory of secularization one step further, Kracauer finds himself and his contemporaries moving in a fragmented world without meaning, the coherent totality of which has been completely lost, producing a fracture between knowledge and existence. Kracauer was not alone in offering such a perspective on the modern world, and similar views were voiced by several key thinkers in the years following World War I. The Marxist critic György Lukàcs, for example, in his *Die Theorie des Romans* (Theory of the Novel, 1920), dates the birth of the novel to the loss of meaning in the world and the break between internal and external reality.

The same division between the world and the subject reappears in *Soziologie als Wissenschaft: Eine erkenntnistheoretische Untersuchung* (Sociology as Science: An Epistemological Investigation, 1922), in which Kracauer finds this separation to be the cause for the emergence of modern science: "Not until the world divides into a reality stripped of meaning, on the one hand, and the subject, on the other, does the latter fall prey to evaluating reality or investigating its being, to elucidating universal laws underlying occurrences, or to grasping, describing and interrelating in some way the occurrences which he experiences as discrete events." Sociology has to face a multiplicity of phenomena by relinquishing its pretense to universal knowledge. Such knowledge would be possible only in a world replete with meaning, while Kracauer defines the task of sociology in the 1920s as that of explaining the fragmentation of contemporary society.

Sociology focuses on the "world of socialized man" and addresses those principles that emerge from the processes of socialization. Because its purpose is the exploration of social reality as manifested in everyday life, sociology cannot rely on abstract conceptualizing. On the contrary, its starting point must be the object itself: "The empirical-sociological procedure is naturally unable to afford an overview of the flow of time, let alone stop it. Proceeding from individual (randomly selected) points of diversity, as it were, it always only describes precisely those individual points; it can never cover the entire reach of reality." These lines enunciate the method adopted by Kracauer in his major, later essays, in which he starts from individual observations and phenomena, gathering evidence without attempting an overall synthesis. In this respect, he has assimilated Simmel's lesson. Significantly, in his monograph "Georg Simmel" (1919), of which only the introductory chapter was published in 1920, Kracauer points out that Simmel's sociology privileges the small detailed element and describes the author of "Die Großstädte und das Geistesleben" (1903; translated as "The Metropolis and the Mental Life," 1936) as a master in the explanation of the fragmented images of the world.

After the war Kracauer regularly contributed reviews and articles to the *Frankfurter Zeitung* and finally became editor of its arts section in 1921, thus relinquishing completely the hated profession of architect. The majority of the pieces written for the *Frankfurter Zeitung* is concerned with the emergence of urban space and the growth of the metropolis as manifestations of modernity. These articles explore the social labyrinth of the city and run parallel to Kracauer's writings of the mid 1920s on the detective novel, which focus on a more formal and intellectual type of labyrinth. According to Frisby, the articles themselves represent "fragments of modernity" at both the levels of form and of content. They are broken images of urban life and space, and Kracauer never tries to make them fit into a wider and overall urban theory. They are fleeting remarks that put their author at the center of the experience of modernity as defined by Marshall Berman in his study *All That Is Solid Melts into Air: The Experience of Modernity* (1982): "to be modern . . . is to experience personal and social life as a maelstrom, to find one's world and oneself in perpetual disintegration and renewal, trouble and anguish, ambiguity and contradiction."

The absence of meaning from the contemporary world is the focus of Kracauer's study on the detective novel. Composed between 1922 and 1925 and first published in volume one of Kracauer's *Schriften* (Writings, 1971–1990), *Der Detektive-Roman: Ein philosophischer Traktat* (The Detective Novel: A Philosophical Tract) is one of the first studies of the genre, and one can detect in it echoes of Lukàcs's *Die Theorie des Romans* and the beginnings of the work of the Frankfurt School on popular culture. The study is one of Kracauer's first attempts to investigate the superficial elements of bourgeois culture, an investigation to which he later returned in the essays collected in the volume *Das Orna-*

SOZIOLOGIE
ALS WISSENSCHAFT

Eine
erkenntnistheoretische
Untersuchung

von

SIEGFRIED KRACAUER

IM SIBYLLEN-VERLAG ZU DRESDEN
1 9 2 2

Title page for the book in which Kracauer locates the emergence of modern science in the division between the world and the individual subject (Jean and Alexander Heard Library, Vanderbilt University)

ment der Masse (1963; translated as *The Mass Ornament: Weimar Essays,* 1995) and that became a leitmotiv of his later research. The only section of *Der Detektive-Roman* published during Kracauer's lifetime, "Die Hotelhalle" (The Hotel Lobby, 1925), with its well-known comparison of a church and a hotel lobby, already points to a major feature of the volume: the discovery of hidden links between such a codified genre as the detective novel and theology. It is a theology of nothingness, of an empty world, where the detective, always a celibate just like the priest, moves through hotel lobbies celebrating the rites of an all-pervading reason.

Structured through different sections that illustrate the agents and the locales of the genre (for example, "Detective," "Police," "Criminals," "Trial"), *Der Detektiv-Roman* goes back to a central motif of Kracauer's earlier writings, which is here applied to literary analysis: the opposition between an authentic community of fulfilled individuals that is only possible in a world endowed with meaning and an artificial society where people move like atoms in an empty space devoid of meaning. The detective novel is concerned with this latter lower sphere of reality and unmasks its lack of meaning through the character of the detective. He is the only one to be able to make connections that remain hidden to others and is the embodiment of the governing principle of higher reason and rationality.

To make clear the distinction between an authentic community and the merely formal relationships linking the protagonists of the detective novel, Kracauer draws a comparison between the church and one of the most common environments where the action of the detective novel unfolds, the hotel lobby. In both places individuals enter as guests, yet in the hotel lobby people do not establish meaningful relationships with each other as they do in a religious congregation. On the contrary, the meetings taking place in the lobby are "*vis à vis de rien*" (face to face with nothing): the lobby is an empty space. Relationships become merely a game, and Kracauer invokes Simmel's definition of society as a game of socialization. The banality of the conversation in the hotel lobby is contrasted to the unifying thrust of the act of praying in the church.

Paradoxically, the detective, as an embodiment of reason, can only be a god in a world that has forsaken God. The detective, as a personification of rationality, is not to be confused with the police forces, who merely represent legality: "The stylistic device by means of which the detective expresses his sovereignty vis à vis the police is irony, which brings rationality to bear against legal force." On the contrary, the detective is able to solve the mystery precisely because of his ability to transgress the boundary between the legal and the illegal and to relate himself both to criminals and policemen alike. Significantly, the detective never arrests the criminal: this act is something that he willfully leaves to the police. Such a description will undoubtedly ring familiar to those acquainted with the narrative patterns and characterization of American film noir of the 1940s and 1950s, a genre that is said to have had its roots in the cultural milieu of the Weimar Republic, where Kracauer was active.

The rational analysis of the data through which the detective arrives at the solution of the crime becomes an end in itself, more important than the actual mystery. The legacy of the detective proved essential methodologically for Kracauer's future oeuvre as a whole. The task of the author in the works that followed *Der Detektiv-Roman* was precisely that of penetrating the unknown layers of social reality. As late as his last monograph, *History: The Last Things before the Last,* Kracauer describes the experience of his own exile in terms fit for the actions of a detective. According to

Kracauer, the exile has ceased to belong to a definite world, so his mode of existence is that of stranger who has to face the task of penetrating exterior appearances.

During the early 1920s Kracauer met the members of what became the Frankfurt School, and he became close friends in particular with Theodor W. Adorno (with whom he studied the philosophy of Immanuel Kant on Saturdays) and Leo Lowenthal. Kracauer maintained these friendships for the rest of his life but was never part of the core group of intellectuals associated with the Frankfurt Institute for Social Research. In 1930 Kracauer married Elisabeth Ehrenreich, a librarian at the institute. The couple moved to Berlin, where Kracauer joined the local editorial team of the *Frankfurter Zeitung*. Kracauer's contributions to the newspaper during the years 1931–1933 often focused on, and criticized, the Universumfilm Aktien Gesellschaft (UFA), the German consortium of movie companies established after World War I to boost the cinematographic means of Germany. Kracauer's target in these pieces is represented by a shift at UFA toward increasingly more nationalistic film productions.

The essays written in the 1920s and early 1930s, edited by the author and collected in *Das Ornament der Masse,* subject to scrutiny the surface phenomena of mass culture. They show Kracauer's increasing interest in the culture and tastes of the masses and also his concern about the means deployed to divert the attention of vast sectors of society from their actual living conditions. Taking up typical themes of modernity, such as isolation and alienation, urban culture and the relation between the group and the individual, Kracauer investigates a multiplicity of topics, ranging from locales of modernity such as shopping arcades and hotel lobbies to cultural manifestations such as the cinema, best-sellers and their readers, photography, and dance. Taken as a whole, the essays collected in *Das Ornament der Masse* assume that the most revelatory facets of modern life lie on the surface, in the ephemeral and the marginal. According to Gertrud Koch's definition in *Siegfried Kracauer: An Introduction* (2000), Kracauer analyzes the visible world as "a figure of thought."

The methodology informing Kracauer's investigation of the mass cultural phenomena of modernity is enunciated from the first section of *Das Ornament der Masse:*

> The position that an epoch occupies in the historical process can be determined more strikingly from an analysis of its inconspicuous surface-level expressions than from that epoch's judgment about itself. . . . The surface level expressions, by virtue of their unconscious nature, provide unmediated access to the fundamental substance of the interpretations of these surface-level expressions. The fundamental substance of an epoch

and its unheeded impulses illuminate each other reciprocally.

Judgments of an epoch about itself tend to be partial because they lack an overarching perspective. Surface manifestations, however, grant access to life behind the scenes, to the mechanisms at work within social conditions, and, in that way, to underlying meanings and unconscious truths. For Kracauer the *Oberfläche* (surface) constitutes a site where social reality manifests itself most dramatically and instructively. The surface is not just a locus of appearance and superficiality; rather, it represents a plane of configurations that demands investigation and analysis. Such spaces are to be read as signs of time: they offer crucial insights into the dynamics of the present. What is crucial for Kracauer is the observation of the phenomena of daily life, focusing on the configurations of modernity that are, by their nature, ephemeral and culturally marginal spaces, media, and rituals of an emerging mass culture.

The surface phenomenon that Kracauer chooses to exemplify the physiognomy of the era is a product of the American entertainment industry: the Tiller Girls, evidence of the fascination that the country to which he eventually immigrated was already exerting on him. The dance performed by the Tiller Girls is geometrically arranged and reflects the arrangement of the masses looking at them: "The regularity of their patterns is cheered by the masses, themselves arranged by the stands in tier upon ordered tier." In this way, the mass observes itself in the mass ornament without being able to see through itself. Koch has thus summarized the dialectics involved between the mass and its ornament: "The mass on the bleachers has a vantage point from which it can see the mass ornament in the playing field of the stadium, but it has no perspective on itself." The comment builds on Kracauer's observations that "although the masses give rise to the ornament, they are not involved in thinking it through." The masses participate in and partake of the mass ornament as an audience. Yet, they do not create it. The more regular and geometric the design, the further removed it becomes from the minds of those who constitute it.

The rationality of the mass ornament mirrors the contemporary reality of capitalist production. This stage of Kracauer's argument is obviously where a surface phenomenon such as the Tiller Girls is linked to a deeper understanding of the economic and cultural mechanisms of the epoch. Capitalism takes control of the organic world through the reification and exploitation of nature and human personality in the name of profit:

DIE ANGESTELLTEN
AUS DEM NEUESTEN DEUTSCHLAND

VON
S. KRACAUER

1930
SOCIETÄTS-VERLAG / FRANKFURT AM MAIN

Title page for Kracauer's study of office workers (translated as The Salaried Masses: Duty and Distraction in Weimar Germany, *1998), based on a "mosaic" of conversations, newspaper articles, advertisements, and personal correspondence (Ellis Library, University of Missouri–Columbia)*

The structure of the mass ornament reflects that of the entire contemporary situation. Since the principle of the *capitalist production process* does not arise purely out of nature, it must destroy the natural organisms that it regards either as means or as resistance. Community and personality perish when what is demanded is calculability. . . . A system oblivious to differences in form leads on its own to the blurring of national characteristics and to the production of worker masses that can be employed equally well at any point on the globe.

The capitalist production process, like the mass ornament, is an end in itself. The workers on the assembly line of Taylorism, the industrial system devised to produce more with less cost, are like dancers in the mass ornament; both perform "a partial function without grasping the totality." In Kracauer's reading, the mass ornament functions as an aesthetic extension of the prevailing economic capitalist order. Yet, Kracauer does not suggest any moral judgment: he does not indict the Tiller Girls as a mindless mass diversion or as fraudulent escapism, and he actually criticizes "certain intellectuals" who "have taken offense" at the Tiller Girls. These dancers enact the reality of modern times, embodying life under capitalism in their physical demonstrations. This configuration reveals the reality of capitalism, which is precisely the kind of "surface-level expression" Kracauer refers to in the introductory methodological remarks to the essay.

"Das Ornament der Masse," a crucial essay in Kracauer's production as a whole, echoes Weber's conception of capitalism, but it also anticipates the main concern of critical theory and specifically of Adorno and Max Horkheimer's *Dialektik der Aufklärung: Philosophische Fragmente* (1947; translated as *Dialectic of Enlightenment,* 1972): the persistence of mythological thought in contemporary society and the truncated rationality of capitalism, in which enlightenment and myth have become intertwined. In the concluding sections of the essay, Kracauer predicts the key traits of National Socialism, with its sanctification of natural laws and irrational powers as well as the fierce anti-intellectualism of the system. According to Kracauer, nature constantly seeks to defend itself against the interventions of reason in the guise of mythological thinking. History has involved a constant struggle between mythological illusions and the power of reason. As the struggle continues, nature loses its magic and should become more readily understandable through reason. Capitalism is an advanced stage in a process of questioning mythological thinking. Yet, such a mode of production does not adopt a complete reason but rather an obscured—"murky" is the adjective Kracauer uses—reason that "does not encompass man." The mass ornament mirrors the inability of capitalism to realize fully the power of reason as it marks a regression to mythology without the symbolic immediacy of mythology. The mass ornament is a godless mythological cult devoid of reason. The production and the consumption of mass ornaments divert attention from the changes in the social world and prevent reason from penetrating the masses, who otherwise might set about to change the status quo. In truth, the mass ornament only perpetuates the status quo, its social meaning being "equivalent to that of the Roman circus games which were sponsored by those in power."

During the 1920s and 1930s Kracauer also devoted a whole series of articles in the *Frankfurter Zeitung* to the expanding class of office workers, the main characters in the new social and cultural dynamics that were developing in the Weimar Republic. The pieces were eventually turned into the book *Die Angestellten: Aus dem neuesten Deutschland* (1930; translated as *The Salaried Masses: Duty and Distraction in Weimar Germany,* 1998). The volume avoids both the instruments of traditional sociological inquiry (although some critics cite it as one of the first examples of the technique of participant-observation) and those of journalistic reportage, drawing instead on conversations, newspapers, advertisements, and personal correspondence. Kracauer's aim is to provide a "mosaic" rather than a "photograph" of office workers, a definition that points once again to the fragmentation of modernity and to the attempt to reconstruct reality through juxtaposition of different points of view and perspectives.

Kracauer himself provides the link between the main themes and concerns of *Das Ornament der Masse* and *Die Angestellten,* citing in the latter two essays that he collected in the former: "Die kleinen Ladenmadchen gehen ins Kino" (The Little Shop Girls Go to the Movies), which has stirred a series of responses from feminist critics in one of the most interesting attempts to update the reception of Kracauer's oeuvre, and "Film 1928." Office workers cease to be merely a new type in a taxonomy of the workplace and become instead yet another representation of the rationality of capitalism, an equivalent to the ornamental display of the masses. The study contends that these masses of salaried workers that populate the cities of the Weimar Republic are not satisfied with the outdated high culture of the bourgeoisie as it does not correspond to their needs and thus does not satisfy their requests for empathy. On the contrary, office workers demand a more specific form of cultural sustenance that suits their tastes. Spiritually homeless, lacking in cultural customs and traditions of their own, these white-collar workers seek refuge in entertainment—or the "distraction industries," analyzed in a chapter significantly titled "Asyl für Obdachlose" (Shelter for the Homeless). Office workers are seen as consumers becoming the champions of a middle-class ideology at a historical point when the high rate of inflation characterizing the post–World War I German economy made the differences between white- and blue-collar employees increasingly less identifiable. The aspirations of office workers point to social mobility even when this new status is a mere masquerade: department stores and the Sunday schools of this new class, according to Kracauer's ironic definitions, display cheap clothes disguised as elegant through the use of elegant decorations. Building on the analysis of Blaise Pascal offered by Lowenthal in his critique of the entertainment industry, *Die Angestellten* is an indictment of the Weimar culture of consumption. The study points to the salaried masses of office workers as composed of individuals unable to live their lives and forever trying to escape the bareness of their world through distraction. Such escapism mirrors a denial of their own transience and eventual death.

If the intellectual stimuli of Frankfurt social and cultural life marked the first part of Kracauer's life, the experience of exile, and of what he ironically called in a quasi-prophetic letter to Lowenthal and Adorno in the 1920s "transcendental homelessness," were to characterize the second part of his biography. On 28 February 1933, the day after the burning of the German Reichstag at the hand of the Nazis, Kracauer and his wife left for Paris, where he struggled to find any work. While in Paris, he completed his novel *Georg* and his study on *Jacques Offenbach und das Paris seiner Zeit* (1937; translated as *Offenbach and the Paris of His Time*, 1937). He was also commissioned to do a study on the social history of German motion pictures, which eventually became his study *From Caligari to Hitler: A Psychological History of the German Film* (1947), by the Library of the Museum of Modern Art.

Ginster, published anonymously in 1928 but heavily revised for the 1963 edition, and *Georg,* completed in 1934 and published posthumously in volume seven of *Schriften,* can be considered as reflections on Kracauer's own existence and as fictional extensions to his intellectual achievements (significantly, several sentences in the novels return in Kracauer's monograph on Offenbach). Kracauer's point of view starts in his own life to then encompass his contemporary society as a whole. Similarly, the monograph on Offenbach is not limited to the figure of the composer himself: the book was, in fact, badly received even by friends of Kracauer, such as Adorno, for its lack of focus on the music of Offenbach. *Jacques Offenbach und das Paris seiner Zeit,* as its title makes clear, is also a study of the social and cultural milieu of a particular city at a particular historical juncture. It is a biography of a specific society that, according to Kracauer, was best embodied by the Jewish operetta composer Offenbach.

In the preface to *Jacques Offenbach und das Paris seiner Zeit,* translated for the first time in the 2003 edition of *Jacques Offenbach and the Paris of His Time,* Kracauer clearly states that the volume is not intended as an orthodox biography of an individual. Far from being a "photographic portrait" where the background is blurred, *Jacques Offenbach und das Paris seiner Zeit* is not limited to the life of the Jewish composer. It is also a biography of the society in which he worked and that influenced him, although critics have challenged the volume precisely on the grounds that it ignores the Marxian dialectic between use value and exchange value that would have allowed Kracauer a fuller understanding of the mystifications of the Second Empire (Walter Benjamin, in his 1971 monograph on Charles Baudelaire, was able to address these mystifications

more fully than Kracauer). The book uses the life and work of Offenbach as a focal point for a broad portrayal of Second Empire Paris. This historical depiction does not simply have a documentary value. On the contrary, Kracauer explains the contemporary importance of his research by pointing out that the modes of thought of his epoch derive in part from those produced in the France of the Second Empire, and in particular, in Paris, the only city whose history is marked by a European dimension.

Although Kracauer takes Offenbach's operettas as mirroring and, to an extent, as creating the society in which they were written, he challenges the view that the composer of *Les Contes de Hoffmann* (The Tales of Hoffmann, first performed in 1881) simply produced works fitting into the pattern of historical amnesia and escapism pervading Paris after the revolutionary thrusts of 1848. On the contrary, the study argues that Offenbach's productions must be reassessed as more than dazzling distractions. Offenbach comes across as an ironist who mocks, through his work, the pomp and the pretense surrounding the apparatuses of power. Offenbach's operettas create a reversal of values where what is thought of as great and mighty is ridiculed. At the same time, Kracauer also discovers that Offenbach's dreamworlds are the embodiment of a utopian essence indicting the deception and corruption of the times.

At the outbreak of World War II, the Kracauers moved to Marseille and prepared to immigrate to the United States. After considerable difficulties the couple managed to get through Spain and Portugal and finally arrived in New York at the end of April 1941. Kracauer became an American citizen in 1946 and published the following year his history of German movies, *From Caligari to Hitler,* with Princeton University Press. Funded by the Museum of Modern Art, *From Caligari to Hitler* can be seen as an outgrowth of Kracauer's concern in *Jacques Offenbach und das Paris seiner Zeit* for the institutions of mass culture. In his psychological history of German cinema, Kracauer leaves the nineteenth century to focus again on the phenomena of modernity of the twentieth century, with a more specific interest in how propaganda influences the establishments and the products of mass culture. The book has become one of the best known by Kracauer, and his central thesis argues that surface cultural manifestations such as movies can in fact reveal the spirit of an era. Thus, the German cinematic production of the first decades of the twentieth century is viewed as filled with premonitions about the totalitarian regimes that were to come into being in the 1930s. Adolf Hitler's dictatorship arose as a resolution to psychological dilemmas that had been reflected in the German movies of the interwar period. Kracauer constructs movie history as a history of the

Siegfried Kracauer

Das Ornament der Masse

Essays

Suhrkamp Verlag

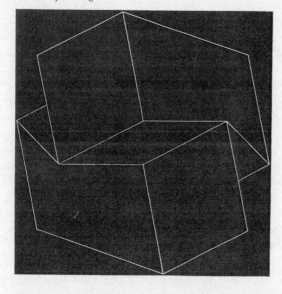

Paperback cover for Kracauer's 1963 collection of his essays from the 1920s and 1930s (translated as The Mass Ornament: Weimar Essays, *1995) on the superficial aspects of mass culture (D. H. Hill Library, North Carolina State University)*

world visions held by people at different historical epochs. The inner dispositions of the German people, those that allow one to understand the rise in power of Hitler and the inefficacy of the opposition, are encoded in the motion-picture texts of the time. Kracauer's primary concern is not to read the movies he selected (and to which, problematically, he had scarce access in the United States) according to aesthetic categories but to treat them as symbols of a collective consciousness, as "visible hieroglyphics" of the "unseen dynamics of human relations."

Kracauer's analysis of director Fritz Lang's production reveals his suspicion for the aesthetic equation of beauty with truth and good. Even though Lang made aesthetically superior movies, their ideological premises remain dubious. Lang was certainly not involved in making propaganda for the Nazi regime, yet Kracauer treats him as a case in point to illustrate

the ambiguities that pervaded also the works of even those directors who did not accept the diktats of the Nazi style. Lang's *Das Testament des Dr. Mabuse* (The Testament of Dr. Mabuse, 1933), for example, is read as illustrating a type of sterile resistance that finally surrenders to the fascination of the führer:

> Dr. Goebbels undoubtedly knew why he banned the film. However, it is hard to believe that the average German audience would have grasped the analogy between the gang of screen criminals and the Hitler gang. And had they even been aware of it, they would not have felt particularly encouraged to stand up against the Nazis, for Lang is so exclusively concerned with highlighting the magic spell of Mabuse and Baum that his film mirrors his demoniac irresistibility rather than the inner superiority of their opponents. . . . This anti-Nazi film betrays the power of the Nazi spirit over minds insufficiently equipped to counter its peculiar fascination.

As this excerpt indicates, *From Caligari to Hitler* is much more than a volume of motion-picture history. It also charts the decline of the individual as an independent thinking entity and his/her surrendering to subordination.

The thesis of *From Caligari to Hitler* has proved influential and has been challenged only much later. According to Thomas Elaesser's revisionary account *Weimar Cinema and After: Germany's Historical Imaginary* (2000), Kracauer's study, together with *L'Ecran démoniaque* (1952; translated as *The Haunted Screen,* 1969) by Lotte Eisner, another exiled critic, has dominated for better or worse the general understanding of Weimar cinema. Elaesser suggests a new reading of *From Caligari to Hitler* centering on the biographical contingency of Kracauer's exile. Thus the relation between Weimar motion pictures, social upheaval, and Nazism posited by the book would be the outcome of the position of its author as an intellectual in exile, trying to mediate between a hated national identity and a suspicious audience of non-German readers.

In 1951 Kracauer was appointed research director of the Empirical Social Research Department at Columbia University. During the 1950s he worked mainly on empirical research and completed his *Theory of Film: The Redemption of Physical Reality* (1960), the genesis of which dated back to his days in Marseille. In her introduction to the 1997 edition of the book, Miriam Bratu Hansen reports an interesting comment by Benjamin, who was in Marseille at the same time, on Kracauer's despairing attitudes toward exit visas. Asked about what was to be done had the exit papers continued to fail to materialize, Kracauer chillingly replied: "We will all have to kill ourselves here." Yet, Benjamin had noticed how involved Kracauer had become in his new project on motion-picture aesthetics (the nucleus of *Theory of Film*) so that he thus comments on Kracauer's reply: "What will happen to us cannot be easily predicted. But of one thing I'm sure: if anyone will *not* kill himself, it's our friend Kracauer. After all, he has to finish writing his encyclopedia of film. And for that you need a long life." Kracauer indeed took a long time to complete his project: he resumed working on the book only in November 1948, after his arrival in the United States and after the publication of *From Caligari to Hitler*. The study went through several editing stages and, although the advance contract with Oxford University Press was signed in 1949, *Theory of Film* was not published until 1960.

Like another important proponent of realism in motion-picture theory, André Bazin, Kracauer links cinema and photography, the latter being the immediate forebear of the former. "Photography . . . has a legitimate claim to top priority" among the various disparate elements that, in combination, have contributed to the formation of the cinematic medium as it is known. The fundamental characteristic of photography is its ability to reproduce material reality: it both records its immediate aspects and discloses those features that are not easily perceivable at first sight. The basic properties of cinema are identical with those of photography, and Kracauer argues that "film . . . is uniquely equipped to record and reveal physical reality and, hence, gravitates toward it." As a consequence of this obligation to gravitate toward physical reality, Kracauer makes aesthetic satisfaction derive from the adherence of a specific oeuvre to the fundamental characteristics of the medium. Therefore, the aesthetic potentials of the medium are best realized when it follows the path of realism so that those cinematic products "almost devoid of creative aspirations, such as newsreels, scientific or educational films, artless documentaries, etc., are tenable propositions from an aesthetic point of view." Motion pictures echo the interest for photography in nature with its penchant for the unstaged: the best movies are those in which the mise-en-scène tends to disappear in favor of a total illusion of reality. The stress of photography on the fortuitous and random events ("the very meat of snapshots") is also mirrored by movies such as American silent comedies, full of incidents and disasters, or by later movies filmed among the chaotic life of the street. What cinema has in addition to the properties of photography is its ability to render the flow of life, so that it represents "the stream of material situations and happenings with all they intimate in terms of emotions, values, thoughts."

The list of subjects that Kracauer considers more filmable than others confirms the task of cinema to

become a more faithful witness of reality than photography. It is no coincidence that Kracauer cites D. W. Griffith's statement that "the task I'm trying to achieve is above all to make you see." According to *Theory of Film*, the polemical target of which is Sergei Eisenstein and his theory of montage, there are subjects that could be termed "cinematic" because of the attraction that they exert on the medium. These include, for example, images that create an impression of concreteness such as inanimate objects. Such objects often "stand out as protagonists and all but overshadow the rest of the cast"; this overshadowing is the case with the cruiser *Potemkin* in Eisenstein's *Bronenosets Potyomkin* (Battleship Potemkin, 1925) and the dilapidated kitchen in Vittorio De Sica's *Umberto D.* (1952), with "the powerful presence of environmental influences in *The Grapes of Wrath*," and with "the interaction between the marshland and the guerrilla fighters in the last episode of *Paisan*." Also labeled as cinematic are those subjects that give the impression of movement, such as dances and chases.

Cinema becomes for Kracauer a documentation of the world and is comparable to science for its analysis of people and events. Yet, the charges of naive realism that have been leveled at the book only have a partial justification. As Hansen explains in her critical introduction to *Theory of Film*, during the Weimar period Kracauer's attention to the surface of things implied an ideal of "transparency": "accordingly, the project of registering and transcribing the surface phenomena of everyday life was often linked to an allegorizing mode of reading and critiques of ideology." In *Theory of Film*, on the other hand, what interests Kracauer is the opacity and the indeterminacy of surface reality, "not just a multiplicity and changeability of meanings but the possibility of a basic indifference to sense and legibility." Such indeterminacy is precisely one of the elements of contemporary interest that Hansen detects in Kracauer's book and that she finds as much a product of overdetermination as one of underexposure: "it is the aura of history's vast refuse or debris, the snowy air reflecting the perpetual blizzard of media images and sounds, the 'hyperindexicality' that at once distinguishes and threatens to defeat cinematic representation."

In the later years of his life Kracauer made several trips to Europe. He died of pneumonia in New York on 26 November 1966. Kracauer's last book, *History: The Last Things before the Last*, published posthumously in 1969 and completed by Paul Oskar Kristeller, was both a defense of historiography and a reflection of Kracauer's own condition of exile. In order to understand historical phenomena, the historiographer has only the option of "self-eradication," of becoming an exile from his or her contemporary world:

> I am thinking of the exile who as an adult person has been forced to leave his country or has left it of his own free will . . . and the odds are that he will never fully belong to the community to which he now in a way belongs. . . . Where then does he live? In the near vacuum of extra-territoriality, the very no-man's-land. . . . The exile's true mode of existence is that of a stranger. . . . There are great historians who owe much of their greatness to the fact that they were expatriates.

The historian can only commune with the material of his historical research through this state of homelessness and self-effacement. His task coincides with the task of exile, that of going beyond superficial appearance "so that he may learn to understand that world from within."

History: The Last Things before the Last casts a skeptical look to those attempts to write history chronologically as an illustration of a logical development toward a certain progress. Instead, it pays close attention to microhistories and their specific contexts, the only locations that can endow them with meaning. The book presents several motifs that have made it of interest for contemporary debates about history versus histories and about what Hayden White has termed the inescapability of discourse and tropes in historiographical narratives. Kracauer stresses, for example, that a great deal of the meaning achieved by history depends on the language used by the historian, "to formal expedients involving structure and composition."

Siegfried Kracauer's writings investigate a world that has lost its totality and has broken down into fragments that do not have any higher meaning. Consequently, he adopts a "from below" perspective, centering his analysis of modernity on its debris and refuse, on its apparently insignificant phenomena, in which instead he was able to reveal the spirit of the time. Benjamin's description of Kracauer as a chiffonier (cabinet), therefore, is not a pejorative one. As Frisby concluded in his critical portrait of Kracauer, the chiffonier is able to save the fragments of history, those surface phenomena that reveal the underlying forces of an epoch, and fit them in their context so as to compose an intelligible mosaic.

Letters:

Walter Benjamin, *Briefe an Siegfried Kracauer: Mit vier Briefen von Siegfried Kracauer an Walter Benjamin*, edited by the Theodor W. Adorno Archive (Marbach am Neckar: Deutsche Schillergesellschaft, 1987);

Volker Breidecker, ed., *Siegfried Kracauer–Erwin Panovsky: Briefweschel 1941–1966* (Berlin: Akademie Verlag, 1996).

Bibliographies:

Thomas Y. Levin, "Kracauer in English: A Bibliography," *New German Critique,* 41 (1987): 140–150;

Levin, *Siegfried Kracauer: Eine Bibliographie seiner Schriften* (Marbach am Neckar: Deutsche Schillergesellschaft, 1989);

Soziographie, 7, nos. 1–2, 8–9 (1994).

References:

Theodor W. Adorno, "The Curious Realist: Siegfried Kracauer," *New German Critique,* 54 (Fall 1991): 159–160;

Dagmar Barnouw, *Critical Realism: History, Photography and the Work of Siegfried Kracauer* (Baltimore: Johns Hopkins University Press, 1994);

Marshall Berman, *All That Is Solid Melts into Air: The Experience of Modernity* (New York: Simon & Schuster, 1982; London: Verso, 1983);

Kenneth Scott Calhoon, ed., *Peripheral Visions: The Hidden Stages of Weimar Cinema* (Detroit: Wayne State University Press, 2001);

Thomas Elaesser, *Weimar Cinema and After: Germany's Historical Imaginary* (London & New York: Routledge, 2000);

David Frisby, *Fragments of Modernity: Theories of Modernity in the Work of Simmel, Kracauer, and Benjamin* (Cambridge: Polity Press, 1985; Cambridge, Mass.: MIT Press, 1986);

Sabine Hake, "Girls and Crisis: The Other Side of Diversion," *New German Critique,* 40 (Winter 1987): 145–164;

Miriam Bratu Hansen, "America, Paris, the Alps: Kracauer (and Benjamin) on Cinema and Modernity," in *Cinema and the Invention of Modern Life,* edited by Leo Charney and Vanessa Schwartz (Berkeley: University of California Press, 1995), pp. 326–402;

Hansen, "Decentric Perspectives: Kracauer's Early Writings on Film and Mass Culture," *New German Critique,* 54 (Fall 1991): 47–76;

Hansen, "Mass Culture as Hieroglyphic Writing: Adorno, Derrida, Kracauer," *New German Critique,* 56 (Spring 1992): 43–73;

Martin Jay, "Adorno and Kracauer: Notes on a Troubled Friendship," *Salmagundi,* 40 (Winter 1978): 40, 42–66;

Jay, "The Extraterritorial Life of Siegfried Kracauer," *Salmagundi,* 31–32 (Fall 1975–Winter 1976): 31–32, 49–106;

Jay, *Permanent Exiles: Essays on the Intellectual Migration from Germany to America* (New York: Columbia University Press, 1985), pp. 217–236, 310–313;

Jay, "Politics of Translation: Siegfried Kracauer and Walter Benjamin on the Buber-Rosenzweig Bible," *Yearbook of the Leo Baeck Institute,* 21 (1976): 3–24;

Michael Kessler and Thomas Y. Levin, eds., *Siegfried Kracauer: Neue Interpretationen* (Tübingen: Stauffenburg, 1990);

Gertrud Koch, *Siegfried Kracauer: An Introduction,* translated by Jeremy Gaines (Princeton: Princeton University Press, 2000);

Levin, "The English-Language Reception of Kracauer's Work: A Bibliography," *New German Critique,* 54 (1991): 183–189;

Inka Mülder, *Siegfried Kracauer: Grenzänger zwischen Theorie und Literatur: Seine frühen Schriften 1913–1933* (Stuttgart: Metzler, 1985);

New German Critique, special Kracauer issue, 54 (1991);

Patrice Petro, *Joyless Streets: Women and Melodramatic Representations in Weimar Germany* (Princeton: Princeton University Press, 1989);

Petro, "Modernity and Mass Culture in Weimar: Contours of a Discourse on Sexuality in Early Theories of Perception and Representation," *New German Critique,* 40 (Winter 1987): 115–146;

Heide Schlüpmann, "Phenomenology of Film: On Siegfried Kracauer's Writings of the 1920s," *New German Critique,* 40 (Winter 1987): 97–114;

Text+Kritik, special Kracauer issue, 68 (1980);

Meir Wigoder, "History Begins at Home: Photography and Memory in the Writings of Siegfried Kracauer and Roland Barthes," *History and Memory,* 13, no. 1 (Spring/Summer 2001): 19–59.

Papers:

Siegfried Kracauer's papers are housed at the Deutsche Literaturarchiv in Marbach am Neckar, Germany. The holdings include diaries, correspondence, notebooks, manuscripts, drawings, and drafts.

Jacques Lacan

(13 April 1901 – 9 September 1981)

Karl Edward Jirgens
Laurentian University

BOOKS: *De la psychose paranoïaque dans ses rapports avec la personnalité* (Paris: Le François, 1932); enlarged as *De la psychose paranoïaque dans ses rapports avec la personnalité suivi de Premiers écrits sur la paranoïa* (Paris: Seuil, 1975);

Ecrits (Paris: Seuil, 1966; revised and republished as *Ecrits I* [1970] and *Ecrits II* [1975]; partially translated by Alan Sheridan as *Ecrits: A Selection* (New York: Norton, 1977);

Les quatre concepts fondamentaux de la psychanalyse, 1964 (Paris: Seuil, 1973); translated by Sheridan as *The Four Fundamental Concepts of Psycho-analysis* (London: Hogarth, 1977; New York: Norton, 1978);

Télévision (Paris: Seuil, 1974); translated by Denis Hollier, Rosalind Krauss, Annette Michelson, and Jeffrey Mehlman as *Television: A Challenge to the Psychoanalytic Establishment,* edited by Joan Copjec (New York: Norton, 1990);

Les écrits techniques de Freud, 1953–1954 (Paris: Seuil, 1975); translated by John Forrester as *Freud's Papers on Technique, 1953–1954* (New York: Norton, 1988; Cambridge & New York: Cambridge University Press, 1988);

Encore, 1972–1973, edited by Jacques-Alain Miller (Paris: Seuil, 1975); translated by Bruce Fink as *On Feminine Sexuality: The Limits of Love and Knowledge* (New York: Norton, 1998);

Le moi dans la théorie de Freud et dans la technique de la psychanalyse, 1954–1955 (Paris: Seuil, 1978); translated by Sylvana Tomaselli as *The Ego in Freud's Theory and in the Technique of Psychoanalysis, 1954–1955* (New York: Norton, 1988);

Les psychoses, 1955–1956 (Paris: Seuil, 1981); translated by Russell Grigg as *The Psychoses* (New York: Norton, 1993; London: Routledge, 1993);

L'Ethique de la psychanalyse: 1959–1960, edited by Miller (Paris: Seuil, 1986); translated by Dennis Porter as *The Ethics of Psychoanalysis, 1959–1960* (New York: Norton, 1992);

Le transfert: 1960–1961, edited by Miller (Paris: Seuil, 1991);

Jacques Lacan (© COLLECTION CORBIS KIPA)

L'envers de la psychanalyse: 1969–1970, edited by Miller (Paris: Seuil, 1991).

Collection: *Écrits inspirés* (Besançon: Arep, 1977).

Edition in English: *Feminine Sexuality: Lacan and the Ecole freudienne,* edited by Juliet Mitchell and Jacqueline Rose, translated by Rose (New York: Norton, 1982).

PRODUCED SCRIPT: "Radiophonie," radio, RTB (Belgium), 5, 10, 19, 26 June 1970; ORTF, 7 June 1970.

OTHER: "Les Complexes familiaux en pathologie," in *La vie mentale,* Encyclopédie Française, volume 8 (Paris: Larousse, Société de gestation de L'Encyclopédie Française, 1938), pp. 842.1–842.8;

"Fetishism: The Symbolic, the Imaginary and the Real," by Lacan and Vladimir Granoff, in *Perversions, Psychodynamics, and Therapy,* edited by M. Balint (New York: Gramercy Books, 1956), pp. 265–276;

"Of Structure as an Inmixing of an Otherness Prerequisite to Any Subject Whatever," translated by Anthony Wilden, in *The Language of Criticism and the Sciences of Man: The Structuralist Controversy,* edited by Richard Macksey and Eugenio Donato (Baltimore & London: Johns Hopkins University Press, 1970), pp. 186–200;

Le Scission de 1953: La communauté psychoanalytique en France I, edited by Jacques-Alain Miller (Paris: Ornicar? 1976)–includes statutes proposed for the Institut de Psychanalyse by Lacan;

"C'est à la lecture de Freud," in Robert Georgin, *Lacan: Théorie and pratiques* (Lausanne: L'Age d'homme, 1977).

TRANSLATION: Martin Heidegger, "Logos," translated by Lacan and A. Botond, *La Psychanalyse,* 1 (1956): 59–79.

SELECTED PERIODICAL PUBLICATIONS–UNCOLLECTED: "Structures des psychoses paranoïaques," *Semaine des hôpitaux de Paris,* 7 (July 1931): 437–445;

"Le Problème du Style et la conception psychiatrique des formes paranoïaques de l'expérience," *Minotaure,* 1 (1933): 68–69;

"Hiatus irrationalis," *Le Phare de neuilly,* 3/4 (1933): 131;

"Some Reflections on the Ego," *International Journal of Psycho-Analysis,* 34 (1953): 11–17;

"La Chose freudienne, ou Sens du retour à Freud end psychanalyse," *Evolution psychiatrique,* 1 (1956): 225–252;

"Fonction et champ de la parole et du langage en psychanalyse: Discours du congres de Rome et Reponse aux interventions," *La Psychanalyse,* 1 (1956): 81–166; translated by Wilden as *The Language of the Self: The Function of Language in Psychoanalysis* (Baltimore: Johns Hopkins University Press, 1968);

"Situation de la psychanalyse et formation du psychanalyste en 1956," *Etudes philosophiques,* 4 (1956): 567–584;

"Le séminaire sur 'La lettre volée,'" *La Psychanalyse,* 2 (1957): 1–44; translated by Jeffrey Mehlman as "Seminar on 'The Purloined Letter,'" in *The Purloined Poe: Lacan, Derrida, and Psychoanalytic Reading,* edited by John P. Muller and William J. Richardson (Baltimore: Johns Hopkins University Press, 1988), pp. 55–76;

"Les Formations de l'inconscient," *Bulletin de Psychologie,* 12 (1957–1958): 250–256;

"Hommage fait à des étudients en philosophie sur l'objet de la psychanalyse," *Cahiers pour l'analyse,* 3 (1966): 5–13;

"De Rome 53 à Rome 67: La Psychanalyse. Raison d'un échec," *Scilicet,* 1 (1968): 42–50;

"Radiophonie," *Scilicet,* 2/3 (1970): 55–99;

"Lituraterre," *Littérature,* 3 (1971): 3–10;

"Aimée," *L'Arc,* 58 (1974): 4–14;

"Introduction a cette publication," "Séminaire du 19 decembre 1974," and "A la lecture du 17 decembre 1974," *Ornicar?* no. 2 (March 1975): 87–105;

"Le séminaire de Jacques Lacan–séminaire du 14 janvier 1975" and "Le séminaire de Jacques Lacan–séminaire du 21 janvier 1975," *Ornicar?* no. 3 (May 1975): 97–110;

"Le séminaire R.S.I. (11 et 18 février 75)," *Ornicar?* no. 4 (1975): 91–106;

"Un ratage dans l'établissement d'une figure de noeud / Le noeud borroméen orienté," "Une proprieté non démontrée," "R.S.I. séminaire du 11 mars 1975: Le pathème du phallus," "R.S.I. séminaire du 18 mars 1975: Dans l'imaginaire on y est," "R.S.I. séminaire du 8 avril 1975: Rectifier le non-rapport sexuel?" "R.S.I séminaire du 15 avril 1975: Trou de réel, trou du symbolique," and "R.S.I. séminaire du 13 mai 1975: Il n'y a pas d'état d'âme," *Ornicar?* no. 5 (Winter 1975): 3–66;

"Séminaire du 18 novembre 1975: Le sinthome et le Père," "Séminaire du 9 décembre 1975: Symbole et sinthome," *Ornicar?* no. 6 (March–April 1976): 3–20;

"Séminaire du 16 décembre 1975: Le pourquoi de ma recherche," "Séminaire du 13 janvier 1976: Vérités premières," and "Séminaire du 20 janvier 1976: Remerciements à J. Aubert," *Ornicar?* no. 7 (16 October 1976): 3–18;

"Séminaire du 10 février 1976: Les embrouilles du vrai" and "Séminaire du 17 février 1976: Paroles imposées," *Ornicar?* no. 8 (Winter 1976): 6–20;

"Le sinthome, séminaire du 16 mars 1976: Bouts-de-réel," *Ornicar?* no. 9 (April 1977): 32–40;

"Le sinthome, séminaire du 13 avril 1976: Le réel est sans loi," *Ornicar?* no. 10 (July 1977): 5–12;

"Le sinthome, séminaire du 11 mai 1976: L'ego de Joyce," *Ornicar?* no. 11 (September 1977): 3–9;

"Desire and the Interpretation of Desire in *Hamlet,*" translated by James Hulbert, *Yale French Studies,* 55/56 (1977): 11–52;

"L'insu que sait de l'une bévue s'aile a mourre: Séminaire du 16 novembre 1976" and "L'insu que sait de l'une bévue s'aile a mourre: Séminaire du 14 decembre 1976," *Ornicar?* nos. 12/13 (December 1977): 5–16;

"L'insu que sait de l'une bévue s'aile a mourre: Effets de signifiants: Séminaire du 11 janvier 1977," *Ornicar?* no. 14 (Easter 1978): 4–9;

"L'insu que sait de l'une bévue s'aile a mourre: Le réel continue l'imaginaire: Séminaire du 18 janvier 1977," *Ornicar?* no. 15 (Summer 1978): 5–9;

"Nomina non sunt consequentia rerum," *Ornicar?* no. 16 (1978): 7–13;

"Vers un signifiant nouveau," *Ornicar?* nos. 17/18 (Spring 1979): 7–23;

"Une pratique de bavardage," edited by Miller, *Ornicar?* 19 (Autumn 1979): 5–9;

"Lettre de dissolution," "L'Autre manque," "D'éco-lage," and "Monsieur A.," *Ornicar?* nos. 20/21 (Summer 1980): 9–20; "Lettre de dissolution" and "L'Autre manque" translated by Jeffrey Mehlman as "Letter of Dissolution" and "The Other Is Missing," in *Television: A Challenge to the Psychoanalytic Establishment* (New York: Norton, 1990), pp. 128–133;

Opening address to Conference of International Lacanian analysts in Caracas, Venezuela, *L'Ane,* 1 (April–May 1981): 30–31;

"Lumière!" and "Le malentendu," *Ornicar?* nos. 22/23 (Spring 1981): 7–14;

"Hamlet: I–Le canevas" and "Hamlet: II–Le canevas," *Ornicar?* no. 24 (9 September 1981): 7–31;

"Hamlet: III–Le désir de la mère" and "Hamlet: IV–Il n'y a pas d'autre de l'autre," *Ornicar?* no. 25 (1982): 13–36;

"Hamlet: V–L'objet Ophélie," "Hamlet: VI–Le désir et le deuil," and "Hamlet: VII–Phallophanie," *Ornicar?* nos. 26/27 (Spring 1983): 7–44.

UNPUBLISHED SEMINARS: Seminar V: *Les formations de l'inconscient* (1957–1958);

Seminar IX: *L'identification* (1961–1962);

Seminar X: *L'angoisee* (1962–1963);

Seminar XII: *Problèmes cruciaux pour la psychanalyse* (1964–1965);

Seminar XIII: *L'objet de la psychanalyse* (1965–1966);

Seminar XIV: *La logique du fantasme* (1966–1967);

Seminar XV: *L'acte psychanalytique* (1967–1968);

Seminar XVI: *D'un Autre à l'autre* (1968–1969);

Seminar XVIII: *D'un discours qui ne serait pas du semblant* (1970–1971);

Seminar XIX: *. . . ou pire* (1971–1972);

Seminar XXI: *Les non-dupes errent* (1973–1974);

Seminar XXVI: *La topologie et le temps* (1978–1979).

Jacques Lacan occupies a fundamental position in French psychoanalytic theory. Lacan's reinterpretation of Freudian psychoanalytic theory as influenced by Fer-dinand de Saussure's structural linguistics has profoundly influenced contemporary critical theory. His opaque style presents a hurdle for many and deliberately engages his audience in a construction of meaning analogous to psychoanalytical self-examination. The response to Lacan is as broad as it is controversial and extends beyond psychoanalytical circles to include reactions from experts in Marxist, feminist, cinematic, social, architectural, media, and literary theory.

Elisabeth Roudinesco documents Lacan's life in *Jacques Lacan: Esquisse d'une vie, histoire d'un système de pensée* (1993; translated as *Jacques Lacan: Outline of a Life, History of a System of Thought*), and *La bataille de cent ans: Histoire de la psychanalyse en France* (1986; translated as *Jacques Lacan & Co.: A History of Psychoanalysis in France, 1925–1985,* 1990). Jacques-Marie Emile Lacan was born in Paris on 13 April 1901. He was the eldest son of middle-class parents: Alfred Charles Marie Lacan, a tradesman, and Emilie Philippine Marie (née Baudry). His sister, Magdeleine-Marie Emmanuelle, was born 25 December 1903. Marc-Marie (later changed to Marc-François), Lacan's youngest sibling, was born 25 December 1908. Lacan's childhood included an oppressive Christian atmosphere with regular domestic squabbles often involving his grandparents and his in-laws, who lived on the same block in Paris. The neighborhood was middle-class, and the family was well known in the food business as purveyors of vinegar, pickled foods, mustard, imported brandy, rum, and coffee. Lacan's paternal grandfather, Emile Lacan, had tyrannical tendencies, although Alfred Lacan was affectionate and tolerant. Lacan was named partly after his grandfather, and the elder Emile may have inspired young Jacques-Emile's recognition of the dictatorial notion of the "Name-of-the-Father" that informs his psychoanalytic theory and his literary interpretations.

Lacan was awarded his *diplôme de médicine légist,* qualifying him as a forensic psychiatrist, in 1931, and his *doctorate d'état* in 1932. Early in his career he was influenced by modern art and, in turn, inspired many artists, particularly from the Surrealist school. As a clinical psychologist he was accused of using unorthodox methods. His seminar series, offered from 1953 onward, usually at the Hôpital Sainte-Anne, established Lacan's reputation by attracting many French and international intellectuals. Each "seminar" consisted of a series of public lectures spanning almost one year. Jean-Bertrand Pontalis was authorized by Lacan to write summaries of some of the unpublished seminar lectures for the *Bulletin de Psychologie.* Jacques-Alain Miller, Lacan's son-in-law, was also authorized to publish edited transcripts of the seminars, and almost half have been released either in book form or in Miller's journal, *Ornicar?.* Lacan's entry into cultural criticism, and in particular his analyses of literary works, gained him international attention. His unorthodox views, however, leave unresolved questions concerning his theory and practice. Lacan's attitude toward feminine sexuality, his infamous arrogance, and his intellectual prowess fed the controversy that surrounds him. In *Jacques Lacan: The Death of an Intellectual Hero* (1983), Stuart Schneiderman (Lacan's only American analysand) comments that Lacan's deliberately obtuse style is akin to that of a Zen master. Like Sigmund Freud, Lacan challenged the humanist notion of free will, but unlike Freud, he rejected the idea of an integrated self. Where Freud believed that speech is the manifestation of a biological need, Lacan claimed that speech revealed unconscious anxieties and desires.

Lacan argues that the human psyche is shaped in its early years by an encounter with a mirror (or some reflective surface). The mirror encounter involves two recognitions. First, the subject as a child recognizes its own physical unity in the mirror for the first time. The subject's first encounter with this idealized self-image is fundamentally narcissistic. The mirror encounter serves a catalytic function that initiates a development of the ego and sense of self-awareness. Second, through an act of projection, the subject typically misidentifies the spectral "other" in the mirror as the object of desire. This *méconnaissance,* or misunderstanding, of the mirror image contributes to the *Spaltung* (gap or split) in the subject's psyche.

Simultaneous to the mirror stage is the subject's acquisition of language. Lacan maintains that the subject defines its identity on the level of discourse. Language as a structure serves a metonymic function analogous to the mirror encounter insofar as the spectral image is a representation of the subject but is not the subject itself. Similarly, words stand in for things but are not the things themselves. Within this formulation, the signified is not a thing but an aspect of language. Lacan's reference to the sliding of the signified under the signifier indicates that language often signifies something other than the literal. Desire evokes metonym. The subject (unconsciously) pursues the ever elusive object of desire through an endless metonymic or signifying chain of discourse (linguistic expression). Thus, by studying a subject's dreams and speech patterns (recurring figures of speech, malapropisms, slips of the tongue, flashes of wit) one can illuminate unconscious patterns of desire and anxiety defining the split or gap in the subject's "imaginary."

Like Freud, Lacan contends that individuals are socialized by the triadic Oedipal complex: in the "seduction" phase the subject is attracted to the object of desire or mother, in the "primal stage" the subject is aware of the mother's sexual intercourse with the father, and in

Lacan with his mother, Emilie; his sister, Magdeleine-Marie; and his father, Alfred, around 1907 (from Elisabeth Roudinesco, Jacques Lacan & Co.: A History of Psychoanalysis in France, 1925–1985, translated by Jeffrey Mehlman, 1990; Thomas Cooper Library, University of South Carolina)

the "castration" phase the father's "No!" or law prohibiting sexual access to the mother is accompanied by threat of castration. The father's "law" or the "Name-of-the-Father" deflects desire from the "mother" to what Lacan calls the *grand Autre* (great Other). Hence, the "Other" always implies a gap or lack. Lacan divides the term into two parts as follows: apart from a condition of difference in the conventional sense, the *petit autre* (small other) is an extension of the unconscious of the ego (in other words, the imaginary) and is misrecognized as one's mirror image. The *petit autre* is the site upon which desire can be projected. The *grand Autre* is rooted in the symbolic (conscious realm of language) and can be thought of as the locus of both speech and desire. This Other is a hypothetical place or space, that of a pure signifier, rather than a physical entity that resides in the subject's imaginary but manifests itself in the symbolic. Lacan has contended that the unconscious is the discourse of the Other. This Other can never be grasped, because the nature of desire is such that the object of desire is always out of reach. Unfulfilled desire leads to a *Spaltung* in the subject's psyche. Lacan does not read Freud's theory of the Oedipal complex biologically, however. Rather, he views the Oedipal complex with reference to language. For example, the "law" in the "Name-of-the-Father" is a linguistic phenomenon that socializes the subject.

For Lacan, the three Oedipal phases are indirectly related to three psychic levels or "registers." The "imaginary" corresponds to variations in the unconscious (for example, memory, dreams, and hallucinations) initiated by the formation of ego that results from the mirror stage. The imaginary is structured like a language. If one reads the rebus-like patterns of the unconscious, then it is possible to identify the desires, anxieties, and traumas of the subject or analysand (the imaginary does not correspond in meaning to *imagination*). The symbolic level is the field of conscious discourse (either spoken or thought), which corresponds to the metonymic substitutions of the conscious mind and its linguistic order and thus permits the subject's entry to society through speech (the symbolic does not correspond with *symbolism* as it is commonly understood). The final level, the real, serves a function of constancy and lies beyond speech; it is the ineffable and, in some cases, the hallucinatory. The real is a kind of false dialectic with a Möbius topology combining material with psychic, explainable with unknowable, *Innenwelt* (internal) with *Umwelt* (external). It can be thought of as the ineffable world of objects and experiences, as well as that which is lacking in the symbolic order. Therefore, the real is approachable but never grasped (this term has little to do with the conventional sense of "reality").

For Lacan, all language is defined in reference to the phallus. Thus, the phallus becomes a universal signifier. Unlike Freud, by *phallus* Lacan does not mean the male sexual organ. Rather, it is understood linguistically and metonymically as a presence, which in turn is indicative of the *manque à être* (absence at the core of being) that can only be fulfilled by the (forever unattainable) object of desire. This *manque à être* applies to either masculine or feminine experience. It is through language that the subject seeks to evoke the presence of the absent object of desire. Hence, language as "Other" serves as a fetish when it evokes the object of desire. Lacan explains that the linguistic locus of the Other is the site where the question of the subject's existence may be recognized during psychoanalysis.

Lacan's contribution to literary criticism is limited but important. His analyses of notable literary texts include the writings of Sophocles *(Oedipus Rex, Antigone),* considered with reference to enigmas and ethics; William Shakespeare's *Hamlet* (1600–1601), examined in

terms of the mother as Other or object of desire; and James Joyce's *Finnegans Wake* (1939), interpreted as a *jouissance* (enjoyment) of language in response to the paternal "law" or the "Name-of-the-Father." Lacan's 1955 seminar on Edgar Allan Poe's "The Purloined Letter" (1845), "Le séminaire sur 'La lettre volée,'" argues that fiction generates its own rules and exemplifies the workings of the "symbolic" or human consciousness as it tries to systematize language into an intelligible order. Lacan has also commented on a host of other literati, including Samuel Beckett, Roland Barthes, Jacques Derrida, and Michel Foucault.

Apart from Freud, Lacan's thinking was influenced by Sophocles, Quintilian (rhetorical form), Benedict de Spinoza (ethics), Immanuel Kant (truth and reason), Marquis de Sade (desire), Georg Wilhelm Friedrich Hegel (dialectics), Ferdinand de Saussure (the relationship between signifier and signified), André Breton (Surrealism), Roman Osipovic Jakobson (linguistics), Martin Heidegger (*Dasein*/Being), Kurt Gödel (mathematics and topology), and Claude Lévi-Strauss (structuralist anthropology), to name a few. Lacan has influenced the theories of many poststructural literary critics. Deconstructivist thinkers such as Derrida, Paul De Man, Geoffrey Hartman, and Gayatri Chakravorty Spivak have mixed responses to Lacanian theory. In different ways, both Derrida (in "The End of the Book and the Beginning of Writing" in *Of Grammatology,* 1976) and Lacan (in "The Function and Field of Speech and Language in Psychoanalysis" in *Ecrits* [1966; translated as *Ecrits: A Selection,* 1977]) address questions of subjectivity and consciousness in interpretations based on language, meaning, and the primacy of the text. Marxist critic Louis Althusser applies Lacanian theories on the relationship between language and power in society in his essay "Ideology and Ideological State Apparatuses: Notes Towards an Investigation" (collected in *Lenin and Philosophy,* 1971). Lacan's notion of the Other is relevant to discussions of postcolonial literature. Gilles Deleuze and Félix Guattari have taken antipsychoanalytic positions (in *L'Anti-Oedipe* [1972; translated as *Anti-Oedipus,* 1977]) in partial response to Lacan's theories. Many Parisian authors associated with the journal *Tel Quel* under the editorship of Philippe Sollers were inspired by Lacan, Barthes, Derrida, and Julia Kristeva.

In his youth Lacan frequented Adrienne Monnier's famed bookshop, Shakespeare & Co. Through books and Monnier's reading series, he discovered the authors André Gide, Jules Romains, and Paul Claudel. Intrigued by Dadaism and Surrealism, Lacan discovered the literary review *Littérature* and met radical writers such as Breton and Philippe Soupault. Lacan first heard readings of Joyce's *Ulysses* (1922) at Shakespeare & Co. He soon became rebellious and rejected Chris-

Lacan around 1925 (from Elisabeth Roudinesco, Jacques Lacan & Co.: A History of Psychoanalysis in France, 1925–1985, *translated by Jeffrey Mehlman, 1990; Thomas Cooper Library, University of South Carolina)*

tian values. Around 1923 he discovered Freudian theory and was impressed by the ideas of Charles Maurras, founder of the right-wing group Action Française. Around 1925 Lacan's rejection of religion was reinforced by his readings of Friedrich Nietzsche. Incensed by his younger brother Marc-Marie's aspirations to the Benedictine monkhood, he felt that he had failed in guiding him.

At this time medical and intellectual views of Freudian psychoanalysis were in conflict. Medical psychoanalysis included dynamic psychiatry (the Zurich school), Pierre Janet's mode (a rival to the Freudian school), and Henri Bergson's approach (a variation on Freud's theories). Following World War I, France resisted Germanic viewpoints. Freud's teachings on sex were considered to represent a Germanic, not a global, psyche. Lacan studied neurology, then psychiatry, and, from 1927 to 1931, clinical treatment of cephalic and mental disorders at psychiatric hospitals in Paris. He joined a small group of young medics who fancied themselves elitists. This intellectual group was unimpressed by organicist views of psychology and instead contemplated revolutionary political models. Members of this group chose an elevated speaking style that set them apart from fellow students. Lacan's interrelations with teachers were intense. His instructor Gaëtan

Gatian de Clérambault agreed with both Freud and the Surrealists on connections between madness and truth, reason and unreason, coherence and delirium. Clérambault influenced Lacan's first theoretical text, "Structures des psychoses paranoïaques" (Structures of Paranoid Psychosis), published in July 1931 in *Semaine des hôpitaux de Paris* (Weekly Bulletin of the Paris Hospital). Upon publication of the article, Clérambault accused Lacan of plagiarism, but Lacan rebutted, claiming that it was Clérembault who had plagiarized him.

During the 1930s Lacan pursued Surrealism, Salvador Dali's theories on paranoia, and Breton's manifestos. By 1931 he had synthesized clinical psychiatry, Freudianism, and Surrealism. Influenced by Georges Politzer's *Critique des fondements de la psychologie* (Critique of the Foundations of Psychology, 1928), Lacan formulated a theory of paranoia following Freud's view that the psyche is shaped by the conscious and unconscious engaged in dialectical play with the social environment. His successful doctoral thesis in psychiatry, *De la psychose paranoïaque dans ses rapports avec la personnalité* (Paranoid Psychosis and Its Relation to Personality), published by Librarie E. Le François in 1932, analyzes the case of "Aimée" in terms of a paranoia that led to self-punishment, the result of a psychotic superego. Lacan applied a phenomenological method, inspired by the *Ethica*

(1677) of Spinoza. Lacan's connections between physical phenomena and psychic events led him to the notion of the "Other." Lacan's thesis received praise from intellectuals and psychologists who relished his attack against conservative values. He became the darling of Parisian dissidents, including pataphysicians, Marxists, and Surrealists. Dali commended Lacan's antimechanistic posture in the first issue of the Surrealist journal *Le Minotaure* (1933). Lacan responded by publishing articles on paranoia in the journal. In 1933 he attended Alexandre Kojève's seminars on Hegel. Lacan, as well as Parisians such as Georges Bataille and Raymond Queneau, were impressed by Kojève's lectures on Hegel's phenomenology. Riding on the success of his thesis, Lacan saw fit to enter into marriage. In spite of his anti-Christian convictions, he agreed to a church wedding with Marie-Louise (Malou) Blondin on 29 January 1934.

In 1934 Lacan entered a tempestuous analysis under Rudolph Loewenstein, one of the finer Freudian training analysts in the Societé Psychanalytique de Paris (Psychoanalytic Society of Paris, or SPP). Lacan became an active member of the SPP and opened a private practice. In 1936, at the Fourteenth International Psychoanalytic Association (IPA) in Marienbad, Czechoslovakia, Lacan read his paper "Le stade de miroir," (The Mirror Stage). After ten minutes, he was out of time and was duly cut off by the IPA president, Ernest Jones. To Lacan's frustration, little discussion of his paper followed. During the time he was writing this paper Lacan and his wife conceived their first child, Caroline Marie Image (born 8 January 1937), whose name refers to the *imago,* a key element in Lacan's paper. "Le stade de miroir" was published in the first volume of Lacan's *Ecrits* (Writings, 1966).

During the mid 1930s Nazism threatened the largely Jewish psychoanalytic world. Lacan, raised a Catholic, was educated by Jesuits, and his theorizing revealed a Christian ethos. Thus, Lacan was within and outside the movement. His detachment suited his renegade posture inspired by Surrealists and other artists. The condition of being both within and without recurred throughout his life and manifested itself in his dissident "excommunicated" situations. As Nazism rose, the psychoanalytic establishment retreated. Freud fled Vienna on 3 June 1938, leaving Jones solely in control of the IPA. In 1938, with the pressure of imminent war, and in spite of controversy over unorthodox methods of analysis, Lacan was granted the status of training analyst in the SPP.

World War II decimated the SPP. An underground of intellectuals, including Albert Camus, Jean-Paul Sartre, and Simone de Beauvoir, began gathering at the Café de Flore. Other Parisians soon joined, including Lacan, Sollers, Bataille, Pablo Picasso, Henri Ey, Alberto Giacometti, André Malreaux, Maurice Merleau-Ponty, and Maurice Blanchot. Intellectual ferment was juxtaposed with growing military aggression. Freud's writings were censored. Lacan published nothing during the war. Most of the SPP members fled France before the arrival of the Germans, and only Françoise Dolto and John Leuba remained in Paris. Resentfully, Lacan worked at the military psychiatric ward at Val-de-Grâce hospital. He argued later that rhetorical debate in France during the war was akin to language used by neurotics as a defense against reality. Thibaut, Lacan's second child, was born on 27 August 1939, and shortly after, on 23 September, Freud died in London. Sibylle, Lacan's third child with Marie-Louise, was born on 26 November 1940. In 1941 Sylvia Bataille, estranged wife of Georges Bataille, gave birth to Judith, Lacan's fourth child. Marie-Louise Lacan requested a divorce.

The second period of Lacan's work dates from 1948 to around 1960. Lacan began to focus on linguistics. In 1948 he tried to exploit the rivalry between Melanie Klein and Anna Freud. Klein's innovative methods appealed to Lacan. Anna Freud, Freud's daughter and the guardian of so-called legitimate Freudianism, perceived Kleinian psychology as a deviation. Lacan approached Klein to support his talk "on the progress of psychoanalysis," aimed at the psychoanalytical establishment. Thus, slipping past Anna Freud, in May 1948 he presented "L'Agressivité en psychanalyse" (Aggressivity in Psychoanalysis) at the eleventh Congrès des Psychanalystes de Langue Française (Congress of French-Speaking Psychoanalysts) in Brussels, in which he offered theories on the mirror stage, the paranoiac structure of the ego, and Oedipal identification with the father. At the 1949 IPA conference in Zurich, Lacan returned to discussions of the mirror stage with "Le stade de miroir comme formateur de la fonction du Je" (The Mirror Stage as Formative of the Function of the I). He attacked the ego-psychology of the "Anna Freudians," including the assertion of the primacy of the ego over the id. Diplomatically, he supported Anna Freud's views of ego-based defense mechanisms. Neither Freud nor Klein embraced Lacan's views, but Klein sensed a potential alliance. Lacan's self-serving attitudes worked against him, however. He offered to translate Klein's *Die Psychoanalyse des Kindes* (The Psychoanalysis of Children, 1932) from German into French, but had René Diatkine, one of his analysands, translate the first half. Klein engaged Françoise Boulanger and Jean-Baptiste Boulanger to work on the second half, but when the Boulangers attempted to cross-reference their translation with Lacan's, he could not produce it. He had lost the translation. When Klein learned of this, Lacan lost credibility, and any imagined alliance collapsed.

In 1951, Lacan became vice president of the SPP and began to deliver a series of weekly seminars at Sylvia Bataille's apartment in Paris. His clinical work became increasingly controversial with the SPP and the IPA. His sessions of variable and abbreviated lengths resulted in the SPP insisting that he regularize his practice. Although he promised to do so, he ignored the instructions. Lacan's life underwent important changes in 1953. Following his divorce, he married Bataille. In the wake of Sacha Nacht's ousting as president of the SPP, Lacan became interim president. That same year, controversy and inner politics within the SPP created student unrest, with Lacan as a target of criticism. Amid discussion of a motion of no confidence in Lacan's presidency, several of his supporters, including Daniel Lagache, Juliette Favez-Boutonier, and Dolto, resigned from the SPP to form the Société Française de Psychanalyse (SFP). Lacan soon quit the SPP to join the SFP, where he delivered an important lecture, "Le symbolique, l'imaginaire et le réel" (The Symbolic, the Imaginary, and the Real, 1953). These three fundamental registers provided the foundation for his definition of the psyche.

Lacan's unorthodoxy was noted by psychoanalytic associations, and in 1953 he was informed by the IPA that his membership had lapsed with his resignation from the SPP. In September 1953 a rebellious Lacan presented his paper "Fonction et champ de la parole et du langage en psychanalyse: Discours du congres de Rome et Reponse aux interventions" (The Function and Field of Speech and Language in Psychoanalysis: Discourse at the Congress in Rome and Answer to the Interventions) at the sixteenth Congrés de la Société Française de Psychanalyse. The paper rebuked his critics and called for allies, but it was too long to be read aloud and was distributed to participants. The "Rome Discourse" or "Rome Report" extolls variable-length or "punctuated" analytical sessions and links psychology with linguistics, mathematics, and structural anthropology. The essay was published in the journal La Psychanalyse in 1956 and later translated by Anthony Wilden as The Language of the Self: The Function of Language in Psychoanalysis (1968). The report also reassesses relationships between analysts and subjects, claiming that the (listening) silence of the analyst results in an act of "transference" in which the subject seeks to turn the analyst into an interlocutor. Lacan's views appealed to younger academics and emphasized linguistics, signifying systems, and the function of the unconscious.

In November 1953 Lacan delivered the first of his public seminars, which continued for twenty-seven years. These seminars helped to gather audiences and establish his reputation. The first, Les écrits techniques de Freud, 1953–1954 (published in book form in 1975 and translated as Freud's Papers on Technique, 1953–1954, 1988), is marked by an eloquent wit and focuses on Freud's case studies and questions of resistance, transference, analytic technique, and the mirror stage within the contexts of linguistics, philosophy, theology, and mysticism. Lacan was trying to confirm his views on the subversiveness of Freudian psychology as suggested to him by the Surrealists, Georges Bataille, and his readings of Friedrich Nietzsche. In 1954 he visited Freud's renegade student Carl Gustav Jung. Upon his return Lacan remained silent about the visit. In 1954–1955 Lacan presented the second seminar, Le moi dans la théorie de Freud et dans la technique de la psychanalyse, 1954–1955 (published in 1978; translated as The Ego in Freud's Theory and in the Technique of Psychoanalysis, 1954–1955, 1988). This paper ignored the focus of the conference, on Freud's Jenseits des Lustprinzips (1920; translated as Beyond the Pleasure Principle, 1922), Massenpsychologoie und Ich-Analyse (1921; translated as Group Psychology and the Analysis of the Ego, 1922), and Das Ich und das Es (1923; translated as The Ego and the Id, 1927), and instead offered an eclectic mix of thought drawing from Plato, the Bible, Molière, Poe, Søren Kierkegaard, Martin Heidegger, Lévi-Strauss, and cybernetics to present his "Schema L" (later developed in "Le séminaire sur 'La lettre volée'").

Schema L aimed to displace Freud's triadic formation of ego, id, and superego. The refined schema developed from this initial formation takes the shape of a Z and is named for its resemblance to the Greek letter lambda. The schema links the subject (S) to the ego (o), to the small other (o'), and to the grand Other (O) and recognizes the subject (or analysand) as decentered (that is, the subject is located not only at point S but also over the entire schema). In this schema the analysand is always blocked by the imaginary axis between ego and specular image. The symbol S is a deliberate pun on the German Es (in Freudian terms, the id). Lacan reminds that the drives of the id define the subject and reveal themselves through dreams, flashes of wit, and unconscious use of language, for example, slips of the tongue. Because it has to pass through the imaginary "wall of language," the discourse of the Other reaches the subject in an interrupted and inverted form. Schema L identifies the opposition between the imaginary and the symbolic, a cornerstone of Lacan's theory. This scheme also identifies the site of the analyst during therapy as within the locus of the grand Other, or O. Lacan explains that the maternal figure initially occupies the locus of the Other because she first intercommunicates with the child. During the

*Lacan and Marie-Louise Blondin on their wedding day,
29 January 1934 (Collection of Sibylle Lacan; from
Elisabeth Roudinesco,* Jacques Lacan: Outline of
a Life, History of a System of Thought, *translated by Barbara Bray, 1997; Thomas
Cooper Library, University
of South Carolina)*

Oedipal complex and the castration phase, however, the child discovers that the maternal figure is without a penis, which initiates what Lacan defines as an awareness of a lack in the Other (the symbol for the castrated or incomplete Other is the capital *O* with a bar through it). Schema L provided an integral base for Lacan's theory. Although his theories were well received, Lacan remained under attack for his variable-length analytic sessions, which contravened IPA standards.

In 1955, as part of Seminar II, Lacan presented to the SFP "Psychanalyse et cybernétique, ou, De la nature du langage" (Psychoanalysis and Cybernetics, or, On the Nature of Language), a paper on cybernetics and the process of abstraction that explains that primordial language is akin to cybernetic language (employing the units 0 and 1, or principles of presence and absence). Digital-media theorists, such as Richard Coyne in his *Technoromanticism: Digital Narrative, Holism, and the Romance of the Real* (1999), have responded to Lacanian theory.

Soon after, Lacan presented "La Chose Freudienne, ou Sens du retour à Freud en psychanalyse," published in *Evolution Psychiatrique* in 1956 and later translated as "The Freudian Thing, or The Meaning of the Return to Freud in Psychoanalysis" in *Ecrits*. This paper combines Freudian theory with Saussurian linguistics and includes Lacan's anecdote on Jung and Freud's 1909 journey to New York. Freud, upon sighting the Statue of Liberty, purportedly said to Jung, "They don't realize we're bringing them the plague." Freudian scholars are unable to confirm or deny this anecdote. Actual or not, the account reveals Lacan's subversive attitude and alludes to the function of the analyst who during a session must "cadaverize" his or her position by maintaining silence, thereby suggesting the presence of death. This allusion gestures both to the "dead Father" of the Oedipal complex and to Freud as the "dead Father" of psychoanalysis. Lacan's unsubstantiated reference to psychology as a plague reveals his own pataphysical and Surrealist attitudes toward the conservative machinations of the psychoanalytic establishment.

Having caught the attention of the intelligentsia, Lacan proceeded to the topic he was most interested and knowledgable in: paranoia. In 1955–1956 he presented his third seminar, *Les Psychoses, 1955–1956* (published, 1981; translated as *The Psychoses,* 1993), which considered the "Nom-du-Père" (Name-of-the-Father) as a fundamental signifier defining psychodynamics. In earlier writings, during the 1950s, the phrase "name of the father" (unhyphenated and not capitalized) refers to the father prohibiting incest during the Oedipal complex. This concept derives from the mythical father in Freud's *Totem und Tabu: Einige Übereinstimmungen im Seelenleben der Wilden under der Neurotiker* (1913; translated as *Totem and Taboo: Resemblances between the Lives of Savages and Neurotics,* 1918). By 1956, in *Les Psychoses,* Lacan capitalized and hyphenated the phrase, indicating that the "Nom-du-Père" was to be understood as the fundamental signifier that permits all other signification to proceed. The Name-of-the-Father confers identity on the subject (by naming him and placing him within the symbolic and social order of language) as well as signifying the paternal Oedipal "No." Lacan argues that Freud links the signifier of the Father (as the author of the Law) to death. The murder of the Father is also the fruitful moment of the debt through which the subject binds himself for life to the Law. Thus, the symbolic Father, insofar as he signifies this Law, is also the "dead father." Lacan states that for psychosis (or paranoia) to exist, the subject must have a psychotic structure wherein the Name-of-the-Father is in symbolic opposition to the subject. Lacan bases his analysis on Daniel Paul Schreber, an appeals court judge in Dresden who kept a memoir of his paranoid delusions. Freud's analysis of this memoir was studied by Lacan, who concluded that Schreber's psychosis was triggered by his failure to produce offspring coupled with his election to the high court. The subject's lack of paternity and his authority in the Name-of-the-Father entered into symbolic opposition.

Later, in the twelfth seminar, *Problèmes cruciaux pour la psychanalyse* (Crucial Problems for Psychoanalysis, 1964–1965), with reference to the triadic Borromean knot, Lacan explains that in a psychotic structure the real, the symbolic, and the imaginary are no longer linked. For psychotic or paranoid subjects there is a slippage of the signified under the signifier until the two are stabilized in delusional metaphor. The slippage of signification finds a parallel in Derrida's discussions of *mythos* and *logos* through his allegory of "La Pharmacie de Platon" (Plato's Pharmacy) in the Winter–Spring 1968 issue of *Tel Quel*. Lacan concludes that the neurotic inhabits language, but the psychotic is possessed by language. He warns against the "talking cure" for psychotic patients, because free association triggers latent psychosis. All treatments should begin with face-to-face interviews to determine the likelihood of psychosis. Alternate methods of treatment are necessary for psychotic patients. Like Freud, Lacan maintains a distinction between paranoia and schizophrenia, but Lacan's predilection for linguistics is revealed in his fascination for paranoid subjects.

Lacan's focus on signification and language emerges in his "Le séminaire sur 'La lettre volée,'" which was first published in *La Psychanalyse* in 1957. Analyzing the deflation of authority in the Name-of-the-Father in Poe's short story, this seminar offers a poststructural literary critique of experience as set into motion by language itself. The seminar examines the role of the gaze and displacement of the letter as signifier. Lacan's insistence on the autonomy of the signifying system leads him to reinterpret the "letter" not only as an epistle but also as an alphabetical character, a secret pact, a phallus, and a female body. Lacan argues that just as ancient Egyptian hieroglyphics eluded understanding for centuries, so displaced letters are meaningless in themselves. Thus, any signifier persists as a meaningless "letter" until deciphered by the subject/analysand. Lacan concludes that a letter always reaches its destination because messages inevitably return to their sender in inverted form (after passing through conditions defined in Schema L). Lacan's psycholinguistic reading of Poe becomes an allegory of psychoanalysis itself. His frame of reference and view of sexuality drew a deconstructive attack by Derrida in his "Le facteur de la vérité" (The Purveyor of Truth), published in the journal *Poetique* in 1975. Derrida rejects Lacan's valorization of the phallus as the universal or transcendental signifier, arguing that Lacan's reading gives priority to a revelation of truth through speech. Derrida further criticizes Lacan's de-emphasis of the importance of features of narcissism and the "imagi-

nary." Lacan's seminar is the subject of John P. Muller and William J. Richardson's *The Purloined Poe: Lacan, Derrida, and Psychoanalytic Reading* (1988), in which an English translation of the seminar appears. "Le séminaire sur 'La lettre volée'" succeeded in expanding his audience beyond psychoanalytic circles.

During the 1950s and 1960s Lacan nurtured relationships with Parisian intellectuals such as Kojève, Heidegger, Lévi-Strauss, Jean Hyppolite, Paul Ricoeur, Althusser, Foucault, Deleuze, Derrida, and Roman Jakobson. It was a commonplace among linguists and structuralists that language was a product of the unconscious. Although Jakobson's antipsychological view of the unconscious was not Freudian, it nonetheless followed Edmund Husserl's view of the subliminal as the repository of unconscious knowledge. In response to Jakobson, Lacan developed a theory of the signifier linked to the Name-of-the-Father. This linkage explained paternal authority and filial response in a case that puzzled even Freud. In *La Psychanalyse* in 1959 Lacan published these findings as "D'une question préliminaire à tout traitement possible de la psychose," collected in *Ecrits II* (1975) and later translated as "On a Question Preliminary to Any Possible Treatment of Psychosis" in *Ecrits: A Selection*.

Lacan's interest in the Name-of-the-Father evidently had its roots in his memories of his dictatorial grandfather, Emile Lacan. His exploration of the subject continues in his fourth seminar, "La relation d'objet et les structures Freudiennes" (Object Relations and Freudian Structures, 1956–1957), which attacks the SPP focus on object relations by arguing that Freud is not concerned with the object but its lack. Lacan discusses the lack or gap with reference to castration, the Law (in the Name-of-the-Father), and the phallus as signifier, which he also relates to the movement of the maternal figure from the symbolic (realm of language) to the (ineffable) real. He addresses homosexual relations, linking the "lack" to the father figure, but only speculates on how women experience object relations.

In 1957–1958 Lacan presented his fifth seminar, *Les formations de l'inconscient* (The Formations of the Unconscious), unpublished but significant for introducing his *graphe du désir* (graph of desire) in response to Freud's theory of jokes as verbal enunciations. For example, Lacan refers to Freud's play on words *famillionär* from *Der Witz und seine Beziehung zum Unbewussten* (1905; translated as *Wit and Its Relation to the Unconscious*, 1916) as a conjunction of two terms (*familiar* and *millionaire*). Issues such as overdetermined, elliptical, or polysemous meaning figure in the graph of desire. The elementary cell of the graph features a curved line indicating a diachronic signifying chain intersecting with a horseshoe-shaped line marking the subject's intentional-

Lacan and Sylvia Bataille, who became his second wife in 1953
(from Elisabeth Roudinesco, Jacques Lacan & Co.: A
History of Psychoanalysis in France, 1925–1985,
translated by Jeffrey Mehlman, 1990; Thomas
Cooper Library, University of South Carolina)

ity. The intersection of the two lines illustrates an Oedipal formation in which two prohibitions are forwarded in the Name-of-the-Father. The first prohibits maternal reintegration with the child as phallic object. The second prohibits the (male) child from (sexual) relations with the mother. The threat of castration is given an alternative path out of the Oedipal complex if the child adopts the ideal of the paternal ego by accepting an androcentric social law or order. Language is fundamental to this order, and the graph illustrates the divided subject (a subject pressured into displacing the maternal object of desire). Lacan returns to this graph in his colloquium of 19–23 September 1960, "Subversion du sujet et dialectique du désir dans l'inconscient freudien" (Subversion of the Subject and the Dialectic of Desire in the Freudian Unconscious), presented at Les colloques philosophique internationaux (The International Philosophical Colloquium) in Royaumont and published in *Ecrits II*. In this colloquium Lacan adopts an anti-Hegelian posture and argues that in psychoanalysis a synthesis is ultimately impossible. He improves the graph of desire, stating that the subject is forever divided in the Name-of-the-Father by the emergence of the signifier (which is indicative of a split between signifier/signified, or the enunciation of desire as opposed to the object of desire).

The third and final period of Lacan's work lasts roughly from 1960 to 1980 and is characterized by a shift in focus from the graph of desire back to the notions of the imaginary, symbolic, and real. Although Lacan tends to leave the graph of desire aside in later deliberations, the Freudian base set forth in "Les formations de l'inconscient" shapes much of his thinking that follows. For example, Lacan discusses *Hamlet* as a tragedy of desire in his sixth seminar, "Le Desir et son interpretation" (Desire and Its Interpretation), some sessions of which were published in *Ornicar?* between 1981 and 1983. He argues that Hamlet's dead father is on an impossible quest for redemption. The dead father as Other (site of language and locus of truth) lacks the signifier that names the real and ensures truth. Lacan reads Gertrude's maternal desire as gluttony and Ophelia's entrapment within a web of masculine desire as symptomatic of the *object a* (or small other, the object of desire and phallic signifier). Hamlet and Ophelia experience an *aphanisis* (loss of desire) accompanied by death. Here, Lacan establishes a phallocentric, hence asymmetrical, mapping of masculine/feminine desire.

The question of ethical behavior raised in *Hamlet* inspired Lacan's seventh seminar, *L'Ethique de la Psychanalyse: 1959–1960* (1986; translated as *The Ethics of Psychoanalysis, 1959–1960,* 1992), in which he attempts to establish ethical foundations for psychoanalysis and contemporary society. *L'Ethique de la psychanalyse* was published by Editions du Seuil in 1986. Here, Lacan situates desire through the fault (both crime and gap), noting that sin is ubiquitous. The task of analysis is to enable the analysand's confrontation with his or her own id in order to discover the truth of his or her desire. In this seminar Lacan draws on Freud, Oedipus, *Hamlet,* Martin Luther, and a monotheistic Judeo-Christian tradition to define the "Thing." Within a linguistic context, the "Thing," akin to the real, is an unknowable *x,* beyond symbolization or signification (with affinities to Immanuel Kant's *ding an sich* [thing itself]). Within the context of *jouissance* (the libidinal pleasure principle), the "Thing" is a composite of the object of desire, the lost object that must be found, the primal Other, the forbidden object of incestuous desire, and the Mother. Further, the "Father" is understood symbolically, as a disincarnate object of faith. Lacan raises philosophical and hedonistic questions regarding Kant and the Marquis de Sade, explaining that sublimation, particularly among artists, marks a creative quest to encounter the Thing. *L'Ethique de la psychanalyse* examines diverse questions including the death of God, the death drive, and the condition of Antigone. Lacan pursued his seminar on ethics further with the publication of "Kant avec Sade" (Kant with Sade) in the April 1962 issue of the journal *Critique*. This text was originally written as a preface to Sade's *La Philosophie dans le boudoir* (The Philosophy of the Bedroom, 1795) and offers a joint reading of Sade's views with Kant's *Kritik der praktischen Vernunft* (Critique of Practical Reason, 1788). In this provocative analysis, Sade's notion of "evil" is read as an equivalent to Kant's notion of "good," insofar as Sade's imperative dictating *jouissance* corresponds to Kant's view on the repression of desire. Lacan's eccentric questions on ethics in Seminar VII and discussions of "good" and "evil" in "Kant avec Sade" found strong and mixed reactions in a Europe still reeling from the totalitarian regimes of Nazism and Stalinism.

In Seminar VIII, *Le transfert dans sa disparite subjective* (Transference in Its Subjective Disparity, 1960–1961; published by Editions du Seuil as *Le transfert: 1960–1961,* 1991), Lacan again draws from Freud and identifies three modes of identification. The first, prior to the Oedipal contest, is based on primitive, ideal, ego-identification with the father as Ur-father. The second is a regressive identification with the (maternal) object of desire, which refuses itself to the subject. Although an identification occurs with the maternal object, Lacan stresses that masculine relations (master/student, father/son) of the small other and the phallus are still operational. The third identification is a hysterical one in which the subject recognizes his own condition in that of the small other. Seminar VIII includes analysis of Plato's *Symposium* and the relationships of Socrates, Alcibiades, and Agathon. In his analysis of the *Symposium,* Lacan addresses matters such as sexual difference, homosexuality, and the notion of the *agalma,* or fetish (object of desire/phallus), as well as the idea of female lack or *manque à être* as forwarded by "Diotima" (a woman representing Socrates' "feminine" voice). The seminar on Plato's text concludes with a discussion of the phallus as the signifier of signifiers. Lacan's response to homosexuality was relatively liberal. Unlike Freud and the larger psychoanalytical establishment, which, at the time, considered homosexuality to be a form of social deviance, Lacan was tolerant and accepted homosexual patients when other analysts refused them simply on principle. He did not go out of his way to become a champion of homosexuality, however.

In Seminar IX, *L'identification* (Identification, 1961–1962), Lacan focuses on the direct relationship between the subject and the signifier. Lacan's use of the term *sign* refers to that which represents something for someone. Alternately, he uses the term *signifier* to indicate that which represents a subject for another signi-

fier. While de Saussure felt that signifier and signified constitute an unbreakable bond, Lacan insists there is rupture and slippage between the two. For Lacan, signification is a metonymic process because meaning lies in the interplay of signifiers within a signifying chain (as in a sentence). Thus, one signifier always refers to another signifier, and the meaning of any signifier depends upon its location within a metonymic order. Lacan now designated the signifier by the symbol s in his topological charts. Shortly after, in Seminar IX, he includes discussion of the differences between preverbal and verbal phases, arguing that the effects of the signifier on the subject define or constitute the unconscious. The signifier, as fundamental unit of the conscious (symbolic) register, is also indicative of a particular order. In other words, the signifier *is* the grand Other (or the *Autre*). Here, Lacan introduces co-relative, mathematically based topologies that correspond to his theorems. Throughout his career, Lacan reconsidered topological figures such as the torus, the Klein bottle, the Möbius strip, and the Borromean knot. This search for appropriate topological representation occupied him until his death.

Lacan's Seminar X, *L'angoisee* (Anguish, 1962–1963), focuses on anxiety. Here, he builds on earlier writings linking anxiety to the *corpse morcelé* (fragmented body), which he discusses in reference to the mirror stage. He links anxiety to the "real" or that which cannot be defined or categorized. The "real" is the supreme object of anxiety. Drawing on his ideas from 1953–1955, Lacan reformulates the "real" as one of the three registers along with the imaginary (unconscious) and the symbolic (conscious). In his first seminar he named the real as that which resists symbolization absolutely (that is, the real is constituted by all that which exists or subsists outside of symbolization). By Seminar XI, *Les quatre concepts fondamentaux de la psychanalyse* (1964; published in book form by Editions de Seuil in 1973 and translated as *The Four Fundamental Concepts of Psycho-analysis,* 1977), Lacan appropriates his earlier definition of the Thing into the real (including the algebraic *x* or Kantian *ding an sich*) and redefines the real by linking it to the impossible (that is, the impossible to imagine, impossible to conceive of, and impossible to symbolize). There are links with the real and hallucination (some physical phenomena are impossible to symbolize and so they enter the real). The real represents an interconnectedness between *Innenwelt* and *Umwelt*. Thus, psychic and physical reality are interwoven. He explains that the real is the locus of the object of desire (including the perception/conception of that object). Lacan now uses the term *real* as an adjective to denote that which is lacking in the symbolic order of language, specifically, the residue of all articulation, the foreclosed element that may be approached but never grasped, the umbilical cord of the symbolic. It is worth noting that the three registers of the imaginary, the symbolic, and the real are profoundly heterogeneous. Yet, the fact that Lacan links the three establishes a commonality.

He addresses this commonality with reference to Borromean topologies in Seminar XXII, "R.S.I." (Real, Symbolique, Imaginaire, 1974–1975), which privileges the real over the symbolic and imaginary. Freud indirectly defined anxiety through a condition of emptiness; however, in Seminar X Lacan argues that anxiety has an object, but that object is undefinable. The *objet a* (small other) connects anxiety with desire. Arguably, the small other is the cause of desire just as it is the *residue* of projected narcissistic desire following the mirror stage, a kind of psychic placenta or, as Lacan puns later in Seminar XXIII, "Le sinthome" (The Symptom, 1975–1976), *l'hommelette* (little man or omelet). Alternately, Lacan suggests that desire and anxiety are linked to the imminence of the object of desire. Through the interlocked frisson between death and sex drives, this imminence inspires anxiety through alternating pulsations of presence and absence.

Lacan's seminars found success during the period from 1953 to 1963, but his career suffered when the IPA denied the request for affiliation by the newly formed SFP. Finally, in 1963, after many interviews and reports, the IPA granted the SFP affiliation on condition that Lacan and two other analysts be removed from the list of training analysts. The report further decreed that Lacan's training activity be banned and that trainee analysts be forbidden to attend his seminars. Later, this decree came to be known as Lacan's "excommunication." At issue was his insistence on variable-length psychoanalytic sessions. In 1963 Lacan resigned from the SFP and, by 1964, moved his seminar to the Ecole Normale Supérieure, where he founded his own group, the Ecole Freudienne de Paris (EFP). As a result of these changes, the SFP was dissolved in 1965.

In 1964 Lacan presented his Seminar XI, *Les quatre concepts fondamentaux de la psychanalyse*. Lacan had been ostracized by the IPA, his teachings declared anathema. The IPA as "Name-of-the-Father" had spoken, and Lacan responded with spleen, comparing his condition to the excommunication of Spinoza from the synagogue in 1656. Nonetheless, Lacan found new support and acclaim. His audience changed. He spoke to fewer psychoanalysts and to more philosophers, linguists, structuralists, and anthropologists. *Les quatre concepts fondamentaux de la psychanalyse* revisits Freudian theory and considers psychoanalytical praxis in terms of four concepts: the unconscious, repetition, transference, and drive. Lacan already elaborated the first three in previous talks. Here, he connects sex and death drives refer-

ring to Heraclitus's discussion of the archer's bow, which is ascribed a "life" value, with a deadly function. Soon after, he presented Seminar XII, "Problèmes cruciaux pour la psychanalyse," addressing psychoanalytic practice with reference to Klein bottle configurations. In 1965–1966 Lacan presented Seminar XIII, "L'objet de la Psychanalyse" (The Object of Psychoanalysis), in which he commented on the Other/other with reference to mathematical topologies and *mathemes,* Lacan's term for a mathematical model for illustrating psychoanalytic theory. His audiences grew.

During the 1960s Althusser saw a potential ally in Lacan. Althusser defended Lacanian views, and through him Lacan met Miller, who married Judith Bataille Lacan in 1966 and became a spokesperson who coherently explained Lacan's theories in structuralist terms. Miller's well-organized interpretations served to contain Lacan's theories within themselves, thereby reducing some of the subtleties. His hyperlogical interpretations of Lacan's theory were ameliorated by Lacan's own interest in arithmetic, mathematics, and topology. Miller noted that Lacan excluded consciousness from any definition of the subject (analysand) and gave the name "suture" to the relationship between the subject and the subject's signifying chain of discourse. Lacan immediately re-revised his theory of the signifier, applying the Millerian concept of the "suture." It is difficult to say how much Miller and Lacan influenced each other. Lacan's theory relied increasingly on mathematical systems borrowed from thinkers such as René Descartes, George Boole, Bertrand Russell, and Gödel. After reading Ludwig Wittgenstein's *Tractatus Logico-Philosophicus* (1922), Lacan developed his idea of the *matheme*. He concluded that a purely scientific consideration of psychology demonstrates that psychology is *not* a pure science.

Lacan's 1966 visit to Johns Hopkins University in Baltimore revealed how his theory integrated with his personal experience. Roudinesco recalls the event in her *La bataille de cent ans*. Lacan was to present a paper that was awkwardly titled: "Of Structure as an Inmixing of an Otherness Prerequisite to Any Subject Whatever" (published in *The Language of Criticism and the Sciences of Man: The Structuralist Controversy,* 1970). The presentation had a sense of provisionality. Shortly before the talk, Anthony Wilden was suddenly recruited to polish Lacan's English translation. Lacan's appearance marked a transitional point both in his life and in the development of twentieth-century theory. The term "post-structuralism" was introduced by the American press to describe this rare meeting of Continental and North American thought. Wearied by the battles with the SPP and IPA and feeling his age, Lacan was self-conscious, simultaneously sensing imminent fame and his own mortality. At dawn, he gazed out his hotel window at the neon lights and traffic of Baltimore and entered a reverie on *Dasein,* a state of thought thinking itself, without consciously knowing it. He included a realization from this reverie in his talk: "The most synthetic image I can give you of the unconscious is Baltimore in the very early morning." Lacan spoke on the fact that he felt close to a breakthrough, but sensed his own mortality and increasing difficulty in progressing. Although his lecture inspired enthusiastic discussion, "Lacanianism" failed to have an immediate impact in the United States. He returned to Paris temporarily deflated. Years later, however, his influence was felt profoundly in North America.

Back in Paris, Miller succeeded in making Lacan's perplexing seminars accessible to broader audiences. In 1966 *Ecrits* was published, presenting a selection of Lacan's seminars as well as twenty-eight articles by Lacan written and published between 1936 and 1966. The book became a best-seller. The initial print run of five thousand copies sold out, and a reprint was ordered within the year. Later, Editions de Seuil republished a condensed version in two volumes (*Ecrits I* and *Ecrits II*), reducing the number of texts to five and seven, respectively. *Ecrits* encompasses the work of some thirty years, presented in nonchronological order. The collection was influential among nonpsychoanalyst scholars and helped to define Lacan's fundamental theories. The *Ecrits* volumes remain problematic to readers because of a lack of conventional linearity in expression. Translators such as Muller and Richardson (in *Lacan and Language: A Reader's Guide to Ecrits,* 1982) suggest that Lacan's writing is a type of rebus or linguistic puzzle. Even the title of the book, *Ecrits,* is a misnomer. The chapters are often based on transcripts of talks given by Lacan. They are not "writings," nor do they represent a well-organized whole. Lacan claimed he structured his talks in imitation of shifting patterns in dreams and the unconscious. He intended that the complexity of reading and understanding texts should inspire a journey similar to that of the analysand trying to find meaning while undergoing psychoanalysis. Lacan's predilection for language play, puns, and associative leaps in logic illustrated the discourse of the unconscious and, with effort, yielded to critical analysis.

Ecrits excluded some of Lacan's important talks, seminars, and papers; nonetheless, the collection drew an enthusiastic following, although it was not without critics. Jean-François Lyotard criticized Lacan for his overly linguistic interpretation of dreams. Lacan's view of language was accused of being overly phallologocentric by Luce Irigary in her *Speculum, de'lautre femme* (Speculum: Of the Other Woman, 1974), and Lacan admitted that he had focused primarily on male experi-

Lacan with his daughter Caroline Marie Image, June 1958 (Collection of Cyril and Fabrice Roger-Lacan; from Elisabeth Roudinesco, Jacques Lacan: Outline of a Life, History of a System of Thought, *translated by Barbara Bray, 1997; Thomas Cooper Library, University of South Carolina)*

ence without fully accounting for the formation of the female psyche and feminine desire. A similar attack was launched by Hélène Cixous and Catherine Clément in *La jeune née* (The Newly Born Woman, 1975). Lacan anticipated some of these matters in *Feminine Sexuality: Lacan and the Ecole freudienne* (1982), but with limited success.

Perhaps it is fair to say that Lacan's megalomania increased during these later years. In 1967, he presented "De Rome 53 à Rome 67: La Psychanalyse. Raison d'un échec" (From Rome 53 to Rome 67: Psychoanalysis, the Reason for Failure), a lecture at the University of Rome (published in *Scilicet* in 1968), which includes a rare mention of Foucault, as well as an allusion to Derrida, whose important notion of *différance* Lacan described as Aphrodite rising out of the foam of Lacanian discourse. It is revealing to know that in classical myth, Aphrodite was born out of the sea when Chronos (Saturn) deposed his father (Uranus) and hurled his scrotum into the ocean. The associated images of castration, the death of the father, and the goddess of love imply that Lacan was taking on the authority of the "Name-of-the-Father" and, through his conjunction of images suggesting death and sex drives, alluded unflatteringly to purported imitators of his ideas.

In Seminar XIV, *La logique du fantasme* (The Logic of Fantasy, 1966–1967), Lacan developed mathematical formulas and grappled with Möbius strip and Klein bottle topologies while suggesting a new flexible approach to logic itself. This seminar plays with versions of Descartes's *Cogito ergo sum* and arrives at theorems such as *Cogito ergo es* ("I think therefore you are"), which includes a German pun on *Es* (the *id;* hence, "I think therefore id"). This seminar is the first to include Marxist notions of value and exchange. Unlike Jakobson, Lacan believes some elements avoid signification. It also includes Lacan's important view that on the symbolic level, there is no sexual act, only sexuality. The sexual act involves a signifying doubling that permits the subject to narcissistically inscribe himself in a metonymic chain that refers back to himself. Lacan picks up on this notion in Seminar XV, *L'acte psychanalytique* (The Psychoanalytic Act, 1967–1968). Seminars XIV, XV, and XVI, collectively titled "D'un a l'Autre" (From One to the Other, 1968–1969), are chaotic and come just prior to the suspension of Lacan's teaching privileges at the ENS. "D'un a l'Autre" argues for the importance of articulating psychoanalysis as a knowledge that can be taught at a university.

May 1968 was a time of great social unrest. The women's movement, student riots, and the "May events" in Paris reshaped France. On 13 May, one million workers demonstrated in the streets. On 18 May, ten million French workers went on strike, and the factories were occupied. The social unrest provided an appropriate backdrop to Lacan's eccentricity, evident with the inception of *Scilicet,* the journal of the EFP. *Scilicet* had a bizarre editorial policy that permitted only articles by Lacan to be ascribed to the author. All other articles were to be published anonymously. In 1967 there was a growing internal controversy in the EFP over Lacan's idea of a procedure named "the pass," in which members who were undergoing analysis could "testify" before their superiors about their progress and thus end their analysis to become full-fledged analysts. Lacan defended his controversial method, arguing that to become an analyst was analogous to becoming a poet. The EFP remained divided over this matter. In 1971 Lacan published "Lituraterre" in the journal *Littérature,* commenting on avant-garde writers such as Beckett, Barthes, and Joyce. He also quipped provocatively that while psychoanalysis was based on the Oedipus complex, it had nothing to say about Sophocles. The comment was bizarre coming from the same ana-

lyst who arrived at remarkable conclusions about Joyce as a "symptom" after reading *Finnegans Wake.*

In the informative Seminar XVII, *L'envers de la Psychanalyse: 1969–1970* (The Inverse of Psychoanalysis, 1969–1970; published in book form in 1991), Lacan establishes the fundamental four discourses (the discourse of the master, the hysteric, the university, and the analyst). Included in this discussion is the role of the university, the place that students hold within it, and Lacan's own position as analyst. This seminar comments on master/slave relations, Marxism and the proletariat, the dead father, and Freud's case study of Dora (and subsequent discussion of hysteria). Lacan states that the discourse of the analyst surrounds the other three discourses without resolving them. The inverse of psychoanalysis, then, is the discourse of the master, which functions as a foil to the subject. Alternately, the inverse of psychoanalysis can be the unconscious discourse that convolutes social "right" and "wrong" in a Möbius-like configuration. Bruce Fink offers an illuminating critical interpretation of this seminar in *The Lacanian Subject: Between Language and Jouissance* (1995). Seminar XVII coincides with the release of *Ecrits* by Editions du Seuil and "Radiophonie," Lacan's 1970 radio broadcast with Robert Georgin broadcast in Belgium by ORTF, published that same year in *Scilicet.* "Radiophonie" served to broaden Lacan's notoriety and further his discussion of the modes of discourse, while identifying similarities and differences between Lacan, de Saussure, and the Prague circle. The Prague Linguistic Circle was inaugurated in 1926 by Vilém Mathesius and his colleagues, Roman Jakobson, Bohuslav Havránek, Bohumil Trnka, and Jan Rypka. The circle grew to include international scholars such as Jan Mukarovsky and René Wellek. The published version also offers mathematical schemes of the four major discourses discussed in Seminar XVII.

Lacan developed the topology of the Borromean knot in Seminar XVIII, *D'un discours qui ne serait pas du semblant* (Of a Discourse That Would Not Be on Semblance, 1970–1971). A Borromean knot is made up of three rings, and Lacan began with this formation but later played with it, adding other rings while allowing the rings themselves to flex. The topology of a ring, with its inner and outer sides representing the subject's *Innenwelt* and *Umwelt,* appealed to Lacan.

The notions of "inside" and "outside" could be convoluted in reference to rings just as they could be in psychology. Here again, Lacan's personal life brushes up against his theory. Continually finding himself both within and without the psychoanalytic establishment, Lacan evolved a theory that explains the psyche and serves as an analog for his troubled professional relationships. Lacan concludes that the psyche is structured like a series of chains or knots. He assigns values to the three rings in terms of the three psychic "registers," the "imaginary," the "symbolic," and the "real." Alternately, he varies the ring's values as psychoanalytical theory, psychoanalytical practice, and the "real" of the psychoanalyst him- or herself. Thus, the rings could be thought of as polysemous or sliding signifiers. The interlinking or mutual interdependence of the rings indicated the manner in which the three registers connected in human experience. The linking of psychic registers was desirable, and through psychoanalysis an adjustment could be made to the psyche by an unknotting and re-knotting of the three registers. He added that in schizophrenics an extended unknotting occurs, signifying a psychic breakdown. Lacan continued to illustrate his theories with such knots and drawings of knots until his death.

D'un discours que ne serait pas du semblant identifies semblance (an element of the signifying order) as the point of organization of the four discourses. Semblance is also co-relative to truth and is a form of ineffable discourse that, Lacan suggests, may emerge through the unconscious, the situation of the analyst, or the process of analysis itself. Lacan admits that this discourse avoids firm definition because it addresses the real, which is always ineffable. Lacan comments on *jouissance* and the absence of a signifier for sexual difference. Seminar XIX, . . . *ou pire* (. . . or worse, 1971–1972), was delivered upon Lacan's return to teach at the Hôpital Sainte-Anne. The seminar is summarized in a 1975 issue of *Scilicet*. Here, Lacan reiterates that there is no sexual relation among speaking beings. He relies on logic and mathematical formulas to discuss sexuality and the unconscious, concluding that, in psychoanalytic discourse, the signifier is *jouissance,* while the phallus is merely the signified.

Seminar XX, *Encore* (1972–1973), is one of Lacan's best known. Published, after being shortened and reorganized by Miller, by Editions de Seuil in 1975 and translated as *On Feminine Sexuality: The Limits of Love and Knowledge* (1998), this seminar includes commentary on femininity and was presented during protests against the psychoanalytical establishment by the Mouvement de Libération des Femmes (Women's Liberation Movement). Using language play, logical systems, and knotted ropes to demonstrate topological relations, this seminar summarizes Lacan's theories, adding that women only enter sexual relations as mothers, while men enter only under constraint of castration. Given this impossible condition, actual sexual relations are displaced and defined by love and speech. Thus, women hold a direct relation with God, who is aligned with the "Name-of-the-Father," and so have a privileged position

Lacan and Philippe Sollers, novelist and editor of the influential Parisian journal Tel Quel *(from Elisabeth Roudinesco,* Jacques Lacan & Co.: A History of Psychoanalysis in France, 1925–1985, *translated by Jeffrey Mehlman, 1990; Thomas Cooper Library, University of South Carolina)*

on the side of truth. Lacan maintains that men are uncertain how to address this feminine verity.

Throughout his career Lacan presented sporadic talks on feminine sexuality. These talks were later translated into English by Jacqueline Rose and published as *Feminine Sexuality.* There is some overlap with this book and the publication of Lacan's Seminar XX. *Feminine Sexuality* includes chapters dealing with the topics of God, transference, the significance of the phallus, the castration complex, and female *jouissance.* Some of the chapters are reprints of talks or seminars given as far back as 1952.

While some feminist critics have argued that any Lacanian interpretation of feminine sexuality is inevitably phallocentric, Lacan's discussions of feminine sexuality are concerned with the concepts of both "man" and "woman" as constructs, or categories within language. *Feminine Sexuality* includes "Guiding Remarks for a Congress on Feminine Sexuality," written in 1958, two years before a colloquium on feminine sexuality organized by the Société de Psychanalyse in Amsterdam. There, Lacan challenged women to articulate their sexuality. David Macey, in *Lacan in Contexts* (1988), identifies a Surrealist iconography in *Feminine Sexuality,* influenced by Lacan's earlier encounters with Surrealist artists such as Dali and Breton. Macey suggests that the seminar reveals a perverse nostalgia for the subject of hysteria, a topic fundamental to Lacan's doctoral thesis on "Aimée."

The reaction to *Feminine Sexuality* ranged from an engaged acceptance to aggressive criticism. It is sometimes difficult to separate Lacan the theorist and Lacan the man. He had a reputation for elitism as well as womanizing. His attitude found little sympathy within the psychoanalytic establishment or with prominent female colleagues such as Anna Freud and Melanie Klein. Schneiderman, in *Jacques Lacan: The Death of an Intellectual Hero,* comments that his mistresses were almost as numerous as his followers. Lacan's personal life and his insistent phallocentrism inspired resistance and mixed reactions to his theories.

A strong feminist response to Lacanian theory can be attributed to the view that the nonbiological notion of the Other as it relates to a sense of *manque à être* is universally applicable. Feminist critics acknowledge that Lacan raised the important issue of subjectivity in psychoanalysis and language, albeit from a phallocentric perspective. Those who embrace Lacan's views remind others that his notion of the phallus is strictly a signifier and therefore applicable to both masculine and feminine experience. Critics such as Jane Flax (in her "Lacan in a Feminist's Gaze," included in *Criticism and Lacan: Essays and Dialogue on Language, Structure, and the Unconscious,* 1990), however, note that Lacan's linguistic orientation is still founded on the incest taboo rooted in patriarchal, biological familial relations. Furthermore, for Lacan, the Other is defined as the other sex, which is female for both male and female subjects. The male plays a pivotal role, and women play the role of Other for themselves as well as for men. It was this point that many feminists found unacceptable.

Thinkers such as Jane Gallup, Kristeva, Juliet Mitchell, Cixous, and Irigaray developed analytical methods in reaction to Lacan and his notion of the signifier as phallus. In *Reading Lacan* (1985) Gallup offers a comprehensive plurality of interpretive possibilities. Kristeva extols the virtues of a heterogeneity of language in her semanalyses, and *le sémiotique* in regard to unconscious patterns of language and the destabilization of the "thetic" subject in literature. She distances herself from Lacan's patriarchal position in books such as *Desire in Language: A Semiotic Approach to Literature and Art* (1980) and articles such as "Il n'ya pas de maître à

langage" (1979; translated as "Within the Microcosm of 'The Talking Cure,'" 1983). Mitchell, in the introduction she wrote as co-editor of *Feminine Sexuality,* addresses how phenomena such as hysteria in narration reveal the subject-in-process in reaction against patriarchal capitalism. Cixous's theory responds partly to Lacan's "imaginary" register, where a prelinguistic unity exists between mother and child. She rejects the Lacanian concept of desire arising from lack, however, and in articles such as "La Sexe ou la tête?" (1976; translated as "Castration or Decapitation," 1981) she shares with Irigaray the notion that a potent feminine challenge to phallic authority is through laughter, indifference, and the disinvestment of interest. Irigaray's discussion of power politics and the sexualization of discourse in her book *Ce sexe que n'en est pas un* (1977; translated as *This Sex Which Is Not One,* 1985) attacks Lacan's phallocentrism and masculine orientation toward language as contributing to the oppression of women's discourse. Within the context of this phallocentric theory, Lacan's views are not particularly amenable to discussions of lesbian sexuality. In "Lacan and Feminism," an essay in *Jacques Lacan: A Feminist Introduction* (1990), Elizabeth A. Grosz offers an overview of feminist responses to Lacanian theory and explains that Lacan permits alternate critical perspectives precisely because he articulates presumptions that were socially dominant but that remained largely unspoken prior to his commentary.

Lacan's *Télévision* (1974; translated as *Television: A Challenge to the Psychoanalytic Establishment,* 1990) includes a defense of his own psychoanalytic methods as well as a critique of the psychoanalytic establishment. The book is a transcription of Lacan's first appearance on television, in 1973 on the two-part program *Psychanalyse,* produced by Benoît Jacquot. He was interviewed by Miller, who published the transcription with Editions du Seuil the following year. An English translation was published along with "A Challenge to the Psychoanalytic Establishment," which is a compilation of controversial items, including the July 1953 report from Heinz Hartmann, president of the International Psychoanalytic Association, as well as letters that trace Lacan's expulsion from the IPA, the introduction to Lacan's Name-of-the-Father seminar (1963), and the text to the Founding Act of the EFP. The program addressed most of the key issues in Lacan's methodology, including his doctrine, psychoanalysis as an institution, and the seminars. Marcelle Marini, in *Jacques Lacan: The French Context* (1992), suggests that the program revealed little that was new and was a contrived device to popularize Lacanian theory while raising the prestige of the interviewer. This form of presentation was the norm for French television at the time, however, and Lacan may simply have done what was expected. The second half of the book features a challenge by Lacan to the psychoanalytic establishment and includes a "dossier on the institutional debate," as well as items such as the July 1953 report from the president of the IPA. This portion of the book presents some of Lacan's responses to the controversy surrounding him since his expulsion from the IPA in 1953 and his so-called excommunication in 1963. *Télévision* reveals the autocracy of Freudian theory and Lacan's situation after challenging the authority of the IPA. His concern for the informing yet perplexing instability of language is revealed in his oft-quoted opening comments on the television program: "I always speak the truth. Not the whole truth, because there's no way to say it all. Saying it all is literally impossible: words fail. Yet it's through this very impossibility that the truth holds onto the real." Lacan contended that all of society is shaped and affected by language and urged further study of *logos*. Critical reception to the book was unexceptional insofar as the ideas had circulated earlier. Significantly, Lacan has inspired a spectrum of media critics. Television and movie critics such as Elizabeth Cowie, Ann Kaplan, and Christian Metz investigate Lacanian perspectives in journals such as *Screen, Ciné-tracts, camera obscura, Film Forum,* and *Filmwork.* Slavoj Žižek has also applied Lacanian theory to cinema, notably the works of Alfred Hitchcock, in *Enjoy Your Symptom! Jacques Lacan in Hollywood and Out* (1992), and *Everything You Always Wanted to Know about Lacan: But Were Afraid to Ask Hitchcock* (1992).

In Seminar XXI, *Les non-dupes errent* (The Non-Dupes Wander, 1973–1974), Lacan reemphasizes Borromean linkages of the imaginary, the symbolic, and the real under the auspices of the Name-of-the-Father. In 1974, the Department of Psychoanalysis at Vincennes was reorganized and renamed "Le Champ Freudien," and Lacan was named the scientific director, with Miller the president. The institute stressed a mathematical formalization of psychoanalytic theory. In 1975 Lacan gave a series of talks at Yale University and the Massachusetts Institute of Technology. Among other things he affirmed the notion raised in Seminar XIII that linguistics permitted psychoanalysis a grasp of science but that psychoanalysis itself was a practice and not a science.

Seminar XXII, "R.S.I.," privileges the real in its discussion of mathematical formulas and psychodynamic Borromean topologies that define the "phallus" (as signifier) and symptom, as well as defining "woman" as an empty set. Lacan's latter seminars are rich in examples of language play that are often untranslatable. Some can be comprehended in English: for example, *Je persevère* (I persevere) and *père sévère* (severe father), or *Pere-version* (Father/version/perversion). At this time, Lacan's language play provided a

Lacan leaving one of his seminars, March 1980 (Gamma Agency photograph by Maurice Rougement; from Elisabeth Roudinesco, Jacques Lacan: Outline of a Life, History of a System of Thought, translated by Barbara Bray, 1997; Thomas Cooper Library, University of South Carolina)

hurdle for himself and English-speaking audiences during his lecture series in the United States.

Seminar XXIII, "Le sinthome," was edited by Miller and published in *Ornicar?* in 1976–1977. Here, Lacan links his investigations of the topology of Borromean knots with his discourse on Joyce, which addresses matters of desire, *jouissance,* the Name-of-the-Father, and logic freed of spatial and temporal constraints. Lacan argues that Joyce himself can be understood as a symptom, or *sinthome* (an antiquated spelling of the French *symptôme*), which could also be a pun for *synthe-homme* (synthesized man) or *saint-homme* (holy man). Lacan plays on the notions of an *hommelette,* a little man or omelet (a mixture of ingredients). Such extended punning is the rule more than the exception in Lacan's later seminars and offers a *jouissant* revelry in the multiple meanings, or what Lacan sometimes called *lalangue* (with the feminine article *la* a reference to the roots of language in the maternal figure). Lacan claimed that associative connections in the meanings of words through puns, homonyms, and synonyms, for example, typified the workings of the human unconscious, and whenever possible he peppered his lectures with examples of polysemous language, much to the mixed consternation and delight of audiences. In this seminar the Joycean notion of "epiphany" is interpreted as both revelation and manifestation of the mind and language itself. Lacan devotes considerable attention to *Finnegans Wake* and *Ulysses* to arrive at an analysis defining madness, with Joyce himself as the "symptom." Lacan's reading of Joyce was unprecedented and drew broad attention from international literary scholars.

Seminar XXIV, "L'insu que sait de l'une-bévure, s'aile a mourre" (The Unknown That Knows through Blundering Flights into the Guessing Game, 1976–1977), was edited by Miller and published in *Ornicar?* over five issues in 1977–1979. The English translation of the title cannot convey the many puns in the French title. This seminar reviews previous themes based on the symptom and unsuccessfully pursues a new signifier that, like the real, would be without meaning. The first session of Seminar XXV, "Le moment de conclure" (The Time to Conclude, 1977–1978), was also edited by Miller and published in *Ornicar?* in 1979. In this seminar Lacan wearily admitted that language is often inadequate to the task at hand. He offers an inversion to Freud, suggesting that life is comic, not tragic, and that Freud was incorrect in choosing the Oedipus complex to define human psychology.

Seminar XXVI, *La topologie et le temps* (Topology and Time, 1978–1979), Lacan's last seminar, featured many mathematical formulas written on the board, lengthy silences, and weary, opaque comments. Delivered during Lacan's terminal illness, the title alludes to his own demise and the question of how time itself can be introduced to topological interpretations. Soon after, at the Conference Chez le Docteur Deniker a l'Hôpital Sainte-Anne (Lecture at Doctor Deniker's at the Hospital of Saint Anne), Lacan hinted that his lengthy attention to structure and language may have been strategically unwise, because regardless of the logic one applies to relations between signifier and signified, the unconscious remains haphazard, disorienting, and, ultimately, ineffable. This sense is confirmed in "C'est à la lecture de Freud" (Upon Reading Freud), the preface to Georgin's *Lacan: Théorie and pratiques* (Lacan: Theory and Practices, 1977), in which Lacan repeats his primary premise that the unconscious is structured like a language but adds that the unconscious is the real, an element that is impossible to fully signify in language. This sentiment is echoed at the Seminar XXVII, "Dissolution!" (1980), which appeared in *Ornicar?* in 1980–

1981 and was partly translated in *Television: A Challenge to the Psychoanalytic Establishment*. This seminar closes with allusions to the Dadaist Tristan Tzara and Lacan's exclamation that "L'homme nait malentendu" (Man is born misunderstood/misheard). Lacan's Le Seminaire de Caracas (Caracas Seminar) was not truly a seminar. Rather, his brief opening statement that it is up to others to be Lacanians and that he defines himself as a Freudian lends support to readings of Lacan as an analyst who forwards his views as an analysand. In other words, Lacan's self-analysis can also be understood as a form of autobiography.

In 1980, after intensive internal disputes, Lacan unilaterally announced the dissolution of the EFP and invited any who wished to join him in a new venture to identify themselves. In place of the EFP, Lacan announced the foundation of La Cause Freudienne. In 1981 La Cause Freudienne was dissolved, and the Ecole de la Cause Freudienne (ECF) replaced it. Lacan died at the age of eighty in Paris on 9 September 1981 as a result of complications arising from an intestinal operation.

Following Lacan's death, battles erupted among the Lacanian factions that have yet to be settled. Miller, as executor and sole legal representative of Lacan's works, was assigned to oversee and publish Lacan's papers and seminars in any manner he chose as appropriate. He has also transcribed sections from Lacan's seminars in his review *Ornicar?*. His control of the papers resulted in controversy between pro- and anti-Miller factions. Lacan's lifelong phobia about being plagiarized may have influenced this publishing policy. Miller's defenders argue that he has been unfairly ostracized by factions of zealous Lacanians. Nonetheless, Lacanian legitimism, although not as intensive as Freudian legitimism, still retains a tight control. Until 1989 the Champ Freudien, directed by Judith Miller (Lacan's daughter), linked Lacanian groups throughout the world. Many factions have emerged worldwide since Lacan's death. In the autumn of 1990 Miller initiated the Ecole européenne de psychanalyse (EEP) to further Lacanian studies. In spite of the many controversies, or perhaps because of them, scholarly and critical interest in Lacan and his views continues to expand steadily. With his challenges to the psychoanalytic establishment and his innovative research, Lacan stepped outside of the psychoanalytic frame to emerge as a leading figure in world critical theory.

Interviews:

Madeleine Chapsal, "Clefs pour la psychanalyse," *L'Express*, 31 May 1957; reprinted in Chapsal, *Envoyez la petite musique . . .* (Paris: Grasset, 1984), pp. 38–66;

Gilles Lapouge, "Un psychanalyste s'explique. Auteur mystérieux et prestigieux: Jacques Lacan veut que la psychanalyse redevienne la peste," *Le Figaro littéraire,* 1 December 1966;

Lapouge, "Sartre contre Lacan: Bataille absurd," *Le Figaro littéraire,* 22 December 1966;

Fiera letteraria (1967): 11–18;

François Wahl, *Bulletin de l'Association freudienne,* 3 (1968): 6–7;

R. Higgins, "Jacques Lacan commente la naissance de *Scilicet,*" *Le Monde,* 16 March 1968;

"Freud y el psicoanalisis," *Biblioteca Salvat,* 28 (1975): 10–19.

Bibliographies:

Michael Clark, *Jacques Lacan: An Annotated Bibliography,* 2 volumes (New York: Garland, 1988);

Joël Dor, *Bibliographie des travaux de Jacques Lacan* (Paris: InterEditions, 1983); revised edition (Paris: EPEL, 1994).

Biographies:

Catherine Clément, *The Lives and Legends of Jacques Lacan,* translated by Arthur Goldhammer (New York: Columbia University Press, 1983);

Elisabeth Roudinesco, *Jacques Lacan: Esquisse d'une vie, histoire d'un système de pensée* (Paris: Fayard, 1993); translated by Barbara Bray as *Jacques Lacan: Outline of a Life, History of a System of Thought* (New York: Columbia University Press, 1997; Cambridge: Polity Press, 1999).

References:

Louis Althusser, "Freud and Lacan," in *Lenin and Philosophy, and Other Essays,* translated by Ben Brewster (London: New Left Books, 1971; New York: Monthly Review Press, 1972);

Jacques Aubert, ed., *Joyce avec Lacan* (Paris: Navarin, 1987);

Bice Benvenuto and Roger Kennedy, *The Works of Jacques Lacan: An Introduction* (London: Free Association Books, 1986);

Richard Boothby, *Death and Desire: Psychoanalytic Theory in Lacan's Return to Freud* (New York & London: Routledge, 1991);

Malcolm Bowie, *Freud, Proust and Lacan: Theory as Fiction* (London: Cambridge University Press, 1988);

Hélène Cixous, "La Sexe ou la tête?" *Cahiers du GRIF,* 13 (October 1976): 14; translated by Annette Kuhn as "Castration or Decapitation," *Signs,* 7, no. 2 (1981);

Cixous and Catherine Clément, *La jeune née* (Paris: Union générale d'éditions, 1975);

Joan Copjec, *Read My Desire: Lacan against the Historicists* (Cambridge, Mass.: MIT Press, 1994);

Richard Coyne, *Technoromanticism: Digital Narrative, Holism, and the Romance of the Real* (Cambridge, Mass.: MIT Press, 1999);

Robert Con Davis, *Lacan and Narration: The Psychoanalytic Difference in Narrative Theory* (Baltimore: Johns Hopkins University Press, 1983);

Davis, ed., *The Fictional Father: Lacanian Readings of the Text* (Amherst: University of Massachusetts Press, 1981);

Gilles Deleuze and Félix Guattari, *Anti-Oedipus: Capitalism and Schizophrenia,* translated by Robert Hurley, Mark Seem, and Peter R. Lane (New York: Viking, 1977);

Dylan Evans, *An Introductory Dictionary of Lacanian Psychoanalysis* (London & New York: Routledge, 1996);

Richard Feldstein, Bruce Fink, and Maire Jaanus, eds., *Reading Seminars I & II: Lacan's Return to Freud* (Albany: State University of New York Press, 1996);

Feldstein, Fink, and Jaanus, eds., *Reading Seminar XI: Lacan's Four Fundamental Concepts of Psychoanalysis* (Albany: State University of New York Press, 1995);

Shoshana Felman, *Jacques Lacan and the Adventure of Insight: Psychoanalysis in Contemporary Culture* (Cambridge, Mass.: Harvard University Press, 1987);

Felman, "Turning the Screw of Interpretation," *Yale French Studies,* 55/56 (1977): 94–207;

Felman, ed., *Literature and Psychoanalysis: The Question of Reading, Otherwise* (Baltimore: Johns Hopkins University Press, 1981);

Fink, *A Clinical Introduction to Lacanian Psychoanalysis: Theory and Technique* (Cambridge, Mass.: Harvard University Press, 1997);

Fink, *The Lacanian Subject: Between Language and Jouissance* (Princeton: Princeton University Press, 1995);

Barbara Freedman, *Staging the Gaze: Postmodernism, Psychoanalysis, and Shakespearean Comedy* (Ithaca, N.Y.: Cornell University Press, 1991);

Jane Gallup, *Reading Lacan* (Ithaca, N.Y.: Cornell University Press, 1985);

Robert Georgin, *Lacan: Théorie et pratiques* (Lausanne: L'Age d'homme, 1977);

Jeanne Granon-Lafont, *La topologie ordinaire de Jacques Lacan* (Paris: Point Hors Ligne, 1985);

Elizabeth A. Grosz, *Jacques Lacan: A Feminist Introduction* (London & New York: Routledge, 1990);

Geoffrey H. Hartman, *Psychoanalysis and the Question of the Text* (Baltimore: Johns Hopkins University Press, 1978);

Patrick Colm Hogan and Lalita Pandit, eds., *Criticism and Lacan: Essays and Dialogue on Language, Structure, and the Unconscious* (Athens: University of Georgia Press, 1990);

Linda Hutcheon, *Formalism and the Freudian Aesthetic: The Example of Charles Mauron* (Cambridge & New York: Cambridge University Press, 1984);

Luce Irigaray, *Ce sexe que n'en est pas un* (Paris: Editions du Seuil, 1977); translated by Catherine Porter and Carolyn Burke as *This Sex Which Is Not One* (Ithaca, N.Y.: Cornell University Press, 1985);

Fredric Jameson, "Imaginary and Symbolic in Lacan: Marxism, Psychoanalytic Criticism, and the Problem of the Subject," *Yale French Studies,* 55/56 (1977): 338–395;

Jameson, "Postmodernism and Consumer Society," in *The Anti-Aesthetic: Essays on Postmodern Culture,* edited by Hal Foster (Port Townsend, Wash.: Bay Press, 1983), pp. 111–125;

Alain Juranville, *Lacan et la philosophie* (Paris: Presses Universitaires de France, 1984);

William Kerrigan and Joseph H. Smith, eds., *Interpreting Lacan* (New Haven & London: Yale University Press, 1983);

Angèle Kremer-Marietti, *Lacan ou la rhétorique de l'inconscient* (Paris: Aubier-Montaigne, 1978);

Julia Kristeva, *Desire in Language: A Semiotic Approach to Literature and Art,* translated by Thomas Gora, Alice Jardine, and Leon S. Roudiez, edited by Roudiez (New York: Columbia University Press, 1980);

Kristeva, "Il n'ya pas de maître à langage," *Nouvelle revue de psychanalyse, regards sur la psychanalyse en France,* 20 (Autumn 1979): 119–140; translated by Gora and Margaret Waller as "Within the Microcosm of 'The Talking Cure,'" in *Interpreting Lacan,* edited by Kerrigan and Smith (New Haven & London: Yale University Press, 1983), pp. 33–48;

Jonathan Scott Lee, *Jacques Lacan* (Boston: Twayne, 1990);

Anika Lemaire, *Jacques Lacan,* translated by David Macey (London & Boston: Routledge & Kegan Paul, 1977);

Jean-François Lyotard, *The Lyotard Reader,* edited by Andrew Benjamin (Oxford: Blackwell, 1989);

Colin MacCabe, ed., *The Talking Cure: Essays in Psychoanalysis and Language* (London: Macmillan, 1981);

Juliet Flower MacCannell, *Figuring Lacan: Criticism and the Cultural Unconscious* (London: Croom Helm, 1986);

Macey, *Lacan in Contexts* (London & New York: Verso, 1988);

Marcelle Marini, *Jacques Lacan: The French Context,* translated by Anne Tomiche (New Brunswick, N.J.: Rutgers University Press, 1992);

James M. Mellard, "Lacan and the New Lacanians: Josephine Hart's *Damage,* Lacanian Tragedy, and the Ethics of *Jouissance,*" *PMLA,* 113, no. 5 (May 1998): 395–407;

Toril Moi, "Patriarchal Thought and the Drive for Knowledge," in *Between Feminism and Psychoanalysis,* edited by Teresa M. Brennan (London & New York: Routledge, 1989), pp. 185–205;

Moi, *Sexual/Textual Politics: Feminist Literary Theory* (London: Methuen, 1985);

John P. Muller and William J. Richardson, *Lacan and Language: A Reader's Guide to Ecrits* (New York: International Universities Press, 1982);

Muller and Richardson, eds., *The Purloined Poe: Lacan, Derrida, and Psychoanalytic Reading* (Baltimore: Johns Hopkins University Press, 1988);

Steve Pile, *The Body and the City: Psychoanalysis, Space, and Subjectivity* (London & New York: Routledge, 1996);

Ellie Ragland-Sullivan, *Jacques Lacan and the Philosophy of Psychoanalysis* (Urbana: University of Illinois Press, 1986);

Ragland-Sullivan and Mark Bracher, eds., *Lacan and the Subject of Language* (New York: Routledge, 1991);

Elisabeth Roudinesco, *La bataille de cent ans: Histoire de la psychanalyse en France,* volume 2 (Paris: Seuil, 1986); translated by Jeffrey Mehlman as *Jacques Lacan & Co.: A History of Psychoanalysis in France, 1925–1985* (Chicago: University of Chicago Press, 1990);

Madan Sarup, *Jacques Lacan* (Toronto & Buffalo: University of Toronto Press, 1992);

Stuart Schneiderman, *Jacques Lacan: The Death of an Intellectual Hero* (Cambridge, Mass. & London: Harvard University Press, 1983);

Martin Stanton, *Outside the Dream: Lacan and French Styles of Psychoanalysis* (London & Boston: Routledge & Kegan Paul, 1983);

Sherry Turkle, *Psychoanalytic Politics: Freud's French Revolution* (New York: Basic Books, 1978);

Elizabeth Wright, *Psychoanalytic Criticism: Theory in Practice* (London & New York: Methuen, 1984);

Slavoj Žižek, *Enjoy Your Symptom! Jacques Lacan in Hollywood and Out* (New York: Routledge, 1992);

Žižek, *Looking Awry: An Introduction to Jacques Lacan through Popular Culture* (Cambridge, Mass.: MIT Press, 1991);

Žižek, ed., *Everything You Always Wanted to Know about Lacan: But Were Afraid to Ask Hitchcock* (London & New York: Verso, 1992).

Papers:

Jacques Lacan's papers are held by his son-in-law, Jacques-Alain Miller.

Emmanuel Lévinas

(12 January 1906 – 25 December 1995)

James E. Faulconer
Brigham Young University

BOOKS: *La théorie de l'intuition dans la phénoménologie de Husserl* (Paris: Alcan, 1930; revised edition, Paris: Vrin, 1963); translated by André Orianne as *The Theory of Intuition in Husserl's Phenomenology* (Evanston, Ill.: Northwestern University Press, 1973);

De l'existence à l'existant (Paris: Fontaine, 1947; revised edition, Paris: Vrin, 1978); translated by Alphonso Lingis as *Existence and Existents* (The Hague: Nijhoff, 1978);

Le temps et l'autre (Montpellier: Fata Morgana, 1947); translated by Richard A. Cohen as *Time and the Other and Additional Essays* (Pittsburgh: Duquesne University Press, 1987);

En découvrant l'existence avec Husserl et Heidegger (Paris: Vrin, 1949; enlarged, 1967; enlarged again, 2001);

Totalité et infini: Essai sur l'extériorité (The Hague: Nijhoff, 1961); translated by Lingis as *Totality and Infinity: An Essay on Exteriority* (Pittsburgh: Duquesne University Press, 1969);

Difficile liberté: Essais sur le judaïsme (Paris: Albin Michel, 1963; revised and enlarged, 1976); translated by Seán Hand as *Difficult Freedom: Essays on Judaism* (Baltimore: Johns Hopkins University Press, 1990);

Quatre lectures talmudiques (Paris: Minuit, 1968); translated by Annette Aronowicz in *Nine Talmudic Readings* (Bloomington: Indiana University Press, 1990), pp. 3–88;

Humanisme de l'autre homme (Montpellier: Fata Morgana, 1972); translated by Nidra Poller as *Humanism and the Other* (Urbana: University of Illinois Press, 2003);

Autrement qu'être; ou, Au-delà de l'essence (The Hague: Nijhoff, 1974); translated by Lingis as *Otherwise than Being: or, Beyond Essence* (The Hague & Boston: Nijhoff, 1981);

Sur Maurice Blanchot (Montpellier: Fata Morgana, 1975);

Noms propres (Montpellier: Fata Morgana, 1976); translated by Michael B. Smith as *Proper Names* (Stanford, Cal.: Stanford University Press, 1996);

Du sacré au saint: Cinq nouvelles lectures talmudiques (Paris: Minuit, 1977); translated by Aronowicz as "From

Emmanuel Lévinas (from Stephan Strasser, Jenseits von Sein und Zeit: *Eine Einführung in Emmanuel Levinas' Philosophie, 1978; Thomas Cooper Library, University of South Carolina)*

the Sacred to the Holy," in *Nine Talmudic Readings*, pp. 91–197;

De Dieu qui vient à l'idée (Paris: Vrin, 1982; revised and enlarged, 1986); translated by Bettina Bergo as *Of God Who Comes to Mind* (Stanford, Cal.: Stanford University Press, 1998);

L'au-delà du verset: Lectures et discours talmudiques (Paris: Minuit, 1982); translated by Gary D. Mole as

Beyond the Verse: Talmudic Readings and Lectures (Bloomington: Indiana University Press, 1994; London: Athlone, 1994);

De l'evasion (Montpellier: Fata Morgana, 1982); translated by Bergo as *On Escape* (Stanford, Cal.: Stanford University Press, 2003);

Transcendance et intelligibilité: Suivi d'un entretien (Geneva: Labor et Fides, 1984);

Hors sujet (Montpellier: Fata Morgana, 1987); translated by Smith as *Outside the Subject* (London: Athlone, 1993; Stanford, Cal.: Stanford University Press, 1994);

A l'heure des nations (Paris: Minuit, 1988); translated by Smith as *In the Time of the Nations* (Bloomington: Indiana University Press, 1994);

Entre Nous: Essais sur le penser-à-l'autre (Paris: Grasset, 1991); translated by Smith and Barbara Harshav as *Entre Nous: On Thinking-of-the-Other* (New York: Columbia University Press, 1998);

Dieu, la mort et le temps, edited, with a preface and a postface, by Jacques Rolland (Paris: Grasset, 1993); translated by Bergo as *God, Death, and Time* (Stanford, Cal.: Stanford University Press, 2000);

Les Imprévus de l'histoire (Saint-Clément-la-Rivière: Fata Morgana, 1994);

Liberté et commandment (Saint-Clément-la-Rivière: Fata Morgana, 1994);

Altérité et transcendence (Saint-Clément-la-Rivière: Fata Morgana, 1995); translated by Smith as *Alterity and Transcendence* (New York: Columbia University Press, 1999);

Nouvelles lectures talmudiques (Paris: Minuit, 1996); translated by Cohen as *New Talmudic Readings* (Pittsburgh: Duquesne University Press, 1999);

Positivité et transcendance: Suivi de Lévinas et la phénoménologie, edited, with an introduction, by Jean-Luc Marion (Paris: Presses universitaires de France, 2000).

Editions in English: *Collected Philosophical Papers: E. Lévinas,* translated by Alphonso Lingis (Dordrecht, the Netherlands & Boston: Nijhoff, 1987);

The Lévinas Reader, edited by Seán Hand (Oxford & Cambridge, Mass.: Blackwell, 1989);

Emmanuel Lévinas: Basic Philosophical Writings, edited by Adriaan T. Peperzak, Simon Critchley, and Robert Bernasconi (Bloomington: Indiana University Press, 1996);

Discovering Existence with Husserl, edited and translated by Richard A. Cohen and Michael B. Smith (Evanston, Ill.: Northwestern University Press, 1998).

TRANSLATION: Edmund Husserl, *Méditations Cartésiennes: Introduction á la phénoménologie,* translated by Lévinas with Gabrielle Peiffer (Paris: Almand Colin, 1931).

Emmanuel Lévinas is perhaps best known for his claim that ethics (literally and more accurately, "the ethical"–*l'éthique*–the domain of human relation rather than that of moral precepts and rules) precedes ontology. As Lévinas says in an autobiographical essay, "Signature" (from *Difficile liberté: Essais sur le judaïsme,* 1963; translated as "Signature" in *Difficult Freedom: Essays on Judaism,* 1990), "The fundamental experience, which objective experience itself presupposes, is the experience of the other person. It is experience *par excellence.*" The encounter with the other person, like the encounter with God, is an encounter with that which is absolutely beyond one's understanding and will remain beyond it, though one may not recognize that it does. But in being beyond one's comprehension, the other person is not also beyond relation.

According to Lévinas, the Western intellectual tradition has understood the other only by means of the self, making the other always no more than a reflection of the self. However, self-knowledge turns in on itself, cutting one off from the other person and alienating one from the other rather than granting one relation to him or her. In contrast, the ethical–the relation to alterity, or otherness–binds one to the other person across their difference. As Lévinas writes later in "Signature," "Moral consciousness is not an experience of values, but access to being that is external to me." Lévinas's work tries to describe the human relation to alterity as the relation of obligation to the other person and to show that that relation is fundamentally nonthreatening as well as the basis for reason, law, and morality.

Emmanuel Levyne was born in Kovno (Kunas), Lithuania, to Yiddish- and Russian-speaking parents, Jehiel Levyne and Deborah Gurvic, on 12 January 1906 (30 December 1905 on the Orthodox calendar). He had two younger brothers, Boris, born 1909, and Aminadab, born 1913. Kovno, a city of approximately one hundred thousand, where his father was a bookseller and stationer, was about one-quarter Jewish, and Jewish culture permeated Lévinas's life there. Lévinas's schooling was double: at home he learned to read the Hebrew Bible (though without the rabbinic commentary that later became important to him); in high school he read the Russian writers Alexander Pushkin, Nikolai Gogol, Fyodor Dostoevsky, and Leo Tolstoy. (Lévinas spoke Russian at home throughout his life.) These writers remained important influences on his thinking throughout his career. He often quoted Dostoevsky's *The Brothers Karamozov* (1879–1880) to summarize his own thinking, as he does in *Autrement qu'être; ou, Au-delà de l'essence* (1974; translated as *Otherwise than Being: or, Beyond Essence,* 1981): "Each of us is guilty before everyone for everyone, and I more than the others."

In 1915, in response to World War I, the Russian government expelled the Jews of Kovno. As a result, in 1916 the Lévinas family found themselves in Ukraine, where, at age eleven, Lévinas attended a Russian-speaking high school in Kharkov. He was one of the few Jews allowed to stand for the entrance examination. In mid 1920, after the revolutions of 1917 and the ensuing anti-Semitic massacres in Ukraine, the Lévinas family returned to Lithuania. On returning, Lévinas decided to continue his studies, but in western Europe. His first intention was to study in Germany because his German teacher had given him a solid grounding in German literature. Because of anti-Semitism, however, he was not accepted to any of the programs to which he applied. Thus, in 1923 he went to France to study Latin, philosophy, and French at the University of Strasbourg. There he became friends with the literary critic and novelist Maurice Blanchot, and their friendship lasted Lévinas's lifetime. Among his favorite professors was the psychology professor Charles Blondel.

In his study of philosophy and through his acquaintance with Blondel, Lévinas became particularly interested in the work of two early-twentieth-century philosophers, the French thinker Henri Bergson and the German Edmund Husserl. In 1928 Lévinas went to the University of Freiburg (in Brisgau), Germany, to study with Husserl. He spent the 1928–1929 academic year there as a guest student, studying first with Husserl for two semesters (and supporting himself as Husserl's French tutor). The courses he attended were on phenomenological psychology and the constitution of intersubjectivity. During the second semester Lévinas also studied with the German philosopher Martin Heidegger (Husserl's assistant), and the impact of Heidegger's seminar was profound, as Lévinas recalls in *Ethique et infini: Dialogues avec Philippe Nemo* (1982; translated as *Ethics and Infinity*, 1985): "With Heidegger, 'verbality' was awakened in the word *being*, that which is event in it, the 'happening' of being. . . . Heidegger accustomed us to this verbal sonority. This reeducation of our ear is unforgettable, even if banal today!" In the same book Lévinas says of Heidegger's first major work, *Sein und Zeit* (1927; translated as *Being and Time*, 1962): "In *Sein und Zeit*'s analyses of anxiety, care, and being-toward-death, we witness a sovereign exercise of phenomenology. This exercise is extremely brilliant and convincing."

Though his own philosophical position came to be profoundly anti-Heideggerian, and though Heidegger's later association with Nazism made Lévinas's personal relationship with him difficult, Lévinas continued to recognize Heidegger as perhaps the most important philosopher of the twentieth century. In *Ethique et infini* he writes: "A person who undertakes to philosophize in

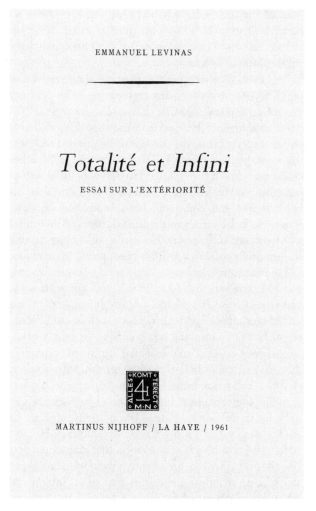

EMMANUEL LEVINAS

Totalité et Infini

ESSAI SUR L'EXTÉRIORITÉ

MARTINUS NIJHOFF / LA HAYE / 1961

Title page for the work on the contrast between the ego and the external world (translated as Totality and Infinity: An Essay on Exteriority, *1969) that eventually established Lévinas as one of the leading philosophers in France (Howard-Tilton Memorial Library, Tulane University)*

the twentieth century cannot avoid going through Heidegger's philosophy, even to escape it. This thought is a great event of our century." In turn, Heidegger seems to have recognized in Lévinas an extraordinary student, for Lévinas was one of only a few invited to participate in the famous 1929 debate between Heidegger and Ernst Cassirer in Davos, Switzerland.

In 1929 Lévinas returned to France and entered the Sorbonne to finish his studies, and in 1930 he published his dissertation, *La théorie de l'intuition dans la phénoménologie de Husserl* (translated as *The Theory of Intuition in Husserl's Phenomenology*, 1973). Jean-Paul Sartre, the French existential philosopher, playwright, and novelist, says that Lévinas's book gave him his first acquaintance with the thought of Husserl and Heidegger. In 1931 Lévinas translated Husserl's *Cartésianische*

Meditationen (Cartesian Meditations) into French for its first publication in book form, further establishing his importance to the development of the phenomenological tradition in France.

Lévinas's interest in the question of otherness and ethics is not obvious in his dissertation. The primary goal of *La théorie de l'intuition dans la phénoménologie de Husserl* is to introduce Husserl to French-speaking thinkers and to explain Husserl's concept of intuition. Thus, it is not a complete overview of Husserl's work, and neither could it be, given the fact that Husserl was still developing his thought in 1930. Lévinas recognizes that his book is not and could not be a complete overview, however, as he writes in the introduction: "We would like to study and present Husserl's philosophy as one studies and presents a living philosophy." In addition, as Lévinas later admits in *Ethique et infini,* his interpretation of Husserl in *La théorie de l'intuition dans la phénoménologie de Husserl* was heavily influenced by his understanding of Heidegger. Nevertheless, the discovery of Husserl's thinking was crucial to his later work.

For Lévinas, the essential truth of Husserl's thought is that radical reflection on the self as self is possible. Following Franz Brentano, Husserl recognizes that the cogito cannot be understood in itself; it can only be understood in its relation to its objects, as always directed at an object, as "intentional." Husserl adds to Brentano's idea the concept that intentional acts always occur within an already-given horizon. Since any object, including the self, is part of an intentional act and the intentional act is made possible by the horizon in which that act occurs, every conscious self and every object of consciousness must be understood, not as simply present to consciousness but as effected in the act of consciousness. Thus, according to Lévinas, Husserl's thinking is important because he asks not only "What is?" but also *"How* is what is?" making Husserl's phenomenology "the first radical contestation in Western thought of the priority of the theoretical," for the theoretical always only asks "What is?" The horizon within which the intentional act occurs gives the *how* of the act, making the *what* of the act possible.

According to Lévinas, Husserl's radical rethinking of intentionality not only breaks with traditional ontology and epistemology. As Lévinas understands that rethinking, it also radically changes the question of transcendence. To use an analogy from Heidegger's 1928 lectures, *Metaphysische Anfangsgründe der Logik im Ausgang von Leibniz* (1978; translated as *The Metaphysical Foundations of Logic,* 1984), Husserl's reflections on intentionality dismiss the traditional question of transcendence, for the traditional question understands the self as a "box," with the ego inside the box and the world outside, and as a result the traditional question takes the question of transcendence to be that of how one can get from the inside of the box to its outside. For Husserl, instead, the question of transcendence is "How does the context make representation possible?"

This reorientation of the question of transcendence provides Lévinas with the insight that he eventually uses to rethink the status of the *I* and the relation to the other person: the problem of transcendence is not how one can relate to a world that is absolutely other than and independent of this one; instead, it is the question of how to understand the horizon within which the representations and relations of this world occur. To that insight Lévinas adds Heidegger's argument that the horizon of intentionality always begins in "average everydayness," something only understood in terms of temporality. At first Heidegger's response to Husserl is sufficient for Lévinas, but World War II and the events leading to it make Heidegger's response complicated.

The same year that Lévinas published his dissertation, 1930, he was naturalized as a French citizen. Then, in 1932, he married Raïssa Marguerite Levi, a pianist and childhood friend from Lithuania and an émigré to France via Vienna. They had a daughter, Simone, in 1935; a second daughter, Andrée Eliane, who died in childhood; and eventually a son, Michaël (born in 1949), who became a prominent musician. Except for the years of World War II, Lévinas and his wife lived in Paris, keeping an observant, kosher home.

After Lévinas received his *doctorat d'université,* a doctorate certified by the university, rather than publishing the additional dissertation required by the state for a *doctorat d'Etat* (a doctorate certified by the state), which would have allowed him to become a professor, he taught at the Ecole normale Israélite orientale de bassin Méditeranéen (Eastern Israelite Normal School of the Mediterranean Basin, or ENIO) in Paris. As the name suggests, ENIO is a school for Jewish students, many of them from traditional backgrounds. It trains students to serve as teachers in the schools of the Alliance Israélite universelle (Universal Israelite Alliance). The alliance was established in 1860, and its original purpose was to encourage the integration of Jews in the states wherever they lived, with the assumed and expected integration of European Jews as its ideal.

Lévinas contributed greatly to the alliance's evolving objective of furthering "the diffusion of a Judaism that is faithful to the tradition, tolerant, and open to the modern world." Under the influence of the turn-of-the-century German-Jewish thinker Franz Rosenzweig, Lévinas understood Jewish integration neither to include nor to foreshadow Jewish assimilation and disappearance. Rather, integration meant the fulfillment of the universalism inherent in Jewish thought, a flowering of Judaism within the secular state and as a contributing part of it. World War II considerably complicated Lévinas's understanding of both integration and universalism, though they remain central to his thinking from beginning to end.

In 1932 Lévinas was drafted into the Forty-sixth Infantry Regiment of the French army. Then in 1933 he received a philosophical shock: Heidegger's collaboration with the Nazis and his rectoral address at the University of Freiburg, an address in which Heidegger spoke of the "inner greatness" of National Socialism and equated labor service and military service with "knowledge service." In spite of his shock, Lévinas's criticism of Heidegger remained mild and indirect. Even his criticism of Adolf Hitler, in "Quelques réflexions sur la philosophie de l'hitlérisme" (Several Reflections on the Philosophy of Hitlerism, published in *Esprit,* 1934), collected in *Les Imprévus de l'histoire* (The Unexpected in History, 1994), was relatively mild. (Lévinas later refused to include that essay in his list of publications on the grounds that it was a mistake to speak of Hitlerism as a philosophy.) Nevertheless, the shock of Heidegger's collaboration led Lévinas to begin truly to go his own way, eventually resulting in *De l'existence à l'existant* (1947; translated as *Existence and Existents,* 1978).

The beginnings of Lévinas's turn from Heidegger to his own thinking are found in an early work, "De l'evasion" (On Evasion, published in *Recherches Philosophiques,* 1935). In that essay Lévinas first asks how thought can escape the domination of being. That question, which reverses the question of how transcendence is possible, dominated his work for the rest of his career.

Before Lévinas could go further with what he began in "De l'evasion," however, World War II interrupted his work. His military unit was mobilized in 1939, and a few months after the mobilization he was captured by the Germans at Rennes. As a French citizen and an army officer, rather than being sent to a concentration camp, Lévinas was interned from 1940 to 1945 in Stalag 1492, a prisoner-of-war camp on the Lünenburger Moor, near Hanover, in northwest Germany. There he performed forced labor in a Jewish labor group of seventy prisoners. He briefly described this time in "Nom d'un chien ou le droit naturel," an essay in *Difficile Liberté* (translated as "The Name of a Dog, or Natural Rights" in *Difficult Freedom*). In the preface to *De l'existence à l'existant,* Lévinas suggests that while in the stalag he continued not only to think about how to deal with the problem that Heidegger's collaboration raised, but that he also continued to write.

Though Lévinas escaped death during the war, his parents and most of his extended family, who had remained in Lithuania, were exterminated by Nazi col-laborators. Through the efforts of Blanchot and other friends, Lévinas's wife and daughter escaped capture by hiding in a convent of the Sisters of Saint Vincent de Paul, near Orléans. On learning of his family's fate after his release from prison camp, Lévinas vowed never to set foot in Germany again.

After the war Lévinas returned to ENIO and became its director, working there for nearly thirty years and making major contributions to its curriculum, shifting it from a curriculum with primarily a secular emphasis to one with more emphasis on the Hebrew language and on Jewish sources. Lévinas himself taught the weekly lessons on the Talmud for many years. This shift of the curriculum reflected his understanding of Europe as "the Bible plus the Greeks."

Also after the war Lévinas was able to complete and publish *De l'existence à l'existant,* his response to Heidegger and the first work that is clearly a step in the development of his own thinking. The question that motivates the book is "What in Heidegger's philosophy could allow him to go so terribly wrong?" As he had suggested in "De l'evasion," Lévinas's answer is that Heidegger can go wrong for the same reason that Western philosophy in general has gone wrong: it has thought that the horizon that gives intentionality meaning is being; as a result, Western philosophy, including Heidegger, has overlooked the significance of the Good. Western philosophy has given ontology precedence over ethics. Lévinas says that *De l'existence à l'existant* is merely a preparatory study, one designed to examine time (Heidegger's touchstone) and the relation to the other person (what Lévinas believes that Heidegger overlooks) against the background of Plato's claim that the Good is beyond being: that which draws one toward the Good is not movement from one level of being to a higher level; instead, it is a "departure from being." Though *De l'existence à l'existant* is only a preparatory study, there are in it intimations of Lévinas's eventual conclusions.

In this first work of his own thought, Lévinas undertakes to reverse Heidegger's way of proceeding (and, he says, that of Western philosophy). He believes that Heidegger begins by reflecting on beings (*l'existant*) and then derives from that his understanding of being (*l'existence*). Lévinas proposes, instead, to begin with being and then, based on that, to derive from its analysis the possibility of understanding beings. To do so, he gives phenomenological analyses of such phenomena as fatigue, indolence, and insomnia in order to show that consciousness has its starting point in its encounter with indeterminacy: the existing being finds itself existing in the field of the elemental, an elemental that is prior to the world and the organization that is implicit in any world, an elemental, therefore, that the person encoun-

PRÉSENCES DU JUDAÏSME

EMMANUEL LÉVINAS

DIFFICILE LIBERTÉ

Essais sur le Judaïsme

ÉDITIONS ALBIN MICHEL

Paperback cover for the 1963 book (translated as Difficult Freedom: Essays on Judaism, *1990) in which Lévinas advocates a rational Judaism and a traditional method of biblical interpretation informed by study of the Talmud (Gumberg Library, Duquesne University)*

ters with horror. As existing beings, however, people find themselves mired in themselves. They find their being to be a burden and they desire to escape it. They desire alterity, something beyond being. Though *De l'existence à l'existant* announced the project that eventually resulted in Lévinas's fame as a philosopher, few paid attention to it. Its style is dense and difficult, and Lévinas was relatively unknown.

In the same year that *De l'existence à l'existant* appeared, 1947, Jean Wahl, a noted French philosopher, a friend of Lévinas, and the founder of a nonuniversity philosophical circle, Collège philosophique, invited Lévinas to give a series of four lectures at the Collège. These lectures were later published as *Le temps et l'autre* (1947; translated as *Time and the Other and Additional Essays,* 1987). These lectures continue the thinking of *De l'existence à l'existant.* Lévinas's thesis is "Time is not the achievement of an isolated and lone subject, but . . . the

very relationship of the subject with the other person." On Lévinas's reading of Heidegger (which is controversial), the horizon of intentionality is temporality, but the human subject is isolated within that horizon. Though the individual does not produce the temporal horizon, the horizon is concomitant with the being of the individual, so the individual has no access to what is beyond his or her own being. In contrast, Lévinas argues that time is the relationship with the other person; it is a relationship given by the other person. Thus, beginning with the ego, seemingly enclosed on itself in being, Lévinas's analysis purports to show how the ego is in fact dependent not only on its relation to the world, but more importantly on its relation to other persons—he moves from the being of the self to the beings of the world and to the other person. Though *Le temps et l'autre* was appreciated by Lévinas's philosophical friends, like *De l'existence à l'existant,* it did not garner him a reputation as a philosopher.

The difficulty of Lévinas's writing and his work at ENIO kept him in philosophical obscurity, but throughout his tenure at ENIO he took part in philosophical discussions, with, for example, Gabriel Marcel (Lévinas was a participant in Marcel's weekly philosophical soirees) and in meetings of the Collège philosophique. He also continued to publish philosophical essays, such as "L'autre dans Proust" (The Other in Proust, published in *Deucalion,* 1947), collected in *Noms propres* (1976; translated as *Proper Names,* 1996); "L'ontologie est-elle fondamentale" (Is Ontology Fundamental, published in *Revue de Métaphysique et de Morale,* 1951), collected in *Entre Nous: Essais sur le penser-à-l'autre* (1991; translated as *Entre Nous: On Thinking-of-the-Other,* 1998); and "La ruine de la représentation" (The Ruin of Representation, published in *Edmund Husserl 1859–1959,* 1959), collected in the second edition of *En découvrant l'existence avec Husserl et Heidegger* (Discovering Existence with Husserl and Heidegger, 1967).

Finally, at the age of fifty-seven and at the urging of his friend Wahl, Lévinas published the work that eventually established him as one of the leading philosophers of France: *Totalité et infini: Essai sur l'extériorité* (1961; translated as *Totality and Infinity: An Essay on Exteriority,* 1969). With the publication of this second dissertation, Lévinas left ENIO to take a professorial position in philosophy at the University of Poitiers.

Besides *De l'existence à l'existant* and *Le temps et l'autre,* Lévinas had already published two essays that anticipate parts of *Totalité et infini:* "Liberté et commandment" (Freedom and Command, 1953) and "Le moi et la totalité" (The Ego and the Totality, 1954). He also had published one essay that gives the outlines of the main threads of his first major work: "La philosophie et l'idée de l'Infini" (Philosophy and the Idea of the Infinite, 1957). *Totalité et infini* brings to fruition Lévinas's argument that if knowledge always presupposes a horizon or context that cannot be given by consciousness and that cannot be made a simple object of consciousness, then there must be something "beyond being."

The title *Totalité et infini* announces that the book will deal with the contrast between totality or being (which Lévinas also calls "the Same") and the Infinite or the other person (which reveals itself in the human face). For Lévinas, this contrast between totality and infinity can also be understood as the contrast between what is confined to the ego and the ego's knowledge, and what is excessive of the ego and its knowledge. Thus, the subtitle, *Essai sur l'extériorité*: to speak of that contrast is to speak of what is exterior to the ego. As in *Le temps et l'autre,* Lévinas's thesis in *Totalité et infini* is that what is exterior, infinite, other, excessive is the origin of what is totalized in being.

The argument of *Totalité et infini* is difficult to follow without considerable background in twentieth-century German and French philosophy. Nevertheless, its lineaments can be sketched: On first analysis the ego is revealed as something that takes itself as a unity and that takes the world as "for me." The ego is separated from everything else and contained in itself. On such a view, however, what is other than the ego—in other words, that which the ego makes a theme in knowledge—"disappears behind its manifestations." The solitary ego knows its representations of the world, but it does not know the world itself; the ego has the phenomenon, but the thing itself is unavailable. If this analysis is correct, then there is no basis for any world except that contained within the ego and its intentions: totality. If the world is confined to the intentional acts of the ego, however, then it is no longer a place in which people seek truth, for there is no truth to be sought outside the ego. The self-contained world of the ego is only a place for enjoyment, a place in which the ego finds what it desires and what it has already produced. Exteriority disappears. It turns out, however, that this analysis is a reductio ad absurdum.

Lévinas argues that, in fact, exteriority does not disappear, for the other person, manifest in the human face, interrupts the ego's enjoyment by undoing its representations of the world. In particular, by being a living presence the face constantly undoes the form in which the ego thematizes it. The face of the other person constantly exceeds the ego's knowledge of the face: infinity. The other person constantly exceeds the ego's knowledge of that person, so the face of the other person (that in which the other person makes himself or herself manifest) is transcendent: exteriority.

This constant disruption and refusal of the ego's thematizing knowledge shows that the other person is absent from the world in which it manifests itself through the face, the world of the ego. As a result, the face is always, essentially, the face of a stranger, the face of someone who comes from another world. The other person is transcendent in that he or she is "destitute," has no properties, because he or she is "in exile," in other words outside the ego's world, with the rights of a stranger. Instead of having properties, the other person requires that the ego give him or her properties. The ego makes this "gift" by thematizing the face of the other person. By appearing as a living face, to which any previous thematizing turns out to have been inadequate, the other person requires the ego to thematize that face again. The appearing of the other person constantly requires the subject to make the other person an object of knowledge. Thus, to recognize the other person is to give him or her properties and to create an object of knowledge—but the gift that the ego gives is given to one who demands that the ego do so. Thematizing is a response to obligation. The totality of the ego is breached by the infinity of the other person, who appears to the ego as one in need or demanding. Lévinas refers to this unavoidable breach of the ego by the other as ethics.

By the word *ethics* Lévinas does not mean "rules for good behavior," however. Instead he means "the relation of the ego to the other person." Thus, the horizon of intentionality, Lévinas argues, is not ontology, for ontology is the realm of the ego in its unity. Instead, the horizon of intentionality is the relation to the other person, for that relation makes knowledge possible. Knowledge is fundamentally the gift that the ego gives the other person, its thematizing explanation of being. Knowledge is an explanation given to another who disrupts one's being, another who, by disrupting one's being, demands an explanation of that being.

Beginning with *Totalité et infini,* Lévinas's renown as a philosopher grew gradually, though it grew more rapidly after the 1968 student revolution, with its violent expression of student disappointment with the established order, a disappointment followed by disappointment in the failed revolution. After giving up on the student revolution, Benny Levy, one of its leaders and, for a time, Sartre's secretary, took great interest in Lévinas's work, as did other important figures among French intellectuals, such as Bernard Henri-Levi and Alain Finkelkraut. Personal friends such as Blanchot and the contemporary French philosopher Jacques Derrida did a great deal to sustain and augment Lévinas's reputation during a time when Marxism rather than either phenomenology or, especially, ethics was fashionable.

Lévinas was not only known as a philosopher, however. After the war and while directing ENIO,

Lévinas also began to engage in Talmud studies, taking an itinerant teacher named Schüler (called "Chouchani") as his master from 1947 to 1951. Schüler was a man of great mystery; his first name is uncertain. It is reported variously to have been Hillel or Mordechai or Moshe or simply unknown. (Elie Wiesel's story "The Wandering Jew" from his collection *Les Chants des morts* [1966; translated as *Legends of Our Time*, 1968] gives a description of the mysterious Chouchani. Wiesel was another of his students.) Chouchani's hermeneutic method emphasized understanding passages from the Bible by putting them in their context but leaving the question of context always open. Lévinas adopted Chouchani's method, interpreting the statements of the Talmud in relation to other Talmudic claims, quotations from the Hebrew Bible, its ethical ground, and nonbiblical learning and contemporary questions. Central to this method is the idea that Israel stands for the whole of humanity, so its stories can be applied universally. Lévinas explicitly reflects on his method in "Terre promise et terre permise" (Promised Land or Permitted Land) in *Quatre lectures talmudiques* (Four Talmudic Lectures, 1968; translated in *Nine Talmudic Readings,* 1990). From 1957 to 1991, each year Lévinas took part in a congress of French-speaking Jewish intellectuals, a congress with a Talmudic text for its theme. The resulting and associated writings form the Hebrew prong of Lévinas's work, with an emphasis on the relevance of Talmudic thought to the rejuvenation of modern culture.

For Lévinas, philosophy and religious teachings are neither reducible to one another nor antagonistic. As he says in *Ethique et infini,* if the biblical and the philosophical traditions harmonize, "it is probably because every philosophical thought rests on pre-philosophical experiences," but his goal is not to harmonize them. Lévinas's trope is that philosophy speaks Greek rather than Hebrew, and by "Greek" he means the prosaic language of clarity, commentary, and hermeneutic. The Hebrew text—in other words, the prephilosophical experience of which the Bible speaks—demands to be translated into Greek again and again. It demands to be secularized and made accessible to modern readers. The Hebrew text does not disappear in those translations, however. Instead, it is revivified by them; it continues to live through the process of translation. On the other hand, as a translation, the Greek text must stand on its own. Though philosophy can translate the religious text, the translation must succeed as philosophy, not requiring one already to know the religious text or already to have the experience or insight that philosophy translates. To the degree that a philosophy requires such a preexisting background to give its own philosophical accounts, it fails as philosophy. Lévinas dis-

cusses the relation of his Talmudic studies to his philosophical work in detail in his 1988 essay "La traduction de l'Ecriture" from *A l'heure des nations* (1988; translated as "The Translation of Scripture" in *In the Time of the Nations,* 1994) as well as the foreword to *L'au-delà du verset: Lectures et discours talmudiques* (1982; translated as *Beyond the Verse: Talmudic Readings and Lectures,* 1994).

In *Difficile liberté,* Lévinas identifies himself as a Pharisee, as one opposed to "enthousiasme" (enthusiasm) in Judaism and in favor of "the face-to-face war that opposes reason with reason" and "the daring of the idea." Thus, though Lévinas's argument that ethics precedes ontology owes much to Martin Buber's thought of the "in-between" that constitutes human relation, Lévinas rejected the Hassidic inclination of Buber's work and his inclination toward scholarly biblical criticism. Lévinas favored a more rational Judaism and a more traditional biblical interpretation informed by Talmud study. His criticism of Buber's philosophy—that Buber's understanding of the I-Thou relation is formal rather than concrete and assumes an unacceptable symmetry of the I and the Thou—can be found in several essays, including "Martin Buber et le théorie de la connaissance" (Martin Buber and the Theory of Knowledge, published in a German translation as "Martin Buber und die Erkenntnistheorie," in *Martin Buber,* 1963), in 1958 and collected in *Noms Propres,* and the first three essays of *Hors sujet* (1987; translated as *Outside the Subject,* 1993).

Lévinas's first book of essays on Judaism and on the contributions that thought about Judaism has to make to contemporary problems was *Difficile liberté.* Not long after its publication, Derrida published perhaps the most important response to Lévinas's work, "Violence et métaphysique: Essai sur la pensée d'Emmanuel Lévinas" (Violence and Metaphysics: An Essay on the Thought of Emmanuel Lévinas) in *L'écriture et la différence* (1967; translated as *Writing and Difference,* 1978). Derrida's criticism takes direct aim at Lévinas's understanding of the relation of his thinking about matters Jewish and his philosophical work. Thus, Derrida's criticisms are directed more at Lévinas's strategy in *Totalité et infini* than at the particular claims that Lévinas makes in that book. According to Derrida, Lévinas claims that the other of philosophy (for Lévinas, Jewish thought) is non-Greek. In other words, it is not philosophy. Derrida questions the possibility of Lévinas's claim, saying that his questions and others like them result from the fact that Lévinas wants to use the language of philosophy ("traditional conceptuality") against philosophy. Derrida is skeptical that one can do that.

Derrida's criticism is important because the questions he raised caused Lévinas to rethink his work, and that rethinking eventually resulted in Lévinas's second major work, *Autrement qu'être*. In the meantime, however, Lévinas took a new professorial position at the University of Paris, Nanterre, in 1967, and in 1968 he published a second volume of essays on Judaism, *Quatre lectures talmudiques,* which particularly focused on his Talmud studies. Then, in 1973 he moved to the University of Paris (Sorbonne).

In 1974, ten years after the appearance of Derrida's essay, Lévinas published the work that resulted from that criticism, *Autrement qu'être*. Though motivated by Derrida's criticism, *Autrement qu'être* does not represent a reversal of Lévinas's thinking or a departure in another direction. Instead, it is a deepening of the insights and claims of *Totalité et infini*.

Lévinas's other philosophical works pale in difficulty when compared to *Autrement qu'être*. Not only is its language extremely difficult, but its organization is unlike any that one might expect of a philosophy book. *Autrement qu'être* begins, without introduction, in medias res. Its first section is "L'argument" (The Argument, though the word *argument* seems to be used not so much in its philosophical sense as in the literary sense of the word, as "plot summary"). Between the argument of the first twenty-three pages and the thirteen pages of the last section, "Autrement dit" (Said Otherwise—a play on a word from the title of the book, *autrement,* and one of its important themes, *le Dit,* "the Said"—translated as "In Other Words"), Lévinas gives his readers several variations on the themes of the beginning and the ending sections. As he says in the end of "L'argument," the necessity of thematizing the various concepts that arise as one tries to speak of transcendence requires that the book be divided into chapters. Those chapters do not correspond to a linear exposition of his argument, however. Instead, they are overlapping excurses on themes raised in the first and last sections. As Paul Ricoeur explains in *Autrement: Lecture d'*Autrement qu'être; ou, Au-delà de l'essence *d'Emmanuel Lévinas* (Otherwise: A Reading of Emmanuel Lévinas's *Otherwise than Being: or, Beyond Essence,* 1997), in the intermediate sections of *Autrement qu'être* Lévinas reveals the major folds of the ethics of responsibility rather than marshaling a phenomenological analysis or a traditional philosophical argument.

Though the language and organization of *Autrement qu'être* are strange, one can identify ideas in it that are central to Lévinas's thinking. For example, he makes much of a distinction that first appeared in *Totalité et infini,* namely the distinction between *le Dit* and *le Dire* (the Saying). The basic idea is that any act of saying does something that is not captured in what is said. Every theme is a Said; every Saying results in a Said that people can then take up, analyze, remember, and use. Signification, a relation to what is otherwise than

EMMANUEL LEVINAS

Autrement qu'être ou au-delà de l'essence

MARTINUS NIJHOFF / LA HAYE / 1974

Title page for the book (translated as Otherwise than Being: or, Beyond Essence, *1981) in which Lévinas uses difficult language and nonlinear exposition to explicate an ethic of responsibility (Jean and Alexander Heard Library, Vanderbilt University)*

being, occurs in Saying, however, since being is always a matter of the Said, of what remains the same. Lévinas also enlarges his claim that the relationship with the other person is a matter of being interrupted or disturbed by the demands of the other, emphasizing the passivity of the encounter with the other person: the other commands before one understands what it is that is commanded. Lévinas conceives of this passive encounter in sensible rather than cognitive terms, however: people are susceptible to being affected.

The notion of substitution is another important theme in *Autrement qu'être*. To find oneself related to alterity is to find oneself commanded and, as Lévinas argued in *Totalité et infini,* it is to find oneself in question: one is commanded to account for oneself before the other person. (According to Lévinas, apology is thus the origin of reason.) One finds oneself not only responsible *before* the other person, but *for* that other person. One is required to give the other person the bread from one's own mouth, to substitute the other person's needs and desires for one's own.

In 1977 Lévinas published another collection of Talmudic essays, *Du sacré au saint: Cinq nouvelles lectures talmudiques* (1977; translated as "From the Sacred to the Holy" in *Nine Talmudic Readings*). He retired from teaching in 1979 but continued to write. Several collections of essays came out after he retired, many of them collections of previously published essays, though he also published several essays for the first time. Examples are three collections of philosophical essays, *De Dieu qui vient à l'idée* (1982; translated as *Of God Who Comes to Mind*, 1998), *Altérité et transcendence* (1995; translated as *Alterity and Transcendence,* 1999), and two collections of essays on Jewish themes, *A l'heure des nations* and *Nouvelles lectures talmudiques* (1996; translated as *New Talmudic Readings,* 1999).

In September 1994 Raïssa Lévinas died, and Lévinas, suffering from Alzheimer's disease, died on 25 December 1995. One of his funeral eulogies was delivered by Derrida. That eulogy, with a memorial address given a year later, has been published as *Adieu à Emmanuel Lévinas* (1997; translated as *Adieu to Emmanuel Lévinas,* 1999).

In an article on 7 January 1997 the *Jerusalem Post* described Lévinas as "one of the greatest Jewish philosophers, perhaps the greatest since Maimonides," though many do not know Lévinas as a Jewish philosopher. In his eulogy for Lévinas, Derrida said, "He overthrew one more time the landscapeless landscape of thought." Lévinas not only introduced phenomenology to French thinkers, but when it fell out of fashion in the 1960s he was among those who brought about its renewal by radically rethinking the fundamental problem of phenomenology as the problem of the other person, or, as that problem is presently described, the problem of transcendence: how can one know, speak of, or relate to that which is radically other than oneself? (Though "radically other" means "irreducible to me" rather than "absolutely unavailable.") Lévinas also changed the landscape of French thought by taking seriously the link between his Jewish thought and his philosophy. Most of the thinkers who have benefited from that element in Lévinas's thinking have been Christians rather than Jews, but more than any other twentieth-century philosopher, Lévinas made it possible for French philosophers to appeal to religion and religious texts. His influence can be seen clearly in works such as Jean-Luc Marion's *Etant donné: Essai d'une phénoménologie de la donation* (Given Being: An Essay on the Phenomenology of the Given, 1997) and Michel Henry's *C'est*

moi la verité: Pour une philosophie du christianisme (translated as *I Am the Truth: Toward a Philosophy of Christianity,* 2002). Though Henry could hardly disagree more with Lévinas philosophically, Henry probably could not have used Christianity as he does in his later work, namely as the explicit philosophical basis of his thinking, were it not for what Lévinas did before him.

Lévinas's claim that ethics precedes ontology has caught the eye of many, so that those writing on literary theory, theology, anthropology, sociology, gay and lesbian theory, and feminism, as well as philosophy, refer to his work. Though Emmanuel Lévinas saw himself as a philosopher rather than a literary theorist or sociologist, his interest in the problem of otherness has aroused the interest of those in disciplines outside of philosophy who are concerned with questions of otherness.

Interviews:

Ethique et infini: Dialogues avec Philippe Nemo (Paris: Librairie Arthème Fayard, 1982); translated by Richard A. Cohen as *Ethics and Infinity* (Pittsburgh: Duquesne University Press, 1985);

Richard Kearney, "Dialogue with Emmanuel Lévinas," in *Dialogues with Contemporary Continental Thinkers: The Phenomenological Heritage: Paul Ricoeur, Emmanuel Lévinas, Herbert Marcuse, Stanislas Breton, Jacques Derrida,* edited and translated by Kearney (Manchester & Dover, N.H.: Manchester University Press, 1984), pp. 49–69;

Is It Righteous to Be? Interviews with Emmanuel Lévinas, edited by Jill Robbins (Stanford, Cal.: Stanford University Press, 2001).

Bibliography:

Joan Nordquist, *Emmanuel Lévinas: A Bibliography* (Santa Cruz, Cal.: Reference and Research Services, 1997).

Biographies:

Maria-Anne Lescourret, *Emmanuel Lévinas* (Paris: Flammarion, 1994);

Saloman Malka, *Emmanuel Lévinas: La vie et la trace* (Paris: J.-C. Lattés, 2002).

References:

Zygmunt Bauman, *Postmodern Ethics* (Oxford & Cambridge, Mass.: Blackwell, 1993), pp. 47–52, 69–77, 84–97;

Bettina Bergo and Diane Perpich, eds., *Lévinas's Contribution to Contemporary Philosophy,* special issue of *Graduate Faculty Philosophy Journal,* 20, no. 2 - 21, no. 1 (1998);

Robert Bernasconi and Simon Critchley, eds., *Re-reading Lévinas* (Bloomington: Indiana University Press, 1991);

Bernasconi and David Wood, eds., *The Provocation of Lévinas: Rethinking the Other* (London & New York: Routledge, 1988);

Maurice Blanchot, *The Writing of the Disaster,* translated by Ann Smock (Lincoln: University of Nebraska Press, 1986), pp. 13–30;

Catherine Chalier, "Emmanuel Lévinas: Responsibility and Election," in *Ethics,* edited by A. Phillips Griffiths, Royal Institute of Philosophy Supplement, no. 35 (Cambridge & New York: Cambridge University Press, 1993), pp. 63–76;

Tina Chanter, ed., *Feminist Interpretations of Emmanuel Lévinas* (University Park: Pennsylvania State University Press, 2001);

Richard A. Cohen, *Elevations: The Height of the Good in Rosenzweig and Lévinas* (Chicago: University of Chicago Press, 1994);

Cohen, ed., *Face to Face with Lévinas* (Albany: State University of New York Press, 1986);

Simon Critchley, *The Ethics of Deconstruction: Derrida and Lévinas* (Oxford & Cambridge, Mass.: Blackwell, 1992);

Colin Davis, *Lévinas: An Introduction* (Cambridge: Polity Press, 1996; Notre Dame: Notre Dame University Press, 1996);

Theodore De Boer, *The Rationality of Transcendence: Studies in the Philosophy of Emmanuel Lévinas* (Amsterdam: J. C. Geiben, 1997);

Jacques Derrida, *Adieu to Emmanuel Lévinas,* translated by Pascal-Anne Brault and Michael Naas (Stanford, Cal.: Stanford University Press, 1999);

Derrida, "Violence and Metaphysics: An Essay on the Thought of Emmanuel Lévinas," in his *Writing and Difference,* translated by Alan Bass (Chicago: University of Chicago Press, 1978), pp. 79–153;

Jean Greisch, "Ethics and Ontology," *Irish Philosophical Journal,* 4, nos. 1–2 (1987): 64–75;

Seán Hand, ed., *Facing the Other: The Ethics of Emmanuel Lévinas* (Richmond, U.K.: Curzon, 1996);

Dennis King Keenan, *Death and Responsibility: The "Work" of Lévinas* (Albany: State University of New York Press, 1999);

Alphonso Lingis, "Face to Face," in his *Deathbound Subjectivity* (Bloomington: Indiana University Press, 1989), pp. 135–155;

John Llewelyn, *Emmanuel Lévinas: The Genealogy of Ethics* (London: Routledge, 1995);

Jean-Luc Marion, *Etant donné: Essaie d'une phénoménologie de la donation* (Paris: Presses universitaires de France, 1997);

Melvyn New, Robert Bernasconi, and Richard Cohen, eds., *In Proximity: Emmanuel Lévinas and the Eighteenth Century* (Lubbock: Texas Tech University Press, 2001);

Adriaan Peperzak, *To the Other: An Introduction to the Philosophy of Emmanuel Lévinas* (West Lafayette, Ind.: Purdue University Press, 1993);

Peperzak, ed., *Ethics as First Philosophy: The Significance of Emmanuel Lévinas for Philosophy, Literature, and Religion* (New York: Routledge, 1995);

Simonne Plourde, *Emmanuel Lévinas: Altérité et responsabilité. Guide de lecture* (Paris: Cerf, 1996);

Paul Ricoeur, *Autrement: Lecture d'*Autrement qu'être; ou, Au-delà de l'essence *d'Emmanuel Lévinas* (Paris: Presses universitaires de France, 1997);

Ricoeur, "What Ontology in View," in his *Oneself as Another,* translated by Kathleen Blamey (Chicago: University of Chicago Press, 1992), pp. 297–356;

Jill Robbins, "An Inscribed Responsibility: Lévinas's Difficult Freedom," *MLN,* 106 (1991): 1052–1062;

Brian Schroeder, *Altared Ground: Lévinas, History, and Violence* (New York: Routledge, 1996);

François-David Sebbah, *Lévinas: Ambiguïtés de l'altérité* (Paris: Les Belles Lettres, 2000);

Sonia Sikka, "How Not to Read the Other: 'All the Rest Can Be Translated,'" *Philosophy Today,* 43, no. 2 (1999): 195–206;

Stephan Strasser, *Jenseits von* Sein und Zeit: *Eine Einführung in Emmanuel Levinas' Philosophie* (The Hague: Nijhoff, 1978);

Merold Westphal, "Lévinas and the Immediacy of the Face," *Faith and Philosophy: Journal of the Society of Christian Philosophers,* 10, no. 4 (1993): 486–502;

Edith Wyschogrod, *Emmanuel Lévinas: The Problem of Ethical Metaphysics* (New York: Fordham University Press, 2000);

Krzysztof Ziarek, "Semantics of Proximity: Language and the Other in the Philosophy of Emmanuel Lévinas," *Research in Phenomenology,* 19 (1989): 213–217.

Papers:

Emmanuel Lévinas's unpublished papers are housed in the Lévinas Center at the University of North Carolina at Charlotte.

Pierre Macherey
(17 February 1938 –   )

Richard L. W. Clarke
University of the West Indies

BOOKS: *Lire "Le Capital,"* 2 volumes, by Macherey, Louis Althusser, and others (Paris: Maspero, 1965; revised edition, Paris: Presses Universitaires de France/Quadrige, 1996);

Pour une théorie de la production littéraire (Paris: Maspero, 1966); translated by Geoffrey Wall as *A Theory of Literary Production* (London & Boston: Routledge & Kegan Paul, 1978);

Hegel ou Spinoza (Paris: Maspero, 1979);

Hegel et la société, by Macherey and Jean-Pierre Lefebvre (Paris: Presses Universitaires de France, 1984);

Comte: La philosophie et les sciences (Paris: Presses Universitaires de France, 1989);

A quoi pense la littérature? Exercices de philosophie littéraire (Paris: Presses Universitaires de France, 1990); translated by David Macey as *The Object of Literature* (Cambridge & New York: Cambridge University Press, 1995);

Avec Spinoza: Etudes sur la doctrine et l'histoire du spinozisme (Paris: Presses Universitaires de France, 1992);

*Introduction à l'*Ethique *de Spinoza,* 5 volumes (Paris: Presses Universitaires de France, 1994–1998);

Histoires de dinosaure: Faire de la philosophie, 1965–1997 (Paris: Presses Universitaires de France, 1999).

Edition in English: *In a Materialist Way: Selected Essays,* translated by Ted Stolze, edited, with an introduction, by Warren Montag (London & New York: Verso, 1998).

OTHER: Renée Balibar, Geneviève Merlin, and Gilles Tret, *Les Français fictifs: Le rapport des styles littéraires au Français national,* introduction by Macherey and Etienne Balibar (Paris: Hachette, 1974);

Renée Balibar and Dominique Laporte, *Le Français national: Politique et pratiques de la langue nationale sous la Révolution française,* introduction by Macherey and Etienne Balibar (Paris: Hachette, 1974);

"Problems of Reflection," translated by John Coombes, in *Literature, Society and the Sociology of Literature: Proceedings of the Conference Held at the University of Essex, July 1976,* edited by Frances Barker and others (Colchester: University of Essex, 1977), pp. 41–54;

"Entre Pascal et Spinoza: Le vide," in *Spinoza nel 350o anniversario della nascità: Atti del congresso internazionale (Urbino 4–8 ottobre 1982),* edited by Emilia Giancotti (Naples: Bibliopolis, 1985), pp. 71–87;

"Déterminisme" and "Dialectique," by Macherey and Etienne Balibar, in *Encyclopaedia Universalis,* volume 7 (Paris: Encyclopaedia Universalis, 1989–1990), pp. 283–288, 359–363;

"Engels (Friedrich)," by Macherey and Etienne Balibar, in *Encyclopaedia Universalis,* volume 8 (Paris: Encyclopaedia Universalis, 1989–1990), pp. 372–374;

"Formalisme et formalisation," by Macherey and Etienne Balibar, in *Encyclopaedia Universalis,* volume 9 (Paris: Encyclopaedia Universalis, 1989–1990), pp. 707–710;

"Marx et marxisme," by Macherey and Etienne Balibar, in *Encyclopaedia Universalis,* volume 14 (Paris: Encyclopaedia Universalis, 1989–1990), pp. 646–656;

"Condillac et Spinoza: Une lecture biaisée," by Macherey and Jacqueline Lagrée, in *Spinoza au XVIIIe siècle,* edited by Olivier Bloch and Hélène Politis (Paris: Méridiens-Klincksieck, 1990), pp. 241–253;

"Les paradoxes de la connaissance immédiate dans la *Korte Verhandeling,*" in *Dio, l'uomo, la libertà: Studi sul Breve Trattato di Spinoza,* edited by Filippo Mignini (L'Aquilà: Japadre, 1990), pp. 203–225;

"Spinoza, la fin de l'histoire et la ruse de la raison," in *Spinoza: Issues and Directions: The Proceedings of the Chicago Spinoza Conference (1986),* edited by Edwin Curley and Pierre-François Moreau (Leiden & New York: Brill, 1990), pp. 327–346;

"From Action to Production of Effects: Observations on the Ethical Significance of *Ethics* I," in *God and Nature: Spinoza's Metaphysics,* edited by Yirmiyahu Yovel (Leiden & New York: Brill, 1991), pp. 161–180;

"A propos de la différence entre Hobbes et Spinoza," in *Hobbes e Spinoza: Scienza e Politica: Atti del Convegno Internazionale–Urbino, 14–17 Ottobre, 1988,* edited by Daniela Bostrenghi (Naples: Bibliopolis, 1992), pp. 689–698;

"L'actualité philosophique de Spinoza," in *Nature, Croyance, Raison: Mélanges offerts à Sylvain Zac* (Fontenay-aux-Roses: Fontenay/Saint-Cloud, 1992), pp. 119–133;

Jules Barni, *La morale dans le démocratie: Suivi du Manuel républicain,* edited by Macherey (Paris: Kimé, 1992);

"La dissociation de la métaphysique et de l'éthique: Russell lecteur de Spinoza," in *Spinoza au XXe siècle,* edited by Olivier Bloch (Paris: Presses Universitaires de Paris, 1992), pp. 285–305;

"Entre la philosophie et l'histoire: L'histoire de la philosophie," in *La Philosophie et son histoire,* edited by Gilbert Boss (Zurich: Grand Midi, 1994), pp. 11–45;

"Spinoza est-il moniste?" in *Spinoza: Puissance et ontologie,* edited by Myriam Revault d'Allonnes and Hadi Rizk (Paris: Kimé, 1994), pp. 39–53;

"Spinoza et l'origine des jugements de valeur," in *Architectures de la raison: Mélanges offerts à Alexandre Matheron,* edited by Moreau (Fontenay-aux-Roses: ENS, 1996), pp. 205–212.

SELECTED PERIODICAL PUBLICATIONS–
UNCOLLECTED: "La philosophie de la science de Georges Canguilhem: Epistemologie et histoire des sciences," *La Pensée,* 113 (1964): 50–74;

"L'analyse littéraire: Tombeau de structures," *Les Temps Modernes,* 246 (1966);

"Sur la littérature comme forme idéologique: Quelques hypothèses marxistes," by Macherey and Etienne Balibar, *Littérature,* 13, no. 4 (1974): 29–48; translated by Ian McLeod, John Whitehead, and Ann Wordsworth as "On Literature as an Ideological Form: Some Marxist Propositions," *Oxford Literary Review,* 3 (1978): 4–12;

"The Problem of Reflection," *Sub-stance,* 15 (1976): 6–20;

"De la médiation à la constitution: Description d'un parcours spéculatif," *Cahiers Spinoza,* 4 (1983): 9–37;

"Leroux dans la querelle du panthéisme," *Cahiers de Fontenay,* 36–38 (March 1985): 215–222;

"La philosophie à la française," *Revue des sciences philosophiques et théologiques,* 74, no. 1 (1990);

"Ethique IV: Les propositions 70 et 71," *Revue de métaphysique et de morale,* 4 (1994): 459–474;

"A Production of Subjectivity," *Yale French Studies,* 88 (1995): 42–52;

"Spinoza, lecteur et critique de Boyle," *Revue du Nord,* 77 (1995): 733–774;

"Choses, images de choses, signes, idées (Ethique II, 18, sc.)," *Revue des sciences philosophiques et théologiques,* 82, no. 1 (1998): 17–30;

"Spinoza, une philosophie à plusieurs voix," *Philosophique,* 1 (1998): 5–22.

Pierre Macherey is professor emeritus in the Unité de Formation et de Recherche (UFR) de philosophie, the faculty of philosophy at the Université Charles de Gaulle, Lille III, where he specializes in aesthetics and the history of philosophy. In "Soutenance," the defense of the entire corpus of his scholarship that he presented in 1991 to a jury of his peers (collected in *In a Materialist Way: Selected Essays,* 1998), Macherey offers this overview of his career: "Three series of questions have . . . preoccupied me. . . . These questions are those of Spinozism, of the relations of literature and philosophy, and of the history of philosophy in France." Macherey's later philosophical explorations, not least his extensive engagement with the philosopher Baruch Spinoza and with the history of philosophy in France, have been all but ignored in the Anglophone world. It can be safely said that for most English-speaking readers, Macherey's philosophical outlook is reducible to the structuralist variant of Marxism synonymous with his mentor Louis Althusser and his major contributions limited to the field of critical theory, rather than philosophy per se. He is best known in this regard for two seminal theoretical works: *Pour une théorie de la production littéraire* (1966; translated as *A Theory of Literary Production,* 1978) and "Sur la littérature comme forme idéologique: Quelques hypothèses marxistes" (1974; translated as "On Literature as an Ideological Form: Some Marxist Propositions," 1978) which was cowritten with his colleague Etienne Balibar.

Macherey was born in Belfort, France, on 17 February 1938. He attended Lycée Louis le Grand in Paris before pursuing studies in philosophy at the celebrated Ecole Normale Supérieure, rue d'Ulm, from 1958 to 1963. There he was awarded the *licence de philosophie* in 1960, the *maîtrise de philosophie* in 1961, and the *Agregé de philosophie* in 1962. The philosopher of science Georges Canguilhem supervised Macherey's thesis for the *maîtrise,* "Philosophie et politique chez Spinoza," the subject of which indicated his keen interest even at this early stage in a philosopher to whom he returned in the later phase of his career. Althusser supervised Macherey's preparation for the *aggrégation,* a competitive examination for admission to posts on the teaching staff of lycées (colleges) and universities. In 1962–1963 Althusser held his celebrated seminar on structuralism, in which Macherey and other colleagues such as Michel

THÉORIE IV.

PIERRE MACHEREY

POUR UNE THÉORIE
DE LA
PRODUCTION LITTÉRAIRE

FRANÇOIS MASPERO
PARIS

*Paperback cover for Pierre Macherey's first book-length work of
critical theory (translated as* A Theory of Literary
Production, *1978), published in 1966, in which
he advocates a rational, deductive approach to
literary criticism (Thomas Cooper Library,
University of South Carolina)*

which appeared in *La Pensée* (Thought), the theoretical organ of the French Communist Party.

Macherey taught at the Prytanée Militaire de la Flèche from 1963 to 1965 and Lycée Descartes in Tours from 1965 to 1966. He participated in Althusser's seminar in 1963–1964 on Karl Marx's *Das Kapital* (Capital, 1867) and contributed, together with Althusser, Balibar, Rancière, and Roger Establet, to the original edition of the seminal *Lire "Le Capital"* (1965; Althusser's and Balibar's contributions, though not Macherey's, were translated as *Reading Capital,* 1970), which resulted therefrom. Althusser and company sought in this work to critique both traditional Marxism and the Hegelian Marxism synonymous with György Lukács by formulating a rapprochement of sorts between structuralism and Marxism. They sought in particular to rewrite both the traditional base/superstructure model and the Hegelian Marxist notion of the expressive totality by arguing that the social formation consists of several "levels" or "practices," the economic, the political, and the ideological, differentiated from or semi-autonomous of each other in a manner analogous to the signs composing the sign system. From this point of view there is no longer any question of the existence of a political and ideological superstructure reflective (in a relationship of effect to cause) of an economic and social infrastructure. By the same token, the various elements comprising the social formation are no longer to be thought of as ultimately expressive (in a relationship of form to content) of the economic totality of which they are part. Rather, the elements composing the social formation are determined by what Althusser termed a "structural effectivity," that is, purely by their relation to each other and the whole formed thereby. Putative processes of reflection or expression are henceforth replaced by an emphasis on the specificity or "relative autonomy" of each practice derived, like signs in the sign system, from their simultaneous difference from and relatedness to each other.

In 1966, in the wake of the success of *Lire "Le Capital,"* Macherey obtained a post in the UFR de philosophie at the Université de Paris I (Panthéon-Sorbonne), where he taught until the early 1990s. That same year he published his first book-length study, *Pour une théorie de la production littéraire,* the focus of which is evidently on critical theory rather than philosophy per se. While it brought Macherey acclaim in his own right, it also brought him (like Althusser) denunciation on the part of diehards and traditionalists within the Marxist camp viscerally opposed to Althusser's rereading of Marx. Its reception in the English-speaking world was certainly facilitated by the indebtedness to it of Terry Eagleton's *Criticism and Ideology: A Study in Marxist Literary Theory* (1976), the publication of which preceded an

Pêcheux, Etienne Balibar, and Jacques Rancière participated. Focusing on philosophers such as Claude Lévi-Strauss, Jacques Lacan, Michel Foucault, and Canguilhem, they paid attention both to what they saw as the beneficial antihumanism of the structuralist enterprise (above all its contribution to the decentering of the autonomous, transcendental subject) and to its principal blind spots, not least the recuperation of the subject in another form: the concept of structure itself. Out of this seminar came Macherey's first publication, "La philosophie de la science de Georges Canguilhem: Epistemologie et histoire des sciences" (1964; translated as "Georges Canguilhem's Philosophy of Science: Epistemology and History of Science" in *In a Materialist Way*),

English translation of Macherey's study by some two years. Eagleton himself, however, in "Macherey and Marxist Literary Theory" (1986) criticized what he considered to be the major defect of the work: the "intrinsicism and formalism" derived from the ahistorical tendencies of structuralism, which undermine the potential inherent in many of its insights into critical practice.

The immense influence of *Pour une théorie de la production littéraire* has made it Macherey's most significant contribution to critical theory. Drawing on the notion of structural effectivity explored in *Lire "Le Capital"* as well as the post-Saussurean critique of traditional referential and expressive models of signification, it offers an important rethinking of both the mimeticism and the expressivism typical of Marxist criticism current to that point. Macherey's project may be reduced to the question: if literary texts, part of the ideological level of the social formation, neither *reflect* the economic and social infrastructure nor *express* the economic totality, what then is the precise nature of their relationship with the other levels of the social formation in which they are produced?

Macherey begins by identifying three major fallacies where criticism is concerned, each predicated on an inductive model of knowledge. The first is the "empiricist" fallacy, which treats the literary work as a mirror held up to reality (that is, as the effect of an absent cause) and views criticism as a secondary mirror held up to the text itself. The second fallacy is the "normative," which informs critical approaches such as structuralist narratology, then in its heyday, and prescriptively measures the conformity of the literary work to an a priori "ideal norm" (from this point of view, the work is the effect of an absent *literary* cause). The third fallacy is the "interpretive," which views the form of the literary work as the material manifestation of the author's intention (which is the content of the work) and criticism as a process of interpretation.

In their place Macherey advocates a "rationalist" approach to criticism, predicated on a deductive model of knowledge, arguing that an objective criticism ought to be founded, like a science, on a certain distance between the literary object per se and critical knowledge about that object. Macherey's view is that, given the nature of signification theorized by Ferdinand de Saussure, the meaning of a literary text is derived neither from mirroring reality in some simplistic way, nor from emulating ideal literary forms, nor from expressing authorial intention. Given the views on the nature of the social formation advanced in *Lire "Le Capital,"* moreover, Macherey argues that a Marxist criticism ought to focus neither on the economic base of which the work is allegedly the ideological effect, nor on the

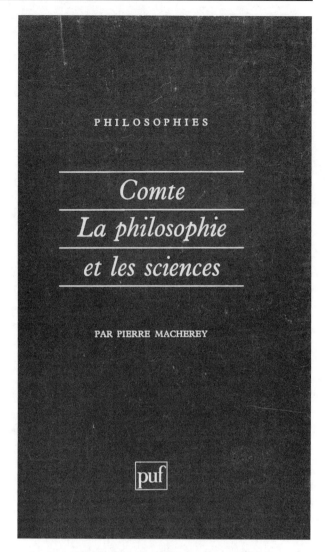

Paperback cover for Macherey's 1989 book, a study of the nineteenth-century French founder of sociology and positivism, Auguste Comte (Thomas Cooper Library, University of South Carolina)

economic totality supposedly expressed or mediated by the form of the work, nor, of course, on literary form to the exclusion of all else. A scientific criticism ought to search, rather, for the "laws" that determine the text. To be precise, the focus must be on the "real and fundamental complexity" of the work itself (which is to be distinguished from the "linear simplicity" of the unfolding of narrative structure that absorbs the attention of narratologists) and in which one must recognize the "signs of a necessity" or, to borrow Althusser's phrase, the determination of a structural effectivity that both complicates simplistic notions of the relationship between text and reality and obviates purely formalistic conceptions of literature.

Macherey argues that the relation of literature to ideology is that of signifier to signified (these are comparable, given Saussure's well-known example, to two sides of a sheet of paper) rather than that of expressive form to expressed content. As merely one form taken by ideology, the ideological specificity of the literary text is determined by both its similarity to and difference from other ideological forms. Through its at least partial departure from dominant ways of conceptualizing reality, therefore, the literary text resists being entirely incorporated into the flow of ideology, functioning in an almost parodic manner to set into relief, and thus provide something close to a scientific knowledge of, the various forms taken by the dominant ideology. As merely one practice within the social formation, the specificity of the ideological is determined in turn by its partial difference from the other practices composing the social formation. The literary text qua ideological form is therefore both related to and different from the political and the economic practices that it sets into relief, rather than simply reflects or expresses. It is for this reason that literature cannot in any way be said to merely mirror reality: it produces, rather, an "effect of reality."

From this point of view, the "laws" that criticism should seek to explicate are those that inform the difference of the literary text both from other ideological forms and from the other practices composing the social formation and which result in the absence of positive presence in the text, its radical otherness, and its consequent decenteredness. Criticism, in other words, ought to be a form of explication designed to describe the silent necessity *(langue)*, determining in this way a given literary text *(parole)*. Rather than serve as an interpretation designed merely to ventriloquize what it does say, criticism ought to seek to explain the mute laws responsible for the existence of the text and thus to describe what the text cannot openly say. There is, thus, an "un-said" that coexists with the "said" of the text, which accordingly cannot speak of the complex of differences that structure it (its "over-determination"). In this way, and not through simplistic processes of overt reflection or expression, history (irreducible to merely literary history) is latently present in the text.

Eagleton argues that "Sur la littérature comme forme idéologique" represents an attempt to correct the formalist deficiencies that mar *Pour une théorie de la production littéraire*. It was arguably motivated by the need to further refine certain aspects of the argument advanced in the earlier study in line with unavoidable developments in post-Saussurean linguistic theory and the Althusserian model of the social formation. It should be noted that if *Pour une théorie de la production littéraire* was influenced by *Lire "Le Capital,"* "Sur la littérature comme forme idéologique" was particularly influenced by Althusser's equally well-known essay "Idéologie et appareils idéologique d'état (Notes pour une recherche)" (On Ideology and Ideological State Apparatuses, collected in *Lenin and Philosophy, and Other Essays*, 1971) not least his view that the cause of ideology (the view, for example, that ideology is a superstructural reflex of the economic infrastructure) may be far less important than its effect: by offering images with which to identify, ideology assigns specific subject positions or roles to individuals and thereby ensures the reproduction of the extant asymmetrical social relations of production. (Althusser gives the name *interpellation* to this process of subject formation.)

Balibar and Macherey begin by pointing out that the Marxist model of literature, in all its various incarnations, revolves around the view that literature, as a form of ideology, is to a greater or lesser degree a reflection of objective reality. This concept of reflection does not do justice, however, to the "relative autonomy" of both the various practices composing the social formation and the elements of which these practices are in turn composed. At stake, therefore, is the indispensability of theorizing both the specificity of ideology in relation to other social practices and that of literature in relation to the other forms, such as moral or political, assumed by ideology. Balibar and Macherey posit that just as ideology is both related to and different from the other practices, so too is literature both related to and different from other ideological forms. The Marxist critic is, hence, no longer confronted with the false dilemma of choosing between intrinsic and extrinsic analysis, that is, whether to "analyze literature on its own ground . . . or from an external standpoint," because to analyze the "ideological specificity" of literature is not to reduce it either to "something other than itself or to itself." Their thesis here is that the specificity of literature is defined less by what it represents (its cause) than by its ideological impact on the reader (effect).

Balibar and Macherey accordingly propose that while literature is not independent of its sociohistorical context, it is to some degree autonomous. Modern French literature, for example, cannot be totally severed from the class struggles that historically accompanied its development and which are encoded in the language that composes it. It is to some degree autonomous of such conflicts, however, which cannot be found there in their original, preliterary form. Balibar and Macherey suggest that such conflicts appear, rather, in a specific literary form designed to provide their solution (or to do away with them altogether) by "substituting imaginary contradictions soluble within the ideological practices of religion, politics, morality, aesthetics and psychology." The biggest shortcoming of *Pour une théorie de la production littéraire* was, they believe, its failure to identify the "specific mechanism of the literary compromise" by which this resolution is accomplished.

Balibar and Macherey argue that the key instrument to this end is characterization, which plays a crucial role in the interpellation of the individual reader. They posit that the subjectification of the reader is accomplished via an "identification effect" similar to that experienced between the individual and the mirror image theorized by Lacan: the "ideological effects of literature . . . materialize via an identification process" that occurs between the audience and the "hero or antihero," leading to the "simultaneous mutual constitution of the fictive 'consciousness' of the character with the ideological consciousness of the reader." In this way literature "unceasingly 'produces' subjects, on display for everyone," thereby transforming "(concrete) individuals into subjects" and endowing them "with a quasi-real hallucinatory individuality." Readers are thus encouraged to take up an "attitude toward imaginary struggles as they would toward real ones." By virtue of inculcating certain attitudes and forms of behavior in the reader, literature is the "privileged agent of ideological subjection" and, thus, one of the most important means by which the dominant ideology is regurgitated and the reproduction of bourgeois society assured.

Macherey engaged intensively with questions of critical theory for much of his early career because he saw a profound link between theoretical and philosophical issues, particularly their "common relation to the truth that governs their respective approaches," as he puts it in "Soutenance." He stresses here too that his interest in the relationship between philosophy and literature was part and parcel of his wider interest in the historical development of philosophy as practiced in France, what he terms *philosophie à la française,* especially during the nineteenth and twentieth centuries. By contrast to those located in the Anglo-American analytic tradition of philosophy, Macherey is keenly interested in questions concerning the history of philosophy that he necessarily views, Marxist that he is, as a socially inscribed practice. Philosophy qua ideological form is not, in Macherey's view, an "independent speculative activity" divorced from real historical conditions. This belief is why Macherey argues that there is intrinsically no such thing as French philosophy per se, at least not "in the sense of a natural datum completely determined by belonging to the land and by the filiation of the people or the race. There is rather what I have proposed to call 'philosophy à la française,' resulting from an institution that has had to be socially elaborated in relation to the transformations of society considered in the totality of its economic, political and ideological structures." The development of modern philosophy in France is thus inextricably linked to the emergence of the French

Paperback cover for Macherey's 1990 book (translated as The Object of Literature, *1995), in which he analyzes French authors such as Gustave Flaubert and Victor Hugo as literary philosophers (Thomas Cooper Library, University of South Carolina)*

nation-state since the revolution of 1789, as a result of which, he argues, the seemingly most "distant and disparate systems of thought" that compose it in fact "reflect the structures and evolutions of the same social formation that give its content to their speculations."

Macherey also emphasizes in "Soutenance" the indispensable contribution made to his own thinking by one philosopher in particular located in the Continental rationalist tradition, Spinoza, who has remained, notwithstanding the occasional interest in other important philosophers or matters of critical theory, Macherey's main interest since the late 1970s. He explains: "I had to set out from the study of Spinoza, because this study gives a support, a basis, and also meaning to the totality of my other inquiries." In 1979, a year after he began to attract attention for his critical theory in the English-speaking world, Macherey returned to his roots with the publication of *Hegel ou Spinoza* (Hegel or Spinoza), the title of which is designed to emphasize the elements of both convergence and divergence that defined Spinoza's philosophy in relation to Georg Wilhelm Friedrich Hegel's. In 1984 he contributed to *Hegel et la société* (Hegel and Society), cowritten by Jean-Pierre Lefebvre. In 1989 he published *Comte: La philosophie et les sciences* (Comte: Philosophy and Science).

Some twenty-four years after the publication of his seminal *Pour une théorie de la production littéraire*, Macherey returned to the issue of literary representation with the publication of his *A quoi pense la littérature? Exercices de philosophie littéraire* (1990; translated as *The Object of Literature,* 1995). Here, Macherey analyzes a series of classic works by French authors from the late eighteenth century to the 1970s, including Germaine de Staël, Georges Sand, Gustave Flaubert, and Victor Hugo. His argument is that literary texts, albeit under varied forms, proffer a particular conception of the relation of the sign to the "Real" and thus are the source of what he calls *une philosophie littéraire,* that is, a characteristically literary manner of philosophizing. From this perspective, literature does not regurgitate key philosophical topoi in some simplistic, unmediated manner. Macherey explains in "Soutenance" that in so arguing it was not his goal to reduce all philosophy to literature, but to widen the traditionally accepted definition of philosophy by stressing that "philosophical ideas do not exist only through the efforts of systematization offered to them by professional philosophers."

In the early 1990s Macherey accepted the post of professor in the UFR de philosophie at the Université Charles de Gaulle, Lille III, where he taught until his retirement in 2003. During this time he pursued the comparative, dialogic spirit of inquiry evident in *Hegel ou Spinoza* in several subsequent studies of Spinoza, including *Avec Spinoza: Etudes sur la doctrine et l'histoire du spinozisme* (In Dialogue with Spinoza: Studies in the Doctrine and History of Spinozism, 1992) and *Introduction à l'Ethique de Spinoza* (Introduction to Spinoza's *Ethics,* 1994–1998), the latter being the culmination of many published papers and presentations on Spinoza at a variety of colloquiums between 1981 and 1991. These works are devoted, he insists in "Soutenance," to clarifying and situating key aspects of Spinoza's thought, especially in relation to its reception, that is, "successive readings, which have in some sense reproduced it by adapting it to theoretical and ideological configurations sometimes very far removed from the conditions in which it was initially produced." Macherey's ultimate goal in so doing was to explore how far Spinoza's philosophy maintains its own identity while being reflected through alternative interpretive prisms. Macherey's argument is that a philosopher's doctrine is not independent of the "history of its interpretations" and that what at first glance might appear to be falsifications of

the true Spinoza are "no less authentic in their own way." Macherey claims that interpretations guilty, paradoxically, of such "true errors" in fact reveal meanings that no one can claim to be "radically foreign" to Spinoza's work and that accordingly testify to its "intrinsic fruitfulness."

Macherey's attempt to situate Spinoza's discourse in a "space of constantly evolving variations" was part of a larger project: to gain insight into the dynamics of its reproduction and, by extension, the process of philosophical history in general. One of Macherey's most important contributions to the study of the history of philosophy may lie in his attempt to formulate a model of intellectual history, one indebted at least in part to his interest in literary history and intertextuality and informed by the Lacanian notion of the mirror stage. "Soutenance" again provides invaluable insights into Macherey's thinking in this regard. For Macherey, philosophy, like literature, is made up of ideas that, far from simply reflecting reality, function to "transform, make, unmake and remake reality." These ideas are not static but have a discernible history: "by following and by making known the shifts, breaches and conflicts of these ideas, this history also reveals their productivity, their fruitfulness." The texts that compose the history of philosophy are, as such, not immune to the process of intertextuality constitutive of literary history, which he is at pains to describe in "For a Theory of Literary Reproduction" (collected in *In a Materialist Way,* 1998), an obvious coda to *Pour une théorie de la production littéraire.* Here, he argues that one never writes on a "completely blank page: the execution of a text necessarily relies on the reproduction of prior texts, to which it implicitly or explicitly refers. Every book contains in itself the labyrinth of a library." From this point of view one "writes on the written," as a result of which the "palimpsest" may be said to define the essence of the literary as much as the philosophical.

Macherey suggests here that this mirror-like relation between texts ought to be conceptualized in terms of the Lacanian notion of the mirror stage: "works are no longer reflected except by being dispersed, and by evoking their internal distance through this dispersion, through effects of mirroring which seem to have not beginning nor end. The notion of an original work succumbs to this splitting. . . . Every style could be explained by the implementation of such a mimeticism." Macherey thus finds it necessary to set the views of philosophers such as Hegel and Spinoza in something of a specular relation to each other. When Hegel reads Spinoza, he argues in "Soutenance," the former is incapable, because of a difference in "philosophical problematic," of "seeing . . . what Spinoza had actually been able to say." As a result, Hegel is obliged to formulate an "imaginary form of thought," the product at least in part of his own doctrine, as a result of which Spinoza's philosophy, "projected outside its own theoretical frontiers, thus plays the role of . . . a mirror, on whose surface conceptions which are apparently the most foreign to his own . . . trace their contours."

This specular relationship, simultaneously one of indebtedness and difference, is not limited to the relation of Hegel and Spinoza alone but is arguably applicable to the dialectical process of intellectual history as a whole. The "strange, and perhaps disturbing, familiarity" characteristic of such "reflections" is arguably true, "beyond their manifest differences," of all the figures who compose the "tortuous, broken . . . discourse of philosophy." Such a view may shed light, for example, on the anxiety of influence, to borrow Harold Bloom's concept, which arguably characterizes the relationship between Macherey and successors such as Eagleton and on the strenuous efforts of all "latecomers" to critique and thus differentiate their own work from that of their precursors.

Although to a large degree overshadowed by his mentor Althusser, Pierre Macherey is certainly an important figure on the French intellectual landscape, especially within philosophical circles, famous not least for his crucial role in the development of what has come to be called Structural Marxism and its application to the study of literature. The importance of Macherey's work on the history of philosophy in general and Spinoza in particular, however, has not received the recognition that it deserves in an English-speaking philosophical world still dominated by the Anglo-American analytic approach and a certain degree of hostility toward the Continental tradition. Moreover, while the groundbreaking nature of his application of poststructuralist Marxist philosophy to critical theory is difficult to underestimate, his name has tended to be overshadowed (at least in the Anglophone world) by those of English-speaking successors whose own contributions would have been impossible without the foundation provided by Macherey.

Interviews:

"An Interview with Pierre Macherey," edited and translated by Colin Mercer and Jean Radford, *Red Letters,* 5 (1977): 3–9;

"Interview: Etienne Balibar and Pierre Macherey," *Diacritics,* 12, no. 1 (1982): 46–51.

References:

Louis Althusser, *For Marx,* translated by Ben Brewster (London: Allen Lane, 1969; New York: Pantheon, 1969);

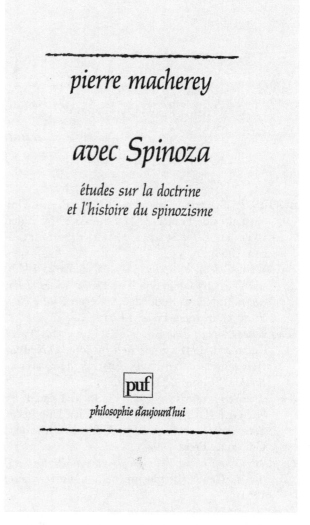

pierre macherey

avec Spinoza

*études sur la doctrine
et l'histoire du spinozisme*

puf

philosophie d'aujourd'hui

Paperback cover for Macherey's 1992 book about Benedict de Spinoza, one of his many works on the seventeenth-century Dutch rationalist philosopher (Thomas Cooper Library, University of South Carolina)

Althusser, "On Ideology and Ideological State Apparatuses (Notes towards an Investigation)," in *Lenin and Philosophy, and Other Essays,* translated by Brewster (London: New Left Books, 1971; New York: Monthly Review, 1972), pp. 127–186;

Frances Barker, "Ideology, Production, Text: Pierre Macherey's Materialist Criticism," *Praxis,* 5 (1980): 99–108;

Terry Eagleton, *Criticism and Ideology: A Study in Marxist Literary Theory* (London: New Left Books / Atlantic Highlands, N.J.: Humanities Press, 1976), pp. 83–84, 89–95, 97;

Eagleton, "Macherey and Marxist Literary Theory," in his *Against the Grain: Essays 1975–1985* (London: Verso, 1986), pp. 9–22.

Maurice Merleau-Ponty

(14 March 1908 – 3 May 1961)

Stuart J. Murray

University of California at Berkeley

BOOKS: *La Structure du comportement* (Paris: Presses Universitaires de France, 1942); translated by Alden L. Fisher as *The Structure of Behavior* (Boston: Beacon, 1963);

Phénoménologie de la perception (Paris: Gallimard, 1945); translated by Colin Smith as *Phenomenology of Perception* (London: Routledge & Kegan Paul / New York: Humanities Press, 1962);

Humanisme et terreur: Essai sur le problème communiste (Paris: Gallimard, 1947); translated by John O'Neill as *Humanism and Terror: An Essay on the Communist Problem* (Boston: Beacon, 1969);

Sens et non-sens (Paris: Nagel, 1948); translated by Hubert L. Dreyfus and Patricia Allen Dreyfus as *Sense and Non-Sense* (Evanston, Ill.: Northwestern University Press, 1964);

Les Relations avec autrui chez l'enfant (cours de 1950–1951) (Paris: Centre de documentation universitaire, 1951);

Elogie de la philosophie, leçon inaugurale faite au Collège de France, le jeudi 15 janvier 1953 (Paris: Gallimard, 1953); translated by John Wild and James M. Edie as *In Praise of Philosophy* (Evanston, Ill.: Northwestern University Press, 1963);

Les Aventures de la dialectique (Paris: Gallimard, 1955); translated by Joseph Bien as *Adventures of the Dialectic* (Evanston, Ill.: Northwestern University Press, 1973; London: Heinemann, 1974);

Les Sciences de l'homme et la phénoménologie (Paris: Centre de documentation universitaire, 1958);

Signes (Paris: Gallimard, 1960); translated by Richard McCleary as *Signs* (Evanston, Ill.: Northwestern University Press, 1964);

L'Oeil et l'esprit (Paris: Gallimard, 1964);

Le Visible et l'invisible, edited by Claude Lefort (Paris: Gallimard, 1964); translated by Alphonso Lingis as *The Visible and the Invisible* (Evanston, Ill.: Northwestern University Press, 1968);

Résumé de Cours, Collège de France, 1952–1960, edited by Lefort (Paris: Gallimard, 1968); translated by O'Neill as *Themes from the Lectures at the Collège de*

Maurice Merleau-Ponty (from <m-pc.binghamtom.edu>)

France, 1952–1960 (Evanston, Ill.: Northwestern University Press, 1970);

L'Union de l'âme et du corps chez Malebranche, Biran, et Bergson, edited by Jean Deprun (Paris: Vrin, 1968); translated by Paul B. Milan as *The Incarnate Subject: Malebranche, Biran, and Bergson on the Union of Body and Soul,* edited by Andrew G. Bjelland Jr. and Patrick Burke (Amherst, N.Y.: Humanity Books, 2001);

La Prose du monde, edited by Lefort (Paris: Gallimard, 1969); translated by O'Neill as *The Prose of the*

World (Evanston, Ill.: Northwestern University Press, 1973; London: Heinemann, 1974);

Merleau-Ponty à la Sorbonne: Résumé de cours, 1949–1952 (Grenoble: Cynara, 1988);

La Nature: Notes, cours du Collège de France, edited by Dominique Séglard (Paris: Seuil, 1995); translated by Robert Vallier as *Nature: Course Notes from the Collège de France* (Evanston, Ill.: Northwestern University Press, 2003);

Notes des cours au Collège de Brace: 1958–1961, edited by Stéphanie Ménasé (Paris: Gallimard, 1996);

Parcours, 2 volumes, edited by Jacques Prunair (Lagrasse: Verdier, 1997, 2000); Sartre and Merleau-Ponty letters from this volume translated by Boris Belay as "Sartre and Merleau-Ponty: The Letters of the Breakup," included in *Merleau-Ponty's Later Works and Their Practical Implications: The Dehiscence of Responsibility,* edited by Duane H. Davis (Amherst, N.Y.: Humanity Books, 2001), pp. 33–59;

Notes de cours sur L'Origine de la géométrie de Husserl, edited by Renaud Barbaras (Paris: Presses Universitaires de France, 1998); translated by O'Neill in *Husserl at the Limits of Phenomenology,* edited by Leonard Lawlor and Bettina Bergo (Evanston, Ill.: Northwestern University Press, 2002);

Causeries: 1948, edited by Ménasé (Paris: Seuil, 2002); translated by Oliver Davis as *The World of Perception* (London & New York: Routledge, 2004);

L'institution dans l'histoire personnelle et publique: Le problème de la passivité, le sommeil, l'inconscient, la mémoire: Notes de cours au Collège de France, 1954–1955, edited by Lefort, Ménasé, and Dominique Darmaillacq (Paris: Belin, 2003).

Editions and Collections: *Les Philosophes célèbres,* edited by Merleau-Ponty, Ferdinand Alquié, and others (Paris: Mazenod, 1956);

Existence et dialectique, edited by Maurice Dayan (Paris: Presses Universitaires de France, 1971).

Editions in English: *The Primacy of Perception and Other Essays on Phenomenological Psychology, the Philosophy of Art, History and Politics,* edited by James M. Edie (Evanston, Ill.: Northwestern University Press, 1964)–includes "The Child's Relations with Others" [*Les Relations avec autrui chez l'enfant*], translated by William Cobb, pp. 96–155; "Phenomenology and the Sciences of Man" [*Les Sciences de l'homme et la phénoménologie*], translated by John Wild, pp. 43–95; and "Eye and Mind" [*L'Oeil et l'esprit*], translated by Carleton Dallevy, pp. 159–190;

The Essential Writings of Merleau-Ponty, edited by Alden L. Fisher (New York: Harcourt, Brace & World, 1969);

Consciousness and the Acquisition of Language, translated by Hugh Silverman (Evanston, Ill.: Northwestern University Press, 1973);

Phenomenology, Language and Sociology: Selected Essays of Merleau-Ponty, edited by John O'Neill (London: Heinemann, 1974);

Texts and Dialogues: On Philosophy, Politics, and Culture, edited by Silverman and James Barry Jr., translated by Michael B. Smith and others (Atlantic Highlands, N.J. & London: Humanities Press, 1992).

In a special memorial edition of *Les Temps Modernes* (Modern Times), published only months after Maurice Merleau-Ponty's death in 1961, the French philosopher Jean Hyppolite wrote of Merleau-Ponty: "His work has become as familiar to us as those landscapes which we no longer see because they are always there, implicated in the way we see . . . presupposed by our research, sedimented in our thought." Philosophers and cultural theorists alike continue to owe a debt to Merleau-Ponty, whose work has informed disciplines across the humanities. Famous as an "existential phenomenologist," he is arguably best known as the philosopher of the body who sought to dismantle the Cartesian legacy in philosophy, a legacy in which mind and body are posited as two distinct substances whose causal interrelation, consequently, proved vexing to philosophers. He worked tirelessly to undermine the binary logic that had come to define philosophy since the ancients, including such presumed dichotomies as mind/body, subject/object, self/world, reason/unreason, thought/language, visible/invisible, and inner/outer. As he remarks in his best-known work, *Phénoménologie de la perception* (1945; translated as *Phenomenology of Perception,* 1962), "Truth does not 'inhabit the inner man,' or more accurately, there is no inner man, man is in the world, and only in the world does he know himself."

Born on 14 March 1908 at Rochefort-sur-Mer, in southwestern France, Merleau-Ponty grew up in a bourgeois family in Paris, where he completed his primary and secondary education at two well-known Paris lycées, Lycée Janson-de-Sailly and Lycée Louis-le-Grand. Along with his brother and sister, he was raised by his mother following the death of his father, an artillery officer, in 1913. Jean-Paul Sartre writes in *Situations IV: Portraits* (1964) that Merleau-Ponty recalled he had "an incomparable childhood": "He had known that private world of happiness from which only age drives us." He studied philosophy at the Ecole Normale Supérieure from 1926 to 1930, graduating with the *agrégation de philosophie*. There he received a solid but conservative education in philosophy, studying René Descartes and Immanuel Kant under the tutelage of the rational idealist Léon Brunschvicg, but his interests soon expanded to include Georg Wilhelm

BIBLIOTHÈQUE DE PHILOSOPHIE CONTEMPORAINE

LA STRUCTURE
DU
COMPORTEMENT

PAR

Maurice MERLEAU - PONTY

PRESSES UNIVERSITAIRES DE FRANCE
108, boulevard Saint-Germain, Paris

1942

Title page for Merleau-Ponty's first book (translated as The
Structure of Behavior, *1963), a critique of behaviorist
psychology (Thomas Cooper Library,
University of South Carolina)*

Friedrich Hegel, Karl Marx, Friedrich Nietzsche, Martin
Heidegger, and Edmund Husserl, whose 1929 Paris lectures, published as *Méditations cartésiennes* (1931; translated
as *Cartesian Meditations,* 1960), he attended. At the Ecole
Normale he made the acquaintance of Sartre, who, in later
years, influenced Merleau-Ponty's philosophy and politics
throughout their friendship and eventual estrangement. In
1930–1931 Merleau-Ponty completed his brief state military service, after which he taught at the Lycée de Beau-
vais from 1931 to 1933. After a one-year fellowship from
the Centre National de la Recherche Scientifique, he once
again taught philosophy, this time at the Lycée de Char-
tres (1934–1935), before returning to the Ecole Normale
in 1935 to teach and to pursue graduate studies. Here he
wrote his *thèse complémentaire* (partial fulfillment of the *doctorat d'état*), which became his first book, *La Structure du com-*

portement (1942; translated as *The Structure of Behavior,*
1963).

During these years, between 1933 and 1939, Merleau-Ponty attended Alexandre Kojève's lectures on
Hegel. These lectures, essentially a humanistic reflection
on Hegel's *Phänomenologie des Geistes* (1807; translated as *The
Phenomenology of Mind,* 1910), were also attended by Raymond Aron, André Breton, Georges Bataille, and Jacques
Lacan. This vibrant French intellectual milieu of Surrealism, psychoanalysis, humanism, and nascent existentialism undoubtedly had a profound influence on Merleau-
Ponty's later work. World War II brought an end to this
Left Bank culture, however. Merleau-Ponty served briefly
as a lieutenant in the infantry in 1939–1940 before taking
a post at the Lycée Carnot in Paris during the German
occupation. Here, he was active, with Sartre, in the Resistance group "Socialisme et Liberté" (Socialism and Liberty); this experience formed the basis of the influential
postwar avant-garde political, philosophical, and literary
journal *Les Temps Modernes.* During this period he wrote his
major work, *Phénoménologie de la perception,* the *thèse principale*
that, submitted along with *La Structure du comportement,*
earned him his doctorate. After the war he taught for four
years at the Université de Lyon. In 1949 he was appointed
to the chair of psychology and pedagogy at the Sorbonne,
where he remained until 1952, when he was appointed to
the chair of philosophy at the prestigious Collège de
France. Details about his life are sparse; according to
Alden L. Fisher in *The Essential Writings of Merleau-Ponty,*
"only a little was written about Merleau-Ponty the man
while he was alive, for he led a quiet and discreet life, in
marked contrast to his sometime friend and collaborator
Jean Paul Sartre." His wife, Suzanne, was a physician and
psychiatrist, and they had one daughter.

Throughout his career Merleau-Ponty was influenced by Gestalt psychology. From the early 1930s he
turned to Gestalt psychology to repudiate the French intel-
lectualist tradition in philosophy, in particular, through the
central claim of Gestalt psychology, that perception is
structured as a "figure on a ground." In the structure of
"figure on a ground," perception of an object is seen as
organized against a background or within a "perceptual
field" whereby the object is not merely the result of
abstract cognitive forces (as in intellectualism) but rather
must be grasped as standing out against the necessary context of a lived world. In other words, the Gestaltists demonstrated that perception is not reducible to mental acts of
thinking or judging; truth does not "inhabit the inner
man." Merleau-Ponty's work develops this basic insight
and describes the body and its intersubjective world,
which together compose the perceptual field. While phenomenology can fruitfully describe perception as organized through Gestalt forces, Merleau-Ponty nevertheless
eschews the hard-line Gestaltist belief that these fields have

particular mechanistic brain correlates that are causal and, thus, in theory fully determinable. He criticizes such a position as naive realism. For Merleau-Ponty, the perceptual field–the world–is suffused with ambiguity, never fully determinate; instead, it is only loosely "determined" by human "motivation," informed by intersubjective and intercorporeal (between bodies) forces within social, cultural, and historical contexts.

Merleau-Ponty's first book, *La Structure du comportement,* deploys Gestalt theory to critique the positivist and reductive approach of psychological "behaviorism" or, in French, *comportement.* By "structure," Merleau-Ponty means nothing like what came to be known as structuralism; for him at this early date, "structure" refers to the holism of Gestalt–or formalist–psychology. He argues that Pavlovian models of stimulus and response are reductionistic and hence an incomplete account of behavior because stimuli and reflex responses are only artificially separated from mental events. Arguments that seek to displace consciousness in favor of a materialist science ultimately fail, Merleau-Ponty claims, because they must presume the consciousness they are seeking to explicate. There is for him something irreducible in consciousness that is the starting point for every investigation, including the scientific. *La Structure du comportement* focuses almost exclusively on the scientific attitude, clearing the way for his next work, *Phénoménologie de la perception,* which performs a similar critique, this time on the natural experience of the perceiving subject–a phenomenology, rather than a discussion of science. In both texts Merleau-Ponty's critique finds its point of departure in the body, since the body is both an object in the world and the conscious subject of one's experience of that world–exactly why consciousness cannot be reduced to either one term or the other, neither a "materialism" nor a "mentalism."

Phénoménologie de la perception steers between these two extremes or schools of thought, which go by various names. Materialism is otherwise known as "empiricism," and its chief proponents are David Hume and behaviorist American psychologist John B. Watson. Mentalism is called "intellectualism" and is better known in the philosophical tradition as rationalism and idealism; its main proponents are Descartes, Kant, and especially Husserl in his early writings. Merleau-Ponty steers between the pillars of objectivism and subjectivism, or, respectively, in Sartre's terminology, between *en soi* (in-itself) and *pour soi* (for-itself). In the simplest terms, for Merleau-Ponty, the focus of empiricism on discrete sensations and causality leaves it unable to account for human intentionality–in effect, the way in which perception is motivated in a thick and complicated manner by the appearance of a preconstituted object against a phenomenal field, and not by a group of so-called pure sensations. Similarly, intellectualism fails because it privileges reason and representational

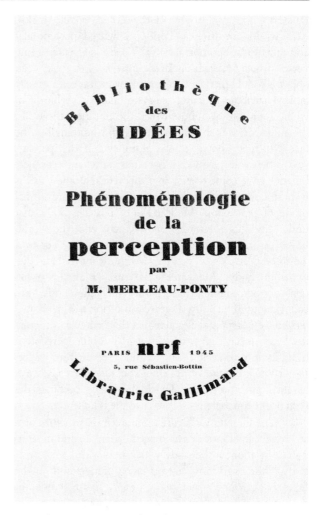

Title page for the book (translated as Phenomenology of Perception, *1962) in which Merleau-Ponty develops a philosophical position distinct from the metaphysical extremes of "materialism" and "mentalism" (Thomas Cooper Library, University of South Carolina)*

consciousness over experience, ignoring human situatedness, or "being-in-the-world." One holds that truth is available through experience; the other, that truth is available through thought–and both presume that such "truth" is objective or independent of the embodied subject who either experiences or thinks it, which amounts to the illusion of objective thinking. In sum, both accounts fail to adequately take account of the body, which plays a key role: "Consciousness is being-towards-the-thing through the intermediary of the body." Here the hyphenation, a practice borrowed from Heidegger, is meant to underscore the inseparability of embodied conscious being and the thing it grasps intentionally–in the world.

Merleau-Ponty develops his concept of "world" in *Phénoménologie de la perception* from Heidegger and from

Husserl's later philosophy of the *Lebenswelt* (life-world). This world, for Merleau-Ponty, is figured perceptually and quasi-anthropomorphically: "To see is to enter a universe of beings which *display themselves* . . . to look at an object is to inhabit it. . . . When I look at the lamp on my table, I attribute to it not only the qualities visible from where I am, but also those which the chimney, the walls, the table can 'see'; the back of my lamp is nothing but the face which it 'shows' to the chimney." If this passage strikes the reader as odd, it is because strict subject-object binaries have come to inform a theoretical attitude that is now second nature, arguably eclipsing a more primordial mode of perception. Merleau-Ponty posits a body that understands its primordial involvement with the world, however, "always already" perceptually given over to a world he describes as "pregnant" with meaning. "The theory of the body," Merleau-Ponty writes, "is already a theory of perception"; perception and the body are coterminous. The body is "geared into" the world, characterized by a corporeal intentionality that remains unthematized or unreflected throughout daily life—"perception hides itself from itself"; people cannot see themselves seeing or touch themselves touching, because there is always an indefinite moment in which the seeing becomes the seen or the touching crosses over to the touched.

The Gestaltists' "figure on a ground" structure provides a means for understanding the intimate and indeterminate relation of the body with the world: "one's own body is the third term, always tacitly understood, in the figure-background structure, and every figure stands out against the double horizon of external space and bodily space." In other words, the body acts as the ground of all perception, invisible to thought and yet presupposed by it, that without which thought would not occur. "My body is the fabric into which all objects are woven, and it is, at least in relation to the perceived world, the general instrument of my 'comprehension.'" The notion of a *schéma corporel* (body schema, misleadingly translated as "body image" in English) is Merleau-Ponty's "third term," comprehensible neither to empiricism nor to intellectualism. What Merleau-Ponty has in mind with *schéma corporel* is a kinaesthetic body, a body actively "polarized by its tasks." Through the body schema, Merleau-Ponty shows that the body does not end at its skin but rather extends into the world. Bodily interactions are neither a question of motor-reflex responses, as empiricism teaches, nor a series of conscious and intentional representations, as intellectualism would have it. The body schema captures the in-between of the body engaged in its world, what Merleau-Ponty calls the body's "motor intentionality."

For example, the amputee's lost limb may still figure in his or her body schema as a "phantom limb"; it can retain an existential validity for that body, neither explicable by reflex responses nor by mere mental representa-

tions. "Consciousness is in the first place not a matter of 'I think that' but of 'I can'"—not abstract thought, but the body-subject's prereflective coping skills. The phantom limb is taken by the body in some sense as still real, still there; it figures in the body schema and in the world of living possibilities that the schema projects by the body's engaged "I can"—a world within the reach of someone who has not lost a limb. Similarly, a blind person's cane cannot be considered a tool; when it is taken up it "has ceased to be an object . . . and is no longer perceived for itself." In the blind person's hand, the cane becomes part of the body, a sensory extension, figuring as part of the body schema always in relation to a world "pregnant with meaning," a perceived world. In a reversal of "common-sense" objective thought, Merleau-Ponty says: "In the exploration of things, the length of the stick does not enter expressly as a middle term: the blind man is rather aware of it through the position of objects than of the position of objects through it."

The body schema concerns concrete involvement in a world that offers both tacit and explicit possibilities to orient a body-subject's intentional behavior. Merleau-Ponty calls this orientation *habitude*, again misleadingly translated as "habit": *habitude* is an ability or tacit knowledge associated with the body schema's motor intentionality, rather than a "habit" performed routinely or customarily. *Habitude* is neither reducible to reflex reactions (empiricism) nor mental representations (intellectualism); it is what the body schema carries with it, much in the way that the body quickly adapts to driving a different car or driving in an unfamiliar city without reflectively taking into account the infinite number of small differences and consciously adapting to each accordingly. So while there are indeed reflex responses, as empiricism maintains, they are inseparable from the representations that intellectualism posits; together, along with the "original text" of the world, Merleau-Ponty conceives of the perceiving body-subject in a life-world replete with significance.

Humanisme et terreur: Essai sur le problème communiste (1947; translated as *Humanism and Terror: An Essay on the Communist Problem,* 1969) comprises a group of essays describing the "inextricable situation" facing postwar France, one that amounted to a virtual political impasse. Merleau-Ponty writes of this impasse: "It is impossible to be an anti-Communist and it is not possible to be a Communist." The impossible alternative seemed set between an American brand of capitalism (anticommunism), whose poignancy in Western Europe was underscored by the introduction of the Marshall Plan in 1947, and a Soviet style of communism, a dogmatic Marxism that was fast proving impracticable in the postwar political landscape of Europe. These two extremes were equally untenable to Merleau-Ponty. The hopes for a revolutionary communism in the Soviet Union had begun to fade because, as

Merleau-Ponty says, "Terror no longer seeks to advance itself as revolutionary terror." What are the conditions of "revolution," if any, under which violence is acceptable or even necessary? What is the relationship between revolution and violence? What is the nature of freedom? If freedom must be purchased, at what cost? *Humanisme et terreur* addresses these questions, directly engaging Sartre's treatment of inescapable freedom in *L'Etre et le néant* (1943; translated as *Being and Nothingness,* 1956). Merleau-Ponty argues that freedom cannot be taken as the original and absolute ground of an individuated subject, as it is for Sartre; similar to his critique of science, Merleau-Ponty demands that freedom presuppose a world that carries significance and lends necessary context. Against Sartre, who contends that humankind is "condemned to freedom," Merleau-Ponty replies instead that "we are *condemned to meaning.*" In other words, the political subject should not be conceived as an abstract, transcendental spectator but rather as an historically and materially situated being whose world is necessarily meaningful. Marx's socio-economic critique is Merleau-Ponty's starting point.

Humanisme et terreur opens with what Merleau-Ponty depicts as the facile characterization of communism—"deception, cunning violence, propaganda"—in contradistinction to the supposed "respect for truth, law, and individual consciousness" represented by democracy. Merleau-Ponty's text deconstructs this abstract opposition, however. Democracies also employ cunning violence and propaganda, often "in the guise of liberal principles." "Respect for law and liberty," he remarks with some irony, "has served to justify police suppression of strikes in America"; moreover, "respect" for law and liberty, and the pursuit of these purportedly pure ideals, is often the justification for violence, such as with American "military suppression in Indochina or in Palestine and the development of an American empire in the Middle East." A Marxist position allows Merleau-Ponty to levy a political critique that is phenomenological, steadfastly refusing to be swayed by idealist arguments—be they in the name of liberalism or communism. "The value of a society," Merleau-Ponty writes, "is the value it places upon man's relations to man." The reference in the subtitle of *Humanisme et terreur* to "the communist problem" does not so much announce the problem with communism as "the problem rightly raised by communism, namely, to establish among men relations that are human."

In this early political work, humanism and terror are not conceived as mutually exclusive. To some extent, a humanistic end justifies the political means—because, as Merleau-Ponty asserts, politics is not ethics, despite claims by democracy of the moral high road. Merleau-Ponty hoped that terror would be employed in the service of a genuine humanism, although the danger was, as Marx indicated, that terror in the name of humanism would

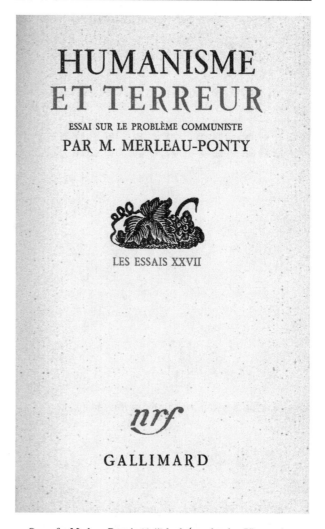

Cover for Merleau-Ponty's 1947 book (translated as Humanism and Terror: An Essay on the Communist Problem, 1969), in which he describes postwar France as caught between American-style capitalism and Soviet communism (Thomas Cooper Library, University of South Carolina)

quickly prove as absolute and as oppressive as that which fomented a revolution in the first place—the "dark side" of communism. To be certain that revolution is not an underhanded and new form of imperialism requires constant vigilance and "critique," in other words, "concrete thinking" as opposed to an abstract "speculative philosophy" or "rigid ethics." Merleau-Ponty still expresses hope that humanity will achieve the Marxist transition from formal liberty to actual liberty, though this faith in a political implementation of Marxism was shaken by the 1950s. Nevertheless, in his adherence to phenomenological principles, Merleau-Ponty postulates the emergence of a "new," critical Left in his critique of American liberalism:

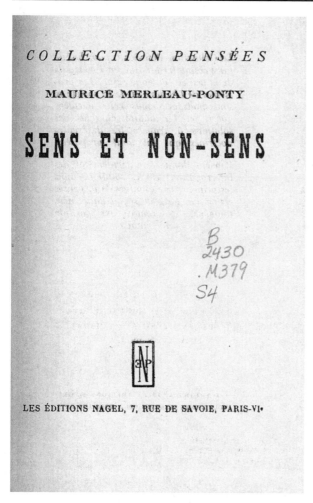

Title page for Merleau-Ponty's 1948 book (translated as Sense
and Non-Sense, *1964), in which he claims that Marxism
has "lost confidence in its own daring" and become no
more than "hierarchy, obedience, myth, inequality,
diplomacy, and police" (Thomas Cooper Library,
University of South Carolina)*

zation, and often utopian: "to recall to Marxists their humanist inspiration, to remind the democracies of their fundamental hypocrisy, and to keep intact against propaganda the chances that might still be left for history to become enlightened once again."

Even as early as 1948, however, Merleau-Ponty expressed doubt about the Marxist vision, claiming in the preface to *Sens et non-sens* (1948; translated as *Sense and Non-Sense,* 1964) that Marxism had "lost confidence in its own daring" and, following brief postwar hopes for a Marxist revival, that Marxism had once again become no more than "hierarchy, obedience, myth, inequality, diplomacy, and police." By the time of the Korean War (1950–1953), Merleau-Ponty had undergone a radical crisis of faith in Marxism–a crisis that precipitated his break with Sartre and his resignation from *Les Temps Modernes* in 1952. Although he then wrote editorials for the socialist weekly *L'Express,* Merleau-Ponty's full reappraisal of Marxism came in 1955 with the publication of *Les Aventures de la dialectique* (1955; translated as *Adventures of the Dialectic,* 1973). In this text he maintains that in a class-structured society, freedom is an empty bourgeois ideal, essentially agreeing with the communists that social change is exigent. This change must not come at any price, however: there must be a limit to violence. As well as being a polemic directed at Sartre, this text reframes a Marxist engagement: "We now know that subject and object, conscience and history, present and future, judgment and discipline, all these opposites decay without one another, that the attempt at a revolutionary resolution destroys one of the two series, and that we must look for something else." Western Marxism, culminating for Merleau-Ponty in György Lukács's *Geschichte und Klassenbewusstsein* (1923; translated as *History and Class Consciousness,* 1971), had by the 1950s proved to be an ineffective political model for anything more than theoretical critique. He writes, pessimistically: "a revolution is proletarian only before it succeeds, in the movement which precedes the taking of power, in its 'ardor,' not in its technique."

The answer is not a "permanent revolution" but a modernization of Marxism in the direction of a "noncommunist left," beyond the alternation of communism and anticommunism, in which the best that can be hoped for is an ever-renewed clash of ideologies (at the time, the Soviet Union and American democratic capitalism). He called his own position "a-communism," a philosophical vigilance through engaged free critique and discussion. Merleau-Ponty had not become apolitical; instead, he had become less certain of the humanistic basis of politics and philosophy. In the early 1950s his philosophy had begun to undergo a shift away from philosophical certainty and perhaps also away from the emphasis on the phenomenological subject. This period was one of personal change and upheaval–including his resignation from *Les Temps Mod-*

"An aggressive liberalism exists which is a dogma and already an ideology of war. It can be recognized by its love of the empyrean of principles, its failure ever to mention the geographical and historical circumstances to which it owes its birth, and its abstract judgments of political systems without regard for the specific conditions under which they develop." The relation of man to man embodies a struggle for recognition, as Hegel argued; but according to Merleau-Ponty, that recognition has, until now, remained implicit "in conflict and the race for power." The alternative–presumably an "explicit recognition"–is not discussed specifically. Merleau-Ponty refrains from offering a prescriptive politics, lest he reduplicate the power structures of which he is critical. His intervention in politics remains marginal, intellectual, without political mobili-

ernes; his break with Sartre; a new appointment to the chair of philosophy at the most prestigious educational institution in France, the Collège de France; and the death of his mother, with whom he had remained extremely close, in 1952. The essays included in *Signes* (1960; translated as *Signs,* 1964), many of which were written in the early 1950s, chronicle the change in Merleau-Ponty's philosophy and political convictions. Merleau-Ponty writes in the introduction to *Signes* that Marxism "is certainly no longer true *in the sense it was believed to be true*"; rather, its value is now secondary: "it can inspire and orient analyses and retain a real heuristic value." He asks: "Is it not an incredible misunderstanding that all, or almost all, philosophers have felt obliged to have a politics, whereas politics arises from the 'practice of life' and escapes understanding?" If one *acts* politically, one does not therefore "have" a politics; instead, one finds politics imbricated with the "practice of life"—an interdependence that frustrates rationalistic modes of comprehension. In other words, politics involves a form of reason that "escapes understanding," as Merleau-Ponty says, "in the exact opposite of a philosophy of God-like survey."

In 1955, toward the end of *Les Aventures de la dialectique,* Merleau-Ponty asks the question that inspired his later philosophy: "The question is to know whether, as Sartre says, there are only *men* and *things* or whether there is also the interworld, which we call history, symbolism, truth-to-be-made." Neither persons nor things can provide the basis of certain knowledge; instead, life takes place in the *inter-monde,* or interworld, where the human subject must search for meaning—between persons, between things. Merleau-Ponty's later philosophy is preoccupied with intersubjectivity and communication, themes he claims are wholly absent in Sartre. For traditional, dualistic philosophies this intersubjective "interworld" spells a crisis of reason, since traditional philosophy is unsure how to conceive "history, symbolism, truth-to-be-made" in either intellectual or empirical terms. It is a marvel, Merleau-Ponty writes in the essay "Einstein et la crise de la raison" (Einstein and the Crisis of Reason) *Signes,* that humans can calculate and speak at all—that algorithms and language put, as he writes in the introduction, "a common domain of thought between us and a third party." Indeed, although meaning relies on this intervening middle term, Merleau-Ponty calls it a "ruse," since it never closes the distance between the self, the other, and things; there is a certain failure to symbolize, to define concretely, without some ambiguity, and it is here in the interworld that the subject finds itself in what he calls the "prose of the world," or, similarly, the universal "flesh of the world." Merleau-Ponty is suggesting a fundamental ontology of the sensible upon which meaning will be founded.

Merleau-Ponty's philosophy of language ultimately relies on his notion of an interworld and intersubjectivity.

He refuses to conceive of language as a code, which, paradoxically, would be "to break it," he says. While common sense suggests that breaking a code will usher in meaning, language itself does not operate through such one-to-one codifications; instead, linguistic meaning inheres in ambiguities and relies on the context, such as with the ambiguous word *break,* which here does not mean to yield meaning (as with a code) but rather to destroy meaningful language. Merleau-Ponty demonstrates in the introduction to *Signes* that there is not a one-to-one correspondence of thought and speech or thought and language. "Thought and speech anticipate one another. They continually take one another's place. They are way-points, stimuli for one another." Speaking is not an act of consciousness: again, there is no place for the interiority of a Cartesian subject. Merleau-Ponty conceives speech along the lines of the operation of the body in the world—it is a capacity, occupied with its tasks, momentarily unreflective in the act of doing, an "I can." Language "promotes its own oblivion," much in the way that when one reads, the words fade from the page and seamlessly usher in a meaning. Language is expressed "Not by a mind to a mind," he says in the introduction to *Signes,* "but by a being who has a body and language." In the essay "Sur la phénoménologie du langage" (On the Phenomenology of Language), he states that language is, as Husserl had suggested, "thought's body." And, indeed, there is the peculiar "anonymity" of the flesh operating here: "things *are said* and *are thought* by a Speech and by a Thought which we do not have but which has us."

The theme of intersubjectivity and the concept of the flesh are developed at greater length in Merleau-Ponty's best-known posthumous work, *Le Visible et l'invisible* (1964; translated as *The Visible and the Invisible,* 1968). The manuscript was left incomplete at Merleau-Ponty's death, on 3 May 1961 at age fifty-three. Whether this text represents a significant departure from *Phénoménologie de la perception* is still debated. Some critics argue that this late work merely elaborates on themes already discussed in 1945: the critique of Sartre, Gestalt psychology, freedom, language, and the body. While an astute reader of *Phénoménologie de la perception* can find there a thread of anonymity and even a collective consciousness or "universal 'We'" that will later gain expression as "flesh," in *Le Visible et l'invisible* Merleau-Ponty is critical of his earlier work, saying that it remains confined within a "philosophy of consciousness"—still too Cartesian. By this time he had moved away from the subjectivism of early French existentialism toward ontological problems. While his early philosophy was concerned with recapturing the prereflective "original text" of perception, he claims that his later philosophy deals with intersubjectivity and communication, precisely insofar as these "take up and go beyond the realm of perception." Merleau-Ponty's final philosophy is

MAURICE MERLEAU-PONTY

LES AVENTURES
DE LA
DIALECTIQUE

nrf

GALLIMARD
5, rue Sébastien-Bottin, Paris VIIe

Title page for Merleau-Ponty's 1955 book (translated as
Adventures of the Dialectic, *1973), in which he
criticizes orthodox Marxism and elaborates a position
he calls "a-communism" (William F. Ekstrom
Library, University of Louisville)*

concerned with the interworld; it is a metaphysics of the
flesh. The body still plays an important role, but it is no
longer the subject's body, as it was in *Phénoménologie de la
perception,* but rather a radically anonymous being that is
not just "pre-personal" but "a-personal." In *Le Visible et
l'invisible,* he relates, "it is not *I* who sees, not *he* who sees,
because an anonymous visibility inhabits both of us, a
vision in general, in virtue of that primordial property that
belongs to the flesh."

Merleau-Ponty returns to his example of two hands
touching. In *Phénoménologie de la perception* the touching hand
takes up the position of "subject," and the touched hand,
that of "object." In *Le Visible et l'invisible,* however, the body
cedes to the flesh: "my body does not perceive, but it is as
if it were built around the perception that dawns through
it." Revisiting the two hands touching, he writes: "If my
left hand is touching my right hand, and if I should sud-

denly wish to apprehend with my right hand the work of
my left hand as it touches, this reflection of the body upon
itself always miscarries at the last moment." This divergence—or "dehiscence"—between the sentient and the sensible is not that between subject and object; Merleau-Ponty
does not duplicate a Cartesian dualism. While the "I" cannot perceive itself perceiving, there is a reversibility of the
touched and touching at work, an "overlapping or
encroachment, so that we must say that the things pass
into us as well as we into the things." The relation is "chiasmatic," from the Greek letter *chi,* representing a crossing
that paradoxically converges and yet maintains distinct-
ness. Hence, the subject's flesh is the flesh of the world,
and the subject is as much its possession as it is his or hers;
subject and object, activity and passivity, are rendered
thoroughly ambiguous.

The two hands touching provide a model for vision,
in terms of the dialectic between the visible and the invisible but also more radically, because there is an "encroachment" and "infringement" between the visible and the
tangible and between the other senses, for sensibility in
general and even for an intersubjectivity in which the self
is chiasmatically related to the other. Merleau-Ponty's
striking example of intersubjective communication is in
the perception of a landscape, already alluded to by Hyppolite in his memorial essay. "For me to have not an idea,
an image, nor a representation, but as it were the imminent experience of them," writes Merleau-Ponty in *Le Visible et l'invisible,* "it suffices that I look at a landscape, that I
speak of it with someone." Communication is not of particulars, however; it is neither through an intellectualism
nor an empiricism but between the self and its interlocutor: "through the concordant operation of his body and
my own, what I see passes into him, this individual green
of the meadow under my eyes invades his vision without
quitting my own, I recognize in my green his green."

Merleau-Ponty sought to overcome these dichotomies—not just mind/body, but also subject/object, self/
world, reason/unreason, thought/language, visible/invisi-
ble, and inner/outer—from the start. Instead of a dialectical
struggle between these binaries, Merleau-Ponty conceives
of them as chiasmatically interrelated, not wholly contradictory. In *Le Visible et l'invisible* he explains these chiasmatic
pairs as examples of a "good dialectic," in which each term
is understood as an abstraction from the whole: "the good
dialectic is that which is conscious of the fact that every *thesis* is an idealization, that Being is not made up of idealiza-
tions or of things said, as the old logic believed, but of
bound wholes where signification never is except in tendency." In such statements, with reference to signification
and "bound wholes," the reader can begin to appreciate
the structuralist influence in Merleau-Ponty's late work.
His philosophy of language is influenced by the linguistics
of Ferdinand de Saussure as well as by the structuralist

anthropology of his friend Claude Lévi-Strauss. Saussure conceived of language as a bound whole or totality, in which meaning is generated within context, through the interrelation of a chain of signifiers, each of which taken in isolation is meaningless. Merleau-Ponty writes in *Elogie de la philosophie* (1953; translated as *In Praise of Philosophy*, 1963): "Just as language is a system of signs which have meaning only in relation to one another, and each of which has its own usage throughout the whole language, so each institution is a symbolic system that the subject takes over and incorporates as a style of functioning, as a global configuration, without having any need to conceive it at all." Merleau-Ponty takes Saussure's linguistics as a model not just for linguistic meaning, but also for those cultural and intersubjective institutions by virtue of whose symbolic system one understands signification directly, tacitly, nonconceptually. There is a marked departure here from the phenomenological subject in favor of structuralism, because that subject cannot be conceived of as the creator of meaning. Meaning does not happen within a subject's mind, but for a body-subject in its larger intersubjective, historical involvement, in the interworld, which is a world of language—not in individuals, but in and between individuals and things. Merleau-Ponty defers to the wisdom of the poets: "In a sense, as Valéry said, language is everything, since it is the voice of no one, since it is the very voice of the things, the waves, and the forests."

Maurice Merleau-Ponty bequeaths to philosophy a manner of rethinking the human subject and its embodiment, its relations with others, the world, and the language through which meaning is conveyed. In such a world, the things, the waves, and the forests are said to "speak," purposely frustrating the attempts of traditional philosophy to impose its abstract reason onto things. Instead, Merleau-Ponty argues that the life-world has a primordial significance of which the human body-subject is an inextricable part, effectively overturning the pretenses of Cartesian mind-body dualism. Merleau-Ponty's philosophy stands as a corrective to the denigration of the body—traditionally conceived in contradistinction to a loftier mind or spirit—in the history of Western thought.

Bibliographies:

François Lapointe and Clara Lapointe, *Maurice Merleau-Ponty and His Critics: An International Bibliography, 1942–1976* (New York & London: Garland, 1976);

Kerry Whiteside, "The Merleau-Ponty Bibliography: Additions and Corrections," *Journal of the History of Philosophy*, 21, no. 2 (1983): 195–201;

Joan Nordquist, comp., *Maurice Merleau-Ponty: A Bibliography* (Santa Cruz, Cal.: Reference and Research Services, 2000).

References:

The Essential Writings of Merleau-Ponty, edited, with an introduction, by Alden L. Fisher (New York: Harcourt, Brace & World, 1969);

Elizabeth Grosz, *Volatile Bodies: Toward a Corporeal Feminism* (Bloomington: Indiana University Press, 1994), pp. 86–111;

Lawrence Hass and Dorothea Olkowski, eds., *Rereading Merleau-Ponty: Essays beyond the Continental-Analytic Divide* (Amherst, N.Y.: Humanity Books, 2000);

Jean Hyppolite, "Existence et dialectique dans la philosophie de Merleau-Ponty," *Les Temps Modernes*, special Merleau-Ponty issue, 17, nos. 184–185 (1961): 228–244;

Martin Jay, "Sartre, Merleau-Ponty and the Search for a New Ontology of Sight," in his *Downcast Eyes: The Denigration of Vision in Twentieth-Century French Thought* (Berkeley: University of California Press, 1993), pp. 263–328;

Richard Kearney, "Maurice Merleau-Ponty," in *Modern Movements in European Philosophy* (Manchester & Dover, N.H.: Manchester University Press, 1986), pp. 73–90;

Thomas Langan, *Merleau-Ponty's Critique of Reason* (New Haven: Yale University Press, 1966);

Christopher Macann, *Four Phenomenological Philosophers: Husserl, Heidegger, Sartre, Merleau-Ponty* (London & New York: Routledge, 1993), pp. 159–201;

Eric Matthews, *The Philosophy of Merleau-Ponty* (Chesham, U.K.: Acumen, 2002);

Olkowski and James Morley, eds., *Merleau-Ponty, Interiority and Exteriority, Psychic Life and the World* (Albany: State University of New York Press, 1999);

Stephen Priest, *Merleau-Ponty* (London & New York: Routledge, 1998);

James Schmidt, *Merleau-Ponty: Between Phenomenology and Structuralism* (London: Macmillan, 1985);

Jon Stewart, ed., *The Debate between Sartre and Merleau-Ponty* (Evanston, Ill.: Northwestern University Press, 1998);

Bernhard Waldenfels, "Merleau-Ponty," in *A Companion to Continental Philosophy*, edited by Simon Critchley and William Schroeder (Malden, Mass.: Blackwell, 1998), pp. 281–291.

Jean-Paul Sartre

(21 June 1905 – 15 April 1980)

LynnDianne Beene
University of New Mexico

and

David W. Frizzell

See also the Sartre entry in *DLB 72: French Novelists, 1930–1960.*

BOOKS: *L'Imagination* (Paris: Alcan, 1936); translated by Forrest Williams as *Imagination: A Psychological Critique* (Ann Arbor: University of Michigan Press, 1962);

La Nausée (Paris: Gallimard, 1938); translated by Lloyd Alexander as *Nausea* (Norfolk, Conn.: New Directions, 1949); republished as *The Diary of Antoine Requentin* (London: Lehmann, 1949);

Le Mur (Paris: Gallimard, 1939); translated by Alexander as *Intimacy, and Other Stories* (New York: New Directions, 1948);

Esquisse d'une théorie des émotions (Paris: Hermann, 1939); translated by Bernard Frechtman as *The Emotions: Outline of a Theory* (New York: Philosophical Library, 1948);

L'Imaginaire: Psychologie phénoménologique de l'imagination (Paris: Gallimard, 1940); translated by Frechtman as *The Psychology of Imagination* (New York: Philosophical Library, 1948; London & New York: Rider, 1950);

Les Mouches (Paris: Gallimard, 1943); translated by Stuart Gilbert as "The Flies," in *The Flies (Les Mouches) and In Camera (Huis clos)* (London: Hamilton, 1946); republished as *No Exit (Huis clos), a Play in One Act, and The Flies (Les Mouches), a Play in Three Acts* (New York: Knopf, 1947);

L'Etre et le néant: Essai d'ontologie phénoménologique (Paris: Gallimard, 1943); translated in part by Hazel E. Barnes as *Existential Psychoanalysis* (New York: Philosophical Library, 1953); complete translation by Barnes as *Being and Nothingness: An Essay on Phenomenological Ontology* (New York: Philosophical Library, 1956; London: Methuen, 1957);

Jean-Paul Sartre (UPI/Bettman; from Christina Howells, ed., The Cambridge Companion to Sartre, *1992; Thomas Cooper Library, University of South Carolina)*

Huis clos (Paris: Gallimard, 1945); translated by Gilbert as "In Camera," in *The Flies (Les Mouches) and In Camera (Huis clos)* (1946); republished as *No Exit (Huis clos), a Play in One Act, and The Flies (Les Mouches), a Play in Three Acts* (1947);

L'Age de raison, volume 1 of *Les Chemins de la liberté* (Paris: Gallimard, 1945; revised, 1960); trans-

314

lated by Eric Sutton as *The Age of Reason* (New York: Knopf, 1947; London: Hamilton, 1947);

Le Sursis, volume 2 of *Les Chemins de la liberté* (Paris: Gallimard, 1945); translated by Sutton as *The Reprieve* (New York: Knopf, 1947; London: Hamilton, 1947);

L'Existentialisme est un humanisme (Paris: Nagel, 1946); translated by Frechtman as *Existentialism* (New York: Philosophical Library, 1947); translated by Philip Mairet as *Existentialism and Humanism* (London: Methuen, 1948);

Explication de L'étranger (Paris: Aux dépens du Palimugre, 1946);

Morts sans sépulture (Lausanne: Marguerat, 1946); translated by Lionel Abel as "The Victors" in *Three Plays: Dirty Hands, The Respectful Prostitute, The Victors* (New York: Knopf, 1949); translated by Kitty Black as "Men without Shadows," in *Three Plays: Crime Passionnel; Men without Shadows; The Respectable Prostitute* (London: Hamilton, 1949);

La Putain respectueuse (Paris: Nagel, 1946); translated by Abel as "The Respectful Prostitute," in *Three Plays: Dirty Hands, The Respectful Prostitute, The Victors* (1949); translated by Black as "The Respectable Prostitute," in *Three Plays: Crime Passionnel; Men without Shadows; The Respectable Prostitute* (1949);

Réflexions sur la question juive (Paris: Morihien, 1946); translated by Mary Guggenheim as *Portrait of the Anti-Semite* (New York: Partisan Review, 1946); translated by Erik de Mauny as *Portrait of the Anti-Semite* (London: Secker & Warburg, 1948);

Baudelaire: précédé d'une not de Michel Leiris (Paris: Gallimard, 1947); translated by Martin Turnell as *Baudelaire* (London: Horizon, 1949; Norfolk, Conn.: New Directions, 1950);

Situations, I: Ouvrage non coupe (Paris: Gallimard, 1947); translated in part by Annette Michelson as *Literary and Philosophical Essays* (New York: Criterion, 1955; London: Rider, 1955);

Les Jeux sont faits (Paris: Nagel, 1947); translated by Louise Varèse as *The Chips Are Down* (New York: Lear, 1948; London & New York: Rider, 1951);

Situations, II (Paris: Gallimard, 1948); translated in part by Frechtman as *What Is Literature?* (New York: Philosophical Library, 1949; London: Methuen, 1950); republished as *Literature and Existentialism* (New York: Citadel, 1962);

L'Engrenage (Paris: Nagel, 1948); translated by Mervyn Savill as *In the Mesh* (London: Dakers, 1954);

Visages, précédé de Portraits officiels (Paris: Seghers, 1948);

Les Mains sales (Paris: Gallimard, 1948); translated by Abel as "Dirty Hands," in *Three Plays: Dirty Hands, The Respectful Prostitute, The Victors* (1949); trans-

lated by Black as "Crime Passionnel," in *Three Plays: Crime Passionnel; Men without Shadows; The Respectable Prostitute* (1949);

Entretiens sur la politique, by Sartre, David Rousset, and Gérard Rosenthal (Paris: Gallimard, 1949);

La mort dans l'âme, volume 3 of *Les Chemins de la liberté* (Paris: Gallimard, 1949); translated by Gerard Hopkins as *Iron in the Soul* (London: Hamilton, 1950); republished as *Troubled Sleep* (New York: Knopf, 1951);

Situations, III: Lendemains de guerre (Paris: Gallimard, 1949); translated in part by Michelson as *Literary and Philosophical Essays;*

Nourritures: Suivi d'extraits de La Nausée (Paris: Damase, 1949);

Le Diable et le Bon Dieu (Paris: Gallimard, 1951); translated by Black as *Lucifer and the Lord* (London: Hamilton, 1952); republished as "The Devil and the Good Lord," in *The Devil and the Good Lord, and Two Other Plays* (New York: Knopf, 1960);

Saint Genet, comédien et martyr (Paris: Gallimard, 1952); translated by Frechtman as *Saint Genêt, Actor and Martyr* (New York: Braziller, 1963; London: W. H. Allen, 1964);

Kean, ou désordre et genie, adapted from the play by Alexandre Dumas *père* (Paris: Gallimard, 1954); translated by Black as *Kean: or Disorder and Genius* (London: Hamilton, 1954); republished as "Kean," in *The Devil and the Good Lord, and Two Other Plays* (New York: Knopf, 1960);

Nekrassov (Paris: Gallimard, 1956); translated by Sylvia Leeson and George Leeson (London: Hamilton, 1956); republished in *The Devil and the Good Lord, and Two Other Plays* (New York: Knopf, 1960);

Transcendence of the Ego: An Existentialist Theory of Consciousness, edited and translated by Forrest Williams and Robert Kirkpatrick (New York: Noonday, 1957); French version published as *La Transcendance de l'ego: Esquisse d'une description phenomenologique* (Paris: Vrin, 1965);

Les Séquestrés d'Altona (Paris: Gallimard, 1960); translated by Sylvia Leeson and George Leeson as *Loser Wins* (London: Hamilton, 1960); republished as *The Condemned of Altona* (New York: Knopf, 1961);

Critique de la raison dialectique, précédé de Question de méthode, volume 1: *Théorie des ensembles pratiques* (Paris: Gallimard, 1960); translated in part by Black as *Search for a Method* (New York: Knopf, 1963); translated by Alan Sheridan-Smith as *Critique of Dialectical Reason: Theory of Practical Ensembles,* edited by Jonathan Rée (London: NLB / Atlantic Highlands, N.J.: Humanities Press, 1976);

Sartre visita a Cuba: Ideología y revolución. Una entrevista con los escritores cubanos. Huracán sobre el azúcar (Havana: Ediciones R, 1960);

Sartre on Cuba (New York: Ballantine, 1961);

Bariona, ou Le Fils de tonnerre (Paris: Anjou-Copies, 1962);

Marxisme et existentialisme: Controverse sur la dialectique, by Sartre and others (Paris: Plon, 1962); translated by John Matthews as *Between Existentialism and Marxism* (London: NLB, 1974; New York: Pantheon, 1975);

Les Mots (Paris: Gallimard, 1964); translated by Irene Clephane as *Words* (London: Hamilton, 1964); translated by Frechtman as *The Words* (New York: Braziller, 1964);

Situations, IV: Portraits (Paris: Gallimard, 1964); translated by Benita Eisler as *Situations* (Greenwich, Conn. & New York: Braziller, 1965; London: Hamilton, 1965);

Situations, V: Colonialisme et néo-colonialisme (Paris: Gallimard, 1964); translated by Azzedine Haddour, Steve Brewer, and Terance McWilliams as *Colonialism and Neo-Colonialism* (London & New York: Routledge, 2001);

Situations, VI: Problèmes du marxisme, I (Paris: Gallimard, 1964); translated in part by Martha H. Fletcher as *The Communists and Peace* (New York: Braziller, 1968); translated in part by Clephane as *The Communists and Peace* (London: Hamilton, 1969);

Il Filosofo et la politica, translated by Luciana Trentin and Romano Ledda (Rome: Riuniti, 1964);

Situations, VII: Problèmes du marxisme, II (Paris: Gallimard, 1965); translated in part by Martha H. Fletcher as *The Communists and Peace* (1968); translated in part by Fletcher as *The Ghost of Stalin* (New York: Braziller, 1968); translated in part by Clephane as *The Communists and Peace* (1969);

Les Troyennes, adapted from Euripides' play (Paris: Gallimard, 1965); translated by Ronald Duncan as *The Trojan Women* (New York: Knopf, 1967; London: Hamilton, 1967);

On Genocide and a Summary of the Evidence and the Judgments of the International War Crimes Tribunal, by Sartre and Arlette Elkaïm-Sartre (Boston: Beacon, 1968);

Les communistes ont peur de la révolution (Paris: Didier, 1968); translated by Elaine P. Halperin as "Communists Are Afraid of Revolution: Two Interviews," *Midway,* 10 (Summer 1969): 41–61;

L'Idiot de la famille: Gustave Flaubert de 1821 à 1857, 3 volumes (Paris: Gallimard, 1971; revised, 1988);

translated by Carol Cosman as *The Family Idiot: Gustave Flaubert, 1821–1857* (Chicago: University of Chicago Press, 1981);

Situations, VIII: Autour de 68 (Paris: Gallimard, 1971); translated in part by Matthews as *Between Existentialism and Marxism* (1974);

Plaidoyer pour les intellectuels (Paris: Gallimard, 1972);

Situations, IX: Mélanges (Paris: Gallimard, 1972); translated in part by Matthews as *Between Existentialism and Marxism* (1974);

Un Théâtre de situations, edited by Michel Contat and Michel Rybalka (Paris: Gallimard, 1973); translated by Frank Jellinek as *Sartre on Theater* (New York: Pantheon, 1976);

On a raison de se révolter: Discussions, by Sartre, Philippe Gavi, and Benny Lévy as Pierre Victor (Paris: Gallimard, 1974);

Situations, X: Politique et autobiographie (Paris: Gallimard, 1976); translated by Paul Auster and Lydia Davis as *Life/Situations: Essays Written and Spoken* (New York: Pantheon, 1977);

Cahiers pour une morale (Paris: Gallimard, 1983); translated by David Pellauer as *Notebooks for an Ethics* (Chicago: University of Chicago Press, 1992);

Les Carnets de la drôle de guerre (Paris: Gallimard, 1983); translated by Quintin Hoare as *War Diaries of Jean-Paul Sartre: November 1939 – March 1940* (New York: Pantheon, 1984); republished as *War Diaries: Notebooks from a Phoney War* (London: Verso, 1984);

Le Scénario Freud (Paris: Gallimard, 1984); translated by Hoare as *The Freud Scenario,* edited by J. B. Pontalis (Chicago: University of Chicago Press, 1985; London: Verso, 1985);

Critique de la raison dialectique (inachevé), volume 2: *L'intelligibilité de l'Historie,* edited by Arlette Elkaïm-Sartre (Paris: Gallimard, 1985); translated by Hoare as *Critique of Dialectical Reason, Volume II: The Intelligibility of History* (London & New York: Verso, 1991);

Mallarmé: La lucidité et sa face d'ombre, edited by Elkaïm-Sartre (Paris: Gallimard, 1986); translated by Ernest Sturm as *Mallarmé, or, The Poet of Nothingness* (University Park: Pennsylvania State University Press, 1988);

Vérité et existence, edited by Elkaïm-Sartre (Paris: Gallimard, 1989); translated by Adrian van den Hoven as *Truth and Existence,* edited by Ronald Aronson (Chicago: University of Chicago Press, 1992).

Editions and Collections: *Théâtre I* (Paris: Gallimard, 1947);

Œuvres romanesques, edited by Michel Contat and Michel Rybalka (Paris: Gallimard, 1981).

PLAY PRODUCTIONS: *Bariona oder Der Sohn des Donners,* Stalag XII-D, Trier/Petriberg (Trèves), France, 25 December 1940;

Les mouches, Paris, Théâtre de la Cité, 3 June 1943;

Huis clos, Paris, Théâtre du Vieux-Colombier, 27 May 1944;

Morts sans sépulture, Paris, Théâtre Antoine, 8 November 1946;

La Putain respectueuse, Paris, Théâtre Antoine, 8 November 1946;

Les Mains sales, Paris, Théâtre Antoine, 2 April 1948;

Le Diable et le bon Dieu, Paris, Théâtre Antoine, 7 June 1951;

Kean, Paris, Théâtre Sarah-Bernhardt, 14 November 1953;

Nekrassov, Paris, Théâtre Antoine, 8 June 1955;

Les Séquestrés d'Altona, Paris, Théâtre de la Renaissance, 23 September 1959;

Les Troyennes, Paris, Théâtre National Populaire, 10 March 1965.

PRODUCED SCRIPTS: *Les jeux sont faits,* motion picture, script by Sartre, dialogues by Sartre and Jacques-Laurent Bost, Gibé-Pathé, 1947;

Les Mains sales, motion picture, dialogue by Sartre, Rivers, 1951;

La Putain respectueuse, motion picture, by Sartre and Bost, Agiman, 1952;

Les Sorcières de Salem, motion picture, adapted from Arthur Miller's *The Crucible,* Borderie, CICC-Pathé (France)/DEFA (Germany), 1957;

Freud, motion picture, original screenplay by Sartre (uncredited), adapted by Charles Kaufman and Wolfgang Reinhardt, Universal International Pictures, 1962;

Le Mur, motion picture, dialogue by Sartre, Procinex-Niepce, 1967;

Sartre par lui-même, motion picture, Institut National de l'Audiovisuel, 1975.

OTHER: Charles Baudelaire, *Écrits intimes: Fusées, Mon coeur mis à nu, carnet, correspondance,* introduction by Sartre (Paris: Point du jour, 1946);

René Descartes, *Descartes, 1596–1650,* introduction by Sartre (Geneva: Traits, 1946);

"Jean-Paul Sartre respond a ses détracteurs," in *Présentation de Colette Audry, un texte de Jean-Paul Sartre,* by J.-B. Lefevre-Pontalis and others (Paris: Atlas, 1948), pp. 181–190;

Hervé Bazin and others, *L'affaire Henri Martin,* with commentary by Sartre (Paris: Gallimard, 1953);

"Doigts et non-doigts," in *Wols en personne: Aquarelles et dessins,* by Wols (Paris: Delpire, 1963); translated by Norbert Guterman as "Fingers and Non-Fingers,"

in *Wols: Watercolors, Drawings, Writings,* edited by Werner Haftmann (New York: Abrams, 1965).

SELECTED PERIODICAL PUBLICATIONS–UNCOLLECTED: "L'Ange du morbide," *Revue sans titre* (1923);

"Légende de la vérité," *Bifur,* 8, no. 169 (1931): 77–96;

"La Structure intentionnelle de l'image," *Revue de Métaphysique et de Morale,* 45, no. 4 (October 1938): 543–609;

"Paris Alive: The Republic of Silence," translated by Lincoln Kirstein, *Atlantic Monthly,* 174 (December 1944): 39–40;

"*Un Collège Spirituel,* fragment d'une etude sur Baudelaire," *Confluences,* 1 (January–February 1945): 9–18;

"The Case for a Responsible Literature," *Horizon,* 9 (May 1945): 307–311;

"Fragment d'un portrait de Baudelaire," *Les Temps Modernes,* 1, no. 8 (May 1945): 1345–1377;

"Forgers of Myths: The Young Playwrights of France," *Theatre Arts,* 30 (June 1946): 324–335;

"American Novelists in French Eyes," *Atlantic Monthly,* 178 (August 1946): 114–118;

"Americans and Their Myths," *Nation,* 165 (October 1947): 402–403;

"Commitment in Literature," *Politics and Letters,* 1 (Winter–Spring 1947): 24–33;

"Présence noire," *Présence africaine,* 1 (November–December 1947): 28–29;

"Freedom of Speech," *Transition,* 48, no. 1 (January 1948): 125–129;

"The Church and French Writers," *Transition,* 48, no. 3 (1948): 129–150; no. 4 (1948): 113–134;

"Drôle d'amitié," *Les Temps Modernes,* 49 (November 1949): 769–806; 50 (December 1949): 1009–1039;

"Chances of Peace," *Nation,* 171 (30 December 1950): 696–700;

"Sur les événements de Hongrie," *L'Express,* 9 November 1956;

"Brecht as a Classic," *World Theater,* 7, no. 1 (1958): 11–19;

"Stocktaking in Philosophy," *Polish Perspectives,* 2 (1959): 6–20;

"Beyond Bourgeois Theatre," translated by Rima Drell Reck, *Tulane Drama Review,* 5 (Spring 1961): 3–11;

"Why I Will Not Go to the United States," *Meanjin,* 24, no. 3 (1963): 340–344;

"'I Always Refuse Distinction,'" *Times* (London), 23 October 1964, p. 12;

"Imperialist Morality," *New Left Review,* 41 (January–February 1967): 3–10.

Sartre at eight with his grandfather Charles Schweitzer; his mother, Anne Marie; Emile Schweitzer; his aunt and uncle Michel and Caroline Biedermann; and his grandmother Louise Schweitzer (from Annie-Cohen Solal, Sartre: A Life, *translated by Anna Cancogni, 1987; Thomas Cooper Library, University of South Carolina)*

More than any other cultural figure of his generation, Jean-Paul Sartre set the tone of intellectual, philosophical, and literary activity both within postwar France and throughout Europe and the United States. Throughout his long writing career, Sartre probed the moral, historical, and philosophical parameters of the twentieth-century search for identity and the nature of existence. Imprisoned in Germany during World War II and later an active participant in the French Resistance, Sartre founded and edited *Les Temps Modernes* (Modern Times), which became the voice of French existentialism. Through this journal and his many novels, plays, and philosophical treatises, Sartre challenged not only contemporary ideas about freedom and human liberation, but also the oppression he found in Western capitalism. His relentless search for freedom gave rise to a process of existential inquiry and reflection. For Sartre, human beings are condemned to make their own destiny. Their burden and their transcendence is the act of making moral judgments. Thus, although he had little hope for the prospects of human institutions, Sartre championed human individuality and universal justice.

Jean-Paul Charles-Aymard Sartre was born in Paris, France, on 21 June 1905. Sartre's father, naval officer Jean-Baptiste Sartre, succumbed to enterocolitis on 17 November 1906, within seventeen months of his son's birth. Without extensive financial means, Sartre's mother, Anne Marie, moved with her infant son, called Poulou, to her parents' home in Meudon, France. The move set in motion Sartre's lifetime association with learning, knowledge, cultural investigations, and iconoclasm, for Anne Marie's father was Karl "Charles" Schweitzer, noted writer, music historian, Albert Schweitzer's uncle, and the major influence on young Sartre. For five years Sartre learned from and rebelled against his strict, pragmatic, bourgeois grandparents. He spent much time alone, for, although his grandfather taught German to French schoolchildren, once classes ended, Schweitzer left school and its inhabitants behind. Sartre had few playfellows other than books and his imagination. Born with strabismus, he was further isolated when at age four he contracted influenza, causing a leucoma in his right eye and destroying the muscles and part of the vision of his eye. For the rest of his life Sartre suffered partial blindness and disfigurement from this errant eye.

Isolated, without typical boyhood experiences, young Sartre learned to read and applied this skill indiscriminately to the works in his grandfather's substantial library. Reading led naturally to writing and, to amuse himself, Sartre wrote stories and impressions in journals. His disapproving grandfather criticized his grandson's efforts and, thereby, made writing even more enticing to the youngster. In his autobiography *Les Mots* (1964; translated as *The Words,* 1964), Sartre reports that he became passionately attached to writing in part to thwart his grandfather's objections. In fact, Sartre began his literary career at just eight years old, writing scripts and staging performances for the puppets his ever-doting mother gave him.

As a writer, Sartre not only created and staged plays for his inanimate actors, he also described living with his grandparents as a sort of playacting. He catered to an alternately warm and stern grandfather and a grandmother who was suspicious of this bookish little boy and usually disapproving of his reading and escapes into fantasy. Sartre played at being good, at being precious, and even at being loved. Like any child, he behaved and spoke in ways that got him their approval while also nurturing his disaffection. Despite his memories of these years as unhappy ones, he reveled in his role as the only child in the home of three adults.

During these years Sartre's mother treated her son as a plaything rather than a child. Anne Marie encouraged his imaginative play and his creative writing; she let his hair grow until his grandfather openly complained that his grandson looked like a sissy and marched him to the barber for a severe haircut. His drastically shorn appearance shocked his mother because his right eye, previously hidden by his hair, was now prominent. Already walleyed, Sartre's right eye looked to the far right. Even Sartre's mother had difficulty hiding her scornful feelings from her already sensitive son.

While in his grandparents' home, Sartre realized their religion was but another form of theater. Watching them as a diffident child does, he concluded that his grandparents and his mother only followed the token strictures of organized religion. His family was a circle of friendless individuals for whom "faith was merely a high-sounding name for sweet French freedom," as he wrote in *Les Mots*. Additionally, Sartre caught his grandfather in many affairs, although his grandmother denied the philandering. By age ten, Sartre wrote, he no longer believed in God.

Despite her financial dependence on her parents, Anne Marie sought to dilute her father's influence over her son. She took Sartre to movies, bought him comic books, and introduced him to American Western fiction, all forms of expression that Sartre exploited as a mature writer. By 1911 Anne Marie tried to escape Schweitzer's influence by fleeing with Sartre to Paris. Yet, Paris was expensive, and Anne Marie had to again accept her father's financial assistance. In 1913 Sartre's grandfather paid to enroll his grandson at Lycée Montaigne, a French secondary school that prepares students for university study, although Sartre was four years younger—and a better reader—than the typical lycée student.

Sartre's term at Lycée Montaigne was short. Although an avid reader, he could not spell. Hence, in 1913 his grandfather, confident Sartre needed basic skills, withdrew him from the lycée and enrolled him in the public school in Arcachon. Sartre's time at Arcachon was equally short, for in 1914 World War I erupted. With few books or supplies, Sartre's schooling languished, and he was forced to stop writing. Schweitzer, ever eager to give his grandson a profitable education, enrolled the ten-year-old boy in the prestigious Lycée Henri IV in Paris, where Sartre again was met with ambivalence. Some schoolmates shunned him because he was walleyed, short, and difficult to get to know. Others became lifelong friends, including many distinguished political activists, thinkers, and writers of the twentieth century, such as Sartre's best friend, Paul Nizan.

By 1917 Sartre was old enough to understand that Schweitzer, in failing health, could no longer provide for his daughter and grandson. Perhaps Anne Marie understood this certainty because she married Joseph Mancy, giving her unpopular adolescent son a new father and another family in which to find a place. Sartre has written of this time that he was anguished with his mother's marriage to Mancy and their move from Paris to La Rochelle, where his new stepfather was head of the naval yards.

Again Sartre found himself in a new school—this time the lycée of La Rochelle—where he learned the meanings of solitude and violence. To buy temporary peace from his schoolmates' taunts, he gave them pastries, purchased with money he stole from his mother. When his grandfather caught him, Sartre experienced the additional humiliation of losing his grandfather's trust. Mancy, in Sartre's eyes, usurped the boy's favored place with his mother and forced science and mathematics on the uninterested adolescent. Household tension grew until Sartre was fifteen years old, and Mancy, unable to control his stepson, sent Sartre back to Paris and to Lycée Henri IV.

Lycée Henri IV proved a turning point in Sartre's literary career. He became a pupil of philosopher and prolific essayist "Alain" (Emile Auguste Chartier). Chartier, a humanist and materialist, attacked official power and promoted pacifism in his essays; he taught his students that opposing authority was politically valuable and philosophically necessary. His influence extended beyond Sartre to biographer and novelist André Maurois, activist Simone Weil, novelist Jean Prévost, and rationalist philosopher George Canguilhem—all of whom influenced and were influenced by Sartre's philosophy.

*Sartre (seated, second from right) in his 1923–1924 class picture at L'Ecole Normale Supérieure. His friends and future
literary colleagues Paul Nizan and Raymond Aron were in the same class: Nizan is seated, second from left,
and Aron is seated next to Sartre, on his left (from John Gerassi,* Jean-Paul Sartre: Hated
Conscience of His Century, *volume 1:* Protestant or Protester? *1989;
Thomas Cooper Library, University of South Carolina).*

Sartre completed his baccalaureate in 1922; he was only seventeen years old. Even though Europe stayed in turmoil, Sartre's formal education continued at the Lycée Louis Le Grand from 1922 to 1924 and at L'Ecole Normale Supérieure (ENS), where childhood friend Nizan joined him for graduate study. He befriended, among others, anthropologist Claude Lévi-Strauss and philosophers Raymond Aron, Maurice Merleau-Ponty, and Jean Hyppolite. At ENS, Sartre continued writing while studying philosophy and preparing for his *agrégation,* the competitive university examinations that determined employment as a teacher. As European turbulence escalated, Sartre wrote, studied, and watched France sink into the political maelstrom.

In 1926 Sartre completed his thesis on the psychology of imagination, published in 1936 as *L'Imagination* (translated as *Imagination: A Psychological Critique,* 1962). Keenly aware of the cultural events and intellectual publications around him, he found himself caught up in these ideas and, as a result, did not pass his 1928 *agrégation.* The failure led to what was probably the

most important personal and philosophical connection he ever made: in 1929, while studying for the examination, he met and fell in love with the twenty-one-year-old future philosopher and feminist Simone de Beauvoir. They became lifetime companions, collaborators, and mutual influences.When they took the examination in 1929, Sartre and Beauvoir placed first and second, respectively.

Sartre and Beauvoir contracted a two-year relationship in which they agreed to be completely open and attached to one another but also to have any or all of the affairs they wanted to have. This relationship lasted his lifetime and defied conventional understanding. Why they were first drawn together, why they became openly lovers but never actually lived together, and why they stayed together until Sartre's death have baffled scholars. Beauvoir, in her memoir *Les Cérémonie des adieux, suivi de Entretiens avec Jean-Paul Sartre* (1981; translated as *Adieux: A Farewell to Sartre,* 1984), creates an intimate but ultimately shrouded history of their relationship. Reportedly, Sartre and Beauvoir always addressed one another formally, but he also called her

Castor (Beaver), a nickname she earned in college owing to her industriousness. Yet, such intimacies were uncharacteristic of their erratic attachment. Beauvoir extended Sartre a deep emotional commitment from their first liaison through the times of divided, German-occupied France, to the political activism of the 1960s and beyond. Sartre, by now known for his caustic personality, seemingly did not reciprocate her loyalty. When he died, his adopted daughter, Arlette Elkaïm-Sartre, was his only companion, and Arlette inherited his unpublished manuscripts, not Beauvoir. If anything, Sartre's and Beauvoir's writings and mutual interviews suggest that the basis for their relationship was rebellion: they were gifted individuals who rejected their privileged class because it depreciated intellectual debate. Always they discussed, wrote about, and fought for the changes they hoped would reform world culture.

Moreover, the changes they wrote for arose from the powerful upheavals they experienced. From 1929 to 1931 Sartre served his compulsory military service in the meteorology unit of the army. At the end of this unpleasant duty he began teaching philosophy at Lycée Le Havre. Beauvoir secured an appointment in Marseilles so that the two could meet, as they frequently did, in Paris. At Le Havre, Sartre returned to developing a treatise on "contingency" that he had carried with him since he was at ENS and studying Friedrich Nietzsche. His childhood experiences with literature, however, never left him. Thus, instead of an analytical philosophical work, Sartre cast his discussion of contingency in a first-person narrative, a journal by the fictional writer Antoine Roquentin. When he asked Beauvoir for her criticism, she suggested many substantive and stylistic changes. This project was the first of their extensive intellectual collaborations.

At a dinner gathering in 1933, Sartre and Beauvoir were joined by friend and former classmate Aron, who was deeply involved at the French Institute in Berlin in phenomenology, a subject that also fascinated Sartre. In one of her memoirs, *La Force de l'âge* (1960; translated as *The Prime of Life,* 1962), Beauvoir describes Aron's comments and Sartre's reaction:

> "You see my dear fellow, if you are a phenomenologist, you can talk about this cocktail and make philosophy out of it." Sartre turned pale with emotion at this. Here was the thing that he had been longing to achieve. . . . Sartre decided to make a serious study of Husserl.

Pursuing this interest meant returning to school; hence, in 1933, Sartre obtained a grant to study at the French Institute in Berlin, where, with Aron's help, he read all of Edmund Husserl's phenomenology. His fascination with philosophy and literature diverted his attention from politics for a time. As Sartre studied Husserl during the day, he rethought his training in philosophy and his place in contemporary political debate, and wrote at night. Now Sartre found his passions for philosophy and for Beauvoir were joined by his familiar passions for politics and other women.

As a philosophy student, Sartre championed René Descartes as the most significant philosophical thinker. Then he read, and met, Husserl, who, he said, was a twentieth-century Descartes. Sartre began to incorporate Husserl's ideas into his philosophical and literary work, but he quickly turned from Husserl to the more complex philosophy of Martin Heidegger. Sartre evidently tried to read *Sein und Zeit* (translated as *Being and Time,* 1962) shortly after it was published in 1927 but found it too dense for his patience and taste. Now after a year's study in Berlin and a more disciplined review of Heidegger's work, Sartre returned to Lycée Le Havre steeped in Husserl's and Heidegger's thought, which formed the bases to his view of existentialism. He also returned to the lycée seeking publication of "Melancholia," his work on contingency, and promoting Olga Kosakiewicz, an eighteen-year-old former pupil of Beauvoir's. Sartre and Beauvoir "adopted" Kosakiewicz to join their household and form what they called "Le Trio." Living with Sartre's demands and ongoing depressions proved too much, and the experiment failed. Sartre recalls in *Les Mots* that he was "at my lowest ebb." He had fallen in love with Kosakiewicz, and, when she left, he temporarily lost the will to write.

Slowly, as he returned to teaching in Leon and Paris, Sartre returned to writing. He revised his thesis and secured its publication in 1936 as *L'Imagination*. *L'Imagination* is as much a study of the psychology of perception as it is a work of philosophy. Here Sartre broaches the distinction between a perception and a recollection of a perception or an image, using not only his general acceptance of most of Husserl's ideas but also his own interpretations. To place *L'Imagination* in perspective, one needs to remember that during Sartre's early schooling, academic philosophy was dominated by at least three major philosophical dualisms. One of these dualisms, the focus on ontology, concerned the philosophical analysis of what there is, of what actually exists. In this debate Western philosophers traditionally settle into two camps: the realists, who believed in independently existing objects, and the idealists, who believed that there is no reality independent of human perception.

Sartre's first philosophical idol, Descartes, twisted the ontological dualism into philosophical deduction. He concluded, through contemplation and deduction,

Sartre in 1929, the year he began the relationship with Simone de Beauvoir that lasted until his death (from John Gerassi, Jean-Paul Sartre: Hated Conscience of His Century, *volume 1:* Protestant or Protester? *1989; Thomas Cooper Library, University of South Carolina)*

demonstration. The empiricists also favor reasoning but rejected deductive reasoning for the inductive: knowledge came about from observing and recording the data of experience.

The foremost early proponent of empiricism, David Hume, held that both a perception of an object and its recalled image were ideas "in the mind"; the difference between any perception and a memory was in how vivid one or the other was. Hume did not doubt that there were real objects, but his theory meant that people only have ideas about objects and not that they actually know the objects themselves. Immanuel Kant, however, took issue with Hume's critique. He believed that humans know more about real things than just ideas. Individuals perceive a *phenomenon,* an object of the world, but cannot know directly a *noumenon,* the actual object.

Kant, in the rationalist tradition, placed more faith in the ability to use deductive logic to analyze the way the world must be. Though he acknowledged deduction, Hume argued that no real existing thing corresponds to causation. Instead, he says, all humans ever actually perceive is the constant conjunction of two events and, thereby, infer a causal connection. Kant flatly rejected this point of view, contending that causation is so uniformly true of human understanding of the world that it must be real. Individuals may not be able to perceive causation but can understand it because they can reason. The human mind creates certain fundamental concepts, or "categories," that are necessarily true descriptions of what is real.

Husserl attempted to correct the apparently intractable dualist problems by attacking their foundations. He held that a person's perception is of two things: the particular objects of the world and the "meanings" of those objects. Hence, objects, properly understood, are not things that exist independently of humans but are constituted by experience. For Husserl, objects are not distinguished from meanings. Rather, meaning is necessary for the experience of objects. Although humans are conscious, their experience of objects comes first and is followed by their paying attention to experience, by reflection about it. When people reflect on their experience, they realize that they were conscious and that consciousness had been at work. On reflection, they learn that consciousness has already constituted a world of meaning and value, without direct awareness of it. These meanings are structures that consciousness imposes on experience and, interestingly, the beginning statement of the existentialist proposition: *existence precedes essence.*

The structures imposed by consciousness are not formally necessary, such as Kant's categories. They do not exist a priori, or independently of experience. In

that two "substances" existed in the world: the mental and the physical. To arrive at a conclusion about something by this approach is called rationalism and is best understood in relation to its opposite theory, empiricism. Rationalists and empiricists differ on two central points: the theory of ideas and the preferred method for investigating philosophical issues. Rationalists argue that ideas, foundational concepts for knowledge, are known intuitively through reason. Descartes described these concepts as innate ideas, the most important being the ideas of oneself, infinite perfection, and causality. Empiricists hold that what humans know is based either on direct perception or on an internal mental experience, such as memory, after the direct experience. The rationalists' method of investigating these issues center on reasoning: humans can deduce truths with absolute certainty from innate ideas. The perfect demonstration of truth is mathematical; hence, mathematical proof should be the model for all other kinds of

this sense Husserl rejected the rationalist tradition. The meanings imposed by consciousness are the result of previous experience and are only materially, or factually, necessary. For Husserl, meaning is the refinement of the experience of an object into an example and, therefore, into an object's essence. Thus, meaning and object are correlatives. Individuals must perceive objects for meaning to exist, and objects have their meaning by virtue of consciousness. Thus, Husserl rejected Hume's argument that humans perceive actual objects and are not limited to perceiving only ideas.

The common use of the term *transcendental,* when Husserl and Sartre were writing, held that aspects of reality are higher than ("transcend") and form the foundation for everyday reality. For instance, a chair is transcendental before users have concepts about it—such as its use or reasons for its name. Husserl used *transcendental* to refer to the archaeology of experience where humans discover the structures or meanings that are imposed on perception by consciousness. Transcendental phenomenology, therefore, investigates and describes the fundamental acts of consciousness that impose meaning on objects. The most fundamental concept is the concept of the object, not some rational category, such as Kant's concept of causation.

Sartre could neither accept nor reject rationalism or empiricism; instead, he tries to find his position as a phenomenologist à la Husserl. He sought other positions on ontology and found in Georg Wilhelm Friedrich Hegel another significant component for his philosophy. Where Husserl shifted the emphasis toward a description of the objects of experience, which were called phenomena, Hegel, in his *Die Phänomenologie des Geistes* (1807; translated as *The Phenomenology of Mind,* 1910), promoted the status of abstractions to the status of real things and actually used the word *phenomenology* to describe a sort of analysis of objects and human perceptions of them. Sartre was, however, even more drawn to Hegel's writing on individual freedom, historical determinism, and his paradigm of all forms of social conflict, in particular the struggle between social classes. Hegel recognized that individuals would come to resent how they were manipulated by history, and he made references to alienation.

In *L'Imagination,* Sartre uses Husserl's phenomenology tools to differentiate perception and image. He rejects the traditional view that the "objects" of a perception are internal and of imagination are external. To some extent he agrees with his first philosophic idol, Descartes, that images have inner causes, whereas perceptions have external causes. Following Husserl, he limits existence to things in the world and to consciousness. Nothing exists only in the mind. Imagining something and seeing something are both ways of being

conscious of the world and of objects. Sartre concluded that imagining a thing means being conscious of it as absent or nonexistent and typifies humans' remarkable capacity to imagine what is not present or does not exist. That capacity expresses individual freedom. When it was published, *L'Imagination* was important for its role in popularizing phenomenology in France.

While he was in Le Havre, Sartre gave lectures on literature and published articles on literary criticism. He spoke and wrote about William Faulkner, Virginia Woolf, James Joyce, Aldous Huxley, and John Dos Passos, whom he labeled "the greatest novelist of our times," as quoted in Annie Cohen-Solal's *Sartre: A Life* (1987). His close friends Nizan and Beauvoir resubmitted his "Melancholia" manuscript to publisher Gaston Gallimard, who praised the book but not its title. He successfully urged Sartre to rename the book and published it the following year as *La Nausée* (1938; translated as *Nausea,* 1949).

Before *La Nausée* was printed, however, Sartre's long essay "La Transcendance de l'ego" (The Transcendence of the Ego) appeared in *Recherches philosophiques* (1936–1937) and marked his philosophical break from Husserl and his first steps toward existentialism. Husserl had taught that when individuals discover structures of meaning through reflection, they discover their individual consciousness behind those structures. Humans find the fundamental "I" in consciousness, which Husserl called the transcendental ego, not in concrete reality. This ego ties everything together; all these perceptions and meanings are personal.

Sartre counters that all acts of consciousness are unified as "objects." Perception is unified from an individual's point of view. Moreover, an individual's perception is sufficient for consciousness of an object; no one need share or confirm a perception. That is, no one need, Sartre argues, posit a subjective, transcendental ego nor a self submerged in consciousness. Instead, the self is like everything else: it is in the world, constituted like all other objects by consciousness. Consciousness, which invents the ego to give it that sense of identity, re-creates its existence continually and without prior reference. In short, the transcendental ego is unnecessary.

"La Transcendance de l'ego" mostly interested students of Husserl and phenomenology. The rest of Europe in 1937 was focused on the increasing threats of Adolf Hilter's Third Reich and the military buildup in Germany. Sartre took a post at Lycée Pasteur.

La Nausée finally appeared in 1938 and is still regarded as Sartre's most enduring work. French critics, such as Amand Robun, hailed it as unquestionably distinct; elsewhere, however, the novel received at best

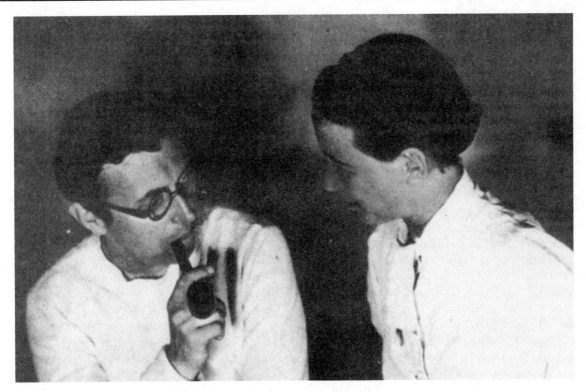

Sartre and Beauvoir in 1939 (from John Gerassi, Jean-Paul Sartre: Hated Conscience of His Century,
volume 1: Protestant or Protester? 1989; Thomas Cooper Library,
University of South Carolina)

lukewarm responses. Russian-born novelist Vladimir Nabokov in *The New York Times Book Review* (24 April 1949) complained that Sartre's powers as a writer were not sufficient to the task he had set himself.

Nonetheless, *La Nausée* illustrates and characterizes Sartre's philosophical development. "The editors" introduce readers to Antoine Roquentin, whose notebooks they are reading. Roquentin writes mainly about his experiences in a fictional town, Bouville, modeled on Le Havre. Shortly after the diary begins, he is troubled by recurring bouts of nausea, feeling ill for extended periods and at odd times. His nausea arises out of his perception of physical objects and his repulsion by the independent reality of those objects. At the same time he is troubled by his developing realization of his own meaninglessness and of his own contingency. Roquentin feels increasingly that his familiar, comfortable world is collapsing into unrecognizable, unrelated things. The familiar characterizations are of the essences of things. When they lose their essences, things just exist. As things lose context, they lose their meaning; nothing is necessary. Roquentin attempts to stop the loss of meaning by capturing his experiences in the diary.

Roquentin has an increasing number of moments when he faces his contingency. In a characteristic description, on a Monday, he is sitting at his writing table but loses his concentration:

> I looked anxiously around me: the present, nothing but the present. Furniture light and solid, rooted in its present, a table, a bed, a closet with a mirror—and me. The true nature of the present revealed itself: it was what exists, and all that was not present did not exist. The past did not exist. Not at all. Not in things, not even in my thoughts. . . . Now I knew: things are entirely what they appear to be—and behind them . . . there is nothing.

With each new description of the actions of other people, Roquentin becomes more neutral, uninvolved, and nonjudgmental. He seems to have no interest in the motives of others. Sitting at a table in a restaurant, he describes people he sees in terms of his life:

> Near the window, a slight dark-complexioned man with distinguished features and fine white hair, brushed back, reads his paper thoughtfully. A leather dispatch case is on the bench beside him. He drinks Vichy water. In a moment all these people are going to leave;

weighted down by food, caressed by the breeze, coat wide open, face a little flushed, their heads muzzy, they will walk along the balustrade, watching the children on the beach and the ships on the sea; they will go to work. I will go nowhere, I have no work.

Roquentin discovers that things divorced from their names surround him. He is overwhelmed by all of the existence around him; the presence of things suffocates him and he feels ill. At that moment, he has an epiphany. He no longer has to fear the illness, the nausea that has been bothering him, because that nausea is not something imposed on him: he is the nausea.

The diary ends without resolution, climax, or denouement. Roquentin, determined to leave Bouville, waits for his train in a café, listening to the saxophone and lyrics of a jazz song, "Some of these days you'll miss me, honey." Without analysis, he concludes that only this music, this creative act, endures. While the music plays, he loses his nausea.

In Europe, Sartre's attention turned to politics. When Hitler invaded Poland in 1939, Sartre returned to active military service as France struggled to prepare for the inevitable. He was dispatched to the meteorological corps, for which his duties included launching weather balloons. For nearly a year he participated in and argued against what he called the "phony war." He wrote prodigiously in anticipation of future publication. He poured all his feelings into notes that he kept in journals, some that he gave to Beauvoir, only five of which still exist. These notes were later included in such works as *L'Etre et le néant: Essai d'ontologie phénoménologique* (1943; translated as *Being and Nothingness: An Essay on Phenomenological Ontology,* 1956), *L'Age de raison* (1945; translated as *The Age of Reason,* 1947), *Les Mots,* and the posthumously published *Les Carnets de la drôle de guerre* (1983; translated as *War Diaries of Jean-Paul Sartre: November 1939 – March 1940,* 1984).

In late 1939 Sartre's short-story collection *Le Mur* (translated as *The Intimacy, and Other Stories,* 1948) was published. The title story fictionalizes Sartre's antiwar fears in its protagonist, Pablo, who has been captured along with other supposed Basque separatists by an unidentified military force seeking rebel Ramon Gris. In the twenty-four-hour period in which the story takes place, different men are interrogated; yet, none divulges what, if anything, he knows about Gris. As they stand in front of "the wall," the men believe they will be executed by a firing squad. One by one they share their fears about dying, about pain, and about disfigurement. With dawn approaching, Pablo "didn't want to think any more about what would happen at dawn, at death. It made no sense. I only found words or emptiness. But as soon as I tried to think of anything else I saw rifle barrels pointing at me. Perhaps I lived through my execution twenty times." Pablo survives for another interrogation after other rebels have been led away and, presumably, shot. He knows and despises Gris, but he willfully resists his interrogators. Gris, he lies, is hiding in a cemetery; he enjoys seeing the soldiers preparing for what he knows will be a wasted trip even though he realizes they will return angry and execute him. To his surprise, the soldiers release him. In a moment reminiscent of O. Henry, he learns that Gris had, quite unexpectedly, gone to the cemetery and was killed by the soldiers. Pablo can only laugh at the absurdity.

Sartre and his meteorology corps comrades were captured by the Germans in June 1940. While in prison camp, Sartre learned to respect his fellow soldiers–people he would have belittled outside the camp. His sense of the importance of political action linked to his philosophical taste for freedom. He translated Heidegger's *Sein und Zeit* and started work summarizing his own philosophy, *L'Etre et le néant.* In March 1941, using a fake medical certificate, Sartre was released from the prison camp, and he returned to Paris to publish and to resist.

With the 1942 publication of *L'Etranger* (translated as *The Stranger,* 1946), Albert Camus was intellectually joined with Sartre in part because their creative output took parallel forms–philosophy, novels, plays, short stories, and streams of articles–and in part because they shared philosophical positions. From their first meeting in June 1943, Camus and Sartre found common ground. Yet, their friendship died as quickly as it came about. Sartre forces readers into the despair of the absurd existence. His interpretation of existentialism is broad, ideologically rigid, but endurable. Crippling self-hatred and nausea of the individual, such as Roquentin's, in the face of the absurdity of life can be redeemed. Camus finds meaning, never redemption, through revolt. In the face of the Nazi threat, the friends argued over communism, an ideology Sartre endorsed wholeheartedly but Camus disparaged. The two writers quarreled in 1951 over Camus's *L'homme révolté* (translated as *The Rebel,* 1953) and never reconciled. Camus died in a car crash with his friend and publisher Michel Gallimard in 1960, without ever communicating with Sartre again.

In 1943 Sartre published his most significant and influential philosophical work, *L'Etre et le néant,* an answer to Heidegger's *Sein und Zeit.* Heidegger had sought to find the meaning of Being by recasting Hegel's alienation as the recognition of death. Being, or *Dasein,* is situated in the world and not somehow independent of the world; it is being that exists for itself. The most significant metaphysical question for Heidegger is "Why is there something rather than nothing?" Heidegger skirts answering his question to consider

Sartre during his service in the French army meteorological corps, 1939 (from John Gerassi, Jean-Paul Sartre: Hated Conscience of His Century, *volume 1:* Protestant or Protester? *1989; Thomas Cooper Library, University of South Carolina)*

instead how humans are characterized by their angst about their deaths. For Heidegger, one's attitude toward death is what allows one to have authenticity.

L'Etre et le néant is also concerned with "la poursuite d'est" (the pursuit of being) not just as a matter of ontological analysis but, rather, so Sartre can use the tools of philosophy to explore the relationship of being to nothingness. He rejects Platonic forms or divine creators to insist on independent reality: the appearance of a thing is the essence of the thing. Humans can create and re-create themselves. Yet, what is being and what is nothingness? Sartre argues that consciousness and objects are distinct and have their own forms of *being*. The being of consciousness, "l'être-pour-soi" (being-for-itself), or, sometimes, just the "pour-soi" (for-itself) is defined "as being what it is not and not being what it is." "For-itself" is consciousness itself, human potential

to be more than just objects. "Being-in-itself" is nonconscious being, the object of consciousness, and characterized by the way in which it acts: it intends or confers meaning on objects. Sartre admits that his best definitions for these forms are provisional; however, he confirms the contingency of being in itself: "This means that being can neither be derived from the possible nor reduced to the necessary. Necessity concerns the connection between ideal propositions but not that of existents. An existing phenomenon can never be derived from another existent qua existent. This is what we call the contingency of being-in-itself. . . . Being-in-itself is never either possible or impossible. It is."

Sartre broadens his inquiry into the relationship between humans and being (in other words, being-in-itself) by including nothingness, the traditional complement of being set out by Descartes and Hegel. Being-in-itself cannot be the source of nothingness; "Being can generate only being." Humans, however, can create nothingness by an act of consciousness. As Descartes argues, this act of negation by the being-for-itself is an act of freedom in which consciousness separates itself from being.

Because people are human and not simply objects, they are free to make any choices they want to make. In line with Camus and others of his era, Sartre rejects determinism for free will. By an act of negation, or through nothingness, being-for-itself severs itself from its past, apprehends objects, and sees itself because consciousness also includes self-consciousness.

Learning they are free to act, humans fear freedom and the choices they have to make. Humans anguish and, consequently, automatically and involuntarily try to deny that freedom. Sartre agrees with both Søren Kierkegaard and Heidegger that such anguish is the self's discovery that it faces nothingness in the past and the future, that it may annihilate itself because it finds no relief from the responsibility for making choices. To flee these realizations, the self may seek reassuring myths, a state of consciousness Sartre calls "la mauvaise foi" (bad faith). Bad faith prevents an individual from being himself and seeks to make him a thing, a being-in-itself. Sincerity is the antithesis of bad faith. Sartre concludes that one feature of human reality is unhappiness because of its imperfect state. This unhappiness expresses the negation from which being-for-itself arises and regarding which being-for-itself strives to transform itself.

Sartre turns to the problem of other minds, noting that Husserl established the possibility of other consciousnesses, not their existence. Heidegger suggested that humans presuppose other consciousnesses but did not claim proof of their existence. Sartre agrees that he cannot prove other conscious minds exist by inductive reasoning, but he says that humans cannot doubt the existence of other consciousnesses any more than they doubt their own existence. The act of reflection that reveals the being-for-itself also reveals what he calls "le pour-autrui" (being for others). This being comes about by encounters with the other; individuals do not constitute the other.

As an example of being-for-others, Sartre considers how observing a man in a park changes everything for an observer. Before the man arrives, the observer apprehended everything as being organized around the observer. Once the man is in the park, that organization "disintegrates" because "it appears that the world has a kind of drain hole in the middle of its being and that it is perpetually flowing off through this hole."

This disintegration of the observer's perceived world arises from a competition between the two consciousnesses, the unreflective consciousness (the pre-reflective cogito of Descartes) and the reflective consciousness (moral consciousness that can expose values). An encounter with the other can be much more uncomfortable, however. The observer must reflect on being perceived by the other. How will the observer appear to the other when the observer cannot control or experience how the other perceives? Sartre suggests that the observer may become ashamed by being observed by the other: the observer experiences self as an object or as being-in-itself.

The experience unreflective and reflective consciousnesses undergo when they encounter one another is competitive, as both the observer and the other seek to maintain their own freedom. It is to the topic of freedom that Sartre turns lastly in *L'Etre et le néant*. Sartre considers causes of human action, one of which is objective, such as a force of nature or a political force. Sartre sometimes refers to this cause as a person's situation, although he also uses the word *situation* in a broader sense. The other cause is subjective or, in Sartre's terms, a motive or a reason. Part 2 of *L'Etre et le néant* centers on how motives (for example, desire) relate to being-for-itself. Now Sartre turns to more immediate concerns.

Consciousness creates a project for itself, conferring meaning on itself. Similarly, for-itself confers on a cause its value as motive. Motives are understood by the negative, by what is not. Sartre says that motive is understood by reference to an "ensemble" of nonexistents. He also refers to an ensemble of projects: "this ensemble is ultimately myself as transcendence; it is Me in so far as I have to be myself outside of myself." Sartre refuses to approve determinism: motives do not cause acts; rather, they are integral parts of an act. Again using the idea of a person's chosen "project" to explain action, he writes that the motive, the act, and

the project are parts of a single upsurge as a person changes in response to a situation.

Objective force, or external cause, cannot change an individual's project (in other words, the meaning one has conferred on oneself), but changes in an environment will clarify an individual's project and lead to evaluating choices. Such choices remain the product of individual freedom, and that ultimate freedom of choice means responsibility. This responsibility leads to one of Sartre's more well-known expressions and his main theme: "man being condemned to be free carries the weight of the whole world on his shoulders; he is responsible for the world and for himself as a way of being."

Casual readers of *L'Etre et le néant* struggle to follow Sartre because he assumes that readers already know much of the history of Continental philosophy, especially phenomenology. He invents terms to replace common words that he thinks are misleading, and he resorts to metaphor as much as to sustained argument. Yet, patient readers have been rewarded by both the sustained analysis of human being and by the persuasive conviction that there is meaning for the secular life.

With France still occupied, Sartre's first play, *Les Mouches* (The Flies), was performed at the Théâtre de la Cité on 3 June 1943. *Les Mouches* uses the classic Oresteian myth as a vehicle to explore and expand the philosophical themes of works such as *L'Etre et le néant* and to rally the French public during wartime. In the play Orestes returns to his homeland, Argos, years after his mother, Clytemnestra, and her lover, Aegistheus, had murdered his father. Parisians quickly connected the dilemma of the play and the moral dilemma of the Occupation and interpreted Orestes' suffering with their daily adversities. When he returns, Orestes finds a people ruled by the tyrant-usurper Aegisthus and his consort, Orestes' mother. Caught between his contempt for the Argos people and his fear of cowardice, Orestes kills for the sake of Argos but is rejected by his sister, Electra, for his violence. Jupiter again intervenes to convince Orestes that he is homeless, an intruder, a splinter in the flesh, a poacher in the lord's forest. Orestes retorts that he is free and can follow only his own laws, even if it means that he must be alone forever.

Nothing is subtle about *Les Mouches*. It is a work to rally resistance to the Occupation. Sartre has Orestes create his own meaning by having him choose and act freely, a theme Sartre continues through most of his remaining works, including *Huis clos* (1945; translated as *No Exit,* 1947).

First performed at the Théâtre du Vieux-Colombier in May 1944, just before the liberation of Paris, *Huis clos* places four characters in a nicely furnished drawing room. The valet and Garcin enter, and Garcin hints at

Sartre at a café in Montparnasse, circa 1964 (from Annie Cohen-Solal, Sartre: A Life, *translated by Anna Cancogni, 1987; Thomas Cooper Library, University of South Carolina)*

the situation by asking, "Do you know who I was?" Shortly, he asks where the instruments of torture are and then complains about missing his toothbrush. Garcin tries to leave but cannot. Soon Inez and Estelle join him, also expecting Gothic, hideous torturers. Instead, as they discover one another's habits, they begin to realize that "each one of us will act as a torturer of the two others." Initially, they try to ignore one another in silence; however, they soon tell how each got there. They form and break alliances with each other and make blatant, crude sexual advances toward one another. At one point Garcin wills the door open but cannot bring himself to leave the two women. Voicing Sartre's existentialism, Inez observes, "One always dies too soon—or too late. And yet one's whole life is complete at that moment, with a line drawn neatly under it, ready for the summing up. You are—your life, and nothing else." Long before the play ends, theatergoers appreciate Garcin's succinct conclusion: "Hell is—other people!"

On 26 August 1944 Paris was liberated, and Sartre watched General Charles de Gaulle and the American Second Armored Division parade along the Champs-Elysées. The new government sought advice on retaining influential administrators or purging those who cooperated with Occupation forces. A Resistance worker and prominent French literary and philosophical writer, Sartre was consulted and stood behind his old friend, Michel Gallimard, who was just publishing Sartre's newest project, *Les Temps Modernes.*

As directed by Beauvoir, Camus, Aron, Jean Paulhan, Albert Olliver, Merleau-Ponty, and Sartre, *Les Temps Modernes* reviewed postwar ideology and offered Sartre's vision of a premier literary, political, and intellectual journal. The first volume set the tone with the "Présentation" (volume 1, no. 1, October 1945) and the essay "La Nationalisation de la littérature" (The Nationalization of Literature, volume 1, no. 2, November 1945). Writers, Sartre proclaims, have their place in the age: "I hold Flaubert and Goncourt responsible for the repression that followed the Commune because they did not write a single line to prevent it." While this manifesto variously irritated and delighted, its principles have continued to guide *Les Temps Modernes.*

In 1946, Sartre, in *L'Existentialisme est un humanisme* (translated as *Existentialism,* 1947), publicly referred to his philosophical work as "l'existentialisme" (existentialism), an ethical humanism. He defends existentialism from claims of immorality or amorality. Sartre acknowledges that existentialists may rely on religious principles or on atheistic or humanistic principles. He, as an atheist, promotes the idea that "there is at least one being whose existence comes before its essence": man. As existence precedes essence, the first principle of existentialism is that "man is nothing else but what he makes of himself." Consequently, existentialism makes humans responsible for themselves and for all people. Sartre refutes claims that existentialists create anguish, despair, and a sense of abandonment by arguing that existentialism offers people a reason to act and be committed in a world without God. Humans are the sum of their actions, freely undertaken. Existentialism inspires and motivates humans by reminding them of their freedom and of their transcendence as an act of surpassing themselves.

A year earlier, in 1945, Sartre published *L'Age de raison,* the first of his projected four-part antinovel, *Les Chemins de la liberté* (The Roads to Freedom). The series illustrates what Sartre described in "Qu'est-ce que la littérature?" (1947; translated in *What Is Literature?,* 1949) as a literature of praxis: "action in history and on history . . . a synthesis of historical relativity and moral and metaphysical absolute." In *L'Age de raison,* philosopher-teacher Mathieu Delarue, a thinly disguised version of Sartre, struggles with his moral responsibility to his pregnant mistress, Marcelle, and his desire to keep his freedom. Unsuccessfully, Mathieu goes to friends, including Ivich, a student he is in love with, to raise Fr4,000 to pay for Marcelle's illegal abortion. One of Mathieu's students, Boris, is involved with a nightclub singer in her early forties, Lola. As in *Huis clos,* Sartre uses conversations between Boris and Lola to explore Mathieu's personality. In one exchange, Lola tries to learn why Boris likes the uninteresting, ineffectual Mathieu. Boris's reply encapsulates Sartre's theme: "'Delarue has his passions,' he said, pursuing his reflections aloud, 'but that doesn't prevent his caring for nothing. He is free.'"

When Mathieu's brother, Jacques, offers him Fr10,000 francs to marry Marcelle, the two engage in an extended argument over Mathieu's refusal to act responsibly. Eventually, Mathieu steals the money from Boris and his homosexual friend Daniel, who impulsively marries Marcelle. Mathieu, alone and discredited, is stunned at Daniel's action: "'Is that what freedom is?' he thought. 'He has acted; and now he can't go back; it must seem strange to him to feel behind him an unknown act which he already almost ceased to understand and which will turn his life upside down. All I do, I do for nothing.'"

Sartre wrote the second novel in the series, *Le Sursis* (1945; translated as *The Reprieve,* 1947), emulating Dos Passos, Faulkner, and Ernest Hemingway. "After reading a book by Dos Passos," Sartre wrote in "American Novelists in French Eyes" for the August 1946 issue of *Atlantic Monthly,* he "thought for the first time of weaving a novel out of various, simultaneous lives, with characters who pass each other by without ever knowing one another and who all contribute to the atmosphere of a moment or of a historical period."

Action in *Le Sursis* takes place in a range of places and characters carried over from *L'Age de raison* in a stream-of-conscious style. During one week in September 1938 the French brace for war, in a way similar to Sartre's participation in "the phony war," and Europe observes the negotiations between England and Nazi Germany. In Berlin a family crouches in fear, waiting for Nazi thugs to arrest them. Almost simultaneously, readers see characters' thoughts and actions, including Mathieu and Odette on the beach and Daniel and Marcelle on a walk shortly before her due date. Through glimpses of words, actions, and thoughts of historical figures, including Neville Chamberlain and Hitler negotiating over the fate of Europe, Sartre presents the evolving attitudes of characters from the first novel, as well as new players. With little didacticism and many sharply juxtaposed images, he dwells on the implica-

tions for freedom in all that is going on around his characters.

Le Sursis ends when, for a brief moment after the Munich Pact is signed, French politicians believe war will not happen. Mathieu thinks of all the men who have been called up or who have volunteered for service and of how all of these men had to struggle with their feelings and their lives and "had made up their minds to die": "Here they were, dazed and baffled, embedded for one more moment in a life that they no longer knew how to use. A day of dupes, he thought."

La mort dans l'âme (1949; translated as *Iron in the Soul,* 1950), the last volume in *Les Chemins de la liberté,* traces soldier Mathieu's intellectual struggles with remorse, action, and being. With vivid detail Sartre paints Mathieu's retreat from the Germans and a host of different soldiers' prewar histories. Each character seems largely disorganized, trying to fall back for what each believes will be demobilization during the coming occupation. Without hope for a cease-fire, a less philosophical Mathieu appreciates his fellow soldiers' personal dilemmas yet demeans the conflict between mindless military hierarchies and the soldiers' needs. News of a possible armistice brings Mathieu passionate disappointment. France should have made the Germans pay for their peace, he rages; everyone should have been involved in politics before the war, and they must now all take responsibility for allowing their defense to have been inadequate. Mathieu at last brings himself to act. In his last moments he finds courage and freedom in defending a small village against advancing Germans and in discrete acts of violence against German soldiers.

Although *La mort dans l'âme* is little more than an apology for the state of French communism, Sartre's *Réflexions sur la question juive* (1946; translated as *Portrait of the Anti-Semite,* 1946) attempts a positive stand against the anti-Semitism then developing in France. Embracing Marxism for the first time in his writings, Sartre narrates four attitudes as characters: an anti-Semite; a democrat; an inauthentic Jew; and an authentic Jew. Sartre, however, based his analyses on evidence gathered from intellectual friends rather than from research on Judaism or current social mores. Hence, he naively asserts: "We find scarcely any anti-Semitism among workers." Then, showing how far he was allowing orthodox Marxism to direct his writing at this stage of his career, he concludes:

The working class . . . sees ensembles in terms of economic functions. The bourgeoisie, the peasant class, the proletariat—those are the synthetic realities with which it is concerned. . . . The majority of the anti-Semites, on the contrary, belongs to the middle class, that is, among

*Sartre at the Paris café La Coupole with his adopted daughter and former lover, Arlette Elkaïm-Sartre, 1965
(from Annie Cohen-Solal,* Sartre: A Life, *translated by Anna Cancogni, 1987; Thomas
Cooper Library, University of South Carolina)*

men who have a life equal or superior to that of the Jews, or, if you prefer, among the "non-producers" (employers, merchants, distributors, members of the liberal professions, parasites).

Réflexions sur la question juive expresses many stereotypes about Jews and French culture that have since been considered unacceptable. For instance, he argues Jews have essentially given up on a religious reason for their Jewishness and are distinctive because of their appearance. He proposes to eliminate anti-Semitism in society by founding a classless society with "collective ownership of the instruments of labor." For all its flaws, *Réflexions sur la question juive* furnishes glimpses of how Sartre personalizes the experience of the French Jewish community at the end of World War II. At a time when such opinions were unpopular, Sartre speaks with passion about real people, not abstractions. He warns the rejoicing French not to forget social conflict and to

remember, in the face of anti-Semitism, the Jews who died in the gas chambers. Talk, discussion, and public action were needed, not silence in the name of national unity. Later, Sartre made this call to action a personal one when he adopted the gifted Jewish Algerian musician Arlette Elkaïm. Like Olga, Arlette had been Sartre's lover. After her adoption in 1962, Arlette remained with Sartre for the rest of his life, much to Beauvoir's disgust.

Sartre turned from fictional philosophy back to theater with the comic satire *La Putain respectueuse* (translated as "The Respectful Prostitute," 1949), first performed at the Théâtre Antoine on 8 November 1946. Abandoning New York for a southern town and a quiet business as a prostitute, Lizzie McKay witnesses the brutal murder of a black man by a senator's son, Thomas. As a cover, Thomas and other white residents concoct a story that two black men had tried to rape the newcomer. Lizzie's goals fit their lie and encourage various white residents to exploit her. Fred, her first customer, tries to bribe her and, failing that, humiliates her. The police threaten to arrest her for prostitution unless she implicates "The Negro." Fred's father, Senator Clarke, assures her that Thomas's mother, the whole town, and her country would honor her for saving Thomas. Confused, Lizzie signs the false report freeing him. *La Putain respectueuse* shows how ironic existentialists can be and how theater can be both funny and chilling. Unlike the dark existentialism of *Huis clos, La putain respectueuse* uses irony and humor to present an individual trying to stay committed to action.

Sartre turned against those who argue that artists, particularly writers, are ethical only when they create for art's sake in his 1948 three-part treatise "Qu'est-ce que la littérature?" In "Qu'est-ce au'écrite?" (What Is Writing?), "Pourquoi écrite?" (Why Write?), and "Pour qui écrit-on?" (For Whom Does One Write?), Sartre answers his rhetorical questions from the stance that the sole, legitimate purpose of writing is to further the freedom of the reader. First, writing, distinct from other arts, uses signs, although Sartre offers no substantive evidence to that effect. The choice of what words to use in prose is different from the choice of, for instance, a color of paint because a writer is not immediately interested in whether the words are pleasing. Rather, the writer is concerned with the action of disclosure. Second, Sartre claims writers compose because they feel a relationship with the world and fulfill that relationship when their words find readers. Writer and readers are freed because they trust one another and place equal demands on one another. Third, Sartre relinquishes literature to Marxism. Writers compose for a classless society, releasing the free judgment of all. Despite the fact that middle-class readers buy literature and, by extension, support writers, Sartre says that the writer must focus on awakening the consciousness of the proletariat.

Sartre's last major philosophical work, *Critique de la raison dialectique, précédé de Question de méthode* (The Critique of Dialectical Reason, Preceded by Question of Method), appeared in 1960 in two parts: *Théorie des ensembles pratiques* (translated as *Theory of Practical Ensembles,* 1976) and *L'intelligibilité de l'Historie* (translated as *The Intelligibility of History,* 1991). Published as the Stalinists were overtaking Yugoslavia, *Critique de la raison dialectique* offers arguments for intellectuals to stay united while the Communist Party reassessed itself. Sartre elevates Marxism and sets existentialism aside. History, he asserts, needed what was to become Stalinism. As a result of what has passed, thinking individuals have "a new moment, more detailed, integrated, and rich of the human adventure." Sartre then turns to a new idea for

him: how the being-for-itself, or consciousness, can be changed by external forces. This transformation requires that Sartre turn his attention to two factors: scarcity and culture. Scarcity, he asserts, explains the possibility of human history, a viewpoint widely different from that in *L'Etre et le néant.* His focus shifts from how the individual perceives the in-itself to how men and women get along when they experience scarcity. This reposition accounts for how Sartre can now talk about constraints on human freedom and, particularly, how he can contemplate the determinism of Marxism.

Sartre outlines types of groups that people forge. The simplest group having a common interest is called a series. This group sustains itself by equating an individual need with a common need. When the series understands the need and the scarcity, the group will act, reacting to the power of circumstances. As a collective the group creates a consciousness that may be acted upon by the external being. Individuals recognize both the scarcity of the resources and the rivalry for those resources. In order to make progress, individuals must learn how to form a fused group; that is, individuals must learn to coordinate action for the common good.

A group most often becomes a fused group in the face of danger. Once the danger has passed, however, the group returns to being a serial group, a group of separate individuals linked but not united. By introducing the possibility of external causes motivating action, Sartre has apparently changed his view about the possibility of action. He argues that since individuals create society and groups, they must, therefore, exercise the freedom that is characteristic of the being-for-itself in that context.

Sartre recognizes two features of action that he did not observe in *L'Etre et le néant:* human freedom has material antecedents, and human freedom may be limited and shaped by ideological influences. To tie these recognitions together, Sartre introduces the heuristic that existentialism offers Marxism a method of discovery of the truth. Sartre's method avoids the simple resort to history that has been the hallmark of Marxism. Instead, he insists that one must also look at the aims of individual human beings. If individuals form groups because of scarcity and out of fear and if scarcity and the causes of fear are removed, individuals remove conflict. Clearly, that change will open up the possibilities for human freedom. Moreover, the circumstances in which individuals find themselves do not determine their actions mechanically; instead, circumstances provide a context for choices that are never arbitrary when viewed against the background of personal and social history.

The editorial board of Les Temps Modernes, *the journal Sartre founded near the end of World War II, in 1978: Jean Pouillon, Benny Lévy, Claire Etcherelli, François George, Andre Gorz, Beauvoir, Sartre, and Claude Lanzmann (from Annie Cohen-Solal,* Sartre: A Life, *translated by Anna Cancogni, 1987; Thomas Cooper Library, University of South Carolina)*

For all intents and purposes *Critique de la raison dialectique* ended Sartre's philosophical writings but not his popularity. He turned during his last years to political action and criticism, cinematic work, and his memoirs. In the years following World War II, Sartre attracted a mass following, particularly among liberal intellectuals, who found him a new phenomenon. Whether seen as the only true philosophy of freedom or as a false consciousness disorienting a whole generation of revolutionaries, Sartre's version of existentialism was identified with freedom and revolution. It stood outside any ivory tower and, thereby, maintained its hold on the youth.

In 1964 Sartre published *Les Mots* and was awarded the Nobel Prize in literature for, in the words of the Nobel Committee, "his work which, rich in ideas and filled with the spirit of freedom and the quest for truth, has exerted a far-reaching influence on our age." Ever confrontational, Sartre declined the Nobel Prize because he saw his task as a writer as one that led him away from such honors. Accepting the Nobel, he felt, would make him "an institution." In refusing the award Sartre could maintain his credibility in a variety of eclectic causes, beginning with Castroism and culminating with Maoism. He received the notoriety he sought for his philosophical and political positions, most importantly, his opposition to the Vietnam War.

From the 1960s until early 1970s Sartre wrote parts of a projected multivolume study, *L'Idiot de la famille: Gustave Flaubert de 1821 à 1857* (1971; translated as *The Family Idiot: Gustave Flaubert, 1821–1857,* 1981), of which he had published only three volumes, 2,130 pages long, by 1971. Sartre sought to present a total biography of Gustave Flaubert—his childhood and adolescence; his fetishes, homoerotic affairs, and masochism; his self-proclaimed desire to be a woman; and his literary career. Sartre sought to present Flaubert through a Marxist lens and Sigmund Freud's concepts of the ego and id. Barring the occasionally dense prose of the work, *L'Idiot de la famille* is a minutely detailed psychoanalytic assessment from a Marxist and existentialist viewpoint. In many ways it summarizes Sartre's career and place in philosophy and literary culture as much as it exposes Flaubert. As a novelist Flaubert perceptively extracted the sociohistorical climate of his class and era. He brought into his fiction, often in thin disguise, the major and minor figures of his time. Much the same is true of Sartre. He lived, as the moral suggests, in interesting times and, using his connections to others in these times and prolific writings, secured his place in twentieth-century culture.

Sartre participated in demonstrations, in the sale of left-wing literature, and in the promotion of revolutionary ideas throughout the 1970s but wrote little after

1971. In 1972 the third volume of *L'Idiot de la famille* was published, but Sartre, now rapidly losing his eyesight, could not finish the dense, detailed project. He was a chain-smoker, and his health deteriorated; on 15 April 1980, with Arlette by his side, he died of a lung tumor. Reportedly, twenty-five thousand people attended his funeral.

The rector of the Caroline Institute, Sten Friberg, who spoke at the Nobel award banquet that Sartre declined to attend, assessed Sartre's place in literature and as an icon of his generation:

> The betterment of the world is the dream of every generation, and this applies particularly to the true poet and scientist. . . . And this is the source and strength of Sartre's inspiration. As an author and philosopher, Sartre has been a central figure in postwar literary and intellectual discussion–admired, debated, criticized. His explosive production, in its entirety, has the impress of a message; it has been sustained by a profoundly serious endeavor to improve the reader, the world at large. . . . Sartre's existentialism may be understood in the sense that the degree of happiness which an individual can hope to attain is governed by his willingness to take a stand in accordance with his ethos and to accept the consequences thereof; . . . In our age of standardization and complex social systems, awareness of the meaning of life for the individual has perhaps not been lost, but it has certainly been dulled; and it is as urgent for us today as it was in Nobel's time to uphold the ideals that were his.

While his works of philosophy are less read today than a generation ago, Jean-Paul Sartre's novels and plays, particularly *La Nausée* and *Huis clos,* remain influential for popularizing existentialism and for their careful debate on the human predicament during a time of immense conflict and change. Yet, as Sartre is quoted as saying in "Sartre at Seventy" (*The New York Review of Books,* 1975), "no man who undertakes a work of literature or philosophy ever finishes." Even in his blindness, Sartre refused to sever himself from the world of ideas, to accept any power over him, or to overlook oppositions. As one of the many artists influenced by Sartre, Beat poet Lawrence Ferlinghetti responded to criticism of his political involvement with a quote from Sartre on the need for engagement: "Only the dead are disengaged." By scope, volume, and acuity of his work, Sartre and his influence live.

Sartre's funeral cortege, 19 April 1980 (from Annie Cohen-Solal, Sartre: A Life, *translated by Anna Cancogni, 1987; Thomas Cooper Library, University of South Carolina)*

ners / Toronto: Maxwell Macmillan Canada / New York: Maxwell Macmillan International, 1993);

Beauvoir, ed., *Lettres à Sartre* (Paris: Gallimard, 1990); translated by Fahnestock and MacAfee as *Witness to My Life: The Letters of Jean-Paul Sartre to Simone de Beauvoir, 1926–1939* (New York: Scribners / Toronto: Maxwell Macmillan Canada / New York: Maxwell Macmillan International, 1992);

Arlette Elkaïm-Sartre, ed., *La reine Albemarle, ou, Le dernier touriste: Fragments* (Paris: Gallimard, 1991).

Interviews:

"After Budapest," *Evergreen Review,* 1, no. 1 (1957): 5–23;

"Interview with Oliver Todd," *Listener,* 57 (6 June 1957): 915–916;

François Giroud and others, "The Theatre," translated by Richard Seaver, *Evergreen Review,* 4 (January–February 1960): 143–152;

Letters:

Simone de Beauvoir, *Lettres au Castor et à quelques autres: 1940–1963* (Paris: Gallimard, 1983); translated by Lee Fahnestock and Norman MacAfee as *Quiet Moments in a War: The Letters of Jean-Paul Sartre to Simone de Beauvoir, 1940–1963* (New York: Scrib-

Oreste F. Pucciani, "Sartre," *Tulane Drama Review,* 5 (Spring 1961): 12–18;

Jacqueline Piatier, "Sartre," *Vogue,* 145 (1 January 1965): 94–95, 159;

Eric Mothram, "The Condition of the Novel: Selection from the Conference of European Writers at Leningrad," *New Left Review,* 29 (January–February 1965): 19–40;

Madeleine Gobeil, "Jean-Paul Sartre–Candid Conversation," *Playboy,* 12 (May 1965): 69–76;

Gobeil, "Sartre Talks of Beauvoir," translated by Bernard Frechtman, *Vogue,* 146 (July 1965): 72–73;

"Imperialist Morality," *New Left Review,* 41 (January–February 1967): 3–10;

"Interview with Michel Contat," *L'Idiot international,* 10 (September 1970);

Michel Contat, "Sartre at Seventy," *New York Review of Books,* 7 August 1975, pp. 10–17;

Benny Lévy, *Le nom de l'homme: Dialogue avec Sartre* (Lagrasse: Verdier, 1984);

Lévy, *L'Espoir maintenant: Les entretiens de 1980* (Paris: Broché, 1991); translated by Adrian van den Hoven as *Hope Now: The 1980 Interviews* (Chicago: University of Chicago Press, 1996).

Biographies:

Simone de Beauvoir, *La Force de l'âge* (Paris: Gallimard, 1960); translated by Peter Green as *The Prime of Life* (Cleveland: World, 1962; London: Deutsch/ Weidenfeld & Nicolson, 1963);

Beauvoir, *Les Cérémonie des adieux, suivi de Entretiens avec Jean-Paul Sartre* (Paris: Gallimard, 1981); translated by Patrick O'Brian as *Adieux: A Farewell to Sartre* (New York: Pantheon, 1984);

Annie Cohen-Solal, *Sartre: A Life,* translated by Anna Cancogni (New York: Pantheon, 1987);

John Gerassi, *Jean-Paul Sartre: Hated Conscience of His Century,* volume 1: *Protestant or Protester?* (Chicago & London: University of Chicago Press, 1989).

References:

David Archard, *Marxism and Existentialism: The Political Theory of Sartre and Merleau-Ponty* (Aldershot, U.K. & Brookfield, Vt.: Gregg Revivals, 1992);

Magin Borrajo, *Moral Perspectives in Jean-Paul Sartre's Existentialism and Authentic Morality* (Manila: UST Press, 1967);

Germaine Brée, *Camus and Sartre: Crisis and Commitment* (New York: Dell, 1972);

Max Charlesworth, *The Existentialists and Jean-Paul Sartre* (New York: St. Martin's Press, 1976);

Nicola Chiaromonte, "Sartre versus Camus: A Political Quarrel," *Partisan Review,* 9, no. 6 (1952): 680;

Andre Gorz, "Jean-Paul Sartre: From Consciousness to Praxis," *Philosophy Today,* 19 (Winter 1975): 287–292;

Maurice Granston, *The Quintessence of Sartrism* (New York: Harper & Row, 1969);

Christina Howells, ed., *The Cambridge Companion to Sartre* (Cambridge & New York: Cambridge University Press, 1992);

Edith Kern, ed., *Sartre: A Collection of Critical Essays* (Englewood Cliffs, N.J.: Prentice-Hall, 1962);

Charles C. Lemert, ed., *Intellectuals and Politics: Social Theory in a Changing World* (Newbury Park, Cal.: Sage, 1991), pp. 47–73;

William L. McBride, *Sartre and Existentialism: Philosophy, Politics, Ethics, the Psyche, Literature, and Aesthetics* (New York: Garland, 1997);

McBride, *Sartre's Political Theory* (Bloomington: Indiana University Press, 1991);

Ronald Santoni, "The Cynicism of Sartre's 'Bad Faith,'" *International Philosophical Quarterly,* 30 (January–March 1990): 3–16;

"Sartre at Seventy," *New York Review of Books,* 22, no. 13 (7 August 1975);

"Sartre on the Nobel Prize," translated by Richard Howard, *New York Review of Books,* 3 (17 December 1964): 5–6;

Michael Scriven, *Jean-Paul Sartre: Politics and Culture in Postwar France* (Basingstoke: Macmillan / New York: St. Martin's Press, 1999);

James F. Sheridan Jr., *Sartre: The Radical Conversion* (Athens: Ohio University Press, 1969).

Papers:

Major collections of Jean-Paul Sartre's papers are the Jean-Paul Sartre Collection of the Beinecke Rare Book and Manuscript Library, Yale University, and the John Gerassi Collection of Jean-Paul Sartre, Beinecke Rare Book and Manuscript Library, Yale University, 1964–1985, which comprises thirty-six interviews from 12 March 1971 to 4 November 1973.

Georg Simmel
(1 March 1858 – 26 September 1918)

Matthew Potolsky
University of Utah

BOOKS: *Das Wesen der Materie nach Kants physischer Monadologie* (Berlin: Druck der Norddeutschen Buchdruckerei, 1888);

Über sociale Differenzierung: Sociologische und psychologische Untersuchungen (Leipzig: Duncker & Humblot, 1890);

Die Probleme der Geschichtsphilosophie: Eine erkenntnistheoretische Studie (Leipzig: Duncker & Humblot, 1892; revised and enlarged, 1905); edited and translated, with an introduction, by Guy Oakes as *The Problems of the Philosophy of History: An Epistemological Essay* (New York: Free Press, 1977);

Einleitung in die Moralwissenschaft: Eine Kritik der ethischen Grundbegriffe, 2 volumes (Berlin: Hertz, 1892, 1893);

Philosophie des Geldes (Leipzig: Duncker & Humblot, 1900); translated by Tom Bottomore and David Frisby as *The Philosophy of Money* (London & Boston: Routledge & Kegan Paul, 1978; enlarged, 1990);

Kant: Sechzehn Vorlesungen gehalten an der Berliner Universität (Leipzig: Duncker & Humblot, 1904);

Philosophie der Mode (Berlin: Pan, 1905); translated as "Fashion," *International Quarterly,* 10 (October 1904): 130–155;

Kant und Goethe (Berlin: Marquardt, 1906);

Die Religion (Frankfurt am Main: Rütten & Loening, 1906); translated by Curt Rosenthal as *Sociology of Religion* (New York: Philosophical Library, 1959);

Schopenhauer und Nietzsche: Ein Vortragszyklus (Leipzig: Duncker & Humblot, 1907); translated by Helmut Loiskandl, Deena Weinstein, and Michael Weinstein as *Schopenhauer and Nietzsche* (Amherst: University of Massachusetts Press, 1986);

Soziologie: Untersuchungen über die Formen der Vergesellschaftung (Leipzig: Duncker & Humblot, 1908); excerpts translated by Kurt H. Wolff and Reinhard Bendix as *Conflict; The Web of Group Affiliations* (Glencoe, Ill.: Free Press, 1955);

Hauptprobleme der Philosophie (Leipzig: Göschen, 1910);

Georg Simmel (from Kurt H. Wolff, ed., Georg Simmel, 1858–1918, *1959; Thomas Cooper Library, University of South Carolina)*

Philosophische Kultur: Gesammelte Essais (Leipzig: Klinkhardt, 1911);

Goethe (Leipzig: Klinkhardt & Biermann, 1913);

Rembrandt: Ein kunstphilosophischer Versuch (Leipzig: Wolff, 1916); translated by Peter Etzkorn and Helmut Staubmann as *Georg Simmel on Rembrandt: A Philosophical Meditation on Art* (London & New York: Routledge, 2001);

Das Problem der historischen Zeit (Berlin: Reuther & Reichhard, 1916);

Grundfragen der Soziologie (Individuum und Gesellschaft) (Berlin & Leipzig: Göschen, 1917);

Der Krieg und die geistigen Entscheidungen: Reden und Aufsätze (Munich: Duncker & Humblot, 1917);

Der Konflikt der modernen Kultur: Ein Vortrag (Munich: Duncker & Humblot, 1918);

Lebensanschauung: Vier metaphysische Kapitel (Munich & Leipzig: Duncker & Humblot, 1918);

Vom Wesen des historischen Verstehens (Berlin: Mittler, 1918);

Zur Philosophie der Kunst: Philosophische und kunstphilosophische Aufsätze, edited by Gertrud Simmel (Potsdam: Kiepenheuer, 1922);

Schulpädagogik: Vorlesungen gehalten an der Universität Strassburg, edited by Karl Hauter (Osterwieck/ Harz: Zickfeldt, 1922);

Fragmente und Aufsätze: Aus dem Nachlass und Veröffentlichungen der letzten Jahre, edited by Gertrud Kantorowicz (Munich: Drei Masken, 1923);

Das individuelle Gesetz: Philosophische Exkurse, edited by Michael Landmann (Frankfurt am Main: Suhrkamp, 1968);

Gesamtausgabe, 19 volumes, edited by Otthein Rammstedt (Frankfurt am Main: Suhrkamp, 1989–   ).

Editions and Collections: *Rembrandtstudien* (Basel: Schwabe, 1953);

Brücke und Tür: Essays des Philosophen zur Geschichte, Religion, Kunst und Gesellschaft, edited by Michael Landmann (Stuttgart: Koehler, 1957);

Philosophische Kultur: Über das Abenteuer, die Geschlechter und die Krise der Moderne: Gesammelte Essais, afterword by Jürgen Habermas (Berlin: Wagenbach, 1983);

Schriften zur Soziologie: Eine Auswahl, edited by Heinz-Jürgen Dahme and Otthein Rammstedt (Frankfurt am Main: Suhrkamp, 1983);

Schriften zur Philosophie und Soziologie der Gesclechter, edited by Dahme and Klaus Christian Köhnke (Frankfurt am Main: Suhrkamp, 1985);

Gesammelte schriften zur religionssoziologie, edited by Horst Jürgen Helle (Berlin: Duncker & Humblot, 1989);

Vom Wesen der Moderne: Essays zur Philosophie und Ästhetik, edited by Werner Jung (Hamburg: Junius, 1990);

Georg Simmel in Wien: Texte und Kontexte aus dem Wien der Jahrhundertwende, edited by David Frisby (Vienna: WUV, 2000).

Editions in English: *The Sociology of Georg Simmel,* translated and edited, with an introduction, by Kurt H. Wolff (Glencoe, Ill.: Free Press, 1950);

Georg Simmel, 1858–1918, edited by Wolff (Columbus: Ohio State University Press, 1959); republished as *Essays on Sociology, Philosophy, and Aesthetics* (New York: Harper & Row, 1965);

The Conflict in Modern Culture and Other Essays, translated, with an introduction, by K. Peter Etzkorn (New York: Teachers College Press, 1968)–includes "The Conflict in Modern Culture" *[Der Konflikt der modernen Kultur: Ein Vortrag],* pp. 11–25;

On Individuality and Social Forms: Selected Writings, edited, with an introduction, by Donald N. Levine (Chicago: University of Chicago Press, 1971);

Georg Simmel: Sociologist and European, translated by D. E. Jenkinson and others (Sunbury-on-Thames: Nelson, 1976; New York: Barnes & Noble, 1976);

Essays on Interpretation in Social Science, edited and translated, with an introduction, by Guy Oakes (Totowa, N.J.: Rowman & Littlefield, 1980; Manchester: University of Manchester Press, 1980)–includes "The Problem of Historical Time" *[Das Problem der historischen Zeit]* and "On the Nature of Historical Understanding" *[Vom Wesen des historischen Verstehens];*

Georg Simmel on Woman, Sexuality, and Love, translated, with an introduction, by Oakes (New Haven: Yale University Press, 1984);

Essays on Religion, edited and translated by Horst Jürgen Helle and Ludwig Nieder (New Haven: Yale University Press, 1997);

Simmel on Culture, edited by David Frisby and Mike Featherstone (London & Thousand Oaks, Cal.: Sage, 1997).

OTHER: "Die Großstädte und das Geistesleben," in *Die Großstadt: Vorträge und Aufsätze zur Städteausstellung,* edited by Karl Bücher and others (Dresden: Zahn & Jaensch, 1903), pp. 185–206; translated by Edward A. Shils as "The Metropolis and Mental Life," in *Syllabus and Selected Readings, Second-Year Course in the Study of Contemporary Society (Social Science II): Syllabus and Selected Readings,* edited by Harry David Gideonse and others (Chicago: University of Chicago Bookstore, 1936), pp. 221–238.

Georg Simmel is one of the more paradoxical figures in twentieth-century thought. Among the founders of sociology as a discipline, and the influential teacher of many of the most important German social theorists of the modern era, Simmel left behind him no students devoted to his project and no school of research. As Jürgen Habermas writes, in his afterword to the 1983 edition of Simmel's book *Philosophische Kultur* (Philosophical Culture, 1911), Simmel "changed the mode of observation, the themes and style of writing of a whole generation of intellectuals." Yet, there remains no consistent academic method that can be traced directly to his teachings. Trained as a philosopher, Simmel is best known for his contributions to the nascent discipline of sociology. He wrote on a remarkably wide range of questions, however–from religion to fashion, ethics to history, flirtation to social conflict, the psychology of urban experience to the philosophy of Immanuel Kant. He was an early advocate of women's rights as well as an apologist for German aggression in World War I. Yet, in few of the fields to which he contributed is his work considered central–or even in many cases recognized at all. Despite the fact that the attentive reader of Simmel can find traces of his thought, and echoes of his ideas, across the breadth of twentieth-century thought, Simmel's name itself is only rarely heard and his reputation has been subject to great fluctuations. The increasing number of English translations of his writings and the ongoing publication of his complete works in German have made Simmel available to more readers. The lasting legacy of his ideas remains uncertain, however.

Part of what makes Simmel's legacy so difficult to pin down is precisely what makes his works so valuable. Unlike his more systematic contemporaries, such as Emile Durkheim and Max Weber, Simmel tends to move from topic to topic. His medium of thought is the brilliant insight, and his preferred literary form is the essay. As a consequence he often sacrifices the overall unity of his arguments to the force of a single penetrating idea, image, or line of thought. Simmel's student György Lukács went so far as to call his teacher a sociological "impressionist," and many commentators have pointed to the fragmentary quality of his writing and thought. His works are not incoherent; however, somewhat like the modern urban milieu he loved and was among the first to analyze, Simmel's writings produce a series of intellectual shocks that are difficult to reconcile with each other. Simmel relies to a great extent–perhaps too great an extent, his critics claim–on the force of metaphor and analogy, a reliance that often brings his works closer to poetry than to cultural theory. These analogies are drawn from a striking range of disciplines. Thus, one finds philosophical terminology in conjunction with insights from experimental psychology, sociological distinctions defined by analogies from aesthetics, and economic claims supported by linguistic concepts. In many ways, the fecundity of his mind and his willingness to join seemingly unrelated schools of thought make Simmel a key forerunner of the interdisciplinary pursuits that have marked so much Western cultural theory since the 1960s.

Despite the variety of his subjects and disciplinary references, though, Simmel does work from a core set of methods that define his thirty-year scholarly career and give an overriding unity to his writings. Simmel's mind is deeply dialectical, always looking for the reciprocal relationships that define seemingly autonomous social phenomena. His essays often seek to demonstrate that concepts taken to be unified (such as value or the social group) are in fact the product of mutually antagonistic forces. Simmel is also consistently interested in the particularities of social interaction. The aim of his studies, he writes in the preface to his book *Philosophie des Geldes* (1900; translated as *The Philosophy of Money*, 1978), is to find "in each of life's details the totality of its meaning." The great interest, as well as the great difficulty, of Simmel's works arguably lies in just this effort to build a bridge between the mundane details of daily life and the totality of the social world.

Georg Simmel was born on 1 March 1858 in Berlin, the child of Edward Simmel, a prosperous local businessman, and Flora (née Bodstein). Simmel was the youngest of seven children, growing up with one brother and five sisters. Both of Simmel's parents were born Jewish, but each converted to Christianity independently (his father was Catholic and his mother Lutheran) before their marriage in 1838. Simmel was raised as a Lutheran, but like so many other assimilated Jews in turn-of-the-century Germany, he suffered from both official and unofficial anti-Semitism throughout his life. When his father died in 1874, Simmel became the ward of a family friend, Julius Friedländer, who owned a music publishing house. Simmel remained distant from his mother for most of his youth. After graduating from gymnasium (roughly the equivalent of an American high school), Simmel enrolled at the University of Berlin in 1876. He concentrated his studies on history and philosophy–he worked with the well-known philosopher Eduard Zeller and the historian Theodor Mommsen–and gained familiarity with a wide range of academic subjects. His second doctoral field was medieval Italian literature, and he was also thoroughly trained in the latest methods of psychology, sociology, anthropology, and art history. In 1881 he received his doctorate in philosophy, on the strength of his thesis, *Das Wesen der Materie nach Kants physischer Monadologie* (The Nature of Matter according to Kant's Physical Monadology). This thesis was in fact the second thesis he submitted to the faculty; his first thesis, an essay on ethnomusicology, was rejected for its aphoristic style and for its many misspellings and grammatical errors.

In 1885 Simmel became a *privatdozent* (an unpaid lecturer reliant on student fees) at the University of Berlin, choosing this less prestigious position rather than leaving his native city for potentially more lucrative possibilities elsewhere. He continued to serve in this position until 1900. Despite his lack of academic recognition, Simmel's courses on logic, ethics, and sociology became highly popular with students, a fact that aroused considerable jealousy among his superiors. In 1887 Simmel began to lecture publicly at the university. According to

8

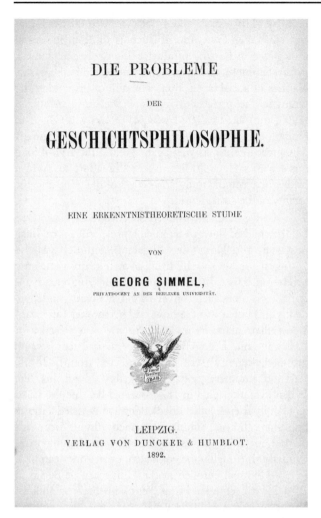

DIE PROBLEME

DER

GESCHICHTSPHILOSOPHIE.

EINE ERKENNTNISTHEORETISCHE STUDIE

VON

GEORG SIMMEL,
PRIVATDOCENT AN DER BERLINER UNIVERSITÄT.

LEIPZIG.
VERLAG VON DUNCKER & HUMBLOT.
1892.

Title page for Simmel's 1892 book (translated as The Problems
of the Philosophy of History: An Epistemological
Study, *1977), in which he attempts to "emancipate the
mind" from the influence of the past (William T.
Young Library, University of Kentucky)*

the recollections of his students, he was a brilliant public speaker, and his lectures on such figures as Kant, Arthur Schopenhauer, Charles Darwin, and Friedrich Nietzsche soon were important intellectual events for the cultural elite in Berlin and were often attended by hundreds of auditors. Simmel was also among the first lecturers in Germany to allow women to attend his university lectures as "guest students." Simmel's lectures, according to one of his students from this period, Arthur Salz, had the quality of improvised soliloquies. "The listener had the impression," Salz recalls in an essay included in the volume *Georg Simmel, 1858–1918* (1959), "that he experienced the finding of truth in *statu nascendi.*"

Although his teaching did not provide a steady stream of income, Simmel's guardian left him a considerable fortune after he died. As a result he was able to live comfortably throughout his life. Secure in his economic

status, in July 1890 Simmel married Gertrud Kinel, the daughter of a railroad engineer, whom he met at the home of a mutual acquaintance. They remained married until Simmel's death and in 1891 had one son, Hans, who later became a professor of medicine at the University of Jena. As his fame grew, Simmel's house became a gathering place for artists and intellectuals in Berlin. His courses remained popular, and he was becoming acquainted with the leading artists and intellectuals in western Europe. Simmel counted among his friends in this period Weber, the philosophers Edmund Husserl and Henri Bergson, and the poets Stefan George and Rainer Maria Rilke. He also corresponded with the French sculptor Auguste Rodin. Gertrud Simmel also was a recognized thinker and published books on religion and human sexuality under the pseudonym Marie-Luise Enkendorf. In the late 1880s Simmel began lecturing on sociology at the University of Berlin, and his earliest publications arose directly out of this context. Two of his earliest books in many ways set out the key sociological topic that occupied Simmel throughout his career: the fate of the individual. Simmel's first major work of social theory, *Über sociale Differenzierung: Sociologische und psychologische Untersuchungen* (On Social Differentiation: Sociological and Psychological Studies, 1890), takes up the question explicitly. Reflecting a broad interest among social thinkers of the period in the division of labor in society and strongly influenced by the social Darwinism of Herbert Spencer, Simmel focuses in this book on the evolutionary processes by which individuals differentiate themselves from and within the social group as a whole. Human beings, he suggests, are basically differentiating animals. Accordingly, any understanding of society must take account of the role that the process of differentiation plays in the development of society. In small groups, Simmel argues, the individual is subsumed under the collective—a family, a tribe, or a guild. Individual and society form an undifferentiated continuum. In larger groups, however, both internal and external competition lead to greater differentiation among individuals and between the individual and society. The larger the social circle, the more individuals must "specialize" in order to distinguish themselves and survive. Both individual and society are not preexisting unities but the products of reciprocal differentiation.

Simmel also brought the question of individuality into his considerations of social theory itself. In his second major work, *Die Probleme der Geschichtsphilosophie: Eine erkenntnistheoretische Studie* (translated as *The Problems of the Philosophy of History: An Epistemological Study,* 1977), first published in 1892 and significantly revised and expanded in 1905, Simmel attempts, in his words, "to emancipate the mind" from the potentially overwhelming force of the past. Arguing against the prevailing historicism of the nineteenth century, he argues that history is as much a creation of individuals as it is the creator of them. In pursuing this claim Simmel follows the lead of one of his main intellectual influences, Kant. Kant was interested in the general conditions for the possibility of knowledge. Knowledge, he argued, is always structured by the powers and limitations of the human intellect. He does not mean that one's image of the world is wholly subjective or biased. Rather, he suggests that knowledge is a product of mental structures rather than a more or less faulty perception of a real world that could be reached by other means. Simmel seeks to apply Kant's insights into individual epistemology to the scholarly study of history. In the preface to the book he argues that, much as Kant freed the ego from the ironclad laws of nature by showing that those laws reside in the mind itself, so historical inquiry must free itself from the idea that history is governed by suprapersonal laws that determine people and limit their freedom. "Consider the stream of existence in which the mind discovers itself," Simmel writes. "It is the mind itself which maps out the shores of this stream and determines the rhythm of its waves. Only under these conditions does the mind constitute itself as 'history.'"

Throughout the 1890s Simmel published essays on a wide range of sociological, political, artistic, and philosophical topics. He also began writing to a more general readership, regularly contributing brief essays, commentaries, reviews, and even original fables to newspapers and popular magazines. His well-known essays on the bridge and the door, on the alpine journey, and on the picture frame originally appeared in these popular forums. In 1892–1893 Simmel published his two-volume work, *Einleitung in die Moralwissenschaft: Eine Kritik der ethischen Grundbegriffe* (Introduction to the Science of Morals: A Critique of the Fundamental Principles of Ethics), the culmination of nearly a decade of teaching courses on ethics. Simmel's next major publication, and arguably his most important and systematic work in cultural theory, was *Philosophie des Geldes*. Published in 1900, Simmel's book measures the social and psychological effects of the money form. Rather than investigating the rise and fall of economic systems or the social effects of economic policies, Simmel looks at the way that money itself—its strange but powerful philosophical status—governs people's relationship to the world. He seeks, in his words, "to construct a new storey beneath historical materialism," to show how the facts of economic life have their ultimate source in human cognition.

Simmel begins by discussing the concept of value and the social practice of exchange. Value, he notes, is a curious phenomenon. People spend their entire lives judging values, but they have little conscious sense of where these values come from and why they seem so important. Although value can only be a subjective feeling, it nevertheless comes to seem an objective property of things. For Simmel, value is an embodiment of desire. People value those things that they want and ascribe higher value to those things that are scarce or that demand some expense of energy to acquire. Over time, the object "absorbs" subjective desire and comes to gain an autonomous significance and an intrinsic value. It represents people's desire to them as an independent and objective quality. This independence of value underwrites what Simmel considers the most basic sociological relationship: exchange. He notes that most human relationships—from conversation to sacrifice and the formation of groups—can be understood in terms of exchange. Exchange is not just a matter of giving and taking, however. Rather, it presupposes the possibility of mediating among values. Two people do not simply exchange things; they exchange things that have equivalent values. Exchange thus arises from and reinforces the objectification of desire that makes value possible in the first place. It gives the fleeting and relative desires of individual humans beings a stable and autonomous existence.

In this context money becomes both possible and necessary. Money is the next stage in the objectification of human desire. Much as desire is "absorbed" by objects, so money comes to absorb value. The process of exchange assumes that different objects are somehow equivalent. As such, it necessitates a measure of value that allows objects to be compared. Money arises as the expression of exchangeability itself. It is, as Simmel writes, "value turned into a substance, the value of things without the things themselves." Money stands "above" valuable objects and turns qualities into quantities. For this reason, money can determine value without itself having any value (as a substance) or having anything in common with the objects for which one exchanges it.

Although it lacks value as a substance, money does produce effects that extend beyond its basic sociological function of enabling exchange. The defining feature of money is its lack of any inner significance. It is, Simmel writes, "an absolute means." Yet, the emptiness of the money form has important sociological consequences. For example, because money can buy anything, the value of a given quantity of money seems to exceed the value of any particular object for which money may be exchanged. It allows people to choose when and where to acquire objects and opens up the possibility of speculation and investment. Money thus increases individual freedom. The ease with which money can be accumulated also allows for social mobility among those for whom the ownership of land or other property is forbidden. The emptiness of money, however, produces new social maladies as well. Instead of remaining a mere means, Simmel suggests, money can be taken as an end

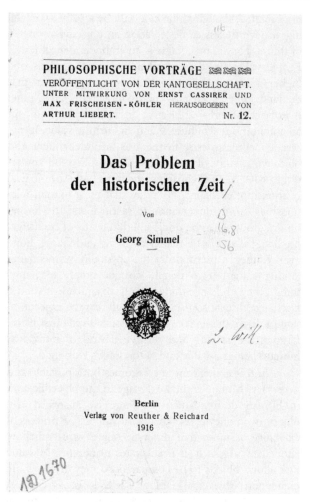

PHILOSOPHISCHE VORTRÄGE
VERÖFFENTLICHT VON DER KANTGESELLSCHAFT.
UNTER MITWIRKUNG VON ERNST CASSIRER UND
MAX FRISCHEISEN-KÖHLER HERAUSGEGEBEN VON
ARTHUR LIEBERT.   Nr. **12.**

Das Problem
der historischen Zeit

Von

Georg Simmel

Berlin
Verlag von Reuther & Reichard
1916

Title page for the first of three essays Simmel published between 1916 and 1918 on the epistemology of history (Thomas Cooper Library, University of South Carolina)

in itself. Both greed and avarice, although psychologically quite distinct, treat money as a final purpose. The same is true of social types such as the miser and the spendthrift, who pathologically overvalue or undervalue money. Cynicism and what Simmel calls the "blasé attitude" are also products of the money form. Both approaches to life refuse to assign a supreme value to anything human; as such, they take a position "above" value that is only made possible by the money form. Indeed, in its emptiness, and in its insistence on the relativity of all values, money is potentially "the most terrible destroyer of form." Money levels distinctions and renders everything potentially the same. Simmel also charts the way that money comes to represent personal values for people. Here he examines, among other social phenomena, monetary payments for murder, the idea of marrying for money, prostitution, bribery, social distinction, and wage labor. In each case, money is made equivalent with human life.

In the final chapter of the book, Simmel charts the relationship between money and the modern "style of life." How, he asks, has money shaped the way people think about their place in and their relationship to the world? Simmel begins by noting the emphasis money gives to intellectual over emotional responses to the world. Like money, the intellect is a characterless tool; it levels, analyzes, and compares. The rise of money thus supports a rise in the value of the intellect. Money transforms the world into units that can be weighed, measured, and calculated. It makes people objective, rational, and abstract. Similarly, money leads to the dominance of what Simmel calls "objective culture" over what he calls "subjective culture." Simmel notes that, while culture is the product of subjective impulses, it seems an autonomous and objective entity. Money accelerates this objectification of culture by its objectification of reality itself. "Cultural objects," Simmel writes, "increasingly evolve into an interconnected enclosed world that has increasingly fewer points at which the subjective soul can interpose its will and feelings." Money represents the preponderance of objective over subjective distinctions and thus sends people constantly in search of new sensations, new ways of trying to overcome the gap between subject and object. Fashion, changes in artistic style, the rapid pace of city life, the rise of leisure travel—all can be traced, for Simmel, to the effect of money on the style of life. In the end, money becomes both the cause and the symbol of the relativity of existence itself. In its leveling, atomizing, and objectifying power, money shapes the nature of reality.

In 1900, after several unsuccessful attempts to gain a more secure academic position at the University of Berlin, Simmel was named *Professor Ausserordentlicher* (Professor Extraordinarius), at the rather advanced age of forty-two. The title was purely honorary and included no salary, but it did at least provide official recognition for Simmel's increasing public profile as a social theorist and public speaker. By this time he was becoming known around the world as a philosopher and sociologist, and his works were being translated into many languages. In 1903 Simmel published a lecture that remains among his best-known contributions to cultural theory, "Die Großstädte und das Geistesleben" (translated as "The Metropolis and Mental Life," 1936). Developing a key thesis from *Philosophie des Geldes*, Simmel argues that the modern city produces a new kind of social relationship and a new kind of person. City life is characterized by shocks of nervous stimulation. Jostled by other people and surrounded by the noise of traffic and industry, the city dweller lives in an entirely different world from the rural resident. As a consequence, city dwellers develop a defensive response to the danger of being overwhelmed by sensation: they react with the head and not the heart, using the distancing power of the intellect to ward off the emotional shocks of the metropolitan world. This recourse to the intellect has, Simmel asserts, many consequences for city life. For example, it helps explain the long association of the city with economic exchange. Like the urban environment, money encourages a rationalization of life; money is thus especially at home in the city. For Simmel, the metropolis also encourages a more cosmopolitan and open-minded relationship to the world. For this reason, the city is commonly associated with personal freedom. Unlike the rural environment, in which everyone knows everyone else, the urban environment allows for anonymity and greater autonomy. The metropolis also creates new kinds of boundaries between individuals, however. Metropolitan interactions are marked strongly by reserve and by the "blasé attitude" Simmel had analyzed in *Philosophie des Geldes*. Both responses allow the city residents to avoid potentially overwhelming emotional interactions with the many people that cross their path. Thus, what seems to be rudeness is in fact part of a complicated defense mechanism. This apparent rudeness is, Simmel suggests, the price one pays for the benefits of urban life.

The period between 1904 and 1908 was a fertile one for Simmel. In addition to two works on major philosophical figures (*Kant: Sechzehn Vorlesungen gehalten an der Berliner Universität* [Kant: Sixteen Lectures Given at the University of Berlin, 1904] and *Schopenhauer und Nietzsche: Ein Vortragszyklus* [1907]) and a book of cultural history (*Kant und Goethe,* 1906), Simmel published influential sociological analyses of religion (*Die Religion,* 1906; translated as *Sociology of Religion,* 1959) and of fashion (*Philosophie der Mode,* 1905; translated as "Fashion," 1904) and continued to write prolifically for newspapers and magazines. In 1908 he made yet another unsuccessful effort to gain a stable academic position. With the support of his friend Weber, Simmel was nominated for the second chair of philosophy at the University of Heidelberg. Although the faculty at the university was favorably inclined toward his candidacy, Simmel's hopes were thwarted by anti-Semitism, as surviving reports make clear. The same year, he published what became his most influential work of social theory, *Soziologie: Untersuchungen über die Formen der Vergesellschaftung* (Sociology: Studies in the Forms of Sociation). Although this book is more essayistic than systematic (it was comprised largely of articles published over the previous fifteen years), it is united by a consistent methodological focus. Accordingly, it became the work that established Simmel's position as a founder of academic sociology.

The introductory chapter, "The Problem of Sociology," first published in a different form in 1894, introduces a concept crucial to Simmel's mature thought: the social form. Every social act, from a casual meeting to the creation of a family, arises from the union of individual interests and motivations with relatively fixed institutions, practices, or patterns of behavior. Simmel calls these fixed and seemingly objective aspects of interaction—the manifold rubrics under which individuals are brought together in groups—social forms. Individual interests and motivations, the "materials" or "contents" of social interaction—love, hunger, desire—are not in and of themselves social. Rather, they become social when they are embodied in a specific form. Hunger alone, for example, is an individual feeling, but embodied in the form of a meal, it becomes the driving force behind a social gathering. Sociation *(Vergesellschaftung)* is the process by which individual motivations are unified in such forms. Simmel argues that both individual contents and social forms are abstractions: forms cannot be discerned apart from the individuals who use them, and individual motivations are incoherent apart from their formal embodiment. Yet, despite their entanglement with individual contents, the forms seem autonomous and objective. The same form can embody radically different motivations, and similar motivations can find expression in a wide variety of different forms. The human experience of social interaction is so determined by social forms, Simmel argues, that "society" as such does not, strictly speaking, exist. There is, in other words, no organic unity called society—only many shifting individual interests embodied in a complicated network of conventional forms. For Simmel, the task of sociology lies above all in the analysis of these forms.

The subsequent chapters in the book examine a broad spectrum of social forms, with often surprising conclusions. Simmel offers "formal" accounts of, among other topics, domination and subordination, the role of numbers in the constitution of groups (including an important analysis of how a "third party" radically changes group dynamics), poverty, the nobility, social space, the senses, hereditary offices, and the self-preservation of social groups. He also returns to two topics first addressed in *Über sociale Differenzierung:* the intersection of social circles and the relationship between the enlargement of the group and the development of the individual.

Two of the most suggestive chapters, "Der Streit" (Conflict) and "Das Geheimnis und die geheime Gesellschaft" (Secrecy and the Secret Society), concern the "forms" of secrecy and conflict. Both secrecy and conflict would seem to be opposed to group formation. Secrecy separates the individual from the group, the private from the public, and conflicts threaten to tear groups apart. For Simmel, however, both forms are in fact essential to the constitution of society. Simmel argues, for example, that all social relationships can be defined in terms of the number and kinds of secrets one keeps from others. Married couples keep fewer secrets from one another than casual acquaintances do, and people share secrets with doctors and lawyers that they may keep from even their closest friends. An awareness of and ability to manage secrecy is, to this extent, essential to the formation of any social group. Secrecy also contributes to people's sense of social status. The secret is a kind of adornment that sets people off from others. Those who hold secrets seem powerful, and the powerful seem more mysterious than other people do. For Simmel, secrecy is thus best understood as a sociological "technique," a form that can contain all manner of individual contents.

Conflict is, likewise, a powerful but unrecognized form of sociation. Most people would acknowledge that conflict is a kind of social interaction, albeit a highly negative one. Simmel argues, however, that conflict in fact has a positive, indeed essential, sociological function. All social groups are made up of widely divergent interests. In fact, the members of a group often have more differences than similarities. Conflict ensures that those differences do not break the group apart. By highlighting the group's distinction from its enemies, conflict allows the group to define itself. The social group, in other words, recognizes itself as a group only by means of its opposition to another group. Opposition does not merely sustain social groups in times of crisis, but actually contributes to their constitution. Common ties alone, Simmel argues, are not enough to form a social structure; rather, such structures only emerge in concert with relations of conflict. Thus, the conflicts that seem to threaten society are instead an indispensable social form.

Soziologie also includes Simmel's influential discussion of the stranger. Although one typically thinks of wandering as the opposite of attachment, Simmel suggests that the sociological form of the stranger is a synthesis of these two tendencies. Strangers are fixed within a group or a spatial circle, but their position is defined by their status as outsiders. The group recognizes the stranger, but only as being outside or other. The stranger is thus an odd union of similarity and difference, insider and outsider, proximity and remoteness. Simmel notes that the stranger is often associated with economic activity and with personal or social mobility. The foreign trader or the Jewish merchant—two classic examples of the stranger—relate to the established social group through money. Each potentially relates to all the individuals in the group, but not by means of locality, kinship, or occupation. The stranger is also often associated with objectivity. As an outsider, the stranger is often called upon, formally or informally, to mediate disputes within the group. Having no definite roots and released from custom and local prejudices, the stranger becomes the recipient of confessions or a source of advice. The synthesis of closeness and distance that marks the

stranger also, Simmel argues, enters into people's most intimate relationships. Love seems to be the closest of human interactions, and yet the feelings that define love are the potential property of all people. Relationships that people feel to be unique, Simmel thus suggests, are always haunted by an element of strangeness.

In the years following the publication of *Soziologie,* Simmel became one of the leading European intellectual figures. His works were widely read, debated, translated, and reviewed, and he was the admired teacher of such students as Lukács, Ernst Bloch, and Karl Mannheim, each of whom later made important contributions to social thought. Through the initiative of the University of Chicago professors Albion Small and Robert Park, he also began to attract attention among American academic sociologists, and many of his important writings in the field were being translated into English. In 1909 Simmel and Weber founded the Deutsche Gesellschaft für Soziologie (German Sociological Association). Yet, Simmel's academic career continued to founder. He was recommended in 1910 for a chair of philosophy at the small Prussian University of Greifswald but was again turned down. In this same year he published one of his major systematic writings in academic philosophy, *Hauptprobleme der Philosophie* (Main Problems of Philosophy, 1910). The following year, Simmel received an honorary doctorate of politics from Freiburg University. This honor, too, led to no professional advancement.

In 1911 Simmel published a collection of essays, *Philosophische Kultur.* This collection, which sold more than ten thousand copies in its first edition, includes essays on the definition of culture, on the artists Rodin and Michelangelo, on the culture of women, and on such other diverse topics as the ruin, the handle, flirtation, the adventure, and the "personality" of God. Simmel explains in his introduction to the volume that the term "philosophical culture" refers not to any theories or dogmas of culture (religious, metaphysical, or artistic) but rather to a critical attitude toward the world that looks at the forms of modern culture, not their established contents. In one of the best-known essays from the volume, "Der Begriff und die Tragodie der Kultur" (The Concept and Tragedy of Culture), Simmel takes up the distinction between "objective" and "subjective" culture that he introduced in *Philosophie des Geldes* to describe the inevitable alienation that marks people's relationship to the social world. Although culture is made up of ideas created by individuals, these ideas come to seem external and objective, independent of any particular person. Much as subjective desires become objective values, so ideas free themselves of their subjective origins. To the extent, Simmel argues, that culture is thus embodied in objects, it can never wholly belong to any individual subject. Objects obey their own developmental logic, and as a result there will always be something alien about culture–the products of human creativity will inevitably come to seem foreign to people. This alienation is what Simmel calls the "tragedy" of culture. Surrounded by the objects of culture, objects created by other human beings, individuals nevertheless feel that culture is never wholly their own.

In 1914 Simmel finally gained a full professorship at the University of Strasbourg, which at that time was in German territory. The move from the metropolitan surroundings of Berlin to the relative isolation of Strasbourg was difficult for Simmel. In 1915 he made one last effort to gain a position at the University of Heidelberg but was again turned down. The outbreak of World War I diverted an entire generation of students from higher education and prevented Simmel from becoming an important figure at his only secure academic position. Yet, unlike many of his fellow intellectuals, and much to the chagrin of his former students and friends, Simmel was a strong supporter of the war. In his period at Strasbourg he published patriotic articles and pamphlets–many of them collected in the volume *Der Krieg und die geistigen Entscheidungen: Reden und Aufsätze* (The War and Spiritual Decisions: Speeches and Essays, 1917)–defending German actions. He also presented a series of lectures on cultural topics for German troops. As the war raged on, however, Simmel became less enthusiastic. Separated from his large student following in Berlin and facing the hostility of some of his colleagues at Strasbourg, he found it more difficult to write. Nevertheless, the war years were a relatively productive time for his scholarship. In addition to a systematic survey of sociological concepts–*Grundfragen der Soziologie (Individuum und Gesellschaft)* (Fundamental Questions of Sociology [Individual and Society], 1917)–Simmel published a book on aesthetics (*Rembrandt: Ein kunstphilosophischer Versuch* [1916; translated as *Georg Simmel on Rembrandt: A Philosophical Meditation on Art*, 2001]), and a work of speculative metaphysics (*Lebensanschauung: Vier metaphysische Kapitel* [Observations on Life: Four Metaphysical Chapters, 1918]). Between 1916 and 1918 he also wrote three substantial essays on the epistemology of history–*Das Problem der historischen Zeit* (1916; translated as "The Problem of Historical Time" in *Essays on Interpretation in Social Science*, 1980), "Die historische Formung" (published in *Logos*, 1917; translated as "The Constitutive Concepts of History" in *Essays on Interpretation in Social Science*), and *Vom Wesen des historischen Verstehens* (1918; translated as "On the Nature of Historical Understanding" in *Essays on Interpretation in Social Science*)–which return to questions he had first addressed in *Die Probleme der Geschichtsphilosophie*. These three essays were most likely intended to form the basis for another book-length study.

During the later war years Simmel also returned to a more general reflection on the nature and limitations of

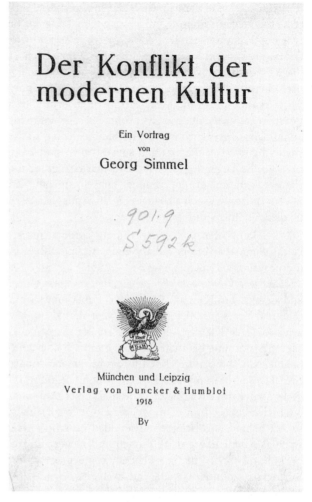

Title page for Simmel's study of modernism as a doomed attempt to free individuals from social, moral, aesthetic, and religious conventions (Delyte W. Morris Library, Southern Illinois University at Carbondale)

culture. One of his final essays, *Der Konflikt der modernen Kultur: Ein Vortrag* (1918; translated as "The Conflict in Modern Culture" in *The Conflict in Modern Culture and Other Essays,* 1968), addresses a paradoxical trend in modern thought. Culture, like all aspects of society, exists by definition only in specific forms–in laws, dogmas, artworks, and technologies, for example. Only in and through such forms can culture be recognized and conveyed. Cultural history, accordingly, is a process by which one form or group of forms is challenged and eventually replaced by another form or group of forms. One artistic style gives way to another style, one set of laws to another. Many modern movements in art, thought, and morals, Simmel notes, seek to free culture from all forms, however, to give immediate expression to life. Expressionist painting, for example, claims to depict the artist's impulses, unconfined by traditional models; pragmatism in philosophy disavows any objective quest for truth outside of daily practices; mysticism tries to separate the religious impulse from conventional dogmas or religious institutions; and critics of marriage seek to free sexual desire from social forms that contain it. Each of these modern trends, Simmel suggests, is doomed to failure. Culture is indeed an expression of life, but it only exists as a specific form; divorced from these forms, life is not more authentic but merely incoherent. The desire for an immediate expression of life, for Simmel, points to the shattering effect of the war and suggests that modernity may be the beginning of a fundamental change in the shape of cultural history. Simmel himself, though, did not survive to see such a change. On 26 September 1918 he died, in Strasbourg, of liver cancer.

"I know that I shall die without spiritual heirs," Georg Simmel wrote in a diary entry first published in the posthumous volume *Fragmente und Aufsätze: Aus dem Nachlass und Veröffentlichungen der letzten Jahre* (Fragments and Essays: Posthumous Works and Publications from the Final Years, 1923), "and that is as it should be. My legacy will be like cash distributed among many heirs, each transforming his share into some profit that is compatible with his nature. But this profit will no longer reveal its source in my estate." To a striking degree, Simmel's analysis of his legacy has been accurate. Although Simmel influenced an entire generation of intellectuals, he left behind no disciples and founded no school. His writings have had a crucial, if often understated, impact on cultural theory in the twentieth century, however. Simmel's accounts of value and exchange, of the city experience, of the stranger, and of the varied forms of social interaction were highly influential during his career and continue to inform contemporary thought. He also strongly influenced some of the key figures of twentieth-century Marxism. Walter Benjamin drew upon Simmel's account of the city experience in his cultural history of nineteenth-century Paris, and Lukács's theory of reification was decisively shaped by Simmel's discussion of the "tragedy" of culture. Although his early influence in American academic sociology was later eclipsed by that of Weber and Durkheim, Simmel's thought was an important influence on the social interactionism of Erving Goffman and others in the 1960s and 1970s. Finally, Simmel remains important for his diagnosis of the atomized "relative spirit" of modern life that was a core tendency of twentieth-century art and thought. As much as any other twentieth-century intellectual, Simmel was closely attuned to the spirit of his age. At his best, he is to social theory what James Joyce is to the novel and Pablo Picasso to the visual arts: at once a reflection of and a decisive influence upon his time. Even where Simmel did not directly influence its writers and thinkers, modernism can hardly be appreciated apart from his ideas and his

example. So although his legacy remains uncertain, Simmel continues to be a valuable resource for cultural theory.

Bibliography:

Kurt Gassen and Michael Landmann, eds., *Buch des Dankes an Georg Simmel: Briefe, Erinnerungen, Bibliographie* (Berlin: Duncker & Humblot, 1958), pp. 311–349.

Biography:

Kurt H. Wolff, ed., *Georg Simmel, 1858–1918* (Columbus: Ohio State University Press, 1959).

References:

Lewis Coser, ed., *Georg Simmel* (Englewood Cliffs, N.J.: Prentice-Hall, 1965);

David Frisby, *Georg Simmel,* revised edition (London: Routledge, 2002);

Frisby, *Simmel and Since: Essays on Georg Simmel's Social Theory* (London & New York: Routledge, 1992);

Frisby, *Sociological Impressionism: A Reassessment of Georg Simmel's Social Theory* (London: Heinemann, 1981);

Frisby, ed., *Georg Simmel: Critical Assessments,* 3 volumes (London & New York: Routledge, 1994);

Jürgen Habermas, "Georg Simmel on Philosophy and Culture: Postscript to a Collection of Essays," translated by Mathieu Deflem, *Critical Inquiry,* 22 (Spring 1996): 403–414;

Fredric Jameson, "The Theoretical Hesitation: Benjamin's Sociological Predecessor," *Critical Inquiry,* 25 (Winter 1999): 267–288;

Michael Kaern, Bernard S. Phillips, and Robert S. Cohen, eds., *Georg Simmel and Contemporary Sociology* (Dordrecht & Boston: Kluwer, 1990);

Siegfried Kracauer, "Georg Simmel," in *The Mass Ornament: Weimar Essays,* edited and translated by Thomas Y. Levin (Cambridge, Mass.: Harvard University Press, 1995), pp. 225–257;

Ralph Leck, *Georg Simmel and Avant-Garde Sociology* (Amherst, N.Y.: Humanity Books, 2000);

Larry Ray, ed., *Formal Sociology: The Sociology of Georg Simmel* (Aldershot, U.K. & Brookfield, Vt.: Elgar, 1991);

Nicholas J. Spykman, *The Social Theory of Georg Simmel* (Chicago: University of Chicago Press, 1925);

Theory, Culture, Society, special Simmel issue, 8 (Summer 1991);

Rudolph H. Weingartner, *Experience and Culture: The Philosophy of Georg Simmel* (Middletown, Conn.: Wesleyan University Press, 1962);

Deena Weinstein and Michael A. Weinstein, *Postmodern(ized) Simmel* (London & New York: Routledge, 1993).

Max Weber

(21 April 1864 – 14 June 1920)

Brian R. Rourke
New Mexico State University

BOOKS: *Entwickelung des Solidarhaftprinzips und des Sond-vermögens der offenen Handelsgesellschaft aus den Hausshalts- und Gewerbegemeinschaften in den italienischen Städten* (Stuttgart: Kröner, 1889);

Die römische Agrargeschichte in ihrer Bedeutung für das Staats- und Privatrecht (Stuttgart: Enke, 1891);

Die Verhältnisse der Landarbeiter im ostelbischen Deutschland: Preußische Provinzen Ost- und Westpreußen, Pommern, Posen, Schlesien, Brandenburg, Großherzogtümer Mecklenburg, Kreis Herzogtum Lauenburg, volume 3 of *Die Verhältnisse der Landarbeiter in Deutschland,* Schriften des Vereins für Socialpolitik, no. 55 (Leipzig: Duncker & Humblot, 1892);

Der Nationalstaat und die Volkswirtschaftspolitik: Akademische Antrittsrede (Freiburg: Mohr-Siebeck, 1895); translated, with an introduction, by Keith Tribe as "The National State and Economic Policy (Freiburg Address)," *Economy and Society,* 9 (1980): 420–449;

Wahlrecht und Demokratie in Deutschland (Berlin: Fortschritt, 1917);

Parlament und Regierung im neugeordneten Deutschland: Zur politischen Kritik des Beamtentums und Parteiwesens (Munich & Leipzig: Duncker & Humblot, 1918);

Der Sozialismus (Vienna: "Phöbus," Kommissionsverlag Dr. Viktor Pimmer, 1918);

Geistige Arbeit als Beruf: Vier Vorträge vor dem Freistudentischen Bund, 2 volumes (Munich & Leipzig: Duncker & Humblot, 1919);

Deutschlands künftige Staatsform (Frankfurt am Main: Frankfurter Societäts-Druckerei, 1919);

Gesammelte Aufsätze zur Religionssoziologie, 3 volumes (Tübingen: Mohr-Siebeck, 1920, 1921);

Gesammelte politische Schriften, edited by Marianne Weber (Munich: Drei Masken, 1921);

Die rationalen und soziologischen Grundlagen der Musik (Munich: Drei Masken, 1921); translated by Martindale, Johannes Riedel, and Gertrude Neuwirth as *The Rational and Social Foundations of Music,* edited by Martindale, Riedel, and Neuwirth

Max Weber (from Jacob P. Mayer, Max Weber and German Politics: A Study in Political Sociology, *1956; Thomas Cooper Library, University of South Carolina)*

(Edwardsville, Ill.: Southern Illinois University Press, 1958);

Gesammelte Aufsätze zur Wissenschaftslehre, edited by Marianne Weber (Tübingen: Mohr, 1922);

Wirtschaft und Gesellschaft, edited by Marianne Weber, volume 3 of *Grundriss der Sozialökonomik* (Tübingen: Mohr, 1922; republished, 2 volumes, 1925);

translated by Ephraim Fischoff and others as *Economy and Society: An Outline of Interpretive Sociology,* 3 volumes, edited by Guenther Roth and Claus Wittich (New York: Bedminster, 1968; revised edition, 2 volumes, Berkeley: University of California Press, 1978);

Wirtschaftsgeschichte: Abriß der universalen Sozial- und Wirtschaftsgeschichte, edited from student lecture notes by Siegmund Hellmann and Melchior Palyi (Munich & Leipzig: Duncker & Humblot, 1923); translated by Frank H. Knight as *General Economic History* (Glencoe, Ill.: Free Press, 1927);

Gesammelte Aufsätze zur Sozial- und Wirtschaftsgeschichte, edited by Marianne Weber (Tübingen: Mohr, 1924);

Gesammelte Aufsätze zur Soziologie und Sozialpolitik (Tübingen: Mohr, 1924);

Rechtssoziologie, edited, with an introduction, by Johannes Winckelmann (Neuwied: Luchterhand, 1960; revised, 1967);

Die protestantische Ethik, 2 volumes, edited by Winckelmann (Munich & Hamburg: Siebenstern Taschenbuch, 1968; revised and enlarged, 1972, 1975; revised edition, Gütersloh: Gütersloher Verlagshaus Mohn, 1978; revised again, 1982);

Zur Politik im Weltkrieg: Schriften und Reden 1914–1918, edited by Wolfgang J. Mommsen with Gangolf Hübinger, volume 15 of Weber, *Gesamtausgabe,* section I (Tübingen: Mohr, 1984);

Die römische Agrargeschichte in ihrer Bedeutung für das Staats- und Privatrecht, edited by Jürgen Deininger, volume 2 of Weber, *Gesamtausgabe,* section I (Tübingen: Mohr, 1986);

Zur Neuordnung Deutschlands: Schriften und Reden 1918–1920, edited by Mommsen with Wolfgang Schwentker, volume 16 of Weber, *Gesamtausgabe,* section I (Tübingen: Mohr, 1988);

Zur Russischen Revolution von 1905: Schriften 1905–1912, edited by Mommsen with Dittmar Dahlmann, volume 10 of Weber, *Gesamtausgabe,* section I (Tübingen: Mohr, 1989); translated as *The Russian Revolutions,* edited and translated by Gordon C. Wells and Peter Baehr (Ithaca, N.Y.: Cornell University Press, 1995; Cambridge: Polity Press, 1995);

Grundriss zu den Vorlesungen über allgemeine ("theoretische") Nationalökonomie (1898) (Tübingen: Mohr, 1990);

Landarbeiterfrage, Nationalstaat und Volkswirtschaftspolitik: Schriften und Reden 1892–1899, 2 volumes, edited by Mommsen with Rita Aldenhoff, volume 4 of Weber, *Gesamtausgabe,* section I (Tübingen: Mohr, 1993);

Zur Psychophysik der industriellen Arbeit: Schriften und Reden 1908–1912, edited by Wolfgang Schluchter with Sabine Frommer, volume 11 of Weber, *Gesamtausgabe,* section I (Tübingen: Mohr, 1995);

Wirtschaft, Staat und Sozialpolitik: Schriften und Reden 1900–1912, edited by Schluchter with Peter Kurth and Birgitt Morgenbrod, volume 8 of Weber, *Gesamtausgabe,* section I (Tübingen: Mohr, 1998);

Börsenwesen: Schriften und Reden 1893–1898, 2 volumes, edited by Knut Borchardt with Cornelia Meyer-Stoll, volume 5 of Weber, *Gesamtausgabe,* section I (Tübingen: Mohr, 1999, 2000).

Collections and Editions: *Gesammelte Aufsätze zur Wissenschaftslehre,* revised and enlarged by Johannes Winckelmann (Tübingen: Mohr-Siebeck, 1951; revised and enlarged, 1968; revised again, 1973; revised again, 1982; revised again, 1985);

Wirtschaft und Gesellschaft: Grundriss der verstehenden Soziologie, 2 volumes, edited by Winckelmann (Tübingen: Mohr, 1956; revised, 1972);

Gesammelte politische Schriften, revised and enlarged by Winckelmann (Tübingen: Mohr-Siebeck, 1958; revised and enlarged again, 1971);

Wirtschaftsgeschichte: Abriß der universalen Sozial- und Wirtschaftsgeschichte, revised and enlarged by Winckelmann (Berlin: Duncker & Humblot, 1958; revised, 1981);

Die Lage der Landarbeiter im ostelbischen Deutschland, 1892, 2 volumes, edited by Martin Riesebrodt, volume 3 of Weber, *Gesamtausgabe,* section I (Tübingen: Mohr, 1984);

Die Wirtschaftsethik der Weltreligionen, Konfuzianismus und Taoismus: Schriften 1915–1920, edited by Helwig Schmidt-Glintzer with Petra Kolonko, volume 19 of Weber, *Gesamtausgabe,* section I (Tübingen: Mohr, 1989);

Wissenschaft als Beruf 1917/1919; Politik als Beruf 1919, edited by Wolfgang, J. Mommsen and Schluchter with Birgitt Morgenbrod, volume 17 of Weber, *Gesamtausgabe,* section I (Tübingen: Mohr, 1992);

Die protestantische Ethik und der "Geist" des Kapitalismus, edited by Klaus Lichtblau and Johannes Weiss (Bodenheim: Athenäum Hain Hanstein, 1993);

Die Wirtschaftsethik der Weltreligionen, Hinduismus und Buddhismus: Schriften 1916–1920, edited by Schmidt-Glintzer with Karl-Heinz Golzio, volume 20 of Weber, *Gesamtausgabe,* section I (Tübingen: Mohr, 1996);

Wirtschaft und Gesellschaft, Die Wirtschaft und die gesellschaftlichen Ordnungen und Maechte, Nachlaß, 2 volumes, edited by Mommsen and others, volume 22 of Weber, *Gesamtausgabe,* section I (Tübingen: Mohr, 1999–2001).

Editions in English: *The Protestant Ethic and the Spirit of Capitalism,* translated by Talcott Parsons (New York: Scribners, 1930);

From Max Weber: Essays in Sociology, edited and translated, with an introduction, by C. Wright Mills and Hans H. Gerth (New York: Oxford University Press, 1946; London: Kegan Paul, Trench & Trübner, 1947);

The Methodology of the Social Sciences, edited and translated by Henry A. Finch and Edward A. Shils (Glencoe, Ill.: Free Press, 1949);

The Religion of China: Confucianism and Taoism, edited and translated by Gerth (Glencoe, Ill.: Free Press, 1951);

Ancient Judaism, translated and edited, with a preface, by Gerth and Don Martindale (Glencoe, Ill.: Free Press, 1952);

Max Weber on Law in Economy and Society, edited, with an introduction, by Max Rheinstein, translated by Rheinstein and Shils (Cambridge, Mass.: Harvard University Press, 1954);

The Religion of India: The Sociology of Hinduism and Buddhism, translated and edited by Gerth and Martindale (Glencoe, Ill.: Free Press, 1958);

Basic Concepts in Sociology, edited and translated, with an introduction, by H. P. Secher (New York: Citadel, 1962);

Max Weber: Selections from His Work, edited, with an introduction, by S. M. Miller (New York: Crowell, 1963);

The Sociology of Religion, translated by Ephraim Fischoff (Boston: Beacon, 1963);

Max Weber on Charisma and Institution Building: Selected Papers, edited, with an introduction, by S. N. Eisenstadt (Chicago: University of Chicago Press, 1968);

Max Weber: The Interpretation of Social Reality, edited, with an introduction, by J. E. T. Eldridge (London: Joseph, 1970; New York: Scribners, 1971);

Max Weber on Universities: The Power of the State and the Dignity of the Academic Calling in Imperial Germany, edited and translated, with an introduction, by Shils (Chicago: University of Chicago Press, 1973);

Roscher and Knies: The Logical Problems of Historical Economics, translated, with an introduction, by Guy Oakes (New York: Free Press, 1975);

The Agrarian Sociology of Ancient Civilization, translated, with an introduction, by R. I. Frank (London: New Left Books / Atlantic Highlands, N.J.: Humanities Press, 1976);

Critique of Stammler, translated, with an introduction, by Oakes (New York: Free Press, 1977);

Max Weber: Selections in Translation, edited by Walter Garrison Runciman, translated by E. Matthews (Cambridge & New York: Cambridge University Press, 1978);

Max Weber on Capitalism, Bureaucracy, and Religion: A Selection of Texts, edited and in part translated, with an introduction, by Stanislav Andreski (London & Boston: Allen & Unwin, 1983);

Political Writings, edited, with an introduction, by Peter Lassman and Ronald Speirs, translated by Spiers (Cambridge & New York: Cambridge University Press, 1994);

Essays in Economic Sociology, edited, with an introduction, by Richard Swedberg (Princeton: Princeton University Press, 1999);

The Protestant Ethic Debate: Max Weber's Replies to His Critics, 1907–1910, edited by David J. Chalcraft and Harrington, translated by Harrington and Mary Shields (Liverpool: Liverpool University Press, 2001);

The Protestant Ethic and the Spirit of Capitalism, translated, with an introduction, by Stephen Kalberg (Chicago & London: Fitzroy Dearborn, 2001).

OTHER: "The Relations of the Rural Community to Other Branches of Social Science," translated by Charles W. Seidenadel, in *Congress of Arts and Science, Universal Exposition, St. Louis,* edited by Howard J. Rogers, volume 7 (Boston & New York: Houghton, Mifflin, 1906), pp. 725–746.

SELECTED PERIODICAL PUBLICATIONS–UNCOLLECTED: "'Römisches' und 'deutsches' Recht," *Die christliche Welt,* 22 (1895): 521–525; translated by Otmar Foelsche as "'Roman' and 'Germanic' Law," *International Journal of the Sociology of Law,* 13 (1985): 237–246;

"'Kirchen' und 'Sekten' in Nordamerika: Eine kirchen- und socialpolitsche Skizze," *Die christliche Welt,* 24–25 (1906): 558–562, 577–583; translated by Colin Loader as "'Churches' and 'Sects' in North America: An Ecclesiastical Socio-Political Sketch," *Sociological Theory,* 3 (1985): 1–13;

"Georg Simmel as a Sociologist," translated, with an introduction, by Donald N. Levine, *Social Research,* 39 (1972): 155–163.

Max Weber has long been recognized as one of the founders of modern sociology. His theoretical works continue to provide elaboration and clarification of the logical and epistemological foundations of social science, while many of the problems he explored have remained central to social research–such as the nature and causes of capitalist development, the sources and forms of political power, and the specific role of ideal or cultural factors as determinants of social action. Weber took pains to define his concepts clearly and precisely, and many of them–for instance, charisma and rational-

*Weber (far right) in 1887 with his parents, Max Weber Sr. and Helene (née Fallenstein), and his siblings
Arthur, Klara, Alfred, Lili, and Karl (from Marianne Weber,* Max Weber: A Biography,
translated by Harry Zohn, 1988; Thomas Cooper Library, University of South Carolina)

ization–have become part of the standard vocabulary of social thought.

Karl Emil Maximilian Weber was born on 21 April 1864 in Erfurt, Germany, the eldest of six children. His father, Max Weber Sr., practiced law and was active in politics. His mother, Helene (née Fallenstein), was well educated, deeply religious, and socially conscious. In 1869 Weber's father took up the post of city adviser in Berlin, and the family moved to Charlottenberg. As a member of the National Liberal Party, he served as a deputy in the Prussian Chamber of Deputies (1868–1882) and later in the German Reichstag (1884–1897). As a result of his father's political prominence, Weber grew up in a home frequented by important politicians and intellectuals, such as Rudolf von Benningsen, Theodor Mommsen, and Wilhelm Dilthey. Weber's parents differed in character and interests, his father having little regard for religion and his mother being out of sympathy with his father's complacent worldliness.

Weber started school in 1870. Though often bored, he read widely in history, classical literature, and philosophy. He completed secondary school in 1882 and moved on to Heidelberg University, focusing on law, economics, and history. Weber returned to Berlin to study in 1884, living with his parents, whose marriage had deteriorated since the death of Weber's sister Helenchen in 1876. After spending the winter term of 1885–1886 in Göttingen preparing for the legal examination that would qualify him as a *Referendar* (junior attorney), Weber continued to study law, history, and economics at Berlin University. He began to pursue a doctorate in law with Levin Goldschmidt, which he completed magna cum laude in 1889. For his dissertation he submitted a chapter taken from a monograph on South European trading companies of the Middle Ages. It was based on extensive research into Italian and Spanish legal documents and shows Weber's early interest in the development of capitalism and the relationship between legal systems and economics. While Weber began work on his *habilitation* he completed his legal training and certification in 1890. In 1891, under August Meitzen, he completed his *habilitation,* titled *Die römische Agrargeschichte in ihrer Bedeutung für das Staats- und Privatrecht* (Roman Agrarian History and Its Importance for State and Civil Law). Weber retained his interest in the social and economic history of ancient societies throughout his career and later contributed a substantial article on the subject, "Agrarverhältnisse im Altertum" (1909; translated as "Agrarian Conditions in Antiquity," 1976) to the *Handwörterbuch der Staatswissenschaften* (Dictionary of Political Science, 1909). Weber continued to pursue both an academic and a legal career, working as a lawyer at the Berlin Supreme Court and lecturing in law at Berlin University. At this time he met Marianne Schnitger, his father's greatniece, and they soon were engaged. They married in 1893. The couple never had any children.

Weber joined the Verein für Sozialpolitik (Association for Social Policy) in 1888 and attended the first meeting of the Evangelish-soziale Kongreß (Evangelical-Social Congress) in 1890. The Verein commissioned Weber to conduct research into the conditions of rural laborers in the East Elbian provinces of Prussia. In September 1892 Weber presented his research and conclusions to the association, which also published his work, titled *Die Verhältnisse der Landarbeiter im ostelbischen Deutschland: Preußische Provinzen Ost- und Westpreußen, Pommern, Posen, Schlesien, Brandenburg, Großherzogtümer Mecklenburg, Kreis Herzogtum Lauenburg* (The Conditions of Agricultural Workers in East Elbian Germany: The Prussian Provinces of East and West Prussia, Pommern, Posen, Schlesien, Brandenburg, the Grand Duchies of Mecklenburg, the Duchy of Lauenberg), as the third volume of a larger work, *Die Verhältnisse der Landarbeiter in Deutschland* (The Conditions of Agricultural Workers in Germany). Weber concluded from his extensive and innovative research that the large estates should be broken up into economically viable plots of land and made available to the workers to encourage them to remain in the area. Weber's conclusions were politically controversial, and they earned him renown within Germany as an expert on rural economics.

In 1894 Weber turned down an offer of a chair in law from Berlin University and accepted a position as professor of political economy at Freiburg University, revealing a shift in his interests from law to economics. Weber's May 1895 inaugural lecture at Freiburg, *Der Nationalstaat und die Volkswirtschaftspolitik* (1895; translated as "The National State and Economic Policy," 1980), courted controversy by advocating nationalism, imperialism, and realpolitik.

Weber succeeded Karl Knies as professor of political economy at Heidelberg University in 1896. In July 1897 his personal life entered a period of crisis that began with a showdown with his father. In a heated confrontation Weber objected strongly to his father's overbearing and arbitrary treatment of his mother. Weber's father died soon afterward, on 10 August, before the break could be mended. Later that year Weber began to suffer symptoms of a nervous disorder that plagued him for the rest of his life. In 1898 he was

only able to fulfill his duties with great difficulty. A series of nervous breakdowns eventually forced Weber to give up regular teaching. He resigned his professorship in 1903. At its worst Weber's condition made him incapable of work altogether. He traveled frequently, which seemed to help somewhat, though he suffered frequent relapses.

Gradually, Weber was able to return to scholarly work. During the first decade of the twentieth century, he started turning his attention to sociology. He began to articulate his innovative approach to the social sciences in a series of methodological essays. In 1904 Weber became an editor of the *Archiv für Sozialwissenschaften und Sozialpolitik* (Archive of Social Science and Social Policy), along with Edgar Jaffé and Werner Sombart. Weber went on to publish much of his work in the journal, which became the most prestigious journal of its type in Germany. In the first issue under the new editorship, Weber included an article titled "Die 'Objektivität' sozialwissenschaftlicher und sozialpolitischer Erkenntnis" (1904; translated as "'Objectivity' in Social Science and Social Policy" in *The Methodology of the Social Sciences*, 1949). He presents his position thoroughly and systematically in this essay, which has been particularly influential. Weber argues that the social scientist's work should be "value-free" neither in the positivistic sense of presuppositionless objectivity nor in the sense of political or ethical neutrality, but rather through a rigorous separation of fact and value, as well as of the explanation of values from the advocacy of values. Against naturalistic scientism and positivism—including Marxian thought and social Darwinism—Weber insists on distinguishing the social sciences, which involve the interpretation of meaningful human action, from the natural sciences. One of the most important tools for such interpretive understanding is what Weber called the "ideal type," in which the distinguishing characteristics of social phenomena are clearly conceptualized and used as analytical tools, rather than hypostatized as metaphysical or natural "laws."

During this period Weber began to focus his attention on religion, considered by him to be one of the most important sources of the meanings and values that inform social action. The first product of this new line of inquiry is probably his best-known work, "Die protestantische Ethik und der Geist des Kapitalismus" (translated as *The Protestant Ethic and the Spirit of Capitalism*, 1930), first published in the *Archiv für Sozialwissenschaften und Sozialpolitik* in 1905 and later included in volume one of his *Gesammelte Aufsätze zur Religionssoziologie* (Collected Essays on the Sociology of Religion, 1920, 1921). It proved to be the first part of a long comparative sociological study of world religions, "Die Wirtschaftsethick der Weltreligionen" (The Economic

Max and Marianne Weber (née Schnitger) in 1893, the year of their marriage (from Marianne Weber,
Max Weber: A Biography, *translated by Harry Zohn, 1988;*
Thomas Cooper Library, University of South Carolina)

Ethic of World Religions), that Weber worked on for the next fifteen years and first published in 1916–1917 in the *Archiv für Sozialwissenschaften und Sozialpolitik.*

Weber defines "the spirit of capitalism" as an ethic explicitly organized around work in a "calling," emphasizing the pursuit of profit and the maintenance of credit. The modern concept of the calling is uniquely Protestant, Weber claims, originating in the works of Martin Luther. Valuing worldly work in one's vocation may appear to be simply a matter of ethics, but Weber argues that the ethical teachings of a religion cannot be separated from its doctrine. The beliefs inculcated by Protestantism, particularly the Calvinist doctrine of pre-destination, exercise their own influence on conduct. Only by grasping the psychological pressure exerted by

the fears and hopes relating to salvation can one under-stand the effect of such a belief on conduct. By illumi-nating the relationship between ideas and conduct, Weber suggests that his study may serve as "a contribu-tion to the understanding of the manner in which ideas become effective forces in history."

Weber's essay concludes on a note of historical pessimism and methodological caution characteristic of much of his work. The construction of the "tremen-dous cosmos of the modern economic order" results in part from the Puritan application of rational Christian asceticism to worldly life. After industrial capitalism becomes dominant, however, it irresistibly imposes its economic conditions and exigencies on humanity with-out the help of the Protestant ethic. The Puritan calling becomes an "iron cage," within which human beings are increasingly subjected to the rule of things. He concludes by recognizing that the influence of social and economic conditions on the development of Protestant asceticism requires investigation and cautions that it is "not my aim to substitute for a one-sided materialistic an equally one-sided spiritualistic causal interpretation of culture and history."

Weber was never reluctant to enter into controversies, and in the years before World War I he was frequently involved in academic controversies, political debates, and lawsuits over matters of honor. Weber attended the Social Democrats' party congress in 1906 and attacked what he saw as its petit bourgeois orientation. At the same time he had no respect whatsoever for the kaiser. He defended the principle of academic freedom from state interference, particularly in confessional and political matters. In 1909 Weber along with other scholars formed the Deutsche Gesellschaft für Soziologie (German Society for Sociology) in order to further the interests of empirical social research in Germany. He resigned from the society after tiring of debates with his colleagues over his principle of value-free social science. During this period Marianne Weber became one of the leaders of the movement for women's rights in Germany, publishing a study of the legal condition of wives and mothers in 1907. In 1910 the Webers moved to a new home in Heidelberg, which they shared with the theologian Ernst Troeltsch. It became a gathering place of intellectuals and writers such as György Lukács, Ernst Bloch, and Stefan George.

In 1909 Weber agreed, on the urging of the publisher of the *Archiv für Sozialwissenschaften und Sozialpolitik,* Paul Siebeck, to update Gustav Schönberg's *Handbuch der politischen Ökonomie* (Handbook of Political Economy, 1882) by producing a new series called *Grundriss der Sozialökonomik* (Outline of Social Economics). Though Weber did not live to see the project through to completion, the volumes he planned to contribute ultimately resulted in the monumental treatise *Wirtschaft und Gesellschaft* (1922; translated as *Economy and Society: An Outline of Interpretive Sociology,* 1968), which Weber was still working on when he died. The work combines a synthesis of Weber's lifelong empirical research with a systematic presentation of his methodology. He completed his first draft of what is now part 2 in 1913 and wrote what is now part 1 in 1918–1920.

As in so much of Weber's work, the precise definition of concepts features prominently in *Wirtschaft und Gesellschaft.* He defines sociology as "a science concerning itself with the interpretive understanding of social action and thereby with a causal explanation of its course and consequences." Behavior becomes action when the actor attributes meaning to it, and action is social when it is oriented toward the action of others. For Weber the task of sociology, broadly speaking, is to understand social action. It thus involves interpretation, and Weber argues that the potential for understanding depends in part upon the degree of rationality informing the action. Though it may be possible to empathize with emotional states or commitments to absolute values, Weber argues that it is methodologically more efficient to understand irrational action as a deviation from forms of rational action conceived as ideal types. This distinction between rational and irrational action informs his entire methodological elaboration.

For example, Weber identifies four types of social action: traditional, affectual, value-rational, and instrumentally rational. The first two Weber describes as being on the border between meaningful action and habitual or automatic behavior. Value-rational action involves rational action governed by or oriented toward some kind of ultimate value or purpose to which other interests are subordinated. Instrumental rationality treats values as personal preferences that can be ranked according to the principle of marginal utility and pursued with the most effective means available. When self-interest is pursued by means of instrumental reason, Weber points out, a uniformity of action develops that often exceeds what can be achieved by the efforts of political or cultural authorities.

Weber concludes his exposition of basic sociological categories by distinguishing political organizations, which make use of physical force within a given territory, from hierocratic organizations, which use psychological pressure, such as religious sanctions. A political organization becomes a state when—according to what has become a famous definition—it achieves "the *monopoly* of the *legitimate* use of physical force in the enforcement of its order" within a territory. A hierocratic organization becomes a church when "its administrative staff claims a monopoly of the legitimate use of hierocratic coercion," such as control over the goods necessary for salvation.

As these definitions show, Weber emphasizes the specific contribution of recognized legitimacy to the maintenance of the established order. He argues that legitimate authority can be based on three distinct foundations: rational grounds, traditional grounds, or charismatic grounds. Recognition of the legality of established rules provides the rational grounds. Traditional authority involves faith in established customs, commonly represented and enforced by a patrimonial ruler. In each case the grounding includes the belief that those who exercise legal or traditional authority have a right to do so. Charismatic grounds are based "on devotion to the exceptional sanctity, heroism or exem-

Weber around the time he became professor of political economy at Heidelberg University in 1896 (from Marianne Weber, Max Weber: A Biography, *translated by Harry Zohn, 1988; Thomas Cooper Library, University of South Carolina)*

plary character of an individual person, and of the normative patterns of order revealed or ordained by him."

"The purest type of exercise of legal authority," Weber argues, "is that which employs a bureaucratic administrative staff." Bureaucracy is a hierarchical organization of appointed, salaried officials who tend to devote their careers to the apparatus. They carry out their duties impersonally within a structure in which each office has its own specific competence. Officials are "separated from ownership of the means of administration" and thus are dependent on the apparatus, within which they are "subject to strict and systematic discipline and control." Bureaucratic organization can be found in any sphere of social life: religion, the economy, or the state. Weber sees bureaucracy as technically superior to other types of administration, and he emphasizes its peculiar durability.

Another important distinction introduced by Weber is the one between classes and status groups.

Classes are determined by conditions of existence and concomitant opportunities. Status is commonly based on "style of life" and "formal education," and status groups form around these distinctions, often attempting to monopolize the sources of their status. Weber insists that while status may be based on class, or vice versa, one is not the function of the other. They are relatively distinct forms of social stratification. The scope of *Wirtschaft und Gesellschaft* extends far beyond these important fundamental concepts, however. It features detailed discussions of law, political organization, intellectuals, ethnicity, economics, and religion—as well as a comparative historical analysis of the city.

In 1911 Weber wrote *Die rationalen und soziologischen Grundlagen der Musik* (1921; translated as *The Rational and Social Foundations of Music,* 1958), his most extended discussion of art. Weber discovers within the structure of Western music rigorous formal rationality in dynamic tension with uncontrollable, irrational elements—both melodic flow and the recalcitrance of harmonic material itself. He explores links between the inner logic of music and its social foundations. Weber argues that the magic and ritual functions of music have often determined its development, while the rationalization of music depends upon its independence from them, as well as on the professional autonomy of musicians. Modern musical notation, without which modern musical composition and performance would be impossible, represents a crucial point in the history of musical rationalization. Weber concludes his study with an examination of the sociohistorical development of musical instruments.

When war broke out in 1914, Weber served on the Reserve Military Hospitals Commission, founding and managing nine military hospitals until 1915. He viewed the war with trepidation at first, but he later became more caught up in nationalist enthusiasm. He continued his scholarly work during the war, focusing particularly on his sociology of religion. Gradually Weber grew more critical of the conduct of the war by the government. He opposed the annexation of conquered territory and criticized the policy of unrestricted submarine warfare, which he warned would bring the United States into the war. In 1917 he began to criticize the German political system as well, arguing in favor of a parliamentary system and against the class-based franchise. He published his political opinions in the *Frankfurter Zeitung,* often attracting the attention of the censor. Weber had mostly recovered from his nervous disorder by 1914, and he felt free to pursue new career opportunities, taking up a position as professor of political economy at the University of Vienna in 1918.

After the defeat of Germany, Weber urged the kaiser to abdicate to save the honor of the Hohenzol-

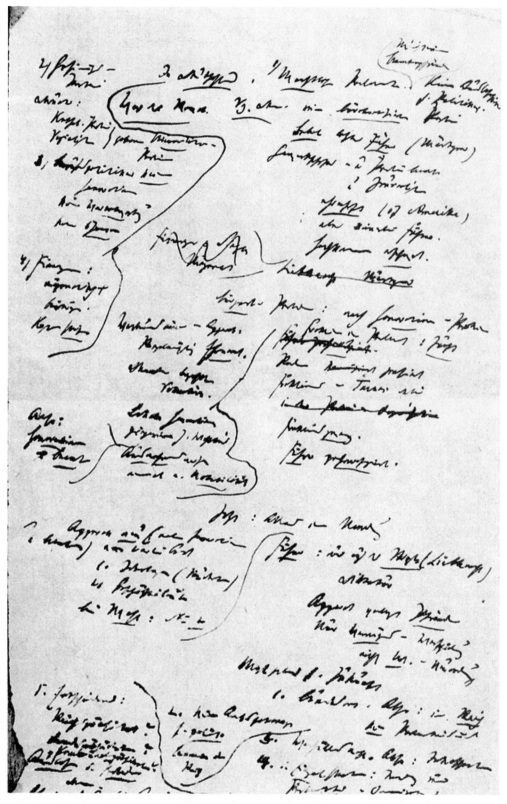

Manuscript page for Weber's lecture Politik als Beruf *(translated as "Politics as a Vocation," 1946), presented to the Federation of Free Students in Munich in 1919 (from Marianne Weber,* Max Weber: A Biography, *translated by Harry Zohn, 1988; Thomas Cooper Library, University of South Carolina)*

Weber's home on the Neckar River in Heidelberg (from Marianne Weber, Max Weber: A Biography, *translated by Harry Zohn, 1988; Thomas Cooper Library, University of South Carolina)*

lern dynasty. He joined the German Democratic Party and stood for election to the Reichstag in the 1919 National Assembly elections, but internal party maneuvering resulted in his having to run on a doomed slate. Marianne Weber, on the other hand, was elected to the Baden Landtag (State Parliament) and served as leader of the Bund deutscher Frauenvereine (Federation of German Women's Associations). The new government considered appointing Weber either as secretary of state for the interior or ambassador to Austria, but he was not offered a position. He did serve as an informal adviser during the drafting of the new constitution. Weber opposed pacifism and Bavarian separatism, and he denounced the 1918 revolution as a "bloody carnival," particularly because he felt that it had weakened Germany in its moment of crisis. Weber served on the German delegation in Versailles, helping to draft the German response to the Allies' war-guilt clause. During this period Weber gave two important lectures in Munich at the invitation of the Freistudentischen Bund (Federation of Free Students): *Wissenschaft als Beruf* (1919; translated as "Science as a Vocation," 1946) and *Politik als Beruf* (1919; translated as "Politics as a Vocation," 1946), in which he presents in condensed form many of his theoretical and political positions.

In 1920 Weber wrote an introduction to his *Gesammelte Aufsätze zur Religionssoziologie,* "Verbemerkung" (1920; translated as "Author's Introduction" in *The Protestant Ethic and the Spirit of Capitalism*), in which he clarifies the fundamental questions motivating the entire project. Instead of a discussion of the nature and function of religion, or an elaboration of the rationales and protocols proper to its comparative study, Weber begins by positing the unique and universal value of Western civilization. Citing examples from science, the arts, and religion, Weber identifies what he sees as distinctively Western forms of rationalization. Weber argues that modern capitalism—defined as the systematic and rational pursuit of profit based on formally free labor—developed only in the West. One may point to the technical exploitation of scientific knowledge and the presence of a rationally calculable legal system as causes of this development, but Weber insists that one must also account for the capacity and inclination of individuals to "adopt certain types of practical rational conduct." Religious belief exercises a powerful influence on conduct, and it has often prevented the adoption of such rational standards. Weber aims to show how religious belief shaped practice, in order to illuminate the character of Western rationality and demonstrate the degree to which it made the development of capitalism possible. The purpose of Weber's studies of ancient Judaism and the religions of India and China, which are much longer than the essay on Protestantism, is thus specific and limited, "oriented to the problems which seem important for the understanding of Western culture from *this* view-point."

Weber considers what might account for this distinctiveness of occidental rationalization. He acknowledges suspecting that heredity probably plays an important role, though he professes skepticism about how that factor could be determined and measured. He argues that social science must explore environmental explanations until they are exhausted, otherwise productive lines of inquiry might be foreclosed in favor of biologistic speculation. Weber's discussion of heredity and his insistence on the unique character of Western rationalism demonstrate that he believed that fundamental differences separated Western culture from all non-Western cultures. He was evidently receptive to the biological racial theories prevalent in Europe at the time. In his later years, both in *Wirtschaft und Gesellschaft* and at meetings of the Deutsche Gesellschaft für Soziologie, he became more critical of attempts to apply racist theory within the social sciences, frequently emphasizing the role of racist ideologies in the legitimation of social stratification.

Weber took up a professorship at the University of Munich in 1919, where he gave a series of lectures on economic history in the winter term. A reconstruction of these lectures, based on students' notes, was published after his death as *Wirtschaftsgeschichte: Abriß der universalen Sozial- und Wirtschaftsgeschichte* (1923; translated as *General Economic History,* 1927). Some of his political stands attracted the hostility of right-wing student groups, who began to disrupt his lectures. During this period he was in the process of completing his *Gesammelte Aufsätze zur Religionssoziologie* and *Wirtschaft und Gesellschaft.* Weber contracted pneumonia in June 1920 and died on 14 June.

While Max Weber's works are viewed as classic foundational texts in the social sciences, his influence has been felt less strongly in the humanities. Nonetheless, several important tendencies within cultural theory owe a great deal to his work. Western Marxist cultural criticism, particularly that of the Frankfurt School, has Weberian roots owing in part to Weber's direct influence on Lukács and Bloch. Phenomenological and existentialist philosophers have shown an interest in Weber, specifically Karl Jaspers—who was a friend of Weber's—Alfred Schutz, and Maurice Merleau-Ponty. The hermeneutic turn in ethnography, which provides much of the conceptual equipment of cultural studies and the new historicism in the United States, has also been influenced by Weber. Pierre Bourdieu's work on the sociology of culture—in particular his analysis of status differentiation in *La distinction: Critique sociale du jugement* (1979; translated as *Distinction: A Social Critique of the Judgment of Taste,* 1984) and his historical investigation into the genesis of intellectual and artistic autonomy in *Les règles de l'art: Gènese et structure du champ littéraire* (1992; translated as *The Rules of Art: Genesis and Structure of the Literary Field,* 1996)—represents a fundamental engagement with and reconstruction of key Weberian problems, specifically the concept of legitimacy, the opposition between class and status, and the theory of sociocultural rationalization. Weber's conception of sociology as a science devoted to understanding the meaning of social action places him at the often contentious border between the humanities and the social sciences, making his work particularly relevant to the study of literature and culture.

Letters:

Jugendbriefe: 1876–1893, edited, with an introduction, by Marianne Weber (Tübingen: Mohr-Siebeck, 1936);

Briefe: 1906–1908, edited by M. Rainer Lepsius and Wolfgang J. Mommsen with Birgit Rudhard and Manfred Schön, volume 5 of Weber, *Gesamtausgabe,* section II (Tübingen: Mohr, 1990);

Briefe: 1909–1910, edited by Lepsius and Mommsen with Rudhard and Schön, volume 6 of Weber, *Gesamtausgabe,* section II (Tübingen: Mohr, 1994);

Briefe: 1911–1912, edited by Lepsius and Mommsen with Rudhard and Schön, 2 volumes, volume 7 of Weber, *Gesamtausgabe,* section II (Tübingen: Mohr, 1998).

Bibliography:

Peter Kivisto and William H. Swatos Jr., *Max Weber: A Bio-Bibliography* (New York: Greenwood Press, 1988).

Biography:

Marianne Weber, *Max Weber: Ein Lebensbild* (Tübingen: Mohr, 1926); translated by Harry Zohn as *Max Weber: A Biography,* edited by Zohn (New York: Wiley, 1988).

References:

Jeffrey C. Alexander, *Action and Its Environments: Toward a New Synthesis* (New York: Columbia University Press, 1988);

Alexander, *The Classical Attempt at Theoretical Synthesis: Max Weber,* volume 3 of Alexander, *Theoretical Logic in Sociology,* 4 volumes (Berkeley: University of California Press, 1983);

Raymond Aron, *German Sociology,* translated by Mary Bottomore and Thomas Bottomore (Glencoe, Ill.: Free Press, 1957);

Aron, *Main Currents in Sociological Thought,* 2 volumes, translated by Richard Howard and Helen Weaver (Glencoe, Ill.: Free Press, 1970);

Reinhard Bendix, *Max Weber: An Intellectual Portrait,* introduction by Guenther Roth (Garden City, N.Y.: Doubleday, 1960);

Pierre Bourdieu, *Distinction: A Social Critique of the Judgment of Taste,* translated by Richard Nice (Cambridge, Mass: Harvard University Press, 1984);

Bourdieu, *The Rules of Art: Genesis and Structure of the Literary Field,* translated by Susan Emanuel (Stanford, Cal.: Stanford University Press, 1996; Cambridge: Polity Press, 1996);

Bourdieu and Jean-Claude Passeron, *Reproduction in Education, Society and Culture,* translated by Nice (London & Beverly Hills, Cal.: Sage, 1977);

Bourdieu, Passeron, and Jean-Claude Chamboredon, *The Craft of Sociology: Epistemological Preliminaries,* edited by Beate Krais, translated by Nice (Berlin & New York: De Gruyter, 1991);

Randall Collins, *Max Weber: A Skeleton Key* (London & Beverly Hills, Cal.: Sage, 1986);

Collins, *Weberian Sociological Theory* (Cambridge & New York: Cambridge University Press, 1986);

Julien Freund, *The Sociology of Max Weber,* translated by Mary Ilford (New York: Pantheon, 1968);

Anthony Giddens, *Capitalism and Modern Social Theory: An Analysis of the Writings of Marx, Durkheim and Max Weber* (Cambridge: Cambridge University Press, 1971);

Giddens, *Politics and Sociology in the Thought of Max Weber* (London: Macmillan, 1972);

Paul Honigsheim, *On Max Weber,* translated by Joan Rytina (New York: Free Press, 1968);

H. Stuart Hughes, *Consciousness and Society: The Reorientation of European Social Thought, 1890–1930* (New York: Knopf, 1958);

Karl Jaspers, *Three Essays: Leonardo, Descartes, Max Weber,* translated by Ralph Manheim (New York: Harcourt, Brace & World, 1964);

Dirk Käsler, *Max Weber: An Introduction to His Life and Work,* translated by Philippa Hurd (Chicago: University of Chicago Press / Cambridge: Polity Press, 1988);

Karl Loewenstein, *Max Weber's Political Ideas in the Perspective of Our Time,* translated by Richard Winston and Clara Winston (Amherst: University of Massachusetts Press, 1966);

Karl Löwith, *Max Weber and Karl Marx,* translated by Hans Fantel (London & Boston: Allen & Unwin, 1982);

Jacob P. Mayer, *Max Weber and German Politics: A Study in Political Sociology,* revised and enlarged edition (London: Faber & Faber, 1956);

Maurice Merleau-Ponty, *Adventures of the Dialectic,* translated by Joseph Bien (Evanston, Ill.: Northwestern University Press, 1973);

Arthur Mitzman, *The Iron Cage: An Historical Interpretation of Max Weber* (New York: Grossett & Dunlap, 1971);

Wolfgang J. Mommsen, *The Age of Bureaucracy: Perspectives on the Political Sociology of Max Weber* (New York: Harper & Row, 1974);

Mommsen, *Max Weber and German Politics: 1890–1920,* translated by Michael S. Steinberg (Chicago & London: University of Chicago Press, 1984);

Mommsen, *The Political and Social Theory of Max Weber* (Chicago: University of Chicago Press, 1989; Cambridge: Polity Press, 1989);

Wolfgang Schluchter, *Paradoxes of Modernity: Culture and Conduct in the Theory of Max Weber,* translated by Neil Solomon (Stanford, Cal.: Stanford University Press, 1996);

Schluchter, *Rationalism, Religion, and Domination: A Weberian Perspective,* translated by Solomon (Berkeley: University of California Press, 1989);

Schluchter, *The Rise of Western Rationalism: Max Weber's Developmental History,* translated, with an introduction, by Guenther Roth (Berkeley: University of California Press, 1981);

Alfred Schutz, *The Phenomenology of the Social World,* translated by George Walsh and Frederick Lehnert (Evanston, Ill.: Northwestern University Press, 1967).

Papers:

The Max-Weber-Archiv is located in Munich. At the end of World War II, Marianne Weber turned the Weber papers that she was holding over to the Preußisches Geheimes Staatsarchiv. Later they were incorporated into the Zentralarchiv der Deutschen Demokratischen Republik, which is now the Historisches Stadtarchiv in Merseburg.

Books for Further Reading

Adams, Hazard, and Leroy Searle, eds. *Critical Theory since 1965*. Tallahassee: Florida State University Press, 1986.

Atkins, G. Douglas. *Reading Deconstruction / Deconstructive Reading*. Lexington: University of Kentucky Press, 1984.

Bayley, John. *The Romantic Survival: A Study in Poetic Evolution*. London: Constable, 1957.

Beauvoir, Simone de. *The Second Sex,* translated and edited by H. M. Parshley. New York: Knopf, 1953.

Bell, Michael Davitt. *The Development of American Romance: The Sacrifice of Relation*. Chicago: University of Chicago Press, 1980.

Belsey, Catherine. *Critical Practice*. London & New York: Eyre Methuen, 1980.

Benjamin, Walter. *Illuminations,* edited by Hannah Arendt, translated by Harry Zohn. New York: Schocken, 1969.

Bennett, William J. *To Reclaim a Legacy: A Report on the Humanities in Higher Education*. Washington, D.C.: NEH, 1984.

Benson, Thomas W., ed. *Speech Communication in the Twentieth Century*. Carbondale: Southern Illinois University Press, 1985.

Benstock, Shari, ed. *Feminist Issues in Literary Scholarship*. Bloomington: Indiana University Press, 1987.

Bloom, Harold, and others. *Deconstruction and Criticism*. New York: Seabury, 1979.

Boone, Joseph A., and Michael Cadden, eds. *Engendering Men: The Question of Male Feminist Criticism*. New York: Routledge, 1990.

Booth, Wayne C. *The Rhetoric of Fiction*. Chicago: Chicago University Press, 1961.

Brandt, Deborah. *Literacy as Involvement: The Acts of Writers, Readers, and Texts*. Carbondale: Southern Illinois University Press, 1990.

Brantlinger, Patrick. *Crusoe's Footprints: Cultural Studies in Britain and America*. New York: Routledge, 1990.

Brodkey, Linda. *Academic Writing as Social Practice*. Philadelphia: Temple University Press, 1987.

Brower, Reuben. *The Fields of Light: An Experiment in Critical Reading*. New York: Oxford University Press, 1951.

Bruss, Elizabeth. *Beautiful Theories: The Spectacle of Discourse in Contemporary Criticism*. Baltimore: Johns Hopkins University Press, 1982.

Bürger, Peter. *Theory of the Avant-Garde,* translated by Michael Shaw. Minneapolis: University of Minnesota Press, 1984.

Butler, Christopher. *Interpretation, Deconstruction and Ideology: An Introduction to Some Current Issues in Literary Theory.* London: Clarendon Press / New York: Oxford University Press, 1984.

Cain, William E. *F. O. Mathiessen and the Politics of Criticism.* Madison: University of Wisconsin Press, 1988.

Calinescu, Matei. *Five Faces of Modernity: Modernism, Avant-Garde, Decadence, Kitsch, Postmodernism.* Durham, N.C.: Duke University Press, 1987.

Caserio, Robert. *Plot, Story, and the Novel: From Dickens and Poe to the Modern Period.* Princeton: Princeton University Press, 1979.

Cavell, Stanley. *The Claim of Reason: Wittgenstein, Skepticism, Morality, and Tragedy.* Oxford: Clarendon Press / New York: Oxford University Press, 1979.

Chamberlain, Mariam, ed. *Women in Academe: Progress and Prospects.* New York: Russell Sage Foundation, 1988.

Chodorow, Nancy. *The Reproduction of Mothering: Psychoanalysis and the Sociology of Gender.* Berkeley: University of California Press, 1978.

Christ, Carol. *Victorian and Modern Poetics.* Chicago: Chicago University Press, 1984.

Christian, Barbara. *Black Women Novelists: The Development of a Tradition, 1892–1976.* Westport, Conn.: Greenwood Press, 1980.

Claridge, Laura, and Elizabeth Langland, eds. *Out of Bounds: Male Writers and Gender(ed) Criticism.* Amherst: University of Massachusetts Press, 1990.

Clifford, James, and George E. Marcus, eds. *Writing Culture: The Poetics and Politics of Ethnography.* Berkeley: University of California Press, 1986.

Cohen, Ralph, ed. *The Future of Literary Theory.* New York: Routledge, 1989.

Collins, Jim. *Uncommon Cultures: Popular Culture and Post-Modernism.* New York: Routledge, 1989.

Conley, Verena Andermatt. *Hélène Cixous: Writing the Feminine.* Lincoln: University of Nebraska Press, 1984.

Connor, Steven. *Postmodernist Culture: An Introduction to Theories of the Contemporary.* Oxford & New York: Blackwell, 1989.

Crews, Frederick. *Out of My System: Psychoanalysis, Ideology, and Critical Method.* New York: Oxford University Press, 1975.

Culler, Jonathan. *On Deconstruction: Theory and Criticism after Structuralism.* Ithaca, N.Y.: Cornell University Press, 1982.

D'Angelo, Frank. *A Conceptual Theory of Rhetoric.* Cambridge, Mass.: Winthrop, 1975.

Davis, Natalie Zemon. *Society and Culture in Early Modern France.* Stanford, Cal.: Stanford University Press, 1975.

Davis, Robert Con, ed. *Lacan and Narration: The Psychoanalytic Difference in Narrative Theory.* Baltimore: Johns Hopkins University Press, 1983.

Delany, Paul, and George P. Landow, eds. *Hypermedia and Literary Studies.* Cambridge, Mass.: MIT Press, 1991.

De Man, Paul. *Blindness and Insight: Essays in the Rhetoric of Contemporary Criticism.* New York: Oxford University Press, 1971.

Donato, Eugenio, and Richard Macksey, eds. *The Languages of Criticism and the Sciences of Man: The Structuralist Controversy.* Baltimore: Johns Hopkins University Press, 1970.

Eagleton, Terry. *Literary Theory: An Introduction.* Oxford: Blackwell, 1983.

Eisenstein, Hester, and Alice Jardine. *The Future of Difference.* Boston: G. K. Hall, 1980.

Ellmann, Mary. *Thinking about Women.* New York: Harcourt, Brace & World, 1968.

Eysteinsson, Astradur. *The Concept of Modernism.* Ithaca, N.Y.: Cornell University Press, 1990.

Fekete, John. *The Structural Allegory: Reconstructive Encounters with the New French Thought.* Manchester: Manchester University Press, 1984.

Felman, Shoshana. *Jacques Lacan and the Adventure of Insight: Psychoanalysis in Contemporary Culture.* Cambridge, Mass.: Harvard University Press, 1987.

Felperin, Howard. *Beyond Deconstruction: The Uses and Abuses of Literary Theory.* Oxford: Clarendon Press / New York: Oxford University Press, 1985.

Fisher, Dexter, ed. *Minority Language and Literature: Retrospective and Perspective.* New York: Modern Language Association of America, 1977.

Frosh, Stephen. *The Politics of Psychoanalysis: An Introduction to Freudian and Post-Freudian Theory.* New Haven: Yale University Press, 1987.

Gallop, Jane. *Reading Lacan.* Ithaca, N.Y.: Cornell University Press, 1985.

Gates, Henry Louis, Jr., ed. *Black Literature and Literary Theory.* London & New York: Methuen, 1984.

Gilroy, Paul. *There Ain't No Black in the Union Jack: The Cultural Politics of Race and Nation.* London: Hutchinson, 1987.

Graff, Gerald. *Literature against Itself: Literary Ideas in Modern Society.* Chicago: University of Chicago Press, 1979.

Hartman, Geoffrey. *Saving the Text: Literature/Derrida/Philosophy.* Baltimore: Johns Hopkins University Press, 1981.

Harvey, Irene. *Derrida and the Economy of Différance.* Bloomington: Indiana University Press, 1986.

Heilbrun, Carolyn G. *Toward a Recognition of Androgyny: Aspects of Male and Female in Literature.* New York: Knopf, 1973.

Hoy, David Couzens. *The Critical Circle: Literature, History, and Contemporary Hermeneutics.* Berkeley: University of California Press, 1978.

Jacobs, Carol. *The Dissimulating Harmony: Images of Interpretation in Nietzsche, Rilke, Artaud, and Benjamin.* Baltimore: Johns Hopkins University Press, 1978.

Johnson, Barbara. *The Critical Difference: Essays in the Contemporary Rhetoric of Reading.* Baltimore: Johns Hopkins University Press, 1980.

Kauffman, Linda, ed. *Gender and Theory: Dialogues on Feminist Criticism.* Oxford & New York: Blackwell, 1989.

Krieger, Murray. *Poetic Presence and Illusion: Essays in Critical History and Theory.* Baltimore: Johns Hopkins University Press, 1979.

Krupnick, Mark, ed. *Displacement: Derrida and After*. Bloomington: Indiana University Press, 1983.

Kuhn, Annette, and AnnMarie Wolpe, eds. *Feminism and Materialism: Women and Modes of Production*. London & Boston: Routledge & Kegan Paul, 1978.

Lemaire, Anika. *Jacques Lacan*. London & Boston: Routledge & Kegan Paul, 1977.

Lentricchia, Frank. *After the New Criticism*. London: Athlone, 1980.

Macdonell, Diane. *Theories of Discourse*. Oxford & New York: Blackwell, 1986.

Macksey, Richard, ed. *Velocities of Change: Critical Essays from MLN*. Baltimore: Johns Hopkins University Press, 1974.

Mann, Paul. *The Theory-Death of the Avant-Garde*. Bloomington: Indiana University Press, 1991.

Marks, Elaine, and Isabelle de Courtivron, eds. *New French Feminisms: An Anthology*. New York: Schocken, 1981.

Megill, Alan. *Prophets of Extremity: Nietzsche, Heidegger, Foucault, Derrida*. Berkeley: University of California Press, 1985.

Miller, D. A. *Narrative and Its Discontents: Problems of Closure in the Traditional Novel*. Princeton: Princeton University Press, 1981.

Mitchell, Juliet. *Psychoanalysis and Feminism*. London: Allen Lane, 1974.

Moi, Toril. *Sexual/Textual Politics: Feminist Literary Theory*. London & New York: Methuen, 1985.

Muller, John P., and William J. Richardson, eds. *The Purloined Poe: Lacan, Derrida, and Psychoanalytic Reading*. Baltimore: Johns Hopkins University Press, 1988.

Nandy, Ashis. *The Intimate Enemy: Loss and Recovery of Self under Colonialism*. Delhi: Oxford University Press, 1983.

Nelson, Cary, and Lawrence Grossberg, eds. *Marxism and the Interpretation of Culture*. Urbana: University of Illinois Press, 1988.

Norris, Christopher. *The Deconstructive Turn: Essays in the Rhetoric of Philosophy*. London & New York: Methuen, 1983.

Ong, Walter J. *Orality and Literacy: The Technologizing of the Word*. London & New York: Methuen, 1982.

Pogglio, Renato. *The Theory of the Avant-Garde*, translated by Gerald Fitzgerald. Cambridge, Mass.: Harvard University Press, 1968.

Poster, Mark. *The Mode of Information: Poststructuralism and Social Context*. Chicago: University of Chicago Press, 1990.

Ray, William. *Literary Meaning: From Phenomenology to Deconstruction*. Oxford: Blackwell, 1984.

Reed, Adolph, Jr., ed. *Race, Politics, and Culture: Critical Essays on the Radicalism of the 1960s*. New York: Greenwood Press, 1986.

Ricoeur, Paul. *Freud and Philosophy: An Essay on Interpretation*, translated by Denis Savage. New Haven: Yale University Press, 1970.

Rimmon-Kenan, Shlomith, ed. *Discourse in Psychoanalysis and Literature*. London & New York: Methuen, 1987.

Robinson, Lillian. *Sex, Class, and Culture*. Bloomington: Indiana University Press, 1978.

Rorty, Richard. *Consequences of Pragmatism: Essays, 1972–1980*. Minneapolis: University of Minnesota Press, 1982.

Ross, Andrew. *No Respect: Intellectuals and Popular Culture*. New York: Routledge, 1989.

Said, Edward. *The World, the Text, and the Critic*. Cambridge, Mass.: Harvard University Press, 1983.

Selden, Raman. *A Reader's Guide to Contemporary Literary Theory*. Brighton, U.K.: Harvester, 1985.

Spivak, Gayatri Chakravorty. *In Other Worlds: Essays in Cultural Politics*. New York: Methuen, 1987.

Sturrock, John, ed. *Structuralism and Since: From Lévi-Strauss to Derrida*. Oxford & New York: Oxford University Press, 1979.

Woodward, Kathleen, ed. *The Myths of Information: Technology and Postindustrial Culture*. Madison, Wis.: Coda, 1980.

Žižek, Slavoj. *The Sublime Object of Ideology*. London & New York: Verso, 1989.

Contributors

Cumulative Index

Dictionary of Literary Biography, Volumes 1-296
Dictionary of Literary Biography Yearbook, 1980-2002
Dictionary of Literary Biography Documentary Series, Volumes 1-19
Concise Dictionary of American Literary Biography, Volumes 1-7
Concise Dictionary of British Literary Biography, Volumes 1-8
Concise Dictionary of World Literary Biography, Volumes 1-4

Cumulative Index

DLB before number: *Dictionary of Literary Biography,* Volumes 1-296
Y before number: *Dictionary of Literary Biography Yearbook,* 1980-2002
DS before number: *Dictionary of Literary Biography Documentary Series,* Volumes 1-19
CDALB before number: *Concise Dictionary of American Literary Biography,* Volumes 1-7
CDBLB before number: *Concise Dictionary of British Literary Biography,* Volumes 1-8
CDWLB before number: *Concise Dictionary of World Literary Biography,* Volumes 1-4

B

ISBN 0-7876-6833-8

90000

9 780787 668334